AF509219

FORGING AN AMERICAN IDENTITY

THE ART OF WILLIAM RANNEY

FORGING AN AMERICAN IDENTITY

By Linda Bantel and Peter H. Hassrick

with essays by Sarah E. Boehme and Mark F. Bockrath

Edited by Kathleen Luhrs

BUFFALO BILL HISTORICAL CENTER

Cody, Wyoming

THE ART OF WILLIAM RANNEY

WITH A CATALOGUE OF HIS WORKS

COPYRIGHT 2006 BUFFALO BILL HISTORICAL CENTER

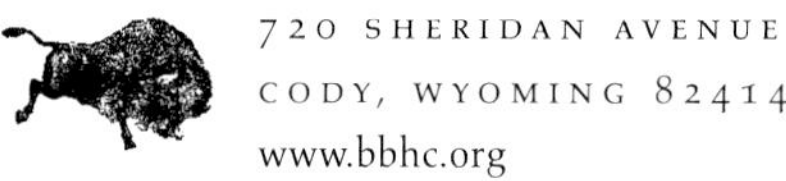

720 SHERIDAN AVENUE
CODY, WYOMING 82414
www.bbhc.org

All rights reserved. No part of this publication may be reproduced or transmitted in any form or by any means, electronic or mechanical, including photocopying, recording, or any information storage or retrieval system, without written permission from the publisher.

Forging an American Identity: The Art of William Ranney with a Catalogue of His Works is supported in part by generous contributions from the Henry Luce Foundation; the 1957 Charity Foundation; Mrs. J. Maxwell (Betty) Moran; Ranney Moran; National Endowment for the Arts, which believes that a great nation deserves great art; and Wyoming Arts Council, through funding from the National Endowment for the Arts and the Wyoming State Legislature.

EXHIBITION ITINERARY

Buffalo Bill Historical Center

Cody, Wyoming
May 13 – August 14, 2006

Speed Art Museum

Louisville, Kentucky
September 29, 2006 – January 1, 2007

Amon Carter Museum

Fort Worth, Texas
February 10 – May 13, 2007

Philadelphia Museum of Art

Philadelphia, Pennsylvania
June 23 – August 26, 2007

LIBRARY OF CONGRESS CONTROL NUMBER: 2006925130

ISBN: 0-931618-61-4

PRINTED IN THE UNITED STATES OF AMERICA

TABLE OF CONTENTS

FOREWORD

With this special exhibition and catalogue raisonné on the art of William Ranney, the Buffalo Bill Historical Center is pleased to advance knowledge through presenting outstanding art and promoting excellent scholarship on the American West. These joint projects of exhibition and publication work together to present a comprehensive look at a versatile American artist, William Ranney, whose artistic works interpret a variety of American subjects and develop concepts of national consciousness. These projects reveal Ranney as a prime figure in the American art canon and a vital player in the art scene of his day.

The exhibition *Forging an American Identity: The Art of William Ranney* presents an inclusive view of this important American artist and provides an opportunity for viewers to see the range of his subjects and stylistic approach. For the Buffalo Bill Historical Center, this project developed from the impetus of the special exhibition *American Frontier Life: Early Western Painting and Prints*, an examination of western genre art that the Center jointly organized with the Amon Carter Museum in 1987. That groundbreaking exhibition presented early nineteenth-century artists, including William Ranney, who portrayed scenes of everyday life in the exotic West, and it highlighted the importance of the narrative tradition in early western art. The research and loan process brought the Historical Center into contact with the great-granddaughter of William Ranney, Mrs. J. Maxwell (Betty) Moran. She supported the museum goals of education and enlightenment and shared her collection first through loans and later through generous donations of important paintings. *American Frontier Life* encouraged new scholarship and pointed to the need for more in-depth research and brought together scholars who would carry out that work. The exhibition *Forging an American Identity: The Art of William Ranney* now presents the first retrospective view of this artist in more than forty years. As the organizing museum for this exhibition, the Buffalo Bill Historical Center is pleased to work within our tradition of mounting exhibitions of important artists such as Frederic Remington and John James Audubon. With this exhibition our audiences will see Ranney's western works in a broader context with his sporting scenes, history paintings, eastern and southern genre scenes, and portraits. We are very pleased as well to share this exhibition with three other important museums and their audiences, the Speed Art Museum, Louisville, Kentucky; the Amon Carter Museum, Fort Worth, Texas; and the Philadelphia Museum of Art.

The research for this exhibition is based on the excellent scholarship of the catalogue raisonné of William Ranney's art, researched and written by scholars Linda Bantel and Peter H. Hassrick. Compiling a catalogue of the complete body of works of an artist, documented with provenance, exhibition histories, and bibliographies, is a cornerstone in art historical methodology, and the Buffalo Bill Historical Center is proud to encourage and support this essential research and is grateful for the excellent work of Linda Bantel and Peter H. Hassrick.

This ambitious project is only possible through generous support and cooperation. We are very grateful for the financial support for *Forging an American Identity: The Art of William Ranney.*

The Henry Luce Foundation, our foundation sponsor, provided important grant support that made it possible to launch the work for this exhibition and publication. Additional significant support came from the 1957 Charity Foundation. Mrs. J. Maxwell Moran and Ranney Moran, descendants of William Ranney, have been invaluable supporters of this project through generous donations as well as their interest and encouragement; we are very grateful to them for their passion and commitment. The exhibition and catalogue also received a significant grant from the National Endowment for the Arts, which believes that a great nation deserves great art. The Cody venue of the exhibition was also enhanced by a grant from the Wyoming Arts Council, through funding from the National Endowment for the Arts and the Wyoming State Legislature.

We are also appreciative of the many museums and collectors who have graciously loaned works of art so that Ranney's paintings may be seen together in this illuminating exhibition. We want especially to thank the staff members of these museums, galleries, and other organizations as well as private collectors, Amon Carter Museum; W. Graham Arader III Gallery, Philadelphia; Brandywine River Museum, Chadds Ford, Pennsylvania; Carnegie Museum of Art, Pittsburgh, Pennsylvania; Corcoran Gallery of Art, Washington, D.C.; Cromwell Historical Society, Cromwell, Connecticut; Dallas Museum of Art; Gilcrease Museum, Tulsa, Oklahoma; Greenville County Museum of Art, Greenville, South Carolina; Haggerty Museum of Art, Marquette University, Milwaukee; Judith Filenbaum Hernstadt; Manoogian Collection, Taylor, Michigan; Merestead, Westchester County Parks Department, Mount Kisco, New York; Morris Museum of Art, Augusta, Georgia; Munson-Williams-Proctor Arts Institute, Utica, New York; Museum of the American West, Autry National Center, Los Angeles; Museum of Fine Arts, Boston; Museum of Fine Arts, Springfield, Massachusetts; Newark Museum, Newark, New Jersey; New-York Historical Society, New York; North Carolina Museum of Art, Raleigh; R. W. Norton Art Gallery, Shreveport, Louisiana; Gerald Peters Gallery, Santa Fe, New Mexico; Princeton University Art Museum, Princeton, New Jersey; Spanierman Gallery, New York; Speed Art Museum, Louisville; Terra Foundation for American Art, Chicago; Virginia Museum of Fine Arts, Richmond; and anonymous private collectors.

At the Buffalo Bill Historical Center, many staff members worked hard and made creative contributions. I want to thank especially, Eugene W. Reber, Robert Pickering, Sarah Boehme, Elizabeth Holmes, Ann Marie Donoghue, Maryanne Andrus, Shelley Leslie, Lynn Pitet, Lee Haines, Christine Brindza, Julie Coleman Tachick, Kimber Swenson, Paul Brock and the Facilities Department, Dean Swift, David Kennedy, Jill Gleich, Anne Marie Shriver, and former interns Susannah Maurer and Thomas Smith. These staff members along with many others have joined with our partners to make possible *Forging an American Identity: The Art of William Ranney*.

Robert E. Shimp
Executive Director
Buffalo Bill Historical Center

PROLOGUE

The American artist William Ranney, the subject of this effort, seems to have had a good life, not long but full of experiences in this new country in the early nineteenth century. Some four generations later, my own quest to learn more about this artist and his life has been fulfilled. I have enjoyed many opportunities to work with scholars and explore my great-great grandfather's life and art. The project has led to new discoveries and insights into William Ranney's work, and we have come closer to the man and how he lived from the 1820s to the 1850s—a sportsman, a traveler with a purpose, a painter, and a friend. A recognized artist in his day, Ranney did his best for his country, family, and himself in his forty-three years.

The research on my part began with just a bit of curiosity and developed with encouragement from our family, especially Elizabeth Ranney Moran, the artist's great granddaughter, followed by the extended Ranney family. Through Richard Ranney and the Cromwell Historical Society in Middletown, Connecticut, where the artist was born, many members of the Ranney clan, no matter their geographical locations, sought to know more about our ancestor the artist.

At first, I was a "green horn" not knowing what to do or how to proceed. Thankfully, through relationships I developed with museums and curators, the project began to grow and gain support. Linda Bantel and Peter Hassrick were approached, and they lent their knowledge and interest. They found Ranney worthwhile, and a publication, the first extensive survey since 1962, seemed possible. Together we have found a number of lost works and uncovered a good deal about Ranney's paintings in general.

Much credit goes to the artist himself. I hope those who see the exhibition and future generations who read this book gain a sense of what life was like at that time in history—it is an interesting story told through art. For Ranney, there were probably many challenges and few rewards, but through his work he showed the best as well as the raw experiences of life at the time. We will probably never really know what was going through his mind as he worked, but fortunately we have been given a taste of life at this period, left to us on canvas and paper.

I do not know precisely what motivated Elizabeth Moran in her willingness to back this project, other than a desire to understand the man and the artist. This project is part of her legacy. Certainly the research started by her father, Claude J. Ranney, made a large contribution to the first Ranney catalogue raisonné written by Francis Grubar. With her quiet understanding, and in all stages of this work, she encouraged us all to proceed. I also want to acknowledge the support of my wife Terri and our children Eliza and Ranney. This project has had a lively momentum and spirit—we traveled all over the country—sometimes to great success and other times not so.

It has been a pleasure to work with people who enjoyed their work and were eager to search for new paintings and information relating to Ranney and his relationship with his contemporaries. Linda Bantel has given her best to research all of Ranney's life. She has made many new discoveries toward bringing him the prestige he deserves. Working together with her I have shared her enthusiasm. Linda has accomplished the most comprehensive analysis of Ranney's work to date and has an appreciation of his simple life. I am very grateful to her for her insight, new research, and accurate testimony of the artist's work.

To Peter Hassrick, who through his knowledge and interest in the American West, goes the credit for spurring a renewed appreciation of Ranney's western paintings. Peter's writings on the artists of the American West have brought Ranney and his contemporaries prominence and understanding over the years. I am very appreciative of Peter's friendship and extremely grateful for his contributions. He has been a great assistance in further establishing Ranney's place in American art history.

Hermann Warner Williams, Jr., wrote in the foreword to the 1962 catalogue of Ranney's work: "This is the definitive catalogue of the paintings and drawings of William Ranney. We feel that the works which have been assembled to form the retrospective study of Ranney's work present him at his best, and it is with the sincerest appreciation that we thank the museums and individual owners for their kindness in allowing these key examples of the artist's work to be more widely known not only to the visitors to the exhibition but to an even wider audience who will refer to this book in the years ahead." This new publication and exhibition reiterates Williams's statement and his wishes. We have, we hope, expanded on and greatly added to the original efforts begun by Claude Ranney and carried out by Francis Grubar.

I particularly want to express my deep appreciation to the Buffalo Bill Historical Center and its entire staff; for, like the Corcoran over forty years ago, they have had the vision to support this new effort by mounting an exhibition and publishing an updated catalogue raisonné.

This new publication and exhibition rests on and corroborates Williams's statement and wishes, confirming the original efforts of Francis Grubar and Claude J. Ranney.

Ranney Moran

ACKNOWLEDGMENTS

The William Ranney project was launched almost a decade ago with the goal of updating and elaborating upon Francis Grubar's 1962 landmark catalogue, *William Ranney: Painter of the Early West*, the publication of which coincided, like this one, with an exhibition. Just as we were fortunate to have the excellent research of Grubar to build upon, Grubar benefited from thirty years of research by the artist's grandson Claude J. Ranney. I fondly recall that a few years ago, while examining photographs at the Frick Art Reference Library, I came across Claude Ranney's name listed as a reference in the early 1950s.

The preparation of a comprehensive catalogue such as this one which lists all the known works of the artist, along with pertinent historical and technical details, analysis and historical interpretations, requires a long-term commitment of energy and time. While exhaustively researched and illustrated surveys such as this one are standard tools for art historians, fewer and fewer organizations or individuals are able to sustain such long term projects. Claude Ranney's daughter, Elizabeth R. Moran, and his grandson, Ranney R. Moran, who I firmly believe will one day become an art historian, are unique exceptions. For their personal commitment, insights, and wit, I am enormously grateful.

A project of this scope inevitably benefited from the support of many colleagues, institutions, and individuals. For their assistance we wish to thank Catherine Beach, Wilmington, North Carolina; Mark Bockrath, paintings conservator; Marisa Bourgoin, archivist, Corcoran Gallery of Art; Lillian Brenwasser, fomerly of Kennedy Galleries, New York; Barbara A. Buckley, paintings conservator; Lee Burke, Dallas, Texas; Carol Clark, Amherst College; David B. Dearinger, formerly of the National Academy of Design; Lydia Dufour, Suz Massen, Jacqueline Rogers, Frick Art Reference Library, New York; Rick Echelmeyer, photographer; Roberts French, Santa Fe; John Dorsey, Boston Public Library; Charles E. Hilburn, Gulf States Paper Corporation Collection, Tuscaloosa, Alabama; John K. Howat, New York; William Johnston, Walters Art Museum, Baltimore; Knoedler Gallery, New York; Martin Kodner, Saint Louis; Harry Lockwood, Cincinnati; James H. Maroney, Jr., Leicester, Vermont; Skip Miller, Enterprise, Oregon; Lilah J. Mittelstaedt, reference librarian, Philadelphia Museum of Art; Merl M. Moore, Jr., Falls Church, Virginia; M. P. Naud, Hirschl and Adler Galleries, New York; James Nottage, Museum of American West, Los Angeles; Arthur J. Phelan, Jr., Chevy Chase, Maryland; Kathleen Rice, Austin, Texas; Megan Rupnik and Judy Throm, Archives of American Art, Washington, D.C.; Linda Simmons, formerly of the Corcoran Gallery of Art, Washington, D.C. Brandon K. Ruud, Joslyn Art Museum, Omaha; Quincy Scarborough, Fayetteville, North Carolina; Julie Schimmel, Gerald Peters Gallery, Santa Fe; Morgan Simpson; Leslie P. Symington, Baltimore; Wendy Shadwell, formerly New-York Historical Society; Mark Simmons, Cerrillos, New Mexico; Rick Stewart, Amon Carter Museum, Fort Worth; Ron Tyler, University of Texas, Austin; Vose Galleries, Boston; William D. Weiss, Jackson, Wyoming.

I am particularly indebted to Mark Thistlethwaite, a generous scholar at Texas Christian University, who, for over thirty years, has contributed such thoughtful work on Ranney. His interpretative art historical approach continues to inspire. I am also grateful to art historian Linda Ayres, whose excellent study of Ranney's western pictures within a literary context and her dogged research on his early Texas experience are invaluable resources.

In addition, I would like to express my appreciation to several researchers, Randall Griffey surveyed the National Archives and the Smithsonian Institution libraries; Jennifer Wagelie and Jennifer Park, conducted newspaper research in New York; Betty L. Krimminger of Chapel Hill, North Carolina, was enormously helpful in discovering new information about the Nott family; B-Ann Moorhouse, Brooklyn, New York, researched the Brooklyn resources and biographies of New York merchants; in Connecticut Gerald M. Cruthers conducted research on the Ranney family in the Archives of the State Library; and Linda Wilhelm who helped with so many organizational details. During the last year of the project, Cynthia H. Sanford was of immeasurable assistance in following up on research inquiries, checking manuscript materials, and proofreading. A talented art historian in her own right, she contributed enormous energy and intellect.

The staffs of the following several institutions were generous with their time and always graciously responded to our many inquiries: The Free Library of Philadelphia, Library Company of Philadelphia, Historical Society of Pennsylvania, New York Public Library, New-York Historical Society, and, in particular, the Frick Art Reference Library in New York. I especially want to extend our deep appreciation to William H. Gerdts and Abigail Booth Gerdts, both generous scholars who so often welcomed us to their home, selflessly shared much information, and allowed us to use their extraordinary research library with its wealth of well-organized primary sources. Without access to the Gerdts American Art Research Library, our task would have been much more difficult.

We have been particularly fortunate that Kathleen Luhrs has been our editor. She has been not only a friend and colleague, but an astute and knowledgeable editor, whose art historical insights have also benefited the entire publication. Thanks also to Deborah Winard for her fine proofreading skills. We owe much to the fine aesthetic sense and organization of Jerry Kelly who designed the catalogue. His good cheer in moments of angst and fortitude at the eleventh hour helped smooth a lot of feathers.

Finally, I wish to thank my husband, David Hollenberg for editing assistance, proofreading, assembling photographs and other materials, computer assistance, and most importantly his wonderful sense of humor and good cheer.

Linda Bantel
William Ranney Catalogue Raisonné Project Director

WILLIAM RANNEY—AMERICAN ARTIST

BY LINDA BANTEL

Possessing a most prolific inventive genius, he was never at a loss for subjects. [1]

William Ranney died at his home in West Hoboken, New Jersey, on November 18, 1857, at the age of forty-four. In spite of a relatively short artistic career of barely seventeen years, he had achieved a significant enough reputation to warrant several lengthy obituaries. These and subsequent articles consistently recognized the artist's native genius and praised his work for its American subject matter and diversity. The *New York Herald* noted that Ranney was "eminent both as a landscape and animal painter, he has illustrated Western life with a graphic truthfulness that entitles him to be placed in the foremost rank of American painters." [2] *Frank Leslie's Illustrated Newspaper* called him "truly an American artist. His pictures were stamped with American character and he chose the most striking features of American scenery for his subjects." [3] The *Home Journal* pointed out: "In portraiture, as well as in his historical efforts, he attained to an enviable reputation." [4] So popular were some of his works, particularly those engraved by the American Art-Union, that they were said to have been widely copied, even during the artist's life time. [5] It is a testimony to Ranney's creativity, energy, and innate talent that, though his work was not always critically acclaimed, he nevertheless achieved considerable respect as an artist during his brief career.

The basic outline of William Ranney's life has been derived from early obituaries as well as the excellent twentieth-century research by Ranney scholars Francis Grubar in 1962, and subsequently by Linda Ayres, who in 1987 added much new information about Ranney's Texas experience. [6] Unlike his contemporaries and friends, such as Arthur Fitzwilliam Tait or William Sidney Mount, for example, Ranney left no inventory of his work, diaries, or letters that would help us gain some insight into his thoughts and inspirations. The list of his work comes almost exclusively from exhibition and sales catalogues. It is through the testimony of a few artists and writers and from family stories that we are able to approach understanding the man himself.

William Tylee Ranney was born on May 9, 1813, in Middletown, Connecticut, the son of William Ranney (1783–1829), a ship's captain, and Clarissa Gaylord (1789–1863). [7] He was the eldest son of four children: the others were Clarissa Gaylord (see cat. no. 5), Richard Atkins (1815–1859) and Elizabeth Nott (1822–1874). He never used Tylee, his middle name, presumably given to him in recognition of this paternal grandmother Hannah Tilley or Tilley (b. 1753) of Saybrook, Connecticut. [8] During the early nineteenth century, Middletown, situated on the west bank of the Connecticut River, was an important inland port from its prosperous shipbuilding and trade in rum and sugar. In 1829, while master of the 139-ton brig *Union*, Ranney's father was lost at sea enroute from St. Croix, Virgin Islands to Boston. [9]

Two years before this, in 1827 at age thirteen, Ranney moved to Fayetteville in Cumberland

County, North Carolina to live with his uncle William Nott, Jr. (c. 1789–1840), who, according to reminiscences of Ranney's wife adopted him after the death of his father.[10] The United States Census of 1830, indicates that Ranney joined a large household of seventeen people. Of these, six were under twenty years old, and, there appear to be two families totaling nine people designated as slaves.[11]

Nott with his wife Elizabeth Gaylord, Ranney's mother's sister, had moved from Middletown in 1817 to establish a business in this bustling and sophisticated town in North Carolina. Because of its location on the Cape Fear River and its accessibility by steamboat just over one hundred miles upriver from the port of Wilmington, Fayetteville was a major commercial gateway from which goods were transported within the South and to the West by covered wagon. Recognizing its financial potential, many Connecticut Yankees were drawn there in the early nineteenth century.

By 1830, Nott had a successful partnership with John D. Starr (d. 1862), also a native of Middletown, Connecticut.[12] The Nott and Starr store advertised its wares in Fayetteville's *Carolina Observer* in 1830, listing a large assortment of items available at wholesale and retail prices: dry goods, hardware, cutlery, shoes, combs, hats, yarn, writing and wrapping paper, spelling books, etc.[13] The business evidently prospered, particularly as new territories in the West were developed. By 1837, the firm had expanded its merchandise selection to include saddles, coffee, tinplate, glass, and an assortment of items imported from England, France, and India.[14] In spite of what was clearly a thriving business, Ranney apparently lacked interest in commerce and was soon apprenticed for the traditional six-year term to either a tinsmith or a blacksmith.[15]

It was in his teenage years in Fayetteville that Ranney's interest in art was kindled. His wife wrote that he "made his first sketches at the home of his uncle."[16] Many of the images and themes which later appear frequently in his work— covered wagons, ferry crossings (cat. no. 23), the Revolutionary War subjects of the South (cat. nos. 8 and 61)—all suggest the artist's indebtedness to his life in North Carolina. Most sources indicate that having completed his apprenticeship around 1833 or 1834, he moved to Brooklyn, New York, to study painting and drawing.[17] No art schools are known to have existed there at the time, and few artists claimed it as their principal residence. It remains a mystery with whom Ranney studied. The most important artist listed in the Brooklyn city directories at that time is James Frothingham, a successful portraitist who had received guidance from Gilbert Stuart, the leading portrait painter of the day. [18]

With the advent in 1836 of the Texas war of independence, Ranney left the New York area to join the Texas Army. [19] Like many young Americans, his sense of outrage and patriotism was fired up after Santa Ana's brutal assault on the Alamo from February 23 to March 6, 1836, in which two hundred Texans were killed, including the fabled and witty frontiersman Davy Crockett. According to Ranney's wife, "during the revolution in Texas, his sympathies being aroused by the sufferings of his countrymen, he . . . joined in the struggle which eventually precipitated the Mexican War and resulted in the annexation of Texas to the United States."[20] One undated account indicates that Ranney went to New Orleans where he enlisted with Captain Hubbel and then preceded on to Texas.[21] Surviving documents confirm that from May 18, until November 18, 1836, he was in

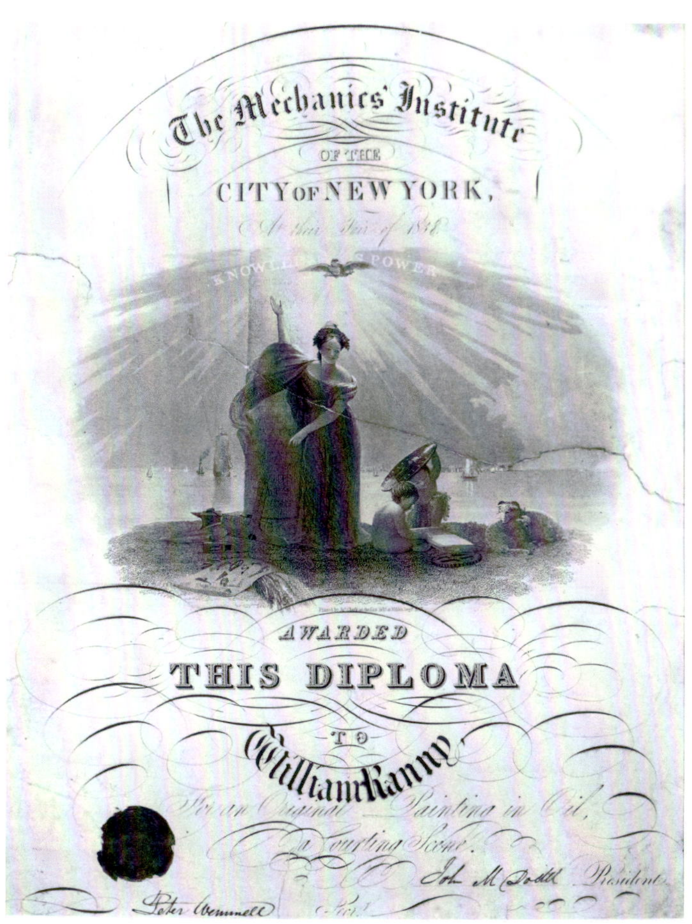

The Mechanics' Institute, New York, "diploma," engraving given to William Ranney in 1838. *Private collection.*

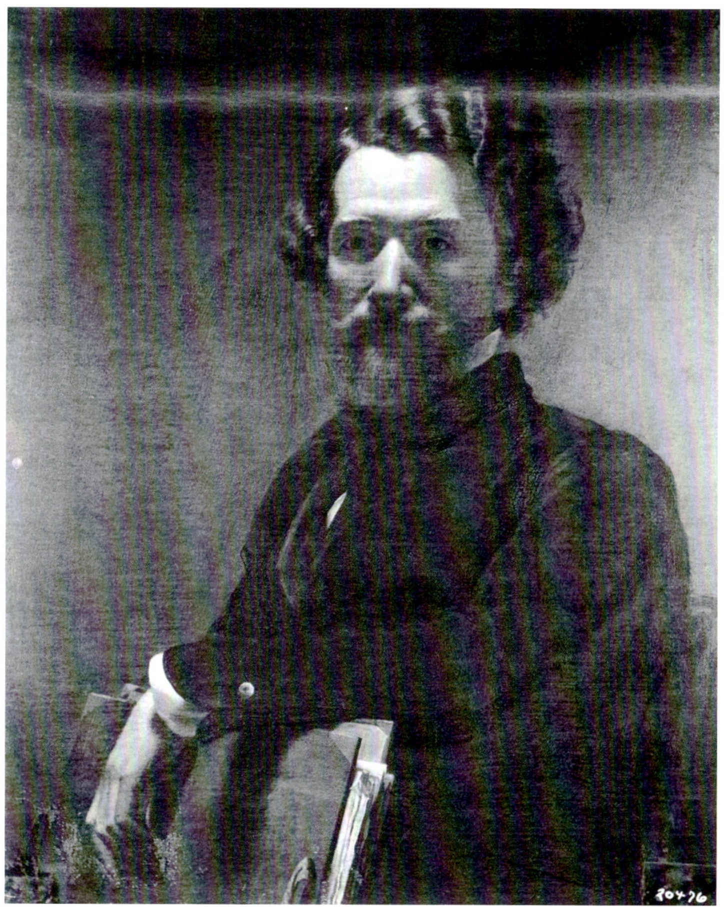

Portrait of William Ranney by James Bogle (1817–1873), c. 1850. Oil on canvas. National Academy Museum, New York. *Photograph courtesy of the Frick Art Reference Library.*

Captain C. A. W. Fowler's company of First Regiment Volunteers. It was based near Columbia (now West Columbia), Texas, the capital of the Republic from September to December 1836. For his service, Ranney was paid a total of forty-eight dollars for six months. [22]

Ranney's Texas adventure was clearly a watershed experience. Unlike many painters who depicted scenes of the West, such as his friend and often imitator Arthur Fitzwilliam Tait, for example, Ranney was one of the few who had actually seen a western landscape and had probably encountered the settlers, trappers, or guides, which he later depicted on his canvases. Again, according to his wife: "He remained in Texas for some time, making sketches for many of his future pictures. He was so charmed with everything he saw; scenes that he long dreamt of were now before his eyes; the wild enchanting prairies, the splendid horses, nature in all her splendor; his poetic mind was filled with the beautiful. He never would have returned North but for the strong love he had for his Mother. . . . On his way home he lingered in a village . . . near where the City of Austin is now situated."[23] While Ranney seems to have sketched in Texas, it remains unclear, whether any of his surviving drawings actually date to 1836, particularly since it was over a decade later, not until 1846, that he painted an obvious western scene, *Hunting Wild Horses* (cat. no. 19). Nevertheless, the visual impact of Ranney's experience must surely have been well etched in his memory for him to re-create such compelling images so many years later.

Sometime in the spring of 1837 Ranney returned to New York, and within a year he had established himself as a professional artist. He is listed in the New York city directories in 1838 and 1839 as a portrait painter at 463 Pearl Street, and he exhibited his first commissioned picture, the now lost *Portrait of Mr. Thompson* (cat. no. 2), at the National Academy of Design in 1838. By specializing in portraiture, Ranney was following the practice of most American artists of his day, who principally supported themselves by catering to a steady demand for likenesses from a variety of patrons. At the National Academy exhibition of 1840, for example, over sixty percent of the works were portraits, and less than nine percent genre paintings.[24] In spite of the apparent lack of taste for genre painting at this time, it is indicative of Ranney's ambitions and future direction that in 1838 he gamely submitted a genre subject to an exhibition of amateur work held at the Mechanics' Institute of the City of New York. This now lost work, *A Courting Scene* (cat. no. 1), was awarded a prize (see illustration p. xv). It is worth noting, that the exhibition catalogue mentioned that Ranney had only been painting for six months.

Ranney's early artistic training remains a mystery. It seems he was essentially self-taught and never when abroad. The Mechanics' Institute may have offered some technical drawing courses, but there are no surviving records to verify whether Ranney attended any courses there. Likewise, his name does not appear on any of the registers of either the National Academy's life class or the antique school during this period or later; although one has to assume he was familiar with the antique cast collection. Moreover, no new information has been discovered to illuminate who, if anyone, may have been his early mentor.

In Ranney's day, North Carolina had only a modest painting tradition and no art schools of note. Charleston, South Carolina, on the other hand, was the artistic center of the South, attracting occasional visits from prominent northern painters, such as Charleston native Thomas Sully, for example. This city sustained the careers of a few resident artists, such as Charles Fraser, Henry Boutheneau, and, in particular, Edward Troye, who was known to paint horses. If Ranney had any

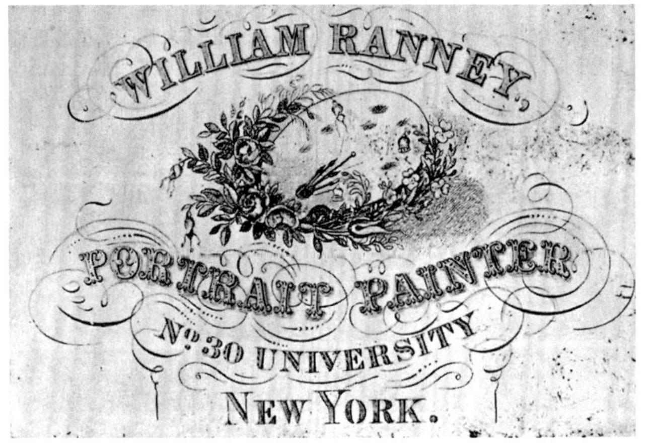

Photograph of William Ranney's business card from the back cover of Francis S. Grubar, *William Ranney: Painter of the Early West* (Washington, D. C.: Corcoran Gallery of Art, 1962).

direct contact with southern artists, the most logical ones were the twins James and Robert Bogle of Georgetown, South Carolina, who, in search of portrait commissions, plied their trade for many years up and down the eastern seaboard. While we have yet to discover evidence of their visiting Fayetteville when Ranney was still living there, a notice appeared in the *Fayetteville Observer* indicating that by December 7, 1838, they had rented rooms and were seeking portrait commissions.[25] James Bogle, who had studied under the prominent portrait painter Samuel F. B. Morse in New York, later painted Ranney's portrait for the National Academy to mark his being named an associate academician (see illustration p. xv).[26] John Crawley, another minor portrait painter, was also in the vicinity of Fayetteville and sometimes traveled with the Bogle brothers. In 1835, a notice appeared in the nearby town of New Bern indicating he was looking for pupils to instruct in drawing and painting.[27]

Ranney must have received some rudimentary training from someone before he arrived in New York, because he was able so quickly to achieve a modicum of success there. Perhaps it was not enough to sustain him; for whatever reason, by late 1839 or early 1840, he decided to return to Fayetteville where he presumably stayed with his aunt and uncle. There he advertised himself as a portrait painter: "Would respectfully inform the inhabitants of Fayetteville and its vicinity, that [William Ranney] will execute Portraits of all sizes, in oil, at moderate prices. Likenesses warranted. He may be seen by enquiring at the Store of Messrs. Nott & Starr."[28] On November 20, 1840, his uncle died, and the business was forced to dissolve.[29] How long Ranney remained in Fayetteville is unknown; we also do not know whether he was successful in his attempts to establish himself as a professional painter. The *Portrait of a Young Man* of 1839 (cat. no. 4) is the only early example of a signed and dated portrait of this period. While following a relatively conventional compositional formula in this picture, Ranney demonstrates a certain amount of individuality in his naturalistic presentation and subtle use of color. In spite of his early emphasis on portrait painting in the South, and subsequently in New York, it is curious that not one signed and dated example by him from 1840 to 1844 has come to light.

By 1843 Ranney had returned to New York and was listed in the city directories, again as a portrait painter at 20 Chambers Street, a neighborhood where several artists' studios and art supply stores were located. Mid-nineteenth artists spaces were, according to one description, "ill lighted dormitories, approached by filthy stairs, and situated in buildings appropriated to different and uncongenial purposes."[30] Ranney obtained better accommodations from about 1845 to 1847, when he was fortunate to be able to rent a studio in the New York University Building at the northeast corner of Washington Square in Greenwich Village (see illustration). Built between 1833 and 1836, the English Gothic style building had rooms in each of the four towers reserved for writers and artists. The painter and inventor Samuel F. B. Morse, one of the building's most renowned tenants, lived there from 1835 to 1843, but he had left by the time Ranney arrived.

During these years, Ranney seems to have been remarkably prolific. One correspondent, reporting on a visit to his studio in 1846, called him a Brooklyn artist and saw a large body of work including western and genre scenes, historical pictures, and "several very good portraits."[31] While there is no mention of Ranney in the Brooklyn city directories of this period, Ranney could easily commute from there by ferry to his Greenwich Village studio. A Brooklyn residency would explain why three of his pictures were lent by private owners to the Brooklyn Art Institute's annual exhibition of 1845 (cat. nos. 15, 16, and 17).

In the mid-1840s Ranney painted what may be his earliest western scene, the unlocated *Emigrants Resting* (cat. no. 15). The Mexican War and the increased migration as a result of westward expansion created a receptive audience for this kind of subject matter, and Ranney had an advantage with the critics who recognized that having been in the West, he had a certain credibility that many of his colleagues lacked. As one writer noted: "we learn that [Ranney] has traveled west, and therefore…understands his subject, which, by the by, is more than we can say of all our painters."[32]

In the National Academy of Design and the American Art-Union publications, Ranney provides a Weehawken, New Jersey, address in 1847 and 1848, the year he married Margaret Agnes O'Sullivan (cat. nos. 66 and 67). He does not give an address again until 1851, by which time he had moved to West Hoboken, the area that is now Union City, where he combined a studio with his home. Perhaps, as Grubar speculated, Ranney built the house himself. Claude J. Ranney, the artist's grandson, reported to Grubar that he had lived in the house until he was about twelve years old. He recalled a spacious two-story structure with about fourteen rooms set within verdant grounds and a large glassed-in studio on the north side. He also said there was a stable nearby for the artist's horses "for he loved to ride as well as to use them for models." In 1867, the art critic Henry T. Tuckerman, having visited Ranney's studio, described it as having been "constructed as to receive animals."[33]

West Hoboken, a brief ferry ride across the Hudson River from New York, was developed in the early nineteenth century as a riverside resort by John Stevens, an attorney and locomotive inventor. For Ranney, its natural setting and access to the Hudson River with its tall ships to the east, the New Jersey marshes with abundant wild life to the west, and the picturesque cliffs of the Palisades nearby, all provided him with a wealth of natural motifs from which he could make sketches. In addition to the marshland settings, other landscape elements specific to his surroundings began to show up in his work, such as, the rocky outcrop in *Boone's First View of Kentucky* (cat. nos. 45). Among the artists who called Hoboken their home in the mid-nineteenth century were Charles Loring Elliott, one of New York's leading portrait painters at the time, and Thomas W. Whitley, a landscape painter and writer on the arts and drama, for the *New York Herald*.

Known as an avid sportsman, Ranney's relocation to this rural setting understandably inspired him to focus on hunting and fishing themes. During this period of urban expansion, many weary middle-class city dwellers yearned for healthy country air and the opportunity to demonstrate their manly self-reliance in the field, as did folk heroes like Daniel Boone or Davy Crockett. Their enthusiasm sparked a wealth of sporting literature beginning in the 1830s that not only codified rules of behavior for the "true sportsman," but also emphasized concerns about loss of habitat and preservation of species. The literature expressed particular disdain for market hunters who over-hunted and commercial fishermen who used nets.[34] Ranney's sporting scenes often share these concerns or anecdotally allude to the sportsman's ethical code (cat. no. 26). Duck hunting does seem to have been his particular passion because of the frequency with which he returned to the theme (cat. nos. 43, 55, 59,72).

West Hoboken not only provided Ranney with the opportunity for seemingly unlimited hunting and fishing, but, thanks to the Stevens family, it also included the Elysian Fields, the home playing field for the New York Cricket Club, of which Ranney was a founder around 1844. Its members shared many of Ranney's sporting interests. Among them were John Richards, the English-born publisher of the *Spirit of the Times*, a periodical with articles on hunting and fishing, its editor, William T. Porter, some members of its staff, and representatives of New York's literary and artistic community.[35] One writer of the period recalled that "some of the most interesting games on record have been those in which the New York Club has taken part."[36]

By the 1840s, the social and artistic climate was much more receptive to artists as well as to a greater variety of expressions. After the financial slump in the late 1830s, New York experienced an economic growth, fueled by increased trade in cotton, corn, and wheat. More professional artists submitted works to the annual exhibitions held at the National Academy, and a subtle, but inexorable shift in subject matter occurred, resulting in the reduced dominance of portraiture and an increased taste for landscape, genre, and history paintings, which particularly appealed to a wealthier and more sophisticated clientele. The local press extensively reported on these exhibitions, often providing enough descriptive material to enable us today to identify lost paintings (see, for example, *Going to Mill* of 1855, cat. no. 105).

Beginning in 1845 until its dissolution in 1852, Ranney benefited from the patronage of the American Art-Union, which was established in New York 1844. While there were other art unions in the country, for instance, in Philadelphia and Cincinnati, New York's was by far the most influential. Founded initially in 1838 as the Apollo Gallery, the Art-Union's nationalistic purpose was to promote the fine arts in the United States by creating a market for American art and elevating artistic tastes. Managed by a civic-minded committee mostly of merchants, bankers, and lawyers, it acquired the work of exclusively American artists, particularly national subjects that celebrated either American history or the American scene and manners. Unlike the National Academy, the Art-Union rarely showed portraits. The organization's business plan was simple: in order to create a fund to purchase art, honorary secretaries based in cities thoughout the country sold annual memberships to their neighbors for five dollars. In return, the members received copies of the Art-Union's publications (periodic *Bulletins* with articles on art and its the annual report, *Transactions*), at least one engraving after a painting purchased each year, and the opportunity to win an original oil painting at a gala affair held annually in December—at which time all the artwork acquired that year was distributed by lottery. Because of the quantity of work it purchased, and the number and geographical range of its membership, the Art-Union's impact was enormous, both in terms of patronage and as a distributor of artworks to the middle class. In 1849, at the peak of its membership, it had 18,960 subscribers nationwide and distributed 1,010 works.

To reinforce its democratic agenda, the Art-Union had a luxurious art gallery furnished with plush ottomans and gaslights at 497 Broadway. Open year-round, it was free to the public and had evening hours so that working people could attend. One newspaper reported that the gallery drew from "every section of the social system . . . from the millionaire of 5th Avenue, to the B'hoy of 3d."[37]

Given the nationalistic goals of the organization, it was not surprising that eight of the twenty-seven paintings Ranney exhibited there were history or historical genre pictures. In response to the Mexican War from 1846 to 1848, an intense period of patriotism and interest in America's past, Ranney created a number of oils casting generalized historical events within a genre mode, such as *First News of the Battle of Lexington* of 1847 (cat no. 31), a subject which resonated with current events in the West. Reflecting the era's obsession with and deification of George Washington, Ranney also depicted at about this same time the hero of the Revolutionary War leading his men into battle on horseback, a style associated with the grand manner of history painting (cat. no. 36). Of all his historical scenes, this is perhaps Ranney's most problematic compositionally and technically: the heroic model seemed alien to his down-to-earth sensibilities, and he never again attempted such a grandiose statement.

The American Art-Union selected three of Ranney's works to be engraved: *Boone's First View of Kentucky, On the Wing,* and *Marion Crossing the Pedee* (see cat. nos. 45, 55, and 61). In addition, the Cincinnati Art-Union engraved the *Trapper's Last Shot* (cat. no. 51). Gift books published during this period also helped disseminate Ranney's work: *Boone's First View of Kentucky* and *On the Wing* were both reproduced in the Appleton's 1855 publication *Ornaments of Memory.* After Ranney's death in 1857, Currier and Ives issued their own versions of Ranney's *Marion Crossing the Pedee* and the *Trapper's Last Shot.* Given this vast distribution of the engravings, it is not surprising that Ranney's works were often copied. Distinguishing copies from what may be his own replicas still remains a challenge. While some scholars have speculated that Ranney may have had studio assistants to help him produce copies, no evidence of such a practice has ever been discovered.

The survival of the American Art-Union papers at the New-York Historical Society provides a unique opportunity to learn just how much Ranney charged for his work. In 1846, for instance, he was paid $75 for *Shad Fishing on the Hudson* (cat. no. 26) and $300 (equivalent to about $6,000 in 2005) for his larger, framed canvas, *First News of the Battle of Lexington* (cat. no. 31). By comparison, that same year George Caleb Bingham received $290 for his slightly smaller picture, *Jolly Flat Boatman* (Manoogian Collection). For his unframed masterpiece *Marion Crossing the Pedee* of 1850 (cat. no. 61), Ranney received $700 (paid over time in $100 installments), an equivalent of about $15,500 in 2005 dollars. In most cases, the Art-Union purchased works from Ranney directly, and in a few instances it bought his pictures from the National Academy's annual exhibitions (see, for example, *The Dead Courser or Charger* [cat. no. 22] and *On the Wing* [cat. no. 55]).

In 1852, a coordinated effort by powerful antigambling forces culminated in a New York State Court ruling that the Art-Union's distributions violated state laws prohibiting lotteries. The business, barely a decade old, was forced to cease all operations and dispose of its 1851 inventory at auction the following year (see cat. nos. 61 and 71). During its short life, this organization had achieved enormous success in heightening public appreciation of art and had played, as well, a

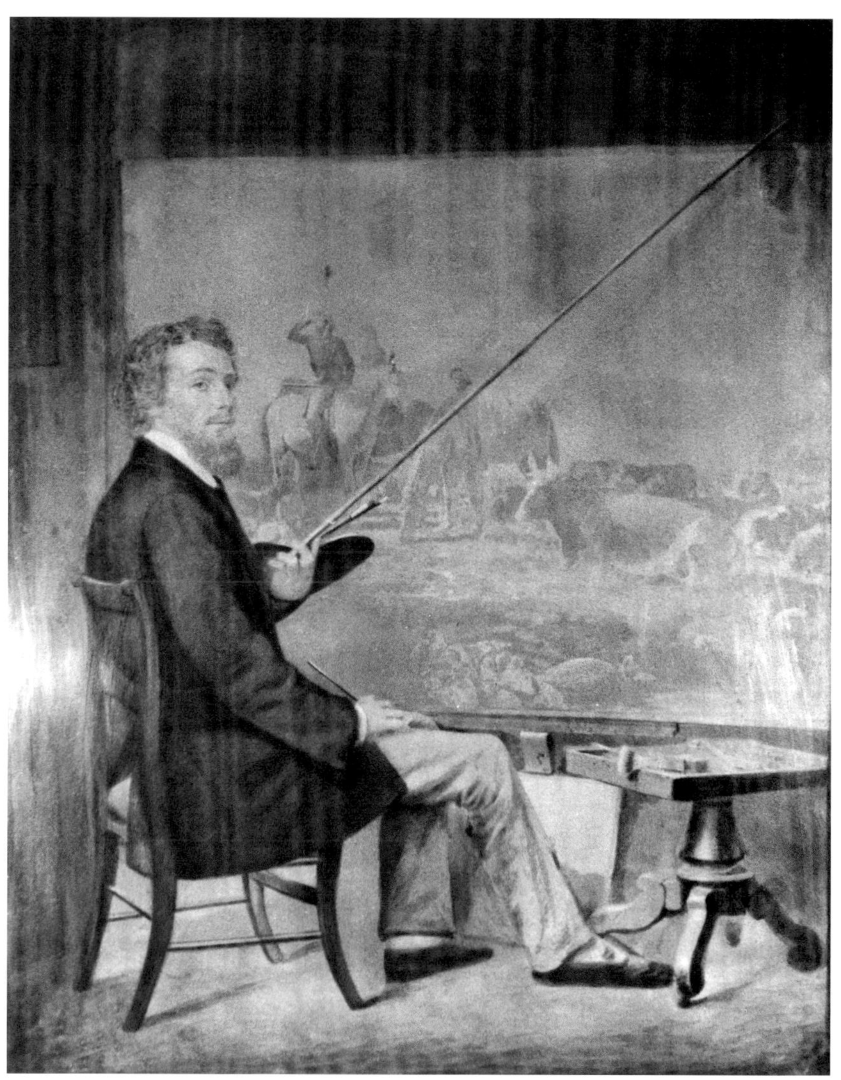

Portrait of William Ranney Painting "Halt on the Plains," attributed to Mathew B. Brady (1823–1896), c. 1856–1857. Salted paper print. *Private collection.*

major role in contributing to the emergence of New York as a significant art center—part of its legacy was stimulating a robust art market of galleries and auction houses.

For Ranney, now at the peak of his career, the loss of this important outlet had to have been a major financial setback, as it surely was for many artists. Almost immediately, however, other galleries, which had emerged in the 1840s, began to fill the vacuum left by the Art-Union. Former artist supply stores had transformed themselves into quasi-galleries to meet the growing demand for art. Two were particularly important for Ranney. By 1851, Williams, Stevens and Williams, located at 343 and 353 Broadway, a block from the Art-Union, advertised itself as a free gallery of fine art and as an art supply store. In 1852 and 1853, this firm held large auctions of paintings which included Ranney's works (cat. nos. 75, 79, 91, 92, and 93). Another artist supply store owner, Samuel N. Dodge, at 189 Chatham Street, may have been collecting Ranney's work or acting as his agent. He is listed as the owner of two paintings at the National Academy's 1855 exhibition (cat. nos. 98 and 108). Dodge also seems to have handled the work of William Sidney Mount. In May of 1858 it was Dodge, who, six months after Ranney's death, tried, apparently unsuccessfully, to sell the remaining works in his studio to help his widow and children.[38]

When Ranney died at the age of forty-four, according to the *New York Times* obituary, he had been "for several years previous to his death . . . gradually succumbing to an incurable malady—consumption."[39] Known today as tuberculosis, this debilitating lung disease was widespread in the nineteenth century. The painting now identified as the lost *Victim* (cat no. 134) is an unusually horrific image, and graphically and metaphorically may represent the intense suffering Ranney endured toward the end of his life. During those final years Ranney presumably was less mobile, because he painted proportionally more landscapes and cattle scenes, themes readily at hand and close to home. His last major picture, however, was a western scene, *Halt on the Plains* (cat. no. 138), a monumental vista, with cattle, horses, mountain guides, and wagon trains. It is a poignant summation of many of the themes he introduced to the American public during his lifetime. A rare,

xxi

now faded image attributed to the well-known mid-nineteenth century photographer Mathew B. Brady, a specialist in professional portraiture, documents Ranney at his easel working on this picture (see p. xxi).

The *New York Herald* obituary described Ranney as "simple minded, honest, and generous to a fault, [who] cared less about his personal advancement than about the esteem and approbation of his friends."[40] The *Crayon* wrote that everyone who knew him recognized "his kindness and gentleness, and [that he possessed] qualities which go to form the true artist everywhere."[41] In May of 1858, an unidentified artist, who years earlier had asked Ranney to critique his work, was moved to write a personal tribute for the *Crayon*. In the piece, he fondly recalled that Ranney "mentioned to me all he knew of the beauties of nature, and the means of rendering them in Art. This was at a time before he had become known to fame, and when he himself stood more in need of an instructor than he was capable of giving instruction."[42] The artist and journalist, Charles Lanman, in an 1847 letter to William Sidney Mount, mentioned meeting Ranney at the National Academy, noting that he admired him "as a man and as an artist. In his manners he is something like you, decidedly original, wearing a sort of I-don't care-what people-think sort of a look."[43]

Though the only fellow-artist who seems to have attended Ranney's funeral at Saint Mary's Catholic Church in Hoboken was Charles Loring Elliott, within a year of his death, a group of friends organized a public sale of the work remaining in Ranney's studio to create a fund to support his family. The project was spearheaded by the painter William Hart, Arthur Fitzwilliam Tait, Ranney's artist-friend and probably also a hunting companion, and the young merchant Nason Collins, who apparently donated much of his time and money to the project.[44] In addition to over one hundred Ranney works, the sale included another hundred paintings contributed by a veritable who's who of the most significant American artists of the period: Frederic Edwin Church, Jervis F. McEntee, David Johnson, Junius Brutus Stearns, James A. Suydam, John S. Casilear, Asher B. Durand, Jasper F. Cropsey, Sanford R. Gifford, Charles F. Blauvelt, Regis Gignoux, James Bogle, and Charles Loring Elliott.

On December 9, 1858, in advance of the sale, the Ranney family friend and prominent lawyer James Topham Brady, who was active in the cultural life of the city, delivered a public lecture on art at Clinton Hall to help raise additional funds.[45] The sale itself took place on December 20 and 21, 1858, at the National Academy of Design, which lent their galleries for the occasion. It was conducted by the auction house of Henry H. Leeds, who declined to take a commission (see Ranney Fund sale).

Both the lecture and the sale were enormously successful, raising, after expenses, over $7,137. To oversee the investments and distribute the interest semiannually to Ranney's widow, the National Academy formed a committee made up of its president, the landscape painter Asher B. Durand, its vice-president, successful banker, and genre painter Francis W. Edmonds, and its treasurer, portrait and miniature painter Thomas S. Cummings.[46]

The sale excited the interest of several important collectors. The most significant for Ranney was someone by the name of Wood, who was probably David A. Wood, a prominent New York carriage maker and patron of William Sidney Mount. He purchased sixteen Ranney works. Dodge is also listed as a buyer, as is one Pepoon, perhaps Marshall who is listed in the city directories as a broker. Someone by the name of Riggs, possibly the prominent Baltimore banker George Washington Riggs, also bought several small pieces, as did the book and art collector William Menzies. The most important known collectors of Ranney's work during his lifetime were Marshall O. Roberts, a wealthy businessman and collector involved in shipping (cat. nos. 19, 70, 111, and 140) and the New York shipbuilder William Henry Webb, (cat. nos. 61 and 75) who, in addition to American works, collected paintings by European masters, with particularly emphasis on the Düsseldorf and Munich schools.

While in the minds of many viewers Ranney is associated primarily with American western painting, those pictures represent less than thirty of the one hundred and fifty oils catalogued in this publication. In modern times, the general public's familiarity with these pictures is partially based on the fact that they were disproportionately preserved, either in museums or private collections, and have been so often reproduced, particularly in the literature on the West. Since Grubar's landmark exhibition at the Corcoran in 1962, however, Ranney's other subjects—genre, animal, history, and sporting pictures—have begun to be better understood, appreciated, and collected. The Brandywine River Museum in Chadds Ford, Pennsylvania, addressed this problem in its important 1991 exhibition *William Ranney: East of the Mississippi,* in which Mark Thistlethwaite effectively broadened the interpretative scope of Ranney's pictures.

To this student of American art, the unfolding of Ranney's life and the discovery of the breadth and integrity of his work have been revelatory. For a self-taught artist who never went abroad to study, Ranney achieved considerable success, both critically and financially. Innately talented and ambitious, he was independent by nature and seems to have been constantly striving for new expressions. In unusually large canvases, he tackled an impressive array of themes, often infused with rich anecdotal details—history, landscape, marines, genre, animal, and sporting scenes as well as western scenes and historical genre subjects. There are few other American artists of his generation whose body of work demonstrates such breadth, quality, and complex figurative compositions. Some critics, who generally admired the tight brushwork of artists of the Düsseldorf school, occasionally complained of his more fluid drawing technique or use of bright colors. But Ranney, ignoring such criticism, continued to apply paint in broken colors, and, in many of his tightly composed works, was able to achieve with that technique rich, tonal atmospheric effects. His intelligence is frequently manifested by allusions to the era's historical, cultural, and social concerns, which he so compellingly imbedded in his narrative scenes. His paintings are for the most part quiet, thoughtful, non-hierarchical images, expressions of the gentle nature, the generosity of spirit, and egalitarianism of the man so admired by his fellow artists.

1. G. H. "Death of William Ranney—1857," undated typescript, Ranney archives.

2. *New York Herald,* December 3, 1858, p. 5.

3. *Frank Leslie's Illustrated Newspaper,* vol. 4 (November 28, 1857), p. 407.

4. *Home Journal,* December 5, 1857, p. 3.

5 Nathan Crosby, *Annual Obituary Notices of Eminent Persons Who Have Died in the United States. For 1857 [–1858],* vol. 1 (Boston: J. P. Jewett and Company, 1858–1859), p. 291.

6. Ayres, "William Ranney," in *American Frontier Life* (New York: Abbeville Press, 1987), pp. 78–107.

7. Charles Collard Adams, *Middletown Upper Houses* (1908; reprint, Canaan, New Hampshire: Phoenix Publishing, 1983), p. 230.

8. Ibid., p. 191.

9. Grubar, pp. 17–19, n. 4, provides extensive records of Captain Ranney's maritime career based on documents in the collection of Mystic Seaport, Mystic, Connecticut.

10. In Margaret Ranney's questionnaire, for *Appletons' Cyclopedia of American Biography,* c. 1883, Artist's file, Art and Architecture Division, New York Public Library.

11. The average slaveholder family in Cumberland County apparently owned two families of slaves during this period. See Roy Parker, Jr., *Cumberland County: A Brief History* (Raleigh: North Carolina Division of Archives and History, 1990), p. 40.

12. For a brief biography of Starr, see John A. Oates, *The Story of Fayetteville and the Upper Cape Fear* (1950: reprint, Raleigh: Fayetteville Woman's Club, 1981), p. 860.

13. *Fayetteville Carolina Observer,* December 2, 1830, p. 4.

14. Clipping, *Fayetteville Observer,* May 31, 1837, Ranney archives.

15. A second William Nott, or perhaps the same man with a second business, had a partnership with Joseph Sumner. An advertisement in the *Fayetteville Carolina Observer* (November 26, 1829), p. 1, indicated they were manufacturers of tinware and sheet iron.

16. Margaret Ranney, questionnaire.

17. Ranney's name was not listed in any of the Brooklyn city directories.

18. Brooklyn Artists Index, lists him at 159 Jay Street from 1835–36, Libraries and Archives, Brooklyn Museum of Art.

19. Ayres, "William Ranney," p. 102–103, n. 2, notes that there was a James Tylee, "a native of New York City who moved to Texas in 1834 to join Stephen Austin's colony [and] died at the Alamo in 1836." Ayres speculated that given Ranney's middle name of Tylee whether the two men might have been distantly related, and that connection "inspired Ranney to join the Texas Army." A connection between the two men has yet to be discovered.

20. Margaret Ranney, questionnaire.

21. G. H., "Death of William Ranney."

22. Grubar, p. 19, transcribes Ranney's military service records located in the Texas State Archives, Austin. Ayres, "William Ranney," p. 103, n. 3, discusses the discrepancies in the interpretation of Ranney's military service, finding no documentation that he returned to Texas in the 1840s, as some scholars suggested. Ayres reported difficulty in confirming whether Ranney, as some writers have asserted, received Texas land grants. She was able to locate documentation indicating that in 1847, Ranney received a bounty land grant of 120 acres in Bosque County for his 1836 service. Other land transactions may have been for different people whose name was similar to Ranney's, but with variant spellings.

23. Margaret Ranney, questionnaire.

24. David B. Dearinger, ed., *Rave Reviews: American Art and Its Critics, 1826–1925* (New York: National Academy of Design, 2000), p. 276.

25. *Fayetteville Observer,* January 2, 1839, p. 4.

26. See William H. Gerdts, *Art Across America: The South and the Midwest. Two Centuries of Regional Painting, 1710–1920* (New York: Abbeville Press, 1990), p. 61, provides an overview of painting in the South.

27. For a discussion of Crawley, see ibid., p. 35, and James H. Craig, *The Arts and Crafts In North Carolina, 1699–1840* (Winston-Salem: Museum of Early Decorative Arts, 1965), p. 10.

28. *Fayetteville Observer,* January 15, 1840, p. 3, and January 22, 1840, p. 1.

29. For William Nott obituaries, see *Fayetteville Observer,* November 25, 1840, p. 3, and *Raleigh Register and North-Carolina Gazette,* November 27, 1840, p. 3. For notice of dissolution of the business, signed by John D. Starr, see *Fayetteville Observer,* December 16, 1840, p. 3.

30. *Crayon,* vol. 5 (January 1858), p. 24, quoted in Annette Blaugrund, *The Tenth Street Studio Building: Artist-Entrepreneurs from the Hudson River School to the American Impressionists* (Southampton, New York: Parrish Art Museum, 1997), p. 11.

31. *Morris's National Press,* February 28, 1846, p. 2.

32. Ibid.

33. Grubar, p. 10, and Henry T. Tuckerman, *Book of the Artists* (1867; reprint, New York: James F. Carr, 1966), p. 431.

34. For a thorough discussion of the sporting literature of the times and the precursors of the conservation movement in the United State, see John F. Reiger, *American Sportsmen and the Origins of Conservation* (3rd rev. ed.; Corvallis, Oregon: Oregon State University Press, 2001), pp. 10–44.

35. George B. Kirsch, *The Creation of American Team Sports: Baseball and Cricket, 1838–72* (Urbana: University of Illinois Press, 1989), pp. 21–22.

36. Charles A. Peverelly, *The Book of American Pastimes Containing a History of the Principal Base Ball, Cricket, Rowing and Yachting Clubs of the United States* (New York: The author, 1866), p. 530.

37. Quoted in Edwin G. Burrows and Mike Wallace, *Gotham: A History of New York City to 1898* (New York: Oxford University Press, 1999), p. 687.

38. *Crayon*, vol. 5 (May, 1858), p. 148.

39. *New York Times*, November 24, 1857, p. 4.

40. *New York Herald*, November 24, 1857.

41. *Crayon*, vol. 5 (January 1858), p. 26.

42. Ibid. (May 1858), p. 148.

43. Quoted in Alfred Frankenstein, *William Sidney Mount* (New York: Harry N. Abrams, 1995), p. 117.

44. Thomas S Cummings, *Historic Annals of the National Academy of Design* (Philadelphia: George W. Childs, 1865), p. 265.

45. Transcript, *New York Times*, December 10, 1858, p. 1.

46. *New York Times*, January 20, 1859, p. 5.

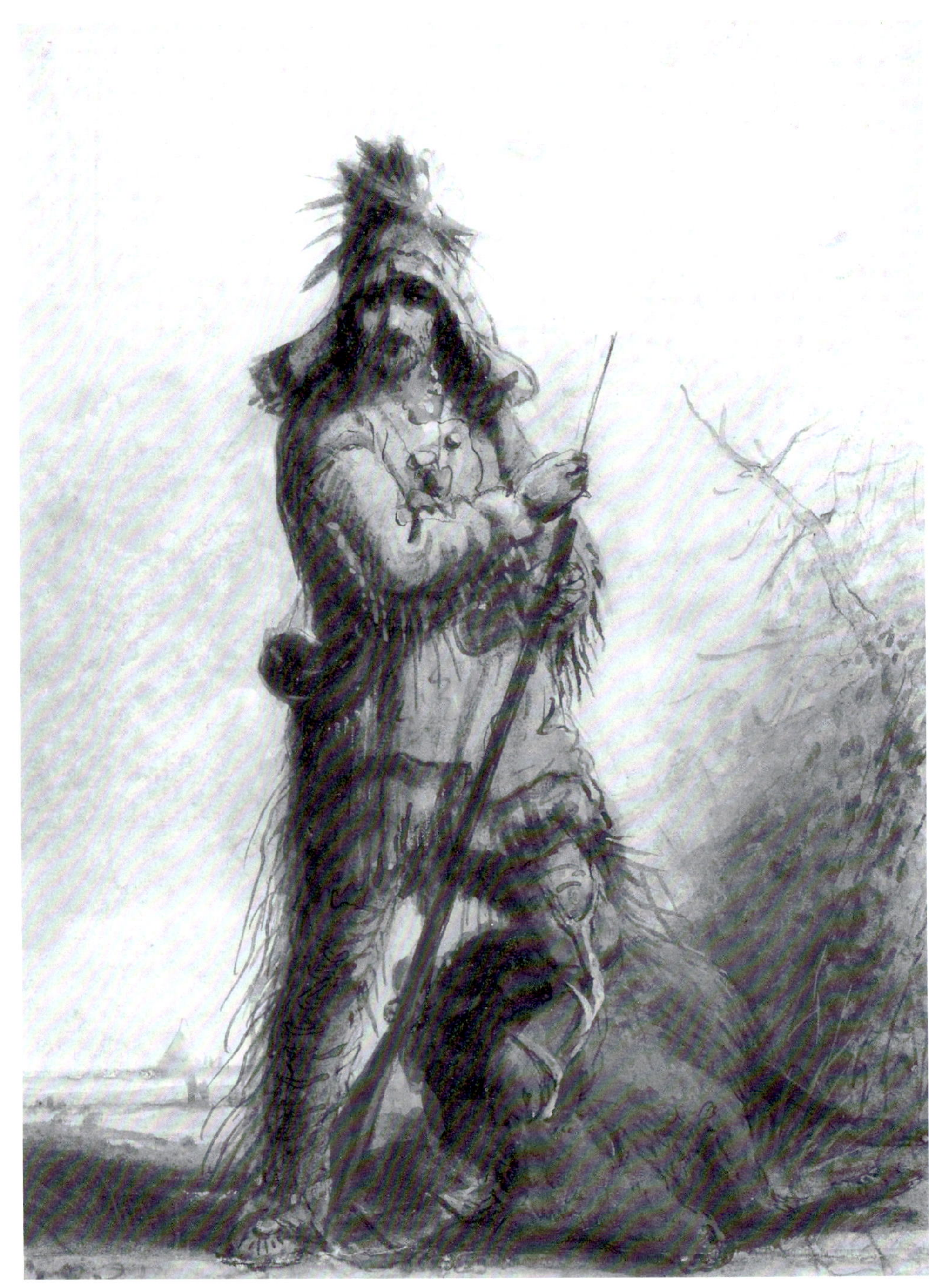

Louis—Rocky Mountain Trapper by Alfred Jacob Miller (1810–1874). Watercolor on paper. *Buffalo Bill Historical Center, Cody, Wyoming, Gift of the Coe Foundation.*

WILLIAM RANNEY AND THE CREATION OF THE FRONTIER IDEAL

BY SARAH E. BOEHME

William Ranney had only one significant experience in the West during his lifetime, and his paintings of western subjects are only one component of his artistic career. Yet Ranney's own identity as an artist is inexorably linked with his western subjects, and some of his strongest portrayals of American identity emerge from his painted western narratives.[1] In these paintings he chose to depict the western types who signified American characteristics such as independence and fortitude. He made his most comprehensive statement in *Advice on the Prairie,* 1853 (cat. no. 81), in which he portrayed the ideals of the frontier narrative. He celebrated first individuality and then community, and thus portrayed the concept of the frontier as a story of American progress. In this view, not only was the frontier moving further west, but waves of people were changing the land from wilderness to settled country.

Ranney's sojourn in the West resulted not from his joining an exploring expedition, as other nineteenth-century artists did, but rather from his enlisting in the military during the Texas Revolution in 1836. Not quite twenty-three years old when he set out for Texas, he had begun to study painting and drawing a few years earlier, but his reason for this trip does not seem to have been an artistic one. His personal motives for joining the Texas Army are not definitively known. He may have been bolstered by youthful idealism, a desire to prove his mettle or a search for adventure. Newspaper accounts of the conflicts between Anglo-American colonists and the governing nation of Mexico with overtones of rebellion against oppression may have precipitated his involvement. Ranney signed up in 1836 and remained in Texas for several months, according to an account written later by his widow.[2] She reported that he made sketches, which were sources for future paintings, and described his experience idyllically, "He was so charmed with everything he saw; scenes that he long dreamt of were now before his eyes; the wild enchanting prairies, the splendid horses, nature in all her splendor;"[3] Although this trip could be seen as a seminal experience, the paucity of drawings that can be associated with Texas and the long period before the experience bore fruit suggest that, while Ranney may have later invoked memories, he also drew upon a variety of other artistic resources to create his works.

Ranney was back in New York by about 1837. Almost ten years passed before he mined his Texas experience in his paintings. In the meantime, he produced history paintings of the American Revolution, but he never directly depicted scenes of the Texas Revolution, with which he had had firsthand experience. Instead his first western subjects, *Hunting Wild Horses* (cat. no. 19) and *The Lasso* (cat. no. 18.), convey the romance of the region in depictions of the individual's struggle to tame the wilderness. The ideology, however, of these paintings, as Peter Hassrick convincingly argues, connects the paintings' overt subjects with the themes of the Texas war for independence. It was in hindsight that Ranney resurrected his memories of the plains and gave them pictorial life, perhaps spurred by the news of Texas's joining the Union in 1845 and then the subsequent war with Mexico. Ranney's time in Texas provided him with one authentic touchstone to the West. This gave him experience and authenticity that separated him from other eastern painters, who portrayed the West but had never seen the region firsthand, such as Felix O.C. Darley or Arthur Fitzwilliam Tait.

Ranney showed his authority on the West in another way, by creating an environment that established an aura of the frontier and firmly placed him in its midst. He filled his studio in West Hoboken, New Jersey, with objects that created a western atmosphere. The critic Henry T. Tuckerman, in his *Book of the Artists*, initiated his discussion of Ranney with a description of the artist's studio, with its "guns, pistols, and cutlasses hung on the walls; and these, with curious saddles and primitive riding gear, which lead a visitor to imagine he had entered a pioneer's cabin or a border chieftain's hut"[4] Tuckerman went on, however, to emphasize that it was noticeably an artist's studio because of the many sketches and studies that were also part of this rugged environment. While conceding that it was the home of an artist, not a "bushranger," he nevertheless pointed out that the objects displayed were characteristic of the occupant's experience and taste. These artifacts served to link Ranney to his western experiences. Tuckerman referred to the artist's service in the army and noted that even though Ranney delayed several years before drawing upon his western experiences, he "had grown familiar with the wilderness, studied the aspects of hunter and aboriginal life, realized the thrill and throe of the explorer's achievements, and came back to the heart of civilization, prepared with subjects and material to make that condition of humanity strongly contrast with primitive life and adventure."[5] Ranney's studio created the idea that the artist had firsthand knowledge of the frontier, providing an aura to impress critics and patrons.

During the last decade of his life, Ranney developed western subjects along with history paintings, genre and sporting scenes—all of which were significant in his work. After his portrayal in *Hunting Wild Horses* of the individual frontiersman struggling with the wildness of nature, Ranney began to depict pioneer families confronting danger in works such at *Stampede* of 1848 (cat. no. 40). These two subjects, the frontiersman and the pioneer, became his primary western types. He returned often to the subject of the frontiersman, especially in scenes of danger. In paintings such as *The Last Shot* of 1850 (cat. no. 52), he portrayed a lone trapper as a monumental figure and a potential martyr making a last stand, a theme reverberating from the Texas war. Ranney's Texas experience could have introduced him to hunters and to adventurers, who joined the Texas army as volunteers. The frontiersmen in Ranney's paintings have a demeanor and wear a style of clothing that link them to the prototype of the mountain man, although it is likely that Ranney himself did not have direct contact with the fur trade. He could have seen the works of Alfred Jacob Miller, who did have direct experience with the fur trade era. Miller had traveled to the Wind River Rendezvous of 1837 as an artist for Scottish adventurer Captain William Drummond Stewart and exhibited his paintings in New York in 1839.[6] Miller's dashing, romantic mountain men with their exotic clothing provided a template.

With his interest in the era, Ranney collected clothing and other items for his paintings, giving a sense of authenticity even to his most dramatic and potentially histrionic works like *The Last Shot*. Such paintings as these influenced other artists' works as well, for example, Tait's *Prairie Hunter— One Rubbed Out!* (Joslyn Art Museum, Omaha). Ranney's collection of trappings also is likely to have impressed other artists. Tait had himself photographed in frontier gear, as a way of creating convincing figure studies for his paintings.[7] He may have borrowed the clothing and objects from his friend Ranney for this purpose (see illustration below left).

Ranney's pioneer figures and his interest in portraying settlers moving west may originally have also been inspired by his Texas adventure. Ranney was exposed in the military environment to independent-minded male figures as well as the prevailing ideology of the Texas war, which was developed from the interests of the Anglo-American colonists who had emigrated from the States into Texas.[8] These settlers brought there eastern American culture, which conflicted with both the wilderness and the culture of Mexico. As Ranney painted in the late 1840s and 1850s, newspaper accounts and published stories from the travelers on the Oregon Trail renewed interest in the subject of western immigration. In such works as *Prairie Burial* (cat. nos. 38 and 39) Ranney depicted scenes in which pioneers or settlers faced danger and hardship. His outlook remained positive in the majority of these scenes; for example in *The Pioneers* (cat. no. 68), the family group crosses the plains in a placid environment, their faces fully expressing optimism.

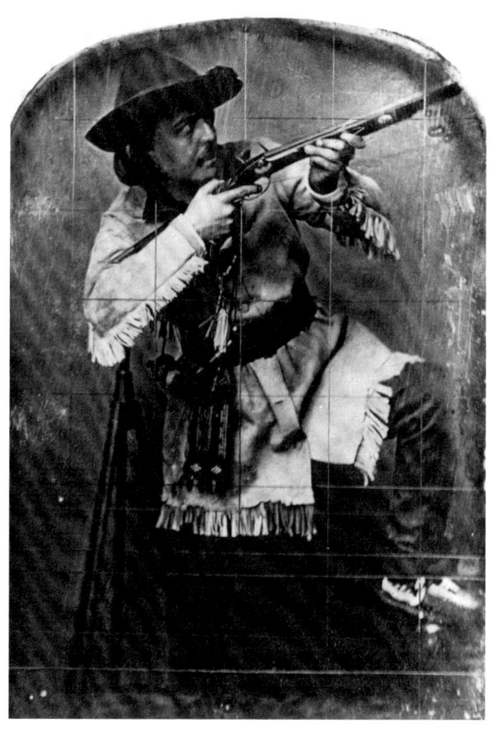

Photograph of Arthur Fitzwilliam Tait (1814–1872) in frontier clothes. *Adirondack Mountain Museum, Blue Mountain Lake, New York.*

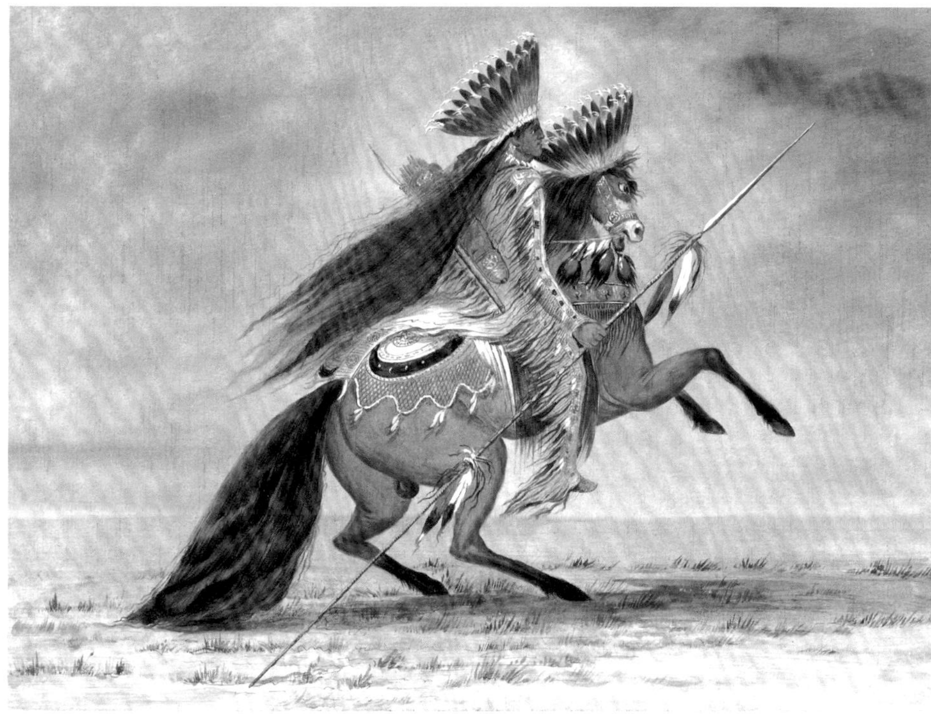

Crow Chief by George Catlin (1796–1872). Oil on paper mounted on board. *Buffalo Bill Historical Center, Cody, Wyoming; Bequest of Joseph M. Roebling.*

In *Advice on the Prairie*, Ranney united the two types, the mountain man and the pioneer, in this frontier theory. He portrays the passing of one era leading to the next and depicts (or, in one instance, suggests) the different types of people who interact, successively in this formulation, with the land.[9] In Ranney's West, the Indian is no longer much of a presence; his day has passed. In contrast to other western artists of the early nineteenth century, Ranney portrayed Indians hardly at all. He lacked the extensive experience with Indian subjects of an artist such as George Catlin, who traveled in the West in the 1830s and devoted his career to recording the appearance and customs of various Indians and tribes (see illustration p. xxix). Catlin was motivated by his belief in "the rapid decline and certain extinction of the numerous tribes of the North American Indians."[10] His primary intention was descriptive, the noting of how persons and objects appeared. He journeyed in the West to record and document, so he often focused on very specific elements. Portraying Indian dances, he repeated the same basic composition and differentiated the dances by detailing specific items of clothing. He did, however, also produce scenes of action and drama, whose compositions possibly influenced Ranney. The impulse to portray native inhabitants of the North American Continent, spurred by a belief that they were disappearing, continued to inspire artists such as John Mix Stanley. Stanley created an Indian gallery of portraits that in size and scope rivaled Catlin's.[11] His *Last of Their Race* of 1857 (see p. xxxi) shares a monumentality with Ranney's *Advice on the Prairie*, but Stanley tells the story of the Indian peoples, pushed to the edge of the continent, with the sun setting in the distance. Whereas in Ranney's view a mother and child hold a prominent place and signal the bright promise of future generations, the mother and child in Stanley's work carry the pathos of finality. Although, of course, Indians did not disappear. In *Advice on the Prairie*, the influence of the Indian is evident in the typical items of the Indian clothing worn by the frontiersman. Ranney depicted the solitary individual, the mountain man, who has taken the dress of the "savage" with his moccasins and fringed buckskins. His clothing attests to his experience; he has encountered Indians. He sits on his saddle with his gear nearby. He is not the mounted leader of equestrian portraiture, but he retains a semblance of that powerful pose. The frontiersman has his musket leaning against his body, close at hand should need arise. He addresses the immigrants with a dramatic gesture, reaching with outstretched arm and open palm, with a sign that almost appears as a blessing. The pioneers in *Advice on the Prairie* are formulated first as a family, with the depiction of the mother and child (with the often-noted comparison to the Madonna and Child), father, older children and extended family of grandfather or uncle. The family circle is flanked by a figure indicating the groups beyond the family. A man, with hat still on his head, stands just outside the circle, and then in the distance appear additional figures. Two covered wagons with several horses bring this community onto the western prairies. *Advice on the Prairie* indicates the contribution that Ranney made to the genre of American western art, for he combined a fascination with the romance of the West with a celebration of its prospects. Ranney created narrative scenes of the West, narratives that not only told stories about life on the prairies, but gave the region significance in the national mythology.

Seth Eastman's 1852 painting *Indian Council* (see p. xxxiii) shares with Ranney's *Advice on the Prairie* the subject of a community listening to wise words from a speaker. Like Ranney, Eastman's

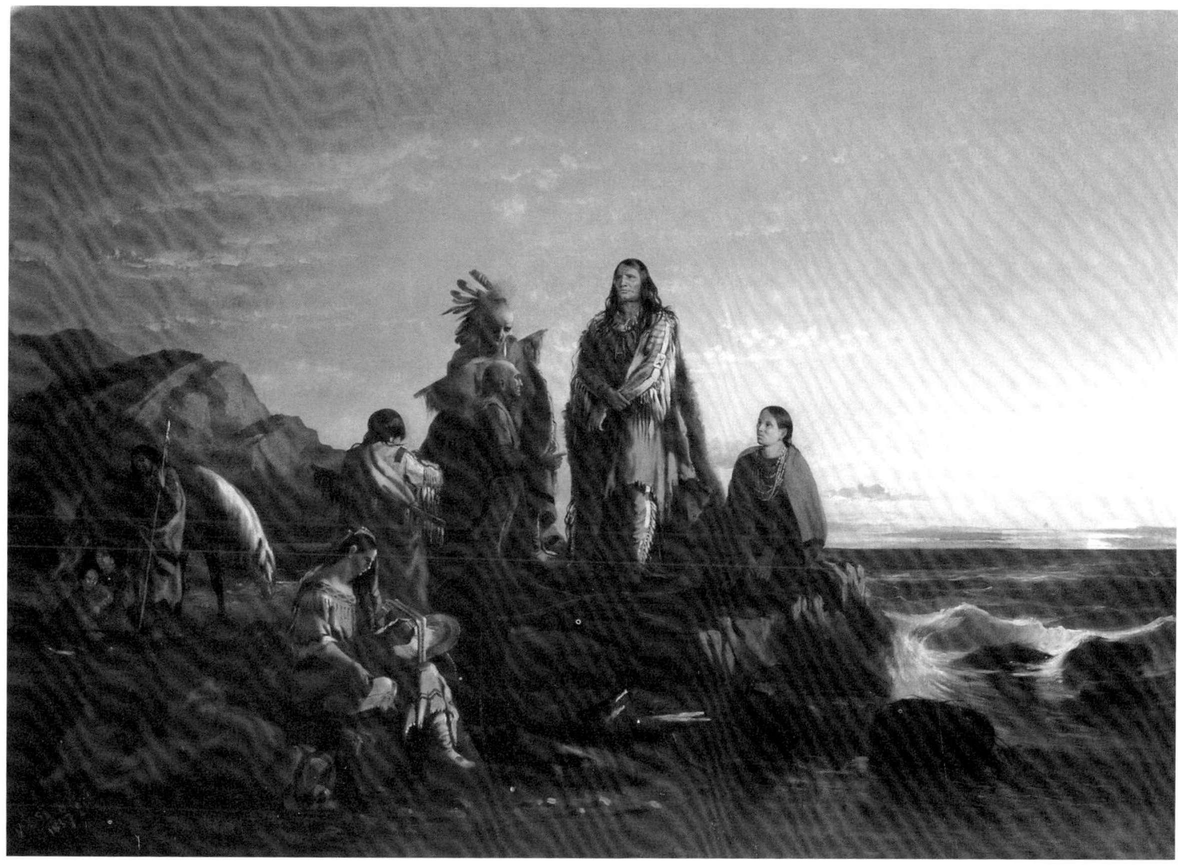

personal experience on the frontier resulted from his enlistment in the military. As an officer in the
United States Army, Eastman was stationed at Fort Snelling in the Minnesota Territory from 1841
to 1848, where he had the opportunity to study the Dakota and Chippewa who lived nearby. He
was perceived by contemporary commentators as a documenter of Indian life, whose knowledge
could be trusted because of his position. Yet, his pictures told stories that often had lessons attached,
lessons that were made explicit by texts written by his wife, the author Mary Henderson Eastman.
She collected oral Indian stories, wrote them down and published them often in gift books that were
illustrated with engravings after her husband's paintings. For his painting of the *Indian Council*,
Mary Eastman provided her own explanation for this depiction of another culture, "The orator,
with his gorgeous head ornament of eagle's feathers, and his robe gathered loosely about him, is
not afraid of interruption while he is delivering to them his sentiments. . . . For we must remem-
ber the Indians are genuine democrats, and would one of them be a leader, he must be guided by
the people."[12] Mary Eastman's commentary emphasizes a democracy of individuals who are united in community and whose leader, although standing in a commanding pose of power, is nevertheless dependent on the consensus of those around him. In Ranney's *Advice on the Prairie*, the
frontiersman maintains the seat of power. As the individual with experience and knowledge of the
frontier, he holds sway over the community. Although the community may eventually settle the
prairies, the independent adventurer is still the leader.

xxxi

In the body of his western scenes, Ranney chose to base his work on experiences that originated from his personal history and his own culture, rather than examining the exotic "other" of Indian culture. He embraced the thrill of excitement and danger on the frontier, and in that element, he shared concerns with artists such as Charles Deas. Ranney's narratives about the settlement of the West, however, indicate his larger concerns with the national story. In his view, not all was golden. *Advice on Prairie* occurs under a darkening sky, and his Prairie *Burial* reminds the viewer that death is present. Yet these elements serve as cautions that temper, but do not quash, the steady and persistent allegiance to and the identification with the West as the ideal of both the past and the future. Within this setting, Ranney's western paintings emerge as history paintings, telling of great deeds, but also depicting the contributions of the common people, rather than those of named heroes such as Generals George Washington or Francis Marion. By focusing on the unnamed figures of history, Ranney's western paintings assert the importance of the average person in nation building. Yet, while the family with its implied domesticity and its structure within a larger community is important, Ranney still maintains identification with the romantic, individualistic frontiersman. He returned often to the subject of the men who traveled in the West seeking fortune and freedom, a type that would in later generations of artists be transformed into the cowboy. Ranney's own hindsight revived his western experience. Today looking back at his narratives we can consider the values implicit in such frontier scenes. His is the aristocracy of adventure, and that may be his most American characteristic.

1. As an example of the identification of Ranney with the West, the first catalogue raisonné of Ranney's work documented the range of subjects he depicted, including portraiture, eastern and southern genre paintings, history paintings, and sporting scenes; yet the subtitle identified Ranney as "Painter of the Early West." Francis S. Grubar, *William Ranney: Painter of the Early West* (Washington, D.C., Corcoran Gallery of Art, 1962).

2. Archival sources documenting Ranney's enlistment are referenced in Linda Ayres, "William Ranney" in *American Frontier Life: Early Western Painting and Prints* (New York: Abbeville Press, Amon Carter Museum, Fort Worth, 1987), 79, 103, and Grubar, *William Ranney*, 6-7, 19.

3. Margaret Ranney, *Appleton's Cyclopaedia of American Biography*, questionnaire, ca. 1883, Artist's file, Art and Architecture Division, New York Public Library.

4. Henry T. Tuckerman, *Book of the Artists* (1867; reprint, New York: James F. Carr, 1967) 431-432.

5. *Ibid.*

6. Ron Tyler, ed., *Alfred Jacob Miller: Artist on the Oregon Trail* (Fort Worth: Amon Carter Museum, 1982).

7. Warder H. Cadbury, "Arthur F. Tait," in *American Frontier Life*, 109-129.

8. Paul D. Lack, *The Texas Revolutionary Experience: A Political and Social History* (College Station: Texas A and M University Press, 1992) and Stephen L. Hardin, *Texan Iliad: A Military History of the Texas Revolution* (Austin: University of Texas Press, 1999).

9. Ranney's painting, in many ways, prefigures elements of Frederick Jackson Turner's frontier thesis delivered in his 1893 address, see Turner, "The Significance of the Frontier in American History," reprinted in *Rereading Frederick Jackson Turner: "The Significance of the Frontier in American History" and Other Essays*, with commentary by John Mack Faragher (New Haven: Yale University Press, 1998).

10. George Catlin, *A Descriptive Catalogue of Catlin's Indian Collection* (London, 1848), p. 2.

11. Julie Schimmel, *John Mix Stanley and Imagery of the West in Nineteenth Century American Art* (Ann Arbor: University Microfilms, 1983).

12. Mary H. Eastman, The *American Aboriginal Portfolio* (Philadelphia: Lippincott, Grambo, 1853), p. 81.

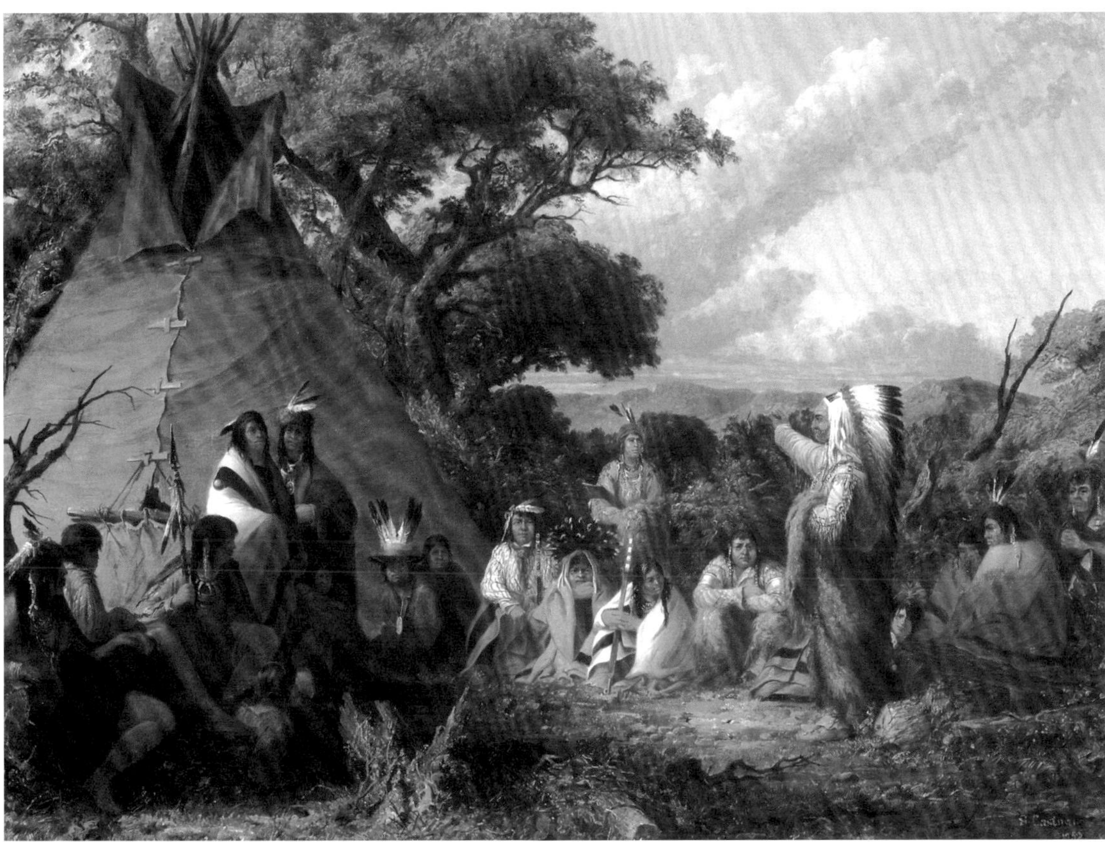

The Indian Council by Seth Eastman (1808–1875). Oil on canvas, 1852. *Gilcrease Museum, Tulsa, Oklahoma.*

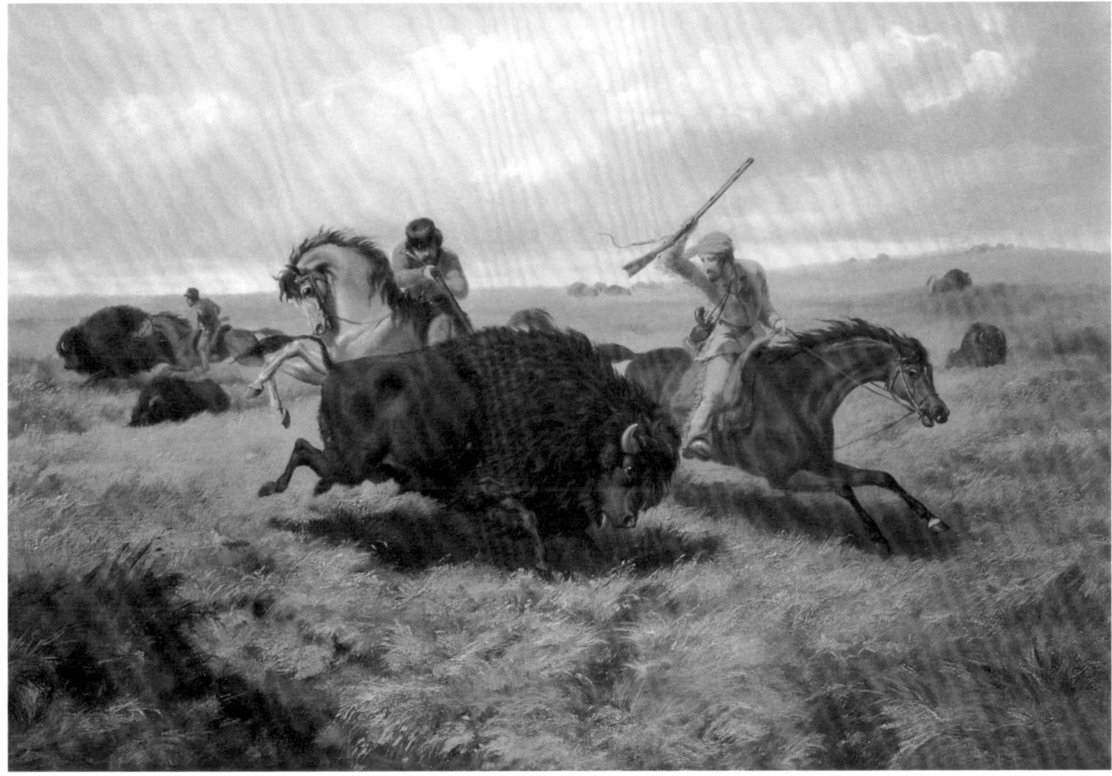

Buffalo Hunt by Arthur Fitzwilliam Tait (1819–1905). Oil on canvas, 1861. *Anonymous collection.*

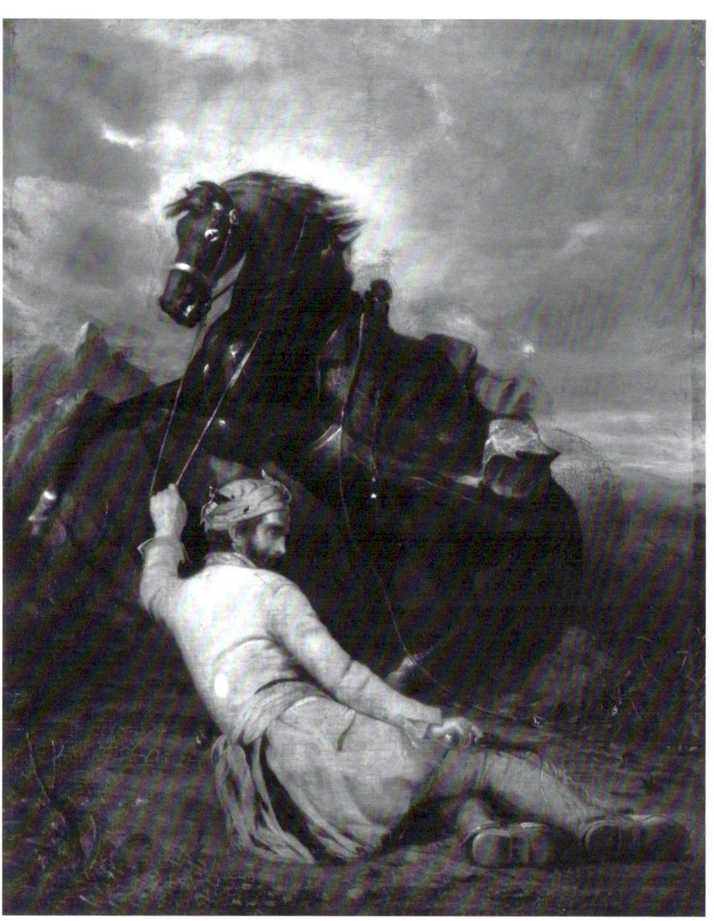

Infrared photograph by Herbert S. Crossan of *The Wounded Trapper,* showing outline of larger horse in lower paint layer.

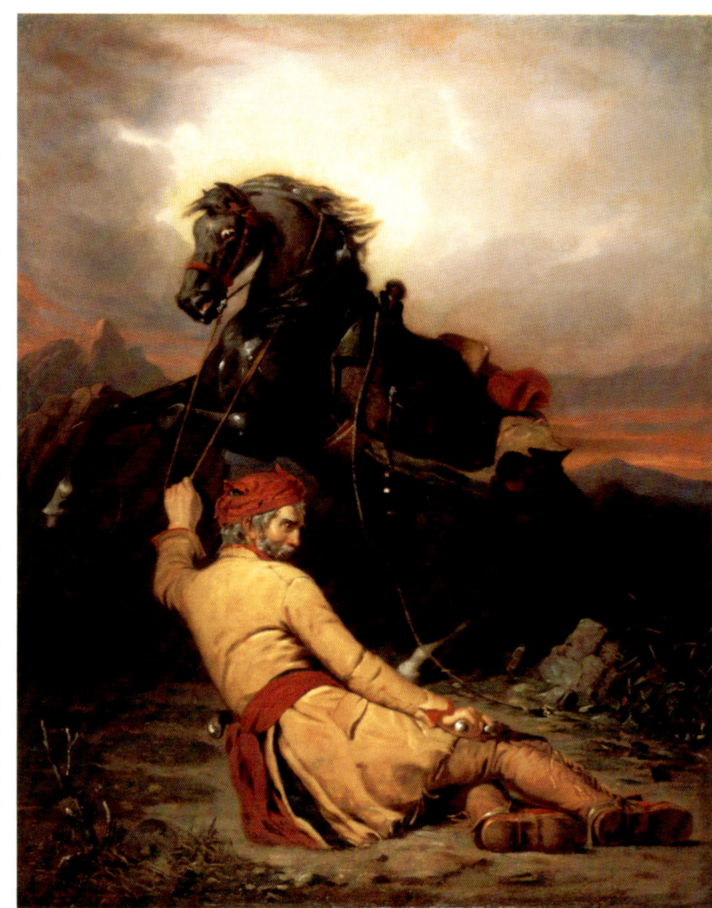

Detail of *The Wounded Trapper* (cat. no. 74).

OBSERVATIONS ON THE PAINTING TECHNIQUES OF WILLIAM RANNEY

BY MARK F. BOCKRATH

The paintings of William Ranney are in many respects typical of American genre paintings of his time, with an emphasis on narrative detail, carefully observed landscape settings, clear colors, and fastidious brushwork. These qualities lend them a kinship to paintings by such contemporaries of Ranney as George Caleb Bingham, Charles Deas, and William Sidney Mount. Furthermore, Ranney's works bear many similarities to those of members of the Hudson River and American luminist schools like Asher B. Durand, Albert Bierstadt, and John Frederick Kensett in the brilliant hues of his sunsets and in the intimately observed details of his foreground foliage and rocks.

It is not surprising, therefore, that the painting materials and techniques employed by Ranney reflect contemporary practice as well. A study of twenty-four paintings by Ranney from all periods of his career shows that he used both finely woven linen plain or "square" weave fabrics and fabrics of twill weave, with its distinctive diagonal pattern. Two self-portraits were examined that were on solid supports. His early *Self Portrait* of 1839 (cat. no. 3) was painted on a three-quarter-inch-thick pine panel, which was coated with a yellow ochre-colored oil ground. The small, late *Self Portrait* of about 1855 (cat. no. 109) is executed on an oval-shaped paperboard primed with a lightly textured off-white oil ground. Ranney preferred off-white or cream-colored oil grounds of commercial preparation for his pictures; these primings can be readily seen on tacking edges.

On the upper corners of *Kit Carson* of 1854 (cat. no. 99), the unpainted cream-colored ground is visible under the curved spandrels of the frame. This painting was clearly composed with a curved frame opening in mind for the upper corners of the picture. This use of curved spandrels to cover the upper corners of a painting was a very popular conceit in the 1850s. Other works by Ranney in this survey that employ spandrels in their designs include *The Stampede* of 1848, *The Duck Shooter's Pony* of 1853, *Halt on the Plains* of 1857, and *Portrait of James Ranney* of about 1855 (cat. nos. 40, 82, 138, and 107). The undated pen-and-ink drawings (D35 and D16) for the paintings *The Retreat* and *On the Wing*, both of 1850 (cat. nos. 60 and 55), are enclosed by the artist with outlines that indicate spandrels in their upper corners, but the oil paintings related to these drawings do not share the spandrel motif.

Ranney painted his works in multiple layers of oil paint that vary in thickness from thin brown washes in foliage to thicker, more fluidly handled paint in highlights. The brown washes of paint are evident in thinly painted passages of many of his paintings and indicate his use of them to block-in his compositions. It is not uncommon to see wide traction cracks in some of his works, suggesting different drying rates for the various paint layers he applied. The quicker drying upper layers have contracted and cracked to expose slower drying underlying layers. Areas where the cracks reveal lower paint layers of markedly different coloration than those in the overlying paint may also suggest areas where he made design changes. Several paintings in this survey show evidence of where he made changes in the composition. Use of an infrared vidicon camera, which penetrates thin layers of paint, revealed a change in the outline of the horse in *The Wounded Trapper* of 1852 (cat. no.74). This was then documented with infrared film. The original position of the horse was higher and the animal was larger. The *pentimento* of the previous position reads as a shadow on the edges of the horse's head and rump when viewed under infrared light (see illustration). In this painting, it is evident that the artist opened up the tacking edges slightly to increase the space between the horse and the edges of the painting, further reducing the animal's dominance of the composition. Similar changes in outlines appear as *pentimenti* in *The First Fish of the Season* of 1849 (cat. no. 44), where Ranney raised the front of the hat brim and the base of the fishing pole from their original positions. In *Sleighing* of about 1847 (cat. no. 34), *pentimenti* showing minor changes in the mane of the black horse, in the outlines of the girl's body at the right, and in the central man's hat are evident. *Pentimenti* also reveal that the artist altered the position of one of the horse's rear legs in *Going to the Mill* of 1855 (cat. no. 105).

On paintings that appeared to retain their original stretchers, the stretchers were all constructed with keyable mortise-and-tenon corner joints, and keyable crossbars on large works. Again this type of construction was very typical of the mid-nineteenth century in the United States.

Firms that sold artists' materials in the nineteenth century often marked their canvases or stretcher bars with stenciled logos. Ranney used such commercially prepared canvases, and the name of the supplier appears on two of the twenty-four paintings in my study. The back of the canvas support for *Portrait of James Ranney* of about 1855 (see cat. no. 107) bears a stencil of the New York colorman's firm S. N. Dodge's Artist & Painter's Supply Store of 189 Chatham Street (see fig. 107.1). *The First Fish of the Season* also bears this stencil.

Like nearly all paintings by artists in Ranney's period, his paintings were finished with a varnish film of natural resins like mastic or dammar. These glossy natural resin varnishes served to increase the brilliance of dried paint and imparted some protection to the paint films.

Ranney's signature appears in a variety of forms, from the white block letters "RANNEY" in the snow beneath the sleigh in *Sleighing* to the florid script of "W. Ranney" in *The Retreat*. Throughout his career, however, Ranney frequently signed his paintings either "Wm. Ranney" or "W. Ranney" with the date quite conspicuous in red or reddish-brown paint in the lower center of the canvas. He sometimes signed and dated paintings in a less obvious manner by incorporating the inscription into a design element, for example in places such as the shadowed bow of the punt in *The First Fish of the Season* or the blanket on the white horse in *Marion and His Men* of 1854 (cat. no. 91).

It is especially fortuitous to find a painting palette used by an artist that still retains a selection of paint colors, and Ranney's palette (see illustration), though much scraped, bears evidence of mixtures of the colors he used in his paintings. A palette knife that bears a stamped "ALPHA" and a crown logo on its blade accompanies the palette. It is interesting to note too that the manner in which the palette was used indicates that Ranney was right-handed. Tiny samples from dabs of paint were removed from the palette and examined under a high-powered microscope with polarized light in order to determine which pigments were present.[1] The following pigments were determined: lead white; bone black; synthetic ultramarine blue; Prussian blue; vermilion; an organic red lake such as alizarin crimson or rose madder, yellow, orange, red, and brown earth colors such as ochres, umbers and siennas; an organic brown earth; and chrome yellow. No brilliant green pigments were found; rather, it was found that greens were made by Ranney from more muted mixtures of blues and yellows. These pigments are typical of the muted earth-toned palettes used by many artists of the period. The brilliant effect of Ranney's color depends on his use of bright yellows, reds, and greens against the background of these earth tones. Though Ranney is allied in his use of painting materials and techniques with his contemporaries, his paintings always display an individual character and original style that are well suited to his lively subjects.

1. I would like to thank painting conservation graduate student Brian Baade for his able assistance in this study.

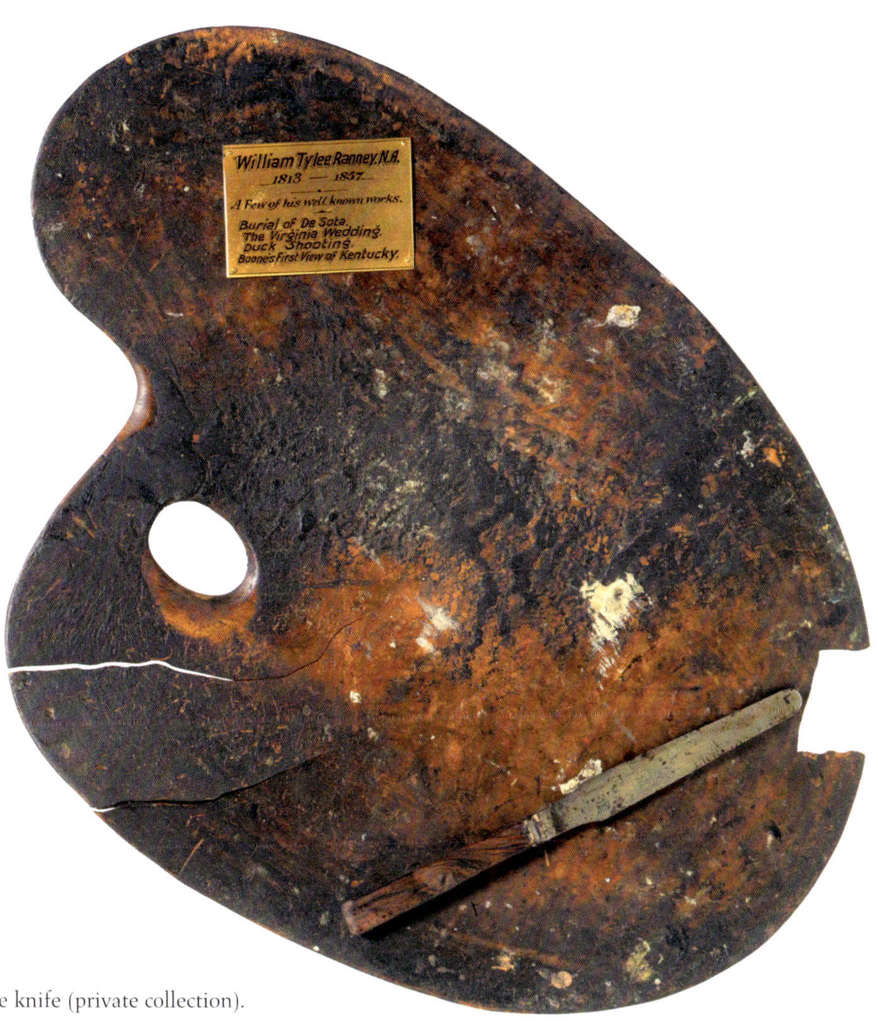

Ranney's palette and palette knife (private collection).

NOTE TO THE READER

The entries are arranged chronologically as best could be determined. Dimensions are given in inches and centimeters, height before width. Signatures, dates, inscriptions, labels, and canvas stamps have been described, again as could best be determined and often after careful examination of the work. The number from Francis Grubar's 1962 catalogue raisonné is included when applicable.

In the PROVENANCE, parentheses indicate an auction house, dealer, or agent.

Regarding REFERENCES, attempts were made to be inclusive for nineteenth-century publications and manuscripts sources; more recent publications, unless they contributed new information, have been excluded. Titles of sales and exhibition catalogues are not generally repeated under REFERENCES, unless they include important added information not annotated under PROVENANCE or EXHIBITIONS.

The entries are signed with the authors' initials, except for those where there is no commentary. Those entries were prepared by Linda Bantel.

Abbreviations and Short Titles precede the SELECT BIBLIOGRAPHY at the back of the CATALOGUE.

The * before a title indicates that the painting was included in the exhibition *Forging an American Identity: The Art of William Ranney.*

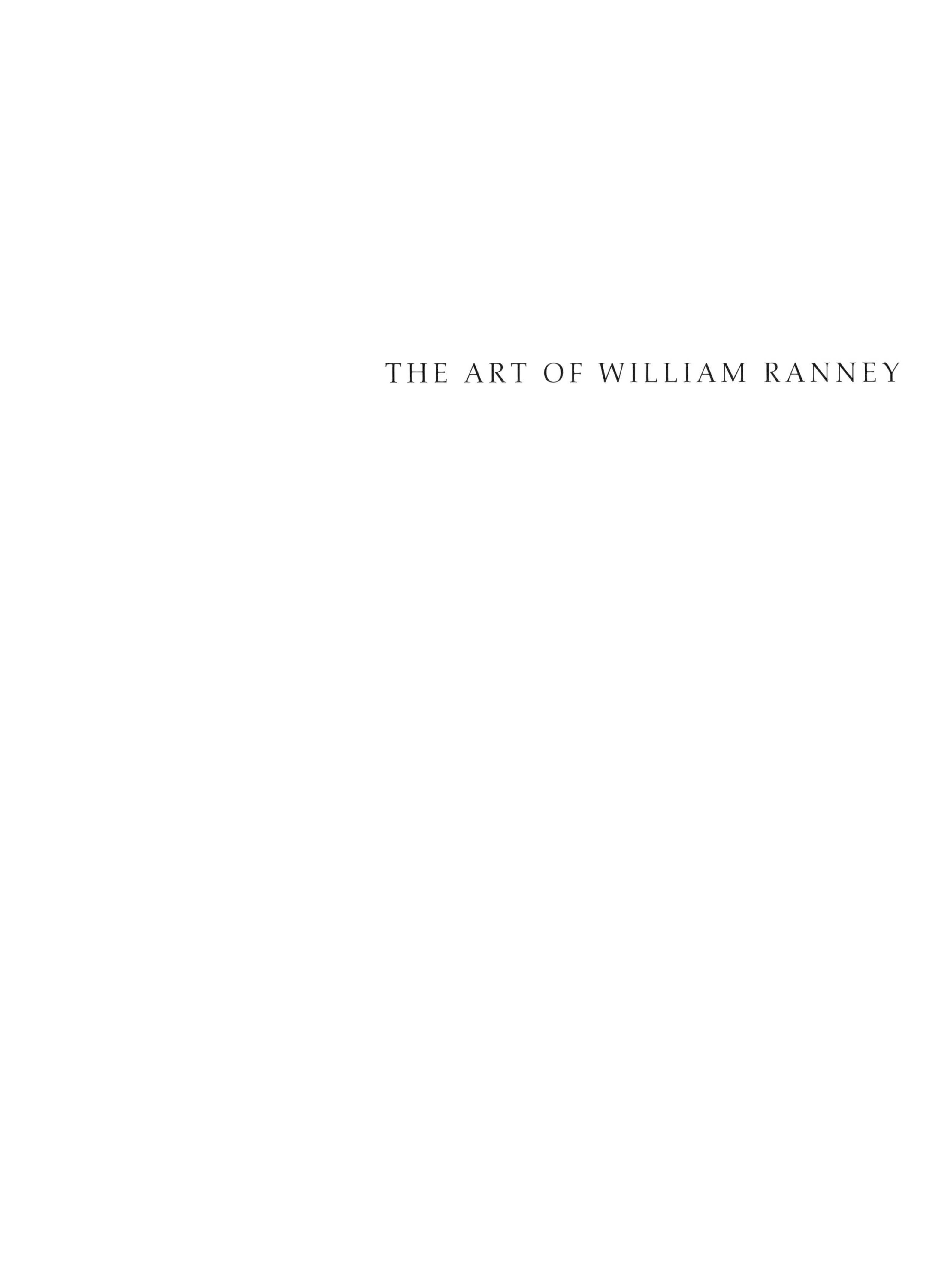

THE ART OF WILLIAM RANNEY

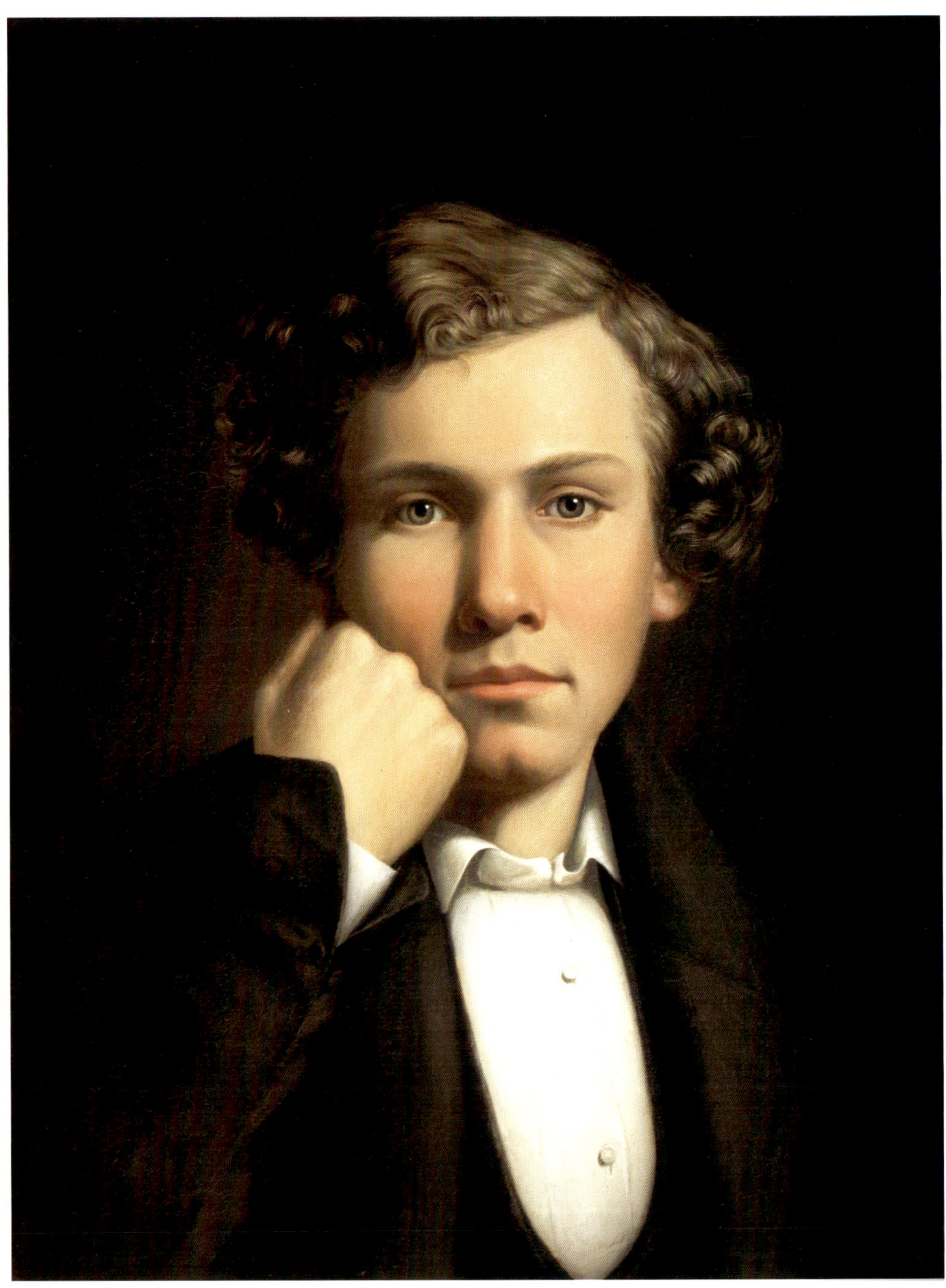

NO. 3

1
A Courting Scene

c. 1838

Oil on canvas

Location unknown

Grubar no. 4

Exhibited: Mechanics' Institute, New York, Fourth Annual Fair, September, 1838.

Reference: "Fine Arts," *Report of the Manager of the Fourth Annual Fair of the Mechanics' Institute, held at Castle Garden, New York,* September 1838 (New York: Mechanics' Institute, 1838), p. 16, provides critical commentary (quoted from Ethan Robey, "The Utility of Art: Mechanics' Institute Fairs in New York City, 1826–1876," Ph.D. dissertation, Columbia University, 2000, p. 260).

Mechanics' institutes, which sprang up in major American cities beginning in the first quarter of the nineteenth century, were modeled on the eighteenth-century British concept of providing education in specific trades. By 1833, the Mechanics' Institute of the City of New York housed five hundred books in its library and sponsored lectures on natural philosophy, chemistry, and architecture. Annual exhibitions were introduced in 1835, though none after 1839 have been documented. While there is no evidence that fine arts were part of the curriculum, they were viewed as integral to the artisan's liberal education, so it was not surprising that a modest selection became part of the annual exhibitions. Diplomas and medals were the two forms of premiums awarded to exhibitors. The "diploma" (see p. xv) awarded to Ranney for *A Courting Scene* corroborates that he exhibited at the fourth annual fair of 1838. In the manager's report of that fair, Ranney's work was praised as having been executed "after only six months' practice in the art, displaying in its composition an unusual degree of ingenuity."

While no separate exhibition catalogue for 1838 has been located, a rare copy of the catalogue of the 1837 fair is preserved in the Boston Public Library. It provides a glimpse of the extensive contents of these extravaganzas, which celebrated American ingenuity. Anticipating the world's fairs which became the rage beginning in the second half of the nineteenth century, the annual exhibitions of mechanics' institutes included hundreds of objects representing a vast array of products and inventions—carriages, sleighs, fire engines, stoves, cabinetry, confections, machinery, honeybees, and musical instruments. The relatively small "Fine Arts" section included paintings as well as a disparate group of works, such as architectural designs, watercolors, specimens of heraldic painting, enamel paintings, lithographic prints, picture frames, window blinds, and miniature paintings.

Unlike the more professional milieu of the National Academy of Design where Ranney exhibited in the spring of 1838, the Mechanics' Institute exhibitions were primarily venues for amateurs or relatively young self-trained artists. Ethan Robey observes, however, that during this period there was less of a distinction between professional and amateur artists than later in the century, and that some interaction between the academies and the mechanics' institutes was common practice (p. 12).

Similar to the practice at the National Academy, an exhibitor probably did not have to be a member of the Mechanics' Institute in order to exhibit there. In any case, no lists of members of the 1830s have survived.[1]

L B

1. This information was provided by Eric Greber, librarian of the Mechanics' Institute, in a telephone conversation with Linda Bantel on February 6, 2001.

2

Portrait of Mr. Thompson

c. 1838

Oil on canvas

Location unknown

Grubar no. 5

P R O V E N A N C E : Merchants' Bank, New York, by 1838.

E X H I B I T E D : NAD, 1838, no. 326, as *Portrait of Mr. Thompson, 35 Years Porter of Merchants' Bank,* lent by Merchants' Bank.

R E F E R E N C E S : *New-York Mirror,* July 7, 1838, p. 15 (quoted in entry). Cowdrey 1943, 2, p. 88.

According to the 1838 National Academy exhibition catalogue, Mr. Thompson was the porter for thirty-five years at New York City's Merchants' Bank, which lent the painting to the exhibition. Porters, traditionally drawn from the lower economic strata, were assigned various menial jobs such as running errands, delivering mail, and taking care of the premises. Longworth's New York City directory of 1835–1836, listed Thomas Thompson, a "colored" porter, who resided at the rear of 71 Sullivan Street and may be the subject of this unlocated painting. Whether white or black, porters would not ordinarily be considered an appropriate subject for the kind of formal portraits so popular with more affluent and influential middle and upper class patrons. Because of the unusual subject, Ranney may have merged portraiture with other narrative elements as, for instance, he so successfully would do later in the *Match Boy* of 1845 (cat. no. 10). In any case, that the bank presumably took the unusual step of commissioning this likeness signifies the esteem in which Mr. Thompson was held. The extraordinary length of his employment, which dated to the bank's founding in 1803, suggests he was in his fifties.

Philip G. Hubert, Jr., the author of the 1903 centennial history of the Merchant's Bank, singled-out the porter (though unnamed) as a notable figure from the bank's early history, who for thirty-five years had occupied the top floor of the bank's first building at 25 Wall Street.[1] Having successfully survived both the Great Fire of December 1835, which destroyed many of their neighbors' buildings in the Wall Street area, and the financial Panic of 1837, the Merchant's Bank was one of the few banks in the late 1830s that was still thriving and whose reputation was intact. In 1838, the year Thompson's portrait was exhibited, the bank sold their modest Federal style building and moved to a larger neoclassical structure at 42 Wall Street, said to have been designed by the noted New York architect Isaiah Rogers (1800–1869). The occasion for the commission of Mr. Thompson's portrait may have been part of the activities marking the bank's history and expansion. How or where it was displayed after its exhibition at the National Academy has yet to be discovered.

The Merchants' Bank is no longer in business, although a similarly named bank founded later in the nineteenth century is still operating in New York City. In a survey of major New York City collecting institutions, no record of such a portrait was found.

Unfortunately this work, one of the young Ranney's earliest known commissions, was not singled out in any review of the exhibition. The critic for the *New-York Mirror* grouped it with several other pictures, dismissing all of them as "none of the first class." L B

1. Philip G. Hubert, Jr., *The Merchants' National Bank of the City of New York: A History of Its First Century Compiled from Official Records at the Request of the Directors* (New York: Merchants' National Bank, 1903), p. 116.

3 *
Self-portrait

c. 1839

Oil on pine

21 1/2 x 16 1/2 inches
(54.6 x 41.9 cm)

Inscribed, lower right
side of panel: Painted
about 1839

Private collection

Grubar no. 1

PROVENANCE: Margaret Ranney, granddaughter of the artist, Union City, New Jersey, d. 1965; her cousin, Claude J. Ranney, grandson of the artist (1883–1971), by c. 1965–1971, Malvern, Pennsylvania.

EXHIBITED: Chadds Ford 1991, cat. no. 1, p. 79, lists it.

REFERENCES: Margaret Ranney estate appraisal, March 22, 1965, no. 1, p. 1, lists, copy in Ranney archives. Thistlethwaite 1991, pp. 17, 18, illus., and 22, discusses redating to c. 1834–1836.

According to family tradition, Ranney painted this portrait when he was eighteen and still in his apprenticeship in North Carolina. Thistlethwaite (1991) argues that the portrait is too sophisticated for an untrained youth to have realized and suggested it is less likely that Ranney painted it in 1831 than between 1834 and 1836, during his first stay in Brooklyn, New York. In the meantime, an 1839 inscription was discovered on the edge of the panel, which suggests an even later and probably more accurate date; indeed, the straightforward handling of facial features and the level of finish relate stylistically to Ranney's recently discovered signed and dated 1839 *Portrait of a Young Man* (cat. no. 4).

The level of sophistication suggests that Ranney may have benefited from at least some informal training during his first New York stay between 1834 and 1836. In New York city directories of 1838–1839 and 1839–1840, Ranney was listed as a portrait painter, and he advertised himself as a portrait painter in Fayetteville in 1840. He may have painted this early self-portrait as an example of his work to show to potential patrons. Unfortunately, it is impossible to determine whether the later inscription was added by the artist or a family member.   LB

(See illustration on page 2.)

4*
Portrait of a Young Man

1839

Oil on canvas

30 x 25 inches (76.2 x 63.5 cm)

Signed, lower left: Ranney, 1839

Private collection

PROVENANCE: James H. Ricau, Piermont, New York, to 1968.

REFERENCE: Hirschl and Adler Galleries, New York, Stuart P. Feld to Mrs. J. Maxwell Moran, November 9, 1988, Ranney archives, mentions that Grubar had seen and authenticated the painting.

Ranney advertised himself as a portrait painter in Fayetteville, North Carolina, between 1839 and 1840, and was listed as a portrait painter in New York city directories from 1838 to 1840, and again from 1843 to 1847. Until the discovery of this picture, however, no example of his early commissioned portraits had been located.

This work provides an opportunity to assess the early artistic career and talent of this largely self-taught artist. Like Ranney's *Self-portrait* (cat. no. 3), this likeness is a refreshingly direct presentation with light focused on and articulating the softly modeled face and hands. With a subtle palette and restrained brushwork, its empathetic realism and formal devices are in the tradition of Ranney's New York contemporaries who were exhibiting at the influential National Academy of Design during this same period. While no nineteenth-century provenance has been discovered, Grubar felt comfortable assigning authorship to Ranney. He could have painted the picture in New York during his stay between 1837 and 1839, or in Fayetteville after he returned there in late 1839 to visit his uncle William Nott. On January 18, 1840, Ranney advertised himself as a portrait painter in Fayetteville's *North-Carolinian.* While the identity of the youth portrayed and his residence have yet to be discovered, his fine garments—a gold silk vest and jaunty bluish black cap—indicate he is a young man of means and social position. The two large tomes atop the side table suggest he is a student, or at least that his parents' had aspirations for him.   LB

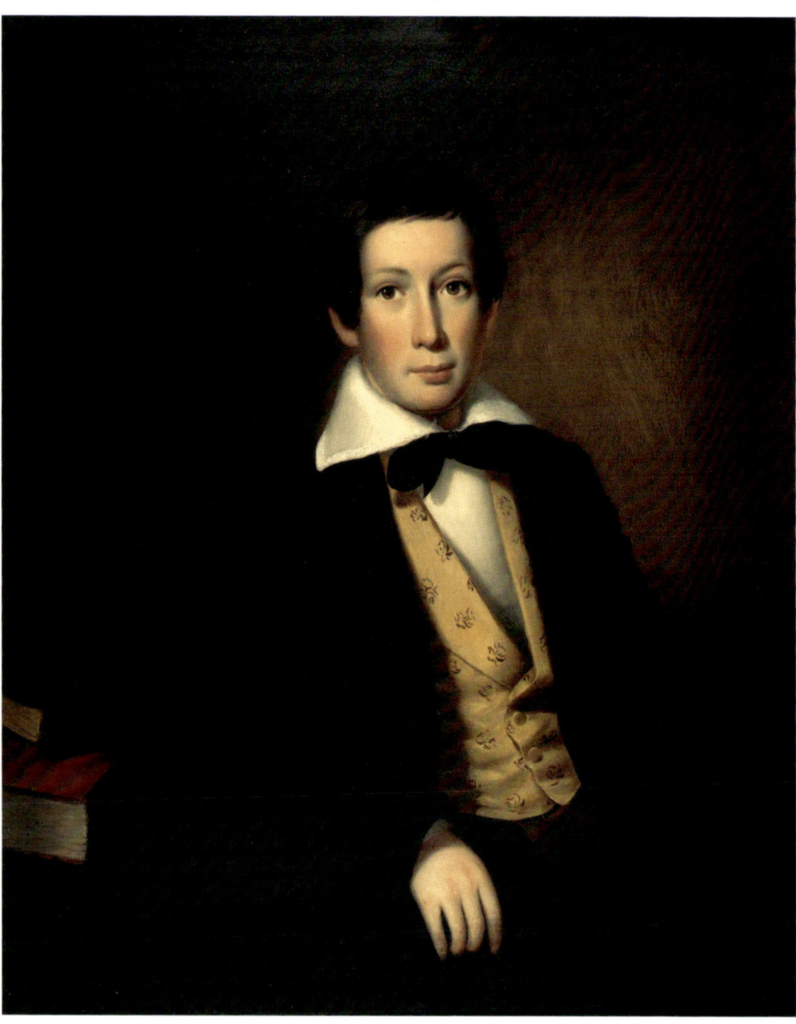

5
Portrait of Clarissa Gaylord Ranney

1835–1840

Oil on copper

12 1/2 x 10 1/2 inches
(31.7 x 26.7 cm)

Initialed, lower right:
W. R.

Private collection

Grubar no. 2

PROVENANCE: Margaret Ranney (d. 1965), granddaughter of the artist, Union City, New Jersey; her cousin, Claude J. Ranney, grandson of the artist (1883–1971), c. 1965–1971, Malvern, Pennsylvania.

EXHIBITED: Chadds Ford 1991, cat. no. 27, p. 82 lists it.

REFERENCE: Thistlethwaite 1991, p. 16 illus., p. 17, discusses style and dating.

This small portrait is in a diminutive format, commonly known as a cabinet picture. Ranney may have been inspired to experiment with this format because of its growing popularity in New York in the 1830s. At that time, one of the foremost masters of cabinet pictures was Henry Inman's student, George Twibill (c. 1806–1836).[1] Another Inman student, William Sidney Mount, was among several artists who regularly exhibited such small pictures at the National Academy of Design, for example, in 1847 (no. 336) and 1849 (no. 259). In Mount's "Catalogue," several cabinet pictures were listed beginning in 1844.[2]

Although cabinet portraits were sometimes painted on wood, in this case Ranney used copper as a support, which creates a particularly smooth flat surface. Ranney's choice of material may have been influenced by his youthful apprenticeship in tinsmithing, a craft that also used a variety of other metals, particularly copper.

A paper document inscribed in ink is glued to the back of the portrait. Signed and dated December 16, 1955, by the artist's grandson Claude J. Ranney, it includes an abbreviated genealogy of the artist's family and identifies the subject as the artist's mother and the "Wife of Captain William Ranney." This inscription is perhaps the source for Grubar's secondary title, "The Sea Captain's Wife."

Since the portrait descended in the Ranney family, Grubar apparently relied on family tradition and the inscriptions on the sheet affixed to the back to identify the sitter as the artist's mother, Clarissa Gaylord (1789–1863). This widowed wife of a sea captain would have been in her mid to late forties at the time the painting was executed. Thistlethwaite (1991) speculated that this likeness was idealized because Ranney painted it from memory between 1827 and 1833 while he was serving his apprenticeship in North Carolina. The portrait is here reassigned to the period 1835–1840 based on the sitter's hairstyle and dress. The hairstyle with its center parting and tight clusters of curls covering the ears and framing the face was fashionable by the late 1830s. And the style of the red velvet gown, with its plunging neckline and sleeves hung low off the shoulder, was popular during this same period.[3]

Because of the sitter's youthful appearance and up-to-date costume, it is likely that the subject is not Ranney's matronly mother, as Grubar suggested, but rather the artist's elder sister of the same name. Clarissa Gaylord Ranney (1809–1886) would have been in her early thirties when this picture was painted. Ranney may have been motivated to paint her portrait amid festive trappings of dress and setting in celebration of her marriage on August 31, 1838, to Zebulon Hale Baldwin (1812–1873), a carpenter and builder from her hometown of Middletown, Connecticut.[4]

Noting the painting's derivative style, Thistlethwaite suggested that perhaps Ranney relied upon an unknown eighteenth-century British print for his inspiration, certainly a common practice of young artists. Grubar observed that "the colors are harsher and less subtle than English artists, recalling perhaps the earlier work of Kneller or Lely" (p. 15). A three-quarter figure seated next to a classical column against a neutral background was not an unusual format, even in the nineteenth century in the United States. The composition was, for instance, employed by leading portrait painters of the time such as James Frothingham, a Gilbert Stuart student who worked in New York from 1826 until his death in 1864, or Henry Inman, whose work Ranney surely encountered in his forays to New York in the 1830s, in particular at the annual National Academy of Design exhibitions to which Inman annually contributed portraits of ladies and gentlemen from

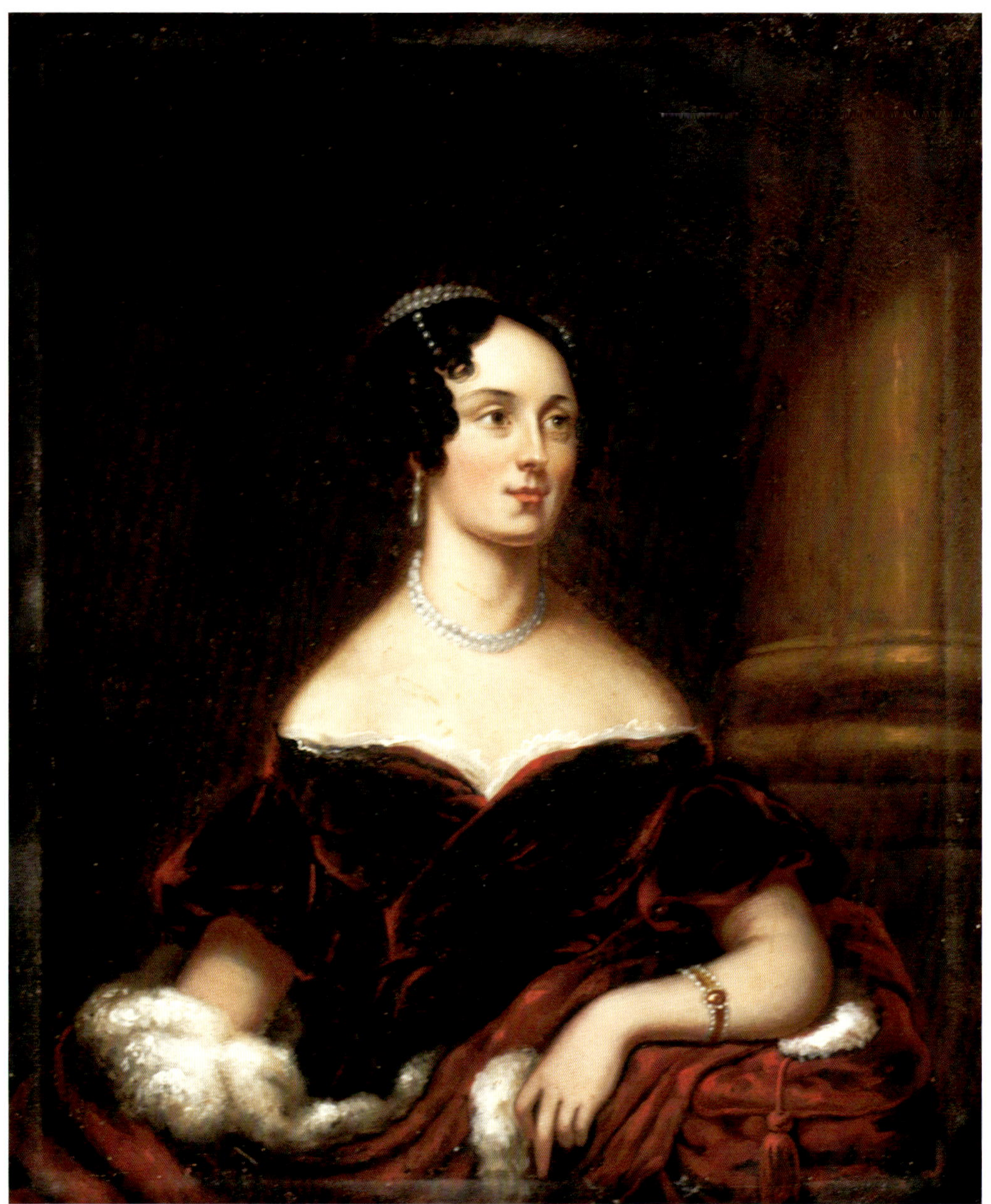

1826 to 1846. If Ranney did rely on a print source rather than firsthand observation, this would account for the sketchiness of the gown and fur boa, which is uncharacteristic of other early works by Ranney, such as his *Self-portrait* (cat. no. 3) or *Portrait of a Young Man* (cat. no. 4).

Clarissa Gaylord has been an enigma within Ranney's work because of the confusion of the identity of the sitter and date. Moreover, the unique use of a copper support and the stylistic idiosyncrasies continue to make it difficult to definitively place the picture within Ranney's known corpus of works.   LB

1. William H. Gerdts, *The Art of Henry Inman* (Washington: National Portrait Gallery, 1987), p. 31.
2. Alfred Frankenstein, *William Sidney Mount* (New York: Harry N. Abrams, 1975), pp. 467–476.
3. Elisabeth McClellan, *Historic Dress in America 1800-1870*. (Philadelphia: George W. Jacobs and Company, 1910), p. 403.
4. Charles Collard Adams, *Middletown Upper Houses* (1908; reprint, Canaan, New Hampshire: Phoenix Publishing, 1983), p. 298.

6
Country Bridge near Middletown, Connecticut

1835–1840

Probably oil on canvas

11 1/2 x 9 inches (29.2 x 22.9 cm)

Signed: Ranney?

Location unknown

Grubar no. 3

PROVENANCE: Margaret Ranney, granddaughter of the artist, Union City, New Jersey, d. 1965

REFERENCE: Letter from Francis S. Grubar appraising Margaret Ranney estate, March 22, 1965, no. 3, lists and describes it, copy in Ranney archives.

This now lost painting is documented by a surviving black-and-white photograph (Ranney archives). The data related to it and its placement in the Ranney chronology are based on the details provided by Grubar, who must have had the opportunity to personally examine the painting prior to the 1962 publication of his Ranney catalogue. Grubar identified the view as an area near Ranney's hometown, which he is said to have left about 1827 after the death of his father to apprentice with his uncle William Nott, a merchant in Fayetteville, North Carolina. In light of the sophisticated handling of the landscape details, the work was probably done well after 1833 or 1834 when Ranney's apprenticeship ended. Unfortunately, there are few known details of Ranney's travels, though he must surely have returned to Middletown from time to time to visit his widowed mother.

In 1846 Ranney exhibited another Middletown, Connecticut, subject at the Brooklyn Institute (see cat. no. 30). The existence of this painting suggests a date when Ranney might have been visiting his Connecticut home. LB

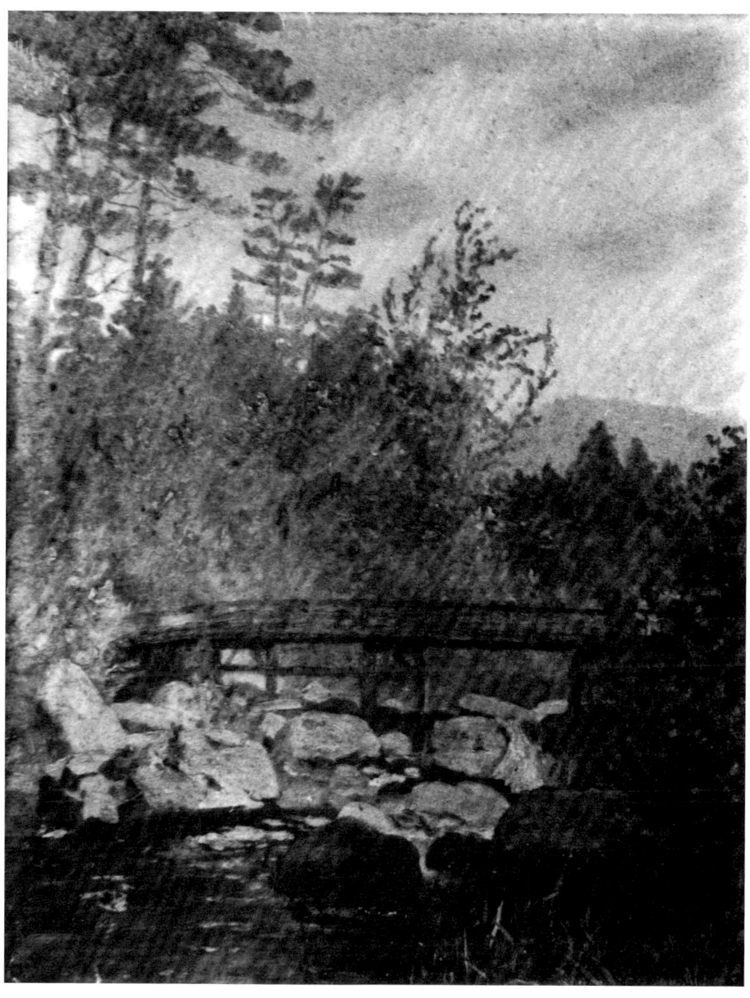

Photograph of no. 6,
Ranney archives.

9

7*
Portrait of a Gentleman

Late 1830s or early 1840s

Oil on canvas

34 x 27 1/8 inches (86.4 x 68.9 cm)

Signed, lower right on chair rail: Ranney

Haggerty Museum of Art, Marquette University, Milwaukee. Gift of Mr. and Mrs. Thomas G. Lamb, 86.45

Grubar no. 109

PROVENANCE: Schuyler Hamilton, New York, d. 1933; (Harry Stone, New York) (Robert C. Vose Galleries, Boston, to 1948) (sale, Parke-Bernet Galleries, New York, February 6–7, 1948, lot 80, as from Massachusetts private collection); the estate of Mrs. Benjamin Sonnenberg (sale, Sotheby Parke-Bernet, New York, December 13, 1980, lot 376) Thomas G. Lamb, Oklahoma City, 1980–1986.

REFERENCE: FARL mount no. 121-7 A, provides provenance. Francis S. Grubar to Mark R. Aldridge, curator, the Lamb collection, December 29, 1982, copy in Ranney archives, authenticates painting and discusses provenance.

In 1962 Grubar listed this portrait of an unidentified elderly man in his catalogue. He only saw and authenticated it, however, in 1982 when it found its way into the Lamb collection. While lamenting how few of Ranney's portraits had survived, he noted that the style of the portrait "compares favorably with what our best known portraitists of the period were doing, particularly Neagle, Healy, Vanderlyn and Elliott." Based on features such as the hairstyle, the rather long sideburns, and the wide stock or cravat revealing the tips of the shirt's collar above, the work dates to the late 1830s or early 1840s, a period during which Ranney advertised himself as a portrait painter. Given its provenance, it is likely the portrait was painted in New York rather than Fayetteville, North Carolina. LB

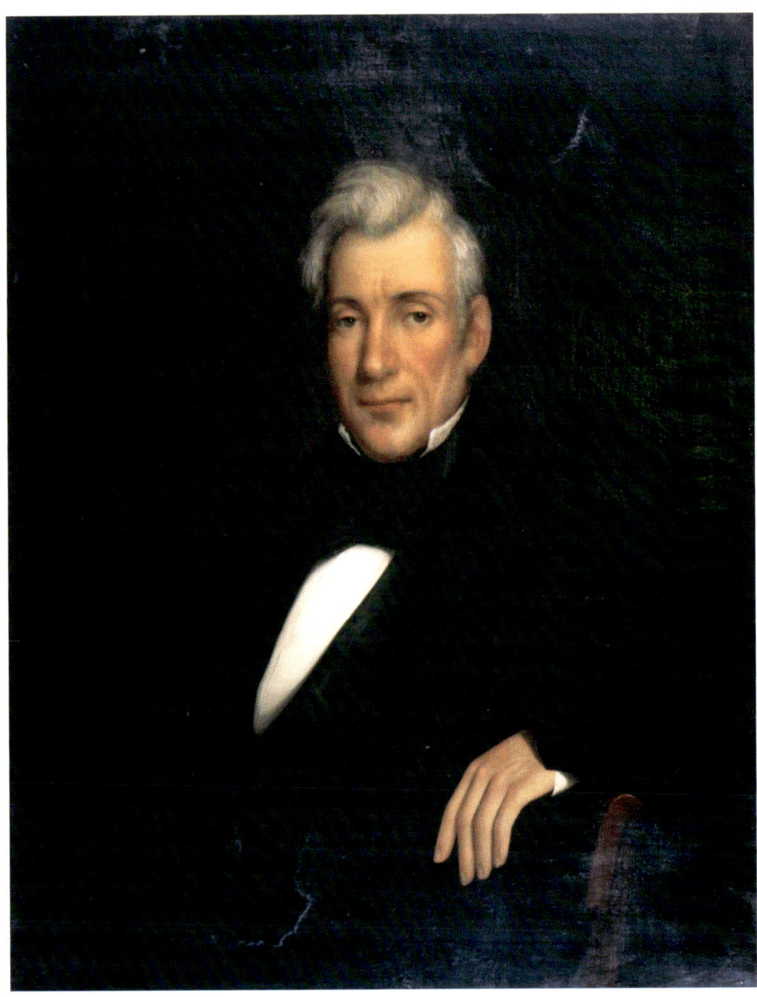

NO. 7

8
Battle of Cowpens

1845

Oil on canvas

36 x 46 inches (91.4 x 116.8 cm)

Signed and dated, lower right: Ranney, 1845

South Carolina Senate, Columbia

Grubar no. 6

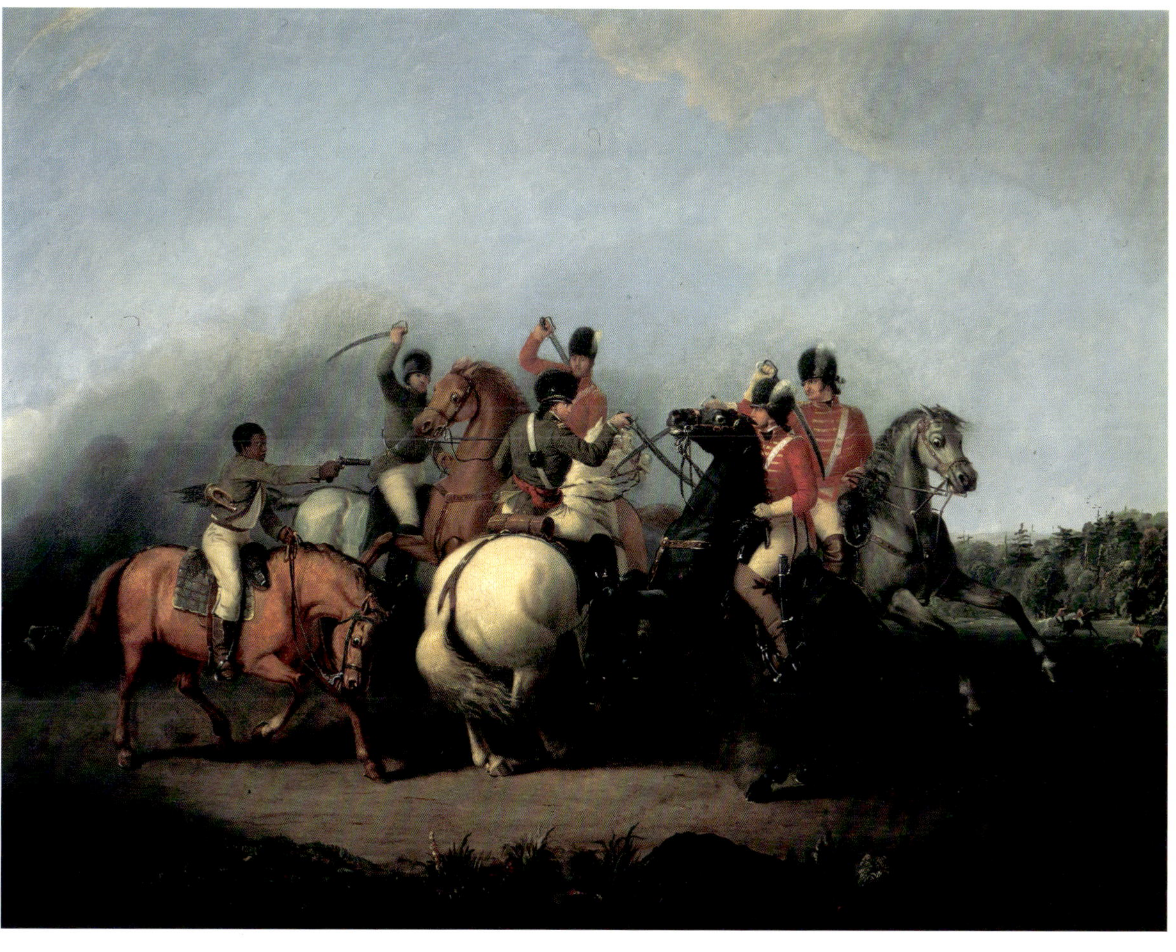

NO. 8

PROVENANCE: M. K. Bridges, 1845; J. K. Paige, 1846–at least 1849; Mr. Acars Rathbun; Miss Anna French, Albany, New York, to c. 1930; her niece, Mrs. Joseph Lewi Donhauser, Albany; her husband, Dr. Joseph Lewi Donhauser, Albany, by 1962; his son, Frederic Donhauser, Alaska, in the custody of his brother, Robert Donhauser, Chevy Chase, Maryland, sold to unknown source, c. 1973.[1]

EXHIBITED: NAD, 1845, no. 206, as Skirmish of Horse, Lieut. Col. Washington in the Midst of the British Dragoons, at the Battle of the Cowpens, owned by the artist. Brooklyn Institute, Brooklyn, New York, October 1845, *Catalogue of Paintings, Sculpture, and Other Works of Art*, no. 61, as owned by M. K. Bridges. Albany, New York. Albany Gallery of Fine Arts, 1846, no. 94, *Catalogue of the First Exhibition*, as owned by J. K. Paige. Albany Gallery of the Fine Arts, *Catalogue of the Fourth Exhibition*, 1849, no. 57, p. 13, listed for sale as Battle of Cowpens.

REFERENCES: *New York Herald*, May 3, 1845, p. 1 (quoted in entry). *Anglo American*, May 17, 1845, p. 93. *Brooklyn Eagle*, October 3, 1845 (quoted in entry). Undated newspaper clipping, c. 1846, Ranney archives (mentioned sold to a gentleman in Albany, New York). *Knickerbocker*, May 1854, pp. 546–547, includes humorous anecdote. Cowdrey 1943, 2, p. 88. FARL mount 114-1c provided provenance, after 1846.

The original title Ranney assigned to this painting when it was exhibited in 1845 at both the National Academy of Design and the Brooklyn Institute was *Skirmish of Horse: Lieut. Col. Washington in the Midst of the British Dragoons at the Battle of Cowpens*. By 1849, however, when it was exhibited and listed as for sale in Albany, the title had been simplified to *Battle of Cowpens*, and that is how it is known today. That historic battle took place in the northwestern section of South Carolina on January 17, 1781, during the wan-

11

ing days of the American Revolution. It was here that the Americans gave the British their most devastating defeat of the southern campaign. Many historians consider this battle and the earlier one at Kings Mountain, South Carolina, in 1780 to be the turning points of the Revolution. Retreating and outnumbered American forces under Brigadier General Daniel Morgan succeeded in taking a stand against the troops of Lieutenant Colonel Banastre Tarleton. The site of the battle was an open field surrounded by trees, which at the time was a pasture for grazing cattle. Morgan capitalized on the terrain's distinctive topography to design his successful line of attack. Against all odds, the Americans completely routed the British and took many prisoners. The dramatic moment portrayed by Ranney occurred near the end of the battle. According to a description in the 1845 exhibition catalogue at the Brooklyn Institute, Ranney's picture is based on an account described in John Marshall's *Life of George Washington*.[2] When defeat appeared inevitable, Tarleton tried to rally his cavalry to support the infantry. As the British stampeded off the field of battle, Tarleton's dragoons ran head-on into the Continental dragoons of Lieutenant Colonel William Washington, second cousin of George Washington.

> In the eagerness of pursuit, Washington advanced nearly thirty yards in front of his regiment. Observing this, three British officers wheeled about, and attacked him; the officer on his left was aiming to cut him down, when a serjeant [*sic*] came up and intercepted the blow by disabling the sword arm, at the same instant the officer on his right was about to make a stroke at him, when a waiter, too small to wield a sword, saved him by wounding the officer with a pistol. At that moment, the officer in the centre, who was believed to be Tarleton made a thrust at him, which he parried, upon which the officer [Tarleton] retreated a few paces and discharged his pistol at him, which wounded him in the knee.

Congress awarded William Washington a silver medal for his valor. Colonel Washington, as the American hero, is represented symbolically on a white horse, while the enemy, the much reviled and vicious Tarleton, whose cruelty was legendary, is riding a black horse. As they raise their swords, Washington's servant, also identified in Marshall's account as a young bugler (notice the bugle strapped over his shoulder), levels his pistol at the British dragoon. While for the most part Ranney followed the historical descriptions rather faithfully, he either knowingly or unknowingly diverged from historical accuracy in his portrayals of the main characters and their uniforms. He depicted, for example, Washington as slender and idealized, although he was known to have been short and stout. Also, the uniforms with their high collars and pinched waistcoats are styles more typical of the 1830s and 1840s than 1781 when the event took place. Moreover, Washington and his sergeant would have been wearing white or buff-colored coats, not green, and the British would have been wearing green, not red. On the other hand, to Ranney's contemporaries "redcoats" would have been instantly recognizable as British, and, even if one did not know the story, the heroes and the villains were clearly identifiable. In spite of these historical lapses, Ranney's selection of this dramatic minor moment captures the essence of the American victory at Cowpens, which represented a significant step on the road to the British surrender at Yorktown and cleared the way for American independence.

The responses of the contemporary critics to the painting were mixed. A reviewer of the National Academy exhibition for the *New York Herald*, for example, admired "the coloring and the grouping" but complained that the scene seemed inappropriately frozen in its action, pointing out that a "battle scene requires all the excitement of the most violent action." When the painting was exhibited later that year in Brooklyn, the *Brooklyn Eagle* correspondent praised it as "one of the best if not *the* best in the collection."   LB

1. Reported by a descendant of Robert Donhauser to Linda Bantel, July 27, 2001.
2. John Marshall, *The Life of George Washington* . . . (Philadelphia: C. P. Wayne, 1805), vol. 4, p. 347 n. The book was republished in 1832 on the occasion of the centenary of George Washington's birth.

9
Deer Hunters

1845

Oil on canvas

20 x 45 inches (50.8 x
114.3 cm)

Signed and dated,
lower left: Ranney
1845

Private collection

Grubar no. 10

PROVENANCE: Descended in the family to present owner, c. 1985.

Based on its subject matter, dimensions, and signature, this recently discovered painting seems to be the one listed in Grubar as no. 10, as location unknown. Dated 1845, it is Ranney's earliest known hunting picture and the only one with a deer. It is also unusual in that it is set in a densely forested area with high mountains in the background. Some of the drawing is less assured than in Ranney's later works, particularly in the rendering of the deer and the dog in the background. This may be partly due, however, to overzealous restorations. So few of Ranney's early genre scenes have survived that it is difficult to fully appreciate his youthful efforts. It is possible that this is the same work entitled *Hunters*, which was exhibited at the Brooklyn Institute in Brooklyn, New York in 1845 (cat. no. 17). LB

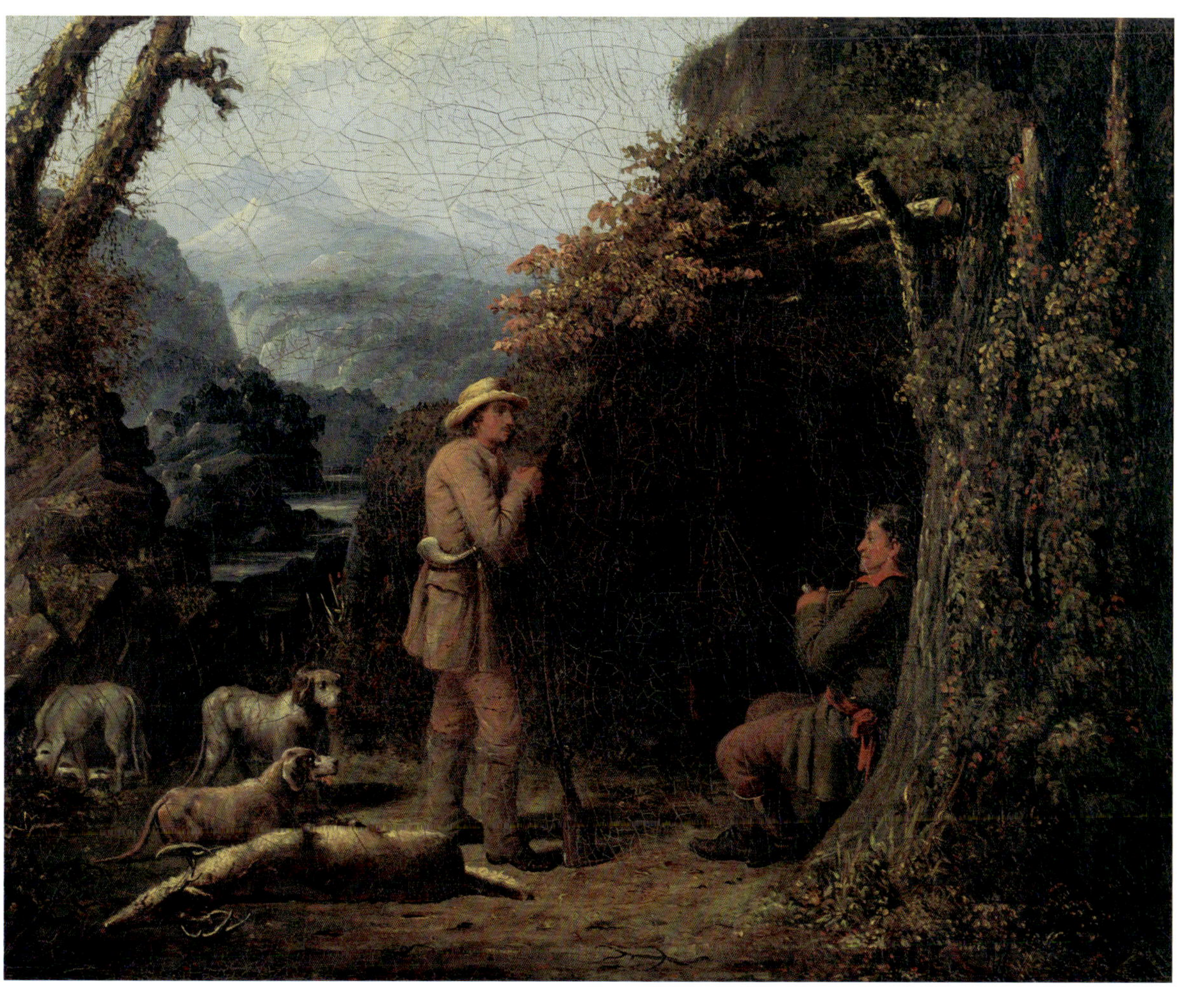

NO. 9

10*

Match Boy

1845

Oil on canvas

30 x 25 inches (76.2 x 63.5 cm)

Signed and dated, center on box: Ranney 1845

Inscribed (on top of box) 11 boxes to...; (above signature) Matches; inscribed in ink on label pasted to stretcher on reverse: R. A. McDonald/Christmas 1904/Jessie & Ralph Dunn."

Private collection

Grubar no. 11

PROVENANCE: Charles L. Vose, New York , by 1846; Jessie and Ralph Dunn; R. A. McDonald by 1904; Dr. Sidney Ulfelder and Mrs. Ethel M. Ulfelder, Maplewood Estate, McLean, Virginia; Francis S. Grubar, Washington, D. C., by 1962–c. 1984; (Vose Galleries, Boston, 1984, as *The Match Seller*, inventory no. 27577).

EXHIBITED: NAD, 1846, no. 192, as Match Boy. Chadds Ford 1991, p. 79, no. 2, listed.

REFERENCES: *New York Herald*, April 21, 1846, p. 2, no. 192 (quoted in entry). *Morris National Press*, vol. 1, no. 6 (May 30, 1846), p. 2 (quoted in entry). *Anglo American*, May 16, 1846, p. 95 (quoted in entry). *Knickerbocker*, vol. 27, no. 6 (June, 1846), p. 556. Cowdrey 1943, 2, no. 192. Thistlethwaite 1991, pp. 26–30, discusses in terms of similar subjects and of Young America movement.

By the mid-1840s the stability and homogeneity of the American middle class was threatened by an expanding and impoverished urban underclass which was fueled by massive numbers of new immigrants. Over one and a half million Europeans, mostly Irish and German, emigrated to the United States between 1840 and 1850. Because cities were unable to fully absorb and support such a large influx of people, there was an increased number of homeless and orphaned children living on the streets or in alleys, many of whom, as petty thieves or pickpockets, terrorized the local populace. Others were forced to work to help support their struggling families by peddling goods such as fruit, flowers, newspapers, or matches. The middle class who patronized artists, and indeed the artists themselves, had divided opinions about these destitute street urchins, and this dichotomy was reflected in the artworks of the period. On the one hand, the more socially conscious and optimistic considered the children hardworking youths who through their own efforts would rise to become the new American middle class. Others felt that the street vendors threatened the very survival of a civilized American society.[1]

A match seller, such as the youth portrayed here by Ranney, was a common sight in New York, particularly beginning in the second quarter of the nineteenth century following the invention of the friction match by the English chemist John Walker in 1827. Numerous innovative copycat versions evolved to meet the demand to more easily light the increasingly popular cigar. By the mid-nineteenth century, a phosphorous match had been developed which could be lit by striking the side of a matchbox, perhaps similar to the one Ranney depicted here.

Match factories in New York apparently used a variety of people to distribute their products. One young man of the period, Johnny Morrow, who published his autobiography in 1860, recalled how he was among at least 150 boys and girls—and apparently even some adults—who daily visited a match factory outlet to buy matches which they peddled for a profit on city streets.[2]

Many artists beginning in the 1830s portrayed these pervasive picturesque urban youth. In the United States, Henry Inman was one of the most notable artists who contributed to the popularity of images of street children with his critically acclaimed *News Boy* of 1841 (Addison Gallery of American Art, Phillips Academy, Andover, Massachusetts). His depiction of a young chap who projected an arrogant self-confidence beyond his tender years was engraved in 1843 by Philadelphia publisher E. L. Carey for *The Gift*. While Inman declined the challenge of creating a whole portrait gallery of street types, his fellow artists had already recognized the inherent marketability of such subjects and filled that need.

Such genre scenes of children selling matches had precedents not only in nineteenth-century American painting but also in eighteenth-century British painting. In 1786, for example, the English artist John Russell (1746–1806) exhibited a *Match Girl* at London's Royal Academy, which at one time was in the William Randolph Hearst collection (FARL mount 228-b). In a composition similar to Ranney's *Match Boy*, a young girl is shown in a three-quarter-length view with a basket full of matches draped over her left arm

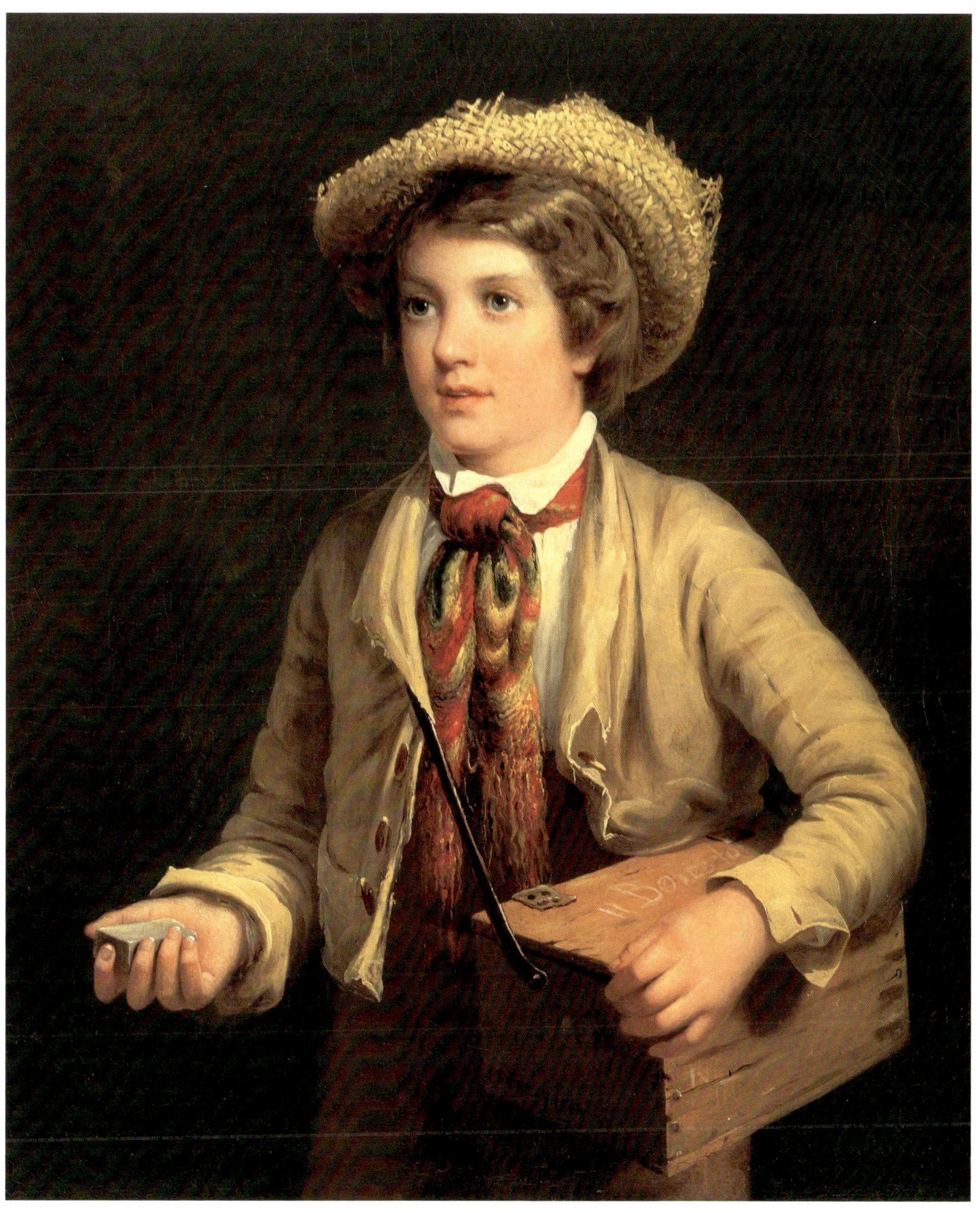

NO. 10

and holding long individual matches in her outstretched right hand. As early as 1834, the American artist George Whiting Flagg painted *Match Girl* (New-York Historical Society) in London for the New York collector Luman Reed. In 1849, Walter Libby exhibited the same theme at the American Art-Union (no. 82, now unlocated). And in about 1856–1865, Pittsburgh artist David Gilmour Blythe painted a similar subject (North Carolina Museum of Art, Raleigh).

With his somewhat idealized child merchant, Ranney seems to adopt a sympathetic and positive view. He portrays a cherub-faced youth with neatly combed hair, rosy cheeks, and bright eyes placed not in an identifiable street environment but emerging from a dark brown background, as though posed in a studio space. He depicts the boy, a wooden matchbox slung over his shoulder, wearing a tattered jacket with a straw hat jauntily askew on his head. The drabness of this ensemble is brilliantly offset by a flamboyant red and yellow scarf knotted atop his white shirt. Narrative content is suggested by the youth's outward gaze, which is seemingly directed toward an unseen customer to whom he offers a box of matches.

Thistlethwaite observed that the *Match Boy* represents a figure doing work, and therefore defines the picture partially as a genre scene. He observes, however, that the figure is relatively inactive and large in relation to the canvas, as in a portrait; he therefore suggests that the work represents a transitional period in which Ranney combined a new interest in scenes of everyday life with that of his earlier experience as a portrait painter.

The *Match Boy* may have been conceived as a companion painting to that of another apparent street peddler, the *Radish Girl* of 1845 (see cat. no. 11). According to a contemporary newspaper account describing that picture, the young girl also wore a straw hat. Both pictures were owned by Charles L. Vose in 1846. (A Charles L. Vose is listed in the New York city directory of 1844–1845 as a commercial merchant at 28 South Street.) A straw hat appears as a prop in several of Ranney's later works, including *Hunters at the Well* (cat. no. 70) and *Going to Mill* (cat. no. 105). The *Match Boy* is the only surviving work in a series of at least five documented pictures of urban workers by Ranney.

Critical responses were mixed. The critic for the *Anglo American* found the painting "well drawn, well coloured, and telling the story admirably." The *New York Herald* reviewer admired the portrait but found it "somewhat etherialised." The more critical observer for the *Morris National Press*, however, pointed out that, while the picture was "capital," Ranney lacks only "a little elementary study to make him an accomplished artist. His conceptions are good and well expressed. But he is sometimes at fault in his perspective, frequently in his anatomy—and his draperies want truth. For example, the coat of the Match Boy. The face is good."   L B

1. See Elizabeth Johns, *American Genre Painting: The Politics of Everyday Life* (New Haven: Yale University Press, 1991), pp. 182–196 for a fuller discussion of this phenomenon.

2. John Morrow, *A Voice from the Newsboys* ([New York], 1860) in Stephen O'Connor, *Orphan Trains: The Story of Charles Loring Brace and the Children He Saved and Failed* (Boston: Hougton Mifflin Company, 2001), p 125.

11
Radish Girl

c. 1845

Oil on canvas

Location unknown

Grubar no. 7

PROVENANCE: Charles L. Vose, c. 1845.

EXHIBITED: NAD, 1845, no. 56, as *Radish Girl*, sold to C. L. Vose.

REFERENCES: *New York Herald*, April 23, 1845, p. 3 (quoted in entry). *Anglo American,* May 17, 1845, p. 93 (quoted in entry). Cowdrey 1943, 2, p. 88.

The writer for the *New York Herald* noted that the artist conceived the figure quite poorly, "crooked in all the joints," as though dependent upon a lay figure. The critic went on, however, to congratulate Ranney on his "taste in gilding." The *Anglo American* reviewer was more complimentary, admiring the *Radish Girl* as "a pretty idea very well carried out; the wretched poverty of the drapery, the broken straw hat, are both in good keeping." The straw hat may have been a prop in Ranney's studio, for a tattered one is also depicted on the head of his *Match Boy* (cat. no. 10), painted in 1845 and exhibited at the National Academy in 1846. Either a study or another version of the *Radish Girl* (location unknown) was listed in the Ranney Fund sale in 1858 as sold to someone named Hurlburt for eleven dollars (lot 153).[1] LB

1. Two other pictures of youths appeared in the same sale—*The Western Girl* (lot 83, sold to unknown buyer for forty dollars) and *Errand Boy* (lot 116, sold to Warner for two dollars and fifty cents).

12
The Wounded Trooper

c. 1845
Probably oil on canvas
Location unknown
Grubar no. 8

PROVENANCE: Am Art-Union, 1845; distributed by lottery to James S. Davis, New York, 1845.

EXHIBITED: Am Art-Union, 1845, no. 35.

REFERENCES: Letter of July 21, 1845, from Ranney to Am Art-Union, Letters Received, February 17, 1845–January 22, 1846, reel 10, Am Art-Union Papers, accepts $60 for Wounded Trooper. Am Art-Union, *Transactions for the Year 1845*, p. 27, no. 35. Cowdrey 1953, 2, p. 294, provides provenance.

13*
Study for Wounded Trooper

c. 1845

Oil on canvas

15 3/4 x 24 inches (40 x 61 cm)

Canvas stamp (before lining): Prepared/by/Edwd Dechaux,/New-York

Courtesy of the Spanierman Gallery, New York and Gerald Peters Gallery, Santa Fe

PROVENANCE: Estate of F. W. Woolworth, Bethlehem, New Hampshire (summer residence) to 1991; private collection, Connecticut, 1991; (Mystic Fine Arts, Mystic, Connecticut, 1991); (Ira Spanierman, New York, jointly with Gerald Peters Gallery, Santa Fe, by c. 1991).

REFERENCE: Copy of August 10, 1991, letter from Francis Grubar to whom it may concern, Ranney archives, authenticates the work and documents canvas stamp.

This painting may be a study for the lost *The Wounded Trooper* (cat. no. 12) exhibited at the American Art-Union in 1845. In addition to pencil sketches related to his major works, a few unsigned oil studies such as this one have survived. While these small, quickly rendered and lively works were often transformed in the final version, they nevertheless provide clues to understanding Ranney's creative process and may in the future also help in identifying lost pictures.

Some studies remained in Ranney's studio until after his death, when they were sold as part of a group of his works and those of other artists to raise money for his widow and children. Grubar in his letter of 1991 suggested that this *Wounded Trooper* in fact may have been a work called *The Wounded Scout*, which was sold in the 1858 Ranney Fund sale (lot 161) for $25 to Wood. That seems unlikely, however, because in addition to having a slightly different descriptive title, the price paid suggests a larger and more finished canvas. Studies and sketches were labeled as such in the catalogue and ranged in price from $3 to $15; paintings from $15 to $340.

Study for Wounded Trooper is a genre scene of ordinary people set within the historical context of the American Revolution. While one soldier reclines beneath a lean-to in the shaded background, a dog and five figures, including the kneeling wounded trooper or soldier, comprise the foreground action. Four of the men are dressed in the casual clothes typical of militia troops. The fifth man tending to the trooper's shoulder, wears a ribboned cocked hat and a blue and buff uniform adorned with gold epaulets, similar to the uniform of an officer of the Continental Army. A sheathed gold-hilted sword hangs at his side, another indication of his rank. That his horse remains saddled in the background suggests he has only recently arrived on the scene. With his grayish white wig, this officer in fact resembles George Washington. He is portrayed as a healer as he gently bandages the left shoulder of the wounded trooper who kneels before him in a quasi-religious allusion to scenes of Christ healing the sick. The religious symbolism is reinforced by the poles of the lean-to which form a cross in the background. By the 1840s a vast literature about Washington had elevated this revered founding father and hero of the Revolution to the level of a minor deity. A related but now lost drawing, *Washington with Soldiers* (cat. no. D27), depicts the general surrounded by three soldiers, all of whom are in various positions of veneration. LB

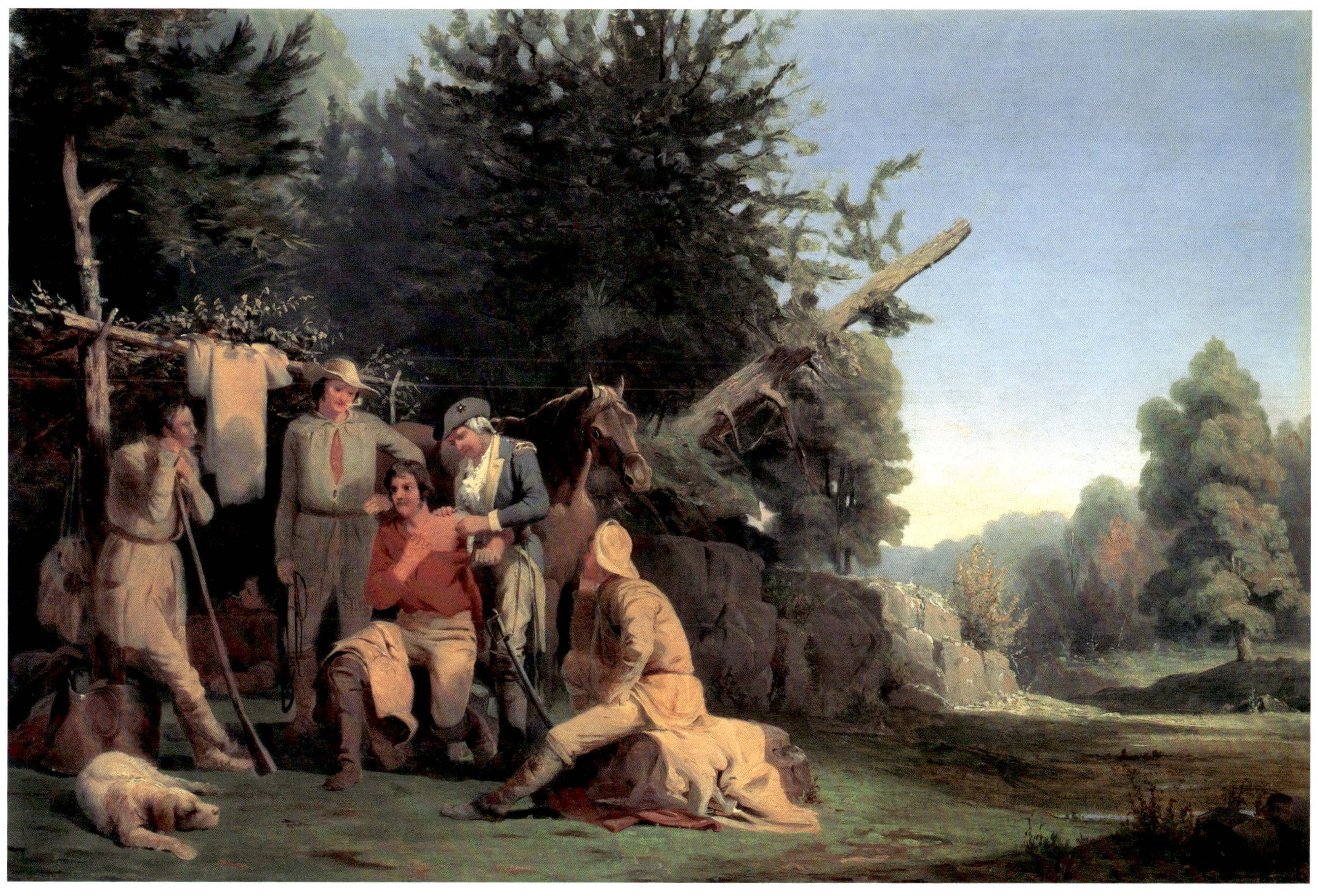

NO. 13

14
Marine View

c. 1845
Location unknown
Grubar no. 9

P R O V E N A N C E : Am Art-Union, 1845; distributed by lottery to George E. Cook, New York, 1845.

E X H I B I T E D : Am Art-Union, 1845, no. 97.

R E F E R E N C E S : Management Committee Minutes, 1839–1855, reel 1, December 8, 1845, Am Art-Union Papers, indicates Ranney was paid $35 for this picture. Am Art-Union, *Transactions for the Year 1845*, p. 29, no. 97, as distributed to George E. Cook, New York. Cowdrey 1953, 2, p. 294.

15
Emigrants Resting

c. 1845
Oil on canvas
Location unknown

P R O V E N A N C E : M. K. Bridges, by 1845.

E X H I B I T E D : Brooklyn Institute, Brooklyn, New York, Fourth Annual Exhibition, October 1845, *Catalogue of Paintings, Sculpture, and Other Works of Art*, no. 70, as owned by M. K. Bridges.

Shortly after the Brooklyn Institute's annual exhibition, *Morris's National Press* reported having visited Ranney's studio in the New York University Building. The writer described what must surely have been the same or a similar picture as "an emigrant family encamping for the night, near what is called 'an oak opening.'"[1] The writer praised the artist for his particular "feeling for nature and truth," noting that unlike many of his contemporaries, the young artist "has traveled west, and . . . understands his subject." He also mentioned having seen "several very good portraits."[2] L B

1. According to the Oxford English Dictionary, an oak opening was defined in the mid-nineteenth century as an opening or thinly wooded space in an oak forest.
2. *Morris's National Press*, February 28, 1846, p. 2.

16
Hay Making

c. 1845
Probably oil on canvas
Location unknown

P R O V E N A N C E : Dr. M. K. Bridges, by 1845.

E X H I B I T E D : Brooklyn Institute, Brooklyn, New York., Fourth Annual Exhibition, October 1845, *Catalogue of Paintings, Sculpture, and Other Works of Art*, no. 88, as owned by Dr. M. K. Bridges.

Later in his career, Ranney returned to this subject (see cat. no. 133). L B

17
Hunters

c. 1845
Oil on canvas
Location unknown

PROVENANCE: O. C. Forsyth, by 1845.

EXHIBITED: Brooklyn Institute, Brooklyn, New York, Fourth Annual Exhibition, October 1845, *Catalogue of Paintings, Sculpture, and Other Works of Art*, no. 88, October 1, 1845, no. 35, as owned by O. C. Forsyth.

This may be the same painting as *Deer Hunters* (cat. no. 9). LB

18*
The Lasso

1846
Oil on canvas
31 1/2 x 42 1/4 inches
(80 x 107.3 cm)
Signed, lower left:
Ranney/1846
Buffalo Bill Historical
Center, Cody,
Wyoming. Gift of Mrs.
J. Maxwell Moran,
22.99.1
Grubar no. 20

PROVENANCE: James Harold Frazer (d. 1913); Mrs. J. H. (Sally Bayly) Crenshaw, Front Royal, Virginia (c. 1913–1951); (T. Gilbert Brouillette, New York, 1951) Claude J. Ranney, Malvern, Pennsylvania, 1951–1971; his daughter, Elizabeth R. Moran, Paoli, Pennsylvania, 1971–1999.

REFERENCE: FARL, supply mount provides provenance. Ayres 1987, p. 83, fig. 47, ill., pp. 84–85, discusses literary sources and calls it a study.

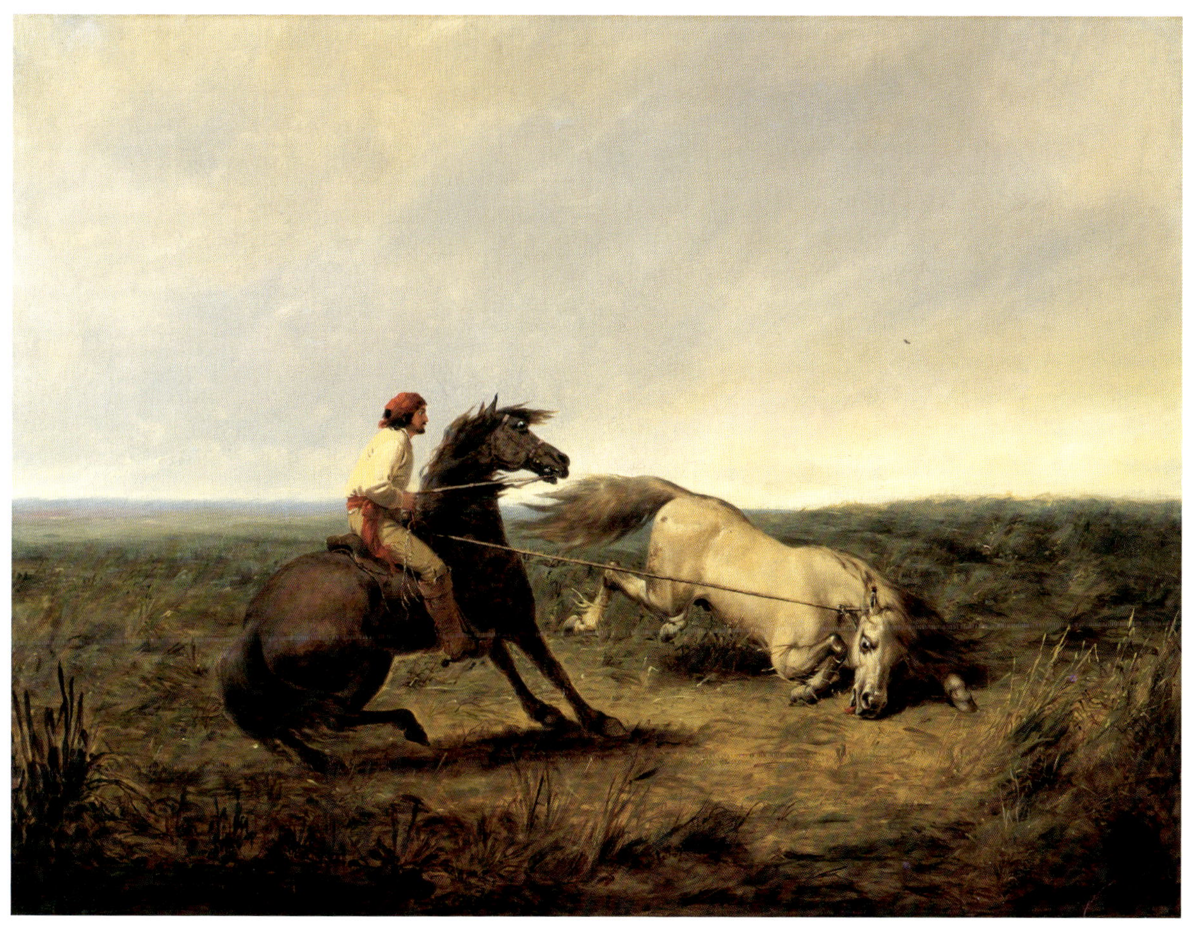

Given its smaller size and similar theme, this painting is considered to be a study for Ranney's *Hunting Wild Horses* (cat. no. 19). Several important differences may be seen between the two works, differences that converge within a more intimate matrix to grant a more commanding presence to the vaquero in the study than in the larger canvas.

The Lasso presents the two primary protagonists alone on the prairie and central in the composition, while in the larger work the vaquero is moved to the left side of the picture, conceding the vortex of the action to the captured white horse. In *The Lasso* only the captor and his horse extend above the horizon line. Moreover, the vaquero is larger in relation to the horse he rides. He leans forward in the saddle, his left hand obscured by his body and the neck of the horse. Both the size of the rider and his position in the saddle appear more naturalistic in the study than in the finished work. In the study, the vaquero is also more in proportion to his mount, and his left hand appears to be controling the dally, which conforms with the normal practice more readily than the arrangement in *Hunting Wild Horses* where the rider has secured the dally and pulls back awkwardly with both hands on the reins.

The forward pitch of the horseman in *The Lasso* would appear to reflect the artist's interest in centering the composition with a circular motion that echoes the curve of the captured horse's neck and the rump of the rider's mount. When Ranney decided to add more horses in *Hunting Wild Horses*, he was forced to reconsider the rider's pose. In order to counterbalance the divergent thrust of the horse on the right side of the picture, the artist positioned his rider to lean backward in the saddle.

Consequent to those elements, *The Lasso* is a more focused work, centered and introverted by comparison. *Hunting Wild Horses*, with its extra dramatic display and added panoramic sweep, transports the viewer into a larger dimension, one that can be read to be more than anecdotal. Even the title *The Lasso* suggests, like the composition, a less ambitious and more closely defined endeavor. The scene is focused on the process of capturing a wild horse rather than the potential and larger implications of such an act.

Many writers of the period relished the opportunity to describe the horse hunters of the western plains. A year after Ranney produced this work, Francis Parkman wrote about several similar episodes that he witnessed. One horse hunter whom he met north of the Arkansas River in 1846 was named Antoine Le Rouge. As in Ranney's painting, Le Rouge wore "loose trousers and fluttering calico shirt. A handkerchief was bound round his head to confine his black shiny hair, and his small eyes twinkled beneath it with a mischievous lustre."[1] PHH

1 Francis Parkman, *The Oregon Trail*, (1849; Boston: Ginn and Company, 1910), p. 265. Parkman's accounts were originally published in serial form in the *Knickerbocker* magazine in 1847.

19*
Hunting Wild Horses

1846

Oil on canvas

36 x 54 1/2 inches
(91.4 x 138.4 cm)

Signed and dated,
lower left:
Ranney/1846

Museum of the
American West, Autry
National Center, Los
Angeles

Grubar no. 21

PROVENANCE: Marshall O. Roberts (1814–1880), New York, by 1856–1880, his widow (sale, Fifth Avenue Art Galleries, *Executor's Sale . . . of the Late Marshall O. Roberts, Modern Paintings*, New York, January 20, 1897, lot 152, p. 49, as Hunting Wild Horses, for $70); (Victor P. Spark, New York, to 1951) (M. Knoedler and Company, New York, 1951–1967, as The Lasso); Northern Natural Gas Co., Omaha, [later Enron Corporation, Houston], 1967–1988.

ON LOAN: Joslyn Museum. Omaha, 1968–1988.

EXHIBITED: United States Sanitary Fair, Philadelphia, 1864, *Great Central Fair*, no. 213, as Catching Wild Horses, lent by M. O. Roberts. Fort Worth 1987, p. 82, no. 46, p. 193, listed.

REFERENCES: *Crayon* 3 (August 1856), p. 249, listed in collection of Marshall O. Roberts, as Wild Horses on the Prairie. Tuckerman 1867, p. 626, listed in the Marshall O. Roberts collection, as Wild Horses. Edward Strahan [Earl Shinn], ed.,*The Art Treasures of America* (Philadelphia: 1879), vol. 2, p. 16, listed in collection of Mrs. Marshall O. Roberts, as The Lasso. *New York Tribune*, January 21, 1897, provides sales information. Larry Curry, *The American West* (New York: Viking Press, 1972), p. 25, calls it a calculated composition. Glanz 1982, pp. 90–97, suggests Homeric influence. Ayres 1987, p. 82, fig. 46; pp. 84–85 discusses. M. Knoedler and Company, telephone conversation, October 16, 2000, provided information on Spark.

"The zoology of the Prairies has probably attracted more attention than any other feature in their natural history," wrote Josiah Gregg in the immensely popular 1844 account of his western travels, *Commerce of the Prairies*. Leading off a chapter on the animals of the Southwest was what Gregg considered "by far the most noble" of the beasts, the "*mustang* or wild horse of the Prairies."[1] The wild horse exemplified the notion of freedom on the expansive western grasslands. Washington Irving, writing about his brief tour to the region nearly a decade earlier, celebrated the wild horse as the "free rover of the prairies" and extolled the innate "pride and freedom of his nature."[2] George Catlin had ridden across the southern plains in 1834 and was, after direct observation, compelled to claim that there existed "no other animal on the prairies so wild and so sagacious as the horse."[3]

Yet other writers of the period viewed the mustang from a different perspective, as an exploitable resource and bounty. The Rocky Mountain adventurer Rufus Sage noted that he "frequently encountered four or five hundred head . . . in a single band," while a travel account by an unknown author of 1834, *A Visit to Texas*, clearly spelled out their economic potential, indicating that at some future date, they might be harvested as a "valuable article of export, as they are innumerable, and cost only the trouble of catching."[4] Thus was revealed one of the fundamental paradoxes of the western experience, the contest between the wild, free element and the usable, tamable and marketable quantity. The tension established by these two opposite views of the West, along with a complex political environment, are what inform one of the earliest western works in Ranney's *oeuvre*, the painting *Hunting Wild Horses*.

In this large and animated tableau, Ranney presents a scene commonly played out on the western plains. Silhouetted against a low horizon line and very close in view is the dramatic interplay of hunter and hunted. The sweeping, thundering dynamic of the wild herd encircles a spotlighted, fallen horse that has been brought to a crippling halt at the end of a vaquero's rope. The downed white steed crumples forward, its tail jetting behind from the force of its interrupted motion. At the other end of the taut rope is the hunter who, leaning back against the jolt, pulls hard with both hands on the reins of his own violently bracing mount. Two other horses dash along the horizon in the distance. All else is steel blue sky and tawny grass plains.

In a calculated composition, Ranney attempts to arrest the action, and, by centering the composition on the captured horse, he focuses the issue of control, while hinting at the sublime, convulsive powers of nature that still lay beyond the reach of this one man and his rawhide lariat. The tension in the picture, conveyed in the bulging eyes of the horses, both tame and wild, suggests not just the physical exertion and danger to all parties involved but plays equally to the pathos inherent in the conquest of nature by man. Poets and fellow artists considered the mustang at once an evanescent form and the purest idea of glorious beauty. The Baltimore painter Alfred Jacob Miller, who rode across the northern prairies in 1837, later recalled their powerful attraction.

> Among the wild animals of the west, none gave us so much pleasure or caused such excitement as the bands of wild horses that at intervals came under our view. The beauty and symmetry of their forms, their wild and spirited action, long full sweeping manes and tails, variety of colour, and fleetness of motion, all combined to call forth admiration from the most stoical.[5]

Others bemoaned the capture, claiming that it meant domestic drudgery, and even death for the hapless victim. It was Washington Irving who most effectively articulated the dismal fortunes of the captured wild horse. When a captive was led into his camp along the Red River one day in 1834, the author, known to be a genre artist in verse, penned the following painterly lament.

> I could not but look with compassion upon this fine young animal, whose whole course of existence had been so suddenly reversed. From being a denizen of these vast pastures, ranging at will from plain to plain and mead to mead, cropping of every herb and flower, and drinking of every stream, he was suddenly reduced to perpetual and painful servitude, to pass his life under the harness and the curb, amid, perhaps, the din and dust and drudgery of cities. The transition in his lot was such as sometimes takes place in human affairs, and in the fortunes of towering individuals:—one day, a prince of the prairies—the next day, a pack horse![6]

Ranney's scene reflects what Americans were weighing in the ongoing deliberations about the future of the western portion of their continent. It speaks also to the fundamental differences between man and nature in the nineteenth-century mind. Man's history, at least the Euro-American chapters, was a linear construct, symbolized in the rigid postures of the hunter and his trained horse as well as the straight horizontal rawhide link between the man and the fallen steed. Nature, on the other hand, was cyclical. Its patterns flowed in seasonal regularity with anticipated regenerative force. Man intrudes on nature, cuts into the circle and extracts what he wants.

The moment that intrigued Ranney was not the rich array of nature's nobility so much as the moment of capture and capitulation. Following Dawn Glanz's suggestion of the influence of the Homeric myth of the Corinthian Bellerophon and the horse Pegasus, in which the horse serves his master in destroying a host of odious adversaries, we can extend this message to Ranney's own day and find many associations. The vaquero is the American Bellerophon and champion of the national will. Athena, who assists Bellerophon, becomes the James Polk administration with its mandate to annex Texas; the white horse represents Texas, the central metaphorical trophy. Once the horse succumbs, then additional spoils on the political horizon, such as California and Oregon, may also yield. In the Ranney portrayal, the horses surrounding the white steed may represent the number of new states that could potentially be carved out of Texas, while the two more distant horses may be the Pacific Coast trophies. Ranney's study for the painting *The Lasso* (cat. no. 18) presents only a single quarry, while *Hunting Wild Horses* features multiple potentials. This suggests that, as the year 1846 unfolded, the western events multiplied from a single issue into a complex and rather dizzying array of options.

While it is not known how Ranney felt about the Mexican War or later the negotiations with England over Oregon, it is probably safe to assume that given his military service in the Texas revolution he harbored sympathies for Polk's expansionist cause. If so, he was among the large segment of the American populace who thought that winning Texas was not just the United States' rightful claim of a deserved bounty in the Southwest, but an expression and preservation of democracy itself. The common man (the Texan), they reasoned, was battling against old world despotism (Mexico). In fact, this movement held broad international political and artistic sway. Take, for example, Emanuel Leutze, living in Düsseldorf at the time, who was soon

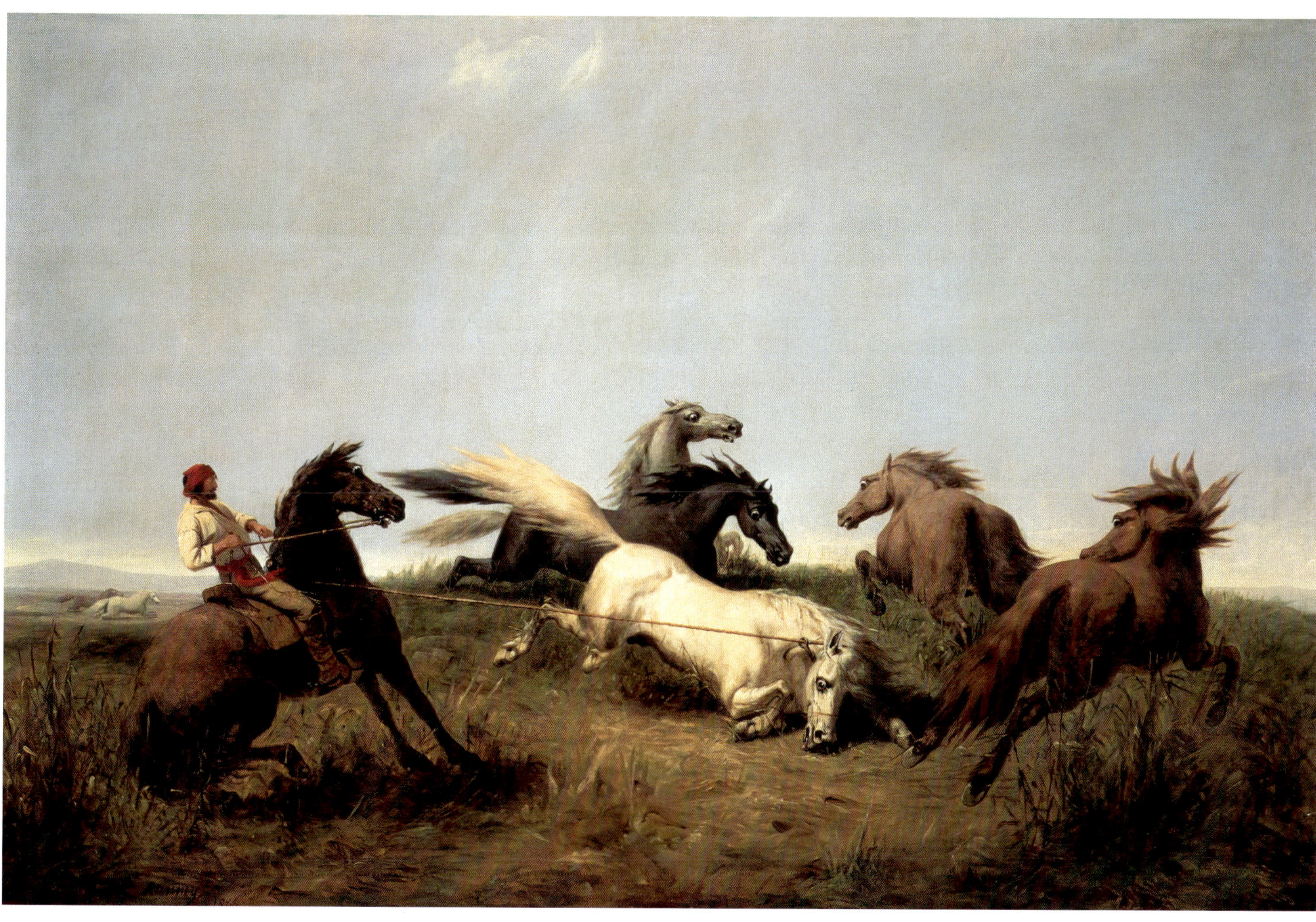

to embark on his *magnum opus, Washington Crossing the Delaware*, as a political statement defending nascent democratic movements in Germany. Hiram Powers's *The Greek Slave* of 1846 articulated similar sentiments about the Greek War of Independence. Ranney's portrayal of conquest may, in this context, be considered a paean to freedom.

Ranney's scene is very likely constructed from personal observation. A number of American artists found the Mexican War to be an appealing subject. Charles Deas, a contemporary of Ranney's and also a soldier in the war, painted several direct views of military life. However, most artists chose to depict the war from afar, showing public reaction to the events rather than the events themselves. For example, Richard Caton Woodville's *War News from Mexico* of 1848 (private collection) and James Goodwyn Clooney's *Mexican News* of 1847 (Munson-Williams-Proctor Institute, Utica, New York) present Americans reading accounts of the war in the newspaper.

Ranney's vaquero is like Ranney, however, an active player—one who determines the outcome of the actions at hand. The artist's experience in the West and his penchant for outdoor life no doubt motivated such a vigorous treatment. He had probably not only witnessed vaqueros at work on the prairie, but also recognized the potency of such imagery in the artworks of other fellow recorders of these scenes. The most commonly quoted influence for Ranney's lassoing paintings is George Catlin, who depicted Comanches in pursuit of wild horses for his famous Indian Gallery. Even if Ranney did not see that vast assemblage of portraits, land-

25

scapes, and scenes of daily life, which enjoyed large audiences in New York during a highly publicized fall exhibition in 1837, he could have viewed such scenes in Catlin's books published in 1841 and 1844. These volumes and prints circulated widely in the United States. [7]

A good number of compositional similarities resonate between Ranney's *Hunting Wild Horses* and Catlin's *Wild Horses at Play*, which was also illustrated in Catlin's 1841 book. Catlin's description of what was involved in catching wild horses fits Ranney's painting as well.

> The usual mode of taking the wild horses, is, by throwing the *lasso*, whilst pursuing them at full speed, and dropping a noose over their necks, by which their speed is soon checked, and they are "choked down." The lasso is a thong of raw hide, some ten or fifteen yards in length, twisted or braided, with a noose fixed at the end of it; which, when the coil of the lasso is thrown out, drops with great certainty over the neck of the animal, which is soon conquered.[8]

He went on to explain that the vaqueros (as pictured in Ranney's work) had learned their trade from the Indians. The "best hunter in these Western regions," according to Catlin, was a Frenchman named Beatte, one of the rangers who served as a guide with the artist on his 1834 southwestern trip and who had grown up among the Osage Indians. He was known for his formidable skills with a lasso and his wiles as a hunter. Irving met the same character a year later and marveled at the spectacle of the "harum-scarum kind of chase" that Beatte led on several occasions in pursuit of wild horses. Carrying a hunting knife in his belt and wearing a handkerchief tied around his head, he was described as part of a "promiscuous throng" who took on heroic stature as the "pell-mell, hurry-scurry, wild buffalo, wild horse, wild huntsman, with clang and clatter, and whoop and halloo, that made the forests ring."[9]

J. T. Hammond's engraved illustration of such huntsmen, *Lazooing a Horse on the Prairie*, which appeared in the 1834 travelogue *A Visit to Texas*, provided an additional pictorial antecedent for Ranney's spirited renditions. A few years later, in 1837, an even more closely allied composition was published by the heirs of Davy Crockett in *"Go Ahead": Davy Crockett's Almanack of Wild Sports in the West*. A wood engraving called *Mode of Catching Wild Horses on the Prairies of Texas* accompanied an article of the same title.[10]

Ranney's *Hunting Wild Horses* was conceived as a purely American exercise. That it represented a statement of national conquest and Yankee capitalist opportunism may be further certified by the work's early ownership. By 1856 the painting was in the collection of the New York financier and art collector Marshall O. Roberts. Owner and art work fit like hand in glove. Roberts, whose fortunes grew to gargantuan proportions by mid-century, had started on his course of success by negotiating important government contracts during the Mexican War. He was also instrumental in building Texas railroads and in establishing transportation systems that served the California gold rush through the Isthmus of Panama. Thus his ties to the West and its rich economic potential provided a natural affinity for Ranney's Texas prairie drama. At the time of his death in 1880, Roberts also owned two other important western genre paintings as part of his sizeable private art collection, Charles Deas's *Long Jakes* of 1844 (Denver Art Museum) and Woodville's *War News from Mexico*.

Although Roberts was involved in numerous business scandals, his munificence as an art patron was highly touted. He opened his art collection free to the public and was known to share his art holding in other ways. In the summer of 1864, for example, he loaned *Hunting Wild Horses* to the Great Central Fair of the United States Sanitary Commission in Philadelphia.

By 1852, only six years after Ranney completed his evocative *Hunting Wild Horses*, the Boston periodical *Gleason's Pictorial* featured an article with an illustration that confirmed the connection between the two themes of wild horse hunting and national expansion. The author notes the broad array of "graceful deer, bounding buffaloes and numerous troops of fine and noble wild horses" available to the settler who selects his spot; builds himself a dwelling in a shady island, and by conforming to certain requisitions of the government, becomes at once the rightful proprietor of nearly as much territory as his eye can at once survey. If he wishes a horse or a drove of horses to ride, to travel, to hunt, to work, he has only to ride into the prairie, and the animals cost him only the trouble of catching them. The horses of Texas are small, run wild in numerous droves over the prairies, and are easily taken and rendered serviceable.[11]

Although the "embodiment of stirring and hazardous adventure,"[12] the securing of wild horses provided the promise of a new life in the West's mythic Eden, where freedom, once surrendered by nature, is perceived of as transferring that freedom to the vanquisher. PHH

1. Josiah Gregg, *Commerce of the Prairies* (New York: Henry G. Langlay, 1844), vol. 2, pp. 206–207.

2. Washington Irving, *A Tour on the Prairies* (London: John Murray, 1835).

3. George Catlin, *Illustrations of the Manners, Customs, and Condition of the North American Indians . . .* (London: Henry G. Bohn, 1857), vol. 2, p. 57.

4. Rufus B. Sage, *Scenes in the Rocky Mountains* (Philadelphia: Carey and Hart, 1846), p. 313, and unknown author, *A Visit to Texas* (New York: Van Nostrand and Dwight, 1836), p. 48.

5. Alfred J. Miller, "Stampede of Wild Horses," *Rough Draughts for Notes to Indian Sketches* (1837–1855) in the manuscript collections of the Gilcrease Museum, Tulsa, Oklahoma, no. 144.

6. Irving, *A Tour of the Prairies*, p. 122.

7. See, for example, William H. Truettner, *The Natural Man Observed: A Study of George Catlin's Indian Gallery* (Washington, D.C.: Smithsonian Institution Press, 1979), p. 126.

8. George Catlin, *Catlin's North American Indian Portfolio: Hunting Scenes and Amusements . . .* (London: G. Catlin, 1844).

9. Irving, *A Tour of the Prairies*, pp. 28, 120, and 149.

10. See J. Fiske, *A Visit to Texas: Being a Journal of a Traveller Through Those Parts Interesting to American Settlers* (New York: Goodrich and Wiley, 1834) and "Method of Catching Wild Horses on the Prairies of Texas," in *"Go Ahead!": Davy Crockett's Almanack of Wild Sports in the West*, vol. 1, no. 3 (1837), pp. 28–30. My thanks are extended to Byron Price for alerting me to the Crockett almanac image.

11. "Catching Wild Horses on a Prairie," *Gleason's Pictorial*, vol. 2, no. 26 (June 26, 1852), p. 1.

12. Ibid.

20
Pennsylvania Teamster

1846

Oil on canvas

29 1/2 x 40 inches
(74.9 x 101.6 cm)

Signed and dated,
lower right:
Ranney/1846

Gilcrease Museum,
Tulsa

Grubar no. 22

PROVENANCE: Am Art-Union, 1847; distributed by lottery to J. J. Haines, New York, 1847; (Kennedy and Company, New York, by 1945–1952, as *Crossing the Ferry*).

EXHIBITED: Am Art-Union, 1847, no. 4 as *Pennsylvania Teamster*.

REFERENCES: Am Art-Union, Executive Committee Minutes, 1846–1854, reel 2, February 26, 1847, Am Art-Union Papers, approved payment of $75.00 for Landscape View in Pennsylvania. Am Art-Union, *Plan of Institution . . . Catalogue of Paintings. . .* , June 1, November 1, and December 15, 1847, no. 4. *Literary World*, October 23, 1847, p. 277 (quoted in entry). Am Art-Union, *Transactions for the Year 1847*, p. 32, no. 4. *Christian Science Monitor*, September 1, 1945, p. 8, illus. as Carting Flour and owned by Kennedy and Company, New York. Cowdrey 1953, 2, p. 294, provides provenance.

When this picture was acquired by the Gilcrease in 1952 it was mistitled *Crossing the Ferry*, a painting exhibited at the National Academy in 1846 as no. 304 and purchased that year by the American Art-Union (see cat. no. 23). Grubar listed three alternative titles: *Going to Mill* (see cat. no. 105), *Carting Flour*, and *Hauling Flour*. A review of the American Art-Union's records indicate that it was first called *Landscape View in Pennsylvania*. When it was exhibited in 1847, however, it was titled *Pennsylvania Teamster*.

Taken together the various titles well describe this scene, which documents commercial activities in early nineteenth-century Pennsylvania. It depicts two wagons; the first, and presumably also the distant second, are loaded with white bags, probably filled with flour. Each wagon and its team of horses is guided by one teamster on horseback. Pennsylvania was so rich in farmland that over one-third of its population was involved in agriculture, the bedrock of its economy. Because of the abundance of grain growing by 1800, the commonwealth led the nation in the production of flour. The mills, primarily based in the countryside, supported many livelihoods, particularly teamsters who transported the processed goods over a well-developed network of roads and turnpikes from remote rural areas to cities like Philadelphia, from which flour was sold locally or shipped abroad. By 1859, flour and meal were the number one ranked businesses in the United States, generating $250 million, or over twice that of the second-ranked cotton textile industry.[1]

While the scene could have taken place anywhere, that it took place in a specific state must have appealed to the nationalistic agenda of the Art-Union, whose purchase committee was particularly interested in scenes that reflected America's unique way of life. While the picture celebrates regional workers, commerce, and transportation, it also echoes much of mid-nineteenth-century imagery, including Ranney's pioneers in wagon trains migrating west.

In reviewing the work when it was exhibited at the Art-Union, the *Literary World* found the picture "free and spirited."[2] LB

1. John A. Garraty, *The American Nation: A History of the United States* (New York: Harper and Row, 1966), p. 337.

2. Quoted in Grubar, p. 28, no. 22.

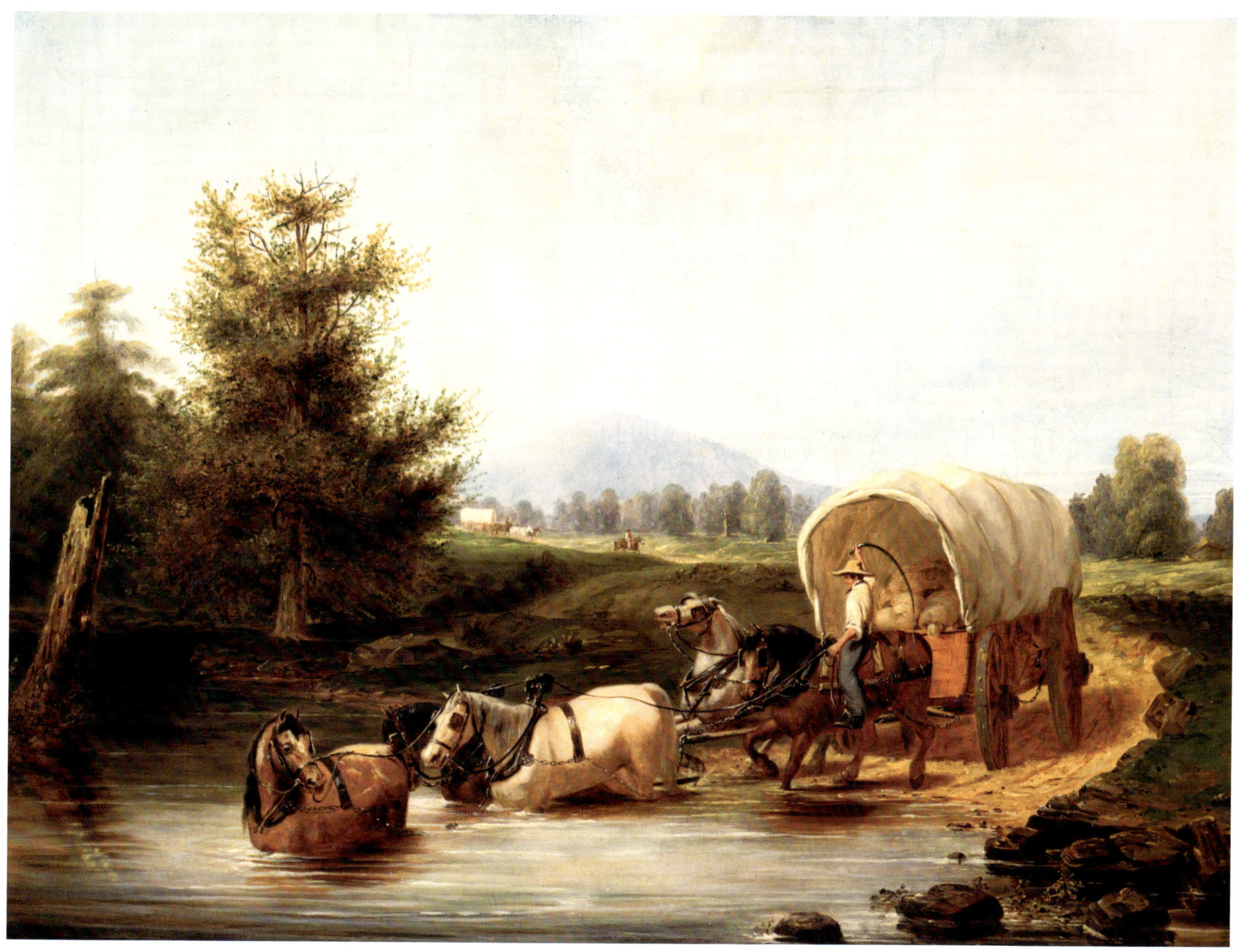

NO. 20

29

21

Coast Scene, with Figures

c. 1846

Oil on canvas

Location unknown

Grubar no. 12

Provenance: Am Art-Union,. 1846; distributed by lottery to Robert Ray, New York, by 1846.

Exhibited: Am Art-Union, New York, 1846, no. 20.

References: Management Committee Minutes, 1839–1855, reel 1, July 24, 1846, approved for payment $50 for frame, Coast Scene; and Executive Committee Minutes, reel 2, December 10, 1846, approved payment of $100 to W. Ranney for Coast Scene, Am Art-Union Papers. *New-York Daily Tribune*, October 1, 1846, p. 2, no. 20, listed as Coast Scene, with figures, purchased for distribution; reprinted in *New York Evening Post for the Country*, October 3, 1846, p. 1. Am Art-Union, *Transactions for the Year 1846*, p. 31, no. 20, as Coast Scene, with figures and as distributed to Robert Ray, New York. Cowdrey 1953, 2, p. 294.

22

The Dead Courser or Charger

c. 1846

Probably oil on canvas

Location unknown

Grubar nos. 13, as The Dead Courser and 14, as The Dead Charger

Provenance: Am Art-Union, 1846; distributed by lottery to D[avid]. A. Wood, New York, 1846.

Exhibited: NAD, 1846, no. 54, as *The Dead Courser*, owned by the artist; Am Art-Union, 1846, no 31, as *The Dead Charger*.

References: *New York Tribune*, April 24, 1846, p. 2 (quoted in entry). *Anglo American* vol. 7, no. 1, (April 25, 1846), p. 22. *Morris's National Press*, vol. 1, no. 12 (May 2, 1846), p. 2. *New York Evening Post for the Country*, October 3, 1846. Am Art-Union, Executive Committee Minutes 1846–1854, reel no. 2, October 29, 1846, approved payment of $150 for Ranney's Crossing the Ferry and Dead Charger, Am Art-Union Papers. Am Art-Union, *Transactions for the Year 1846*, p. 31, no. 3, as distributed to D. A. Wood, New York. *Spirit of the Times*, September 26, 1846, p. 36, provides detailed description of painting (quoted in entry). *United States Magazine and Democratic Review*, January 1847, p. 65. Cowdrey 1943, 2, p. 88. Cowdrey 1953, 2, p. 294.

In his catalogue, Grubar listed *The Dead Courser*, no. 13, and *The Dead Charger*, number 14, as two different pictures. A courser and a charger are synonymous: both words describe a battle horse. Grubar speculated, however, that since no purchaser was listed for the National Academy picture, and the Art-Union regularly bought paintings from their exhibitions, the *Dead Courser* and *The Dead Charger* are in fact the same picture. He further noted that, as was the case with Ranney's *Dead Courser*, an asterisk in the National Academy's catalogue denoted paintings that were purchased by the Art-Union but still hanging in the exhibition. It is now clear from a survey of contemporary descriptions of the picture when it was exhibited at each venue that Grubar's hunch was correct, and that both titles indeed refer to the same object.

The 1846 *New York Tribune* article described *The Dead Courser* when it was exhibited that spring at the National Academy of Design: "This is a small picture by Ranney, and is hung in a low and unfavorable position. But it is a powerful and startling piece, and will hold on the Gallery Walls." Around the same time, *Morris's National Press* described it as a bloody battle scene with a dead courser in the foreground and a bird of prey overhead. The *Anglo American* described the subject as a "dead white horse."

When the picture was shown at the American-Art Union later that year, the *Spirit of the Times* identified the painting as *Ringgold's Dead Charger* and provided the following excerpt detailing the violent narrative of the picture: in the foreground lies the "noble steed. . . . his caparisons [ornamental coverings for a horse] soiled and stained, the pistols fallen from their holsters . . . his neck extended . . . nostrils dilated." The writer goes on to describe the picture in which a wolf tears the flesh of the forlorn horse while trying to keep at bay a vulture sitting atop a shattered cannon wheel in the background, patiently awaiting his opportunity to feast on the remains. He concluded his piece with praise for the painter who so "eloquently and sadly painted" the "gallant steed, thou and thy master alike with this bright world are done—his memory shines proudly on his country's history—the young and kindly painter eloquently and sadly hath pointed to *thy* story."

Such a reaction as well as the assigned title indicate that this writer was reading this painting as a celebration of Major Samuel Ringgold (1800–1846). A graduate of West Point and new national hero, Ringgold headed a unit of light artillery which was known as the Flying Artillery because of the swiftness with which they were able to maneuver their lightweight cannon on wheels. In one of the earliest battles of the Mexican War, Ringgold and his men triumphed at the Battle of Palo Alto (April 26–May 8, 1846), ravaging the Mexicans and forcing them to retreat with heavy losses. In the subsequent confusion and mayhem, many Mexicans, overladen with uniforms and equipment, tragically drowned in the Rio Grande. At the end of the battle, as his triumphant unit approached the Mexican line, both of Ringgold's legs were pierced by cannon balls. He died three days later and became the first hero and martyr of the war. A declaration of war and a call to arms to vindicate the honor of the country was swiftly voted on in Congress. Ringgold was immortalized in song, as well as in printed images in which he was generally depicted as falling off his battle horse or charger. Unfortunately, in spite of this contemporary interpretation, Ranney exhibited *The Dead Courser* at the National Academy beginning in April 1846, a month before Ringgold's death, and could not have anticipated the hero's connection described in the *Spirit of the Times*. It was more likely that Ranney, as was his usual practice, was in fact depicting a generic battle scene which he meant to resonate in general with the current conflicts in the West. It was only later, while the painting was on exhibit at the American Art-Union, that widespread outpouring of grief and outrage resulted from Ringgold's death. The *Spirit of the Times* then co-opted Ranney's horrific image as a springboard to allude to Ringgold's death and eulogize the fallen national hero. LB

23 *
Crossing the Ferry—Scene on the Pee Dee

c. 1846

Oil on canvas

28 1/8 x 42 1/8 inches (71.4 x 107 cm)

Signed on boat: Ranney

Inscribed on American Art-Union label affixed to stretcher: No. 30. Crossing the Ferry/Scene on the peedee/W. Ranney

Morris Museum of Art, Augusta, Georgia, 1993.006.

Grubar no. 15

PROVENANCE: Am Art-Union, 1846; distributed by lottery to A. M. L. Scott, Middletown, New York, by 1846; descended in family to Alexander M. Clark, Newtown, Connecticut (David B. Findlay Galleries, New York, by 1953, as advertised in *Antiques* 63 [February 1953], p. 104).

EXHIBITED: NAD, New York, 1846, no. 304, as Crossing the Ferry; Am Art-Union, 1846, no. 30, as Crossing the Ferry—Scene on the Pee Dee.

REFERENCES: *New York Herald,* April 21, 1846, no. 192, p. 2. *Morris's National Press,* vol. 1, no. 19 (June 20, 1846), p. 4, reviews it (quoted in entry). Am Art-Union, Executive Committee Minutes 1846-1854, October 29, 1846, reel 2, Am Art-Union Papers, approved $150 payment for Ranney's Crossing the Ferry and Dead Charger. Am Art-Union, *Transactions for the Year 1846,* p. 31, no. 30, as distributed to A.M.L. Scott, New York. *New York Tribune,* October 1, 1846. *New York Evening Post for the Country,* October 3, 1846. Cowdrey 1943, 2, p. 88. Cowdrey 1953, 2, p. 294. Estill Curtis Pennington, *Passage and Progress in the Works of William Tylee Ranney* (Morris Museum of Art: Augusta, Georgia, 1993). David Findlay Jr., New York, 1992, provided provenance

This is one of Ranney's earliest surviving pictures of a scene that documents his formative years in rural North Carolina. Although undated, it has been assigned to the year 1846, when it was exhibited in the spring at the National Academy of Design and purchased by the American-Art Union. The fortuitous survival of a rare American-Art Union label, which remains affixed to the stretcher, verifies the title and authorship.

By 1839, Ranney had returned from New York to Fayetteville, North Carolina, probably to visit his maternal aunt and uncle, the Notts, with whom he had lived from 1827 until about 1836. While there he advertised himself as a portrait painter. It is likely that he made sketches of his environs which he later used as sources for finished paintings after returning to New York in 1843, when he is again listed in the city directories.

The source of the Pee Dee River is in the western mountains of North Carolina, from which it winds its way southeast through the South Carolina woods to the sea at Georgetown. About halfway down, it is joined by

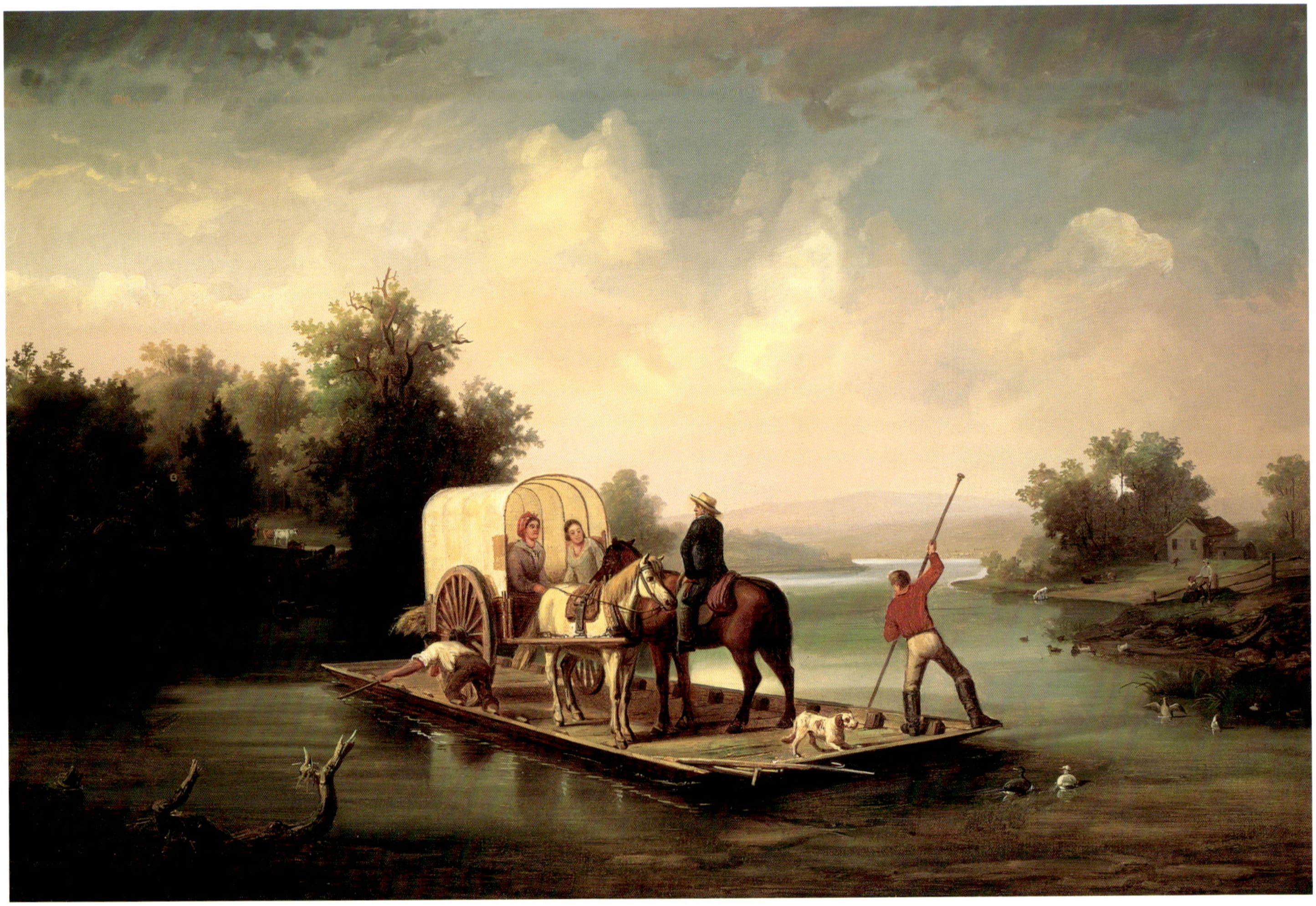

NO. 23

American Art-Union
label.

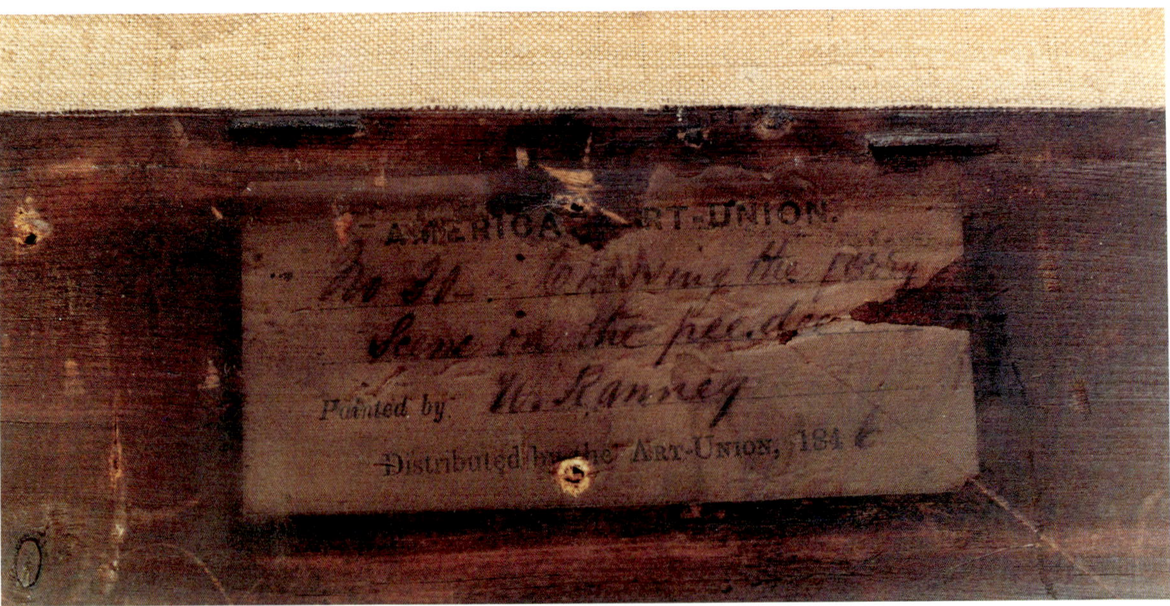

32

a tributary called the Little Pee Dee, which flows out of Cumberland County, North Carolina, where Fayetteville is located.

The ferry crossing, set in a lush landscape, is a typical scene that Ranney must have frequently encountered while traveling in the back country of the Carolinas. In this picture, as so often in his work, there is a central scene surrounded by multiple subthemes, so that the viewer's interest is sustained across the canvas. Here, the major action is the ferry with two flatboat men poling across the river toward the homestead at the right. Two women in a small covered wagon pulled by a single horse appear to be conversing with an elderly man atop a roan horse. Ducks paddle nonchalantly past the ferry, aware of, but ignoring, an agitated canine. Though the dog's instinctual hunting abilities are suggested by its alert pose, it is frustrated by its trapped situation. On the right shoreline, a man and woman appear to be waiting for the ferry. In the left background, a man, apparently in anticipation of a return trip, is herding cattle toward the ferry landing, and a second man stands on the bank in the shadows above two moored skiffs.

While the overall composition is ambitious and teems with spirited narrative detail, the individual figures have been sketchily, almost flatly drawn, with the contours and volume barely defined by light and shadow. Some of this apparent naiveté may be a result of Ranney's immaturity as an artist. On the other hand, a con-servation report of August 10, 1993, in the Morris Museum files indicates that the thinly painted surface has been abraded and that there are retouched areas visible in the faces of the two women, the red shirt of the ferryman, and some patches of the water and trees. Even when it was exhibited at the National Academy of Design in 1846, however, the *Morris's National Press* observed that the painting looked "raw, and the boat makes no ripples in the water." In response to this criticism, Ranney may have reworked the canvas by adding ripples in the water or modifying other details before the picture was bought by the American Art-Union. The technical naiveté of this work, however, does indicate Ranney's youth and lack of formal training.

Grubar listed A. E. Douglass as the owner of this painting in 1857, based on a listing in the sale catalogue of his collection on March 26 of that year at the gallery of Henry H. Leeds and Company, New York City (lot 28). That painting, however, was entitled simply *The Crossing* (see cat. no. 106) and described as an "upright oval" with dimensions of 25 by 30 inches, somewhat smaller, and in a different format than this horizontal painting.[1]

Crossing the Ferry was apparently in continuous family ownership since its acquisition from the American Art-Union in 1846. According to a descendant, the original owner, Alexander McCloud Scott, was a drygoods merchant from Middletown, New York, who lived part-time in New York City. L B

1. That now lost painting was cited in the *Crayon* in May 1857 (p. 158) as having sold for $122. Grubar further speculated that *Crossing the Ferry* may be *The Escape* (cat. no. 116), which he also attributed to the Douglass collection. He inadvertently com-bined two different Leeds sales, however. *The Escape* did not appear in the Douglass sale, but rather was offered two days earli-er on March 24, in a general sale.

24
Jack

c. 1846
Oil on canvas
Location unknown
Grubar no. 16

EXHIBITED: NAD, 1846, no. 20.

REFERENCES: *Morris's National Press*, vol. 1, no. 11 (April 25, 1846), p. 2 (quoted in entry). *The Anglo American*, vol. 7, no. 1, (April 25, 1846), p. 22 (quoted in entry). Cowdrey 1943, 2, p. 88.

The 1846 *Morris's National Press* describes *Jack* as "an ill-looking gentleman of the canine species; a very clever study for an artist, but not a proper subject for an exhibition picture." The *Anglo American* critic clearly had a more positive take. After identifying the dog as a "springer" he calls the painting "one of the freshest, and most spirited things of the kind we have ever beheld." LB

25
Friendship in Adversity

c. 1846
Probably oil on canvas
Location unknown
Grubar no. 17

EXHIBITED: NAD, 1846, no. 332.

REFERENCES: *Morris's National Press*, vol. 1, no. 19 (June 20, 1846), p. 4 (quoted in entry). Cowdrey 1943, 2, p. 88, provides provenance.

Morris's National Press describes this painting as "two old horses, turned out to die, [which] is happy in feeling and very cleverly executed." LB

26

Shad Fishing on the Hudson

c. 1846

Oil on canvas

25 1/2 x 35 inches
(64.8 x 88.9 cm)

Signed on gunwale of
boat: Ranney

New Britain Museum
of American Art,
Connecticut. Harriet
Russell Stanley Fund,
65.9

Grubar no. 18

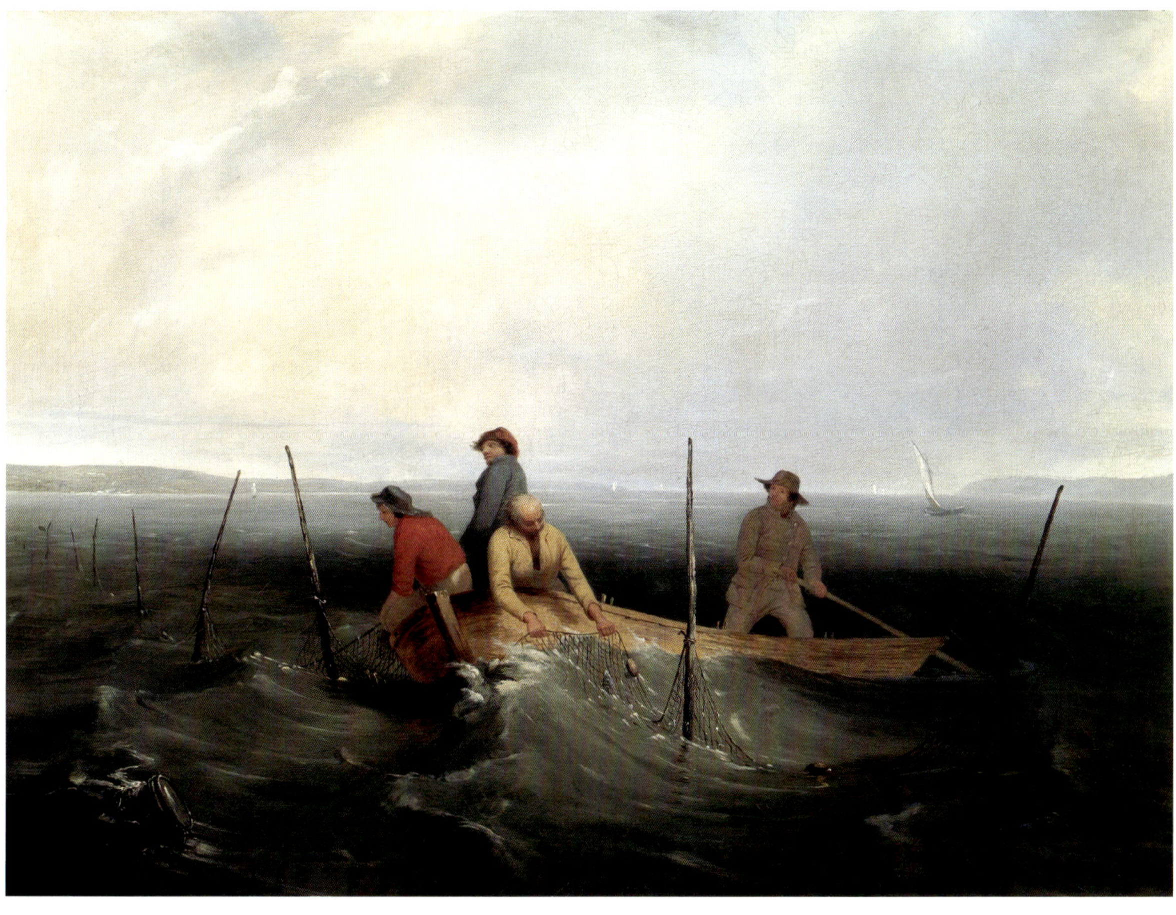

NO. 26

PROVENANCE: Am Art-Union, 1846; distributed by lottery to David T. Valentine, New York, 1846; Nick Sweitzner, to 1962; (Hirschl and Adler Galleries, New York, 1962–1965).

EXHIBITED: Am Art-Union, New York, 1846, no. 44. Hirschl and Adler Gallery, New York, "The Hudson River from New York to Albany," April 14–May 9, 1964, no. 35, illus.

REFERENCES: Am Art Union, Executive Committee Minutes, 1846–1854, reel 2, October 9, 1846, artist paid $75 for this picture, Am Art-Union Papers. Am Art-Union, *Transactions for the Year 1846*, New York, p. 31, "List of Paintings distributed among the members of the American Art-Union at the Tabernacle, New York," December 18, 1846, no. 44, to David T. Valentine. Cowdrey 1953, 2, p. 294. *The New Britain Museum of American Art: Catalogue of the Collection* (New Britain, Connecticut: New Britain Museum of American Art, 1975), p. 35, illus., p. 55, listed.

The scene represented in this painting exemplifies Ranney's early fascination with fishing activities in and around New York and New Jersey. While later in his career Ranney was to earn a reputation for his sporting or leisure scenes, in this genre scene he depicts fishermen at work. Shad, or *Alosa sapidissima* ("the most savory"), was the principal commercial fish in the Hudson River in the nineteenth century. Then, as today, it was prized for its sweet flesh and roe. The fish ranges in size from twenty to twenty-three inches in length and from five to six pounds in weight. In 1859, over a decade after Ranney painted this picture, *Frank Leslie's Illustrated Newspaper* estimated that over three thousand fishermen were involved in the business of shad fishing, excluding merchants and other salesmen.[1] Staples of the American diet, these tasty fish were salted and packed in large barrels and sold in cities from Philadelphia to Boston. In 1867 Thomas De Voe noted that American shad "is a general favorite among all classes of persons, as its flesh is considered among the best, sweetest, the most delicate as well as being the most plentiful when in season."[2] Shad run annually in the Hudson in the spring from mid-March through early June. To spawn in fresh estuary waters as far north as Albany, the Hudson River's mature shad—those born in the river four or five years earlier—work their way upriver 150 miles from the salty waters of the Atlantic Ocean and the tip of Manhattan. During Ranney's time, shad numbered in the hundreds of thousands. Beginning in the mid-nineteenth century, early conservationists began to observe that the number and size of the fish were beginning to decrease because of overfishing.[3]

The method Ranney illustrates in this picture may have directly contributed to this overfishing. Up until about 1810, shad fishermen set either hoop or fyke nets in the shallow waters close to the shore, leaving the Hudson's deep central channel free for multitudes of migrating fish. By the 1840s, these practices were superseded by the more efficient technique shown in Ranney's image—shad poles of about 40 to 120 feet long driven into soft mud. Supported by floats, gill nets were attached to these poles and spread almost entirely across the river's main channel, often disrupting ship traffic. As the shad made their way upstream, they swam head first into the vast nets and were trapped when their gills got entangled. The fishermen, who worked in teams of four to six from a flat-bottomed boat, then lifted the nets and removed the fish by hand. This method, also called pole netting, was used, among other places, on the New Jersey side of the Hudson opposite 125th Street, a short distance south of where the George Washington Bridge is today. In Ranney's time, the fish caught in this way were considered the tastiest,[4] but relatively few were able to avoid the efficiencies of this system.

Characteristically, Ranney has placed the observer in the center of the action, as though sitting in an adjacent skiff in the middle of the river. He probably sketched the original scene from a similar vantage point. As though making a sad commentary on the impact of overfishing, Ranney shows only one shad in the fishermen's nets, hardly the bounty that was reported earlier in the nineteenth century. LB

1. "The Shad Fisher," *Frank Leslie's Illustrated Newspaper*, April 23, 1859, no. 177, vol. VII, p. 324.

2. "The Market Assistant, Containing a Brief Description of Every Article of Human Food Sold in the Public Markets of the Cities of New York, Boston, Philadelphia, and Brooklyn," quoted in John McPhee, *The Founding Fish* (New York: Farrar, Straus and Giroux, 2002), p. 224.

3. McPhee, *The Founding Fish*, p. 224; and, James E. DeKay. *Zoology of New York or the New-York Fauna: Part IV. Fishes*, (Albany: W. and A. White and J. Visscher, 1842), p. 257.

4. "The Shad Fisher," p. 324; see also Robert H. Boyle, *The Hudson River: A Natural and Unnatural History* (New York: W. W. Norton and Company, 1969), p. 110; McPhee, *The Founding Fish*, p. 255.

27
Coast Scene with Fishermen

c. 1846
Oil on canvas
Location unknown
Grubar no. 19

PROVENANCE: Am Art-Union, 1846; distributed by lottery to J. H. Obear, Macon, Georgia, by 1846.

EXHIBITED: Am Art-Union, 1846, no. 121.

REFERENCES: Executive Committee Minutes, 1846-1854, reel 2, vol. 1, July 24 and December 10, 1846, artist was paid $50 for the frame and later $100 for the picture, Am Art-Union Papers. Am Art-Union, *Transactions for the Year 1846*, p. 34; Cowdrey 1953, 2, p. 294, provides provenance.

28A and 28B
Landscape

c. 1846
Oil on canvas
Location unknown

PROVENANCE: James E. Miller, Esq., by 1846.

EXHIBITED: Brooklyn Institute, Brooklyn, New York, *Fifth Annual Exhibition of the Brooklyn Institute*, 1846, no. 58, as Landscape, lent by James E. Miller, Esq., and no. 71, as Landscape lent by James E. Miller, Esq.

REFERENCE: *Catalogue of Paintings: Fifth Annual Exhibition of the Brooklyn Institute* (1846), cats. no. 58 and 71, lists and provides provenance.

29
The Lone Indian

c. 1846
Oil on canvas
Location unknown

PROVENANCE: Bridges and Fisher, by 1846.

EXHIBITED: Brooklyn Institute, Brooklyn, New York, Fifth Annual Exhibition of the Brooklyn Institute. 1846, no. 33.

REFERENCE: *Catalogue of Paintings: Fifth Annual Exhibition of the Brooklyn Institute*, October 27, 1846, no. 33, p. 4, lists painting and provides provenance.

30
Newfield Falls, Middletown, Connecticut

c. 1846
Oil on canvas
Location unknown

PROVENANCE: Bridges and Fisher, by 1846.

EXHIBITED: Brooklyn Institute, Brooklyn, New York, Fifth Annual Exhibition of the Brooklyn Institute, 1846, no. 60.

REFERENCE: *Catalogue of Paintings: Fifth Annual Exhibition of Paintings*, 1846, cat. no. 60, p. 4, lists painting and provides provenance.

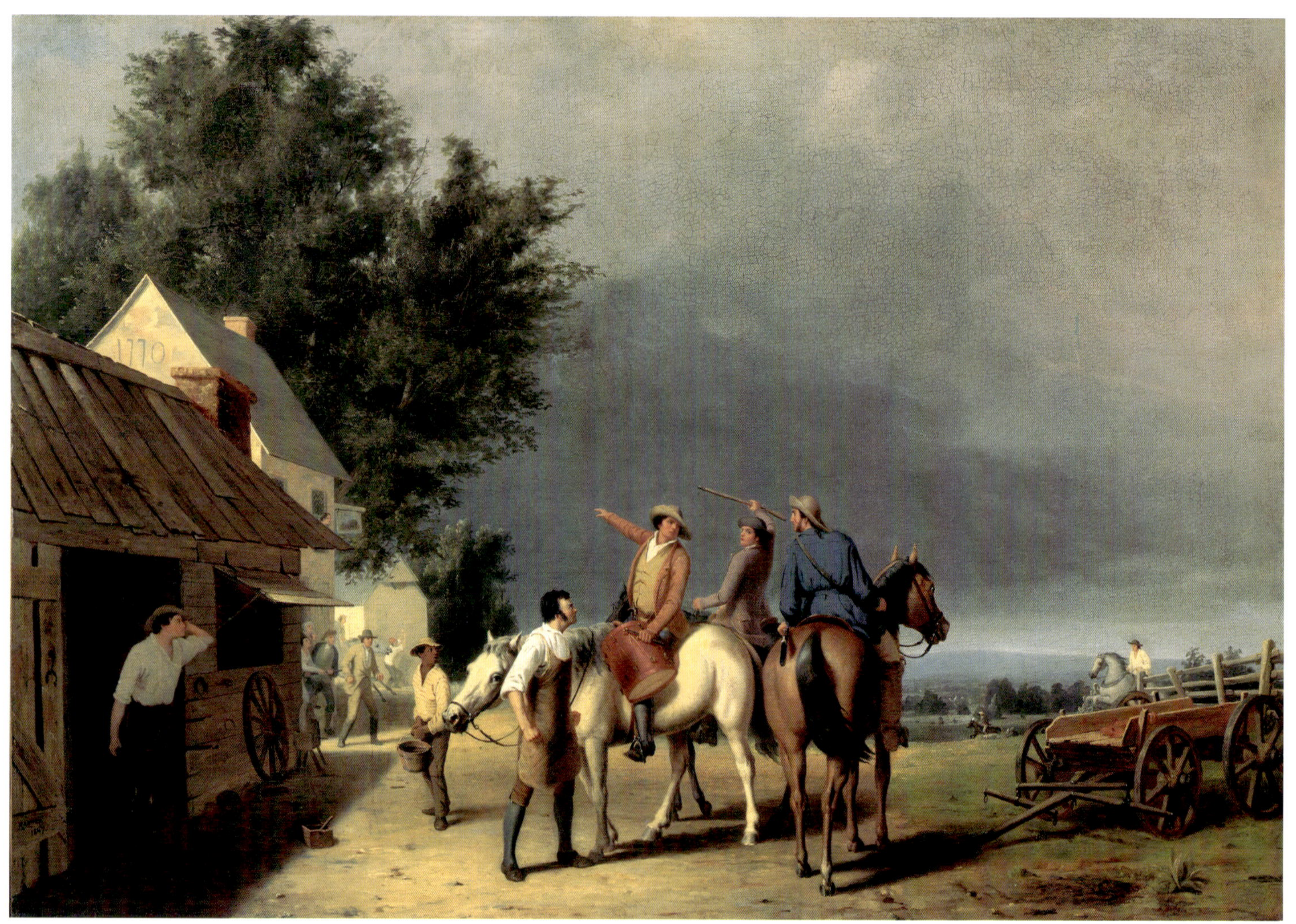

NO. 31

31*
First News of the Battle of Lexington

1847

Oil on canvas

44 1/16 x 63 5/16 inches (111.9 x 160.8 cm)

Signed and dated, on door, lower left: Ranney /1847 and on ground, lower left: W. Ranney

North Carolina Museum of Art, Raleigh. Purchased with funds from the State of North Carolina, 52.9.25

Grubar no. 26

PROVENANCE: Am Art-Union, 1847; distributed by lottery to Mrs. John Stevens Cogdell (nee Maria Gilchrist), Charleston, South Carolina, 1847; possibly bequeathed to her nephew, Robert Cogdell Gilchrist, c. 1858, according to the North Carolina Museum of Art, a transcript of the will signed on May 8, 1856, and probated on December 15, 1858, is in the South Carolina State Archives, Columbia; (John Nicholson Gallery, New York, by 1947 to 1952).

EXHIBITED: Am Art-Union, 1847, no. 149.

REFERENCES: Am Art-Union, Executive Committee Minutes, 1846-1854, December 15, 1847, reel 2, Am Art-Union Papers, approved bill for $300 (framed). *Literary World*, vol. 2 (October 23, 1847), p. 277, and (November 13, 1847), p. 356, includes critical responses (quoted in entry). Am Art-Union, *Plan of Institution . . . Catalogue of Paintings. . . .* November 1 and December 15, 1847, no. 30; *Transactions for the Year 1847*, p. 39, no. 149. *Charleston Courier*, January 31, 1848, p. 2, mentions that Col. John S. Cogdell's widow had acquired the painting. *New York Post*, June 30, 1848, clipping file, NAD, says work is "superior to *Washington Rallying the Americans at the Battle of Princeton.*" *Art Quarterly* 10 (Spring, 1947), p. 154, advertisement provides provenance information. Mark Thistlethwaite, "The Past into the Present: William Ranney's *First News of the Battle of Lexington*," North Carolina Museum of Art *Bulletin* 16 (1993), pp. 1–12, discusses it within its historical context.

A large and ambitious work, the *First News of the Battle of Lexington* was bought by the American Art-Union in 1847. While the most familiar tale associated with that brief but pivotal battle of the American Revolution on April 19, 1775, was Paul Revere's famous ride to warn his countrymen of the imminent British attack, Ranney chose instead to create an imaginary genre scene—a call to arms as it were—set in the conflict's aftermath in which the Massachusetts patriots learned of casualties suffered by their volunteer militia, or minutemen. While accounts differed about who fired the first shot, it is generally agreed that the outrage following this conflict contributed to the American resolve to expand the volunteer army and prepare for the war. According to one account published by Robert Sears in 1848, "The country was alarmed; armed men crowded in from every quarter; and the retreating troops were assailed with an unceasing but irregular discharge of musketry." [1]

Mark Thistlethwaite (1993) points out that comparisons between the American Revolution of 1776 and the Mexican War of 1846–1848 were widespread in the minds of the general public. Both wars relied upon quickly assembling a volunteer army, and scores of young men saw the Mexican War as an opportunity to show their mettle and embrace the spirit of '76.

The 1847 America Art-Union publications included the following description of the *First News of the Battle of Lexington*:

> The tidings spread—men galloped from town to town beating the drum and calling to arms. The people snatched their rifles and fowling pieces, and hurried towards Boston. The voice of war rang through the land, and preparations were every where commenced for united action.

Though a scene with realistic narrative details, Ranney anchored it within a specific historical time frame, and thereby merged two categories of painting—genre and history. The most obvious historical reference is the inscription of 1770 on the wall of the tavern in the left background. The rural clothing worn by most of the men, however, is quite generalized. Only the aproned blacksmith and his assistant emerging from the doorway at the left wear the leggings associated with eighteenth-century period dress. The focal point of the composition is the three messengers on horseback who relate the news of the battle. The young drummer on the white horse points toward the blackened sky as if the flames of war are still visible, smoldering in the background; his compatriot angrily raises his rifle as though urging his countrymen to arm. Another man in the left background is seen ringing the alarm bell as people rush toward the central figures on foot and on horseback to hear the news. The sole disengaged figure in the composition is the African American at the left, who seems to quietly observe the excitement. Did Ranney include him in this imaginary scene of the initial events in America's struggle for independence to allude to the contentious political controversy facing the nation in 1847—whether the new western territory of California would enter the union as a slave state and tilt the balance of power toward the southern slave-owning states? In *The Bigelow Papers* of 1848, the poet, abolitionist, and satirist James Russell Lowell (1819–1891) expressed the distrustful sentiments of many northerners: "They just want this Californy/So' to lug new slave-states in."

Critical reception to Ranney's painting was lukewarm. In November of 1847, when the picture was on view at the American Art-Union, the *Literary World* observed that this was "a more ambitious picture than Mr. Ranney has heretofore painted," but that it was "too sketchy and washy." Since those qualities do not appear to be evident today, it is possible that Ranney subsequently reworked parts of the canvas. This is supported by the numerous adjustments that were revealed in 1999, when David Findley, chief conservator of the North Carolina Museum of Art, undertook infrared analysis. It was during this examination that a second Ranney signature was revealed in the lower left foreground. In his report of April 9, 2001, Findley indicates that Ranney apparently painted out a horse that was drinking from the bucket carried by the African American man. Other less dramatic changes were also discovered, such as numerous repositionings of people and the legs of horses. Also, in the tavern in the background, Ranney simplified the architectural details, eliminating windows and perhaps even a second building. The scope of these changes indicate how much the artist struggled to clearly arrange the several disparate narrative elements across his picture.

Two sketches of the central figures in the painting have survived (cat. nos. D15 and D23). Both represent a figure facing forward with his rifle aloft, astride a horse flanked by two men on the ground. In the final painting this figure has been turned with his back to the viewer and is riding a different horse, and the flanking two men on horseback were added. These drawings and the numerous changes revealed by the conservation assessment indicate that, while Ranney seems to have sketched out his general concept on paper, he developed most of the composition on the canvas. Without the benefit of underdrawing, he used thinly brushed paint strokes to create his picture, making adjustments and refinements as he went along. LB

1. Robert Sears, *Pictorial History of the American Revolution with a Sketch of the Early History of the Country, the Constitution of the United States . . .* (1848; repr., Whitefish, Montana: Kessinger Publishers, 2004), p. 140.

32
The Eagle's Nest

c. 1847

Oil on canvas

Location unknown

Grubar no. 23

PROVENANCE: Am Art-Union, 1847; distributed by lottery to A. B. Matthews, Pontiac, Michigan, 1847 to c. 1876.

EXHIBITED: Am Art-Union, 1847, no. 19. Detroit Art Association, *Second Exhibition*, 1875, cat. no. 10.

REFERENCES: *Anglo American*, February 6, 1847, p. 381 (quoted in entry). Am Art-Union, *Plan of Institution . . . Catalogue of Paintings . . .* , June 1, November 1, and December 15, 1847, no. 19. Am Art-Union, *Transactions for the Year 1847*, p. 33. no. 10. Detroit Art Association, *Catalogue, Second Exhibition . . .* 1875–1876, no. 10, listed as for sale. Cowdrey 1953, 2, p. 294. *Literary World*, October 23, 1847, p. 277 (quoted in Grubar and entry).

The reviewer for the *Anglo American* describes this now lost painting as "particularly remarkable for its originality. On a pyramidical point of rock on which is the Eagle's nest, is seen a hunter clinging to the face of the precipice, and defending himself with the remains of his rifle from the attack of the king of birds, which, in protection of its young, darts upon him. Beneath, on a jutting point of crag lies his dead mate. The rock strikes the eye as being too artificial; nevertheless, it is a good exhibition picture, showing much talent. . . ." The writer for the *Literary World* admires Ranney's conception as free and spirited, and agrees with the *Anglo American* that "the rocks are artificially arranged." LB

33
Washington's Mission to the Indians in 1753

c. 1847

Oil on canvas

Location unknown

Grubar no. 24

PROVENANCE: Am Art-Union, 1847; distributed by lottery to A. G. Carll, Jericho, New York, 1847.

EXHIBITED: NAD, 1847, no. 88, as owned by the American Art-Union. Am Art-Union, 1847, no. 30.

REFERENCES: Am Art-Union, Executive Committee Minutes 1846–1854, March 10, 1847, resolved to purchase painting with frame for $200, and March 19, 1847, approved for payment, reel 2, Am Art-Union Papers. *Literary World,* vol. 1, no. 8 (March 27, 1847), pp. 182–183 (quoted in entry). Am Art-Union, *Plan of Institution . . . Catalogue of Paintings . . . ,* June 1, November 1, and December 15, 1847, no. 30. *New York Anglo American,* March 6, 1847, p. 477, and May 8, 1847, p. 69. *Democratic Review,* May 1847, p. 464. *Literary World,* October 23, 1847, p. 277. *Transactions for the Year 1847,* Am Art-Union, p. 33. no. 30. Cowdrey 1943, 2, p. 88. Cowdrey 1953, 2, p. 294.

Unfortunately, this early history painting has been lost. During its brief period of public exposure, over the year 1847, the painting received wide critical recognition and, given the comments that were published about it, more than likely had a profound effect on Ranney's subsequent efforts as a history painter.

This is one of two known occasions when Ranney treated the subject of Washington's 1753 mission to the Indians. In that year, during the French and Indian War, the French had crossed the Great Lakes from Canada into the Ohio Valley, where they established outposts and tried to convince some of the local Indians to switch allegiances and turn on the British. The colonial governor of Virginia, Robert Dinwiddie, enlisted the aid of Washington, then a young militia officer, to warn the French to desist and to find out what their intentions were. (For more on this subject see cat. no. 98.)

There are a few contemporary descriptions of the painting that give us an idea of what was represented. One is a quote from the well-known author Joel T. Headley (1813–1897) that was cited with Ranney's painting in the 1847 *Catalogue* for the American Art-Union:

> For 750 miles, more than half the distance through an unbroken wilderness, accompanied by only seven persons, across rivers and morasses, over mountains, through fearful gorges, and amidst tribes of Indians, the fearless stripling pursued his way for forty-one days.[1]

The work was purchased by the American Art-Union in March 1847 and put on exhibition at the National Academy that spring. It was the subject of an extensive review in the *Literary World,* admonishing Ranney to devote more attention to details and to improve his drawing considerably. From that opinion we discover that "the picture represents the party struggling over the mountains through a blinding snow-storm." In pointing out the lack of anatomical expression and proportion in the figures of the men and horses, we further learn that Washington is portrayed on horseback.

The comments were not all derogatory. Another writer, in the *Democratic Review,* says that the "snow-storm is so well represented that it appears to be the subject of the picture, and the figures the accessories." Even the critic from the *Literary Review* admired "the overall happy conception and agreeable feeling of the picture," and noted that it "does the artist much credit, and we hail it as the promise of something more complete hereafter."

Ranney seems to have taken these judgments to heart. He went on to tell many more stories in paint and to do so by refining his drawing, among other things, and by becoming a true student, if not a scholar, of nature.

LB/PHH

1. This quote was taken from the then recently published volume by Joel T. Headley, *Washington and His Generals* (New York: Charles Scribner, 1847), vol. 1, p. 21. The trip actually took thirty days.

34*
Sleighing

c. 1847

Oil on canvas

30 3/4 x 42 inches
(78.1 x 106.7 cm)

Signed, lower center, in
white: Ranney

Private collection

Grubar no. 25

PROVENANCE: (McClees Gallery, Philadelphia); Claude J. Ranney, Malvern, Pennsylvania, by 1949 to c. 1956; given to his son-in-law and daughter, Mr. and Mrs. J. Maxwell Moran, c. 1956.

EXHIBITED: NAD, 1847, no. 305, as Sleighing. M. Knoedler and Company, New York, *Opening of the West*, 1949 (no catalogue, lent by Claude Ranney according to FARL photo mount). Chadds Ford 1991, no. 4.

REFERENCES: *Literary World*, June 12, 1847, p. 447. Cowdrey 1943, vol. 2, p.88. Thistlethwaite 1991, p. 22, no. 4, illus.; p. 23, compares to a work by Charles Deas.

This is Ranney's initial exploration of a wintry scene featuring a sled. Six years later he again treated the subject in *The Sleigh Ride* (cat. no. 75). The unusually bold and dramatic composition in *Sleighing* shows the horses flying pell-mell down the center of the canvas. The *Literary World* admired the spirit of the work, although the writer, like so many during this early period of Ranney's work, complained about the drawing. While the horses are more crisply delineated than the rather sketchily rendered riders, they are inaccurately depicted with all fours airborne, a not uncommon technical error of the time. As Thistlethwaite points out, the photographic studies forty years later by Eadweard Muybridge slowed down horses in motion and proved that hooves were in fact on the ground as they galloped.

Thistlethwaite further notes the striking similarity between the poses of Ranney's horses and those in Charles Deas's *The Death Struggle* of c. 1845 (Shelburne Museum, Shelburne, Vermont). In addition, the driver, with his right arm raised high over his head, resembles Deas's knife-wielding trapper. Ranney could have seen Deas's work when it was exhibited at the American Art-Union in the late summer of 1845, or the engraving of it published in New York in 1846.[1] Unlike Deas, who dramatically presents a horrific scene of struggle as the horses soar off a precipice—they and their riders facing certain death—Ranney presents an anxious but more idyllic scene. With a whip snaking emphatically overhead, two young couples seem to be rushing toward an undisclosed destination, probably still five miles away based on the "5 miles to" inscription on the stone marker at the right. Contributing to the excitement is the dog barking at the accelerating bug-eyed steeds.

During the early decades of the nineteenth century, Americans increasingly abandoned their farms to seek their fortunes in crowded cities such as New York. To the weary urban dweller, the youthful sleighing party may have held a nostalgic appeal for a distant and less hectic time and place. LB

1. See Carol Clark, "Charles Deas," in *American Frontier Life: Early Western Paintings and Prints* (Fort Worth, Amon Carter Museum, 1987), pp. 65 and 68.

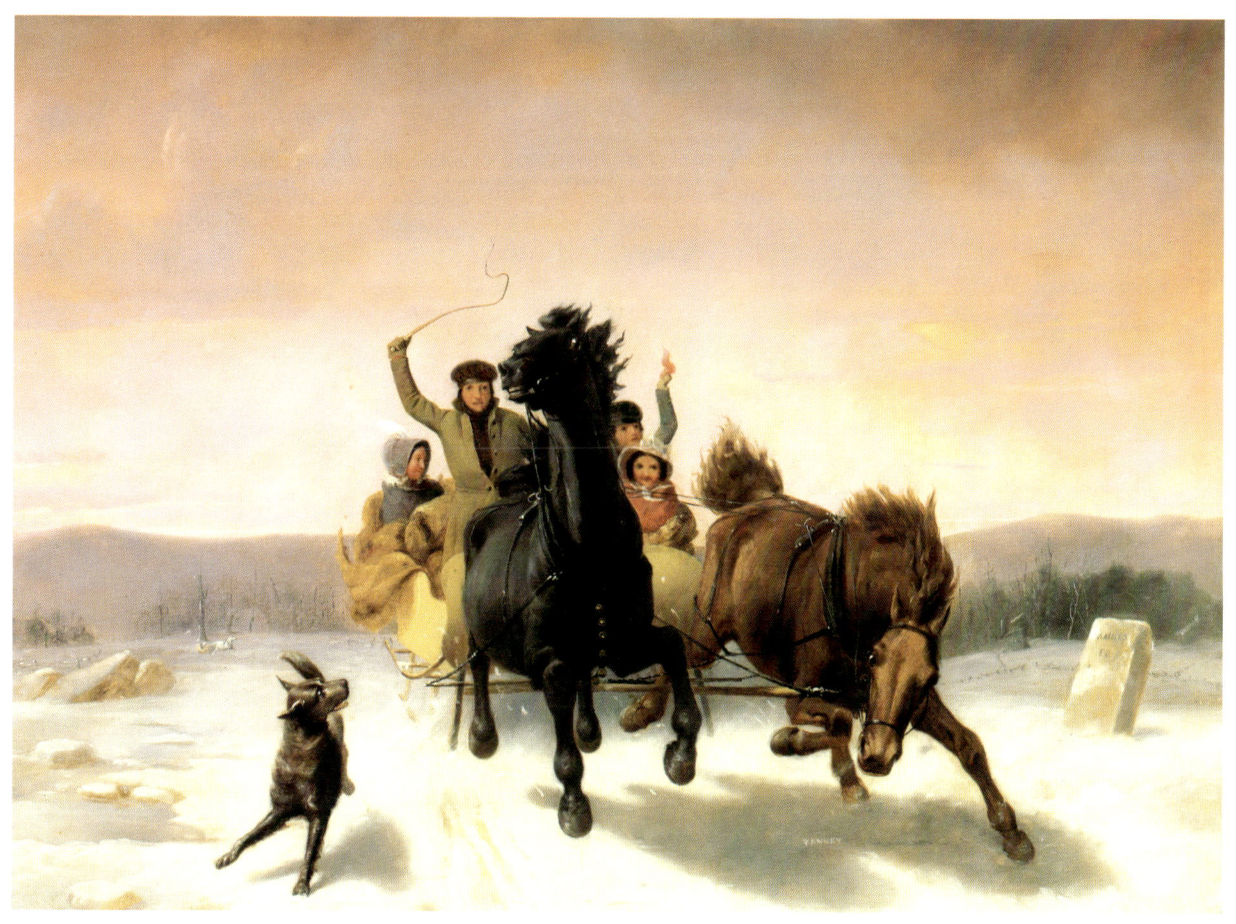

NO. 34

35
Burial of de Soto

c. 1847

Oil on canvas

Location unknown

Grubar no. 27

PROVENANCE: Am Art-Union, 1847; distributed by lottery to George T. Plume, New York, 1847.

EXHIBITED: Am Art-Union, 1847, no. 264.

REFERENCES: Am Art-Union, Executive Committee Minutes, 1846–1854, reel 2, December 24, 1847, Am Art-Union Papers, indicates purchase price of $200 (framed). Am Art-Union, *Transactions . . . for the Year 1847*, p. 43, no. 264, provides provenance. Tuckerman, 1867, p. 432, mentions (quoted in entry). Cowdrey 1953, 2, p. 294, lists and provides provenance.

No contemporary descriptions of this lost oil have been located. It is among several that Tuckerman lists and describes as having "won the common eye and heart, and hav[ing] a genuine American scope and tone."

The subject of this work was an early event in the history of the United States and concerned the dashing Spanish conquistador Hernando de Soto (c. 1500–1542) who explored Florida in search of treasure between 1539 and 1542, and then moved farther west where he encountered and crossed the Mississippi River. By the mid-1840s when Ranney painted this picture, the popularity of nationalistic history paintings was on the rise. Discovery and exploration subjects were particularly popular and were encouraged by the patronage of the American Art-Union. The Philadelphia artist Peter F. Rothermel, for example, painted *De Soto Discovering the Mississippi* in 1843 (St. Bonaventure University Art Collection, Bonaventure, New York). It was exhibited both at the National Academy of Design and the American Art-Union in 1844 and may well have been seen by Ranney who was in the city by that time. A decade later, William H. Powell's version of the same subject was installed in the rotunda of the United States Capitol.

The discovery of the Mississippi River was important not only as a distant historical event of national significance but also because of the widespread recognition in the 1840s of its commercial importance as an essential transportation link to the West. Particularly after the development of steam navigation, hundreds of steamboats plied the river from Louisville to New Orleans, which gave rise to that city's emergence as a major American port. During the Mexican War, the river was indispensable in quickly transporting ordnance—ammunition, food, and clothing—to the Americans fighting in Texas and Mexico. LB

36*
Washington Rallying the Americans at the Battle of Princeton

1848

Oil on canvas

48 1/2 x 64 inches
(123.2 x 162.6 cm)

Signed and dated,
lower center: W.
Ranney /1848;
inscribed, at lower
right: Henry Inman
1834

Princeton University
Art Museum,
Princeton, New Jersey.
Gift of Edward
Wasserman in the
name of his children,
Jesse A., Renee II, and
Edward Wasserman, Jr.,
in 1911

Grubar no. 28

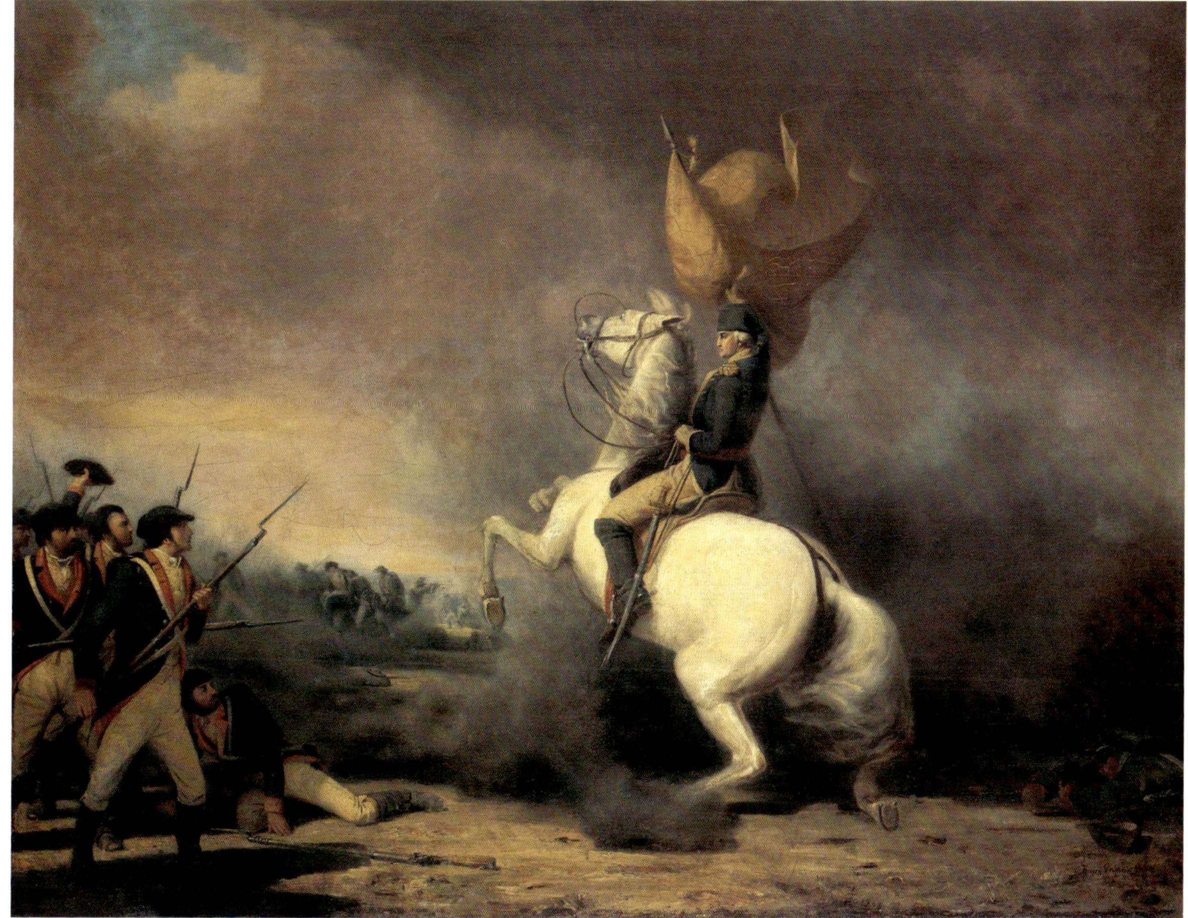

NO. 36

PROVENANCE: Manigault Collection, Charleston, South Carolina; Edward Wasserman, New York; Corcoran Gallery of Art, Washington D.C., to 1911.

Exhibited: NAD, 1848, no. 177, as Washington Rallying the Americans at the Battle of Princeton, after the Death of Mercer.

REFERENCES: NAD, *Catalogue of the Twenty-Third Annual Exhibition*, 1848, p. 16 (annotated copy at NYHS lists price as $350). *New York Evening Post*, May 13, 1848, p. 3. *Family Companion*, vol. 2, no. 2 (May 27, 1848), p. 23 (quoted in entry). *New York Post*, June 30, 1848. Board of trustees, April 17, 1911, Corcoran Gallery of Art, accepts gift of George Washington at the Battle of Princeton by Henry Inman and on November 24 and 25, 1911, arranges to send painting to Princeton. Frank Jewett Mather, Jr., "American Paintings at Princeton University," in *Record of the Art Museum, Princeton University*, vol. 2, no. 2 (fall 1943), p. 7, reports the discovery of Ranney's signature. Cowdrey 1943, 2, p. 88, no. 177, lists as for sale. Thistlethwaite 1991, p. 42, fig. 2, illus. and suggests that Ranney finished Inman's work.

The Battle of Princeton, which took place on January 3, 1777, was the pivotal conflict in George Washington's campaign against the British in New Jersey during the American Revolution. Ranney represented the dramatic moment when General Washington charged into the midst of the battle with reinforcements and rallied the demoralized and underarmed troops after General Hugh Mercer had been severely wounded. Mercer in fact died eight days later, but although the two events are combined in Ranney's original title when it was

45

exhibited at the National Academy, they are not in the picture itself. As a result of Washington's boldness the Americans won a decisive victory, forcing General Charles Cornwallis to retreat and gaining control of most of New Jersey.

Pictorially the Princeton work is unique among Ranney's history subjects in that it does not combine history and genre but rather is in the more elevated grand manner of history painting. He portrays a calm Washington atop a rearing white steed with unmistakable echoes of a long tradition of dramatic and bombastic equestrian figures. Visually the figure relates to iconic images such as the oft-reproduced *Napoleon at Saint Bernard* of 1800 (Musée National de Chateau de Versailles) by the French neoclassical artist Jacques-Louis David. Similarly both mythologize a hero and his exploits.

This painting has been confused in the literature because it bears not only Ranney's signature, which was only revealed in 1920 during a cleaning at Princeton University, but also is inscribed with the name of Henry Inman (1801–1846) and the date 1834. While briefly in the Corcoran's collection, the work was listed as by Inman. The existence of the Inman inscription has led to speculation that Ranney may have finished a work painted by Inman after that artist's death in 1846. A technical examination (February 26, 1998) in the conservation laboratory at the Princeton museum by conservator Norman Muller did indicate extensive overpainting, but it was inconclusive when the Inman name and date were added. Inman expert William H. Gerdts notes that the size, subject, and the content of this painting are totally inconsistent with that artist's known work, and there are no references to such a picture by him in the literature.[1]

Using an infrared vidicom camera to look beneath the upper paint layers, Muller observed several modifications to the scene. The billowing banner or standard carried by Washington, for instance, is dramatically enlarged. Under the dark overpaint is a smaller, more well-defined form. Extensive overpainting is also visible in the cloud of dust underneath the horse's body and in the sky in the upper left corner. The right hind leg of the horse, which looks so impossibly distorted, exhibits a rather surprising lack of anatomical verisimilitude, which is atypical of Ranney's other pictures. Muller also noted that that area appears much more loosely painted than other sections of the canvas. His findings confirm that more than one hand worked on this painting and altered its appearance. When and by whom remains a mystery.

The many modifications to this work indicate that Ranney was struggling technically to realize a heroic concept. His shortcomings were noted by contemporary reviewers, and, based on those descriptions, there is little doubt that this is the painting Ranney exhibited at the National Academy in 1848.[2] The *Family Companion* observed, for example, that "The horse is colossal and ill drawn; the whole is sketchy and unfinished. The artist has placed the hero in dangerous proximity to the Hessian bayonets. If he is leading the Americans to the charge, they are a very respectable distance *en arriere*." Perhaps because of Ranney's early experience as a portrait painter, the most successful part of the painting is the dignified and well-defined likeness of Washington. LB

1. William H. Gerdts in telephone conversation with Linda Bantel, August 2005.
2. It is unlikely that a painting signed by Henry Inman and submitted to the National Academy by Ranney would have gone on exhibition without mentioning Inman.

37*
Veterans of 1776 Returning from the War

1848

Oil on canvas

34 1/4 x 48 5/8 inches
(87 x 123.5 cm)

Signed and dated,
lower left: W Ranney
1848

Dallas Museum of Art.
The Art Museum
League Fund, Special
Contributors, and
General Acquisitions
Fund, 1981.40

Grubar no. 29

PROVENANCE: Am Art-Union, 1848; distributed by lottery to William E. Remsen, Syosset, New York, 1848; Harrison Earl, Philadelphia, by 1851; Henry Paul Beck, Philadelphia, by 1864; Mrs. William H. S. Wells, Philadelphia, by 1976; (Hirschl and Adler Galleries, New York, by 1977 to 1981).

EXHIBITED: Am Art-Union, 1848, no. 110. Pennsylvania Academy of the Fine Arts, Philadelphia, 1851, no. 169 (lent by H. Earl). United States Sanitary Commission, Philadelphia, *The Great Central Fair*, 1864, no. 134, as lent by H. Paul Beck. Pennsylvania Academy of the Fine Arts, Philadelphia, 1865, no. 606; and 1866, no. 516, as lent by H. P. Beck. Pennsylvania Academy of the Fine Arts, Philadelphia, *In This Academy*, 1976, no. 143, p. 113, illus., and p. 292. Chadds Ford 1991, cat. no. 5, p. 41 illus., pp. 42–43, discusses.

REFERENCES: Management Committee Minutes, 1839-1855, reel 1 June 22, 1848, Am Art-Union Papers, agrees to purchase Veterans of 76 at "artist's price, not framed," of $175. Am Art-Union *Bulletin* (appears as no. 110 in the following issues), June 25, 1848, p. 9; July 10, p. 9; July 25, p. 8; August 12, p. 8; August 25, p. 9; September 10, p. 9; September 25, p. 9; October 10, p. 9; October 25, p. 9; November 10, p. 10; November 25, p. 10, 25, and 36, include abridged reprints of reviews from the *New-York Courier* and *Enquirer*, and December 10, p. 10; December 25, p. 11. Am Art-Union, *Transactions for the Year 1848*, p. 57, provides provenance. *Southern Literary Gazette*, November 15, 1848, and *New York Commercial Advertiser*, December 14, 1848 (quoted in entry), from Newspaper Clippings, reel 3, vol. 1, Am Art-Union Papers. *New York Evening Post*, November 16, 1848. *Home Journal*, November 25, 1848, p. 2 (quoted in entry). Cowdrey 1953, 2, p. 294. Mark Thistlethwaite, in *In This Academy* (Philadelphia: Pennsylvania Academy of Fine Arts, 1976), p. 112, discusses in terms of historical genre. Peter Hastings Falk, ed., *The Annual Exhibition Record of the Pennsylvania Academy of the Fine Arts* (Madison, Connecticut: Sound View Press, 1988), vol. 1, p. 177, lists exhibit and lender. Mark Thistlethwaite, "The Most Important Themes: History Painting and Its Place in American Art," in *Grand Illusions: History Painting in America,* 1988, pp. 40–42, excellent discussion of work in terms of historical genre painting. Thistlethwaite 1991, pp. 42–43, discusses; pp. 50–51, discusses current use of slang word b'hoy in the late 1840s, and the merging of historical events with current ones.

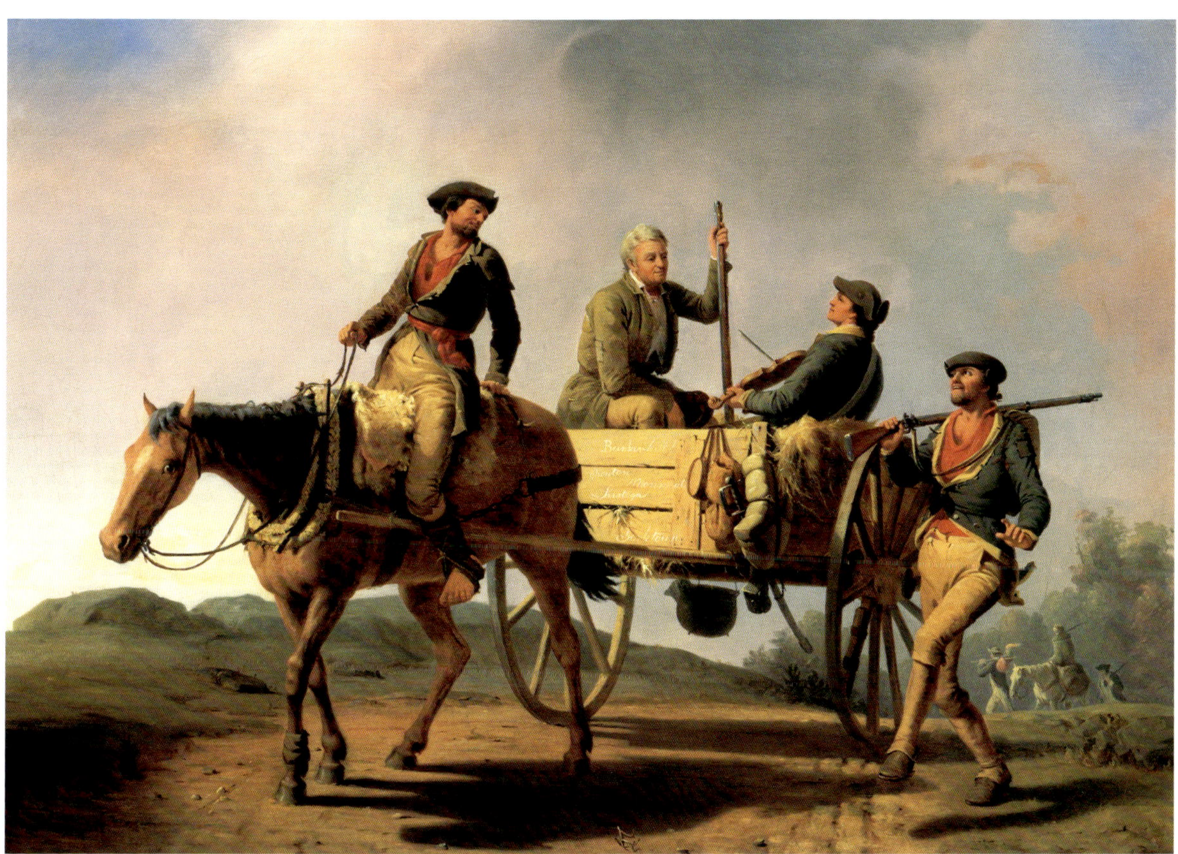

NO. 37

47

This well-documented painting, unlocated at the time of Grubar's publication in 1962, was rediscovered in 1976. It was critically acclaimed at the time it was exhibited at the American Art-Union in 1848. The *Home Journal*, for example, clearly impressed with Ranney's recent efforts, included an unusual number of colorful lines of description: "Jolly old chaps are these hard 'veterans,' poking along in their homely equipage, with the accompaniments of song and dance. The expression of the b'hoy [slang for a jovial fellow and in 1848 a term associated with troops in the Mexican War] dancing so gayly by the side of the cart, to the fiddle of one of his companions, is admirable. Mr. Ranney is always happy in the selection of his themes." The *New York Commercial Advertiser* of September 14, 1848, added its own interpretation of the narrative: "Their merry humor, as they jog so philosophically along, never fails to excite a feeling of joy and sympathy in the heart of the beholder."

The fanciful scene is set in the aftermath of the American Revolution, seventy years earlier. The proud and victorious soldiers, attired in ragged remnants of their military uniforms, appear happy to be headed home. The shabby figure riding the bedraggled horse has even lost his boots. Four famous battles in which the Americans were victorious are inscribed in white on the front of the cart: "Bunker-hill / Trenton / Monmouth / Saratoga / Yorktown." In the right background, the group is followed by stragglers.

This painting's popular appeal was surely partially based on the fact that the scene celebrated ordinary, down-to-earth individuals, participating in recognizable activities—not dissimilar, as Thistlethwaite points out, from other contemporary genre scenes such as *Going to Market* by George Caleb Bingham, painted about 1842 (Virginia Museum of Fine Arts, Richmond). While exemplifying the best of narrative painting of the mid-nineteenth century, the general historical ambiance Ranney created in the *Veterans of 1776* appealed to contemporary Americans' passion for relating the history of the Revolution to events then current in the war with Mexico. In 1848, the same year Ranney painted this picture, for example, the American artist Richard Caton Woodville painted *Young '48 and Old '76* (Walters Art Museum, Baltimore). When Woodville's painting was engraved for the American Art-Union in 1851, the *Literary World*, expressing the pervasive view of history at that time, observed that Woodville's print was "a contrast of the past and present age, the days of Washington and Taylor."[1]

It is within this historical context that the *Veterans of 1776* should be viewed. The fall of Mexico occurred in 1847, and the treaty between the United States and Mexico was signed in February 1848, on the eve of soldiers returning home. Regarding Ranney's picture, as Thistlethwaite posited in 1988, the general public may have associated the elder, distinguished gentleman sitting in the cart with the much beloved, old farmer-general Zachary Taylor (1784–1850), whose heroism and exploits in Mexico earned him national approbation and the Whig nomination for the presidency in 1848. Indeed, though younger and somewhat idealized, the face and styling of the thick gray hair does vaguely resemble contemporary images of Zachary Taylor. Concealing the inner strength of the future president, the casual and rumpled attire is in keeping with how Taylor's troops affectionately described him: "old man in the plain brown coat." In 1991 Thistlethwaite further observes that the "US" brand visible on the horse's rump anchors the painting to current, not past, events because it was a mark common on horses in the Mexican War but not in the Revolutionary War setting suggested by the title of the painting. LB

1. Quoted in Elizabeth Johns, *American Genre Painting: the Politics of Everyday Life* (New Haven and London: Yale University Press, 1991), p. 180.

38*
Prairie Burial

1848

Oil on canvas

28 1/2 x 41 inches
(71.8 x 104.1 cm)

Signed and dated,
lower left: W
Ranney/1848; and on
dirt pile, lower right:
Ranney/[indeciperable
numbers]

Buffalo Bill Historical
Center, Cody,
Wyoming. Gift of Mrs.
J. Maxwell Moran, 3.97

Grubar no. 30

PROVENANCE: Am Art-Union, 1848, distributed by lottery to Charles de Kay, Geneva, New York, 1848; (Harry Shaw Newman Gallery, New York, by 1945–1953) Claude J. Ranney, Malvern, Pennsylvania, 1953 (?) to c. 1954; his daughter, Elizabeth R. Moran, by 1954–1997.

EXHIBITED: Am Art-Union, 1848, no. 328; Fort Worth 1987, p. 193, as private collection.

REFERENCES: Am Art-Union, *Bulletin* (December 10, 1848), p. 15; and (December 15, 1848), p. 20; *Distribution Catalogue*, December 22, 1848, p. 23, no. 328; *Transactions for the Year* 1848, p. 68. no. 328, provides provenance. Harry Shaw Newman Gallery (later Old Print Shop), New York, *Panorama*, vol. 1, no. 1 (October 1945), p. 10, illus., clipping of *Panorama*, in files of the Old Print Shop, annotated "11/18/53 / Sold to individual." Cowdrey 1953, 2, p. 294. Glanz 1982, p. 76 (quoted in entry). Ayres 1987, fig. 49, pp. 85-86, discusses intellectual and art historical context, and illustrates.

Ranney showed four paintings in the 1848 American Art-Union exhibition, two of which were western scenes, this one and *Stampede* (cat. no. 40). According to the *Knickerbocker* magazine, the Art-Union display that year promised to "form the best exhibition of works by American artists ever opened to the public."[1] The organization planned to issue the annual engraving for its membership after Daniel Huntington's highly wrought picture *Queen Mary Signing the Death-warrant of Lady Jane Grey* of 1848 (location unknown). The second version of Thomas Cole's remarkable four-part series *The Voyage of Life* of 1841–1842 (National Gallery of Art, Washington) graced the walls of the gallery as did Frederic E. Church's touching homage to Cole, who had died in February of that year. Referred to as the "charming" *Tribute to the Memory of Cole* of 1848 (Des Moines Women's Club), this latter work was not only an affirmation of Church's adherence to the "higher style of landscape" that was Cole's mandate but, like Huntington's historical trope and Cole's morality quartet, was an exercise in tracing the flux of human fate.[2] Ranney's *Prairie Burial* shared this profoundly serious theme.

The painting was, despite the apparent regional isolation implied by the prairie scene, universal in its theme of pathos and loss. Like Cole's *The Voyage of Life,* it fulfilled the spiritual "requirements" of the general public in the mid-nineteenth century— "a public that placed a high value upon religious sentiment and yet had little taste for traditional religious imagery."[3] And if the Art-Union was intended to perform one primary function, it was to address public taste. In order to accomplish that, it was bent on encouraging both a broad range of artist participation (it claimed "from Maine to Texas") and a breadth of public involvement and appreciation. By 1848 the Art-Union could no longer be considered a "superfluity." It had according to the *Knickerbocker* "become a necessity…a part of the public property as much as the fountains, the parks, or the City-Hall." It drew subscribers from far and wide and played to all manner of folk. "The retired merchant from the Fifth Avenue, the scholar from the University, the poor workman, the news-boy, the beau and the belle, the clerk with his bundle, all frequent the Art-Union."[4]

Paintings like *Prairie Burial* were intended to provide moral lessons for those public audiences, lessons that might assist the community in dealing with the trials and travails of life and the inevitability of mortality. That artists of Ranney's era were specifically called upon to impart moral instruction, and spiritual reinforcement had long been spelled out. In 1847, an Albany, New York, newspaper articulated the message clearly:

> He who learns to look with admiration upon a work of art as a natural consequence must admire and learn to imitate a virtuous action. The painter thus becomes a moral teacher, and under the impulses of his inspired calling may inculcate a lesson which the printed page often fails to convey.[5]

Showing the harsh realities of pioneer life on the American frontier, Ranney's family is presented as a social unit, in which presumably lessons of religious principle and moral values have been imparted and its members are fortified to endure through difficult times. Ranney had married the year he painted *Prairie Burial,*

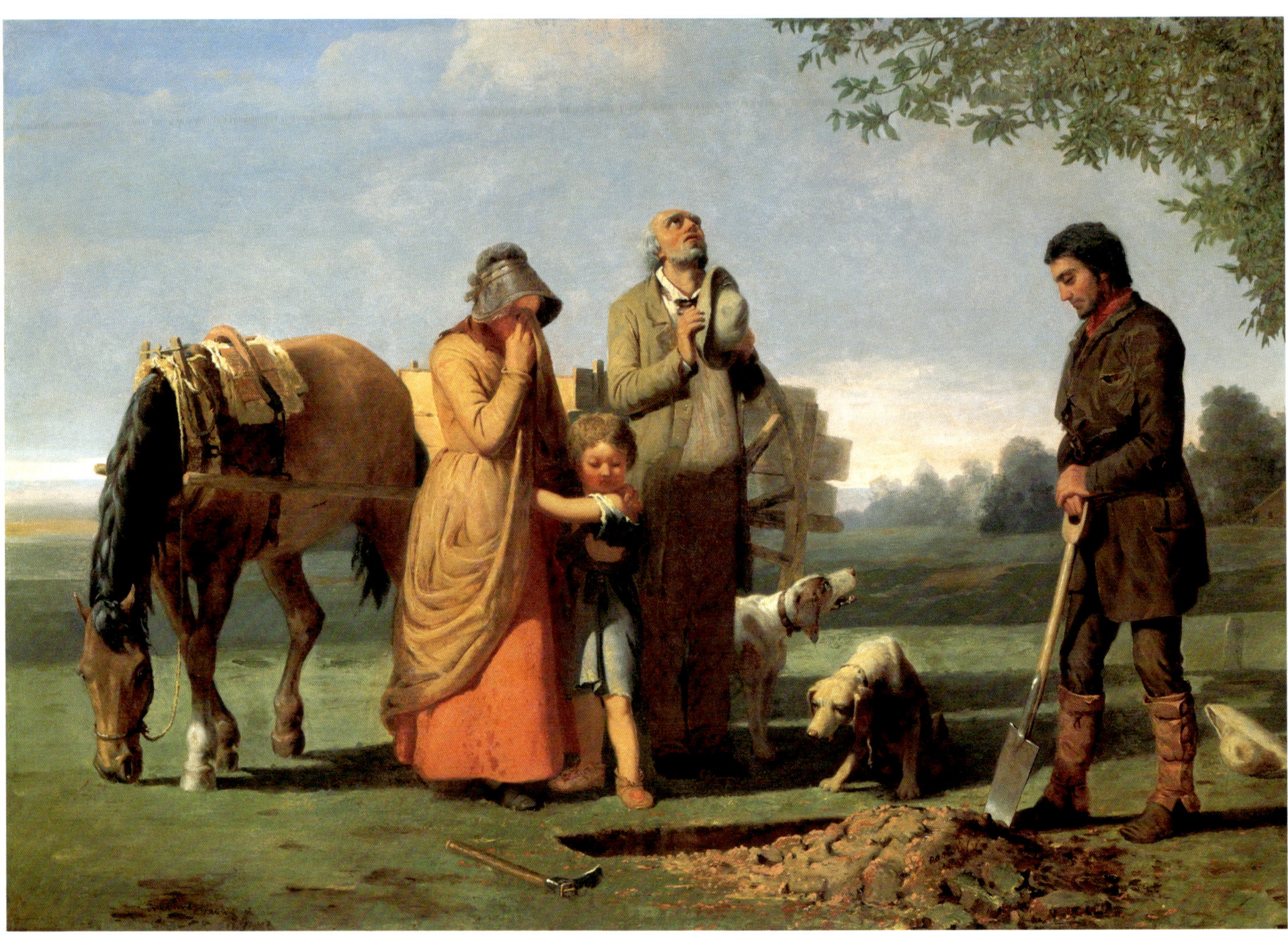

and such values may have begun to bear a special measure of importance in his own personal life.

The art historian Dawn Glanz captures the true moral essence of Ranney's painting when she writes that the "real subject of Ranney's painting . . . was not so much the harshness of frontier life as the patience and per-severance of the Americans who endured it." The painting may also represent something of a metaphorical tribute to the young Americans whose lives had been sacrificed in the Mexican War just recently concluded. But for certain it reflected familial devotion as expressed in "The Pioneers," an essay about a frontier moth-er's travails published in the *Knickerbocker* in 1841.

> Spring came again, and with it also the scourge of a new country, racking agues and burning fevers. The strong man was bowed low; his frame drooped, his eye rolled delirious, and his tongue spake strange things: the tender child too was confined to its couch of pain. Then came the trials of life upon that lone wife and mother. No physician was near, with healing medicine; no friend to keep with her the long watches of the night; but the 'Lord of the whole earth' was there, and He inspired her breast with fortitude . . . Saddest of all, came Death into that lonely abode — and the youngest and fairest child was no more! A rough box was all the coffin its feeble father could make: a few shovels of loose mould was thrown up, and the pale child, borne to its resting place by the hands of

50

its mother, its father faintly following, was covered with moist earth and matted leaves. Not a word was spoken, but tears fell like rain. The scene was more solemn than if loud-sounding requiems had been sung, or long procession drawn out to bid the little sleeper farewell.[6]

In Ranney's painting, the old man looks skyward for heavenly guidance in this moment of grief. The bower of leaves above the father's head and the child's grave suggests the "wooded vales" and "alleys green" that were prototypes of heaven in many views of American cemeteries of the period.[7]

In recent years, Ranney's painting has generally been interpreted as a scene on the Oregon Trail. When included in the St. Louis Art Museum's seminal 1954 exhibition, *Westward the Way*, it was illustrated in the catalogue alongside a quote from Francis Parkman's *The Oregon Trail*, which had been published serially in the *Knickerbocker* over the year 1847: "These were the first emigrants that we had overtaken. . . . Sometimes we passed the grave of one who had sickened and died on the way."[8] More likely the scene depicts pioneer settlers rather than emigrants on the trail. The cabin in the distant right and the additional gravesite, with marker, would suggest that a residence, perhaps only transitory, has been established there on the prairie. A two-wheel cart, while useful to a settler, would have been less common on one of the overland trails.

This painting underwent conservation treatment in the early 1990s at the Twistback Art Conservancy, in Oxford, Pennsylvania. At that time, the new signature at the lower left was revealed as well as the arbor of leafy branches in the right upper corner of the composition below an overpainted blue sky. Those branches, thought to be original to the composition, have been retained. The painting, in its previous state, without the trees, had been illustrated in numerous modern publications.

Recent analysis, by conservator Richard Wolbers, of a paint sample taken from the top edge of *Prairie Burial* shows five paint layers. A layer of sky blue paint has been applied over a green layer of paint and a layer of yellow highlights (the foliage) and appears to be identical to the two layers of original sky blue paint applied by the artist, which are below the layers of foliage. From this analysis, it could be inferred that Ranney himself painted over the foliage (see December 2006 Report, Object File 3.97, Buffalo Bill Historical Center). PHH

1. "The American Art-Union," *Knickerbocker*, vol. 32, no. 5 (November 1848), p. 444.

2. Ibid and Franklin Kelly, *Frederic Edwin Church* (Washington, D.C.: National Gallery of Art, 1989), p. 38.

3. William H. Truettner and Alan Wallach, *Thomas Cole: Landscape into History* (New Haven: Yale University Press, 1994), p. 101.

4. "The American Art-Union," p. 446.

5. Quoted in Lillian B. Miller, *Patrons and Patriotism: The Encouragement of the Fine Arts in the United States, 1790-1860* (Chicago: University of Chicago Press, 1952), p. 294.

6. "The Pioneers," *Knickerbocker*, vol. 43, no. 5 (November 1841), p. 390.

7. Nicholas Powers Tillinghast, "Lines Written on a Visit to Mount Auburn," *Godey's Lady's Book*, vol. 26 (June–December 1843), p. 79.

8. Francis Parkman, *The Oregon Trail* (1849; Boston: Ginn and Company, 1910), p. 48.

39
Prairie Burial

c. 1848

Oil on canvas

14 x 20 inches (35.6 x 50.8 cm)

Initialed, lower center, on dirt pile: W.R. inscribed, on frame: Ogden

The Anschutz Collection, Denver

Grubar no. 31

PROVENANCE: T. H. Ogden, Brooklyn, New York; a descendant of Ogden, Brooklyn; John J. Bowden, Long Island, New York. (T. Gilbert Brouillette, New York, by 1955) (Parke-Bernet, New York, March 16, 1967, lot no. 23, p. 7, illus.) (M. Knoedler and Company, New York, 1967–1973).

EXHIBITED: Charlotte, North Carolina, Mint Museum of Art, *Five Centuries of Selected Paintings from the T. Gilbert Brouillette Gallery in New York*, October 1957 (no catalogue).

REFERENCE: FARL supply file, provides provenance.

With minor modifications of color and scale of the figures in the landscape, this is a smaller version of the *Prairie Burial* (cat. no. 38). Grubar, who provided the exhibition history, suggested it was an oil study. LB

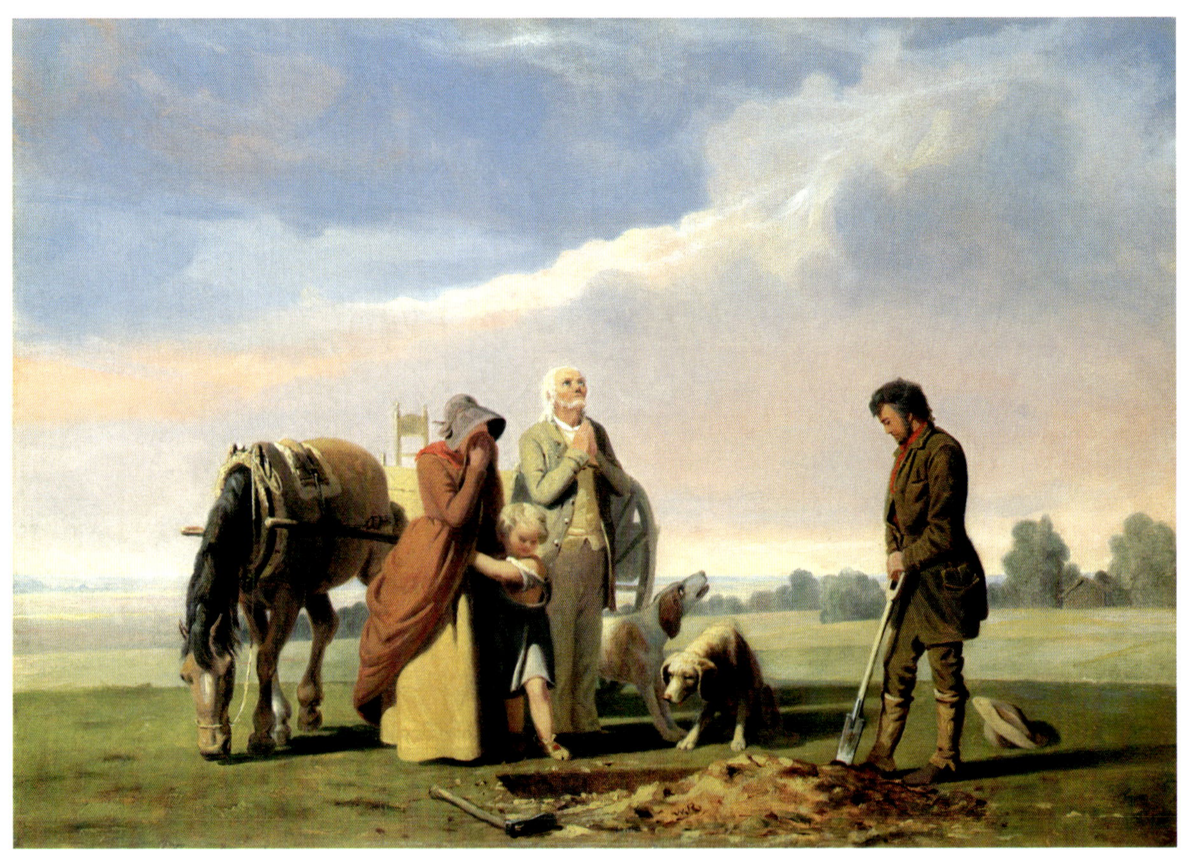

NO. 39

40*

Stampede (formerly *The Prairie Fire*)

1848

Oil on canvas

38 x 60 inches (98.5 x 152.4 cm)

Signed and dated, lower center: Ranney/1848

Private collection

Grubar nos. 32 and 33

PROVENANCE: Am Art-Union, 1848; distributed by lottery to Jacob G. Bedell, Coxsackie, New York, in 1848; Louis Hasbrouck, New York (M. Knoedler and Company, New York) Claude J. Ranney, Malvern, Pennsylvania by 1949–1960.

EXHIBITED: Am Art-Union, New York, 1848, No. 339, as *Stampede*.

REFERENCES: Am Art-Union, *Bulletin* (December 10, 1848), p. 15, lists it; *Distribution* (December 22, 1848), p. 15, listed, and *Bulletin* (December 25, 1848), p. 20 gives provenance. Am Art-Union, *Transactions for the Year 1848*, p. 68. Cowdrey 1953, 2, p. 294. Rena A. Coen, "David's Sabine Women in the Wild West," *Great Plains Quarterly*, vol. 2, no. 2 (Spring 1962), p. 68 (quoted in entry), p. 74, discusses as Prairie Fire and illustrates. Ayers 1987, p. 88, no. 71, illus., p. 87, asserts that the Prairie Fire and the Stampede are one work and that the appropriate title is Stampede.

In many modern sources, this painting carries the title *The Prairie Fire*. In fact, it is quite certain that this is the work known in Ranney's time as *Stampede*, which was exhibited at the American Art-Union in 1848. There is no reference in the press of the day to a painting by Ranney titled *The Prairie Fire*. Given the work's size and its highly developed composition and theme, it is difficult to imagine such a commanding piece being passed over without some comment. The name *The Prairie Fire* was probably affixed to the painting when it emerged on the commercial market in the late 1940s. Although it seems like a suitable enough title, the real action of the scene and its most direct subject are the stampede of horses caused by the approaching fire. It is the horses that present the immediate danger, not the glowing inferno in the distance. By 1848 when Ranney exhibited *Stampede* at the American Art-Union, its central theme of the horrific fires on the western prairies had already been firmly established in American art and literature as one of the quintessential expressions of sublimity in nature. Early men of American letters, like James Fenimore Cooper, exploited such natural dramas in order to enliven reader interest in their descriptions of the otherwise relatively mundane character of the plains. In his first book, *Recollections of the Last Ten Years* of 1826, the Harvard-trained popularizer of western life and Cooper protagonist Timothy Flint professed to be the first writer to take notice of such "impressive" events. He gratuitously applied to them apocalyptic dimensions; for they were, in his estimation, not just "grand" and "terrific" but sufficiently awesome to strike an "image of our" very "conceptions of the final conflagration."[1]

Six years later George Catlin witnessed prairie fires during his western tours. He described them as "war, or hell of fires! where . . . the flames are driven forward by the hurricanes, which often sweep over the vast prairies of this denuded country." Using a standard aesthetic conflation of the period, he discovered in these grassland infernos a unifying force connecting "some of the most beautiful scenes" with "some of the most sublime." He described his painting of 1832 *Prairie Meadows Burning* (Smithsonian Museum of American Art, Washington), for example, as displaying a "swelling flood of smoke that is moving on like a black thunder cloud, rolling on the earth, with its lightning's glare, and its thunder rumbling as it goes."[2]

For artists like Ranney and Charles Deas, who were decidedly nativist in their artistic inclinations, these scenes were also distinctly American in character. In prefatory remarks to a critique of Deas's 1847 dramatic tableau *Prairie Fire* (Brooklyn Museum), a reviewer commented on the importance of such native themes and hoped that the artist would be applauded for according his art "the true spirit of the American school."[3] In his painting *Stampede*, Ranney successfully took advantage of this full range of emotional and national sentiment. What more sublime a scene could be conjured up than the overland emigrants' defending themselves from nature's rage in the form of frenzied horses and the oncoming ravages of smoke, flames, and cinders. Before a relentless onslaught of nature's most formidable forces, a group of pioneers struggles to survive. One man thrusts a flaming log or bundle at the thundering horse herd in an effort to avoid being trampled. Another endeavors to control a rearing steed that may provide hope for their escape. And in the midst of the turmoil hovers a blanket-wrapped woman sheltering an infant from the potential disaster that surrounds them. In the severity of the circumstances rendered here and the height of its sublime spectacle, Ranney's canvas presents the true pioneer Armageddon. "Many travellers, arrested by these burnings, have perished," according to Flint's telling, as "the crimson-coloured flames . . . rise from the earth to the sky."[4] If these travelers were spared, they had indeed been left with visions permanently seared into their memories. The confusion displayed in this work may also reflect the tumultuous and equally unforgettable times that followed the Mexican War. For while the Americans had won the war, vastly expanded their territory, and elected a military hero to the presidency, the newly claimed bounty to the west bode ill for the nation in many ways. Ralph Waldo Emerson would be quoted as saying, "The United States will conquer Mexico but it will be as the man swallows the arsenic which brings him down in turn. Mexico will poison us."[5] The political horizon, with slavery and expansionism mixed in immense and unsavory proportions, loomed as an incendiary veil over the country's future. North and South, not unlike Ranney's two central and desperate pioneer men, would move in opposite directions to assure their survival. And the larger American cultural life, along with future generations represented by the vulnerable mother and child, would be imperiled in the increasingly bitter and inflamed debate that ensued.

Art historian Rena Coen suggested a political flavor to this painting when she revealed formal and thematic associations between it and Jacques-Louis David's classic pictorialization of heroic reconciliation, *The Sabine Women* of 1799 (Musée du Louvre, Paris). If David's historical tribute to feminine endurance and virtuosity served as "an allegorical plea for an end to the internecine bloodshed of the French Revolution," so, too, may Ranney have sounded a prescient warning about the importance of preserving American unity. It is this contextualization of the *Stampede* that may in fact reveal its most national essence.

A generation later, one's travels west could be accomplished by rail and after the blazing sectional battles had been fought, such scenes as *Stampede* were considered the melodramatic exaggerations of sensationalist western writers and painters. Overwrought with romantic imagination, according to William E. Webb in his 1873 travel book, they missed the truth. The prairie fire was

> by no means terrifying to either man or brute. The only occasion when it could possibly prove dangerous is when it reaches, as it sometimes does, some of the narrow valleys where the tall grass of the bottom grows; but even then, a run of a hundred yards will take one to buffalo grass and safety.[6]

As pictorial proof of his sardonic claim, Webb illustrated two wood-engraved images of the prairies ablaze, *Fire on the Plains, According to Novels* and *Fire on the Plains, As It Is*. While Ranney may have witnessed a grassland conflagration, it is likely that he, like Deas, was following the lines of Cooper's or Flint's peppery tales of border adventure. PHH

1. Timothy Flint, *Recollections of the Last Ten Years* (Boston: Cummings, Hilliard, and Company, 1826), pp. 239–40. See also James Fenimore Cooper, *The Prairie: A Tale* (1827; Philadelphia: Carey, Lea and Carey, 1927), 2, pp. 84–85.

2. George Catlin, *Illustrations of the Manners, Customs, and Conditions of the North American Indian* (London: Henry G. Bohn, 1857), 2, p. 19–20.

3. "Mr. Deas," *Literary World*, vol. 1, no. 12 (April 24, 1847), p. 280.

4. Flint, *Recollections*, p. 239.

5 Bernard DeVoto, *The Year of Decision: 1846* (Boston: Houghton Mifflin Company, 1961), p. 214.

6. William E. Webb, *Buffalo Land: An Authentic Account of . . . the Wild West* (Cincinnati: E. Hannaford and Company, 1873), p. 118.

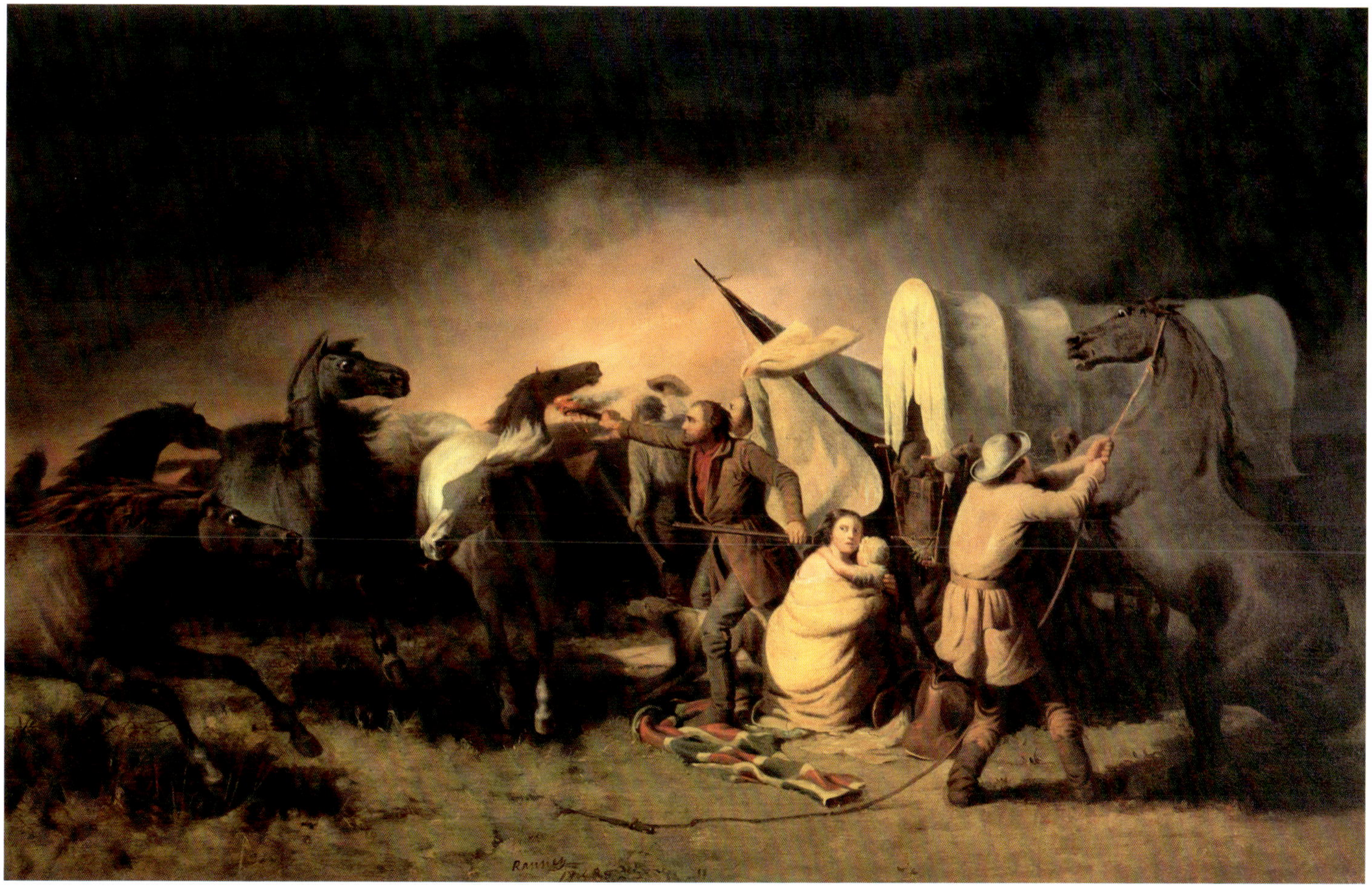

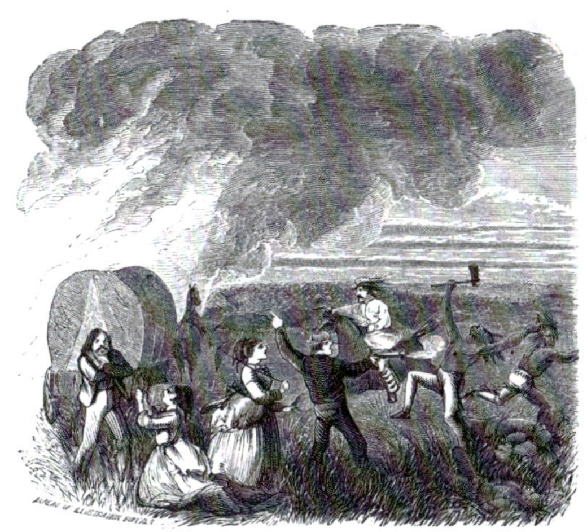

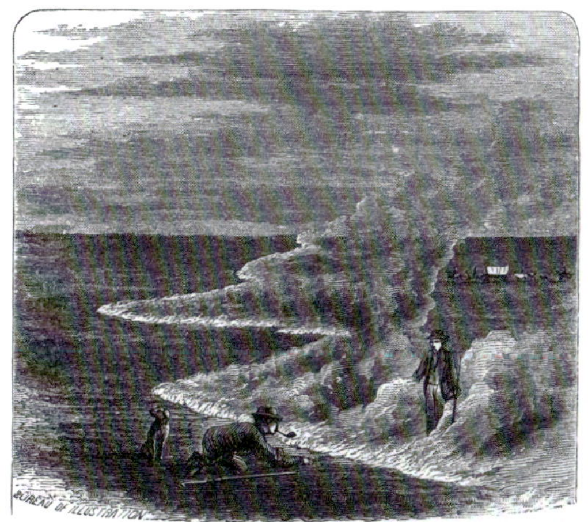

NO. 40

Fig. 40.1
Fire on the Plains, According to Novels and *Fire on the Plains, As It Is,* engraved from drawings by Henry Worrall. From William Edward Webb, *Buffalo Land* (Philadelphia, 1874). Courtesy of the Buffalo Bill Historical Center, Cody, Wyoming.

55

41
The Flight on the Prairie

c. 1848

Oil on canvas

Location unknown

Grubar no. 34

PROVENANCE: J. M. Burt, to 1857 (Henry H. Leeds and Co., New York, November 5, 1857, lot no. 6).

REFERENCES: New York, Henry H. Leeds and Company, New York, *Catalogue of a Splendid Collection of Costly Oil Paintings, Water Colors and Drawings, being the private gallery of J. M. Burt, Esq. . . . ,* November 5, 1857, lot no. 6, p. 1, lists as *The Flight, on the Prairie. Crayon* 4 (December 1857), p. 376, reports sold for $30.

This painting may relate to the *Stampede* (cat. no. 40). The low price earned at the Burt sale suggests this picture may be a rather small canvas. Included in that sale were also works by such landscape artists as Regis Gignoux, John F. Kensett, George Inness, Jasper F. Cropsey, William M. Hart, and Asher B. Durand. The landscapes, which seemed to have fared better than Ranney's picture, ranged in price from a low of $40 to a high of $250 for a Kensett entitled *Mountain Scenery*. LB

42
Fisher Boy

c. 1848

Oil on canvas

Location unknown

Grubar no. 35

PROVENANCE: Am Art-Union, New York, 1848; distributed by lottery to B. Blakeman, Albany, New York, 1848.

EXHIBITED: Am Art-Union, New York, 1848, no. 408.

REFERENCES: Am Art-Union, Executive Committee Minutes, 1846–1854, December 20, 1848, reel 2, vol. 1, Am Art-Union Papers, agreed to purchase Fisher Boy for $75. Am Art-Union, *Bulletin* (December 25, 1848), p. 23, no. 408, *Transactions for the Year 1848*, p. 72, no. 408, provides provenance. Cowdrey 1953, 2, p. 294.

43 *
Duck Shooters

1849

Oil on canvas

26 x 40 1/8 inches (66 x 101.9 cm)

Signed and dated, on side of boat: W Ranney/49

Museum of Fine Arts, Boston. Gift of Maxim Karolik for the M. and M. Karolik Collection of American Paintings, 1815–1865. 48.470.

Grubar no. 36

PROVENANCE: Am Art-Union, 1849; distributed by lottery to A. L. Hatch, Brooklyn, New York, 1849; Milton Rathbun, Mt. Vernon, New York; Alan Rathbun, New York; (T. Gilbert Brouillette, New York and Falmouth, Massachusetts, by c. 1946); (John Levy Galleries, New York, by 1946).

EXHIBITED: Am Art-Union, 1849, no. 13, as *Duck Shooters*. Chadds Ford 1991, cat. no. 8.

REFERENCES: Management Committee Minutes, 1839–1855, reel 1, vol. 2, February 1, 1849, notes agreed to purchase Duck Shooters for $125, framed; and Register Works of Art, 1848–1851, reel 2, July 3, 1849, no. 13, lists it, Am Art-Union Papers. Am Art-Union *Bulletin*, April (quoted in entry) through October and December 1849, no. 13, lists on various pages; November 1849, no. 13, p. 30, describes it and provides dimensions as 26 by 46 inches. Am Art-Union, *Transactions for the Year 1849*, p. 41, lists and provides provenance. *New York Sun*, March 9, 1849 (in Newspaper Clippings, reel 3, vol. 1, Am Art-Union Papers). *New York Morning Courier*, March 28, 1849, p. 3, provides critical response. *Literary World*, vol. 4 (April 14, 1849), p. 342, lists it. *New York Herald*, September 30, 1849 (in Newspaper Clippings, reel 3, vol. 2, p. 33, Am Art-Union Papers). *Catalogue of Paintings, Drawings, Statuary, etc. of the Art Department in the Great Central Fair* (Philadelphia, 1864), no. 510, p. 18, provides provenance. Museum of Fine Arts, Boston, 1949, p. 462, no. 206, as *Duck Hunters on the Hoboken Marshes*, provides specific information about location, individuals, provenance, and the man paddling boat. Cowdrey 1953, 2, p. 294.

This is one of a series of pictures inspired by the rich hunting and fishing areas near Ranney's New Jersey home. In these works he chronicled the activities of the emerging middle class, following in the genre traditions of artists such as William Sidney Mount. The following description of *Duck Shooters* appeared in the American Art-Union's *Bulletin* of 1849:

> A Sportsman, with his gun in hand, is being quietly rowed by an attendant around a small green island, on the other side of which a number of ducks are seen. Both figures express great eagerness. A dog is in the boat, looking as eager as his master. The scenery is low and flat, and the sky bright colored.

As a hunter himself, Ranney could dramatically portray the thrill and tension of the sport. He set the scene against a brilliant pink sky, the whole suffused with subtle coloristic tonalities. In its spare horizontal com-

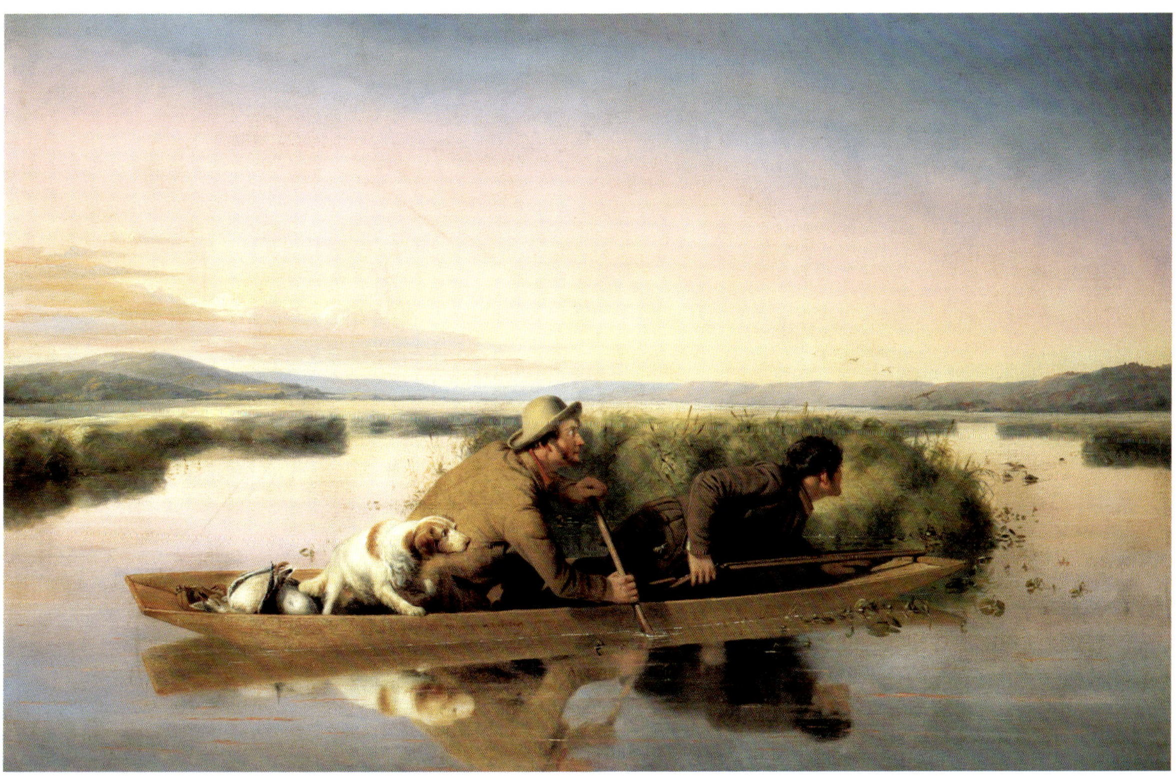

NO. 43

position and the use of poetic atmospheric effects, the work can be placed within the larger context of luminist landscape painting of the mid-nineteenth century. Ranney may also be stylistically indebted to George Caleb Bingham, whose *Fur Traders Descending the Missouri* of 1845 (Metropolitan Museum of Art) he could have seen when it was exhibited at the American Art-Union in 1845.

The presence of the boat and its sharp-eyed hunters are reinforced by the bold reflections in the water. The sportsmen are focused on the three feeding ducks barely visible at the right, presumably waiting for them to take wing. They are accompanied by a brown and white dog resembling a springer spaniel, the preferred gun-dog, then as now, for retrieving dead or crippled birds. While their exaggerated expressions seem to border on caricature, the man paddling, according to the Museum of Fine Arts' files, was in fact said to be a portrait of Nat McIver, a neighbor of Ranney's who worked in a nearby stable. In the boat, the bagged birds, with their white breasts and long slim necks, are similar to marsh ducks known today as northern pintails.

When the painting was exhibited at the American Art-Union in 1849, critical response was very positive. The *New York Sun* of March 9, 1849, found *Duck Shooters* "of striking merit." The writer in the 1849 *New York Herald* admired Ranney's drawing and conception, but noted that the coloring suggests a hot summer day and "to a sportsman [the scene] looks out of season." This remark reflects the era's keen awareness of a strict code of conduct which stipulated that a true sportsman must respect and understand the life cycles of his prey and contribute to its preservation by not hunting during its breeding season. Popular and influential sporting writers, such as Henry William Herbert, who wrote under the pen name of Frank Forester, indicated that the best seasons for hunting waterfowl were in the fall and spring, for about an hour at twilight or early evening. He further advised hunters to use a birch canoe to discover known feeding areas and to shoot the birds on the wing, preferably with a 10-pound, 10-gauge, and 34-inch barrel gun made by John Mullins of New York. The sportsman's code of conduct forbade shooting a bird that was at rest feeding. For humanitarian reasons and to preserve the sense of fair play, the bird must be shot on the wing, preferably on the first shot so that it would not suffer.[1]

Though originally entitled *Duck Shooters* when it was purchased in 1849 by the American Art-Union, the painting had several variant titles, including *Duck Hunters on the Hoboken Marshes*. When Boston acquired the picture in 1948, it was suggested that the view was of the marshes of Penhorn Creek, a Hackensack River tributary near Secaucus, New Jersey. This locale is several miles southwest of the Hoboken marshes near Ranney's home, which seems to have been the inspiration for most of his duck hunting pictures.[2]

A contemporary description that appeared in the *New York Morning Courier* when the painting was exhibited in 1849 clearly describes this scene and its popular appeal:

> One of the most successful pictures on the walls is No. 13, *Duck Shooters*, by W. Ranney. It is excellent in color and drawing; and wariness and restrained eagerness are admirably expressed in the faces and attitudes of men and dog. The very gun seems almost endowed with volition, and to be on the lookout not to "go off" too soon.

It has been noted that the dimensions of the canvas published in the American Art-Union publications differ from those of this work. According to notes from the museum's files, provided by the museum conservators, there is no evidence that the canvas has been cut down. Presumably the Art-Union's information was a typographical error. L B

1. See Frank Forester [Henry William Herbert], *Complete Manual for Young Sportsmen* (1856; reprint, [New York] Westvaco Corporation, 1993), pp. 157–158.

2. It was also suggested that there were silhouetted buildings visible on the hilltop in the upper right, which were said to represent the Passionist mission, St. Michael's Monastery. Those buildings were not constructed, however, until 1861. A recent reexamination of the canvas did not indicate any evidence of buildings. The source for this misinformation seems to be a letter of October 31, 1947, from Norman Hirschl of the John Levy Galleries, New York, to Richard B. K. McLanathan, curator of the Museum of Fine Arts, Boston, copy in the museum files.

44[*]
First Fish of the Season

1849

Oil on canvas

27 x 40 inches (68.6 x 101.6 cm)

Signed and dated, center right, bow of boat: W Ranney/1849

Canvas stamp (before lining): S. N. Dodge, 189 Chatham Street, New York

Private collection

Grubar no. 96

PROVENANCE: Joseph Harrison, Jr. (1810–1874), Philadelphia, by 1867; his wife, Sarah Poulterer Harrison (1817–1906), Philadelphia, 1874–1906 (sale, Philadelphia Art Galleries, Philadelphia, February 23, 24, and 25, 1910, lot no. 103); estate of Ruth Allin John (Vose Galleries, Boston, c. 1980) Edward L. Shein, Providence, Rhode Island; private collection, Colorado; (J. N. Bartfield Art Galleries, New York, by 1984) Mr. and Mrs. Eddy Nicholson, Hampton Falls, New Hampshire, c. 1984–1995 (sale, Christie's, New York, January 27, 28, 1995, lot no. 840).

REFERENCES: Tuckerman 1867, p. 630, lists in the collection of J. Harrison, Esq. *Catalogue of Pictures, Statuary and Bronzes in the Gallery of Joseph Harrison, Jr., Rittenhouse Square, Philadelphia*, 1870, no. 45. Edward Strahan [Earl Shinn], ed., *The Art Treasures of America* (Philadelphia 1879–1880), vol. 3, p. 92, lists in collection of Mrs. Joseph Harrison.

In this work Ranney successfully combines his skills as a portrait, landscape, and genre painter. Suggesting the likeness of a known subject, he portrays a fisherman with spectacles, grayish hair, and in gentlemanly dress offset by a red neck scarf. The dog accompanying him in the wooden skiff appears to be a border terrier. A drawing of two similar terriers is in a private collection (cat. no. D78).

Ranney renders the background landscape, very likely the Hoboken marshes near his home, in the muted colors of early spring, before the fresh green foliage has had a chance to emerge. He suffuses the whole with the delicate pink atmospheric light of early morning hours, which etches clear and bold reflections on the peaceful waters. While sparse pictorially, the scene includes a number of subtle elements that taken together relate a story. The oars at rest, the rope looped across the front of the boat, and the floating bobber are all clues that a good fishing spot has been discovered. The bait bowl and cutting board with a knife stuck upright into it and a few leftover bits tell the viewer that the hook is baited. The anxiety of the wait of this first outing of the season is expressed by the fisherman's tight grasp of the bamboo fishing rod as well as the tense

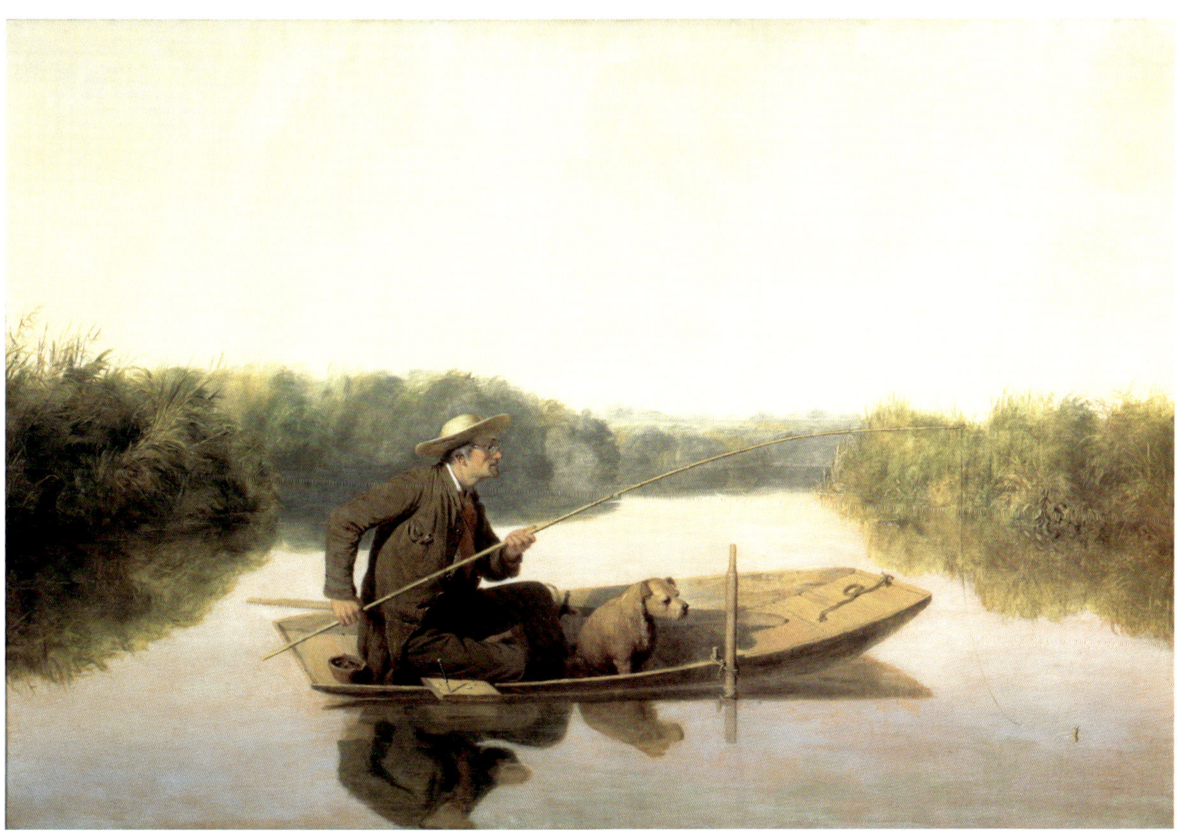

NO. 44

watchfulness of both man and dog for the bobber to disappear underwater, signaling a strike. By his meticulous attention to the realistic details of everyday objects and the likenesses of the figure and his dog, Ranney empathetically conveys the emotional and practical experience of all fishermen.

This painting was in a prominent private collection throughout the nineteenth century. By 1962, it was recorded by Grubar as "location unknown," but it came to light in the early 1980s. In its general subject matter, size, horizontal composition, and atmospheric effects, the work is very similar to Ranney's *Duck Shooters* (cat. no. 43), also painted in 1849. *Duck Shooters*, however, was an American Art-Union exhibition piece in which the expressions of the hunters appear exaggerated, perhaps to appeal to a broad audience. There is no evidence that *First Fish* was ever exhibited during the artist's lifetime, which leads one to assume that it was a private commission, perhaps inspired by the success of the *Duck Shooters*. Whether it was meant as a portrait of a specific individual is not known.

The earliest recorded owner of *First Fish of the Season* was Joseph Harrison, Jr., a mechanical engineer, who achieved his fame and fortune by designing and building locomotives in Russia, where he was decorated by Nicholas I, emperor of Russia. When Harrison returned to his native Philadelphia in 1852, he and his wife built a mansion on fashionable Rittenhouse Square and filled it with art which he had begun collecting abroad.[1] He served on the board of the Pennsylvania Academy of the Fine Arts from 1854 to 1870, and several of the more significant artworks he owned are now in that collection, including Benjamin West's *Penn's Treaty with the Indians* (1771–1772), John Vanderlyn's *Ariadne Asleep on the Island of Naxos* (1809–1814), and Charles Willson Peale's *Artist in His Museum* (1822). In addition to European and early American works, Harrison's collection also included many examples by Ranney's contemporaries, such as Albert Bierstadt, Thomas Cole, Jasper F. Cropsey, and Arthur Fitzwilliam Tait.   LB

1. On April 24, 1849, Harrison wrote a letter from Russia to a George H. Prince in Leeds, England: "I want good or well executed paintings." He forwarded fifty pounds for Prince to draw upon. There is some evidence in several letters in the fall of 1849 that Harrison may have returned briefly to the United States. Either he or an agent in New York could have bought Ranney's picture at that time. See Joseph Harrison Letterbooks, vol. 1 (1844–1851), Manuscript Collection, Historical Society of Pennsylvania.

45 *
Boone's First View of Kentucky

1849

Oil on canvas

36 x 53 1/2 inches
(91.4 x 135.9 cm)

Signed and dated,
lower right, on rock:
W. Ranney/1849

Gilcrease Museum,
Tulsa, Oklahoma.

Grubar no. 38

ENGRAVING: Alfred Jones (1819–1900), *Daniel Boone's First View of Kentucky*, steel engraving, image 5 1/2 x 8 inches (14 x 20.3 cm). Published in the Am Art-Union *Bulletin*, May 1, 1850, opposite p. 17.

PROVENANCE: Am Art-Union, 1850; distributed by lottery to Mrs. John [Daisey Dell] Dillon, Zanesville, Ohio, in 1850; her son, Daniel Dillon, to 1917; Mrs. Lucy H. Yetter, Phoenix, by c. 1917 to c. 1930s; her granddaughter, Mrs. L. Sirotti, California, c. 1930s to c. 1958; (Kennedy Galleries, New York, by 1958); Thomas Gilcrease, Tulsa, 1958–1963.

EXHIBITED: Am Art-Union, New York, 1850, no. 2. Zanesville Industrial Exposition, Zanesville Art Center, Ohio, December 24 , 1873–January 1, 1874, cat. no. 120, p. 11, as *Boone's First View of Kentucky*, lists Mrs. John (Daisey Dell) Dillon as owner.

REFERENCES: Register Works of Art, 1848–1851, reel 2, no. 1458, October 25 [1849], indicates purchased framed, reel 2, Management Committee Minutes, 1839–1855, reel 1, November 1 and 8, 1849, Am Art-Union Papers, discusses possibility of using it as engraving for members in 1850. Am Art-Union, *Bulletin*, August 1849, p. 29, mentions as The Encampment of Boone; and November 1849, as Boone's First Sight of Kentucky from the Cumberland Mountains, p. 18. *Literary World* (August 11, 1849), p. 113. *New York Evening Post* , May 4, 1850, p. 2, mentions engraving. *New York Herald*, September 8, 1850, p. 2, reviews it. *New York Tribune*, December 10, 1850, says Am Art-Union catalogue of works to be distributed; December 21, 1850, p. 4, no. 2, indicates "drawn by a name we missed entirely." Henry T. Tuckerman, "Over the Mountains or the Western Pioneer," in *The Home Book of the Picturesque; or American Scenery, Art, and Literature* (New York: Putnam, 1852), pp. 117-118 (quoted in entry). *Ornaments of Memory . . .* (New York: D. Appleton and Co., 1855), pp.48–52, discusses and illustrates engraving. Cowdrey 1953, 2, p. 294, provides description and provenance. J. Gray Sweeney, *The Columbus of the Woods: Daniel Boone and the Typology of Manifest Destiny* (St. Louis: Washington University Gallery of Art, 1992), pp. 31–39; 73–74, discusses this painting and Ranney's idea of Daniel Boone as a type of national hero.

As part of an extended historical series on the American West, Ranney painted his first major allegory of discovery in 1849. That year he produced not one but two versions of Daniel Boone's initial encounter with the glorious wilderness of Kentucky. This version was sold to the American Art-Union in 1849 and shown in 1850. It revealed, according to their November 1849 *Bulletin*, "a striking delineation of the wilderness and the frank hearty spirit of pioneer life." In order to promote the painting, the Art-Union published an engraving of the work by Alfred Jones (fig. 45.1), which conveyed Ranney's primary theme that historical events could confirm and validate contemporary events. The Mexican War had been concluded with rich rewards for the United States, and gold discoveries in California held such alluring promise that more than eighty thousand Americans had either moved there or were on their way as Ranney completed this painting.

The second version (cat. no. 46), an oil of almost identical size, was probably the product of a private commission spurred by the enthusiastic reaction to the Art-Union's piece. Its palette was considerably fresher, which may have been the result of criticism leveled at the earlier version. The *Herald's* reviewer of the 1850 exhibition had regarded the initial version as "well treated," "spirited," and "as a work of art, . . . among his best." But the critic had also noted that it was wanting of "relief from too much brown. Ranney is too good a painter to throw away his brush so much on buff leather, for which his pictures are all remarkable." Although Ranney would make only moderate adjustments to the pervasiveness of "buff leather," he took major steps in the subsequent interpretation to free the figures from the all-permeating golden brown luminosity that enshrouds the scene. The painting's atmospheric clarity and the cerulean blush of the sky infuse the second painting with an awakened vitality, converting a dreamy, self-absorptive calm to one of cheerful, national ordination.

Ranney wished to suggest a sense of rationality that he no doubt perceived as an important characteristic of the American experience. If such works of historical transference were to instill the public with a feeling of virtue and morality, certainly rational explanations for momentous episodes from the past were called for. This also provides meaning for the calm and revelatory nature of the presentation. The historian Francis Parkman described Boone in 1849 as the "prince of pioneers" whose "quiet and tranquil spirit. . . . remarkably distinguish him."[1] Yet American life was anything but calm in 1849. Rational, nonfrangible decisions affecting the nation's future, from the divisive 1848 election that brought General Zachary Taylor to the presidency to the thousands of broken homes and uprooted families caused by gold fever, were few and far between. Ranney's dip into history, his proclamation of reasoned optimism and ambition, and his case for a composed epiphany for an aspiring people, can be considered as much a salve for wounds of disquiet as a celebration of future hope for the country.

The critic and writer Henry Tuckerman saw the first version of this work on exhibit in 1850. He wrote so affectionately and insightfully about it (published 1852) that his comments are worth quoting in full:

> There hung, for many months, on the walls of the Art-Union gallery in New-York, a picture by Ranney, so thoroughly national in its subject and true to nature in its execution, that it was refreshing to contemplate it, after being wearied with far more ambitious yet less successful attempts. It represented a flat ledge of rock, the summit of a high cliff that projected over a rich, umbrageous country, upon which a band of hunters leaning on their rifles, were gazing with looks of delighted surprise. The foremost, a compact and agile, though not very commanding figure, is pointing out the landscape to his comrades, with an air of exultant yet calm satisfaction; the wind lifts his thick shirt, his easy attitude, the fresh brown tint of his cheek, and an ingenuous, cheerful, determined yet benign expression of countenance, proclaim the hunter and pioneer, the Columbus of the woods, the forest philosopher and brave champion. The picture represents Daniel Boone discovering to his companions the fertile levels of Kentucky.

Ranney had attempted to capture a historical moment, the climactic point at which the young Boone has realized his ambitions of finding new ground. Seeing his future dreams formulated within his gaze, the pioneer has thrown down his hat as a gesture, traditional since the times of the Roman emperors, of claiming the discovered dominion as his home. The Indian trader John Finley (rather than Boone, as Tuckerman suggests) points out to the new territory. As the guide for the group, Finley is given the role as interlocutor figure. Boone's brother-in-law John Stewart is also positioned in a place of prominence. He stands to the left of Boone, leaning contemplatively on his rifle, an appropriate pose as he was known as a superior marksman.[2] But it is Boone—positioned at the center of the group and with a particularly potent stance (legs apart, feet firmly planted, focus forward and rifle pointed diagonally at the sky)—who transports the viewer from the empirical instant of discovery on May 1, 1769, to the abstract notion of discoverability. It is as though all of western America, not just Kentucky, is in his view. It was in Ranney's vision a land filled with similar potential epiphanies for others to share. And it was those broader implications that invited Tuckerman to regard this work as so "refreshing" and "so thoroughly national."

Boone, who like Ranney, had been raised in North Carolina, found a lofty place in the hierarchy of American heroes as a common man with enormous courage and determination. His exploits were considered a backwoods extension of the spirit of the American Revolution. And though he was anything but peaceable, his early biographer, William Henry Bogart, claimed that he "gave to the enterprise the means of furnishing a home for millions, where the arts of peace can illustrate the true destiny of mankind."[3] Boone was regarded as simple, clear sighted, unambiguous, and fully comprehensible by the common people. Art historian Dawn Glanz has concluded that Ranney's depictions of Boone "evened the differences between the common man and the hero."[4]

The distinguished modern historian and literary critic Henry Nash Smith concluded that, to many in the nineteenth century, Boone embodied a dual historical personality. One view of the wilderness hero held that Boone represented the frontiersman who constantly strove to escape civilization. He was the "white Indian" whose life was devoted to testing himself against the wilds and staying beyond reach of the sullying influences of society and culture. The other view envisioned him as a harbinger of the very civilization he

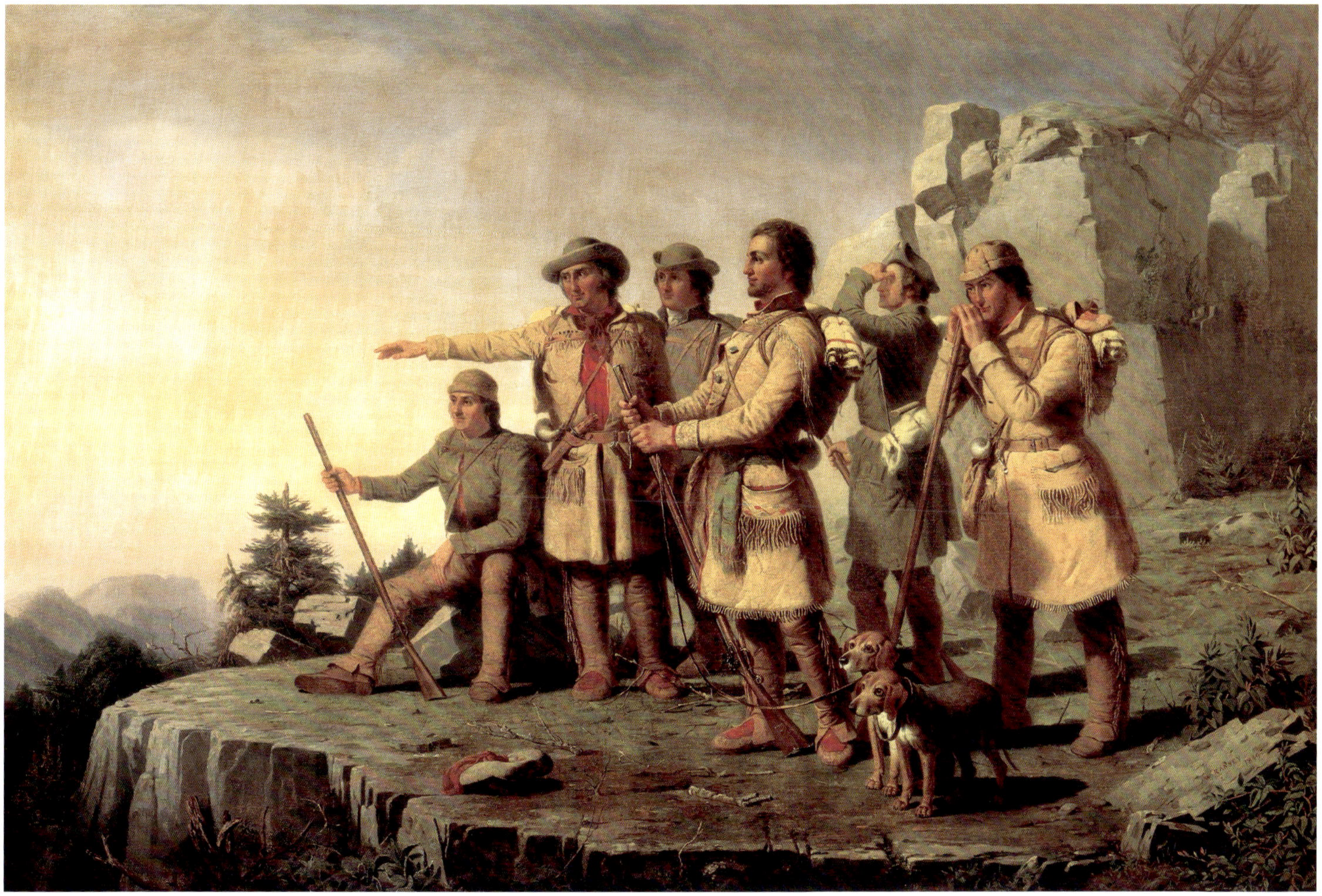

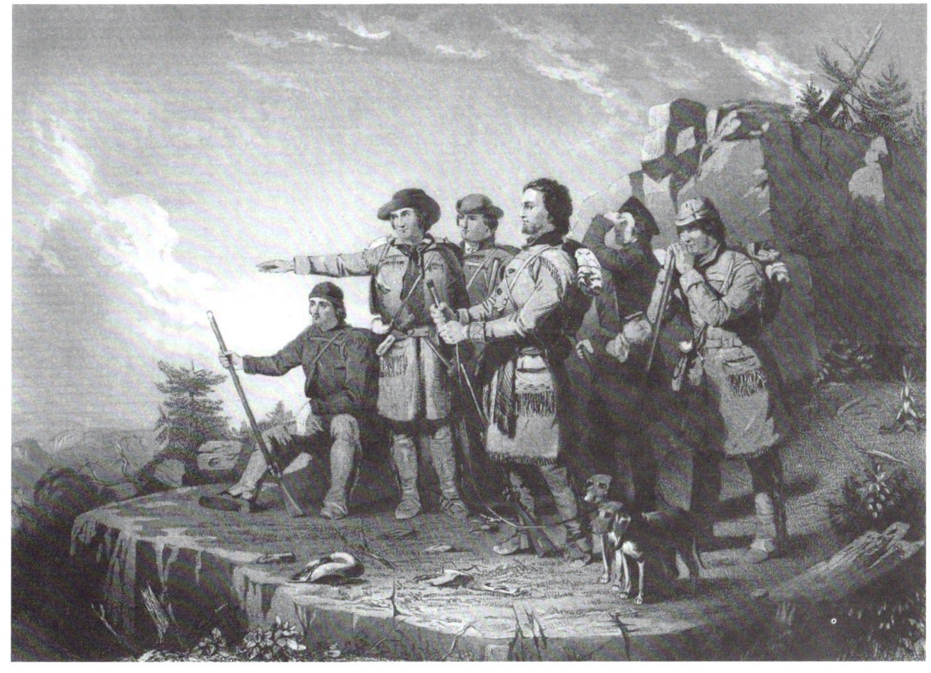

Fig. 45.1

Boone's First View of Kentucky, wood engraving
by Alfred Jones. Library Company of Philadelphia.

eschewed. It was he who would lead the vanguard of America's yeomen into the West. He was America's Moses and Kentucky the American Canaan. Boone's mission was largely considered a holy cause.[5]

Ranney's paintings of Boone represent him most strongly in the first guise. In the initial version of the painting, Boone and his party are clad in buckskins and wear moccasins for the most part. Here Boone is nativism incarnate. Yet he also metaphorically bridges the wilderness from civilization and the future from the past. The ethereal space into which the group stares is essentially formless and unknown. Behind them rises a formidable rock outcropping. A path has led them by it to the ledge on which they stand. The rocks provide evidence of structure and linear order, realities on which they turn their backs, just as they have done to civilization and its constraints. In the later version of the work, Ranney buttresses Boone and his compatriots with a less architectonic backdrop, giving a feeling of all-around wilderness. Yet he suggests an industrial East by selecting manufactured footwear in place of moccasins for each of them.

The true champion of Boone as a leader of, rather than a fugitive from, civilization was the Missouri artist George Caleb Bingham. Soon after Ranney's success with the Boone subject, Bingham produced his famous painting *The Emigration of Daniel Boone into Kentucky*. Although Bingham's message about "manifest destiny" as a signal force in American life mirrors Ranney's, his portrayal of Boone is quite different. Bingham, a resolute member of the Whig Party, saw the West as a place into which civilization must be brought rather than a sanctuary from society.

By comparison to the formal, grand manner history paintings by Emanuel Leutze, Peter Rothermel, and William Powell, Ranney's portrayal of Boone in Kentucky possesses an air of fresh reality that reduces the epic event to normal human scale. Ranney's experience as a portrait and genre painter in fact characteristically caused his history work to relate more to genre painting than to the oversized, overstaged spreads that decorated the United States Capitol's rotunda and other public spaces. In this approach, with its reduced scale and treatment of subjects, Ranney was following a transformation in history painting that had gradually emerged since the 1830s. As Mark Thistlethwaite has noted, American painters of historical scenes in the 1840s and 1850s increasingly represented "incidents rather than major events."[6] And in Europe, French painters like Paul Delaroche were working to demystify major events and personages such as Napoleon by making them more accessible to a public audience. In Ranney's two paintings, Boone is portrayed as a common man, the eighteenth-century equivalent of the Oregon pioneer or the California gold-seeker. And as evidenced by the American Art-Union's patronage of the early rendition, it was conceived as a savory morsel for popular delectation — a painting that someone of common means might win and hang in her or his private home.

For a study of this painting see cat. no. D1. PHH

1. Francis Parkman, *The Oregon Trail*, (1849; Boston: Ginn and Company, 1910), p. 116.

2. For a description of this event and the characters involved, see John Mack Faragher, *Daniel Boone: The Life and Legend of an American Pioneer* (New York: Henry Holt and Company, 1992), pp. 70–78.

3. William Henry Bogart, *Daniel Boone and the Hunters of Kentucky* (Auburn and Buffalo: Miller, Orton & Mulligan, 1854), p. 55.

4. Glanz 1982, p. 19.

5. Henry Nash Smith, *Virgin Land: The American West as Symbol and Myth* (New York: Vintage Books, 1950), pp. 54–63.

6. Gerdts and Thistlethwaite 1988, p. 37.

46
Boone's First View of Kentucky

1849
Oil on canvas
37 5/8 x 54 1/4 inches
(95.6 x 137.8 cm)
Signed and dated,
lower right: W. Ranney
/1849
Anschutz Collection,
Denver
Grubar no. 39

PROVENANCE: Mrs. J. Madden, Greenwich, Connecticut, 1951–1962 (Knoedler and Company, New York, by 1962); National Cowboy Hall of Fame and Western Heritage Center, Oklahoma City, 1972–1980; (Ira Spanierman, New York, by c. 1981–1982).

REFERENCES: Patricia Hills, "Picturing Progress in the Era of Westward Expansion" in *The West as America: Reinterpreting Images of the Frontier, 1820-1920* (Washington: National Museum of American Art, 1991), pp. 110-111, no. 93, illus. and discusses in terms of theme of discovery pictures and identifies Boone as the elder man who like Moses points out "the Promised Land to the advanced guard of his people."

See cat. no. 45 for a discussion of this subject and picture. LB

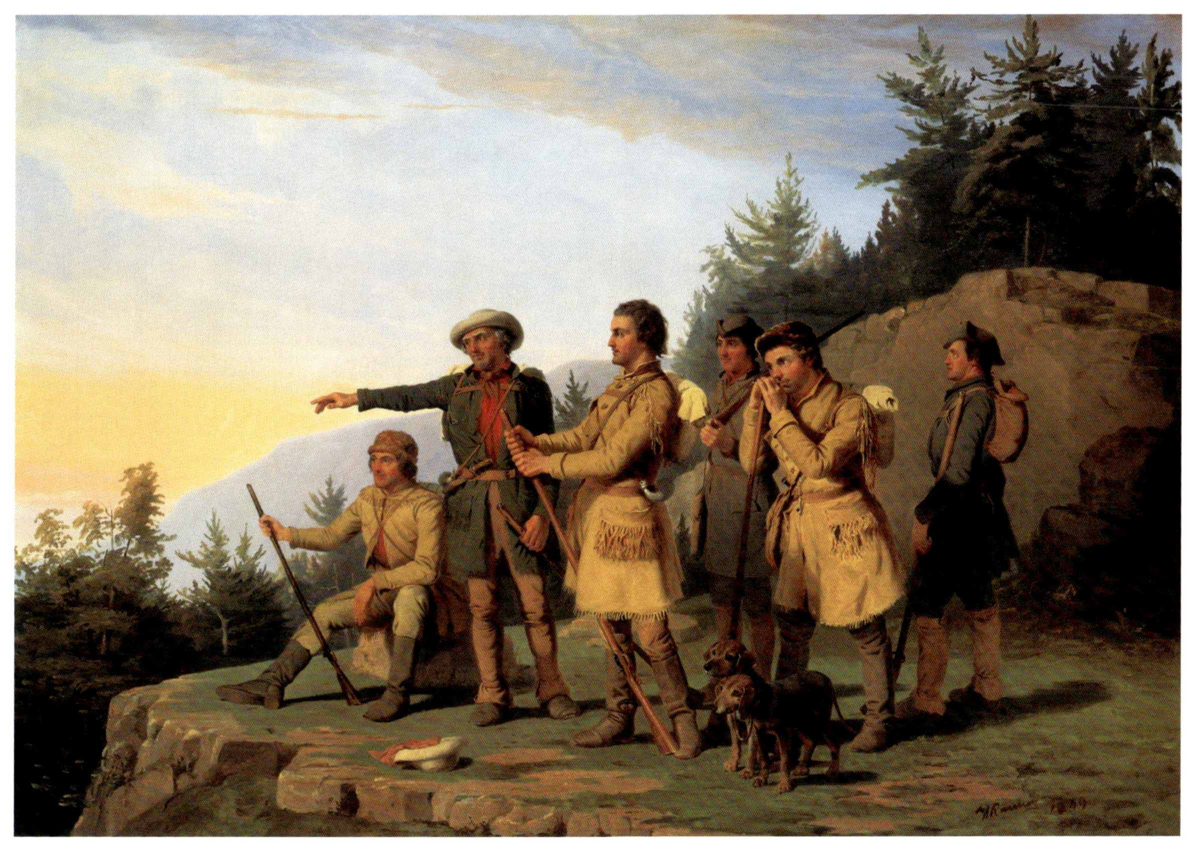

NO. 46

47
A Rabbit Hunter

c. 1849

Oil on canvas

22 x 27 inches (55.9 x 68.6 cm)

Location unknown

Grubar no. 37

PROVENANCE: Am Art-Union, 1849; distributed by lottery to William Waters, Franklin, New York, by 1849.

EXHIBITIONS: Am Art-Union, 1849, no. 142. Franklin, New York, Delaware Academy of Design, *Catalogue of the Second Annual Exhibition*, July, 1857, no. 10, p. 2, as A Winter scene, a hunter with his dog in pursuit of game.

REFERENCES: Register, Works of Art 1848–1851, no. 1045, as Rabbit Hunter purchased June 7, 1849, $80 (framed); and Management Committee Minutes 1839-1855, June 7, 1849, reel 1, Am Art-Union Papers, agreed to purchase no. 1045, for $80 (unframed). Am Art-Union, *Bulletin*, July 1849, no. 142, p. 31. *New York Morning Courier*, August 18, 1849, p. 4, no. 142, listed. *New York Tribune*, September 1, 1849, p. 3, no. 142, listed. Am Art-Union, *Catalogue of Works of Art. Purchased by the American Art-Union . . . , 1849*, no. 142, listed. *American Art-Union Distribution Catalogue*, December 21, 1849, no. 142. Am Art-Union, *Transactions for the Year 1849*, p. 46, no. 142, lists and provides provenance. Cowdrey 1953, 2, p. 294, lists, describes, and provides provenance.

While no contemporary reviews have been discovered describing this lost painting, the American Art-Union publications provided the dimensions and the following description: "A hunter going through the snow with his dog and gun." Two other such subjects entitled *Rabbit Hunting* were sold in the Ranney Fund sale: lot 79 to someone by the name of Eastburn for twenty-one dollars, and lot 182 to someone by the name of Riggs for four dollars.

Grubar notes that the *New York Tribune* of December 22, 1849, listed William Wallace of Franklin, Delaware County, New York, as the recipient of this painting, while the American Art-Union listed the name as William Waters. LB

48
Trappers on the Lookout

c. 1849

Oil on academy board

9 x 11 inches (22.9 x 27.9 cm)

Initialed, lower right, on rocks: W R.

Canvas stamp: Muller-Paris. Small label with the number 56

Location unknown

Grubar no. 40

PROVENANCE: Ranney Fund sale, as Trappers on the Lookout, sold for $21 to Walker; estate of Mrs. Samuel R[illegible], c. 1950s (Meredith Galleries, New York) (Victor Spark, New York, jointly with James Graham and Sons, by 1954 to 1955); (Mortimer Brandt Galleries, New York, by 1962); Carl Schaefer Dentzel, Northridge, California, by 1961 until at least 1978.

REFERENCES: "Stock Book: 1954–1955," Victor Spark Papers, Archives of American Art, Smithsonian Institution, Washington, D.C., lists under stock no. 3198, as Two Frontiersmen with Their Dogs and provides provenance. Irwin Shapiro, *The Golden Book of California from the Days of the Spanish Explorers to the Present* (New York: Golden Press, 1961), p. 26, no. 7, illus. and lists in the collection of Dr. Carl S. Dentzel. William H. Goetzmann, *The Mountain Man* (Cody: Buffalo Bill Historical Center, 1978), pl. 19, illus. and lists in collection of Carl Schaefer Dentzel.

This now unlocated small study, variously titled *Mountain Men with Their Dogs* or *Trappers on the Lookout*, shows two figures and two hounds that are virtually identical to those in Ranney's *Boone's First View of Kentucky*, painted in 1849 (cat. nos. 45 and 46). In the paintings, the two men appear clean-shaven and are separated by other figures. According to Grubar there was affixed to the back of this study "a small, shieldlike label with the number '56' inscribed therein, which corresponds to the Ranney Fund Sale number." At that sale, the work was purchased by someone by the name of Walker for twenty-one dollars. LB

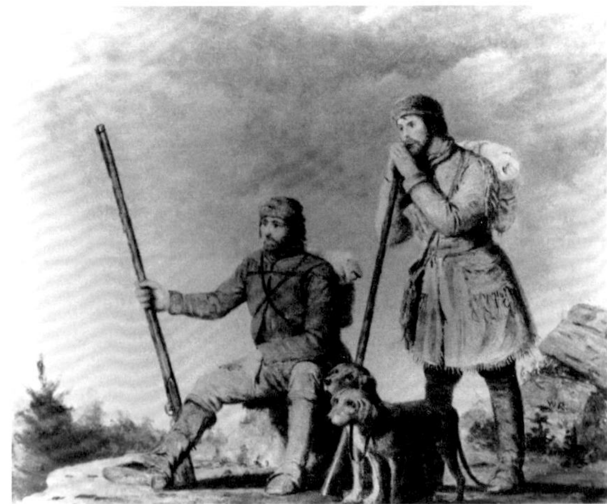

Illustration of no. 48 from Goetzmann (1978), pl. 19.

49*
Wounded Hound

1850

Oil on canvas

30 x 25 inches (76.2 x 63.5 cm)

Signed, lower left: W. Ranney; signed and dated, on the back: W. Ranney/1850

Virginia Museum of Fine Arts, Richmond. The J. Harwood and Louise B. Cochrane Fund for American Art, 2002.538

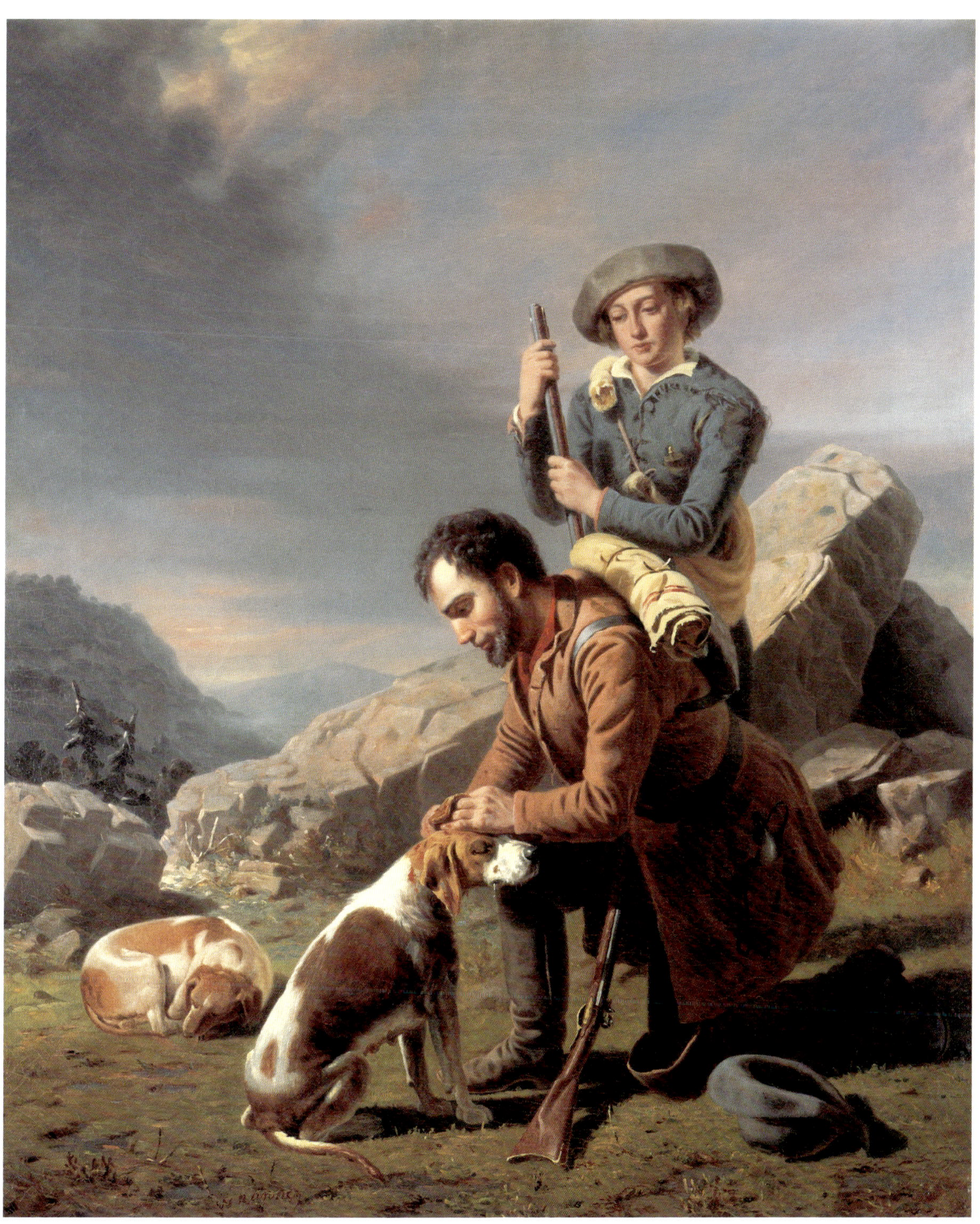

Provenance: Private collection, Hartford, Connecticut, 1890–1995 (Beacon Hill Fine Art, New York, 1995–1996) (Godel Company Fine Art, New York, 1996) (Spanierman Gallery, New York, c. 2001 to 2002).

References: Godel Company Fine Art, *Antiques Magazine*, vol. 150 (November, 1996), p. 633, advertises it. Spanierman Gallery, *The Spirit of America: American Art from 1829 to 1970* (New York: 2002), no. 6 color illus.

In this picture, Ranney represents two hunters and their dogs. The men have interrupted the rigors of the hunt to attend to an unexpected injury. In the background, one dog is curled up napping while the younger hunter leans on his rifle watching, as though admiring the skills of a respected mentor at work. The older kneeling gentleman has laid his hat on the ground so he can more easily attend to the wound near the dog's left ear, which is torn and bleeding. Whether the dog was mistakenly caught in inadvertent cross fire or attacked by an animal in the field is unclear.

As a sportsman himself, Ranney included dogs in many of his works, perhaps using his own dogs as models. The medium-sized hounds in this picture appear to be distant relatives of British foxhounds or beagles. Bred in the United States to accompany hunters on foot, particularly in search of the American hare, they were then as today appreciated not only for their excellent abilities to follow scents but also for their intelligence and amicability.

This scene has the pathos of an everyday hunting drama. To many seasoned sportsmen, however, it would have been recognized as a specific visualization of an important component of the code of ethics promulgated by the extensive sporting literature of the period. Just as the true sportsman must exhibit humanitarianism and restraint in hunting, it was also incumbent upon him to extend that benevolence to the care and treatment of his dogs. He was admonished to provide his dogs with clean lodging and water, excellent bedding, food, bathing opportunities, and daily exercise, and also to be prepared to manage "them in sickness or in health, in the kennel or in the field."[1]

The *Wounded Hound*, which is signed and dated 1850, is one of two versions, both recently rediscovered. Characteristically, Ranney neither signed nor dated what is probably the second version (cat. no. 50) of this subject, now in a private collection. While the dimensions of both paintings are identical, there are subtle compositional and other changes. The figures in this Virginia Museum version, for instance, are smaller in relationship to the picture plane than in the unsigned version, and, although they are apparently the same individuals, they appear younger here because they do not have graying hair and full mustaches and beards. The clothing and background also differ in coloring and minor details. A related pen and ink wash drawing entitled *Mountain Men with Dogs* is in the collection of the Phoenix Art Museum (cat. no. D77). In it, as in the unsigned version of the *Wounded Hound*, the hunters appear to have aged. This age disparity suggests that Ranney revisited this theme, either a few years after he first painted it in 1850, or that perhaps he used different models.

Neither work is known to have been exhibited publicly during Ranney's lifetime. The signed version of *Wounded Hound* was probably sold in 1850, shortly after it was painted, at a time when demand for Ranney's work, particularly the sporting scenes, appeared to have been strong.   LB

1. See Frank Forester [Henry William Herbert], *Complete Manual for Young Sportsmen* (1856: reprint [New York]: Westvaco Corporation, 1993), pp. 23–24 and pp. 50–52.

50*
Wounded Hound

c. 1850

Oil on canvas

30 x 25 inches (76.2 x 63.5 cm)

Private collection

PROVENANCE: Possibly Ranney Fund sale, 1858, lot 24, annotated as sold to Wood for $21; (Kennedy Galleries, New York, to 1979), (James Maroney, New York, 1979).

EXHIBITED: Kennedy Galleries, New York, *Wildlife and Sporting Pictures*, May 1979, no. 11, as attributed to J. F. Herring. Chadds Ford 1991, cat. no. 15.

REFERENCE: James H. Maroney, Jr. to Linda Bantel, December 1, 1998, Ranney archives, provides provenance and notes J. F. Herring apocryphal signature.

This is probably the second version of the painting discussed under cat. no. 49. It is possible this unsigned, possibly later, version of the *Wounded Hound* is the one that remained in the artist's studio until his death and sold for twenty-one dollars at the Ranney Fund sale (lot 24) to someone by the name of Wood who purchased sixteen of the 108 Ranneys in that sale. Two brothers, Charles B. and David A. Wood were New York patrons of Mount. David A. Wood was listed as a prominent carriage maker in the New York city directories of the period.

Before the painting was attributed to Ranney by the American art dealer James H. Maroney, Jr., it was exhibited as the work of J. F. Herring. His signature, which had been added on top of the varnish, disappeared during restoration. The British artist John Frederick Herring (1795–1865) was noted for his sporting pictures as well as farmyard and animal genre scenes. LB

NO. 50

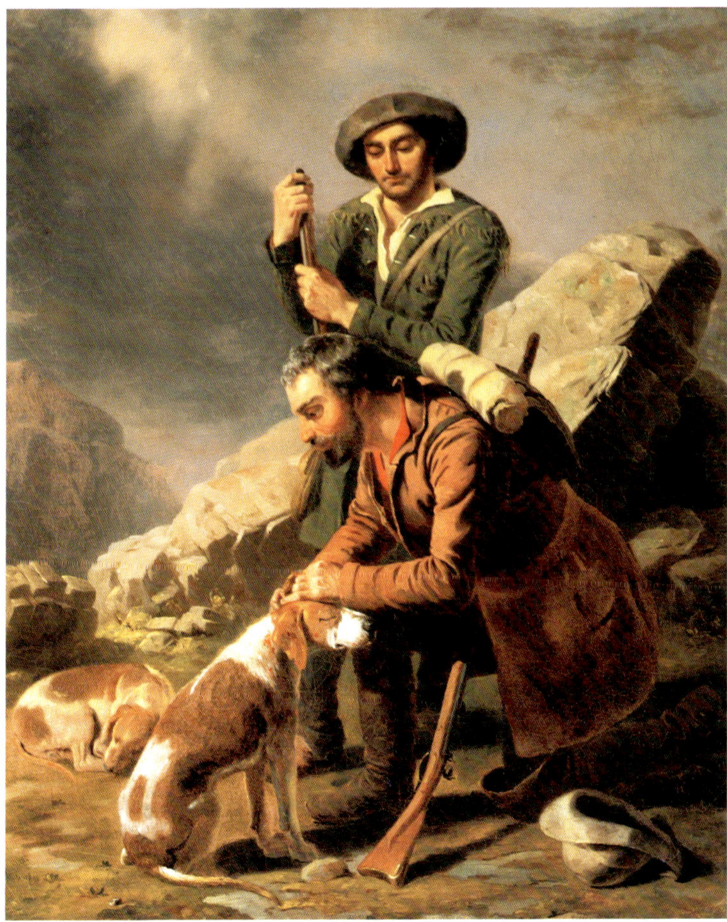

51
The Trapper's Last Shot

1850

Oil on canvas

18 x 24 inches (45.7 x 61 cm)

Signed and dated, lower right: W. Ranney /1850; and on the back: W. Ranney 1850

Canvas stamp: 18–24/ S. N. Dodge's/Supply Store/189 Chatham cor/of Oliver St./N. York

Private collection

Grubar no. 41

Engraving: T. Dwight Booth, *The Trapper's Last Shot*, steel engraving, image 17 3/4 x 23 3/4 inches (45.1 x 60.3 cm), Inscribed "Engraved by T. D. Booth, Cinnt. printed by R. Neale"; and "From the Original Painting Distributed by the Western Art Union 1850"; inscribed in plate, on back of saddle "W. Ranney—1850" and initialed on blanket roll "R." This plate was later reissued by J. M. Emerson and Company, New York.

Provenance: Western Art-Union, Cincinnati, 1850; distributed by lottery to Mrs. C[atherine] E[llicott] Lindley, Indianapolis, 1851; descended to Nelson O. Lindley, Bound Brook, New Jersey, to 1981 (sale 4583M, Sotheby Parke Bernet, New York, April 23, 1981, lot. no. 89); (Vose Galleries of Boston, by 1985 to c. 1987); (W. Graham Arader III, Philadelphia, by 1991); Richard Fox, Chesterbrook, Pennsylvania, 1991–1998.

Exhibited: Western Art-Union, Cincinnati, no. 68, as *The Trapper's Last Shot*. Fort Worth, 1987, lent by Vose Galleries of Boston.

References: Am Art-Union *Bulletin*, April 1850, p. 29, discusses Cincinnati painting and Booth print. *Transactions of the Western Art-Union for the Year 1850*, pp. 15, 20, 71, provides provenance; *Cincinnati Enquirer*, January 22, 1851, documents date of print distribution. The artist Frank Blackwell Mayer, in his diary for May 1851 mentions it as "a good hunting scene" in the Cincinnati exhibition (quoted in Bertha L. Heilbron, ed., *With Pen and Pencil on the Frontier of 1851: The Diary and Sketches of Frank Blackwell Mayer* [St. Paul, 1932]), p. 45. Francis S. Grubar, "Ranney's 'The Trapper's Last Shot,'" in *American Art Journal* 2 (Spring 1970), pp. 92–100, discusses rediscovery of painting. Bernard Reilly, "The Prints of Life in the West, 1840–60," in Amon Carter 1987, pp. 188–190, discusses prints.

The Trapper's Last Shot is one of Ranney's best-known and most popular images. The dramatic portrayal of a western trapper, a romanticized symbol of independence and courage, had particular appeal to contemporary audiences.

In 1962, Grubar recorded *The Trapper's Last Shot* as " location unknown." He knew it was the first version of the subject that Ranney painted early in 1850 and sold to the Western Art-Union in Cincinnati, which then distributed the first engravings of the painting. As Grubar relates in his 1970 article in the *American Art Journal*, he had searched for the lost painting, and, while he found many examples of the scene, all were inferior copies. He then describes how this work came to his attention. The daughter of a descendant of the original owner stumbled upon a copy of Grubar's 1962 book, recognized *The Trapper's Last Shot* as a painting in her family's collection, and mentioned it to her father. He contacted Grubar who, immediately recognizing Ranney's hand, declared that he "was certain the 'lost' Western Art-Union work had indeed been located." Typically, Ranney signed and dated only his first version of the subject.

The Western Art-Union commissioned T. Dwight Booth (active 1830–1857) to execute a steel line engraving in virtually the same size as the canvas and distributed it to its membership of 1850 (fig. 51.1). The same print was later reissued by New York publisher J. M. Emerson and Company without crediting Ranney. A slightly smaller but related lithograph was published by Currier and Ives sometime after 1857. Unlike the original Cincinnati engraving, its only inscription is the "R" on the blanket roll. With so many prints available and because of the popularity of the image, it is not surprising that many copies by unknown painters continue to come to light.

A second larger version of this subject, entitled *The Last Shot* (see cat. no. 52), was purchased later in 1850 by the American Art-Union. A third version, also called *The Last Shot*, was sold at the Ranney Fund sale (lot 178) to someone by the name of Brookings for fifty dollars. Because of this relatively high price, it seems likely that this third version, if it still exists, is a fairly large and finished work. LB

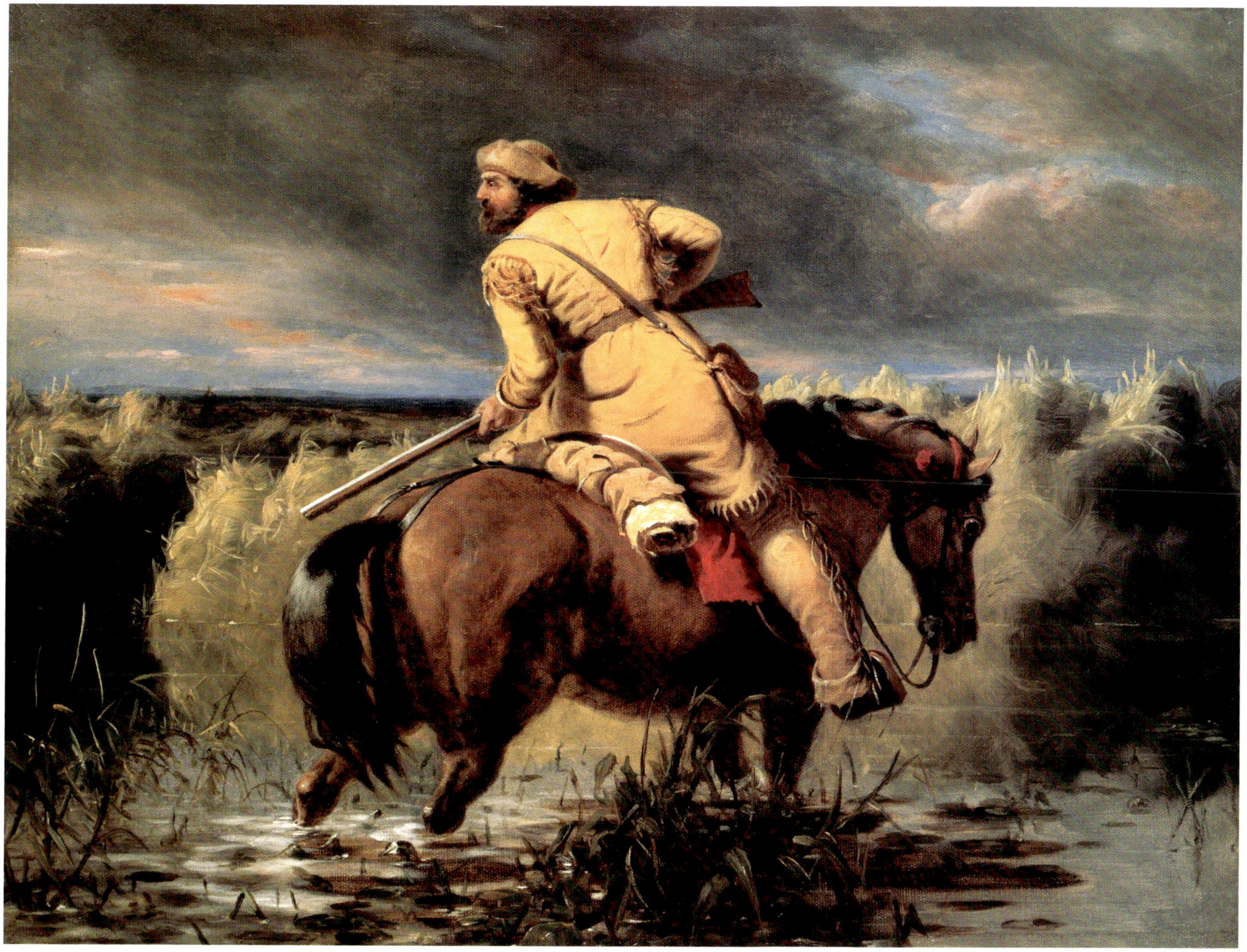

NO. 51

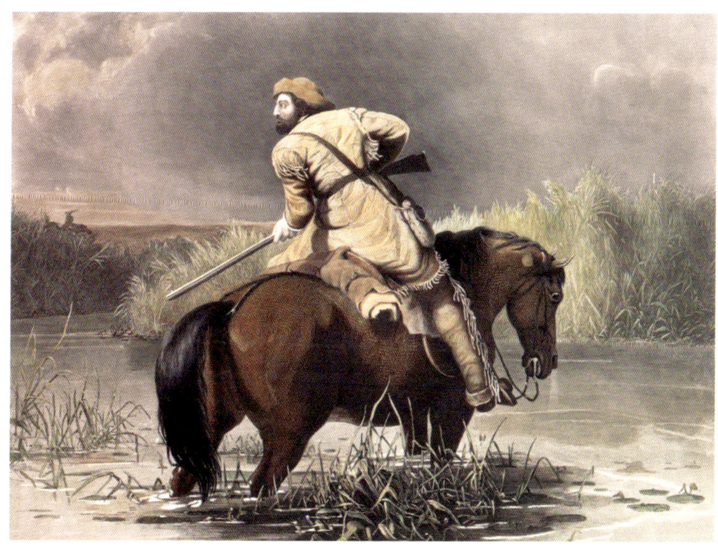

Fig 51.1
The Trapper's Last Shot, engraved by T. Dwight Booth. Steel engraving,
hand-colored. Private collection.

52 *
The Last Shot

c. 1850

Oil on canvas

28 1/2 x 36 inches
(72.4 x 91.4 cm)

Signed on back of saddle: W Ranney

Label (torn) of the Am Art-Union on back

Grubar no. 42

Private collection

Provenance: Am Art-Union, 1850, as The Last Shot; distributed by lottery to Anna E. Lambert, New York, 1850; (sale, *A Large Collection of Superb Oil Paintings*, Henry H. Leeds and Co. Galleries, New York, May 5, 1857, lot 151, may be this work); Charles L. Frost, to 1870 (sale, Leavitt, Strebeight and Co., New York, March 20,1870, as The Trapper's Last Shot, sold for $270) (Harry Shaw Newman Gallery, New York, by 1947); (M. Knoedler and Co., New York, stock no. A-5901, c. 1950–1956); (Edward Eberstadt and Sons, New York, c. 1956); C. R. Smith, New York, by 1962.

Exhibited: Am Art-Union, 1850, no. 91, as The Last Shot.

References: Register, Works of Art, reel 2, Am Art-Union Papers, no. 1876, July 21, 1850, paid $100 (unframed). Am Art-Union, *Bulletin*, April, mentions Ranney working on painting, and November and December, 1850, no. 91. *New York Herald*, September 8, 1850, p. 2, reviews it. *New-York Daily Tribune*, December 16, 1850, "American Art-Union Catalogue," p. 8, no. 91, and December 21, 1850, p. 4, no. 91 (quoted in entry), says distributed to Anna E. Lambert. *New York Evening Post*, March 21, 1870, p. 2, mentions auction and provides provenance. *Art Digest* 21 (September 15, 1947), p. 2, advertised by Harry Shaw Newman Gallery, New York. *Panorama* 3 (February 1948), no. 8. Cowdrey 1953, 2, p. 295.

In 1850 Ranney embarked on a new theme in his art, the pictorial record of the fabled mountain men of the western plains and Rockies. Much had been written about these historical figures; and other artists, especially Charles Deas, had made a success of their depiction. Now it was Ranney's turn. Two of the six paintings that he exhibited at the American Art-Union that year, this painting and *Halt on the Prairie* (cat. no. 54), were devoted to the subject of the fur trappers in the West. Another oil, *The Retreat* (cat. no. 60), which was sold privately, added yet another work to comprise a suite of images on the theme. Of these,*The Last Shot* might be considered the centerpiece. From 1870 until now, the painting has been known as *The Trapper's Last Shot*, now known to be the original title of the earlier version (cat. no. 51).

Although the mountain man's era had concluded some years earlier, contemporary writers were busy developing a romantic literary construct for the public appreciation of these characters. Especially successful were three men who boasted of firsthand experiences in the West and published their own accounts, George F. Ruxton, Francis Parkman, and Lewis H. Garrard. Their books featured the trappers as wilderness heroes, ambitious opportunists, and daring adventurers. On the last point, Parkman wrote, "I defy the annals of chivalry to furnish the record of a life more wild and perilous than that of the Rocky Mountain trapper."[1] Yet the public did not necessarily have to read what curious and colorful figures those mountain men were. They did not have to rely solely on words from the likes of Ruxton that "the trappers of the Rocky Mountains . . . , their lives being spent in the remote wilderness . . . with no other companion than Nature herself . . . assume a most singular cast of simplicity and ferocity."[2] Some of the old trappers could actually be seen and heard in person. The celebrated Joseph L. Meek (1810–1875), for example, was cleaned up and flamboyantly paraded through eastern cities in 1848 as a spokesman for President James K. Polk, to whom he was related by marriage. Meek, who by that date resided in Oregon, regaled audiences with tales of his extraordinary early feats of daring, while promoting the idea of territorial status for Oregon.[3] Here was the living ideal of the wilderness demigod for enthusiasts like Ranney to meet or, at least, see on stage. And even though there exists no direct proof that the two ever crossed paths, there is an uncanny resemblance between Meek's portrait (fig. 52.1) and the central figure in Ranney's painting *The Last Shot*.

The possible connection between this painting and Joseph Meek originated in the first full-length biography of the mountain man, Mrs. Frances Fuller Victor's *River of the West* that was published in 1870.[4] Although attributing authorship to the wrong artist, John Mix Stanley, the writer used Ranney's painting to illustrate an adventure that befell Meek in 1837 on the headwaters of the Madison River in the remote Yellowstone region. Meek was, according to the tale, out to avenge a comrade named Markhead who had fallen at the hands of the Blackfeet. Several skirmishes resulted, including a side-by-side running battle with an Indian

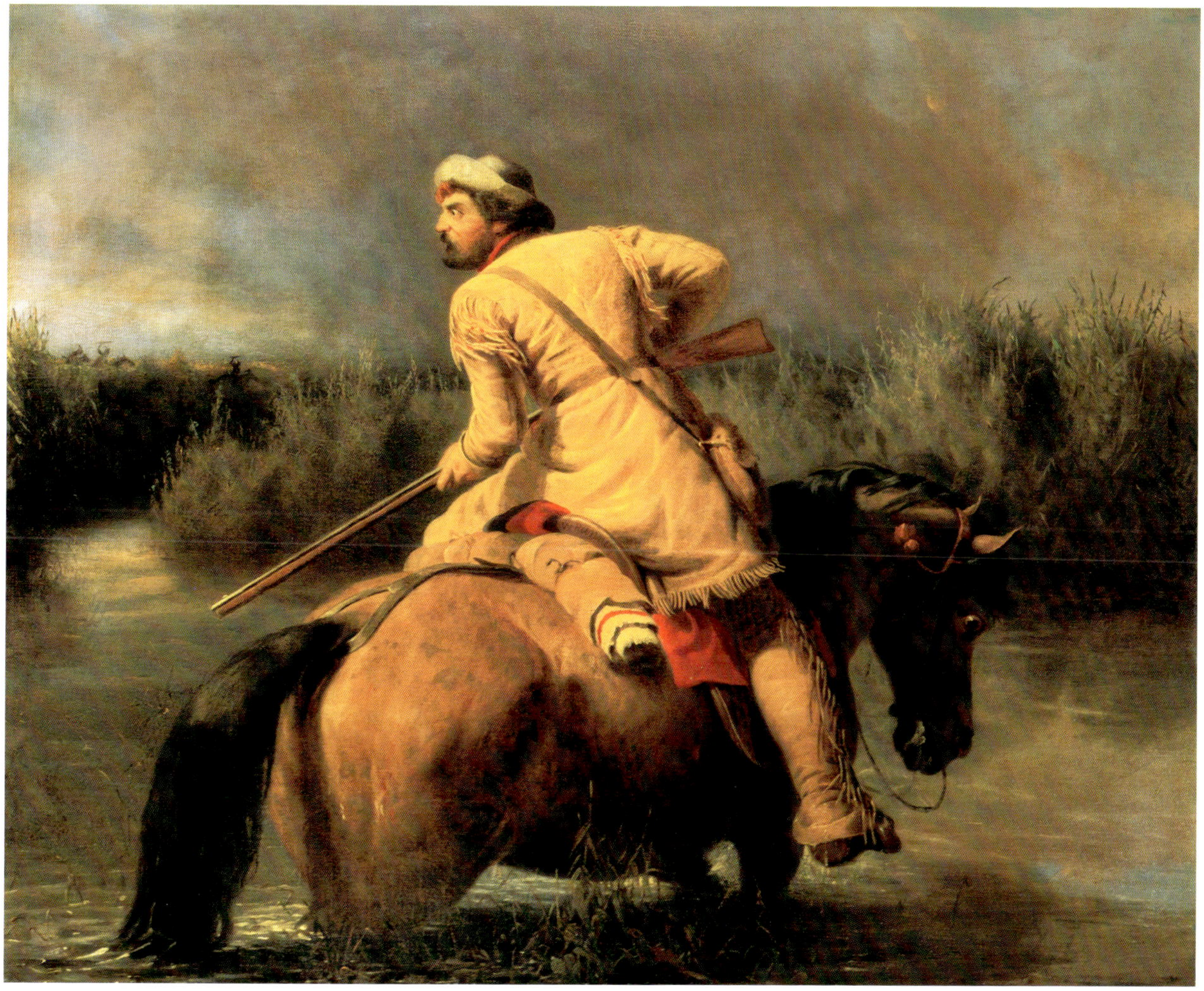

Fig 52.1
Label of the American Art-Union

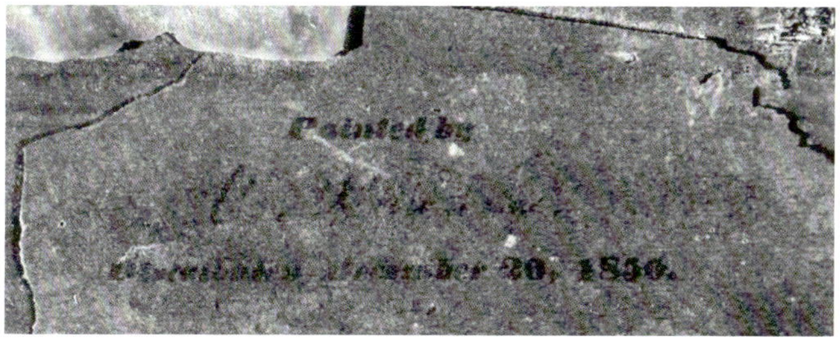

foe. One of the final scenes in that contest, according to Victor, became "the picture which is well known as 'The Trapper's Last Shot,' [that] represents him as he turns upon his horse, a fine and spirited animal, to discharge his last shot at an Indian pursuing."[5] Victor had accumulated hours of personal interviews with Meek in order to compile her biography, so it may be safe to assume that the two of them at least viewed the Ranney image as a credible depiction of that perilous episode.

Whether intended to portray Meek or some anonymous trapper, the Ranney painting addressed dual components in frontier life—risk and stratagem. The tension suggested in the pose, gesture, and expressions of horse and man leads the viewer to identify with the sense of jeopardy inherent in the narrative that is about

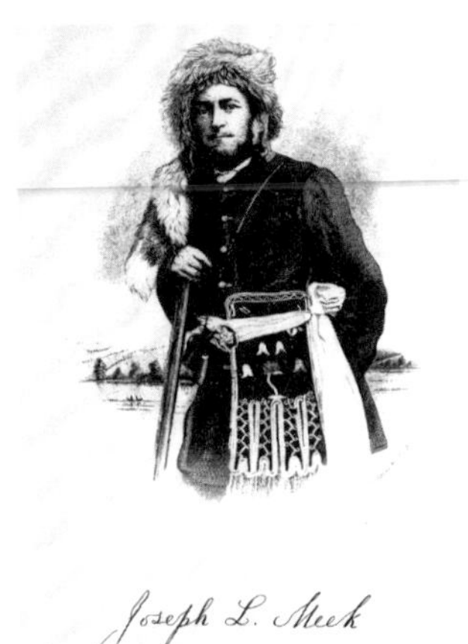

Fig 52.1
Joseph L. Meek (1810–1875).
From Frances Fuller Victor, *The River of the West* (Hartford, 1870). Courtesy of the Buffalo Bill Historical Center, Cody, Wyoming.

to unfold. Moreover, the fact that the horse is mired in water above its hocks implies that escape will be impeded. The trapper is trapped. He who lives in the water pursuing beaver in every possible stream is now a captive of his very resource.

While other paintings in this suite of works allude to alternatives for survival—preparedness in *Halt on the Prairie* and flight in *The Retreat*—the theme and title of *The Last Shot* seems to connote finality; yet there is also a hint at a promise of survival. Through stealth and valor, the trapper may actually escape his fix. In fact, as the western traveler and chronicler Josiah Gregg observed, trappers and hunters caught out alone on the prairies and confronted by hostile Indians could at times persevere by keeping their cool and holding their last shot. The Indians, he noted, are

> loth to charge upon even a single armed man, unless they can take him at a decided disadvantage. Therefore, it is at all times imprudent to fire at the first approach of Indians; for, seeing their guns empty, the savages would charge upon them; while very small bands of hunters have been known to keep large numbers of the enemy at bay, by presenting their rifles, but reserving their fire, till assistance was at hand.[6]

Provided with this explanation of tactical savy, Ranney's painting fits the pattern of a statement of survival. The painting may also provide a metaphor for larger national questions of survival. The United States in 1850 was grappling, and like the trapper, quite desperately so, with the matter of how to politically accommodate the newly acquired western lands without causing the convulsive destruction of the Union. The Compromise of 1850 was a shaky and ephemeral attempt to settle deeply rooted sectional differences. As any number of historians has concluded, it was at best "an artful evasion."[7] The *New-York Daily Tribune*, in an article on the American Art-Union published in December 1850 at the time *The Last Shot* was exhibited, reminded its readership that not only had the sponsoring institution "preferred American subjects" by American artists, but also that it "sought to encourage compositions of national and historical interest." The settlement of the delicate and contentious question about how to deal with slavery in the new western territories commanded nearly everyone's attention, including that of Ranney, who was devoting increasingly more of his creative attention to western subjects. Earlier that fall, on the same day that the *New York Herald* first announced his submission of *The Last Shot* to the 1850 exhibition, they also excitedly reported on the long sought after compromise, with the headline "Settlement of the Territorial Question in Congress." A compromise had been effected. A tactical maneuver, no more certain in outcome than that possibly employed by Ranney's mountain man, had been ventured. And a disastrous confrontation had temporarily been avoided. As the *Herald's* critic said of the painting, "The intense eagerness of the horseman is admirably conveyed." So, one might infer, was the intense eagerness of the nation.

The theme of a single horseman confronted with what Parkman called the "wild and perilous" odds in the Far West caught on quickly among the ranks of Ranney's fellow artists including John Mix Stanley, Alfred Jacob Miller, and Arthur Fitzwilliam Tait. PHH

1. Francis Parkman, *The Oregon Trail* (1849; Boston: Ginn and Company, 1910), p. 125.

2. Ruxton, as quoted in LeRoy R. Hafen, *Ruxton of the Rockies* (Norman: University of Oklahoma Press, 1950), p. 227.

3. Frances Fuller Victor, *The River of the West* (Hartford: R.W. Bliss and Co., 1870), p. 460.

4. Ibid., pp. 225–231.

5. Ibid., pp. 229–230.

6. Josiah Gregg, *Commerce of the Prairies* (New York: Henry G. Langlay, 1844).

7. Mary Beth Norton et al., *A People and a Nation* (Boston: Houghton Mifflin Company, 1998), p. 382.

53
The Lazy Fisherman

1850

Oil on canvas

27 x 34 inches (68.6 x 86.4 cm), sight

Signed and dated, lower left, on tree stump: W. Ranney/1850

Private collection

Grubar no. 43

PROVENANCE: Am Art-Union, 1850; distributed by lottery to Cyrus Cole, Springfield, Massachusetts, 1850; his son, Daniel Pomery Cole (d. c. 1946), Springfield; his daughter, Lucy Cole (d. 1984), Springfield.

EXHIBITED: Am Art-Union, 1850, no. 320.

REFERENCES: Register, Works of Art: 1848–1851, reel 2, no. 2352, September 12, 1850, lists purchase price of $100, unframed (asking price $150); Letters from Artists, reel 6, from John P. Ridner, New York, September 12, 1850, to the Committee of Management, offers *Lazy Fisherman* unframed by W. Ranney for $150; Purchasing Committee Minutes, reel 3, Examining Committee Minutes, September 17, 1850, recommends paintings be "purchased at prices fixed by artists," or $100, unframed, Am Art-Union Papers. Am Art-Union *Bulletin* (August 1850), p. 81 mentions it; and (December 31, 1850), p. 174, describes it. *New York Tribune*, December 16, 1850, mentions distribution date of December 20 and lists it. *New York Herald*, December 17, 1850, p. 3, lists it; and December 21, 1850, p. 5, provides owner's name. Cowdrey 1953, 2, p. 295, no. 320, describes it and provides provenance.

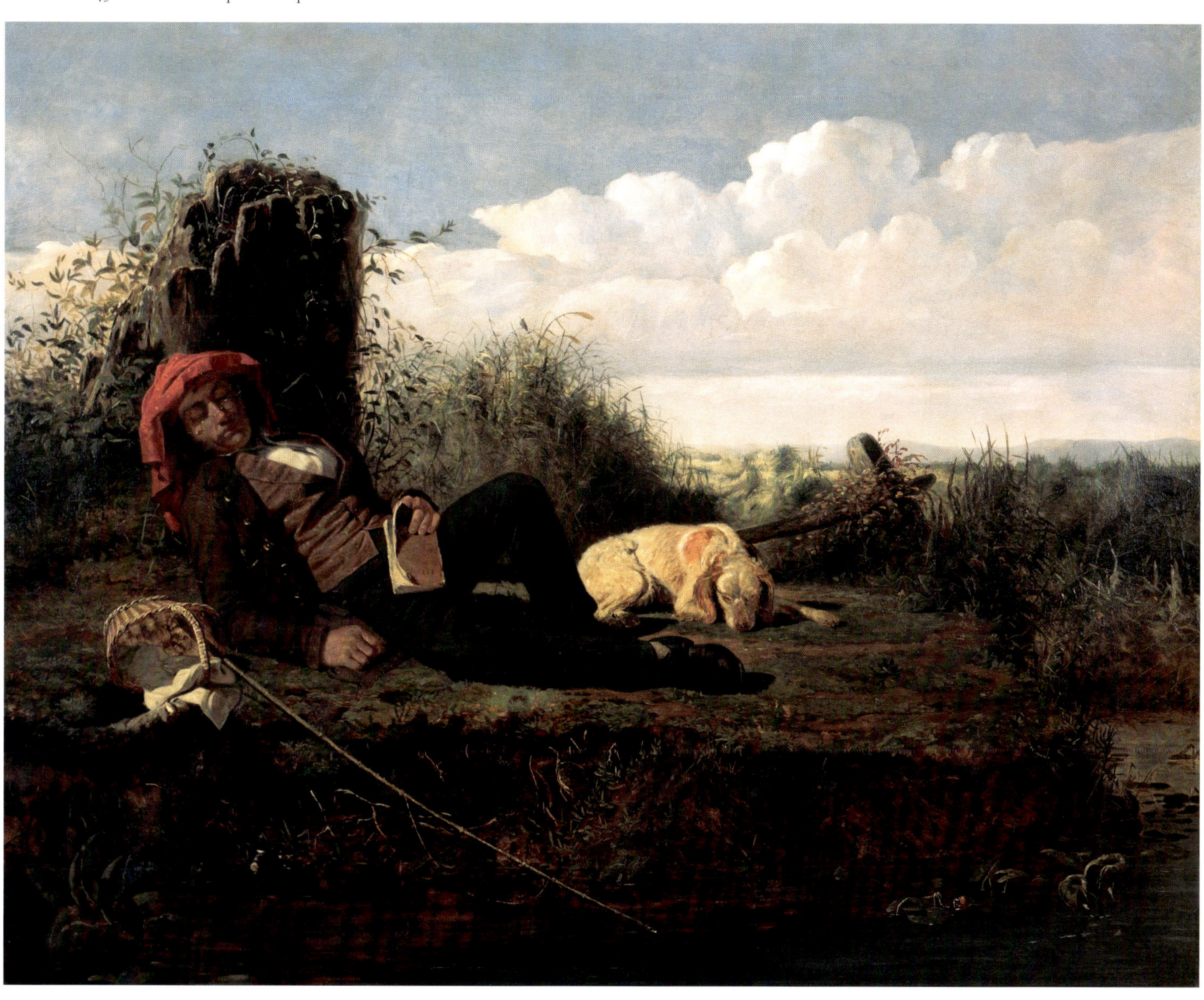

NO. 53

Though only recently rediscovered, the basic image of *The Lazy Fisherman* was known from descriptions that appeared in the Art-Union's *Bulletins* of 1850. In the August issue Ranney's new painting was mentioned as "a close study of nature." Later, in the December issue, it was more specifically described as "'an elderly gentleman' dosing [*sic*] beside a 'murmuring stream,' with a book in his hand, and a rod lying on the ground. Near him is his dog, also taking a nap."

Ranney set this scene along a stream, amidst a flat landscape similar to the distinctive New Jersey marshlands so familiar from his other sporting pictures of this period. Just as the pervasive brown tonality, the puffy cumulus clouds, low water level of the stream, and steep bank indicate the lazy days of late summer or early fall, the red cloth protecting the fisherman's head suggests the intensity of the afternoon sun. Recalling the protagonist in *First Fish of the Season* (cat. no. 44), the fisherman has donned spectacles. Characteristically, Ranney scatters about this idyllic scene a myriad of other homey details to enhance its narrative appeal. That it is past midday is confirmed by the overturned straw picnic basket—its white cloth in disarray revealing only a few leftover scraps from the angler's repast. His sleeping dog is a setter of a type often seen in Ranney's sporting pictures (cat. no. 55). The disengaged fishing rod, the book partially held open on the angler's lap, and the lack of any visible catch, all reinforce the notion that this man has used fishing as a pretext to get away from home or work and leisurely enjoy the countryside rather than land a fish.

The Lazy Fisherman can also be interpreted as a humorous genre piece in which the fisherman not only lacks commitment and perseverance, but also seems ignorant of the widely accepted sporting practices of the day. Unlike a knowledgeable sportsman, he appears to be fishing off season (spring or fall is preferred, when the water is cool and high), at the wrong time of day (early morning is preferred, when the fish are more likely to be feeding), and has clearly not chosen an ideal spot with abundant fish.   L B

54
Halt on the Prairie

1850

Oil on canvas

37 3/8 x 54 5/16 inches (95.9 x 139.1 cm)

Signed and dated, lower center: W. Ranney/50

Jack S. Blanton Museum of Art, University of Texas, Austin. Gift of C. R. Smith, 1985

Grubar no. 44

PROVENANCE: Am Art-Union, 1850, distributed by lottery to Mrs. E. D. Knower, New York, 1850; Randall Collection, Randall's Island, New York; (James Graham and Sons, New York, by 1954); C. R. Smith, New York, by 1962–1985.

EXHIBITED: Am Art-Union, 1850, no. 121.

REFERENCES: William Ranney to the Committee of Management of the American Art-Union, New York, March 7, 1850, Letters from Artists, October 1, 1849–June 28, 1850, reel 5, Am Art-Union Papers, has sent painting called The Halt on the Prairie, and offers it for $300; Purchasing Committee Minutes, reel 3, March 11, 1850, no. 1904, offers $200 (unframed); and Management Committee Minutes, reel 1, vol. 3, p. 67, April 4, 1850, no. 1904, purchases painting for $200. Am Art-Union *Bulletin*, April, p. 15 and December, 1850, p. 169. *Literary World* (April 6, 1850), p. 353, says he has finished this work. *New York Tribune*, November 27, 1850, p. 8 (quoted in entry). *New York Herald*, December 21,1850, p. 5, no. 121 distributed to Mrs. E. D. Noah [Knower?]. Cowdrey 1953, 2, p. 295, provides description and provenance. Glanz 1982, p. 50. Ayres 1987, pp. 95–96, illus. and discusses. Natasha Bartalini, in *Collecting the West: The C. R. Smith Collection of Western American Art* , ed. Richard H. Saunders (Austin: University of Austin Press for the Archer M. Huntington Art Gallery [1988]), pp. 160–161, discusses it. Kathleen Rice, "Representational Images: William Ranney's *Halt on the Prairie*," (unpublished essay, University of Texas, Austin, 1999).

On March 7, 1850, Ranney wrote to the Committee of Management of the American Art-Union offering them a remarkable work for their consideration. In this letter he wrote, "I send herewith a painting called 'The Halt on the Prairie,' which I desire to offer to you for sale. My price for the same is $300." A bargain was struck and the painting was offered in the Art-Union's sale that year. It was exhibited as entry number 121 and described as follows: "Two trappers, each with two horses: one mounted; the other is standing, and engaged in adjusting his saddle-girth. The scene is the broad prairie, and the time is afternoon."

Halt on the Prairie was one of five Ranney paintings presented that year at the American Art-Union, and one of two treating the subject of the western trapper. The other such painting, *The Last Shot* (cat. no. 52), received more critical acclaim than this one but was not as ambitious a work, nor as subtle. These two were, according to the Art-Union *Bulletin* of April 1850, "characteristic scenes" for Ranney. Despite the assessment by the critic for the *New York Tribune* that "Ranney's pictures are all weak in color," they succeeded in narrative strength, vigor of expression, and were "favorites of the public." "'Halt on the Prairie,' the critic noted, "is especially admired, not without reason."

One reason for the popular success of the painting may have been its sense of reserved idealism. Though filled with romantic elements like exotic location, sublime expanses, and remote isolation, there is a quiet dignity about the scene that shows an appreciation for the quotidian nature of work, regardless of where it is performed. The unmounted trapper is stripping leather with his knife, perhaps to alter the cinch. Unlike the rather derivative composition by Arthur F. Tait, *Trappers at Fault* (fig. 54.1) of 1852, Ranney's painting is void of drama. The mounted trapper looks on his comrade's labors with patience, while in Tait's picture the onlooker holds his rifle at the ready, his posture suggesting imminent danger or at least an alertness to impending action. For Ranney, drama is subverted by the mundane. What there is of it seems to be taking place on the left rump of the black horse where playful, boredom-induced nibbling has resulted in some ears-back annoyance that portends a flinch at best and a kick or two at worst. Whatever is occurring in the right background, a prairie fire or perhaps a dust storm, is nonthreatening, for the trappers pay no heed to it.

For American audiences, Ranney's trappers in *Halt on the Prairie* were common men of noble but protean habit. As one modern art historian, Dawn Glanz, has concluded, the spirit of such paintings "is constant with" a "democratic outlook." Ranney's "characters were perceived as fundamentally from the same stock as the American tradesman, artisans, and professionals who comprised his audience at mid-century." Another scholar, Kathleen Rice, has suggested that Ranney's painting broadly hints at growing sectional tensions

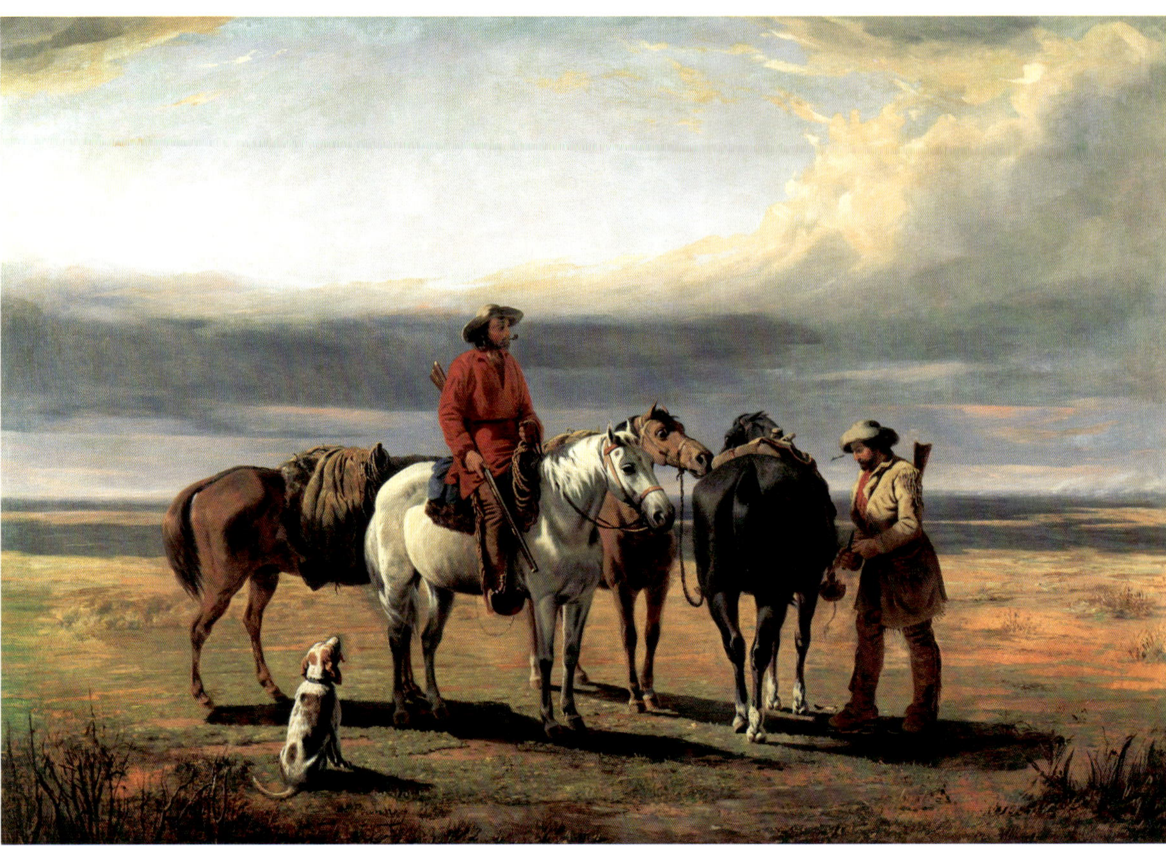

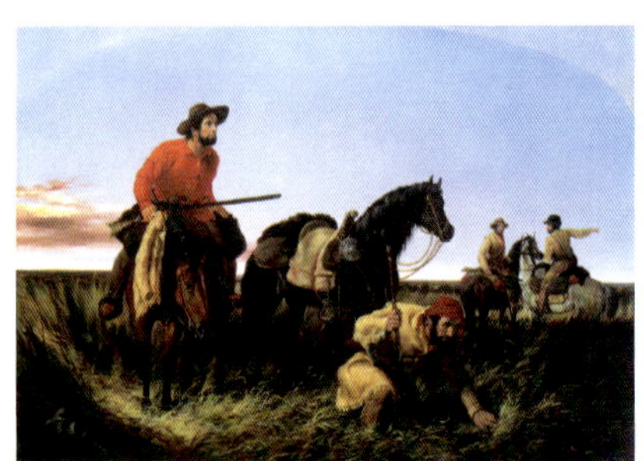

Fig 54.1
Trappers at Fault by
Arthur Fitzwilliam Tait
(1819–1905). Oil on
canvas. Anschutz
Collection, Denver.

within the national body politic. Others contend that such images helped foster a national passion for entrepreneurial zeal, "having an immediate appeal for the merchants and railroad developers of the 1850s."[1] In most any interpretation, this work by Ranney can be construed as a national picture, an unabashed tribute to the then-celebrated pioneer spirit.

Appealing also to American viewers was the painting's uncompromised truth to nature. Ranney clearly intended by this depiction of the starkly barren prairie to avoid presenting the West as overly lush. Tait and other artists, including Frances Flora Palmer, both of whom worked for Currier and Ives, consistently chose to depict the prairie as a tall grass region, which was described by Francis Parkman in 1849, the year before Ranney's painting, as an "interesting country," somewhere at the edge of the frontier before the real prairie began. Parkman noted that this narrow but "fertile belt" answered "tolerably well" to the public's "preconceived ideas of the prairie: for this it is from which picturesque tourists, painters, poets and novelists . . . have derived their conceptions of the whole region."[2] Ranney took heed of such descriptions as limited and fictive. His knowledge of the Texas prairies led him to portray the relatively barren, though far more ubiquitous short grass prairie. In *Halt on the Prairie* he pairs the sweep of a featureless plain with the expansive western sky to accentuate the feelings of remove and isolation. PHH

1. Patricia Hills, "Picturing Progress in the Era of Westward Expansion," in William H. Truettner et al., *The West as America: Reinterpreting Images of the Frontier, 1820–1920* (Washington, D.C. : Smithsonian Institution Press, 1991), p. 112.
2. Francis Parkman, *The Oregon Trail* (1849; Boston: Ginn and Company, 1910), p. 28.

55
On the Wing

1850

Oil on canvas

30 1/2 x 45 inches
(77.5 x 114.3 cm)

Signed and dated,
lower corner: W
Ranney/1850

Private collection

Grubar no. 45

ENGRAVING: Charles Burt (1823–1892), steel engraving, image 5 x 7 3/8 inches (12.7 x 18.7 cm). Inscribed, lower left; painted by Ranney, and lower right, etched by Burt. Commissioned by the Am Art-Union and published in its *Bulletin* (October 1850), facing page 113.

PROVENANCE: Am Art-Union, 1850; distributed by lottery to John Broadhead, Philadelphia, 1850; F[erdinand] J. Dreer (1812–1902), Philadelphia, by c. 1858; his granddaughter, Abigail P. Dreer Read, Philadelphia (by c. 1918–c. 1948); (Newhouse Galleries, New York, by c. 1948 to 1960); Kimbell Art Foundation, Fort Worth, Texas, 1960–1975 (sale, Sotheby Parke Bernet, New York, April 17, 1975, lot 18).

EXHIBITED: NAD, 1850, cat. no. 111, as for sale. Am Art-Union, 1850, no. 224. Philadelphia, 1864, *Great Central Fair*, no. 510, as *Duck Shooters*, lent by F. J. Dreer; Chadds Ford 1991, no. 110.

REFERENCES: *Albion* 9 (April 27, 1850), p. 201, describes and reviews it (quoted in entry). *Literary World* 6 (May 4, 1850), p. 448, reviews it (quoted in entry). Am Art-Union *Bulletin* (May 1850), p. 21, provides detailed description. *New-York Daily Tribune*, June 22, 1850, p. 1, reviews it. Management Committee Minutes 1839–1855, reel 1, vol. 3, June 10, 1850, recommends purchasing On the Wing for $200, and notes work examined at the NAD; Executive Committee Minutes, 1846–1854, reel 2, July 25, 1850, resolves that On The Wing be etched for the *Bulletin* by Mr. Burt; August 8, 1850, bill for $200 for painting approved for payment; August 15, 1850, paid Burt $60 for etching; Am Art-Union Papers. Am Art-Union *Bulletin* (June, September, October, and December 1850), no. 224. *New York Herald*, September 8, 1850, p. 2, reviews it. *New York Tribune*, December 16, 1850, p. 8. *New York Herald*, December 17, 1850, p. 3, lists it. *New York Tribune*, December 21, 1850, p. 5, no. 224, provides provenance. *Ornaments of Memory* . . . (New York: D. Appleton and Company, 1855), illustrates Burt's engraving and provides commentary, facing p. 41. Cowdrey 1943, 2, p. 88, no. 111. Frank Read (husband of Abigail P. Dreer Read) to Bertram Newhouse, copy, January 11, 1948, Ranney archives, provides provenance. Cowdrey 1953, 2, p. 295, no. 224, provides description and provenance.

On the Wing is perhaps Ranney's most successful and well-known sporting picture. The title is an idiom meaning in flight or flying. According to the sense of fair play embodied in the sportsman's code so widely promulgated during this period, shooting birds in flight tested the skill of the shooter while giving the prey a fair opportunity to escape.

Brilliantly colored, the scene is set against an azure sky offset by feathery greenish yellow reeds that encircle the highlighted figures. Within a tightly organized triangular composition, Ranney creates the tension involved in duck hunting by focusing all the psychic and pictorial energy toward the sky in the upper right corner of the canvas. Although the quarry is invisible to the viewer, the hunter, his gun at the ready, spots them. We can see in the foreground that he has already shot four ducks. The man is dressed in a drab brown jacket, pants, and tall boots, which contrast with his bright crimson shirt and orange bandanna—the headgear also worn by the figures in Ranney's *Lasso* and *Hunting Wild Horses* of 1846 (cat. nos. 18 and 19). Crouching behind the hunter in rapt attention is a young boy—perhaps a son being tutored by his father— who grasps the powder horn, seemingly in anxious anticipation of reloading the hunter's percussion shotgun. Equally attentive is the setter, with its characteristic coat of white highlighted with reddish brown spots, a type of large spaniel which, because of the frequency that it appears in his works, suggests it may have been one of Ranney's own dogs. The intelligence, affability, courage, stamina, and beauty of form of the breed particularly endeared these dogs to contemporary sporting writers, who considered them the "first in the list of sporting dogs."[1] The hunter's skill is revealed by the dead common goldeneyes and red neck hens at his feet, their white plumage stained by blood. Goldeneyes winter in salt bays from the Great Lakes to the Gulf of Mexico, a habitat characteristic of the Jersey marshes near Ranney's home. At the right, the back of a skiff and a bit of water serve to further define the marshland environment.

On the Wing was first exhibited at the annual exhibition of the National Academy of Design in 1850. The response of the reviewers was virtually unanimous in its praise. "It is capital in style. Sportsman and dog are both in the best spirits," said the *Literary World*. The painting is a "vigorous production which at once arrests

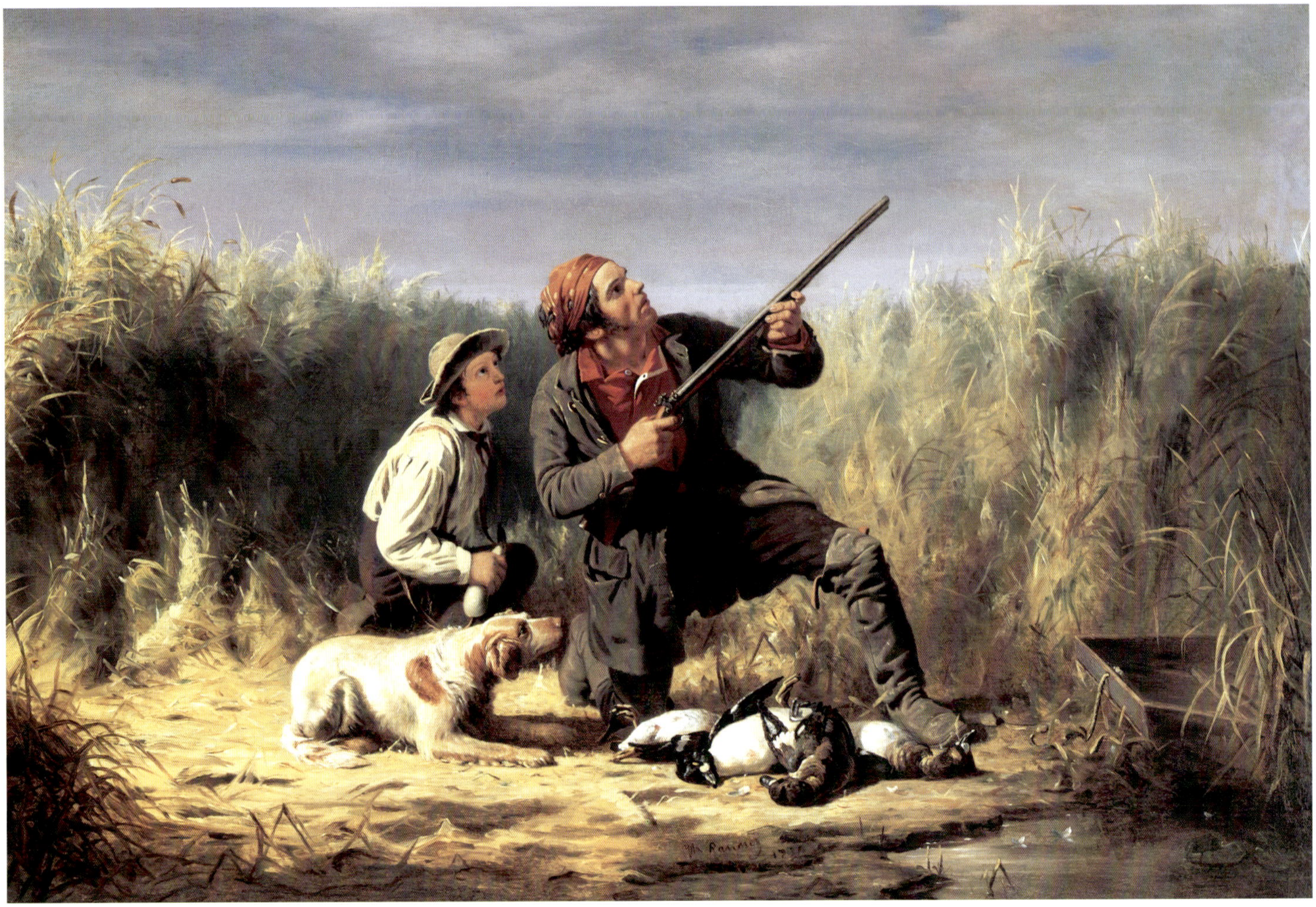

NO. 55

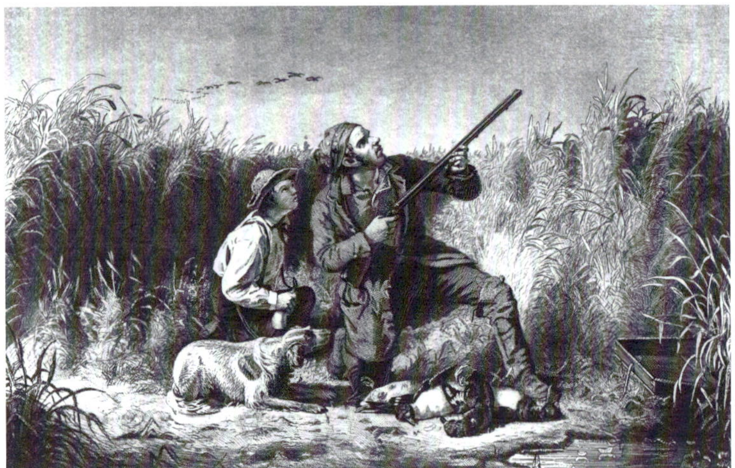

Fig 55.1
On the Wing, engraved by Charles Burt. Library Company of Philadelphia.

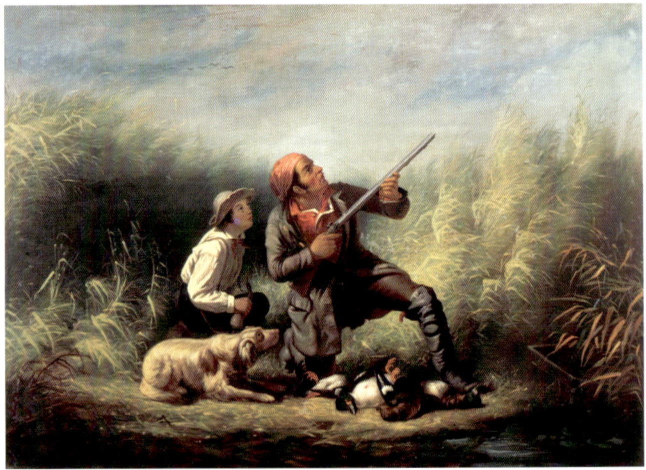

Fig 55.2
On the Wing, attributed to William Ranney, c. 1850. Oil on canvas, 32 x 45 inches. Butler Institute of American Art, Youngstown, Ohio.

the attention," noted another reviewer cited in the Art-Union's May *Bulletin*. The most fulsome piece appeared in the *Albion:*

> One of the very best pictures in the whole collection. It is of moderate size oblong, and rounded at the upper corners. It represents a duck-hunter, with his boy, and his dog, grouped amidst the reeds of a river side. The man is kneeling, gun in hand, prepared to take aim at birds "on the wing." . . . The drawing is good, and the colouring remarkable for its truth and beauty. The reeds and accessories show a masterly hand. . . . we venture to note a fault that the painter might easily amend, before it goes out of his reach. The ear and the neck of the principal figure are defective.

The critic's comment about the "rounded corners" suggests that the picture may have been exhibited in a spandrel frame, a favorite choice of Ranney's at the time. Unlike some of his other works with this kind of frame, such as *Duck Shooter's Pony* (cat. no. 82) for instance, there is no evidence that Ranney painted the curved shape on the canvas itself. There is, however, a related drawing (cat. no. D24), with several variations in the central group, that does have a curved border at the top. Equally interesting is that at the end of the above review the critic suggested that Ranney consider correcting the poorly rendered ear and neck details. There is no evidence that he made any adjustments to the canvas in those areas.

In June 1850 the American Art-Union recommended purchasing *On the Wing* from the National Academy exhibition for two hundred dollars. In July they resolved to commission Charles Burt to engrave it for their membership, and his engraving appeared in the October 1850 issue of the *Bulletin* (see fig. 55.1). In that print, Burt added a seemingly decorative filler—the flock of ducks in the upper left sky—effectively diluting Ranney's original intention of suggesting an off-canvas narrative in the opposite direction. Moreover, perhaps indicative of Burt's lack of intimate knowledge of the specifics of ducks, his airborne birds in their relative size, form, and flight pattern do not appear to be the same species as the stocky goldeneyes Ranney pictured on the ground. Burt also seems to have attempted to address the ear and neck criticism. He completely deleted the ear of the young boy, for example, and created a very prominent, mollusk-shaped ear on the hunter.

One version attributed to Ranney includes all Burt's modifications (fig. 55.2). Because of the popularity of Ranney's image and the widely distributed print, copies of *On the Wing* still turn up in the marketplace.[2] Ironically, when the Kimbell Art Foundation examined this painting in 1972, there were birds in the upper left sky as in Burt's print. Technical analysis revealed, however, that they were later additions.[3]

There are at least three other unsigned copies of this subject (cat. nos. 56, 57, and 58). Grubar authenticated cat. nos. 56 and 57. All three have in common the addition of ducks in the upper left sky but do not include Burt's other alterations. A Philadelphia framer's label of around 1858 on one copy (cat. no. 56), suggests that that copy may have been painted by an unknown artist after Ranney's death. Because we did not have access to all three paintings for comparative purposes, it is still unclear which, if any of these copies, can be confidently attributed to Ranney. LB

1. Frank Forester [Henry William Herbert], *Complete Manual for Young Sportsmen* (1856; reprint [New York]: Westvaco Corporation, 1993), p. 53.

2. An unknown artist by the name of Wilson (perhaps Samuel), for example, with an address in Philadelphia, exhibited "On the Wing—After Ranney" (owned by Harrison Earl[e], at the Washington Art Association, Third Annual Exhibition, no. 157, 1859.

3. Treatment report of Perry C. Huston, January 1972, *On the Wing,* Kimbell Art Museum, registrar's files.

56
On the Wing

c.1850

Oil on canvas

31 1/8 x 43 5/8 inches (79.1 x 110.8 cm)

Jack S. Blanton Museum of Art, University of Texas, Austin, Texas. Gift of C. R. Smith, 1973.

Grubar no. 46

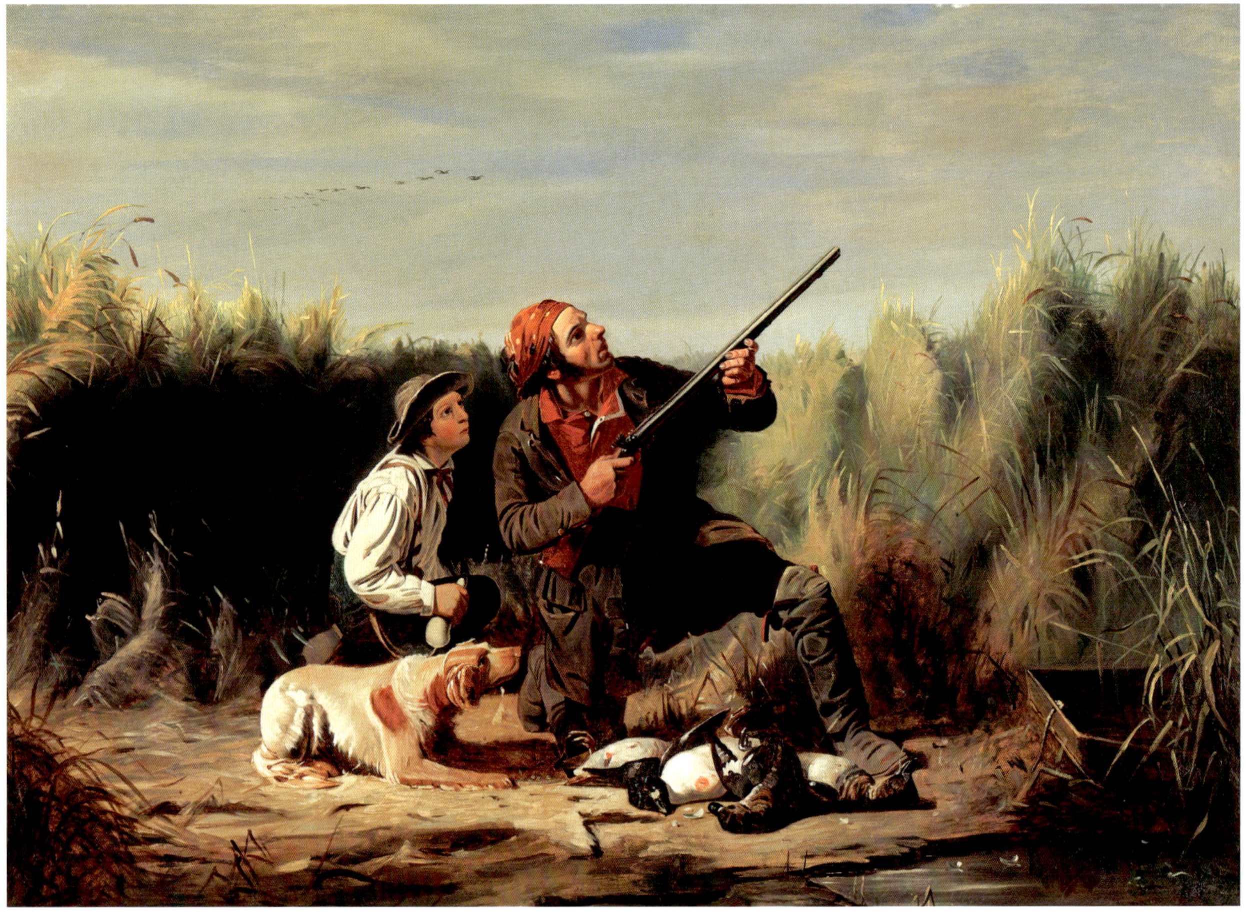

NO. 56

PROVENANCE: R. B. Honeyman, New York; (J. N. Bartfield, New York, by 1959 ~ c. 1965); C. R. Smith, to 1973.

REFERENCES: J. N. Bartfield, advertisement in *Antiques*, vol. 75 (June 1959), p. 530, as On the Wing—Wild Duck Shooting and provides provenance. Natasha Bartalini, in *Collecting the West: The C. R. Smith Collection of Western American Art*, ed. Richard H. Saunders (Austin: University of Austin Press for the Archer M. Huntington Art Gallery, [1988]), p. 162, discusses it and calls it Wild Duck Shooting—On the Wing.

While in the authors' opinion, this example of *On the Wing* lacks the subtlety and refinement of details associated with Ranney's work, Grubar felt that it is "an excellent painting, well within one's expectations of Ranney. The strongly modeled man is especially well done, and the treatment of the foliage and other accessories is consistent with Ranney's manner."[1]

1. Grubar and the museum record a framer's label on the stretcher: "Julius Scholz/No. 115 S. Eighth Street, Philadelphia, Pa. . . ." There was an artist supply store of this name and address in 1858. In 2006, a second painting of the same dimensions as the Blanton Museum's was discovered with an identical framer's label. That both works have this connection raises the question of whether they are copies painted by the illusive Wilson of Philadelphia (see cat. no. 55, n. 2)

57
On the Wing

c. 1850

Oil on canvas

32 1/4 x 45 1/4 inches
(81.9 x 114.9 cm)

Location unknown

PROVENANCE: (Possibly Kennedy Galleries, New York,1924), James H. Watson, by 1924; Meade Alexander, by 1929, descended in the family to unnamed owner, 1991 (sale, Sotheby's, New York, May 23, 1991, lot 13) Mr. and Mrs. Randolph Agley, Grosse Pointe, Michigan (sale, Sotheby's, New York, November 29, 1995, lot 148).

REFERENCE: Francis S. Grubar To Whom it May Concern, copy, April 7, 1991, Ranney archives, authenticates picture.

We have not examined this picture. LB

58
On the Wing

c. 1850

Oil on canvas

31 x 45 inches (78.7 x
114.3 cm)

Private collection

PROVENANCE: Descended in the family to the present owner.

59*
The Retrieve

1850

Oil on canvas

30 1/4 x 40 3/8 inches
(76.8 x 102.6 cm)

Signed and dated,
lower center: W.
Ranney/1850

Corcoran Gallery of
Art, Washington, D. C.
Gift of William Wilson
Corcoran, 69.62

Grubar no. 48

PROVENANCE: William Wilson Corcoran, 1850–1869.

EXHIBITED: NAD, 1850, no. 365, as The Retrieve owned by W. W. Corcoran

REFERENCES: *Catalogue of the Corcoran Gallery*, prepared by Charles Lanman (Washington, D. C.: 1857), p. 9, no. 24, lists as Duck Shooting and describes. Tuckerman 1867, p. 632, lists in Corcoran's collection as Duck Shooting. *Catalogue of the Paintings, Statuary, Casts, Bronzes, &c. of the Corcoran Gallery of Art*, prepared by William MacLeod (Washington, D.C.: 1878), p. 57, no. 45, lists as Duck-Shooting and describes it. Cowdrey 1943, 2, p. 89, lists. *A Catalogue of the Collection of American Painting in the Corcoran Gallery of Art: Painters Born Before 1850*, 1 (repr. 1974: Washington: Corcoran Gallery of Art, 1966), pp. 82–83.

The Retrieve is one of at least three known duck hunting scenes that Ranney painted around this time (cat. nos. 43 and 55). Clearly attuned to the popularity of this subject, he subsequently painted other variations of the theme (cat. nos. 78 and 79). Here, he seems to have drawn his inspiration from both the sporting literature of the day and his own hunting practices. The painting portrays the relationship between the hunter and his springer spaniel, clearly illustrating one of the cardinal rules of working with hunting dogs: When the dog has retrieved a dead bird, it must be trained to deliver it directly into the owner's hand. According to the artist's grandson Claude J. Ranney, whom Grubar interviewed in preparation for the 1962 exhibition, the model for the kneeling figure was the artist's younger brother Richard Ranney (1815–1859), and the standing figure cleaning his gun may have been a neighbor's groom who sometimes posed for Ranney.

The Corcoran's 1878 catalogue noted that *The Retrieve* was a "thoroughly American scene [set] in the Jersey Flats, [and] full of vigor and truth to nature." Like most of Ranney's sporting pictures of this period, the setting probably was indeed the Hackensack meadows near his home and studio. The flat grassy landscape and the telltale skiff—only partially visible along the marsh at the right—are familiar motifs in his work. The brightly illuminated figures and objects are arranged in a typically rigorous triangular composition. Unlike the harmonious palette that characterizes most of Ranney's duck shooting pictures, however, the atmosphere here is chilly, the sky and background unusually dark and foreboding, with a dramatic glow articulating the horizon line. Ranney's use of this new romantic vocabulary in the background of what is essentially a genre scene links him to many of his contemporaries, who in the 1840s and 1850s began to experiment with visual elements that today are considered indicative of the luminist tradition in American landscape painting. In 1850, for example, the same year Ranney exhibited *The Retrieve* at the National Academy, Frederic E. Church exhibited *Twilight, "Short Arbiter Twixt Day and Night"* (Newark Museum, New Jersey), which similarly exploits the poetic effects of twilight.

The description of the painting in the Corcoran's first catalogue in 1857 shows the high regard in which Ranney's work was held at the time: it is a "truly . . . American Picture, and the style is one in which the Artist has attained a high reputation." It is worth noting that the compiler of that catalogue was the multi-talented artist, journalist, and biographer Charles Lanman (1819–1895). It is possible that he met Ranney when he was working in New York in the 1840s and both were exhibiting their work at the National Academy. In fact, by 1857 Ranney's work was known to be represented in Lanman's own collection.[1]

When the painting was exhibited at the National Academy in 1850 it was titled *The Retrieve*. Grubar notes that at some point it was also called *The Retriever*. By 1857, when it was listed in the Corcoran's first catalogue, it had acquired the title *Duck Shooters*, which it carried throughout the nineteenth and the twentieth centuries in the Corcoran's numerous collection catalogues. In 2003, the Corcoran restored Ranney's original title. LB

1. *Crayon*, vol. 1 (February 28, 1855), p. 137, provides a description of Lanman's collection.

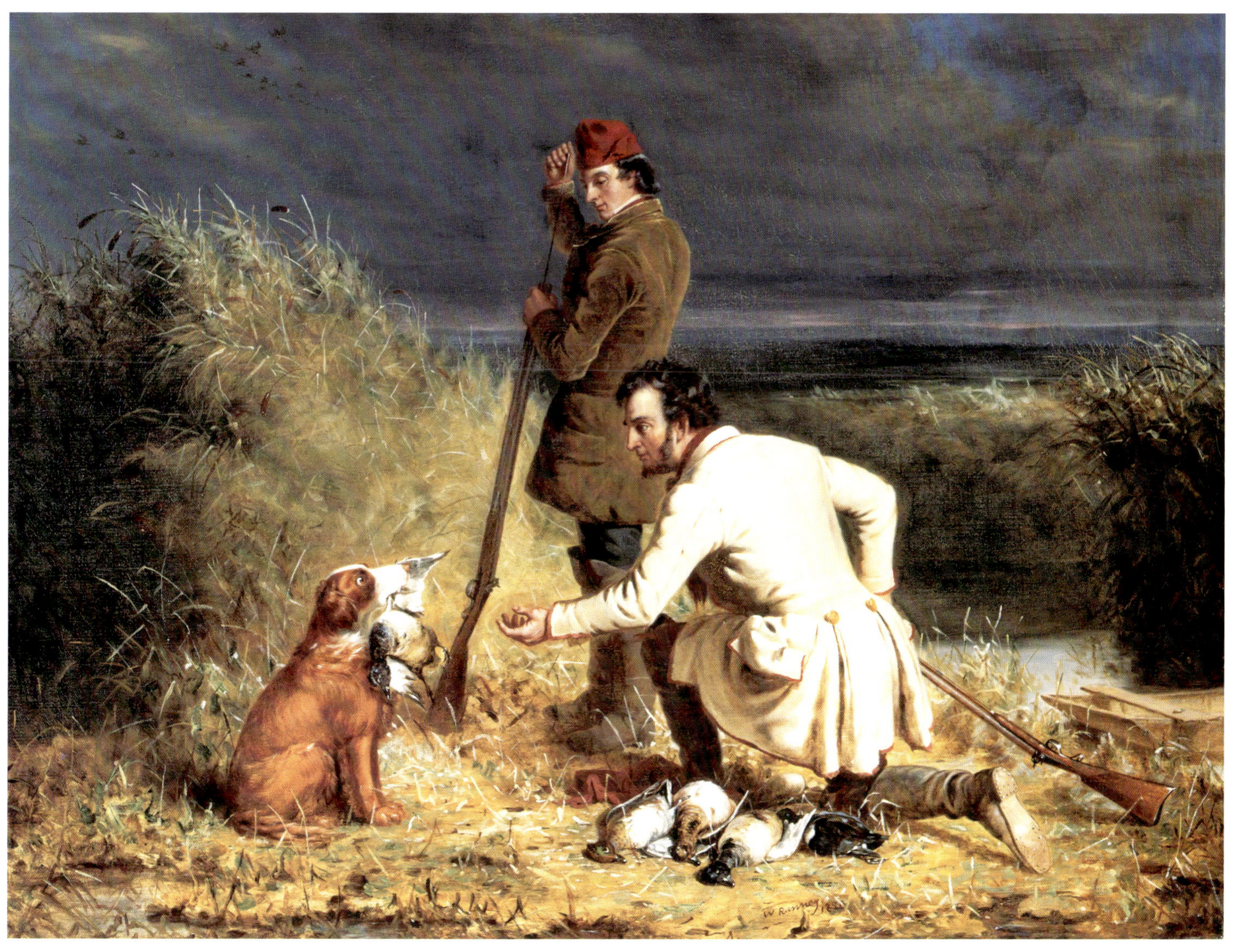

NO. 59

60*
The Retreat

1850

Oil on canvas

30 1/2 x 48 1/2 inches
(77.5 x 123.1 cm)

Signed and dated lower right: W. Ranney/1850; and initialed on rear flank of pack mule: W.R.

Grubar no. 51

Private collection

PROVENANCE: John Wolfe (c. 1821–1894), New York, by 1851; (possibly Henry H. Leeds and Company, New York, *A Large Collection of Superb Oil Paintings*, May 5, 1857, no. 42 1/2, as The Trappers Retreat); (Coleman Auction Galleries, New York, June 2 and 3, 1938); Dr. Frederick H. Wilke, New York; (T. Gilbert Brouillette, New York); Clendenning Ryan, New York; (M. Knoedler and Company, New York, by 1949–c. 1976); (Hirschl and Adler Galleries, New York, c. 1976).

EXHIBITED: NAD, 1851, no. 123, lent by John Wolfe, as The Retreat.

REFERENCES: *Albion* 10 (April 19, 1851), p. 189, provides description and notes "The humour of the piece is seen in the efforts of the fugitives to drag with them a reluctant pack-saddle mule." *New York Tribune*, June 21, 1851, p. 6 (quoted in entry); *New York Sun*, March 28, 1938, mentions Coleman auction. Cowdrey 1943, 2, p. 89. *New York Sun*, February 25, 1949, mentions painting on view at Knoedler.

Ranney produced one of his most dramatic western scenes in 1850. It was purchased by the New York collector John Wolfe who loaned it to the National Academy's annual exhibition in 1851.

A pencil study for this painting (cat. no. D35), perhaps produced to entice a buyer for the work, shows three trappers, two of whom are seen racing across the prairie on their mounts, urging on a heavily laden pack mule to flee with them. The third rider has set himself against some unseen foe. He has lowered and aimed his rifle off to the left, protecting his compatriots and their harvest of furs.

The finished painting mirrors this action but provides a more complex scenario. The bundle of furs on the pack mule has been substantially bulked up. The rifleman guarding the left flank has been incorporated into the thundering central group. At either margin of the focal action are distant figures silhouetted against a violent yellow and orange sky. To the right is a riderless horse, suggesting a fallen comrade. To the left, an outrider prepares to take a shot at a group of three barely visible Indians who gallop toward them, all with weapons held high. The critic for the *New York Tribune* in 1851 found that the whole "scene throbs with characteristic life."

This was Ranney's sequel to *The Trapper's Last Shot* (cat. no. 51), with the tension and drama ratcheted up to a higher level. Yet *The Retreat* is quite different as a subject. The *Tribune's* critic applauded the picture's "action," "good movement," and overall dynamic "spirit," so lacking in the frozen awe of the *The Trapper's Last Shot*, even though he "could have wished a more spacious view of the Prairie," into which "vastness" the drama might unfold. What the critic did not acknowledge was the true focus of the painting, the white mule and its hefty burden. It is the pack animal that holds the prominent spotlight and most central placement in the composition. That same mule, surrounded by the three mounted figures, is deliberately guarded from the unwelcome advances of the impending foe. Certainly the men wish to escape, but they refuse to relinquish, yanking and prodding the treasure of furs hidden beneath the matrix of half hitches and crimson cloth. In this work, Ranney was speaking to the matters of danger and physical isolation, but he was also addressing the notion of a bountiful West, exploitable by those who were sufficiently intrepid, perseverant, quick-witted, and agile.

Various literary sources have been ascribed as this painting's inspiration. Charles Webber in 1848 and Francis Parkman a year before each recount narratives of such harrowing adventures and describe similarly desperate and exotic characters.[1]

The most probable origin for Ranney's canvas, however, was most likely the highly popular fictionalized adventure story *The Lost Trappers* by David H. Coyner. In romantically fanciful detail, Coyner elaborated on a true-life tale of an early fur trapper, Captain Ezekiel Williams, and his fellow explorers of the western reaches. Williams's party of twenty had split in half. One group, impressed with the prairie richness—"a perfect Elysium," abounding with "buffalo, elk, antelope, white and black-tail deer"—turned from trapping for a day to take advantage of the buffalo hunting. In their zeal for exhilarating sport, they fell prey themselves to a large group of Blackfeet who resented the intrusion onto their land.

> A company of Black-feet, numbering at least one hundred, suddenly appeared on horses from behind a covert of trees and undergrowth, and dashed toward the men as they were scattered over a plain pursuing and shooting the buffalo. Five of the men being on fast horses, and flying at the top of their speed, were able to effect their escape, but the others were intercepted by the savages, and their escape to the camp cut off. They . . . were killed by that tribe.[2]

PHH

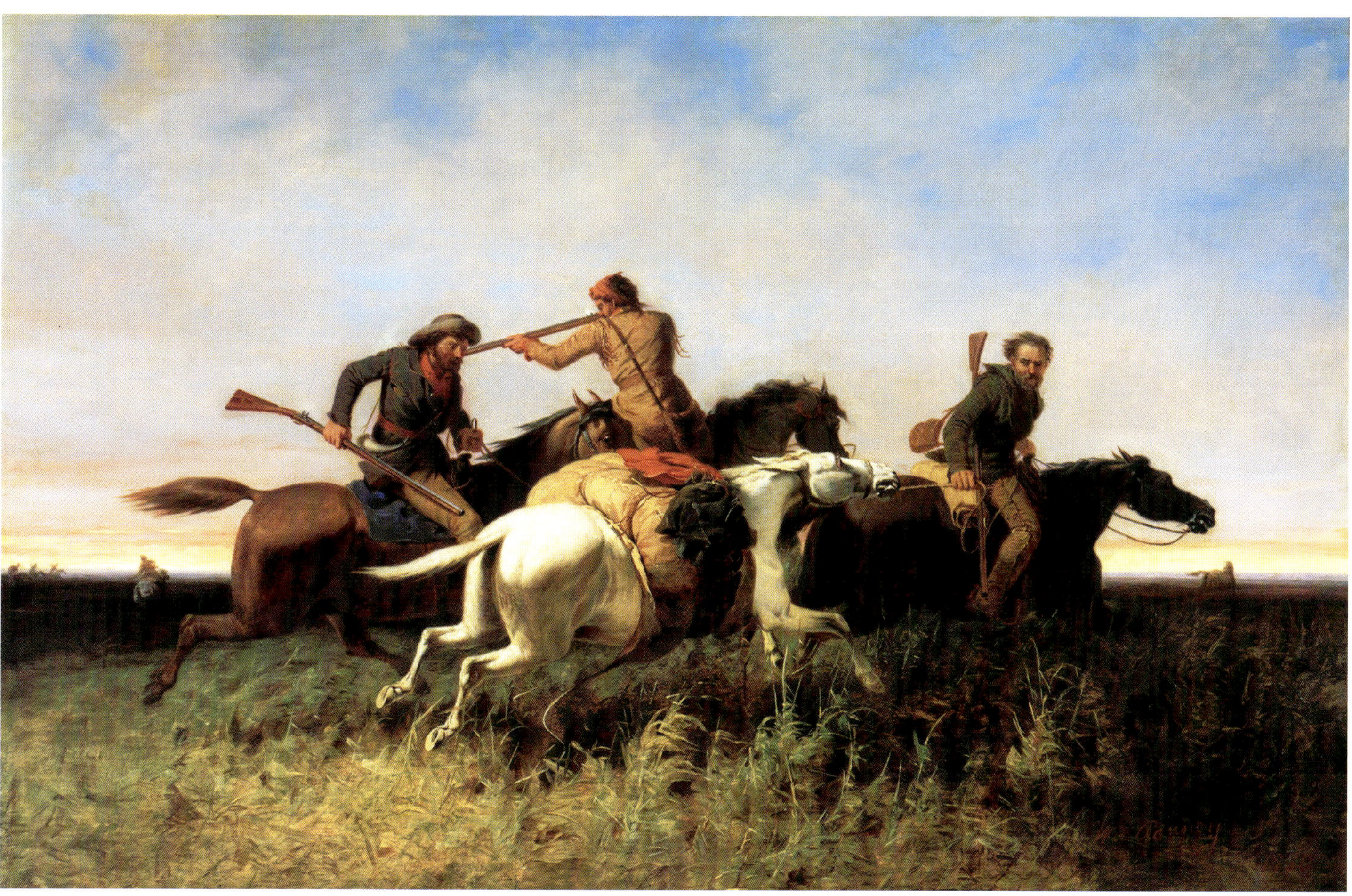

NO. 60

1. Charles W. Webber, *Old Hicks the Guide, or, Adventures in the Camanche Country in Search of a Gold Mine* (New York: Harper & Brothers, 1848), p. 336, and Francis Parkman, *The Oregon Trail* (1849; Boston: Ginn and Company, 1910), pp. 281–282.
2. David H. Coyner, *The Lost Trappers* (Cincinnati: E. D. Truman, Publisher, 1850), pp. 88–90. A full chapter is devoted to Coyner and his fictive account of Williams and his troop of fur trappers in Hiram Martin Chittenden, *The American Fur Trade of the Far West* (Stanford, Calif.: Academic Reprints, 1954), vol. 2, pp. 651–664.

61*
Marion Crossing the Pedee

1850

Oil on canvas

50 1/8 x 74 3/8 inches
(127.3 x 188.9 cm)

Signed and dated,
lower center, on side of
boat: W Ranney/1850

Amon Carter
Museum, Fort Worth,
Texas. 1983.126

Grubar no. 56

ENGRAVING: Charles Burt (1823–1892), steel engraving, sheet size 14 1/2 x 18 3/8 inches (36.8 x 46.7 cm); image size 8 7/8 x 11 7/8 inches (22.5 x 30.2 cm). Inscribed on side of boat: W Ranney; at lower left: Painted by W. Ranney; lower right, Engraved by C. Burt. Inscribed Marion Crossing the Pedee / Engraved from the original painting in possession of the American Art Union / American Art Union 1851. Printed by J. Dalton. Unauthorized Currier and Ives print, after 1872. Marion's Brigade Crossing the Pedee River, S. C., 1778. On their Way to Attack the British force under Tarleton. (See Harry T. Peters, *Currier & Ives: Printmakers to the American People* [New York: Doubleday, Doran and Company, 1942], pl. 47.

PROVENANCE: Am Art-Union, 1851 (sale, Am Art-Union, David Austen, Jr., New York, December 15, 16, and 17, 1852, p. 13, no. 348, sold for $900) William H. Webb (1816–1899), New York, 1852–1876 (sale, Miner's Art Galleries, New York, *William H. Webb's Collection of Works of Art*, March 29 and 30, 1876, lot 43, p. 16, sold for $525); Mr. and Mrs. Willard T. Evenson, Clatskanie, Oregon, c. 1945–1964; Dr. and Mrs. Franz R. Stenzel, Portland, Oregon, 1964–1979 (Vose Galleries, Boston, 1979–1980) Koffler Corporation, Providence, Rhode Island, by 1980–1983.

ON LOAN: Los Angeles Country Museum of Art, 1974–1979.

EXHIBITED: Am Art-Union, 1852, no. 348. Metropolitan Fair, New York, 1864, *Exhibition at the Metropolitan Fair in Aid of the U.S. Sanitary Commission*, New York, 1864, no. 129, p. 10, as Marion and His Men Crossing the Pedee, lent by W. H. Webb. Chadds Ford 1991, cat. no. 9.

REFERENCES: Am Art-Union *Bulletin* (August 1850), p. 81 (quoted in entry); and (November 1850), pp. 138–139, mentions Ranney working on picture. *New York Evening Post*, November 12, 1850, p. 2 (quoted in entry). *Home Journal* (November 23, 1850), p. 3 (quoted in entry). *Harper's New Monthly Magazine*, vol. 2 (December 1850), p. 131, mentions it. Executive Committee Minutes, 1846–1854, reel 2, vol. 2, March 27, 1851, Am Art-Union Papers, resolves to purchase picture, unframed for $700. Am Art-Union, *Bulletin* (April 1851), p. 17; and (May 1851), p. 35, describes it and mentions engraving. *New York Herald*, May 1, 1851, p. 6, mentions engraving. *New York Tribune*, May 7, 1851, p. 1, mentions engraving. *Home Journal* (August 9, 1851), p. 3, includes critical commentary. *New York Evening Post*, September 23, 1851, p. 2, includes critical comment, p. 3, mentions engraving. Am Art-Union, *Bulletin* (November 1851), p. 135, describes it. *New York Herald*, December 3, 1851, p. 1, mentions distribution; December 10, 1851, p. 5, mentions engraving. *New York Tribune*, December 15, 1851, p. 8, mentions engraving. Am Art-Union *Supplementary Bulletin* (December 1852), includes auction catalogue, p. 7, no. 348 (quoted in entry). *New York Evening Post*, December 13, 1852, p. 2, mentions auction. *Catalogue of Pictures and Other Works of Art: The Property of the American Art-Union, to be Sold at Auction by David Austen, Jr., at the Gallery, 497 Broadway, on Wednesday, the 15th, Thursday 16th, and Friday 17th, December 1852*, p. 13, no. 348. *New York Tribune*, December 18, 1852, p. 7, notes W. H. Webb purchased painting for $900. *New York Daily Times*, December 18, 1852, p. 6, says sold for $900, estimate was $745. *Literary World* (December 25, 1852), p. 406, mentions Webb and purchase price. *New York Evening Post*, March 14, 1876, p. 4, discusses Webb collection; and March 30, 1876, p. 2 (quoted in entry). *New York Commercial Advertiser*, March 18, 1876, p. 3, discusses it in Webb's collection. Cowdrey 1953, 2, p. 195. Linda Ayres et al., *American Paintings: Selections from the Amon Carter Museum* (Birmingham, Alabama: Oxmoor House, 1986), p. 34. Thistlethwaite 1991, pp. 61–65, provides thorough discussion of literary, biographical background, and artistic contexts.

This picture is perhaps Ranney's most celebrated, and, up to this point in his career, the most ambitious in size and figurative complexity. The first public notice of his working on the scene appeared in August 1850 in the American Art-Union's Bulletin:

> Ranney . . . is engaged in a large picture the drawing and composition of which are praised. We have always thought that the War of the Revolution at the South, and particularly the incidents in the partisan operations there, afforded many excellent subjects for the artist. The display of the nude, which the climate permitted, and the necessities of the troops required, the service of the blacks, and the half-sportsman, half-warrior character of the people engaged, suggest many picturesque combinations."

In November, the *New York Evening Post* reported that Ranney "has on his easel, and nearly completed, a large picture representing Marion and his men crossing the Pedee. It is an admirable work in every way, and will add much to the growing reputation of this able painter."

On March 27, 1851, the American Art-Union resolved to purchase the picture, unframed, for seven hundred dollars, the most money they had ever paid for one of Ranney's pictures. It was one of five images selected by the Art-Union to be engraved for its Gallery of American Art series. The painting itself was slated for distribution in 1851, but before that took place the New York Supreme Court ruled that the Art-Union's distributions were illegal lotteries, and the organization was forced to cancel the distribution. Instead, Ranney's painting, along with all the Art-Union's 1851 pictures, were sold at auction the following year. It was bought by the successful New York shipbuilder William Henry Webb for nine hundred dollars, along with Richard Caton Woodville's *Old '76 and Young '48* of 1848 (Walters Art Museum, Baltimore) and other works. Twenty-five years later, in 1876, the *New York Evening Post,* in reporting on the results of the sale of Webb's collection, seemed surprised that Ranney's painting was sold "for the insignificant sum of $525." After this sale, its location was unknown until it reappeared in a private West Coast collection in the second-quarter of the twentieth century.

By the time Ranney painted this picture, there was widespread national interest in the history of the American Revolution, and Francis Marion was a recognized figure in the pantheon of national heroes whose exploits were regularly related in numerous general histories. Marion himself, like George Washington and others, was also the subject of several biographies. In 1824, for instance, Parson M. L. Weems, Washington's biographer, wrote *The Life of General Francis Marion,* loosely based on notes by Marion's friend and fellow officer Peter Horry, who repudiated the biography as highly embellished. In 1832, the renowned Massachusetts poet William Cullen Bryant immortalized him in "The Song of Marion and His Men." And in 1844 the respected Charleston author William Gilmore Simms (1806–1870), who had romanticized Marion beginning in 1836 in the *Partisan,* a series of southern stories of the Revolution, published a new biography, *The Life of Francis Marion.*

These literary sources notwithstanding, Ranney probably had a more direct knowledge of Marion. From at least 1827 to 1834, Ranney lived in the South, where Marion was a recognized regional hero. According to Marion's twentieth-century biographer Robert D. Bass, in the heady days following the war, Marion's exploits were often retold in the South and soon became part of the local folklore. To some Carolinian patriots, Marion was a latter-day Robin Hood; to Marion's comrade-in-arms Peter Horry, the brilliant and brave warrior was "the Washington of the South."[1] Like Horry, Bass, also a southerner, called Marion "a hero of the Revolution second only to George Washington."[2] In fact, there is evidence that at least some of Marion's band of patriots were from Fayetteville, North Carolina, where Ranney lived from about 1827 to 1834.[3] There Ranney must have heard the tales oft repeated, perhaps even from men with firsthand knowledge of Marion's escapades.

Francis Marion (c. 1732–1795), a successful planter and Indian fighter, was the South's most famous hero of the American Revolution for good reason. When the British gained control of the South after the fall of Charleston in 1780, he was one of the few officers of the Continental Army left in the area who had not been captured, and he took it upon himself to organize and lead small ragtag groups of patriots. These self-supporting bands of guerrillas tormented and harassed the British with midnight raids and hit-and-run tactics, effectively disrupting their communication and supply lines. His archenemy, the notorious Banastre Tarlcton, dubbed him the Swamp Fox because of his uncanny ability to disappear with his men into the swamps and bogs of the Pee Dee and Santee Rivers, successfully eluding and infuriating the superiorly armed, clothed, and fed British forces. Their sustained efforts helped deny the South to the British and contributed to the American victory.

Ranney represented Marion and his men traversing the river, an imaginary re-creation of a recurring event rather than a specific historic battle. The Amon Carter Museum's catalogue suggests that the small band are leaving their hideout on Snow's Island in South Carolina, between the Lynches and Pee Dee Rivers. The presumed time period for the scene is about 1780 when Marion's Brigade was formed. The Art-Union publications called it "one of the very best works of the artist" and provided the following description in December

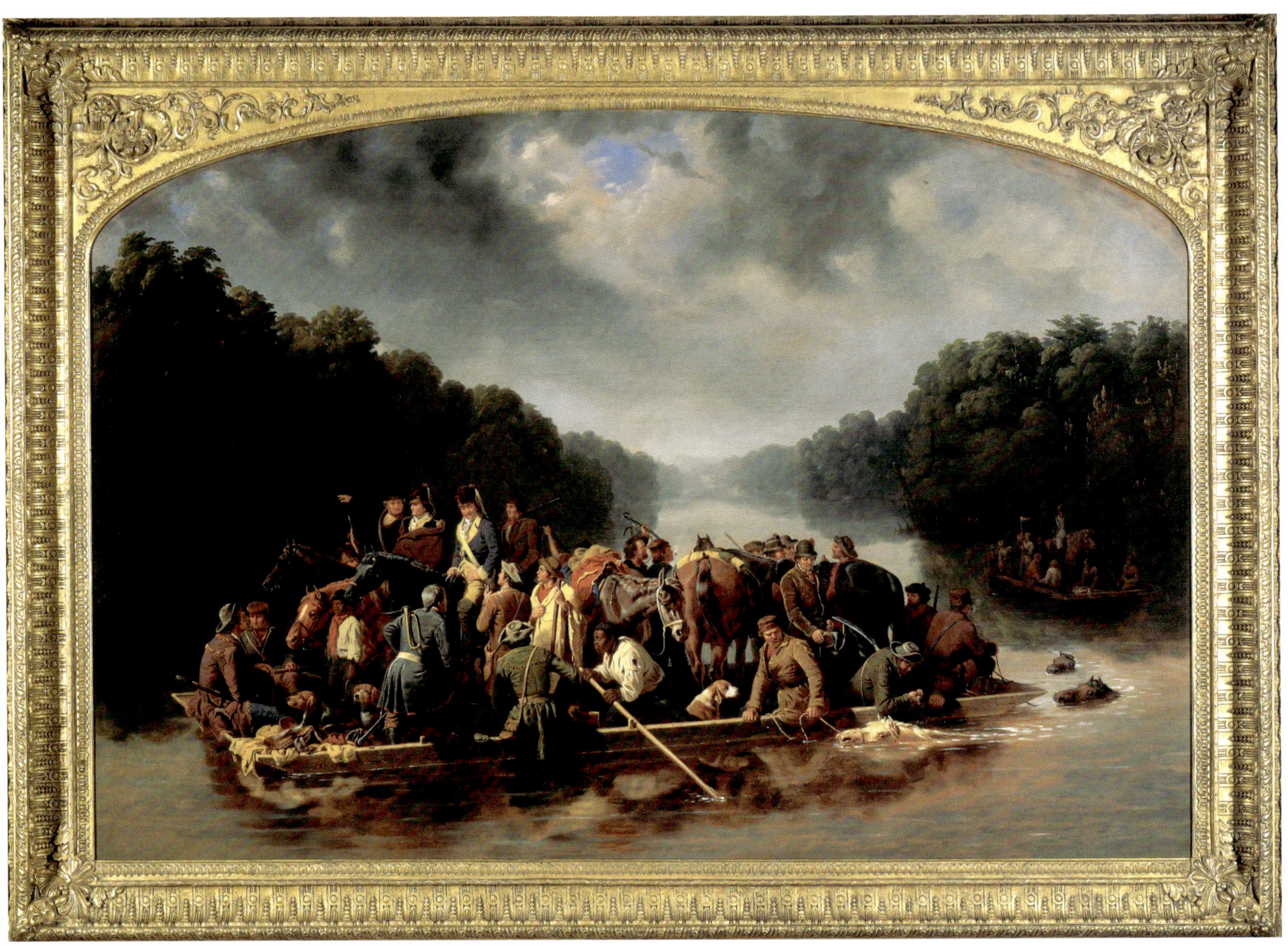

1852: "It represents Marion and his men, with their horses and attendants, crossing the river in a large scow, while some of the troopers are swimming their horses beside it. In the distance are other boats and men preparing to embark."

Ranney places Marion at the far left, integrated within the overall composition. He is flanked by two men on horseback: The one pointing appears to be a guide, and the officer on Marion's left may be Peter Horry, a colonel when Marion's Brigade was formed. Marion, who became a brigadier general of the militia in August 1780, is the central figure at the left on horseback. His shoulder is adorned with officer's epaulettes, and he is enveloped by a great brown cloak, which art historian Mark Thistlethwaite noted as "indicative of authority." He sits astride a sorrel horse, the type, which, according to legend, was captured from the British colonel John Coming Ball, after whom it was named. Marion's likeness compares favorably with a contemporary's description of his appearance around 1780: Marion was then about forty-eight years old, "lean and swarthy," and "had a countenance remarkably steady; his nose was aquiline."[4]

Ranney represents a cross section of types: Marion's motley band were short-term volunteers, often farmers who rarely had uniforms and generally provided their own firearms. The flat-bottomed boat is congested with this array of men in various forms of dress—from buckskins to tattered shirts, to natty jackets—

90

along with horses, pack horses, hounds, and saddles, all enriched and augmented by realistically rendered details. Interestingly, however, the most dominant figures pictorially are two African Americans. Isolated at the far left is a young boy wearing a bright red neck scarf and holding the reins of Marion's horse. In the foreground is an older man who is emphasized not only by his central position in the composition but coloristically by his starkly white ragged blouse. He apparently is the sole oarsman in charge of the seemingly impossible task of transporting the overladen vessel across the river, only assisted by a man, partially visible in the background, poling. The oarsman also functions as a visual link between the group of uniformed soldiers at the left and a nondescript group of men at the right. Unlike any other figure in the picture, all of whom relate to either Marion or one another, this robust individual is isolated spatially and socially shunned, not only by all the men on the scow, but by the animals as well, for example, the pack horse at his back that separates him from the figures to his right and behind him. Even the dog profiled behind him pointedly looks in the opposite direction.

Marion Crossing the Pedee might therefore be interpreted not merely as a celebration of the American Revolution, but as a poignant visualization of the controversy sweeping the nation at the time Ranney conceived the picture—whether the newly annexed western territories should or should not allow slavery. The Compromise of 1850 and its updated Fugitive Slave Law, a pastiche of concessions to the North and South, seemed to address these regional disputes, at least temporarily. Alas, in New York, however, the city where Ranney's work was exhibited, this legislation almost immediately ignited bitter disputes between abolitionists and antiabolitionists. As historian David Quigley points out:

> At mid century, New Yorkers occupied a strange space apart from America's deepening sectional divisions. As North and South grew further apart, New Yorkers tried to carve out an economic and political middle ground . . . the enactment of the federal Fugitive Slave Law of 1850 forced issues of slavery, race, liberty, and home rule to the surface . . . In the struggles over fugitive slaves, new voices came forward . . . suggesting that some New Yorkers would question the persistence of the city's special relationship with the slaveholding South.[5]

Unfortunately no records have been discovered to clearly give us Ranney's personal view about these pressing matters. On the one hand, it could be argued that Ranney included African Americans for the artistic purpose of realistically representing their significant presence in the South; his portrayals, however, are so extraordinarily deliberate and sympathetic, and so dominant visually, that it is hard to imagine that he was not only alluding to the major social and political concerns of this period, but that he himself was deeply sympathetic to the antislavery cause.

Because of the subject matter, unmistakable compositional parallels, and the coincidence of production, art historians, such as Mark Thistlethwaite in 1991, have often compared Ranney's *Marion Crossing the Pedee* to Emanuel Leutze's *Washington Crossing the Delaware* of 1851 (Metropolitan Museum of Art, New York). Indeed, both artists similarly portrayed their hero wrapped in a great cloak, crossing a body of water on a boat. Either consciously or unconsciously Ranney seems to have incorporated some of the specific details of Leutze's picture as described in the American Art-Union's *Bulletin*: "The great leader's gaze is fixed on the distant shore. . . . Other boats follow close, some with horses and artillery."[6]

In spite of some similarities, however, overall Ranney's considerably smaller easel-sized picture has little in common with the heroic style epitomized by Leutze's epic-sized canvas with its life-sized figures. Unlike Ranney, Leutze focuses his scene on a specific rather than generalized historical event: Washington, at the apex of the pyramidal composition, is the central idealized presence in the romantic and dynamic composition. Eschewing Leutze's grand manner theatrics and drama, Ranney presents a rather low-keyed genre scene with several narrative details that suggest the diversity and background of the various participants in Marion's band, most of them ordinary men. In fact, Ranney so effectively integrated Marion into the ensem-

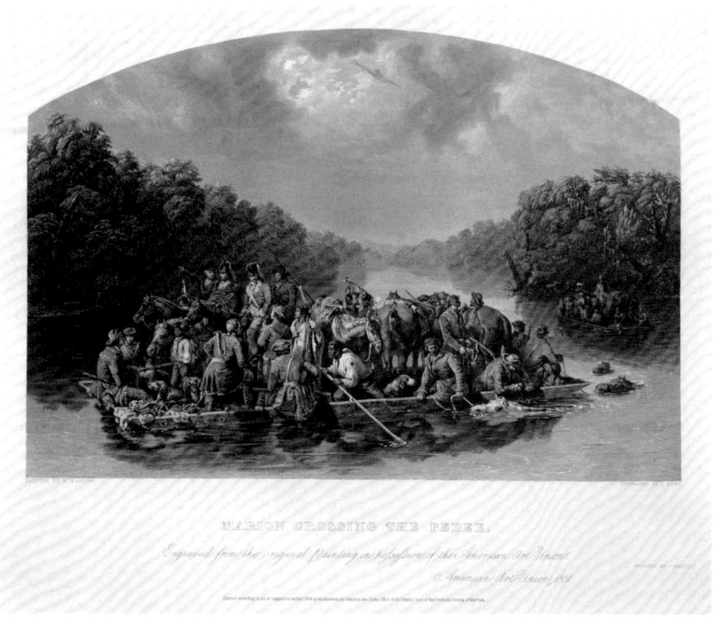

Fig 61.1

Marion Crossing the Pedee, engraved by Charles Burt. New-York Historical Society, gift of the American Art-Union, 1863.

ble that, unlike Leutze's Washington, Marion is not readily distinguishable or identifiable. Here, as in most of his successful paintings, Ranney characteristically relied upon his skill as a storyteller to render the more human aspect of the Marion legend and, as in William Cullen Bryant's poem, expressed the shared experiences of Marion and his men.

In 1849, the year before Ranney began his painting, enthusiastic accounts chronicling Leutze's progress on *Washington Crossing the Delaware* had begun to arrive from Düsseldorf. Although a detailed description of that work appeared in the American Art-Union's *Bulletin* of October 1850[7], Ranney could not have seen the actual painting until after he finished his own painting in the spring of 1851. Leutze's first version was so damaged in a fire in his studio in November 1850 (and later destroyed in World War II) that he had to paint a second copy, the one now in the Metropolitan Museum of Art. It was shown in New York in November 1851. Coincidentally, a third copy, painted by Leutze and Eastman Johnson (Manoogian Collection), on which the engraving was based, was purchased by William Webb, the collector who also bought Ranney's *Marion Crossing the Pedee*.[8]

While Leutze's painting itself may not have been an inspiration, the periodic reports about it may have piqued Ranney's regional pride and played a role in his choice of Marion as a subject. In addition, if his shrewd choice of subject matter in the past is any indication, Ranney was keenly attuned to American taste and in particular the Art-Union's interest in purchasing pictures that represented national historical events. Certainly aware of the eagerness with which the general public was anticipating the arrival of Leutze's painting, Ranney may have decided to capitalize on that excitement to create a composition whose subject matter and title, so similar to the Leutze, would have equally resonated with the American public.

Because of the widespread distribution of the engraving based on this picture (fig. 61.1), numerous later copies in oil continue to be discovered. Ranney himself painted a second version of the scene (see cat. no. 62). Also, two other later variations on the theme of Francis Marion have recently been discovered (see cat. nos. 93 and 94). LB

1. Peter Horry and Parson M. L. Weems, *The Life of General Francis Marion . . .* (1854; reprint Winston-Salem, N.C.: John F. Blair Publisher, 2000), Peter Horry preface, n.p.

2. Robert D. Bass, *Swamp Fox: The Life and Campaigns of General Francis Marion* (1959); (Orangeburg, S. C.: Sandlapper Publishing Co., 1974), pp. 3–4.

3. John A. Oates, *The Story of Fayetteville and the Upper Cape Fear* (1950; reprint Raleigh: Fayetteville Woman's Club, 1981), p. 33.

4. Quoted from W. Gilmore Simms, *The Life of Francis Marion* (New York: Henry G. Langley and Astor House, 1844), p. 121.

5. David Quigley, "Southern Slavery in a Free City: Economy, Politics, and Culture," in *Slavery in New York*, ed. Ira Berlin and Leslie M. Harris (New York: New Press, 2005), p. 280.

6. Correspondent of the *Literary World*, "American Artists Abroad," in American Art-Union, *Bulletin* (October 1850), p. 117.

7. Ibid.

8. See Natalie Spassky, *American Paintings in the Metropolitan Museum of Art, Volume II: A Catalogue of Works by Artists Born between 1816–1845* (New York: Metropolitan Museum of Art, 1985), pp. 13-24, provides a complete chronology of the development of Leutze's painting.

62*
Marion Crossing the Pedee

c. 1850

Oil on canvas

16 x 21 inches (40.6 x 53.3 cm)

Signed, lower center, on side of boat: W. Ranney

Greenville County Museum of Art, Greenville, South Carolina. Gift of Dr. and Mrs. DeWitt Harper

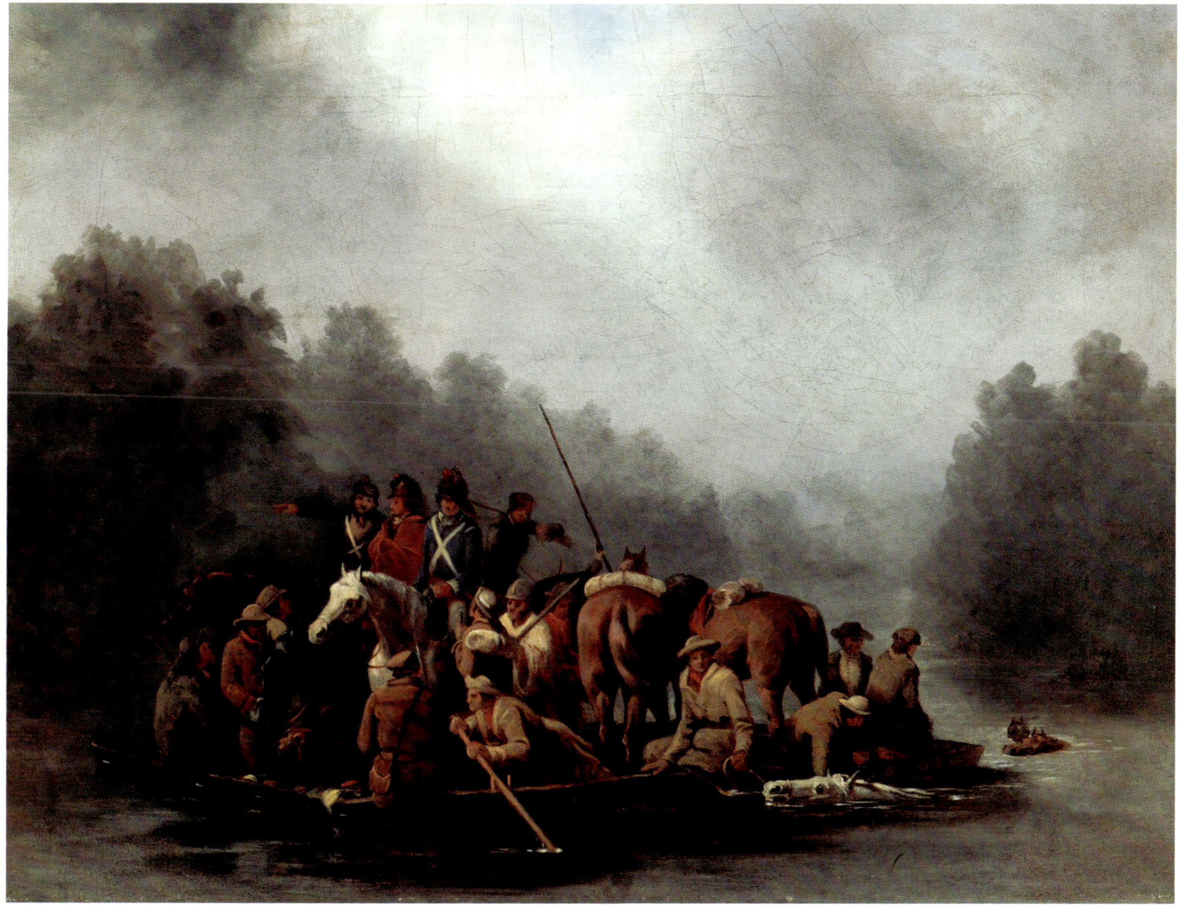

NO. 62

PROVENANCE: Descended in the family to Doris Brewster Meeker, Brunswick, Maine (sale, Barridoff Galleries, Portland, Maine, September 28, 1985, lot no. 42) (Spanierman Gallery, New York, 1985–1986).

Because this small, signed but undated painting was only discovered in 1985, it was not included in Grubar's 1962 catalogue. An uncharacteristically dark canvas for Ranney, it is a variation of his large *Marion Crossing the Pedee* (cat. no. 61). In addition to the color, there are several notable differences between the two paintings. Here there is only one boat, and it is less populated than in the larger canvas. There are also many variations in the details of the clothing. The most striking variance, however, is that the foreground oarsman in this picture is a white man, not a black man as in Ranney's 1850 canvas. Whether this is the artist's initial concept for his 1850 canvas or a variation of the later work related to a now unlocated canvas of 1853 (see cat. no. 93), is unclear. [1] LB

1. See Henry H. Leeds and Company, New York, *Catalogue of Williams, Stevens and Williams, Second Great Annual Sale...*, November 10 and 11, 1853, p. 87, no. 490.

93

63
Portrait of Ambrose Jordan Clark

c. 1850

Oil on canvas

24 x 29 1/2 inches (61 x 74.9 cm)

Signed, lower left: Ranney

Jane Forbes Clark

P R O V E N A N C E : Caroline (d. 1874) and Edward Clark (1811–1882); their son Alfred Corning Clark (1844–1896); his son Frederick Ambrose Clark (1880–1964), Cooperstown, New York.

R E F E R E N C E : Emmanuel Jay Rousuck, *The F. Ambrose Clark Collection of Sporting Pictures* (New York: 1958), pp. 222, 223 illus.

Ambrose Jordan Clark (1836–1880) was the first-born child and eldest son of Edward and Caroline (nee Jordan) Clark. Edward Clark, after graduating from Williams College in 1827, spent three years studying law with Ambrose L. Jordan. In 1835, he married Jordan's eldest daughter Caroline and joined Jordan's law firm in Hudson, New York. There, the following year Ambrose Clark was born and named after his maternal grandfather. By 1838, his father's law firm relocated to New York City. Edward Clark eventually became the attorney for Isaac Singer, who developed the sewing machine. Through Clark's shrewd business advice, both men acquired considerable wealth.[1]

How Ranney came to know the Clark family is not known. However, according to Francis Grubar's notes documenting an interview conducted with the artist's grandson Claude J. Ranney on April 19, 1961, Edward Clark (whom Claude Ranney misidentified as Alfred Corning Clark) was a legal adviser to the family. After the artist's death, Clark apparently advised his widow Margaret on estate matters, helping her to establish a trust fund which supported her for the rest of her life.[2]

While Ranney in his early years was primarily known as a portrait painter, few examples of this aspect of his work are known today. This picture, presumably commissioned, is a rare surviving example of a known subject. The painting demonstrates the caliber of Ranney's technical abilities in combining portrait, genre, and animal painting. He portrays Ambrose Jordan Clark, who is probably in his early or mid teens, in the manner of late eighteenth- and early nineteenth-century informal English portraiture and sporting pictures. Casually attired, the young man wears no jacket and has cavalierly tossed his hat on the ground. Like a squire enjoying his country estate, he is pictured against the backdrop of a low stone fence amidst a lush and light-filled landscape—undoubtedly a known spot on the Clark's property in upstate New York. Ranney represents the moment when the youthful equestrian has put his left foot in the saddle's stirrup to mount his horse, which family tradition identified as his favorite gray Welsh pony. The horse's pose, with head down and right front leg raised, is virtually identical to that represented in Ranney's drawing *Dragoon with His Charger* (cat. no. D11).

By the 1870s, Ambrose Clark owned land on the western side of Lake Otsego, near the family estate in Cooperstown, New York. Called Fenimore Farm, it was stocked with sheep and short-horn and Jersey cattle, which both he and his father raised.[3] Ambrose Clark, a bachelor, died suddenly in New York at the age of forty-three. He is buried in Cooperstown. LB

1. For biographical information on the Clark family, see Edgar W. Clark, *History and Genealogy of Samuel Clark, Sr.* (St. Louis: Nixon-Jones Printing Company, 1892), pp. 39–41 and *Encyclopaedia of Contemporary Biography of New York* (New York: Atlantic Publishing and Engraving Company, 1882), vol. 2, pp. 191–194.

2. Francis Grubar, "Notes from 2nd visit to Claude J. Ranney, Malvern, Pa., April 19, 1961," p. 2, copy in Ranney archives.

3. See *Pedigrees of Short-Horn Cattle, the Property of Ambrose J. Clark* (Cooperstown, N. Y., 1877). Copy of pamphlet in the New York State Historical Association, Cooperstown.

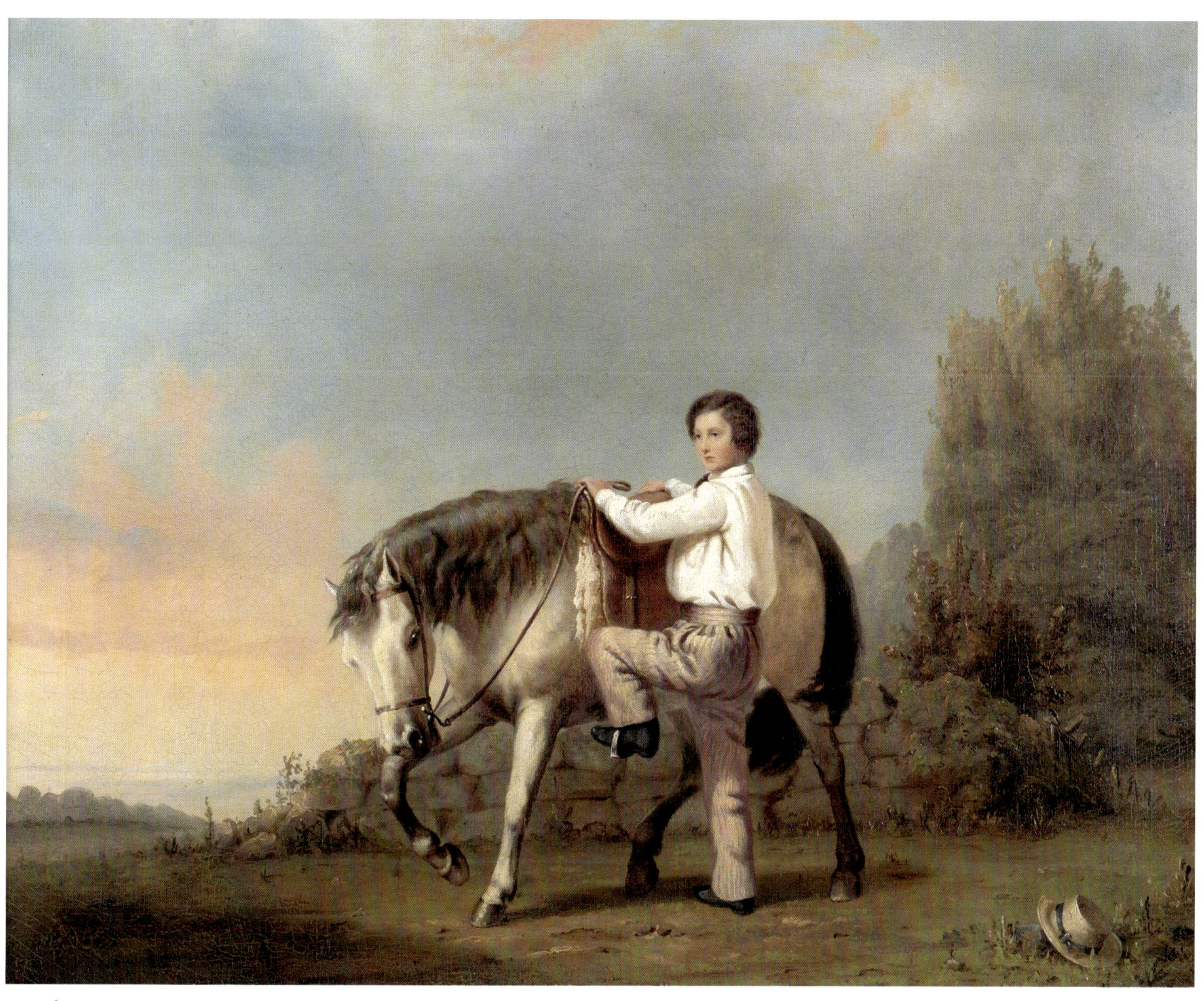

NO. 63

64
The Post Rider

c. 1850

Oil on canvas

17 x 14 inches (43.2 x 35.6 cm)

Location unknown

Grubar no. 50

PROVENANCE: Am Art-Union, 1850; distributed by lottery to Isaac Stebbins, Chelsea, Massachusetts.

EXHIBITED: Am Art-Union, 1850, no. 349, as The Post Rider.

REFERENCES: Register, Works of Art: 1848–1851, reel 2, September 12, 1850, price of $25, unframed, reel 2; Examining Committee Minutes, reel 3, September 17, 1850, recommends purchasing for $25; Committee of Management, September 19, 1850, reel 1, vol. 3, agrees to purchase The Post Rider for $25, *Am Art-Union Papers. Am Art-Union Bulletin* (December 31, 1850), p.175, no. 349. *New York Tribune*, December 16, 1850, p. 8, no. 349. *New York Herald*, December 17, 1850, p. 3, no. 349, and December 21, 1850, p. 5, no. 349. *New York Tribune*, December 21, 1850, p. 5, no. 349, lists it and provides provenance. Cowdrey 1953, 2, p. 295, gives dimensions.

This was the sixth and smallest of Ranney's works purchased in 1850 by the American Art-Union. The Art-Union's December *Bulletin* described the picture as "a man on horseback, riding through the snow, and among bleak and wild hills." (See cat. no. 65 for more complete information.) LB

65
The Express Rider

1850–1857

Oil on canvas

16 1/2 x 13 1/2 inches (41.9 x 34.3 cm)

Signed, lower left: W. Ranney

Location unknown

Grubar no. 50

PROVENANCE: (Fridenberg Gallery, New York); (sale, Possibly Savoy Art and Auction Galleries, New York); (Parke Bernet, New York, January 11 and 12, 1950, sale no. 1115, lot 352, as Pony-Express Rider, sold for $100); Louis Oakes, Greenville, Maine; Gerald D. Hamilton, Bingham, Maine, by 1962; Christopher L. Huntington, Mt. Vernon, Maine, by 1966; (sale, Parke Bernet, New York, October 24, 1968, pp. 24–25, lot. 43 as The Express Rider and illus.); (sale, Sotheby's, New York, December 4, 1986, lot. no. 111, as The Express Rider, property of a New England collector).

EXHIBITED: Erich-Newhouse Galleries, New York, *Early American Genre Paintings: Third Annual Exhibition*, December 19, 1934–January 5, 1935, n.p., lists it.

REFERENCE: Christopher Huntington, letters, December 26, 1966, January 13, 1967, and November 9, 1995, Ranney archives, discusses provenance.

The only visual source for this now unlocated work is an old, undated black-and-white photograph. It shows a lone mailman on horseback, called in the eighteenth and nineteenth centuries either a post or express rider, framed and illuminated by a dramatic sky, his isolation pictorially suggested by the stark and barren landscape. Ranney expresses the urgency and determination of the effort to deliver the mail both by delineating the man's scarf as though soaring in the wind behind the rider and by depicting the neck of the airborne galloping horse as tensely extended.

Synonymous with speed, the fastest riders could cover about twelve miles an hour. With the introduction of the electric telegraph in the mid-1840s, however, the express riders began to lose their "preeminent position in the transmission of information relating to commerce and public affairs."[1] As a result, when Ranney recorded this subject in 1850, the important role held by these early mailmen in everyday life had begun to wane, and they were already becoming romantic figures of America's past. Even the legendary Pony Express, which tried to introduce fast relay messenger service in 1860 (years after Ranney painted this picture) to carry mail from Missouri to California, could not compete and was out of business in less than two years.

This writer has not had the benefit of personally examining this now lost picture and has had to rely on the photograph. Grubar, who had presumably seen the actual painting, assumed it was the work exhibited at the Art-Union in 1850 (see cat. no. 64). Although signed and of about the same dimensions as that picture, it seems unlikely that the sketchily rendered image shown in the photograph would have met the standards of finish generally demanded by the Art-Union, particularly when compared with the other works by Ranney

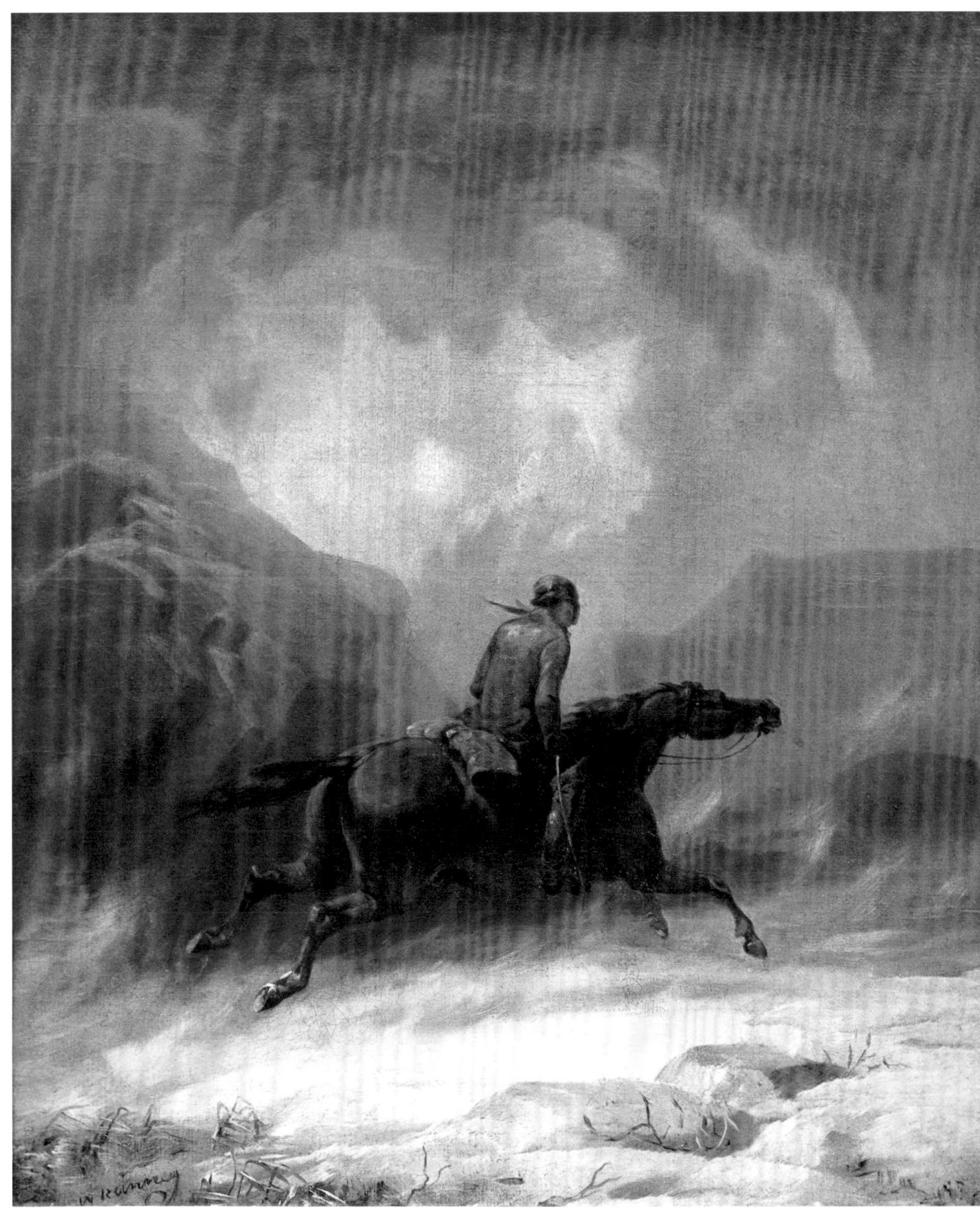

they had purchased. The specifics of the horseman's anatomical features and details of the clothing are unusually vague, and the horse is uncharacteristically ill-conceived. Because of these stylistic inconsistencies, it is doubtful that this is the painting that was shown at the Art-Union, although it does pictorially match the contemporary description (see cat. no. 64) of that picture. Furthermore, most twentieth-century references use the title *The Express Rider,* suggesting it could be the lost painting of that title which remained in Ranney's studio until his death. It was sold in the Ranney Fund sale (lot 138) to Nason Collins for twelve dollars. L B

1. Richard R. John, *Spreading the News: The American Postal System from Franklin to Morse* (Cambridge: Harvard University Press, 1995), p. vii.

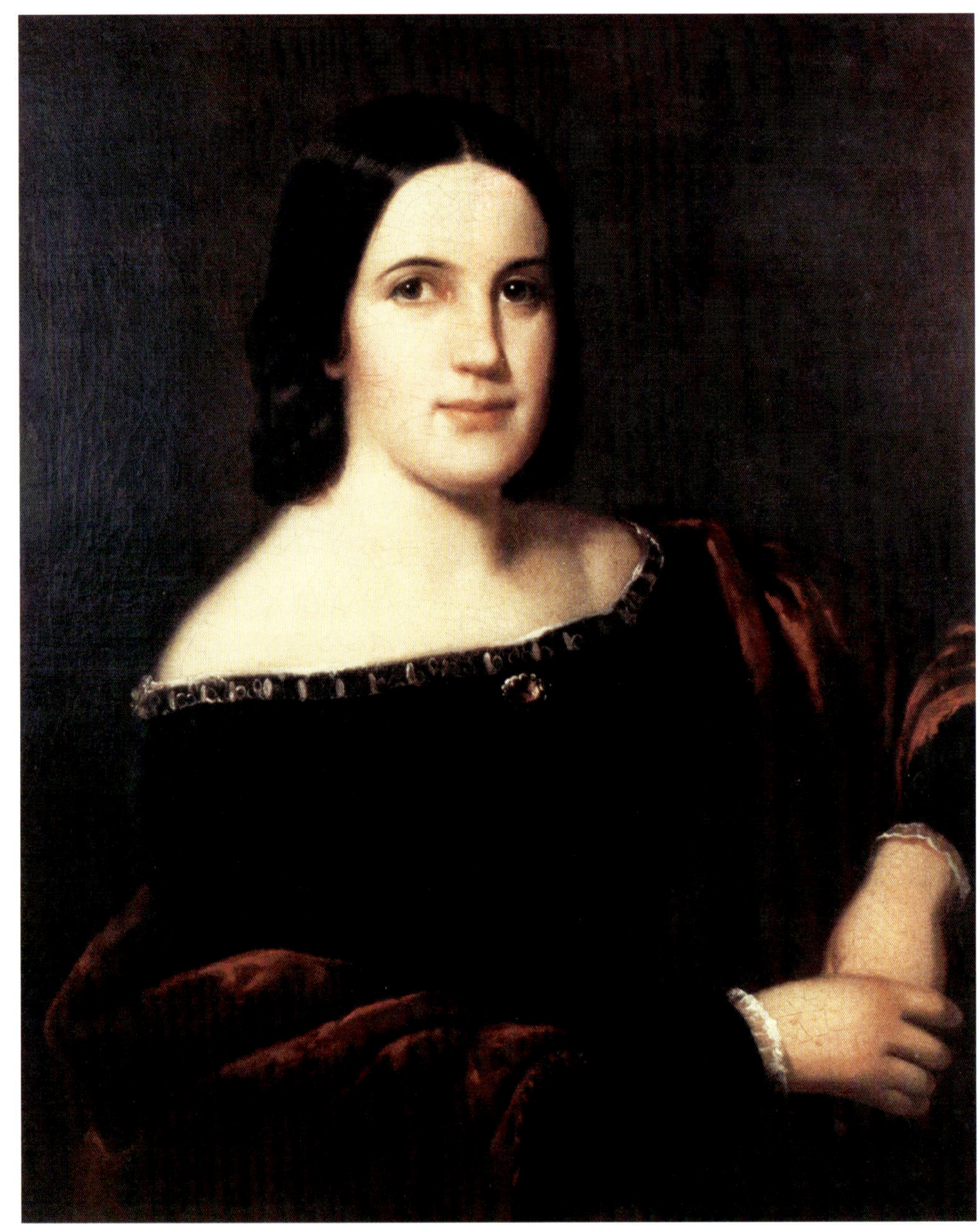

NO. 66

66*

Portrait of Margaret Ranney

c. 1850

Oil on canvas

30 x 25 1/2 inches
(76.2 x 64.8 cm)

Cromwell Historical
Society, Cromwell,
Connecticut

Grubar no. 52

PROVENANCE: Descended in the artist's family to his grandson Claude J. Ranney (1883–1971), Malvern, Pennsylvania, his daughter, Elizabeth R. Moran, Paoli, Pennsylvania, by 1971–1999.

EXHIBITED: Chadds Ford, 1991, cat. no. 13.

REFERENCE: Thistlethwaite 1991, p. 17, discusses painting.

In his few known formal portraits such as the 1839 *Portrait of a Young Man* (cat. no. 4) or the slightly later portrait *Ambrose Jordan Clark* (cat. no. 63), Ranney creates a rather fully developed setting filled with various details, which identify the sitter's interests. In this straightforward and unassuming portrait, one of two portrayals (see cat. no. 67) of his wife Margaret (1819–1903), Ranney presents her matter-of-factly, as though in a studio, set against a nondescript mottled brown background. She is seated in a relaxed pose and gazes amicably at the viewer. In a palette dominated by reds and browns, recalling Ranney's portrait of his sister (cat. no. 5) painted a decade earlier, he depicts Margaret Ranney wearing a long-sleeved black gown trimmed with lace at the neckline and sleeves, an amber brooch at her throat, the whole further accessorized by a red velvet shawl.

The Ranneys were married in New York in 1848 and had two children. According to their grandson Claude J. Ranney, who inherited this picture, Mrs. Ranney was well read and could quote Shakespeare and the Bible.[1] She was born Margaret Agnes O'Sullivan in Cork, Ireland, on January 7, 1819. Her father was an ironmaster who died in 1845.[2] Her death certificate of August 19, 1903, indicates she had lived in New Jersey for fifty-seven years, or since about 1846. It is not known just when she arrived in the United States. For various reasons—ongoing political unrest, economic depressions, and general discontent under British rule—large numbers of Irish had been emigrating throughout the nineteenth century. It is possible she was part of the massive wave of people who fled their homeland in response to the potato famine which brought more than a million Irish to these shores, beginning in 1845.[3]   LB

1. Copy of notes by Grubar during a visit with Claude J. Ranney, April 19, 1961, p. 2, Ranney archives, and Grubar p. 8.
2. Charles Collard Adams, *Middletown Upper Houses*, (1908: Canaan, New Hampshire, repr. 1983: Phoenix Publishing), p. 298.
3. George Brown Tindall, *America: A Narrative History*, 2nd ed. (New York: W. W. Norton, 1988), vol. 1, p. 475.

Portrait of Margaret Ranney

c. 1850s

Oil on canvas

30 x 25 inches (76.2 x
62.2 cm)

Private collection

Grubar no. 53

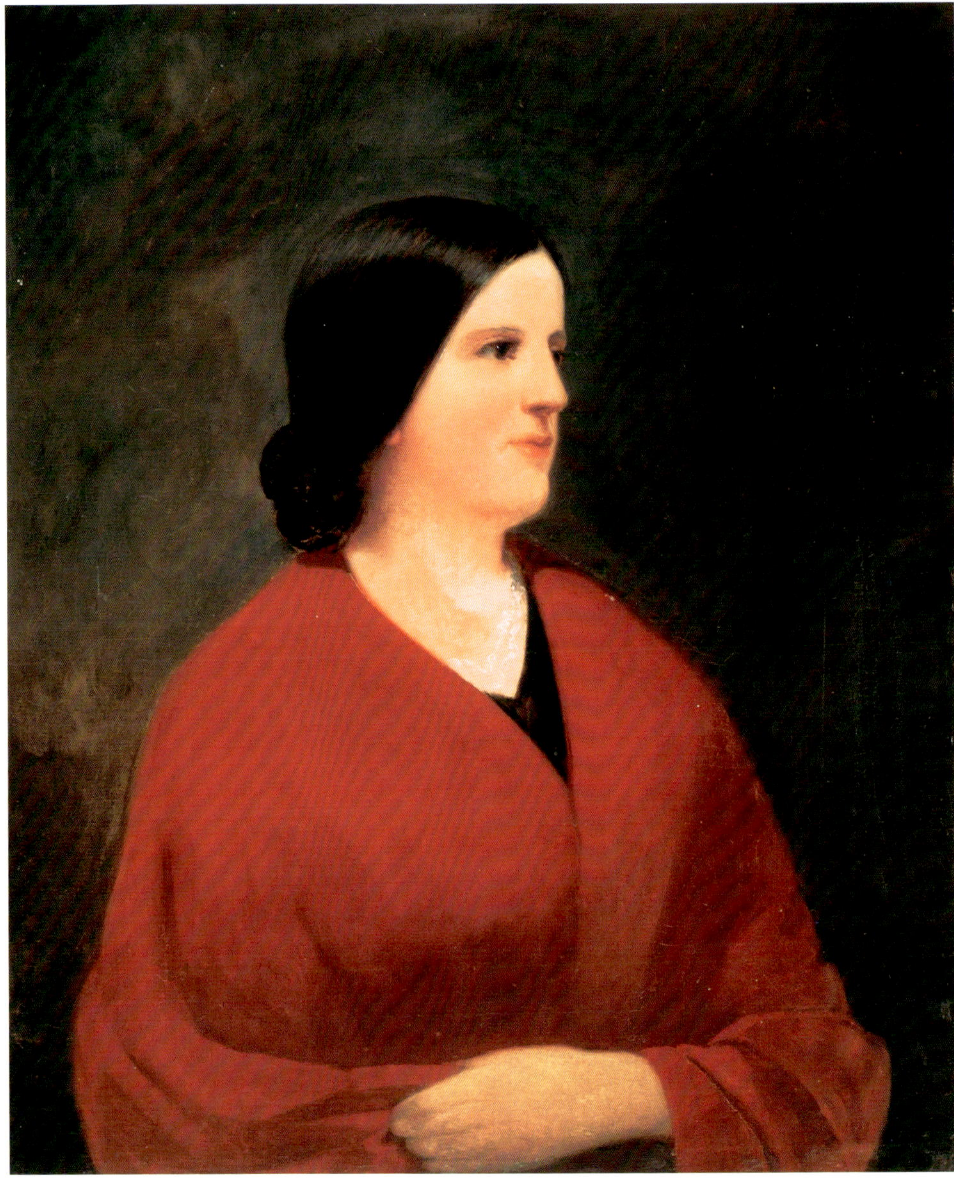

PROVENANCE: Descended in the family to artist's granddaughter Margaret Ranney (d. 1965), Union City, New Jersey; her second cousin Elizabeth R. Moran, Paoli, Pennsylvania by c. 1965.

The visual impact of this second painting of the artist's wife (see cat. no. 66 for biographical details) has been compromised due to overcleaning and paint losses. There is a considerable loss of definition, particularly in the areas around the hand and under the chin. The figure seems to be dwarfed by the expanse of vertical space over her head. While now framed rectangularly, an old photograph shows that at some time the canvas was framed in an oval spandrel, a favorite format of the artist. The earlier enclosure gave the figure greater presence and more intimacy. LB

68
The Pioneers

c. 1850–1857

Oil on canvas

24 x 36 inches (61 x 91.4 cm)

Signed (in another hand), lower right: W. Ranney

Inscribed on stretcher: Brady

Grubar no. 47

Warner Collection of Gulf States Paper Corporation, Tuscaloosa, Alabama

Provenance: James Topham Brady (1815–1869), New York, c. 1859–c.1862; his nephew, Nathaniel Jarvis, by 1862; Brady's daughters to Michael de Sherbinin, New York; (sale, American Art Association, Anderson Galleries, New York, January 27, 1938, p. 36, no. 51, as *Pioneers with Covered Wagons*) (Mortimer Brandt Galleries, New York, for \$325); (McClees Gallery, Philadelphia); J. Clifton Buck; his son-in-law, Claude J. Ranney, Malvern, Pennsylvania, by 1949–1972; his brother, William G. Ranney, Doylestown, Pennsylvania, to 1973 (M. Knoedler and Company, New York, by 1973); Stanley Joselson, Bala Cynwyd, Pennsylvania, to 1990 (Gerald P. Peters Gallery, Santa Fe, 1990–1993).

On loan: Westervelt Warner Museum of American Art, Tuscaloosa, Alabama

Exhibited: Possibly Artists Fund Society, New York, *Catalogue of the Third Annual Exhibition at the Gallery of the Fine Arts*, 1862, cat. no. 72, as *Emigrants on the Prairie* and lists M. Jarvis as owner.

References: Claude Ranney, catalogue sheet, provides provenance and inscription information, Ranney archives. Rena A. Coen, "David's Sabine Women in the Wild West, *Great Plains Quarterly*, vol. 2, no. 2 (Spring 1982), pp. 73–74, discusses. Ayres 1987, p. 89.

By 1850 much had been written in the popular literature about the pioneer life, especially family life, and the experience of moving west on the overland trail. Francis Parkman's famous account, *The Oregon Trail*, had first been serialized in the *Knickerbocker* in 1847, published in book form in 1849, and made for exciting reading. He described many scenes along the road west, but found one train of emigrants from Illinois particularly appealing.

> A multitude of healthy children's faces were peeping out from under the covers of the wagons. Here and there a buxom damsel was seated on horseback, holding over her sunburned face an old umbrella or a parasol. . . . The men, very sober-looking countrymen, stood about their oxen. [1]

Trekking the Oregon Trail was essentially a family business. John C. Fremont had camped with a family of emigrants on his second expedition west in 1845. He was struck by the "fine appearance" of their stock and the prim aspect of their camp. Although it was strange in his estimation "to see one small family travelling alone through such country, so remote from civilization," they seemed naturally connected to this foreign land. They "presented a picture of home beauty that went directly to our hearts."[2]

In Ranney's *Pioneers*, the characters act out their prescribed social roles. The father marches determinedly forward, seeking the goal of some "Promised Land." Since it was generally the restless man's decision to resettle, he is portrayed, rifle in hand, intent on fulfilling and protecting that right of passage. The children and a woman, sheltered from the elements by the wagon's canopy, appear to relish the experience. And the mother, on her sturdy gray horse, appears to cast a long glance over the viewer's shoulder toward her future home. The painting is about that woman's reaction and about pioneer women in a larger sense. It is about the woman's experiencing the alien land she is seeing for the first time and about her hopes for a new home. It is also about the responsibilities that frontier families shared and the woman's role, as much as the man's, in binding the family together and helping the members adapt to the process of moving and to what lay ahead. Ranney's pioneer mother is, as Linda Ayres (1987) has observed, a hint above the mere mortal pioneer woman. She is a prairie Madonna. Her broad, approving visage, her radiant countenance and graceful pose provide the central feminine presence for what Ayres finds reminiscent of a biblical Rest on the Flight into Egypt. In 1850, the year that Ranney's first child, William, was born and the year that the largest number of emigrants would move west along the overland trail (estimated at 55,000), the artist had artfully connected personal and national milestones under the rubric of divine sanction.

In addition to being a tribute to motherhood and Manifest Destiny, this painting exudes a quality of sensate pleasure. The atmospheric clarity and sun-dappled highlights establish a feeling of joy and optimism. Mrs. Thomas Farnham, wife of one of the early writers of overland trail guides, waxed eloquently in 1845 about her recollection of a spring morning on the Illinois prairies, that "vast ocean, teeming with life;—redolent of sweet odors!"

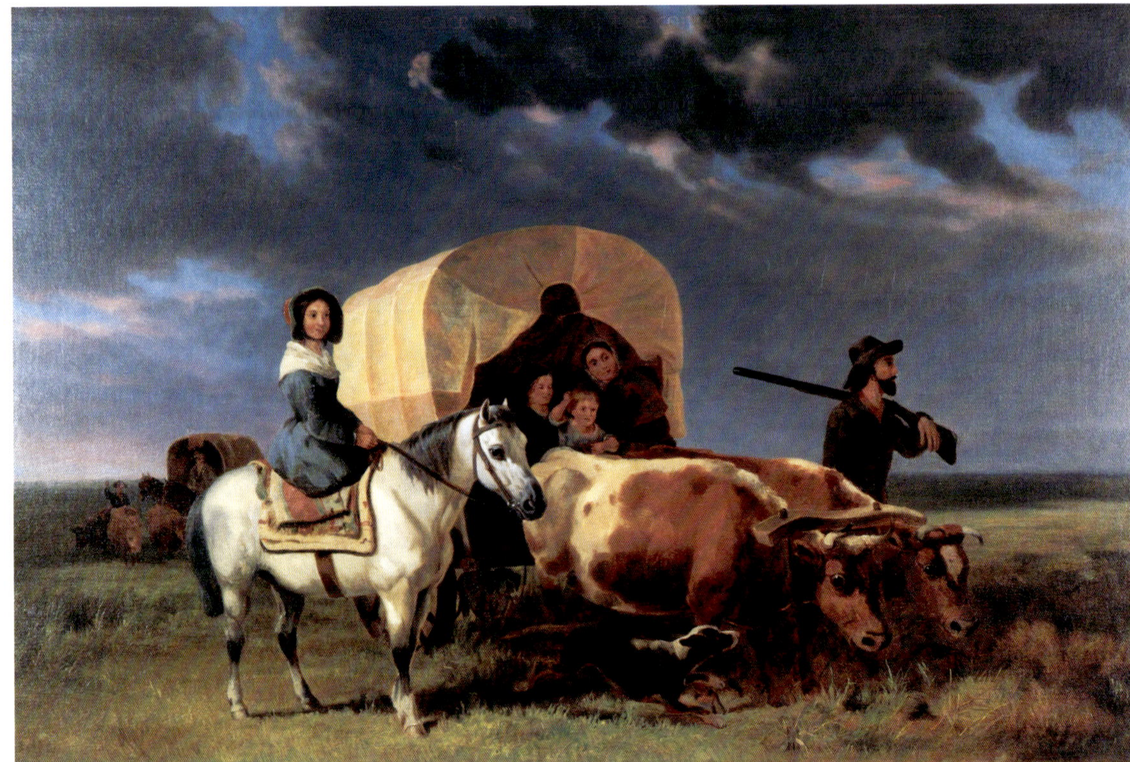

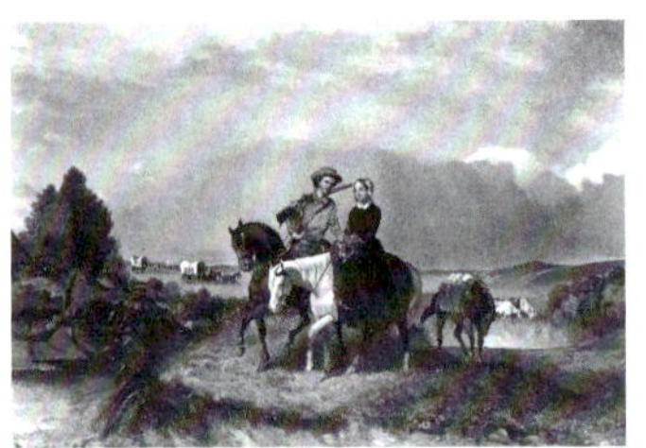

Fig 68.1
Betrothal on the Plains,
attributed to John Mix
Stanley (1814–1872), c. 1850.
Oil on canvas. Location
unknown. Photograph cour-
tesy of the Buffalo Bill
Historical Center, Cody
Wyoming.

I wish I could find language that would convey to the mind of the reader an adequate idea of the deep joy which the soul drinks in from every feature of this wonderful scene! If he could stand where I have often stood when the rosy clouds were piled against the eastern sky, and the soft, tremulous light was streaming aslant the dewy grass, while not a sound of life broke on the ear . . . so much in harmony with the whole of visible nature, he would feel one of the charms which binds the hearts of the sons and daughters of this land.[3]

Ranney was not alone in his celebration of youth, family unity, and the westward migration. One of the country's most highly touted illustrators and the artist who embellished the first edition of Parkman's *Oregon Trail* (1849), Felix O. C. Darley, articulated the same message in his pictorial tribute *Emigrants Crossing the Plains.* Here, as in Ranney's *Pioneers,* the family is pictured together as not just travelers embarking on a physical journey but indeed as exemplars of a spiritual one that is promising, uplifting, and unifying.

Another contemporary artist, John Mix Stanley, painted at least one recollection of an 1846 trip he took on the Santa Fe Trail, which has been titled *Betrothal on the Plains* (Fig. 68.1). There Stanley brought to center stage the affectionate interplay of a young emigrant couple. Such images of pioneers moving west left no doubt in the American mind about the sanctity that family harmony and the westward movement shared.

According to Ranney's grandson Claude J. Ranney, *The Pioneers* did not leave the artist's possession until after his death. This, however, cannot be substantiated. The picture was first in the possession of the lawyer and art patron, James Topham Brady, who delivered a lecture on American art to help promote the Ranney Fund sale in 1859 to raise money for Ranney's widow and her children. PHH

1. Francis Parkman, *The Oregon Trail* (1849; Boston: Ginn and Company, 1910), pp. 5–6.
2. John C. Fremont, "Captain Fremont Reports," *Niles' National Register* (September 20, 1845), p. 44.
3. Mrs. Thomas J. Farnham, "Life in the Prairie Land," *United States Magazine and Democratic Review,* vol. 17, no. 87 (September 1845), p. 222.

102

69
Halt on the Prairie

c. 1850-1857

Oil on paper, mounted on paperboard

8 1/2 x 14 1/2 inches (21.6 x 36.8 cm)

Joslyn Art Museum, Omaha. Bequest of Mrs. John F. Merriam, 1998.25

Grubar no. 49

PROVENANCE: (Victor Spark, New York, by 1951) (M. Knoedler and Company, New York, 1951–1953, as Halt on the Prairie) Mr. and Mrs. John F. Merriam, Omaha, Nebraska, by 1953; Mrs. John F. Merriam, to 1998.

REFERENCE: Perry T. Rathbone, *Westward the Way: The Character and Development of the Louisiana Territory as Seen by Artists and Writers of the Nineteenth Century* (St. Louis: City Art Museum, 1954), pp. 182 and 268, titles it Caravan on the Prairies, provides period description of construction of wagons and cites provenance.

Grubar notes that this small, fluidly painted, variously titled sketch is probably a study for a larger work. Its wagon train subject matter, however, does not relate to Ranney's similarly titled work of 1850 (cat. no. 54). Grubar further suggests that it may be Ranney's *Sketch for Picture, Halt on the Prairie*, which was sold to someone by the name of Wood[1] for eight dollars in the Ranney Fund sale (lot 93). If that is true and the work was in Ranney's studio until his death in 1857, it seems equally likely that it was painted after 1850, the date Grubar assigned to it. Possibly it is a preliminary idea related to Ranney's last monumental western scene, *Halt on the Plains* (cat. no. 138) of 1857. LB

1. See cat. no. 50 for information on Wood.

NO. 69

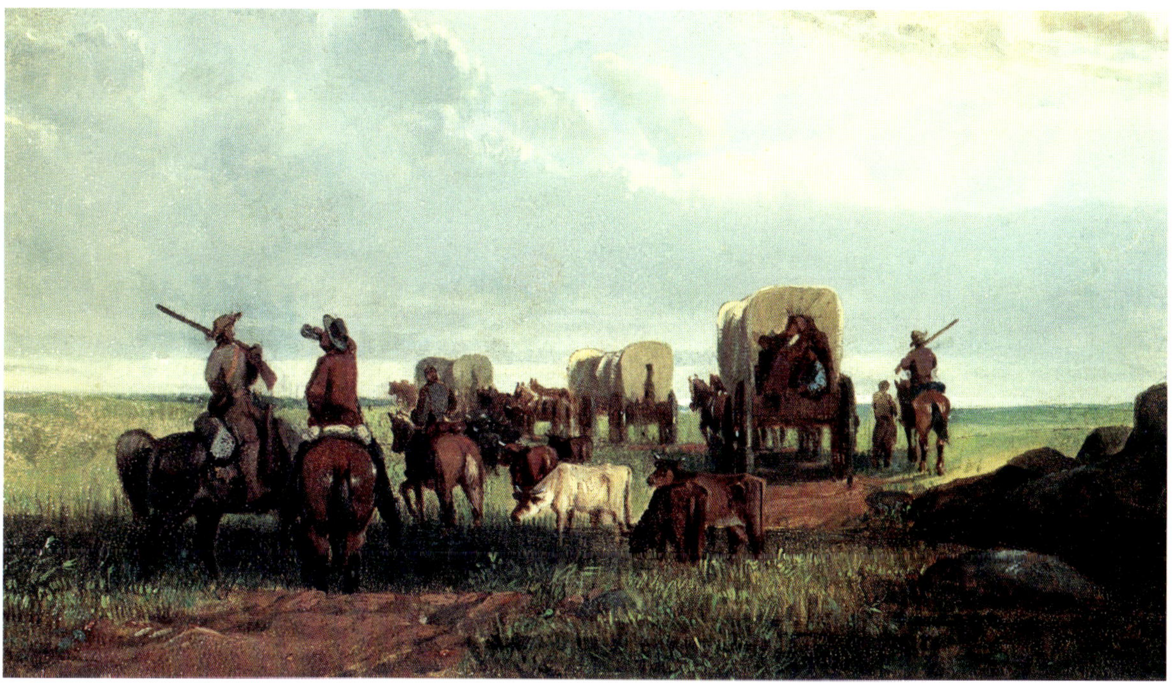

70*
Hunters at the Well

1851

Oil on canvas

20 x 24 3/4 inches
(50.8 x 62.9 cm)

Signed and dated,
lower left:
W. Ranney/51

Carnegie Museum of
Art, Pittsburgh.
Howard N. Eavenson
Memorial Fund for the
Howard N. Eavenson
Americana Collection,
1972

Grubar no. 59, as The
Old Oaken Bucket *

PROVENANCE: (John P. Ridner, New York, 1851) Am Art-Union, 1852; Marshall O. Roberts (1814–1880), New York, by 1856; his widow (sale, Fifth Avenue Art Galleries, New York, *Executors' Sale . . . of the Late Marshall O. Roberts*, January 19, 20, and 21, 1897, lot 237, p. 69, as The Sportsman's Halt at the Well, for $42); (John Levy Galleries, New York, 1951–1953) (M. Knoedler and Company, New York, 1953–1972, as Hunter's Pause at the Well.)*

EXHIBITED: Chadds Ford 1991, cat. no. 17.

REFERENCES: John P. Ridner to Andrew Warner, corresponding secretary, November 13, 1851, Letters from Artists, January 1, 1851–December 29, 1851, reel 7, p. 426, Am Art-Union Papers, offered for sale as *Hunters at the Well* by Wm. Ranney for $100; and Register, Works of Art 1848–1851, reel 2, reg. no. 3352, Am Art-Union Papers, as *Hunters at the Well*, W. Ranney, J. P. Ridner, $100 (unframed), Apr 29/52. *Crayon*, vol. 3 (August 1856), p. 249, lists it as *The Old Oaken Bucket* in the collection of Marshall O. Roberts. Tuckerman 1867, pp. 432 and 626, as *The Old Oaken Bucket* in Roberts collection. Edward Strahan [Earl Shinn], ed., *Art Treasures in America* (Philadelphia: George Barrie, 1880), vol. 2, p. 16, as *The Sportsmen's Halt at the Well* in the Collection of Mrs. Marshall O. Roberts. Thistlethwaite 1991, p. 29, no. 17, illus. pp. 30, 32, discusses it. *American Paintings and Sculpture to 1945 in the Carnegie Museum of Art* (New York: Hudson Hills Press, 1992), pp. 390–391, catalogued.

In this richly colored genre scene, full of realistic details, Ranney portrays a boy and a man interrupting their outing to quench their thirst at a country well. The man, having removed his hat and placed it along with his rifle and pouch on the ground, eagerly tilts the bucket of water to his mouth. As though patiently awaiting his turn, the boy leans on the side of the well and watches, holding his straw hat in one hand and, in the other, the results of the day's hunt—a beige rabbit and a fluffy-tailed gray squirrel. Each of the dogs seemingly echoes the role played by its owner in the picture: one slurps from a puddle of water on the ground while the other stands quietly nearby. In the background, the resting cow and the shed indicate that this is a farm setting. Characteristically, Ranney focuses light on the central foreground to emphasize the main action of this story. He enhances that emphasis by visually isolating each figure—the boy framed by the shed, and the man silhouetted against the sky.

In his re-creation of this ordinary event, Ranney responded to the pervasive mid-century taste for recognizable and distinctively American subject matter, the simple stories which helped to define national character. Ralph Waldo Emerson was one of many writers who extolled Americans to "embrace the common . . . and sit at the feet of the familiar."[1]

Similar genre themes by Ranney's contemporaries were often represented in the National Academy and Art-Union exhibitions during this period. Ranney's friend, the Long Island artist William Sidney Mount, for example, painted at least two such subjects in 1848: *The Well by the Wayside* (location unknown) and *At the Well* or *Sportsman at the Well* (New Britain Museum of American Art, Connecticut). Like Ranney's work, *At the Well* is essentially a hunting scene, although without the detail of the dead animals. It shows a mustached man at a well, his gun propped up by his side, preparing to drink from the bucket as his dog reclines nearby.

For many years, in spite of the obvious sporting imagery, this painting was titled *The Old Oaken Bucket*. It was thought that Ranney's choice of subject had been inspired by the similarly titled poem written by Samuel Woodworth in 1818 and later set to music by Frederick Smith. Woodworth's plaintive lyrics lamenting the lost days of youth and romanticizing the well of his childhood and its sweet waters became one of the country's most popular songs. Indeed, as early as 1856, when the canvas is first reported in the collection of Marshall O. Roberts, Ranney's painting was titled *The Old Oaken Bucket*, and in the twentieth century was published as such by Grubar and by the Carnegie Museum of Art. Its title has now been changed.

Grubar himself expressed uncertainty over the connection of Ranney's painting and Woodworth's poem. Because of the recent discovery of the 1851 letter from John P. Ridner to the American Art-Union, which lists a Ranney painting *Hunters at the Well*, it now seems likely that there indeed was no connection, and that

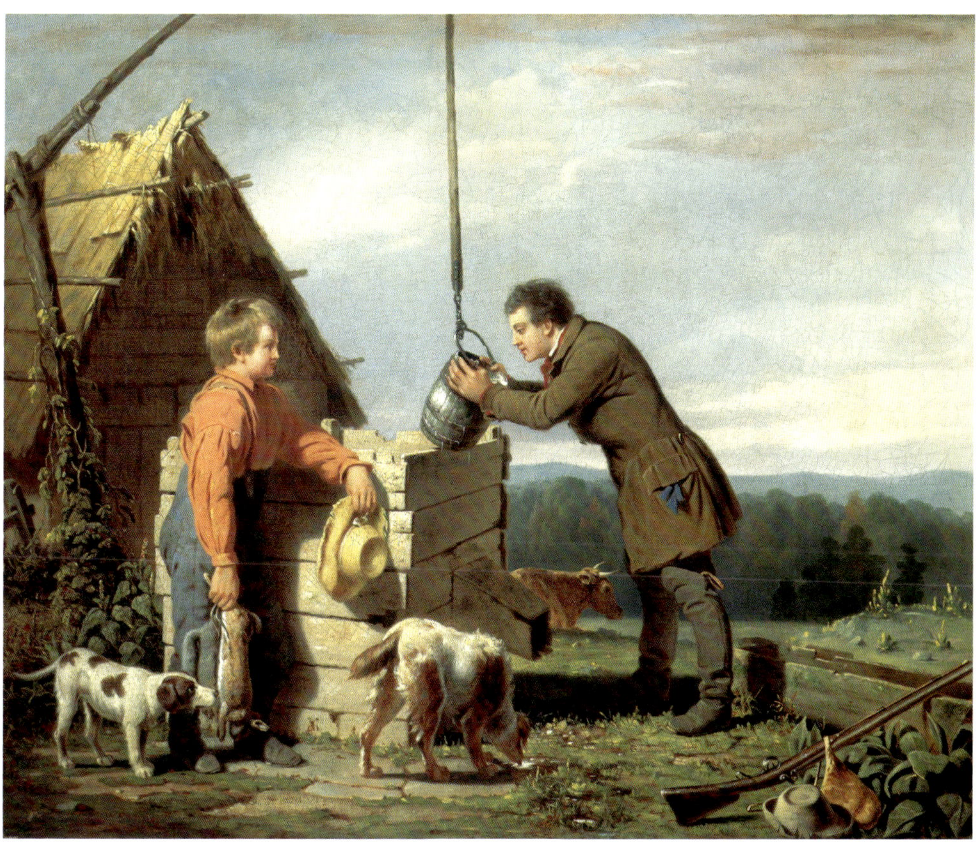

Ranney provided one of his characteristic descriptive titles. Ridner, who offered the painting to the Art-Union for one hundred dollars, was a New York merchant and at that time a member of the Art-Union's Committee of Management. Art-Union records indicate that the painting was purchased on April 29, 1852. Unfortunately, in 1852 the New York Supreme Court ruled the Art-Union's lottery system illegal, forcing it to discontinue its operations, and all the paintings in its possession were sold later that year at auction rather than distributed by lottery. According to the *New York Daily Times* report of the sale, "several other pictures, the property of individuals, were disposed of."[2] Unlike those works purchased and itemized for the 1851 distribution and sold in the 1852 auction, a complete detailed list of those miscellaneous items may not exist.[3]

In any case, by the time Roberts's collection was published in 1880, perhaps the popularity of the song had waned, because the title was listed as *The Sportsmen's Halt at the Well*, closer to Ranney's original. It was similarly listed in Roberts's 1897 estate sale. In the twentieth century it was called *The Hunters Pause at the Well*. A small unlocated drawing entitled *At the Well* (cat. no. D84) was in the collection of a James M. Burt in 1887 and may be related.[4] LB

* It should be noted that Grubar relied on Knoedler's inaccurate dimensions of 14 1/2 x 19 1/4 inches.

1. Quoted in Patricia Hills, *The Painters' America: Rural and Urban Life, 1810–1910* (New York: Praeger Publishers, 1974), p. 24, from Emerson's Phi Beta Kappa address delivered at Harvard College on August 31, 1837. Hills provides a good discussion of nationalism in art of this period.
2. *New York Daily Times*, December 18, 1852, p. 6.
3. There are also no Ranney paintings listed in the American Art-Union's *First Annual Sale of Paintings by American and Resident Artists, Exclusively*, September 15–December 15, 1853.
4. See Moore's Auction Galleries, New York, *Catalogue of the Private Collection Belonging to Mr. James M. Burt of Brooklyn*, November 16, 17 and 18, 1887, lot 186, p. 13.

71
The Scouting Party

1851

Oil on canvas

22 x 36 inches (55.8 x 91.4 cm)

Signed and dated, lower center: W. Ranney / 1851

Carmen Thyssen-Bornemisza Collection on loan at the Museo Thyssen-Bornemisza, Madrid

Grubar no. 60

Fig 71.1
The Scouting Party, engraved by James H. Richardson. Library Company of Philadelphia.

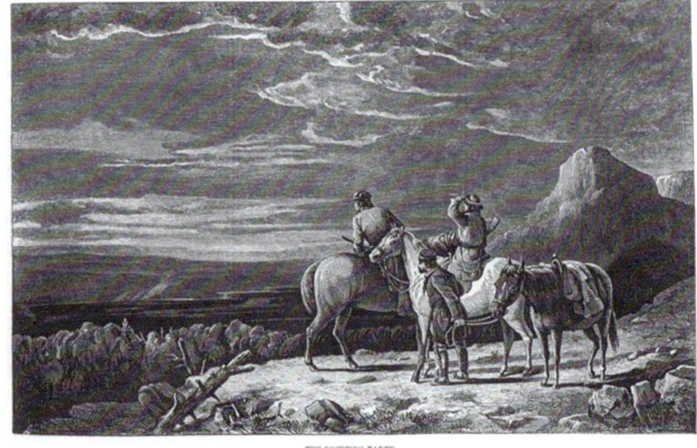

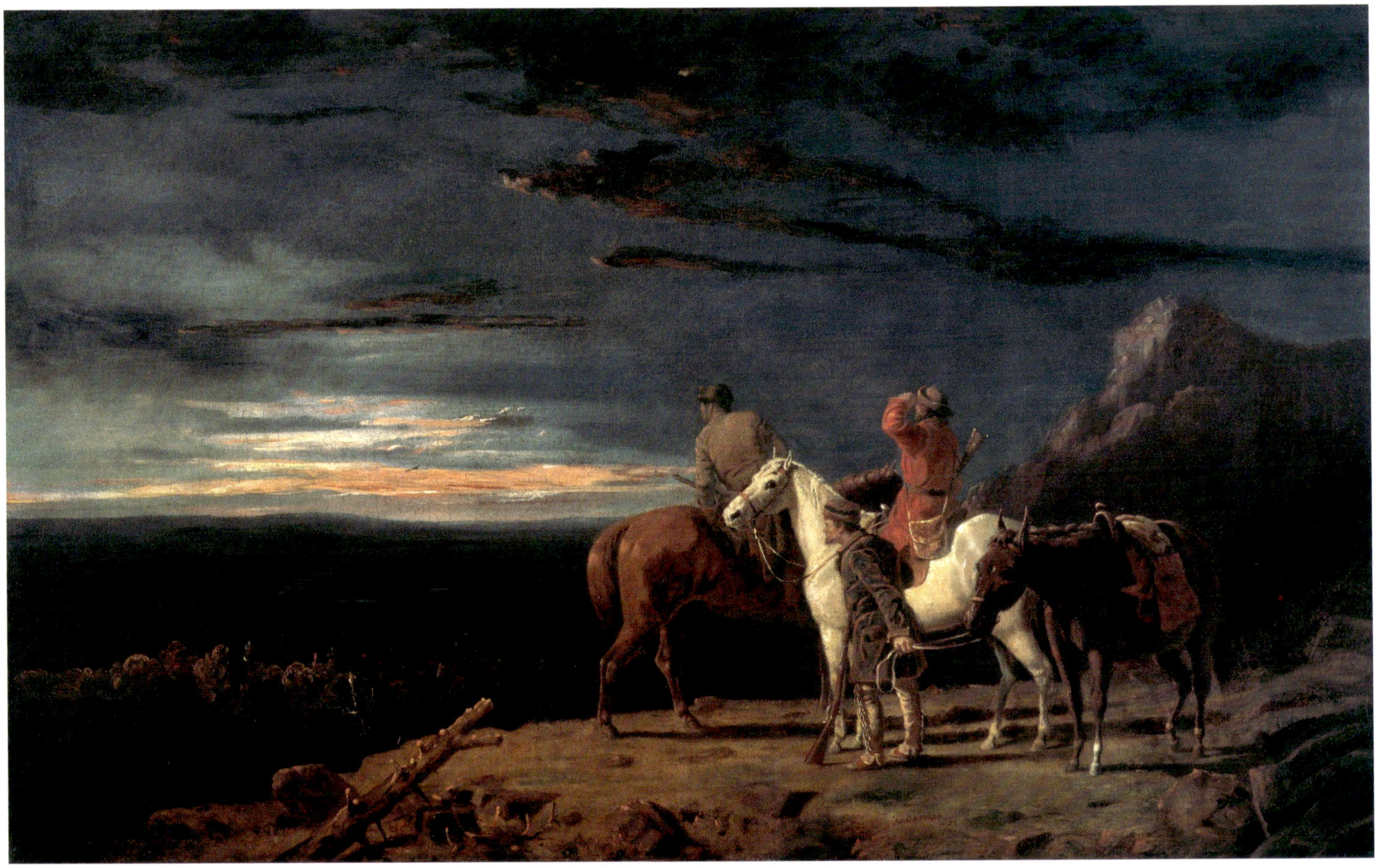

NO. 71

Wood engraving: [James H.] Richardson from a drawing by [William R.] Miller, 4 1/2 x 7 1/4 inches (11.4 x 18.4 cm). Included in Am Art-Union *Bulletin* (September 1, 1851), p. 89. Inscribed: The Scouting Party./Drawn on wood by Miller, from the original by Ranney, and engraved by Richardson.

Provenance: Am Art-Union, 1851–1852 (American Art-Union sale, December 15, 16 and 17, 1852, no. 228, sold for $95) J. Yeoman, by 1852; Fred N. Maloof, Washington, D.C.; (M. Knoedler and Company, New York, by 1962, as Scouts); National Cowboy Hall of Fame and Western Heritage Center, Oklahoma City by 1973; Private collection, St. Louis; Richard Manoogian, Detroit; (Andrew Crispo Gallery, New York to 1980) Thyssen-Bornemisza Collection, by 1980.

On loan: Museo Thyssen-Bornemisza, Madrid.

Exhibited: NAD, 1851, no. 201 as *The Scouting Party*; Am Art-Union, 1851, no. 252, and 1852, no. 228 as *The Scouting Party*. Fort Worth, 1988, p. 193, lists in private collection.

References: *Albion* 10, (April 19, 1851), p. 189, calls it "a more ambitious attempt than those usually undertaken by this artist, being a sunset piece with strong effects of light and shade." Am Art-Union, Management Committee Minutes, 1839–1855, June 19, 1851, reel 1, Am Art-Union Papers, reported that the painting was purchased from the NAD for $100. Am Art-Union *Bulletin* (September 1, 1851) mentions and reproduces woodcut engraving, p. 85, p. 89, illus., and *Supplementary Bulletin* (December 1, 1852), p. 5, no. 228 lists and describes it (quoted below), and p. 8, no. 469, lists woodcut; *Catalogue of Pictures and Other Works of Art. To be sold at Auction by David Austen, Jr. at the Gallery, 497 Broadway, on . . . [15th, 16th and 17th] December 1852 . . .* , p. 9, no. 228, lists painting, and p. 15, no. 1, lists woodcut. *New York Evening Post*, December 16, 1852, p. 2, reports on results of sale. *New York Tribune*, December 17, 1852, p. 3, notes buyer. *New York Herald*, December 17, 1852, p. 7, as sold to J. Yeoman for $95. Cowdrey 1943, 2, p. 89, no. 201, as for sale. Cowdrey 1953, 2, p. 295, no. 228, provides description and provenance. Frank Getlein, *The Lure of the Great West: Painters from Catlin to Russell* (Waukesha, Wisconsin: Country Beautiful, 1973), pp. 116–117, provides provenance. Ayres 1988, pp. 98-99, discusses and illus. fig. 62. Elizabeth Garrity Ellis, in Barbara Novak, *The Thyssen-Bornemisza Collection: Nineteenth Century American Painting* (London: Philip Wilson Publishers for Sotheby's Publications, 1986), pp. 196–197, discusses and illustrates.

Early in his career, when he first chose to add western subjects to his work, Ranney seems to have made a conscious decision not to paint Indians. No doubt this decision was reached on practical grounds. Unlike George Catlin or Alfred Jacob Miller, he had no real experience among native peoples. Unlike Catlin, Charles Deas, and John Mix Stanley, he made no attempt to assemble an Indian gallery and record their likenesses and ways of life. In his paintings, the Indian was afforded only a hint of presence and then, almost exclusively, he appeared as a phantom foe.

By 1851, the year that Ranney painted *The Scouting Party*, Indian subjects in American art were rather less pervasive than in previous decades. Despite the fact that Stanley's Indian Gallery opened to considerable fanfare at the Smithsonian Institution in Washington early the next year and was regarded as an exercise in national pride, public attention had been on the wane since the 1840s.[1] A review of Stanley's display that appeared in the Washington press at the time highlighted 4 paintings out of 130 works as deserving special mention. One was a dramatic equestrian portrait of 1846 of *Black Knife, An Apache Warrior* (Smithsonian American Art Museum), one was a landscape *View on the Gila River* (an 1855 version hangs in the Phoenix Art Museum), and two works represented "the chase of the trapper by the Indians, and his successful escape."[2] So even in the midst of a gallery almost exclusively filled with paintings of Indians, it was two pictorial episodes about a mountain man that won critical notice.

Although in *The Scouting Party* Ranney's dramatic focus is on Indians, in reality the Indians are nowhere to be seen. Only some smoke from distant fires suggests their proximity. Nonetheless, the smoke is enough to throw the scene into confusion, as three trappers twist and strain to interpret the diaphanous signal. One has even dismounted, attempting to gain a better perspective on the situation. They are spotlighted on a small promontory and somewhat trapped there by their uncertainty as well as the rocky escarpment to the right and the fallen tree that provides a potential impediment on the left. Clouds swirl above them, and the valley below is dark and ominous.

Scenes like this filled the literature of the day. Washington Irving had described such incidents as commonplace on the western prairies in the 1830s. The question whether such signs portended friend or foe was raised nearly on a daily basis, with travelers "traversing these perilous wastes."[3] Irving's novel *The*

Adventures of Captain Booneville of 1837 is said to have inspired Ranney's contemporary Alvan Fisher to paint a similar episode in 1842, *Trappers Discover Smoke of an Indian Camp* (Mead Museum, Amherst College, Williamstown, Massachusetts).[4] Fisher's trappers respond to the situation in a similar way to Ranney's. One has dismounted, perhaps in some way feeling he can better reconnoiter. Although Fisher's men look up the hill and Ranney surveys the scene from above, they are both alike in being stopped in their tracks and frozen in anticipation. They are cast equally in incertitude and vulnerability.

The Scouting Party was exhibited at the National Academy of Design and the American Art-Union in 1851, and it appeared in the Art-Union's final sale the following year. At the last venue it was described as "a party of trappers with their horses on a high bluff watching the movements of Indians who are betrayed by fires in the prairie below."

Although there are no evident references in the Ranney painting to the gold fields of the distant Sierras, these scouts may well be headed for California. The smoke, the Indians, and the ominous darkened valley are merely impediments to the larger goal of the country's quest for the riches of California. The year before, Ranney's friend William Sidney Mount had painted a tongue-in-cheek account of gold fever, *California News*, 1850 (Museums at Stony Brook, New York), in which he made a careful and revealing study of human nature in its most fatuous manifestation, as tested by anticipation of future wealth. Farther from home, an American sculptor living in Florence, Hiram Powers, was working on his polished marble personification of *California* 1850 (Metropolitan Museum of Art, New York) at this time. The expatriate artist described his work in progress as

> an Indian figure surrounded with pearls and precious stones. A kirtle surrounds her waist, and falls with a feather fringe down to just above the knee. The kirtle is ornamented with Indian embroidery, with tracings of gold, and her sandals are tied with golden strings. At her side stands an inverted cornucopia, from which is issuing at her feet lumps and grains of native gold, to which she points with her left hand, which holds the divining rod. With her right hand she conceals behind her a cluster of thorns.[5]

In both the Mount painting and the Powers sculpture, the road to El Dorado, while glorious to imagine as a potential realization, lay obstructed by hidden impediments—the foible of errant cupidity that might lead one to ruin or the metaphorical thorns that may inevitably savage ideal beauty. For Ranney's scouts, though they can see the hint of gold in the sky before them, their path is uncertain, and their vulnerability before nature's force is omnipresent. PHH

1. Brian W. Dippie, *Catlin and His Contemporaries: The Politics of Patronage* (Lincoln: University of Nebraska Press, 1990), p. 282. Elwood Perry in *The Image of the Indian and the Black Man in American Art: 1590–1900* (New York: George Braziller, 1974), p. 104, suggests that national attention on abolition and slave-related issues accounted for much of the diminished stature of Indians as subjects for American art in the 1850s.

2. "Indian Gallery of Paintings," Washington *National Intelligencer,* February 23, 1852, p. 4. For a listing of these four paintings, see John M. Stanley, *Catalogue of Portraits of North American Indians, with Sketches of Scenery, etc.* (Washington, D. C.: Thomas McGill, 1853), nos. 98, 99, 59, and 60.

3. Washington Irving, *A Tour on the Prairies* (London: John Murray, 1837), pp. 155–156.

4. Irving, *The Adventures of Captain Bonneville, U.S.A., in the Rocky Mountains and the Far West* (Paris, 1837). See Fred Barry Adelson, "*Alvan Fisher (1792–1863): Pioneer in American Landscape Painting,*" Ph. D. diss., Columbia University, 1982, pp. 523-524.

5. "Literature, Science, Art, Personal Movements, etc.," *Harper's Monthly* 3 (June 1851), p. 136. The finished statue was considerably changed. See Richard P. Wunder, *Hiram Powers: Vermont Sculptor, 1805–1873* (Newark: University of Delaware Press, 1991), 2, pp. 124–126.

72
Dogs in Repose

c. 1851

Oil on canvas

Location unknown

PROVENANCE: (John P. Ridner, New York, by 1851) Am Art-Union, by 1852.

REFERENCES: John P. Ridner to Andrew Warner, corresponding secretary, November 13, 1851, Letters from Artists, January 1, 1851–December 29, 1851, reel 7, offers Ranney's Dogs in Repose for $25; and Register, Works of Art 1848–1851, reel 2, no. 3355, $25 (unframed) to JPR, and to JPR, March 24, 1852, Am Art-Union Papers.

73
Dead Game

c. 1851

Oil on canvas

Location unknown

PROVENANCE: (John P. Ridner, New York, by 1851)

REFERENCES: John P. Ridner to Andrew Warner, corresponding secretary, November 13, 1851, Letters from Artists, January 1, 1851–December 29, 1851, reel 7, offers Ranney's Dead Game for $20, and Register, Works of Art, 1848–1851, reel 2, no. 3356, $20 (unframed) and "re[turned] JPR March 23/52," Am Art-Union Papers.

While no contemporary description of this painting has been located, it may have depicted dead fowls hanging from a nail against a blank background. This kind of trophy theme was especially popular with mid-century American artists, particularly Ranney's friend Arthur F. Tait, who listed several similarly titled subjects in his notebooks beginning in 1853.[1] Ranney's painting was offered by John P. Ridner for sale to the American Art-Union, but according to its register of works of art it apparently was not purchased and was returned to him. LB

1. See "A Checklist of His Works," in Warder H. Cadbury and Henry F. Marsh, *Arthur Fitzwilliam Tait* (Newark: University of Delaware Press, 1986) pp. 124–130.

74[*]
The Wounded Trapper

1852

Oil on canvas

35 x 29 1/4 inches
(88.9 x 74.3 cm)

Signed and dated lower center, W. Ranney.52; and visible above that under infrared light: Wm Ranney

Inscribed on an old paper label affixed to stretcher: From the collection of L. R. Nightingale/Paston House/Elm Hill/Norwich; Artist's Name—Delacroix

Private collection

PROVENANCE: (William, Stevens and Williams, New York) (sale, Henry H. Leeds and Company, New York, October 27, 28, and 29, 1852, no. 79, as Wounded Trapper); possibly B. F. Bush, by 1853; L. R. Nightingale, Norwich, England, c. 1967; unknown dealer (Sotheby Parke Bernet, New York, April 23, 1982, no. 100, as The Fallen Trapper); Harry J. Renker, Sebring, Florida, by c. 1982–1999.

EXHIBITED: Possibly Detroit, Michigan, Firemen's Hall, *Catalogue of Articles on Exhibition at the Gallery of Fine Arts*, February 7, 1853, no. 356 as The Wounded Trapper, lent by B. F. Bush.

REFERENCES: Henry H. Leeds and Company, New York, *Catalogue of William, Stevens and Williams Great Annual Sale . . .* 1852, p. 7, no. 79, describes as "The convulsive grasp of the dying man, and his glazing eyes are extremely well done. The attitude of the horse very spirited"; and gives dimensions as 44 x 36 inches. (The difference in size may be a mistake or framed size. A recent conservation examination revealed that the canvas was not cut down and that Ranney actually expanded his image to the canvas edges as he reworked the composition.) Francis S. Grubar to Sotheby's New York, April 19, 1982, copy, Ranney archives, authenticates painting.

Ranney is generally thought to have avoided the sentimental dramatizations characteristic of the Düsseldorf Academy and the theatricality of the French romantic painters in order to appeal to his American middle-class audience. Even when compared to fellow American artists, he is said to have stood apart as a voice of calm. In his paintings of mountain men, according to Dawn Glanz, he abstained from "the theatrics that give Deas's trappers an aura of Napoleonic heroics and the romanticization that renders [Alfred Jacob] Miller's western characters as exotic as Delacroix's Arabs."[1] The painting *The Wounded Trapper* appears as a clear exception to that claim and probably for several good reasons.

For one thing, Ranney's ties to the country's popular American audience were abruptly severed in 1851, two years before he produced this work. The American Art-Union was, on dubious legal and political grounds, brought to its demise. The concluding Art-Union sale, held in December of 1852, was referred to in the press as "a final act of triumph" amid the profound loss of the "decided prestige it has given to American art."[2] Artists like Ranney viewed this as the end of an era, realizing that no other institution would come forward to replace it and to sponsor an art program that implicitly promised "to do something for the public good."[3] The trauma of this change could easily explain the especially histrionic tenor of *The Wounded Trapper*. And Ranney's change of mood may also represent an attempt to reach a new English or European audience.

Many of the most celebrated attributes of the romantic military hero that appeared in French painting during the first half of the nineteenth century seem to resurface in Ranney's fallen trapper. Art historian Holly Richardson has succinctly summarized the artistic legacy of the French soldier.

> The soldier confronted key romantic dilemmas. War evoked the "sublime," that peculiar quality in violence and terror that attracted the romantic imagination. Pervasive throughout the period, war also fulfilled the romantic compulsion to address modern issues. Finally, the romantic artist was concerned with the problem of alienation, and the soldier often was as isolated in society as he was when facing death on the battlefield.[4]

Certainly these are qualities that resonated for Ranney. The mountain man era had come to a close during the previous decade. His place in literature and history had definitely verged on the sublime, and his passing, as well as the triumphs and tragedies of the Mexican War, transformed such modern issues into armatures on which this narrative could be draped. Similarly, Ranney, along with a host of his fellow artists, surely felt alienated from society by the sad fate of their cherished patron, the Art-Union.

In pose and spirit, *The Wounded Trapper* resembles one of the most celebrated of the French romantic military paintings, Théodore Gericault's *The Wounded Cuirassier* of 1814 (Musée du Louvre, Paris). Aside from compositional similarities between the two works, which suggest that Ranney probably had seen one of the

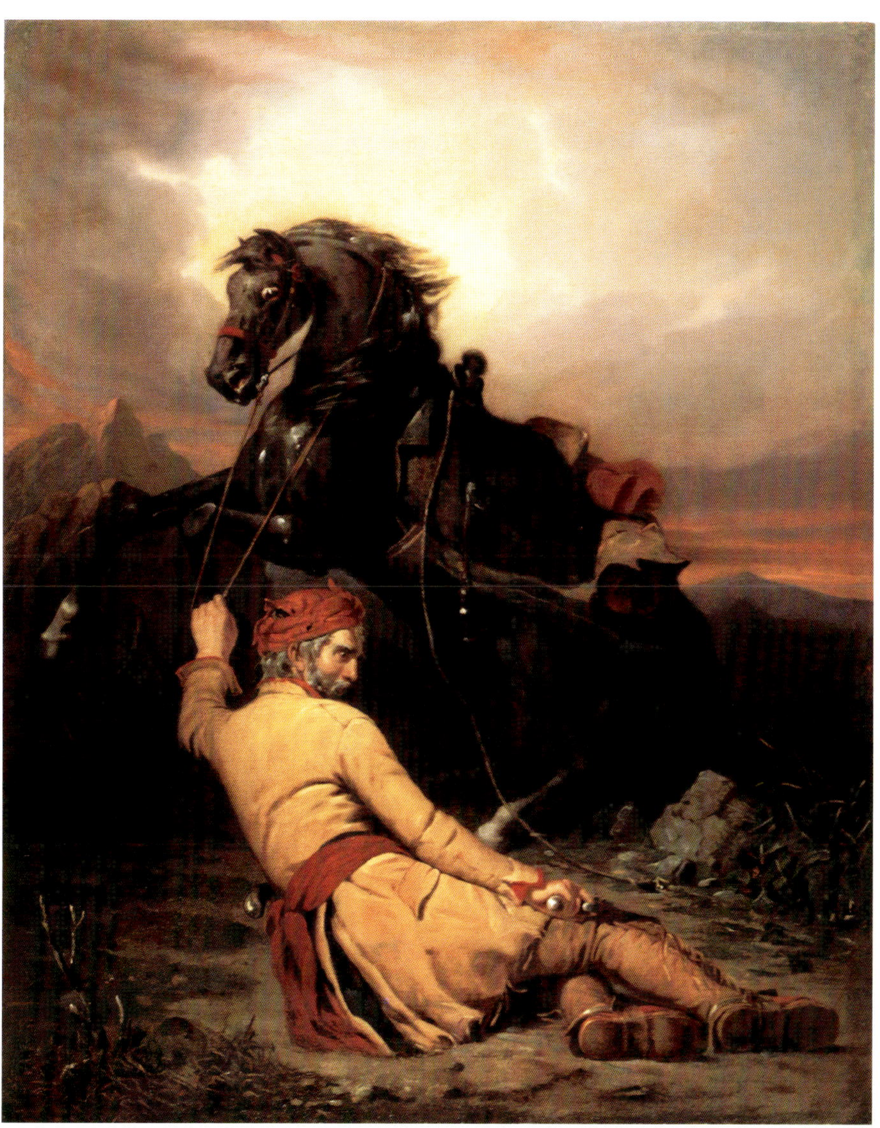

lithographs of Gericault's famous painting issued in 1822, there are the shared messages of defeat and the changing fortunes of heroic characters. Gericault's cavalryman looks back over his shoulder, wearing an expression of loss, resignation, and stoic acceptance. Ranney's trapper, who looks back down a trail, seems defiant and vulnerable, if not helpless. The lead rope from his pack animal has been broken. It hangs, snapped in two, from the saddle horn. He still controls his own mount, but his packhorse or mule has disappeared. He and his once-lucrative enterprise, just like the American Art-Union and the once burgeoning program of public art for the nation, appear to be lost causes.

This painting signaled the close of a chapter in Ranney's career as well. After the American Art-Union's final sale, Ranney seems never again to have exhibited a western work in a juried public venue. PHH

1. On the latter point, see Glanz 1982, p. 50.
2. "Literature—Books of the Week, Etc.," *Literary World*, vol. 11, no. 308 (December 25, 1852), p. 406.
3. Ibid.
4. Holly Richardson, "The Military Hero in the Romantic Imagination," in *All the Banners Wave: Art and War in the Romantic Era 1792–1851* (Providence: Brown University, 1982), p. 8.

75*
The Sleigh Ride

1852

Oil on canvas

30 1/8 x 40 1/8 inches
(76.5 x 101.9 cm)

Signed and dated on
stone, lower left: W.
Ranney/1852

Manoogian Collection

Grubar no. 64

PROVENANCE: Williams, Stevens and Williams, New York, 1852 (Henry H. Leeds and Company, New York, *Williams, Stevens and Williams Great Annual Sale . . .* October 27, 28, and 29, 1852, lot 295, p. 22, lists and describes it [quoted in entry]; sold for $350) Dr. Gardiner, by 1852; William H. Webb (1816–1899), New York, by 1864–1876 (*Catalogue of a Very Fine Assemblage of Works of Art . . . of Mr. Wm. H. Webb . . .* Miners Art Galleries, New York, March 29 and 30, 1876, lot 15, p. 9, as The Sleigh Ride. Returning from School); Jordan L. Mott, New York; Mrs. McLean, New York; Dr. Edward Perkins, Brooklyn, New York; Miss Clara Perkins, Riverhead, New York; Mrs. George Perkins, Riverhead, New York; Suffolk County Historical Society, Long Island, New York, by 1962 to 1980 (Sotheby's, New York, November 17, 1980, no. 137, provides provenance.) (Alexander Gallery, New York, by 1980).

EXHIBITED: NAD, 1852, no. 100, as for sale. Alexander Gallery, New York, *American Genre Paintings,* February 14 to March 14, 1984, discussed. Chadds Ford 1991, no. 18.

REFERENCES: *New York Herald,* April 21, 1852, p. 3, describes it (quoted in entry). *Albion,* vol. 11 (May 1, 1852), p. 214, provides critical review (quoted in entry). *New York Evening Post,* November 2, 1852, p. 2, provides provenance and price paid at auction. William Young, *Lights and Shadows of New York Picture Galleries: Forty Photographs by A. Turner* (New York: D. Appleton and Company, 1864), xxix, provides literary description, suggests influence of German art (quoted in entry), and lists it in the collection of William H. Webb, Esq., illus. on facing page, plate 29. Cowdrey 1943, 2, p. 89, no. 100, lists it. Advertised by Alexander Gallery, New York, in *Magazine Antiques* (February 1981), vol., 119, p. 270, and (January 1984), vol. 125, p. 57. Thistlethwaite 1991, pp. 23–24, 26, cover illus., discusses in terms of child-rearing practices of the day and political context. Franklin Kelly in *American Paintings from the Manoogian Collection* (Washington: National Gallery of Art, 1989), no. 24, pp. 68–69, discusses it.

In 1852, when this painting was offered for sale by Williams, Stevens and Williams, the following description appeared in the catalogue:

> Admirably composed, and excellent in color. A subject we should hardly have supposed the artist would have attempted, yet one in which he has as usual been completely successful. A benevolent old farmer has turned out after a fall of snow, with oxen and sled, to carry home from the distant school as mischievous and happy a group of urchins as one can well remember to have seen. In the distance the *master* is seen just locking the door of the schoolhouse, standing a little out of the woods.

Following on the critical success of his *Marion Crossing the Pedee* of 1850 (cat. no. 61), Ranney again created a complex figurative scene, his second sleigh ride theme (see cat. no. 34). Compared to the popular genre scenes of children at play or engaged in other activities painted by Ranney's fellow artists such as William Sidney Mount or James G. Clonney, *The Sleigh Ride* has far more participants and is more ambitious in size. In terms of its formal design, it seems to have more in common with the artists associated with the Düsseldorf school. In fact, in 1864 William Young in *Lights and Shadows* observed: "The careful drawing . . . and the genial sentiment that pervades [the picture], recall certain familiar acquaintances that German schools of Art send hither." As art historian William H. Gerdts has observed, the influence of these German artists on American artists was particularly palpable in the mid-nineteenth century after the establishment in 1849 of the Dusseldorf Gallery in New York City. For almost a decade, a rich array of contemporary German paintings, along with works by American artists studying abroad, most significantly, Emanuel Leutze, were shown there to great critical acclaim. Claiming the Italian Renaissance as its model, the art was characterized by tranquility, balance, and harmony.[1] To some extent, Ranney, who surely visited the gallery and was aware of the popularity of the pictures with New York audiences, may have been inspired to incorporate these qualities into his own work.

Within his characteristic rigorous triangular composition, Ranney, having just recently become a young father, seems to delight in depicting this upbeat celebration of rural childhood. He effectively captures the contagious energy of the band of young students, who on a snowy afternoon are released from the confines of their one-room school, leaving their teacher to lock up. With snowballs in hand, sporting an impressive display of clothing, and in a variety of poses, the enthusiastic boys rush and tumble as they crowd atop the

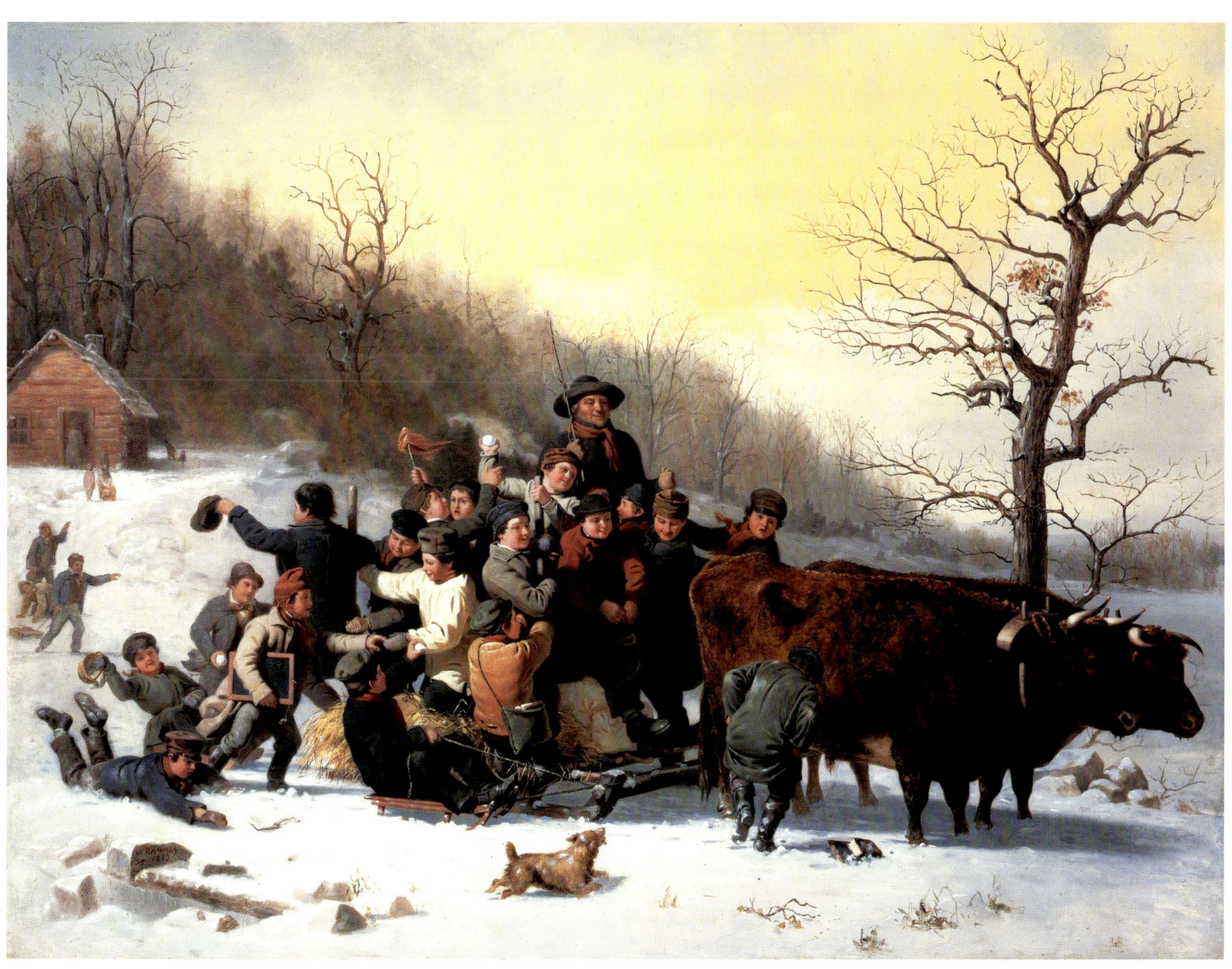

NO. 75

large sleigh pulled by two oxen and driven by a kindly looking old gentleman. Other children hasten from behind to catch up with the melee, while the youth at the right, his back to the viewer, seems to dance a jig. A plethora of details—other small sleds, blackboards, books, book bags, and a dog yapping so excitedly his tongue is hanging out—not only add to the sense of confusion but also create a sense of compelling realism and spirited ambiance. The whole is suffused in a warm atmospheric glow of blues, yellows, and pinks.

When *The Sleigh Ride* was exhibited at the National Academy, the reviews were overwhelmingly favorable. The *New York Herald* noted: "This is an animated and a well painted piece. The countenances of the occupants of the sleigh, especially the old driver [are] harmoniously natural." The *Albion* called it "a successful venture upon new ground," adding that "there is much spirit running through it; and it shows moreover unusual care in the finishing."

Thistlethwaite, who discusses several publications of the period that stress the importance of unfettered play in raising and nurturing children, interprets the painting as both an "enjoyable and believable depiction of a rural winter afternoon and as a reinforcement of the naturalness of children engaged in play." To Ranney's urban patrons, perhaps recently transplanted, the idyllic rural scene and carefree children may have evoked childhood memories. They themselves may have nostalgically recalled their own one-room school and just such an outing.

The modern viewer, however, should be aware that access to education in the early 1850s was primarily limited to middle and upper class children, mostly white boys, as Ranney illustrates in this picture. This scene does not represent the reality of the masses: Most youngsters attended little, if any, school. The practice of providing universal public education, as we know it today, was still in its infancy. Ironically, it was in response to the burgeoning immigrant underclasses in northeastern cities that reformers may have been induced to promote compulsory, publicly supported educational programs as a means of creating social harmony and establishing a uniform code of moral conduct in support of democratic ideals. LB

1. William H. Gerdts, "The Düsseldorf Connection," in William H. Gerdts and Mark Thistlethwaite, *Grand Illusions: History Painting in America* (Fort Worth: Amon Carter Museum, 1988), provides a thorough discussion of the impact of the Düsseldorf school on American painting, pp. 128, 136.

76
Landscape with School House

c. 1852
Oil on canvas,
unmounted
10 1/2 x 14 5/8 inches
(26.7 x 37.1 cm)
Location unknown
Grubar no. 65

PROVENANCE: Claude J. Ranney (1883–1971), Malvern, Pennsylvania, by 1962.

Grubar suggests that this now lost painting was possibly a study related to *The Sleigh Ride* (cat. no. 75).
LB

77*
Squire Boone Crossing the Mountains with Stores for His Brother Daniel, Encamped in the Wilds of Kentucky

1852

Oil on canvas

36 x 32 1/2 inches
(91.5 x 83.5 cm)

Signed and dated,
lower right: W.
Ranney/'52

Grubar no. 66

Museum of Fine Arts,
Springfield,
Massachusetts. Gift
from the Estate of
Amelia Peabody

PROVENANCE: Edward D. Nelson (d. 1871), by 1853; descended in family to his great-granddaughter, to 1955; (Vose Galleries, Boston, 1955) Amelia Peabody, Boston, 1955–1984.

EXHIBITED: NAD, 1853, no. 80, lists as *Squire Boone Crossing the Mountains with Stores for His Brother Daniel, Encamped in the Wilds of Kentucky* and Edward D. Nelson as owner. Vose Galleries, Boston, *A Loan Exhibition Honoring Robert Churchill Vose*, March 7–25, 1961, no. 27.

REFERENCES: *Home Journal*, April 30, 1853, p. 2, no. 80, provides critical description (quoted below); *New York Herald*, May 23, 1853, p. 3, provides critical review and description (quoted in entry). Vose Galleries, Boston to Linda Bantel, December 9, 1997, Ranney archives, provides provenance.

In 1852, Ranney completed this work, thematically related to his 1849 paintings of *Boone's First View of Kentucky* (cat. nos. 45 and 46). It shows a single figure, a rather matter-of-fact equestrian portrait of Daniel Boone's brother Squire (1744–1815), as this stalwart sibling crests a rise along a wilderness mountain trail. He leads a heavily laden white packhorse whose head is bowed under the weight of his burden. A conical peak appears in the distance behind them.

The scene was one frequently visited by the literature of the day. In 1769–1770, the Boone brothers had spent months alone in the Kentucky wilderness. As spring approached, they began to run low on provisions, especially ammunition. Squire was sent east for supplies, while Daniel remained behind to continue hunting and to protect their perceived rights to the newly explored hunting grounds. Their plan was to rendezvous in July, their stores freshened by Squire's efforts. The brothers, once reunited, continued their hunting and exploring. Ranney depicts Squire returning to the wilderness with that fresh stock of necessities. One of the primary motivations of this mission, the wooden powder keg is plainly seen on the right side of the pack.

Much has been made of this episode, particularly the part about Daniel's period of isolation, and his physical as well as psychological adaptation to those lonely and perilous months.[1] It was during that wilderness exposure that he experienced a mythic epiphany of self-discovery. And, on a more pragmatic level, the solitude afforded him an opportunity to experience this new land so that as later pioneers arrived he might be able to assist their settlement. And indeed it proved to be a lucrative business.

Ranney chose to disregard the self-discovery element and also to avoid the characteristic presentation of the "savage" wilds as they would have appeared before white settlement. Typical of Ranney, his work is very different than contemporary depictions that focused on Daniel Boone and more dramatic events, such as George Caleb Bingham's *Daniel Boone Escorting Settlers through the Cumberland Gap* of 1851–1852 (Washington University Gallery of Art, St. Louis). Instead his work presented a fairly tame topography and included Native

115

Americans only by inference. The *New York Herald* reviewer of the work suggested that Squire's focused gaze and alert pose evidenced a need for him to be "listening around if any Indians are near." But beyond this, Ranney used Squire to represent the larger symbolic vanguard of civilization and a view that implies that the East would be the provider for the West. Squire seems to supply not only the practical necessities for survival in the far reaches but the resolution and fortitude that were thought to be required to deal with the Kentucky region. The painting carried the same or similar message as Bingham's but in a quieter way.

Ranney's painting was owned by the amateur artist Edward D. Nelson (d. 1871) in 1853 when it was exhibited at the National Academy of Design. Ranney's presentation of Boone garnered praise as a "spirited and pleasing picture." According to the *Home Journal:*

> The gallant backwoodsman is mounted, and is leading a pack horse. He sits in the attitude of one who, knowing himself to be in a dangerous country, has just heard, or fancied he heard, a suspicious noise. The face is an open and bright one; the horses are excellent; the accoutrements and dress of the rider are exceedingly good. We could wish the design of the artist had comprehended a wider expanse of country, or that he had made the scenery a little more distinct and characteristic.

PHH

1. John Mack Faragher, *Daniel Boone: The Life and Legends of an American Pioneer* (New York: Henry Holt and Company, 1992), pp. 84–85.

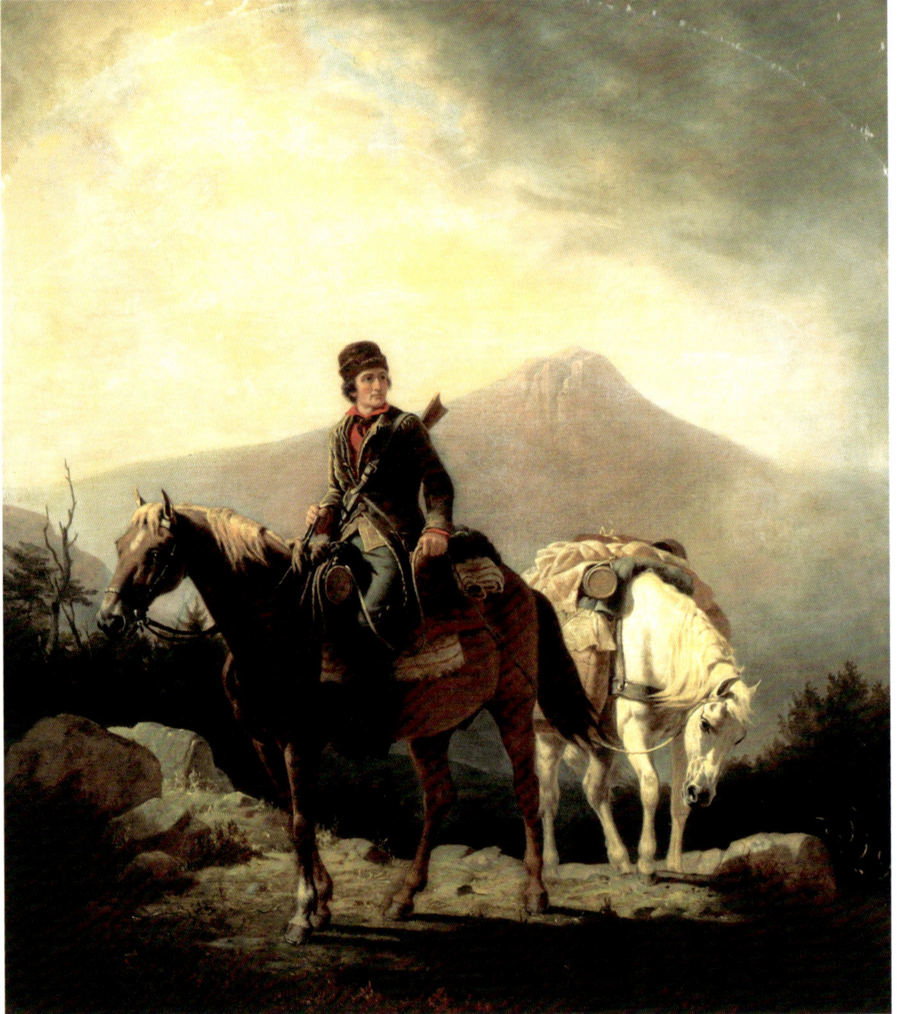

78
The Retrieve

c. 1852
Oil on canvas
Location unknown
Grubar no. 62

PROVENANCE: D[avid] L[ydig] Suydam (d. 1884), 1852.

EXHIBITED: NAD, 1852, no. 340, as lent by D. L. Suydam.

REFERENCES: *New York Herald*, April 21, 1852, p. 3, no. 340 (quoted in entry); Cowdrey 1943, 2, p. 89, no. 340, lists it and provides provenance.

This unlocated oil painting was shown at the National Academy's 1852 exhibition. It carries the same title as the painting in the Corcoran Gallery of Art (cat. no. 59), which was exhibited at the National Academy in 1851. Whether it is a replica of the earlier painting or a variation on Ranney's popular duck hunting theme is unknown. Only a partial description appears in the 1852 *New York Herald:* "the figure of the dog deserves special notice." LB

79
Duck Shooting

c. 1852
Oil on canvas
12 x 18 inches (30.5 x 45.7 cm)
Location unknown
Grubar no. 63

PROVENANCE: (Williams, Stevens and Williams, New York, by 1852).

REFERENCES: Henry H. Leeds, New York, *Williams, Stevens and Williams Great Annual Sale,* October 27, 28, and 29, 1852, lot 133, p. 11, lists it and provides dimensions. *Literary World,* vol. 11 (November 6, 1852), p. 300, indicates sold for $42.50.

According to the 1852 auction catalogue this was "the original sketch—preferred by many to the finished picture." While the title *Duck Shooting* does not conform specifically to a known picture, this picture was probably an oil sketch for Ranney's most celebrated duck hunting picture of this period, *On the Wing* of 1850 (cat. no. 55) rather than the less well-known or reproduced versions of the duck hunting theme (see cat. nos. 59 and 78). A painting also entitled *Duck Shooting* was sold in the Ranney Fund sale (lot 118) for twenty-seven dollars to someone by the name of Wood, who purchased sixteen of Ranney's works from this sale.[1] LB

1. See cat. no. 50 for information on Wood.

80
Winter in New Jersey

c. 1852

Oil on canvas

Location unknown

Grubar no. 67

PROVENANCE: Am Art-Union, 1852 (sale, American Art-Union, Artists' Sale: *Catalogue of Very Valuable and Choice Paintings, Recently Selected from the Studios of the Most Distinguished American and Resident Artists, David Austen, Jr.,* New York, December 30, 1852, no. 170, p. 10, lists it as Winter in New Jersey, by Kanny [sic]).

81
Advice on the Prairie

c. 1853

Oil on canvas

38 3/4 x 55 1/4 inches
(98.4 x 140.3 cm)

Signed and dated,
lower right: W.
Ranney./ ..53

Buffalo Bill Historical
Center, Cody,
Wyoming. Gift of Mrs.
J. Maxwell Moran,
10.91

Grubar no. 68 also
titles it The Old
Scout's Tale and The
Frontiersman

PROVENANCE: Henry Sampson, Sr., New York; his son, Henry Sampson, Jr., Douglaston, New York; Paul H. Bilhuber, Douglaston; Claude J. Ranney (1883–1971), Malvern, Pennsylvania, 1959–1971; his daughter, Elizabeth R. Moran, Paoli, Pennsylvania, 1971–1991.

EXHIBITED: Fort Worth, 1987, p. 193 lists it in private collection.

REFERENCES: Catalogue sheet, Claude J. Ranney provides provenance, Ranney archives. Grubar, p. 41, notes that according to Ranney family tradition, the figures at right were friends of the artist, and that it has also been said the scout was James Bridger (1804–1881). Ayres 1987, p. 89, discusses painting and role of women and children in western imagery, fig. no. 53, p. 91, illus. Patricia Hills, "Picturing Progress in the Era of Westward Expansion," in *The West as America: Reinterpreting Images of the Frontier, 1820–1920,* ed. William H. Truettner (Washington: Smithsonian Institution Press, 1991), pp. 112–113, discusses it, fig. 95, illus., discusses in terms of cohesive family unit and Christian imagery.

In the late spring of 1852, the *Literary World* critiqued one of Ranney's sporting paintings, *Duck Shooting* (cat. no. 79), which was on display at the National Academy of Design. Although the critic lavished approbation on the "character of individuality" that he found in Ranney's work, he also sounded a cautionary note. Such pictures were, he wrote, "becoming painfully conspicuous in our exhibitions and shop windows, of which glaring red shirts, buckskin breeches, and very coarse prairie grass are essential ingredients."[1]

When, the following year, Ranney embarked on *Advice on the Prairie*, one of his major artistic achievements, he made special efforts to mitigate such a reaction. In this tribute to the pioneering spirit, he also sought an opportunity to claim higher moral ground and a more nationalistic spirit. Each of these aspirations had a good deal to do with trends in the American art scene of the day. The *Literary World* article had, beyond admonishing Ranney for repetitiousness, waxed enthusiastically about what they viewed as redeeming virtues in current American art. Ranney's contemporary Daniel Huntington received praise for displaying a scriptural composition, *Tribute Money*, that was welcomed as an "attribution through humanity of the great attributes of the religious mind." In the same galleries of the academy hung two genre pieces by George Baker, *Going to School* and *Summer Hours*, that garnered the claim of "exquisite" in their dreamy evocation of childhood and the expectations of the seasons. These were praised for the poetic nature of their conception, the simplicity of their treatment, and the unaffected pleasantness that they projected—"precious" qualities in a day when "our artists run mad with [Thomas] Couture and the charlatans of the European schools," in response to which "we cannot value too highly the feeling that preserves its own originality and purity."[2]

American paintings that stood for home and church were, in the reviewer's mind, at least, affirmations of national cultural priorities as well as uniqueness. They existed on a higher moral plane than such Thomas Couture's canvases as *Romans of the Decadence*, 1847 (Musée du Louvre, Paris) with its sweaty, lascivious swoon that had provided earthly delectation for audiences at the Paris Salon a few years before. Any self-respecting, not to mention self-righteous, American would eschew such displays. Characteristic of the endur-ing Second Great Awakening, they would look to Huntington, Baker, Ranney, and others to steer a loftier, more spiritually efficacious course.

Advice on the Prairie speaks to these issues on several levels. At first blush, it appears as a fairly straightfor-ward narrative. A scout, perhaps hired by this immigrant troop or perhaps pausing in his own journey, takes an opportunity after the evening supper to give an earnest and heedful young family counsel on what lies ahead. Or maybe the group was simply listening with rapt attention to a mountain man's yarns of the West. A guidebook with which Ranney may well have been familiar, Thomas Farnham's *Travels in the Great Western Prairies* of 1843, recounted such a scene.

> We . . . staked down our animals near at hand, and prepared and ate in the usual form, our evening repast. Our company was divided into two messes, seven in one, and eight in the other. On the ground, with each a tin pint cup and a small round plate of the same material; the first filled with coffee, tea or water, the last with fried side bacon and dough fried in fat; each with a butcher-knife in hand, and each mess sitting, tailor-like, around its own frying pan, eating with the appetite of tigers, was, perhaps, the toute-ensemble of our company at supper on the banks of the Osage. There were encamped near us some wagoners on their return to Missouri. . . . With these men we passed a very agreeable evening; they amused us with yarns of mountain-life which from time to time had floated in, and formed the fire-side legends of that wild border.[3]

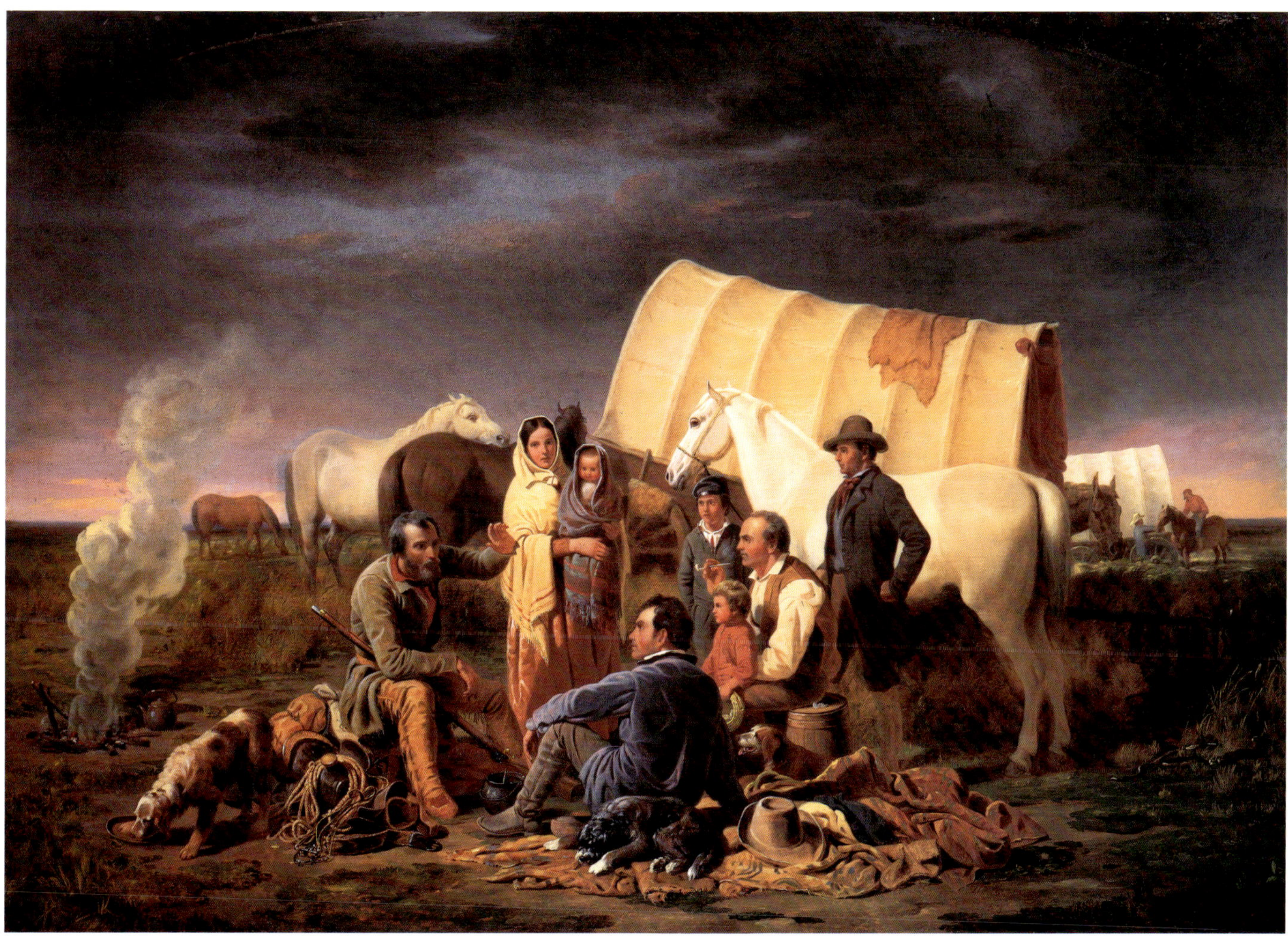

NO. 81

119

But more than simple narrative, this work bears a hefty moral message. It has to do with the nature of advice. When, for instance, the advice was flawed, through ignorance or disingenuousness, the results could be tragic. Such was the case of the infamous immigrant guide, Lansford Warren Hastings, whose cavalier behavior and scam of a guidebook had sent many in the Donner party to a snowy, highly publicized Sierra grave in 1846.[4] Ranney may have had this in mind when he painted this oil.

The second inculcation was somewhat pious. Though not so overt, the Ranney painting was, like Huntington's, another "attribution through humanity of the great attributes of the religious mind." The Second Great Awakening, though winding down by the early 1850s, had revised public spiritual expectations of a second coming or, short of that, the establishment of the kingdom of God on earth. That hope, combined with the belief common among the zealous that they shared a right to individual self-improvement, explains much about Manifest Destiny and the western movement at mid-century. The family in Ranney's painting provides a pictorial embodiment of the supposed sanctity of expansion. It is not just an American family; it is a metaphor for the Holy Family on its way to the Promised Land. The divine nature of their task is especially well marked in the woman who fills the role of what in later years would be called the "Prairie Madonna." She and her baby are raised to a level above the human plane—she into a spiritual and ethereal sphere that touches the sky—while the men are posed close to the ground in a corporeal, earthly location that speaks of business and mundane practicalities. The Prairie Madonna with her baby is clad in garments of red, white, and blue, each with a headcover that resembles a halo. They are mixed with the animals, as in the Christmas story, and flanked by two white mares of angelic beauty. The mother's gaze, which may just have caught the scout's gesture, has moved off into another place. With her mind fixed in the abstract, she embodies one of the prime messages of the picture—that, as art historian Annette Stott has concluded, "the western enterprise had the blessing of God and that woman's role was to bring the double salvation of Christianity and Anglo-American civilization to the western plains."[5] The clouds have parted just above her, and a golden horizon awaits as if to assure the verity of this context. The scout's gesture establishes a third important focus for the painting. In it can be read hope. The hand suggests onward motion and a lift that might imply surmounting or overcoming something in the course of that action. Perhaps he signals the crossing of the Continental Divide or the Sierras. In any event, it connotes accessibility and promise. PHH

1. "The Fine Arts," *Literary World*, vol. 9, no. 274 (May 1, 1852), p. 316.

2. Ibid.

3. Thomas J. Farnham, *Travels in the Great Western Prairies . . .* (New York: Greeley and McElrath, 1843), p. 7.

4. Lansford Warren Hastings, *The Emigrants' Guide to Oregon and California* (Cincinnati: G. Conclin, 1845). See also Edwin Bryant's, *What I Saw in California in 1848* (Philadelphia: D. Appleton and Company, 1848), pp. 127, and 250–265 and J. Quinn Thornton, *Oregon and California in 1848* (New York: Harper and Brothers, Publishers, 1849), vol. 2, pp. 95–240.

5. Annette Stott, "Prairie Madonnas and Pioneer Women: Images of Emigrant Women in the Art of the Old West," *Prospects*, vol. 21 (1996), p. 301.

82

Duck Shooter's Pony

1853
Oil on canvas
33 1/2 x 55 inches
(85.1 x 159.7 cm)
Signed and dated,
lower center: W.
Ranney/.53
Private collection
Grubar no. 70

PROVENANCE: Henry C. Coit, 1853; Mr. and Mrs. George Bernard Wagstaff, New York, by 1937; unknown private collection; (Meredith, Long and Company, Houston, by 1974) (Davis and Long Company, New York, 1974) (Hirschl and Adler Galleries, New York, to 1975).

EXHIBITED: NAD, 1853, no. 40, as owned by Henry C. Coit. Metropolitan Museum of Art, New York, *Sporting Prints and Paintings*, March 1–April 25, 1937, listed as Duck Shooting in addendum to catalogue and lent by Mr. and Mrs. George Barnard Wagstaff. Chadds Ford 1991, no. 19.

REFERENCES: *New York Herald,* May 8, 1853, p. 7 (quoted in entry). Cowdrey 1943, 2, p. 89. FARL photo mount, no. 120–21D, provides provenance and exhibition history. Thistlethwaite 1991, p. 33, illus., p. 35, discusses.

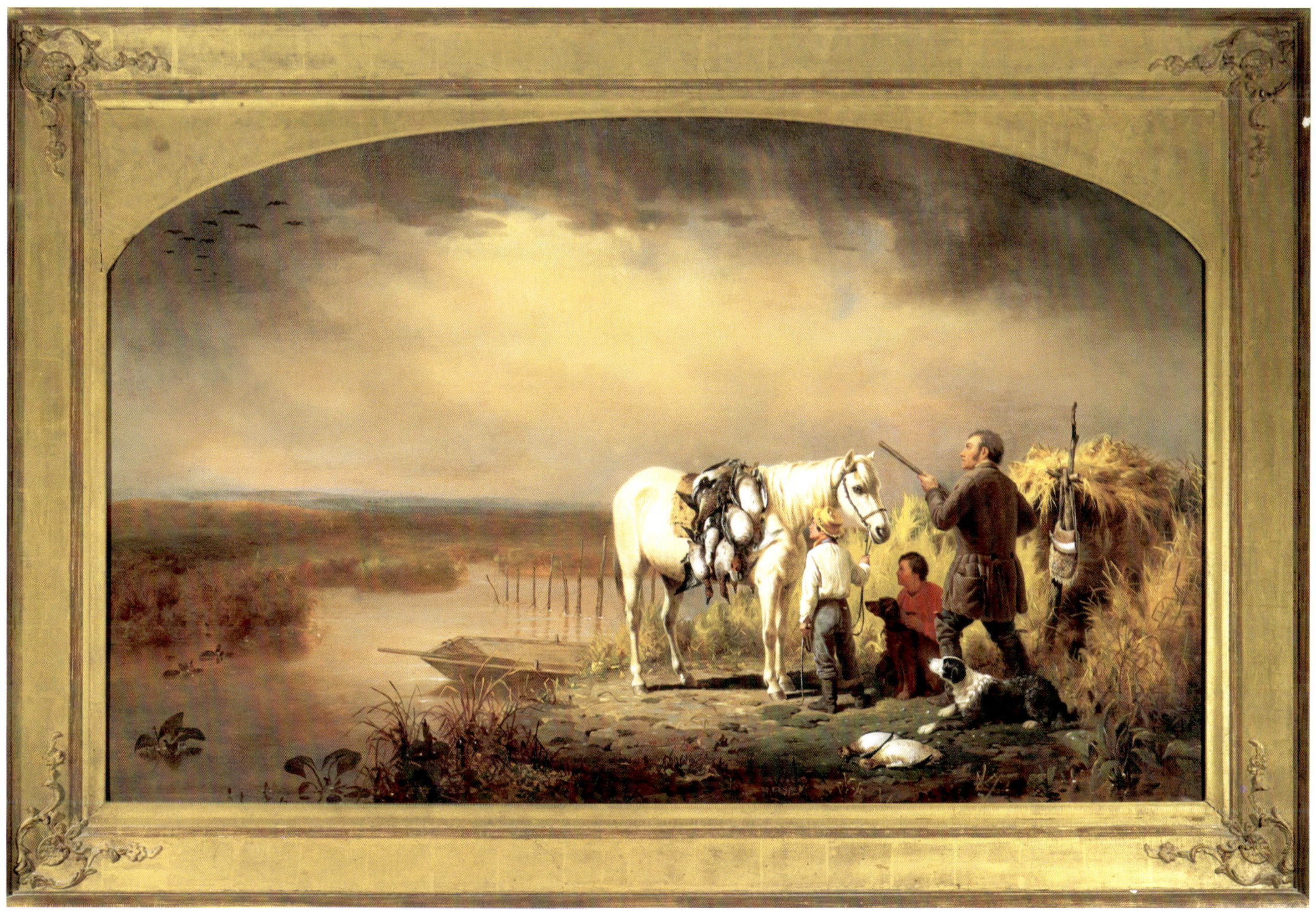

NO. 82

Duck Shooter's Pony is a variation of the duck hunting theme which Ranney first explored in *Duck Shooters* of 1849 (cat. no. 43) and the following year in his highly successful *On the Wing* (cat. no. 55). Like his other sporting scenes, this one appears to be set in the familiar New Jersey salt water marshes near his home and studio. But unlike those earlier versions, here Ranney includes a young boy who leads an overladen pack horse with the hunter's dead game and shifts the focus from the center of the canvas to the duck blind at the far right. He also reduces the size of the figures relative to the rest of the composition. The result is that over half of the scene is devoted to the landscape itself, an emphasis that reflects the increasing taste of artists and collectors for this subject.

At this time, the popularity of landscape painting was becoming so pervasive that one reviewer of the National Academy exhibition of 1853 felt compelled to point out that of the 442 works: "Portraits and land-scapes almost equally divide the Catalogue of the Exhibition this year. There are certainly far fewer attempts than usual at what are called historical pictures, and figure pieces of the domestic class are quite as rare on the walls."[1]

A detailed description of *Duck Shooter's Pony* appeared in the *New York Herald*'s review of the same exhibition. It provides not only a positive critical response to Ranney's work of this period, but also, in its specific observations about seasons appropriate for duck hunting and the use of firearms, it indicates how widespread knowledge was, at least in certain circles, of sporting practices of the day:

> This is a picture of considerable merit—it shows the hand of a draftsman. The old pony, with a large bunch of canvass back ducks, or redheads, on his back, stands patiently, while the old man, his two boys and dogs are engrossed with the approach of a flight of ducks—the old man has seized his gun and all eyes are fixed, on the nearing of the fowl. In our judgment, we should say the artist has made the weather appear too warm: the scene is evidently intended for the fall, and the gunners seldom find ducks until much colder weather. We should also say, from the small size of the fowling piece in the hands of the old gunner, that the ducks must have been very accommodating, if we may judge from the large quantity killed. The artist has been very happy in giving a lifelike interest to the whole scene: the dogs, in particular, are very natural, with their eyes fixed on the flying ducks, awaiting only the discharge of the gun to receive orders to fetch the game. It is a very interesting picture—only a little too warm.

On the back of a drawing by Ranney entitled *Cows in the Hackensack Meadow* (cat. no. D72), there is a sketch of the figural grouping in this picture. LB

1. Quoted in *Literary World*, vol. 12 (April 30, 1853), p. 358.

83 *
A Trapper Crossing the Mountains

1853

Oil on canvas

29 x 24 inches (73.7 x 61 cm)

Signed and dated, lower right: W Ranney/1853

Speed Art Museum, Louisville, Kentucky. Museum purchase, Mrs. Elizabeth J. Bohon Fund, 1949.29

Grubar no. 71

PROVENANCE: (John Levy Galleries, New York, 1948 to 1949, as *Squire Boone Crossing the Mountains into Kentucky*).

REFERENCES: J. B. Speed Art Museum, *Bulletin*, 11 (February 1950), n.p., as *Squire Boone Crossing the Mountains into Kentucky*. Grubar no. 71, gives incorrect dimensions of 38 x 33 inches (96.5 x 23.8 cm).

In 1858 the Baltimore painter Alfred Jacob Miller began work on a brilliant set of watercolors for the noted art patron from his city, William T. Walters. Among the two hundred views of Rocky Mountain scenery and Native American life was an uncharacteristically static, neoclassically inert, and formal depiction of a Sioux family entitled *Camp Scene*. It showed a young man, statuesquely posed, with his horse and emblems of war, as part of a domestic ensemble, grouped with his wife and child. Their home, a buffalo-hide tepee, fills the composition to the right. For Miller, this was a scene of familial accord. When he came to write about it in the text notation that accompanied the watercolor, he used it as an opportunity to proclaim the West as the perfect studio and its inhabitants as equally perfect subjects for the artist.

> American sculptors travel thousands of miles to study Greek statues in the Vatican at Rome, seemingly unaware that in their own country there exists a race of men equal in form and grace (if not superior) to the finest beau ideal ever dreamed of by the Greeks. . . . Most unquestionable, that sculptor who travels here,—and models from what he sees (supposing him to have equal power and genius), will far excel any other who merely depends upon his own conception of what it ought to be.[1]

Ranney's painting *A Trapper Crossing the Mountains* of 1853 effectively redirects that plea. In Ranney's vision, the mountain man rather than the Indian embodied those ideals. When he elected to portray this unknown trapper, his footstep quieted by a muffled cushion of fresh snow, he invested the figure with a conventional aesthetic purity that called on the classical traditions as forcefully as had Miller. For underneath the trapper's quotidian garb—his red woolen shirt, buckskin leggings, moccasins, and red-sashed leather coat—is the body of a Greek athlete reminiscent of *The Doryphorus*, immortalized in marble by Polykleitos of Argos in the fifth century BC. That figure, which survived in a number of Roman copies, was known to most art students of Ranney's day. As Polykleitos' statue had attained a new height in artistic achievement with his poise, relaxation of attitude, and resultant harmony of design,[2] so too did Ranney's effort strive to imbue an otherwise humble American figure with ideal form.

A few years before Ranney completed this painting, perhaps around the time he began to sketch his initial study for the work (cat. no. 84), the young Francis Parkman penned a tribute to "those rude and hardy men, hunters and traders, scouts and guides," who had ranged beyond the border that separated the provinces of "barbarism and civilization."

> Even now, while I write, some lonely trapper is climbing the perilous defiles of the Rocky Mountains, his strong frame cased in time-worn buck-skin, his rifle gripped in his sinewy hand. Keenly he peers from side to side, lest Blackfoot or Arapahoe should ambuscade his path. The rough earth is his bed, a morsel of dried meat and a draught of water are his food and drink, and death and danger his companions. No anchorite could fare worse, no hero could dare more; yet his wild, hard life has resistless charms.[3]

Ranney's trapper crossed the mountains with a good deal more than antiquity's grace, Parkman's charms, and the supplies bundled in the bulging tan panniers on his mule. For not only is this trapper the pictorial equivalent of Parkman's American hero and the bearer of stores requisite for survival in the wilderness, he is the sponsor of a larger iconographical message as well.

In 1850, Woodbury Langdon of New York had purchased, amid considerable public fanfare, Paul Delaroche's

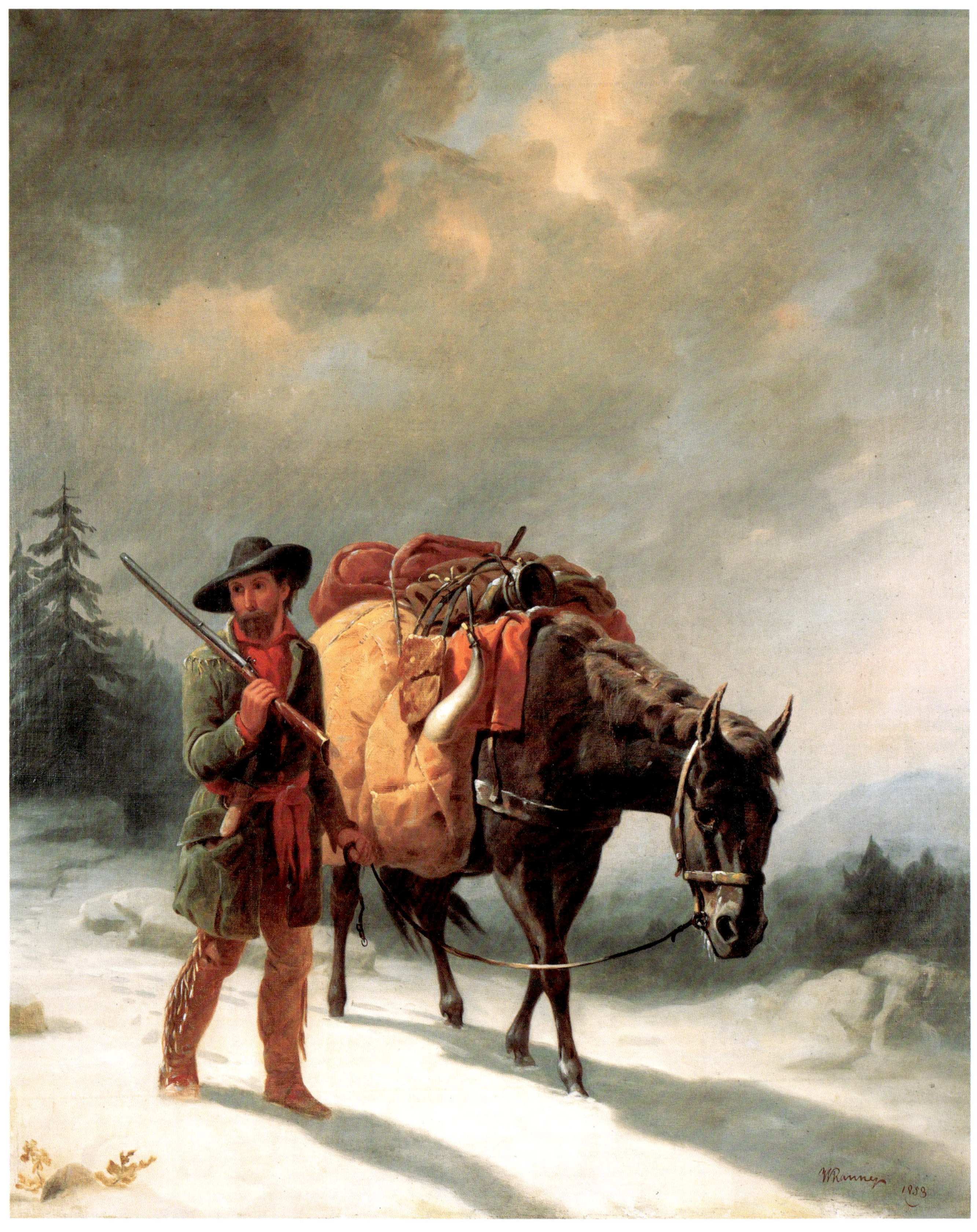

NO. 83

124

Napoleon Crossing the Alps. Ranney would have known of this noteworthy acquisition of French art as it was heralded in the *American Art-Union Bulletin* that year (p. 150). He had very likely seen the lithograph after this work (fig. 83.1).He would have recognized, too, that this work represented a triumph of romanticism over classicism, as an *au courant* retelling of Jacques-Louis David's earlier rendition of the same episode, *Napoleon Crossing the Alps* of 1801 (Château de Malmaison, Paris). Thought to be something of a historical corrective, Delaroche's revisionist take on the event showed not a demigod in heroic action but an emotive, internally absorbed victim of excessive ambition being led into his destiny on a mule with blinders. As in Ranney's painting, the mule transports the burden of history, and as art historian Stephen Bann has pointed out, Delaroche intentionally chose to present a moment in Napoleon's career that revealed "a man who has both created and destroyed himself, rising above all pre-existing authority but for that very reason uniquely aware of his own failure."[4]

The mountain man's journey is no less mythical than Napoleon's and no less wrought with human failings. Parkman's cantation to his "rude and hardy men," quoted above, goes on to reveal their fundamentally human weaknesses. He invites his reader to travel with the trapper to the rendezvous. There, the reader could review, along "with all its ancient energy, that wild and daring spirit, that force and robustness of mind which marked our barbarous ancestors of Germany and Norway," the profoundly self-destructive nature of the beast. "Here, rioting among his comrades, his native appetites break loose in mad excess, in deep carouse, and desperate gaming. Then follow close the quarrel, the challenge, the fight,—two rusty rifles and fifty yards of prairie."[5]

Like Delaroche's Napoleon, Ranney's trapper wears a shroud of melancholy introspection. At once he bears the hopes of civilization in his stride and also the paradox that accompanies the effort. The wilds that he claims as his new home will inevitably suffer spoliation at the hands of those who follow his trail through the mountain fastness. And the mountain man himself, through his want of excess, will be rendered an ephemeral though romantic figure in art and history.

In 1853, the year this work was painted, a picture by Ranney called *The Pack Mule* with very similar dimensions was sold in New York (see cat. no. 91) and could be this one or the other undated version in the Anschutz Collection (cat. no. 84). PHH

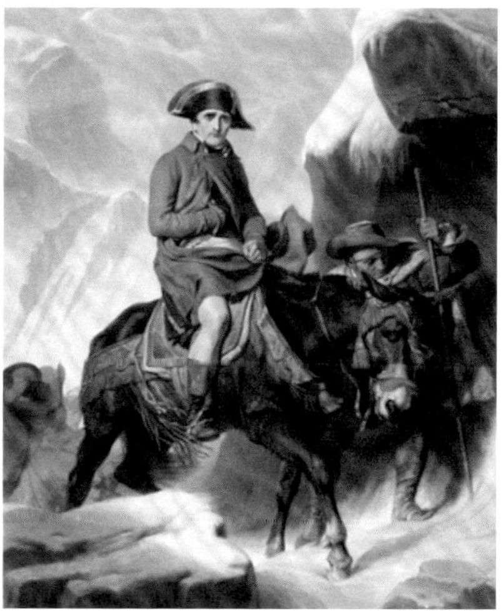

1. Quoted in Marvin C. Ross, *The West of Alfred Jacob Miller* (Norman: University of Oklahoma Press, 1968), op. p. 64.
2. Gisela M.A. Richter, *A Handbook of Greek Art* (New York: Phaidon Publishers, 1960), p. 110.
3. Francis Parkman, "The Wilderness and Its Tenants," *Literary World*, vol. 9 (August 30, 1851), p. 170.
4. Stephen Bann, *Paul Delaroche: History Painter* (Princeton, N. J.: Princeton University Press, 1997), p. 253.
5. Parkman, "The Wilderness and Its Tenants," p. 170.

Fig 83.1
Engraving (1850) of *Napoleon Crossing the Alps* by Paul Delaroche (1797–1859). Old Print Shop, Kenneth M. Newman, New York.

84
A Trapper Crossing the Mountains

c. 1853

Oil on canvas

30 x 25 1/4 inches
(76.2 x 64.1 cm)

Anschutz Collection,
Denver

Grubar no. 72

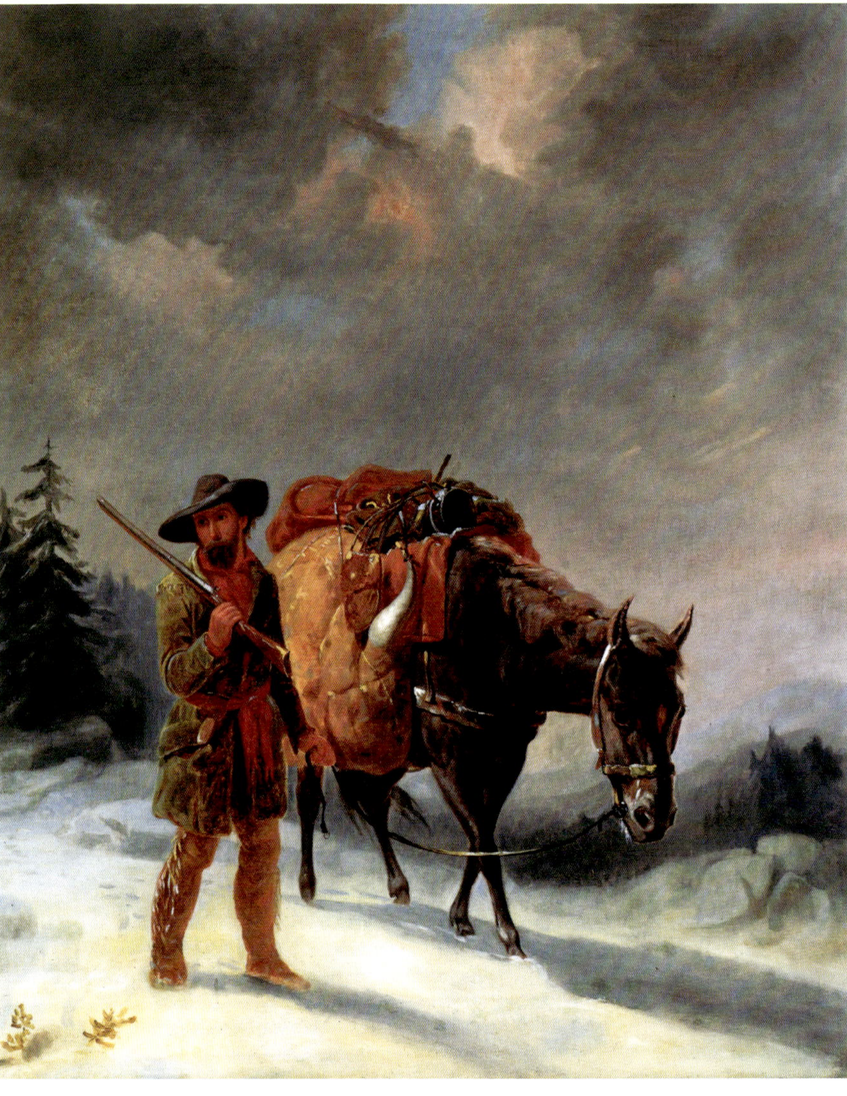

PROVENANCE: Private collection, Boston; G. Harry Adalian, Newton, Massachusetts; his wife, Mrs. G. Harry Adalian, Newton, to c. 1954 (T. Gilbert Brouillette, New York, and Falmouth, Massachusetts, by 1954); Mr. and Mrs. M. D. Johnston, Los Angeles, by 1962; (Terry DeLapp Gallery, Los Angeles); (Ira Spanierman, New York); (Nicholas Woloshuk, Santa Fe, to 1972).

REFERENCE: FARL photo mount no. 114-1 D, mistitles it *Squire Boone Crossing the Mountains*, provides provenance to 1954, and notes: "The artist's brother was used as the model for the picture." Ayres 1987, fig. 63. pp. 99–100, illus. and notes that the image is the only winter scene from the trappers series.

For a full discussion of this painting's subject see *A Trapper Crossing the Mountains* of 1853 (cat. no. 83). Grubar suggests that this virtually identical though larger version of that signed and dated oil may be a similarly titled work that was sold at the Ranney Fund sale (lot 38) to someone by the name of Walker for seventeen dollars. Two other works by Ranney, both identified as *The Pack Mule*, were also sold at auction, one in 1853 and another in 1854 (see cat. nos. 91 and 103), either of which may be this painting. LB

85
Old Scout's Tale

c. 1853

Oil on canvas

14 x 20 inches (35.6 x 50.8 cm)

Initialed, lower center: Wm. R

Gilcrease Museum, Tulsa

Grubar no. 69, as Advice on the Prairie

PROVENANCE: Claude J. Ranney (1883–1971), Malvern, Pennsylvania; (Russell W. Thorpe, New York); (John Levy Galleries, New York, by 1944); (C. W. Lyon, New York, to 1944); Gilcrease Foundation, 1944–1955.

EXHIBITED: Robert Fridenberg, New York, c. 1918. Frederic Frazier Gallery, New York, *An Exhibition of American Genre*, April 20–May 20, 1938, no. 13, as Advice on the Frontier (annotated typescript in Frick Art Reference Library, indicates "not owned by Frederic Frazier Gallery"). Russell W. Thorpe, New York, *Exhibition of American Genre Paintings*, April–May, 1940, cat. no. 20, as The Old Scout's Tale. John Levy Galleries, New York, *America in the 19th Century*, May 16–June 9, 1944, no. 22, as The Old Scout's Tale (Western Scene).

REFERENCE: FARL mount, 120-a, provides provenance.

This is a smaller version of, or study for, *Advice on the Prairie* (cat. no. 81). Since 1940, it has been called *Old Scout's Tale*, and, at some point, according to Grubar, it was also known as *The Frontiersman*. LB

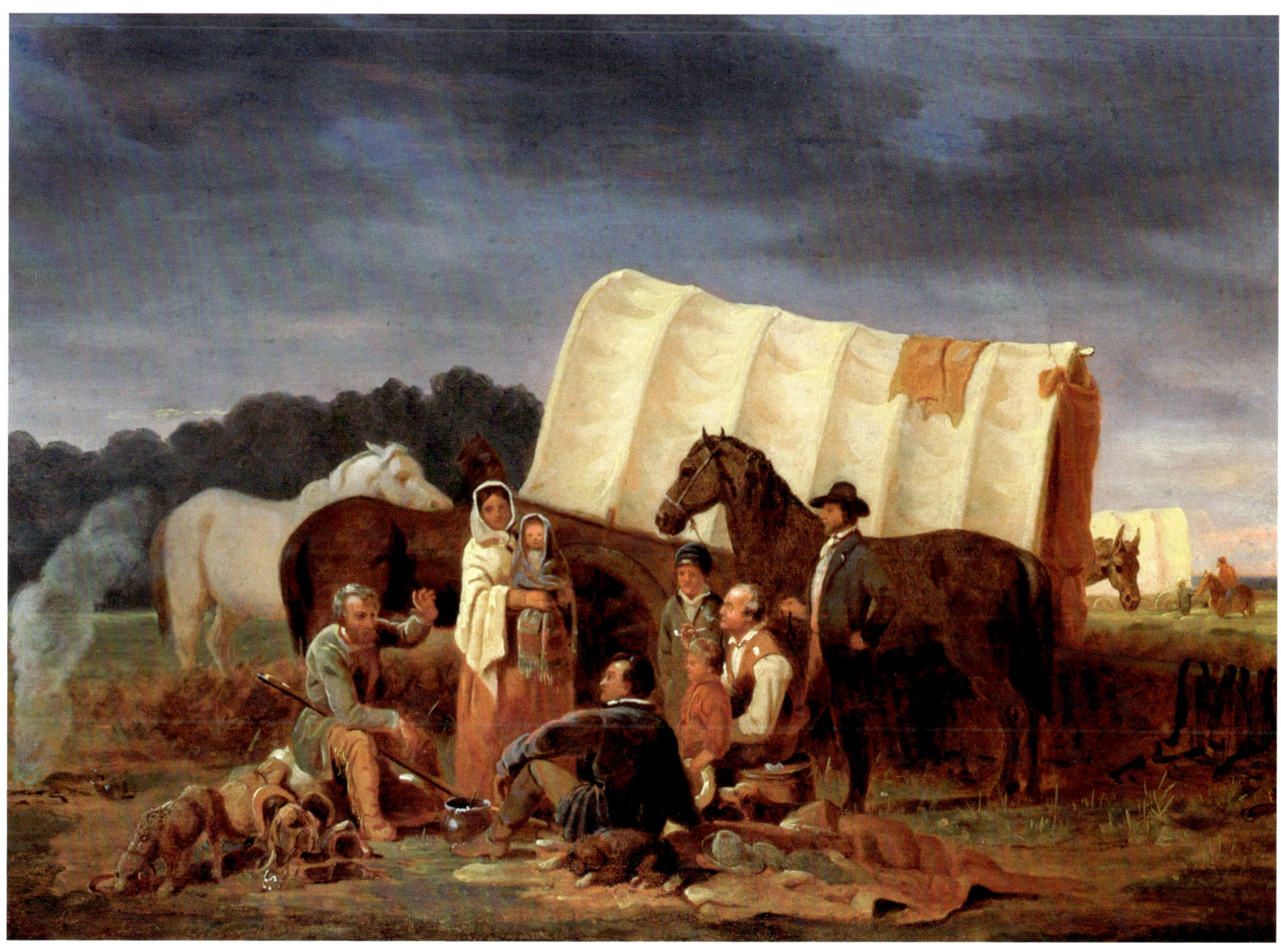

86
Study for a Large Picture

c. 1853

Oil on canvas

Location unknown

Grubar no. 73

PROVENANCE: John B. Moreau, by 1853.

EXHIBITED: NAD, no. 348, as owned by John B. Moreau

REFERENCE: Cowdrey 1943, 2, p. 89, no. 348, lists it and provides provenance.

87
Purchase of Manhattan Island from the Indians by the Dutch in 1626

c. 1853

Oil on canvas

48 x 68 inches (121.9 x 172.7 cm)

Signed, lower center: W. Ranney

Location unknown

Grubar no. 74, as The Sale of Manhattan by the Indians

PROVENANCE: Dr. James Anderson, New York, by 1853; Rutgers University, New Brunswick, New Jersey, by 1923.

EXHIBITED: NAD, 1853, no. 71.

REFERENCES: *Catalogue of the Twenty-Eighth Annual Exhibition of the National Academy of Design*, 1853, p. 14, no. 71, describes it (quoted in entry). *Literary World*, vol. 12 (April 30, 1853), p. 359, mentions it. *Home Journal*, April 30, 1853, p. 2, describes and critiques it (quoted in entry). *Literary World*, vol. 12 (May 7, 1853), no. 326, p. 359, mentions it. *New York Herald*, May 23, 1853, p. 3. *Crayon*, vol. 5 (January 1858), p. 26, discusses figures and costumes (quoted in entry). Tuckerman 1867, p. 432, mentions it. James G. Wilson, ed., *The Memorial History of the City of New-York* (New York: New-York History Company, 1892–1893), vol. 1, p. 152, engraved illus., p. 156, n. 1, identifies Anderson. Alexander Stuart Graham, "The Story of a Picture and an Artist: An Original Painting by William Ranney Discovered at Rutgers," *Rutgers Alumni Monthly*, vol. 4, no. 6 (March 1925), cover illus., p. 174, recounts discovery of picture and indicates there is no record of how long it had been at Rutgers. Cowdrey 1943, 2, p. 89. Undated catalogue sheet includes descriptive notes by Claude J. Ranney (quoted in entry), Ranney archives.

Purchase of Manhattan Island is one of only nine historical paintings shown at the National Academy in 1853. The catalogue of the exhibition provides the following description:

> The picture represents the purchase by the Dutch West India Company, of the Island of Manhattan, from the native Indians, in the summer of 1626. The principal figure is Peter Minuit, the Director General of the New Netherlands. Behind him is Isaac De Rasieres, the Provincial Secretary. On Minuit's right, is Sebastian Jansen Kiol, "Krank-besoekee," whose duty it was to visit the sick and read the Scriptures and creeds to the people on Sunday.

Grubar pointed out that this painting's obvious compositional and design antecedent is Benjamin West's *Penn's Treaty with the Indians* of 1771–1772 (Pennsylvania Academy of the Fine Art, Philadelphia), a well-known image that was so popular that copies of it were widely dispersed in a variety of media. Like West, Ranney took great care to include historically accurate details. For instance, he depicts fabrics and other trinkets, which the Dutch were said to have used to pay the Indians. In the background he shows a large ship, suggesting the type of vessel the trading company used to transport shipments of furs, lumber, and other goods back to the Netherlands. The artist also took particular care in rendering period dress. According to an account that appeared in the *Crayon* of 1858: "The costumes were carefully studied from prints drawn from authentic sources."

Critical responses to this unusual subject were mixed. Some admired the grouping of the figures but complained of the "gaudy" color. The *Home Journal,* while admiring the artist's ambition, observed that "A group of very red and very stiff Indians stand in proximity to a group of highly-coloured Europeans."

The painting's subject was likely selected and defined by Dr. James Anderson, a physician and an elder of New York's Dutch Reformed Church, who probably commissioned the painting because it was he who lent it to

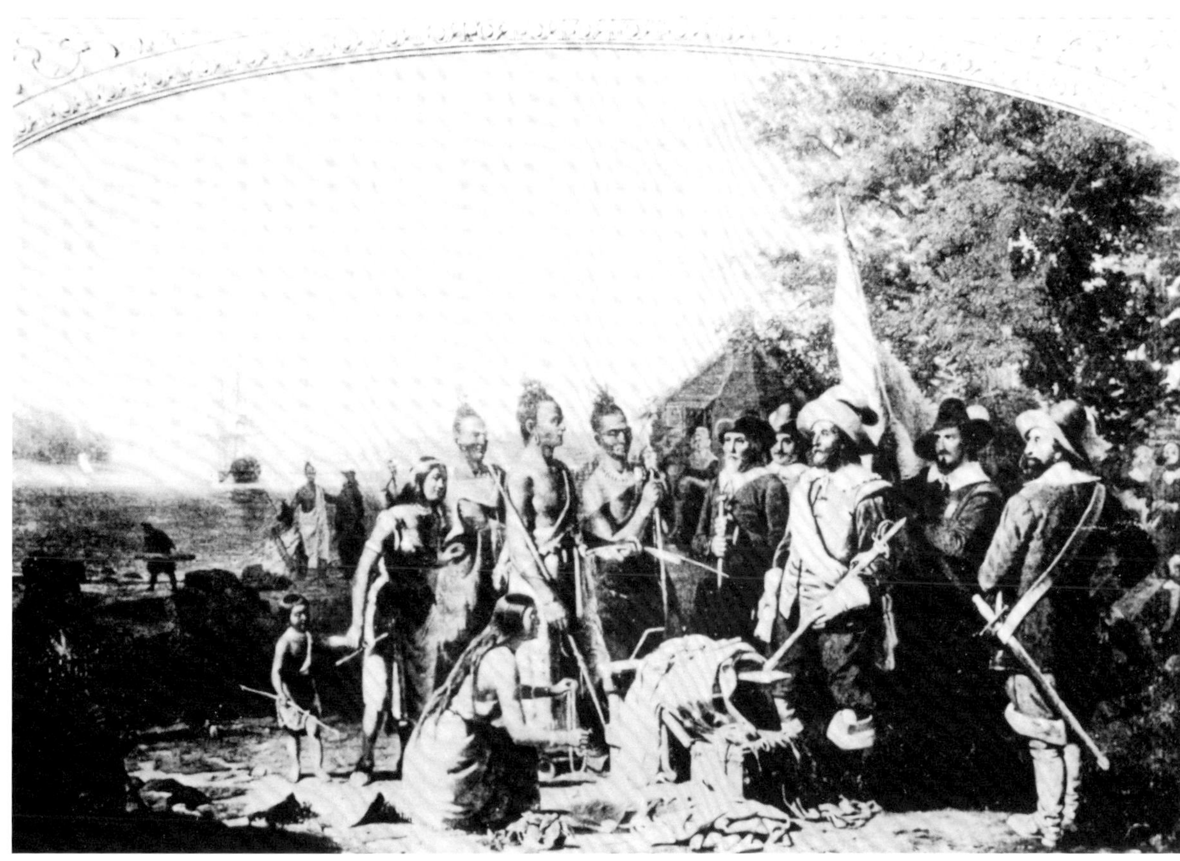

the National Academy's exhibition. While *Purchase of Manhattan Island* may have commemorated and celebrated the establishment of the Dutch colony of New Netherland (today New York), it may also have symbolized to Dr. Anderson the birth in the United States of the Dutch Reformed Church, the established religion of the colony until the British conquered New Netherland in 1664.

In 1766, the Dutch Reformed Church's governing body, or classis, secured a charter for Queens College (now Rutgers University) in New Brunswick, New Jersey. That historic connection between the church and the university may explain why the painting ended up at Rutgers University. In 1925, Alexander Stuart Graham reported in the *Rutgers Alumni Monthly* that Ranney's canvas had been identified two years earlier, that it had hung for many years in the center hall of the Queen's Building (now administrative offices), and that no one knew where the picture came from or how long it had been owned by the college. While Grubar seems to have seen it in 1962 when he published his catalogue, the location of the painting is now again unfortunately unknown.

Luckily, an undated black-and-white photograph has survived to document its appearance. In addition, Claude J. Ranney's undated notes provide a hint of some of its colors: "The center figure, Peter Minuit, is dressed in rose-colored breeches, tan and yellow jacket, yellow sash, white ruffled lace-collar, gray hat with golden yellow plume. Four companions have . . . costumes in slate, brown, and dark blue. One is carrying the Dutch flag."

There is a closely related oil study (see cat. no. 88). There is also an engraved version in the *Memorial History of the City of New-York,* of 1892 (vol. 1, p. 152). LB

88

Study for "Purchase of Manhattan Island from the Indians by the Dutch in 1826"

c. 1853
Oil on canvas
14 1/2 x 22 1/2 inches
(36.8 x 57.2 cm)
Alexander Galleries,
New York

PROVENANCE: Possibly Ranney Fund sale, as *Sale of Manhattan to Dutch*, no. 50, 1858; possibly Pepoon, 1858; (Kennedy Galleries, New York, by 1996–2005).

This oil study may be the painting purchased from the Ranney Fund sale (lot 50) by someone named Pepoon for twenty-six dollars. It closely relates to the now unlocated painting (see cat. no. 87) in its composition, figural types, and costume elements. The colors of the clothing are also consistent with those described by Claude J. Ranney in that entry. LB

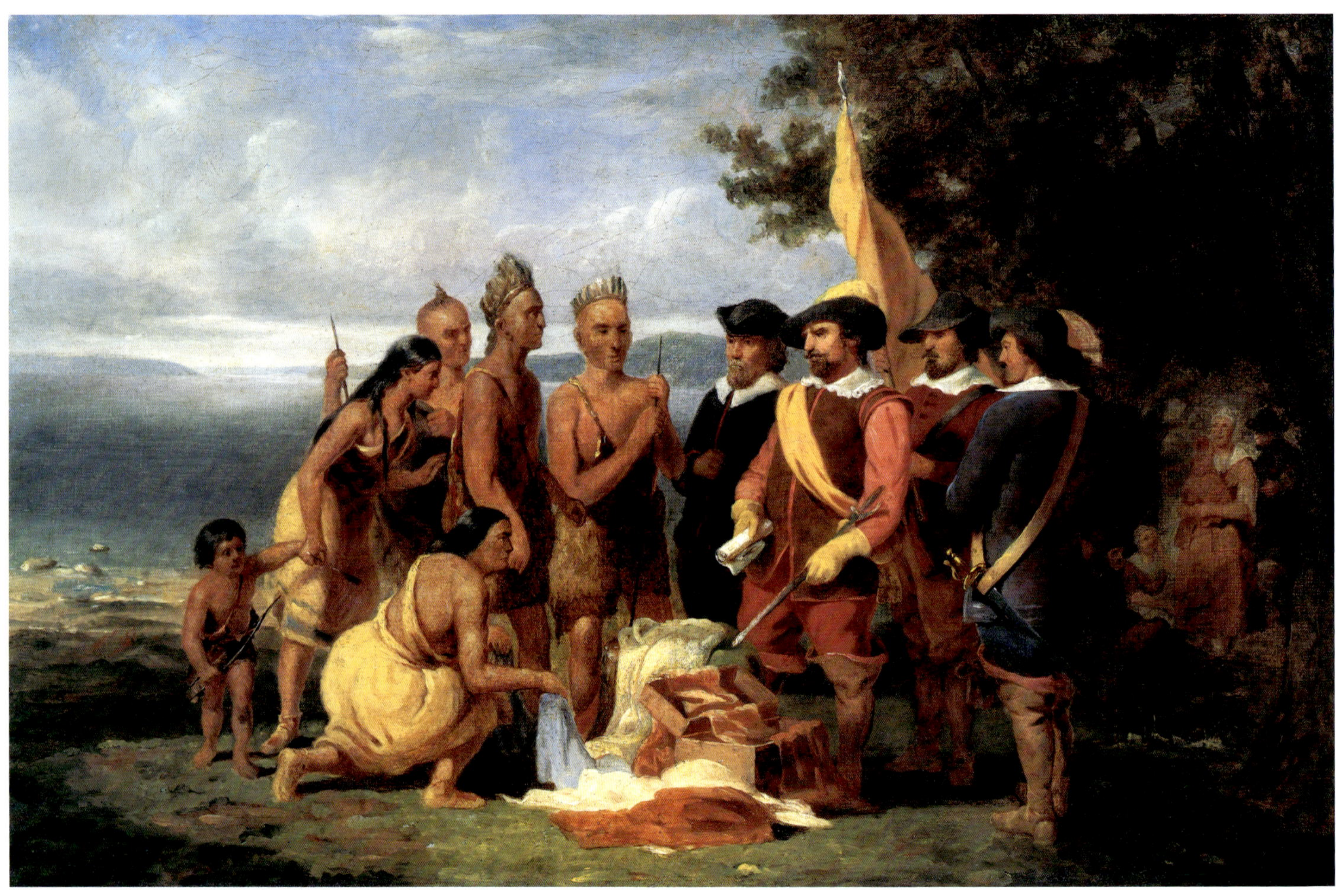

NO. 88

89

Backwoodsmen

c. 1853
Oil on canvas
Location unknown
Grubar no. 75

PROVENANCE: Possibly American Art-Union, 1853.
REFERENCE: Claude Ranney notes, Ranney archives.

90
Cowboys—The Banditti of '76 Fighting Over Their Spoils

c. 1853

Oil on canvas

Location unknown

Grubar no. 76

PROVENANCE: Thomas W. Phelps, by 1853.

EXHIBITED: NAD, 1853, no. 420, as owned by Thomas W. Phelps.

REFERENCE: Cowdrey 1943, 2, p. 89.

Although no contemporary reviews have been discovered which describe this painting, the title does define the subject matter. During the Revolution, banditti—bands of marauders and thieves, often composed of disgruntled ex-soldiers—operated between the British and American lines, where they plundered the countryside and terrorized the citizens who had no protection. In New York there were two rival factions: the Skinners, who were patriots, and the Cowboys, apparently the subject of this painting, who were Tories. Both groups were feared and hated by the populace. According to one account, they infested almost all of Westchester County, in New York, "and made it a political and social hell for the dwellers. Many left it; and allowed their lands to become a waste, rather than remain in the midst of perpetual torments."[1]

In 1858, *A Study for Large Picture of Cow Boys Quarreling over their Plunder* was sold at the Ranney Fund sale (lot 28) to Menzies, probably the book collector William Menzies (1810–1896), for twenty-two dollars. [2]

LB

1. Benson J. Lossing, *The Pictorial Field Book of the Revolution* (New York: Harper and Brothers, 1851–1852), vol. 2, p. 185, quoted from this book, which was owned by Ranney. See also Harry M. Ward, *Between the Lines: Banditti of the American Revolution* (Westport, Connecticut: Praeger, 2002), which provides contemporary accounts of the activities of the banditti.
2. No Ranney painting of this title, however, appeared in the 1876 sale of the Menzies' collection (sale, Messrs. Leavitt, New York, *Catalogue of a Collection of Fine Modern Paintings . . . Belonging to William Menzies, Esq. . . . ,* April 18 and 19, 1876).

91
The Pack Mule

c. 1853

Oil on canvas

30 x 25 inches (76.2 x 63.5)

Location unknown

Grubar no. 77

PROVENANCE: Williams, Stevens and Williams, New York, 1853. no. 115.

REFERENCE: Sale, Henry H. Leeds and Company, New York, *Catalogue of Williams, Stevens and Williams Second Great Annual Sale of 500 of the Most Valuable Oil Paintings in This Country . . . and about 100 paintings of the Düsseldorf School to be Sold at Auction, November 10 and 11, 1853,* p. 10, no. 115, provides dimensions (quoted in entry).

This is the first of at least two versions of this subject (see cat. no. 103). It is possible that this painting is the work we now know as *A Trapper Crossing the Mountains* (cat. no. 83) of 1853, which has close to the same dimensions.

The Williams, Stevens and Williams catalogue encouraged buyers with the following words: "Recollect the artist's reputation and the price his pictures brought at the last sale." The *New York Herald* of November 11, 1853, in reporting on the results of the sale, described this painting as "a clever picture; coloring very good. Sold at $95. He should have finished the background" (quoted from Grubar, p. 43). LB

92
The Emigrant's Halt

c. 1853

Oil on canvas

40 x 56 inches (101.6 x 142.2 cm)

Location unknown

Provenance: Williams, Stevens and Williams, New York, 1853, no. 350.

Reference: Sale, Henry H. Leeds and Company, New York, *Catalogue of Williams, Stevens and Williams Second Great Annual Sale of 500 of the Most Valuable Oil Paintings in This Country . . . and about 100 Paintings of the Düsseldorf School to be Sold at Auction, November 10 and 11, 1853,* p. 27, no. 350, provides dimensions and description (quoted in entry).

The Williams, Stevens and Williams catalogue described this large, now unlocated painting as "a scene of every day life in the West." LB

93
Marion and His Men

c. 1853

Oil on canvas

36 x 50 inches (76.2 x 127 cm)

Location unknown

Provenance: Williams, Stevens and Williams, New York, 1853.

Reference: Henry H. Leeds and Company, New York, *Catalogue of Williams, Stevens and Williams, Second Great Annual Sale of 500 of the Most Valuable Oil Paintings in This Country . . . and about 100 Paintings of the Düsseldorf School to be Sold at Auction, November 10 and 11, 1853,* p. 87, no. 490, as Marion and His Men, mentions (quoted in entry).

This newly discovered unlocated work was described as "Just finished. Never before exhibited, and the best example of color the artist has produced." Whether it relates to *Marion Crossing the Pedee* of 1850 (cat. no. 61) or the other later version of *Marion and His Men* (cat. no. 94) is unknown. LB

94*
Marion and His Men

1854

Oil on canvas

35 1/4 x 50 inches
(89.5 x 127 cm)

Signed and dated, center on saddle blanket of white horse: W Ranney 1854

Private collection

PROVENANCE: John James Herrick (1817–after 1885), Brooklyn, New York, and Tarrytown, New York, probably by at least 1859; his son, George Taylor Herrick (1862-1942), Pittsburgh; his son, John James Herrick (1889–1962), Pittsburgh, by 1928; his son, George H. Herrick, Washington D.C., and daughter, Mary H. Lisensky, Portland, Oregon (Sotheby's, New York, sale 7737, November 28, 2001, lot 176, as *Revolutionary Militia Crossing a River*).

REFERENCE: Copy of October 9, 1995, letter from Mary H. Lisensky to Sotheby's, Ranney archives, details provenance and includes biographical information on John J. Herrick from Herrick genealogy.

This recently discovered Revolutionary War subject is said to have descended in the Herrick family since the mid-nineteenth century. John J. Herrick, a prosperous New York City flour merchant and collector, was active in New York's business, social, and political life. He was one of the founders of the New York Mercantile Library and one of the ten governors of the almshouse, among other civic responsibilities.

For many years, according to Herrick family tradition, this picture was entitled *Marion Crossing the Pedee* (cat. no. 61). While there is no pictorial connection to Ranney's iconic image of river passage of 1850, the painting includes enough visual evidence to suggest that it does indeed relate to General Francis Marion. Known as the "Swamp Fox," this hero of the American Revolution was lionized because of his notorious guerilla activities in the South, particularly during the fall of 1780.

The wooded landscape setting of this painting evokes the swamps and creeks in which Marion was known to have hidden when he crisscrossed South Carolina, successfully taunting the British and eluding capture. As

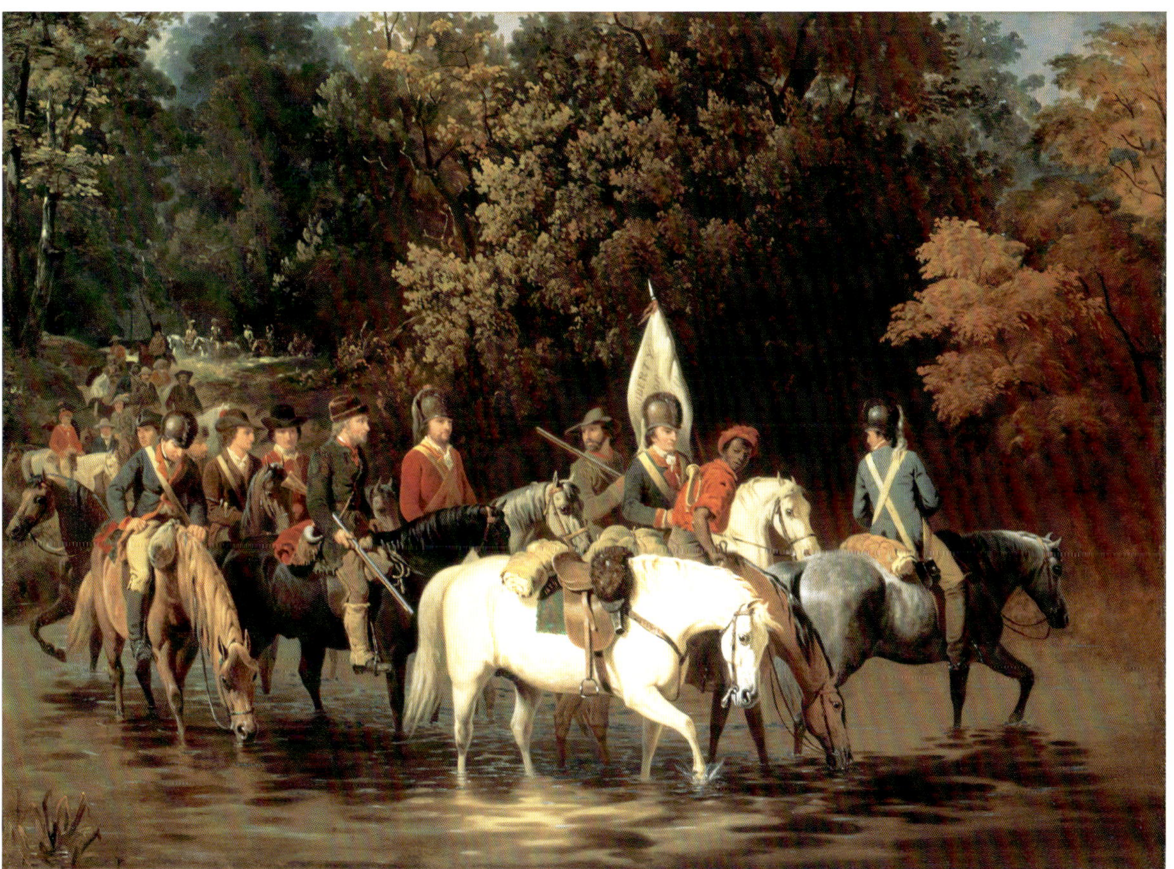

NO. 94

133

he did in *Marion Crossing the Pedee,* Ranney presents a group of men in a variety of colonial garb—Continental Army soldiers in full uniform and militiamen informally dressed—which typify the cross section of Marion's poorly supplied troops. Also following along on horseback in the languorous procession of men appears to be a British soldier or redcoat, perhaps meant to suggest the common practice of victors escorting prisoners of war to a central prison site or, alternatively, accepting into the ranks a captured soldier who decided to switch sides.

In the background, behind the young black man with a bugle, a man carries a regimental flag inscribed "Liberty or [Dea]th," the final words from Patrick Henry's emotionally charged and influential speech delivered to the Virginia Convention in 1775. This motto, while a common rallying cry of the American Revolution, was particularly associated with Marion's second regiment of Carolinians and was inscribed on a silver crescent on their leather helmets.[1] The question is, of course, which figure is Marion? It is tempting to suggest he is the uniformed figure whose head is framed by the flag, but no man particularly stands out.

The pictorial focus of the scene is not the hero but rather the centrally placed riderless white horse. Whether Ranney intended this image to symbolize the hero, a horse captured from the enemy, or that of a comrade lost in action is unclear. The bearskin draped across the front of the saddle is the most identifiable gear. While some American officers used this kind of protective cover for saddle-mounted pistol holders, the fact that it was standard issue for calvary troops of the British Legion suggests that this is a captured horse. Americans regularly supplemented their meager supplies by capturing prized British horses with their saddles along with other military materiel. In the short Battle of Black Mingo Creek on the night of September 28, 1780, for instance, Marion captured and rode thereafter Colonel John C. Ball's charger. If the riderless horse, however, represents the death of a comrade in arms, the most compelling incident mentioned in Marion's biography was the brutal murder of his beloved nephew Gabriel in mid-November 1780. Marion is said to have grieved for the boy as though he was his only son.[2]

The title assigned to this painting, which is dated 1854, is based not only on its historical and iconographic connections with Francis Marion, but also on the recent discovery of evidence indicating that Ranney in fact explored the Marion theme anew in 1853. In its sales catalogue that year, Williams, Stevens and Williams listed a work by Ranney entitled *Marion and His Men* and described it as "Just finished. Never before exhibited, and the best example of color the artist has produced." (see cat no. 93). The dimensions listed for that painting are identical with this painting's. Because of the coincidences of dates and sizes, *Marion and His Men* could be either that unlocated painting, which Ranney for whatever reason reworked the following year, or a closely related second version, which was subsequently commissioned.

The pose of the horse relates in reverse to the one depicted in Ranney's drawing, *Dragoon with His Charger* (cat. no. D11). LB

1. William Gilmore Simms, *The Life of Francis Marion* (New York: Henry G. Langley and Astor House, 1844), p. 121.
2. Roger D. Bass, *Swamp Fox: The Life and Campaigns of General Francis Marion* (Orangeburg, South Carolina: Sandlapper Publishing Company, 1974), p. 90.

95 *
The Fowler's Return

1854

Oil on canvas

19 x 27 inches (48.3 x 68.6 cm)

Signed and dated, lower center: Wm. Ranney /1854

Private collection

Grubar no. 79

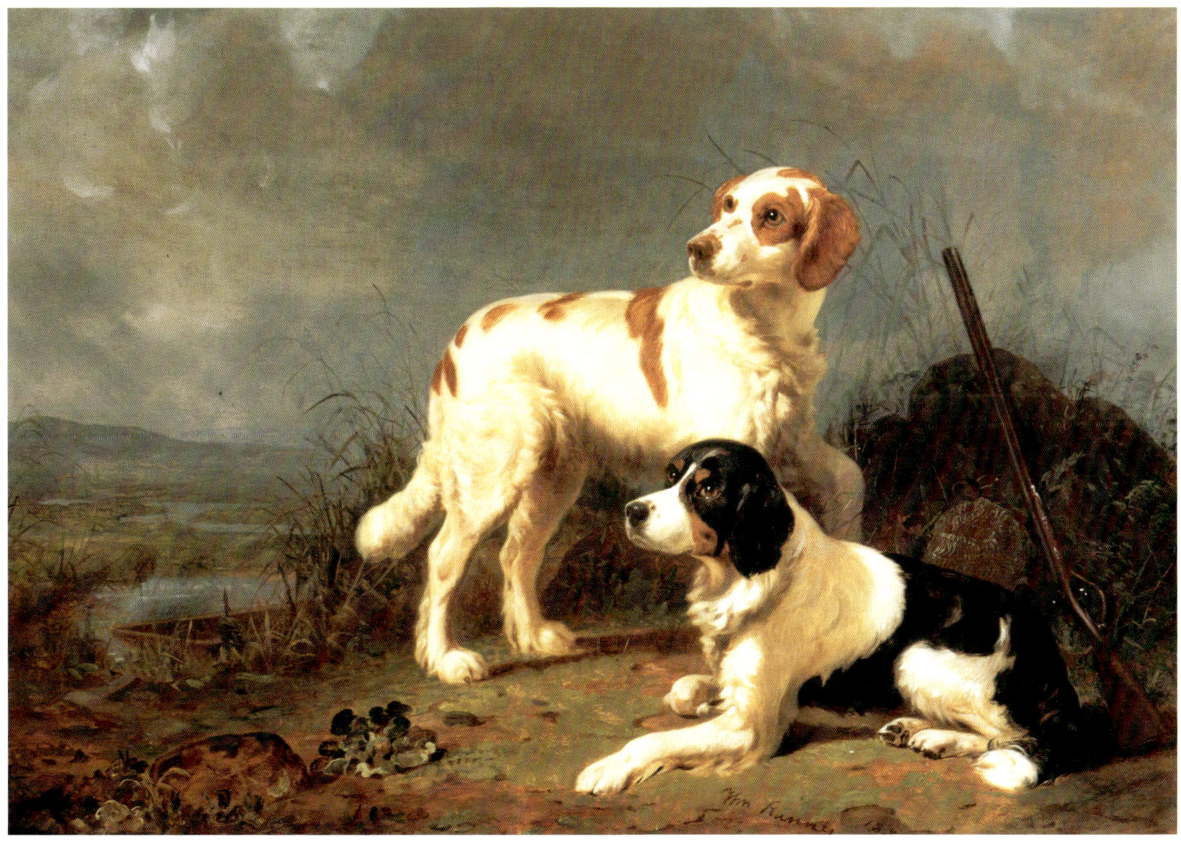

NO. 95

PROVENANCE: (Hirschl and Adler Galleries, New York, to c. 1982).

EXHIBITED: NAD, 1854, no. 229, as for sale. Chadds Ford 1991, no. 20.

REFERENCES: Cowdrey 1943, 2, p. 89. Thistlethwaite, 1991, p. 32 (quoted in entry).

The Fowler's Return, listed as unlocated by Grubar in 1962, is likely this recently discovered painting whose subject so closely relates to that title. Set within Ranney's typical marshy landscape, two setters, perhaps the artist's, await the return of their owner. The fowler of the title is in fact unseen, but his presence is implied by visual clues—a telltale skiff in the background, a rifle propped vertically at the right, and the obedient, almost wistful, gundogs that stare eagerly toward the left, clearly indicating his general whereabouts off-canvas. Early in his career, Ranney successfully introduced into his work this characteristic method of creating an off-canvas narrative, most notably, for instance, in *Match Boy* of 1845 (cat. no. 10) or *On the Wing* of 1850 (cat. no. 55).

The Fowler's Return is a particularly effective example of the off-canvas narrative technique. In addition, it demonstrates how skillful Ranney was at portraying dogs realistically. He enhanced their presence by capturing their traits and projecting their personalities. In this scene, he celebrates the strong and affectionate bond of the dogs to their owner. Mark Thistlethwaite (1991) observes: "Ranney inflates the dogs to heroic proportions and imbues them with sentimentality, an approach that calls to mind the works of the best-known animal painter of the nineteenth century, British artist Edwin Landseer." LB

135

96*
Virginia Wedding

1854

Oil on canvas

54 1/8 x 82 1/2 inches
(137.5 x 209.6 cm)

Signed and dated,
lower right: Wm.
Ranney, 1854

R.W. Norton Art
Gallery, Shreveport,
Louisiana

Grubar no. 80

PROVENANCE: Dr. Thomas Edmondson (1808–1856), Baltimore, his daughter Mary (Mrs. Samuel J.) Hough (1846–1920) and her husband, Baltimore, by 1874, their daughters, Mary, Ethel, and Anne E. Hough, all of Baltimore, to 1954, Maryland Historical Society, Baltimore, 1954–c. 1975 (Hirschl and Adler Galleries, New York, by c. 1975) Amon Carter Museum, Ft. Worth, Texas, 1975–1996.

ON DEPOSIT: Maryland Historical Society, Baltimore, by c. 1900–1954.

EXHIBITED: Maryland Historical Society, *Sixth Annual Exhibition,* 1858, no. 49. Maryland Historical Society, *Charity Art Exchange Exhibition,* 1874, no. 239, as lent by Samuel J. Hough. Virginia Museum of Fine Art, Richmond, *An Exhibition of Nineteenth Century Virginia Genre,* January 17–February 13, 1946, no. 50. Chadds Ford 1991, no. 22, lent by the Amon Carter Museum.

REFERENCES: *Home Journal,* December 5, 1857, p. 3, mentioned as commissioned (quoted in entry). *Catalogue of Paintings, Engravings, etc. at the Picture Gallery of the Maryland Historical Society, Sixth Annual Exhibition, 1858* (Baltimore, 1858), no. 49, p. 4, lists it. *Art Gallery of the Maryland Historical Society, Catalogue of Paintings, Statuary, etc.* (Baltimore, 1901), no. 259, p. 12, lists it as owned by Mr. Hough (1839–1911); ibid., 1904, and 1907. Thistlethwaite 1991, no. 22, p. 44, illus., pp. 67–68, 70, discusses it.

With the figures dressed in late eighteenth-century attire, *Virginia Wedding* is one of Ranney's largest historical genre paintings. This nostalgic scene captures the festive mood of a wedding set on a modest southern plantation during the early years of the Republic. Traditionally, the bride and groom have been identified as the couple pictorially highlighted at the left, astride the white horse, leading the serpentine line of mounted youthful revelers. They are met by an elderly gentleman, presumably one of the parents, who welcomes them with outstretched arms: his social rank is suggested by the finery of his formal dress and wig. The woman's prominently displayed wedding band indicates that the ceremony has already taken place.

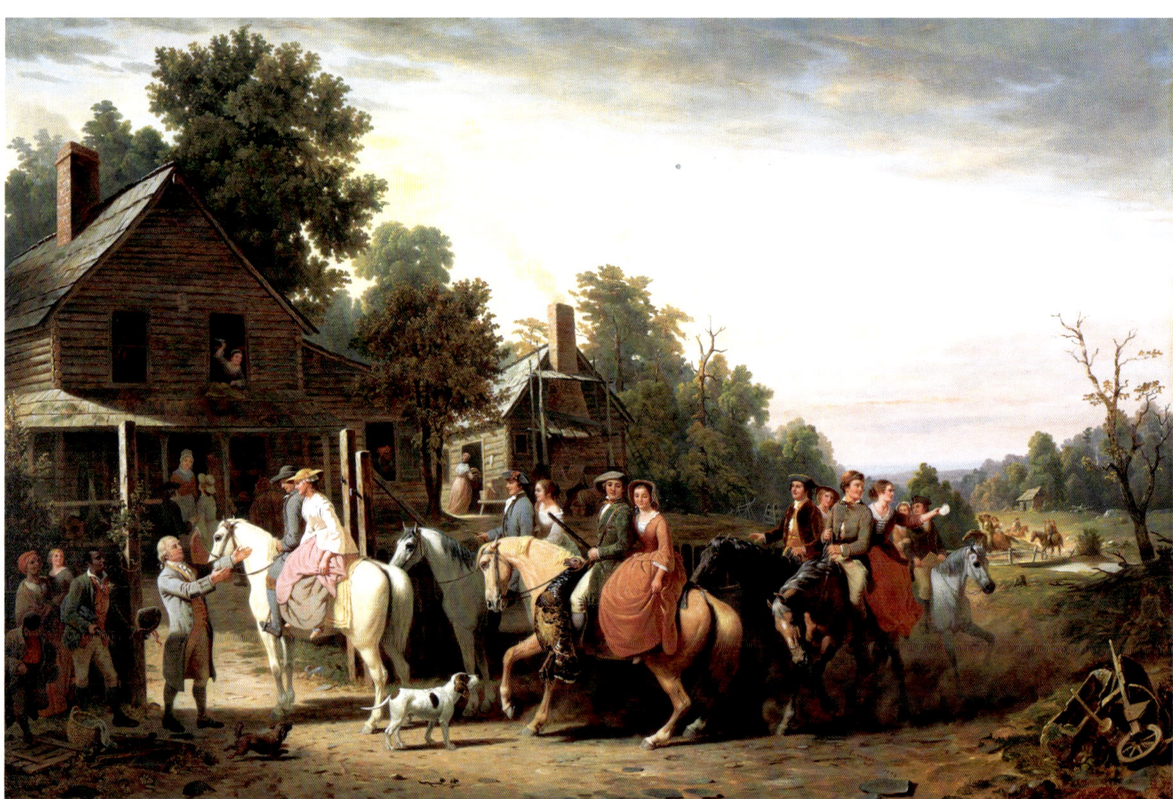

NO. 96

136

The actual identification of the newlyweds, however, is somewhat ambiguous. It is curious, for example, that the happy couple behind the assumed bride and groom are more ostentatiously dressed than others in the picture: The man's tricorn hat is ornamented with a red ribbon, and, unlike the traveling clothes worn by her female companions, the woman wears a white gown and her hair is bejeweled. Prominently featured in the center of the composition, a couple on horseback, the man with his hunting rifle, transport a dead wild turkey, perhaps a gift for the anticipated feast.

The excitement of the ensuing celebration is captured by the many individuals seen scurrying throughout the background. A woman waves from the second floor of the house, while a second hastens into the kitchen (the outbuilding in the background, with the smoke rising from the chimney). At the left corner, a black musician carries a fiddle and a youngster, in eager anticipation, is already dancing a spirited jig. At the right corner, a butter churn, remnants from a broken wheelbarrow, and a feed trough form a still life of farm implements celebrating country life.

Unlike other mid-nineteenth recreations of historical wedding scenes, such as *The Marriage of Washington to Martha Custis* of 1849 (Virginia Museum of Fine Arts, Richmond) painted by Ranney's contemporary Junius Brutus Stearns, *Virginia Wedding* appears to be a generalized historical scene, set outdoors and, given its title, chronicling a rather specific regional tradition, as described, for instance, by Henry Howe in his *Historical Collections of Virginia of 1852:* "A wedding engaged the attention of the whole neighborhood and the frolic was anticipated by old and young with eager expectation."[1] It is unclear whether or not neighborhood celebrations like these still took place as late as 1854 when Ranney painted this picture, but it is interesting to note that by that time the wild turkey had become virtually extinct.

Scholars have speculated that Ranney's selection of this subject was based, like many of his historical subjects, on an as yet to be identified literary source, particularly since there is no evidence he spent any time in Virginia. While that certainly is a possibility, a Ranney obituary in the *Home Journal* of 1857 includes a statement that the canvas was commissioned by "a wealthy and liberal patroness of the arts." This undoubtedly refers to the young wife of Dr. Thomas Edmondson, who was the earliest known owner of the picture. Mary Howell (born 1822) predeceased her husband in 1853. She or he presumably defined the scene for Ranney, based on either personal family recollections or on a literary source. Dr. Edmondson received his medical degree from the University of Maryland in 1834, and, according to the November 26, 1856, obituary which appeared in the *Baltimore American*, he "was a gentleman of liberal education and refined tastes and contributed with a generous hand and sound discriminating judgment to the advancement of Science and the Arts in this community."

No record has been discovered to indicate whether *Virginia Wedding* was ever exhibited publicly during Ranney's lifetime. Grubar, however, quotes an undated clipping from the Ranney scrapbook (New-York Historical Society) that suggests it was shown somewhere: "[Ranney's] *Virginia Wedding* exhibits his powers to advantage. What a pleasant cavalcade is that of the youths each with a partner pillioned behind. The horses enter the spirit of the scene, and seem to enjoy their double burdens as much as the bridegroom his duplicated responsibilities" (pp. 43–44).

A Study for *Virginia Wedding* was sold at the Ranney Fund sale (see cat. no. 97). L B

1. Henry Howe, *Historical Collections of Virginia* (Charleston, South Carolina: W. R. Babcock, 1852), p. 198, quoted in Thistlethwaite 1991, p. 68.

97
Study of Picture, Virginia Wedding

c. 1854

Oil on canvas

Location unknown

PROVENANCE: Ranney Fund sale, no. 174, as sold to Menzies for $30; William Menzies, 1858–1876 (sale, Messrs. Leavitt, Auctioneers, New York, April 18 and 19, 1876, no. 62, as Virginia Wedding).

REFERENCE: *Catalogue of a Collection of Fine Modern Paintings . . . Belonging to William Menzies* (New York, 1876), no. 62, p. 11.

98
Washington and Gist Crossing the Allegheny River

1854

Oil on canvas

39 x 55 inches (99.1 x 139.7 cm)

Signed and dated, lower left: Wm. Ranney/1854

Richard King Mellon Foundation, Pittsburgh

Grubar no. 81

PROVENANCE: S. N. Dodge, New York, 1855; Mr. M. Hold, New York; Louisa B. Holt, Summit, New Jersey; (John Levy Galleries, New York, by 1947); (Vose Galleries, Boston, by 1948) (McCaughen and Burr, St. Louis, by c. 1949–1955).

EXHIBITED: NAD, 1855, no. 95, as owned by S. N. Dodge; Robert C. Vose Galleries, Boston, *American Landscape and Figure Paintings: From 1800 to 1890 . . .* Summer, 1948, no. 36; Chadds Ford 1991, no. 23.

REFERENCE: FARL mount, provides provenance. Thistlethwaite 1991, pp. 55–59 and 61, discusses, p. 56. illus.

This is a sequel to Ranney's painting *Washington's Mission to the Indians in 1753*, exhibited at the National Academy in 1847 (see cat. no. 33). Like that earlier work, *Washington and Gist Crossing the Allegheny River* portrays an event which occurred during the French and Indian War, when George Washington, then a twenty-one-year-old major in the Virginia militia, was sent west over the Alleghenies by Virginia governor Robert Dinwiddie to gather military intelligence and to admonish the French not to intrude on lands that Virginia claimed as part of its 1609 charter. As a representative of British interests, Washington was also asked to meet with the Indians in the region, especially the Iroquois confederacy, to try and win their allegiance.

On November 15, 1753, with the tough and knowledgeable backwoodsman Christopher Gist as his guide, Washington set out toward the divide between the Shenandoah and Ohio valleys. Being in the midst of extreme wintry weather, the expedition, according to Washington's legendary and creative biographer, Parson Weems, "was as disagreeable and dangerous as Hercules himself could have desired."[1] Washington recalled the "excessive rains and a vast quantity of snow."[2]

One hundred years later, Ranney depicted this historic event, which occurred in early January of 1754, in the area of present-day Pittsburgh. Having completed his negotiations with the French and Indians, Washington and his companions began their return journey to Williamsburg, Virginia, five hundred miles away. By then, however, the snow was so deep that the horses were unable to proceed, and Washington and Gist were forced to trek through the wilderness on foot. They hoped that by the time they reached the Allegheny, it would be frozen over so they could walk across. But instead, they found the river dangerously high and teeming with ice floes. With one hatchet between them, they constructed a small raft. As Washington later recounted: "Before we were halfway over, we were jammed in the ice, in such a manner that we expected every moment our raft to sink and ourselves to perish. I put out my setting pole to try to stop the raft . . . when the rapidity of the stream threw it [the pole] with such violence . . . that it jerked me out into ten feet of water."[3] The two shivering travelers found their way to an island in the river, where they spent the night. They awoke the next day to find the river frozen and were able to walk across and complete their journey.

Mark Thistlethwaite (1991) notes that in the mythology introduced initially by Parson Weems in the early 1800s and well codified in the literature by the mid-nineteenth century, Washington's survival was indicative of his being "divinely protected" and reinforced the notion that "his life and greatness were foreordained by Providence."

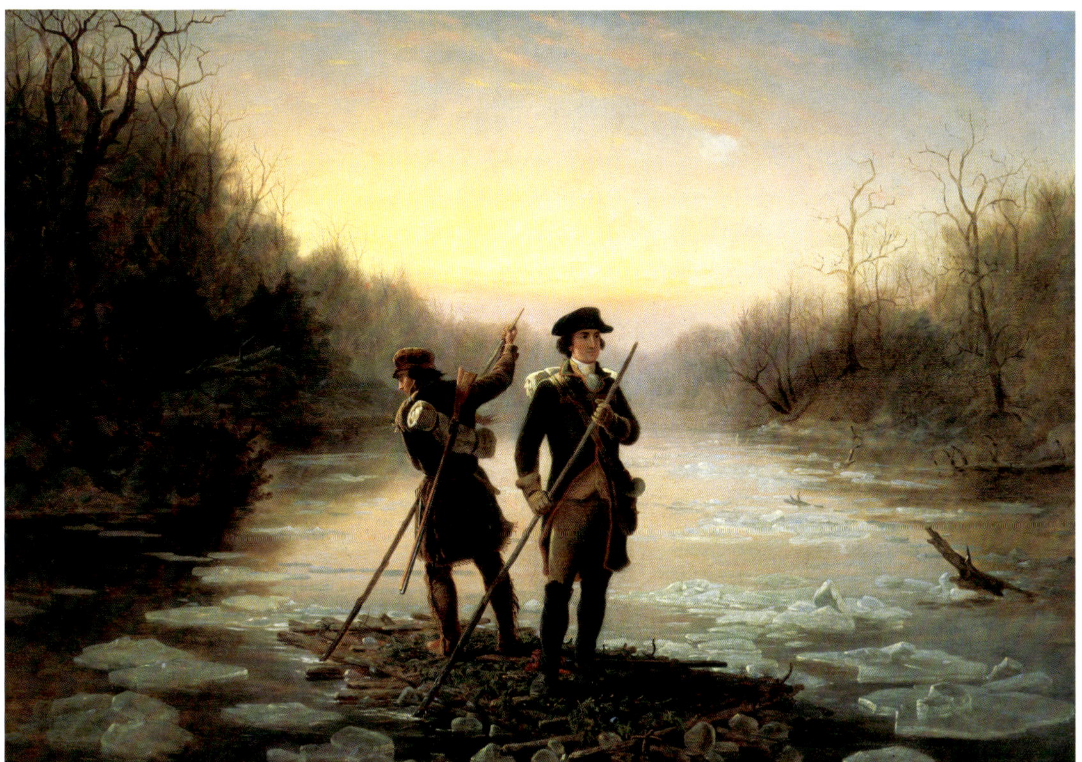

It was thus not surprising that the subject of Washington and Gist was a popular one for artists at the time. Typically the travelers were depicted on the raft, before Washington falls off. Thistlethwaite cites in particular Daniel Huntington's painting of 1843, which subsequently appeared as an engraving in several magazines which Ranney might have seen.[4] In Huntington's dynamic version of the subject, Washington is shown as an idealized hero who, with Gist, seems to exert all his strength to pole the tiny raft across the treacherous waters. In Ranney's less dramatic interpretation, Washington, in the uniform of the Virginia militia, stands erect as though a captain of a ship, while Gist, whose face is barely visible, does the poling. In 1863, Ranney's friend William Sidney Mount painted a similar subject, *Washington Crossing the Allegheny* (private collection).

In addition to a very finished and similarly titled watercolor and ink study (cat. no. D80) and a pencil drawing (cat. no. D65) both of which are related to this work, there are also two small pencil sketches (see cat. nos. D20 and D21). These sketches, however, illustrate a different and later aspect of the story. Unlike *Washington and Gist Crossing the Allegheny River*, in which Ranney depicts the national hero in a statuesque pose suggesting authority and power, in his alternative scenes he shows a soaking wet, faceless Washington—only the top of his head visible—being pulled from the water by Gist. While this down-to-earth interpretation of the story may be a more accurate representation of the event, the loss of dignity implied in this image compromises Washington's omniscient mythological stature and may not have been as appealing to the general public. Whether this was a preliminary and rejected idea, or Ranney was planning another sequel, is unknown.

A probable related work, *A Study for Picture, Washington Crossing the Susquehanna,* was sold in the Ranney Fund sale to someone named Wood[5] for seventeen dollars (lot 89). LB

1. Mason L. Weems, *The Life of Washington*, ed. by Marcus Cunliffe (1809; reprint, Cambridge, Massachusetts: Belknap Press of Harvard University Press, 1997), p. 30.
2. Quoted in James Thomas Flexner, *George Washington: The Forge of Experience (1732–1775)* (Boston: Little, Brown and Company, 1965), p. 60.
3. Quoted ibid., p. 76.
4. Thistlethwaite, p. 58, notes that the Huntington engraving appeared in the *Columbian Magazine* (1844), *The Gift* (1845), H. Hastings Weld's *Life of Washington* (1845), and T. Addison Richard's *Romance of the American Landscape* (1854). Grubar also noted that a modified version of the engraving appeared in *Graham's Magazine* (August 1855).
5. See cat. no. 50 for information on Wood.

99*
Kit Carson

1854

Oil on canvas

29 x 24 1/2 inches
(73.7 x 62.2 cm)

Signed and dated, lower center: Wm Ranney/1854

Private collection

PROVENANCE: Herman Eldridge Giffin (b. 1829) and Anna Christina (Gordon) Walker Giffin (b. 1833), New York, and San Francisco, by c. 1876–1877; their son, Oscar F. Giffin (1861–1952), San Francisco; his widow; her niece, Dorothy Carson, and her husband, Walter G. Carson, by c. 1953–1984, Santa Barbara, California (Vose Galleries, Boston, 1984) (Country Store Gallery, Austin, 1984); Cliff Logan, Austin; (Rosenstock Arts, Denver, to 1984) John F. Eulich, Dallas, 1984–1998 (Sotheby's, New York, *The American West: The John F. Eulich Collection,* May 20, 1998, lot 59).

EXHIBITED: Mechanics' Institute of the City of San Francisco, *Fifteenth Industrial Exhibition of the Mechanics Institute,* August 10–September 11, 1880, no. 176, p. 54, lists it as Kit Carson, lent by Giffin. Los Angeles County Museum of Art, *Western Scene,* October 14–December 14, 1975, n. p., no. 35, lists it as Kit Carson, misdates it 1853, lent by Mr. and Mrs. Walter Carson, Santa Barbara.

REFERENCES: Walter G. Carson to Mrs. J. Maxwell Moran, June 9, 1975, Ranney archives, describes how it descended in his wife's family, calls it The Pioneer Kit Carson. Undated copy of a history of the painting compiled by Walter G. Carson, ibid., titles it Kit Carson and provides provenance and exhibition details. Francis S. Grubar to Walter G. Carson, December 26, 1976 (copy), ibid., authenticates picture with title Kit Carson and redates 1854. Rick Stewart with Don Hedgpeth, *The American West: Legendary Artists of the Frontier* ([Dallas]: Hawthorne Publishing Company, 1986), p. 84, discusses it, p. 85, illus. Vose Galleries to Linda Bantel, December 9, 1997, Ranney archives, titles it Kit Carson and provides further provenance.

NO. 99

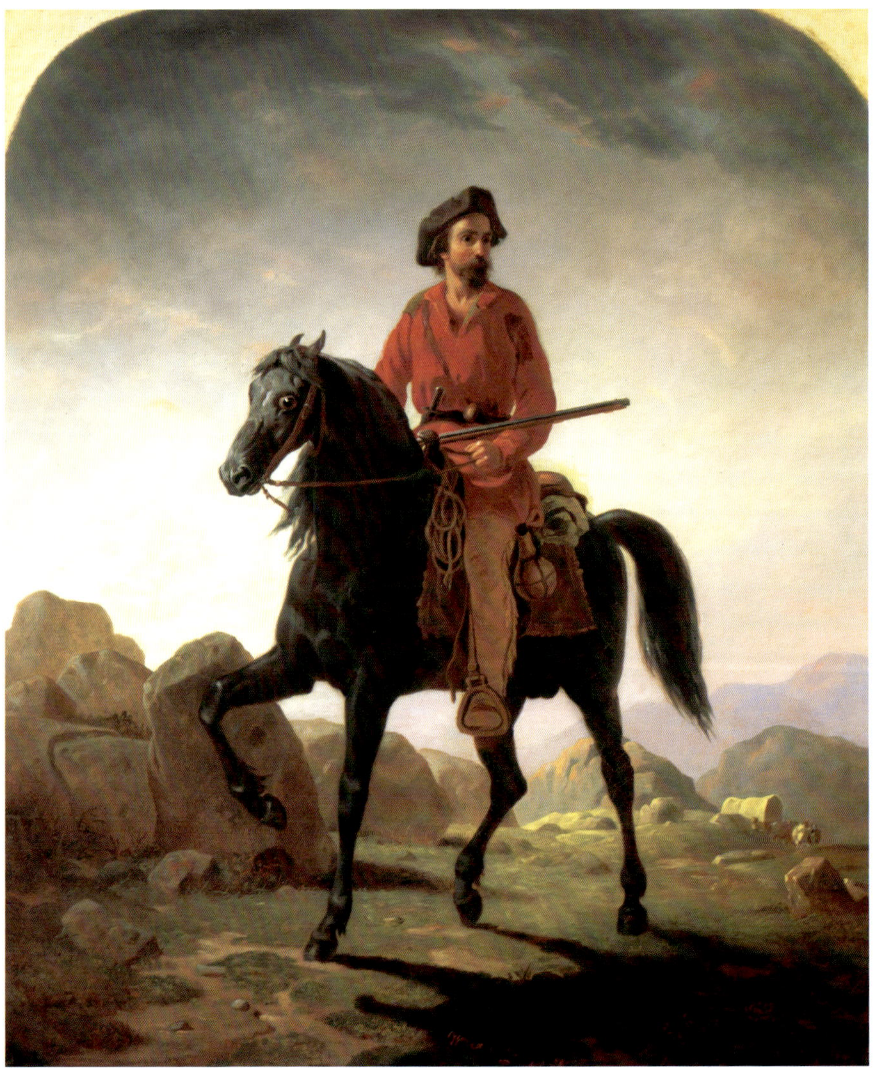

One of the early, if not the original owners of the painting, the Herman Eldridge Giffin family of New York and later (after 1877) of San Francisco, knew it as *Kit Carson*. They loaned it to the Mechanic's Institute exhibition in San Francisco in 1880 with that title. As such, it descended in the family and was accepted by Ranney scholar Francis S. Grubar in 1976, shortly after the painting again came to public notice.

Christopher "Kit" Carson (1809–1868) was certainly a man who would have come to Ranney's attention in the 1850s when he painted this oil. By then Carson was well on his way to becoming a mythic figure in the history of the American West. As a youth raised in Missouri, he had been apprenticed to a saddlemaker, but soon was lured west on the Santa Fe Trail. He settled in Taos, then an important trading spot, and took up the life of a trader and trapper. Over the years he gained substantial knowledge and experience on his many forays into the Rockies and beyond. So reliable and well versed was he with the geography of the West that he functioned as a guide for the celebrated explorer John C. Fremont on several occasions from 1842 to 1845. He was a federal Indian agent and served in the military in campaigns against the Indians during the Civil War, after which he attained the rank of brigadier general.

In Ranney's day, Carson figured prominently in several well-publicized western accounts, including the Mexican War memoirs *General Scott and His Staff* of 1848, which included a portrait of Carson, and an article by fellow artist and adventurer George D. Brewerton for *Harper's New Monthly Magazine* in 1853.[1]

Despite the long history of this painting's association with Kit Carson, concerns about such an attribution of identity have arisen in recent times. Most modern Carson scholars contend that the Ranney depiction of Carson looks nothing like the historical figure.[2] Portraits of Carson in the 1840s and 1850s show him as a beardless man with tight lips, a prominent nose and narrow, piercing eyes.[3] In addition, he was a stocky fellow with short legs. None of these characteristics resemble the individual portrayed by Ranney. Moreover, Ranney's figure wears an eighteenth-century tricornered hat, a historical detail that is difficult to explain. Thus, if Ranney really intended this to be Carson, he was doing so in the most general of terms. The painting might best be viewed as the artist's attempt at a heroic and symbolic characterization rather than as a specific portrait of the man. It is perhaps most prudent to consider it as a metaphor and tribute to Carson's heroic pathfinder legacy. PHH

1. *General Scott and His Staff: Comprising Memoirs of Generals Scott, Twiggs, Smith, Quitman, Shields* (Philadelphia: Grigg, Elliot and Co., 1848), and George D. Brewerton, "A Ride with Carson Through the Great American Desert and Rocky Mountains," *Harper's New Monthly Magazine*, vol. 7, no. 39 (August 1853), pp. 306–334.

2. I am grateful to Skip Miller, past director of the Taos Historic Museums (fomerly the Kit Carson Historic Museums), and two prominent independent Carson scholars and historians, Mark Simons of Taos and Lee Burke of Dallas, for their insights into the Carson likeness.

3. See, for example, Brewerton, "In the Buffalo Country," *Harper's New Monthly Magazine*, vol. 148, no. 25 (September 1862), p. 307, for a written description of Carson.

100

When Shall We Three Meet Again?

c. 1854

Oil on canvas

Location unknown

PROVENANCE: A. Robeson, Jr., Newport, Rhode Island, by 1854.

EXHIBITED: Providence, the Rhode Island Art Association, 1854, no. 121.

REFERENCE: *Catalogue of the First Exhibition of Paintings, Statuary, and Other Works of Art*, by the Rhode Island Art Association, at Westminster Hall, Providence, September, 1854, cat. no. 121, lists owner as A. Robeson, Jr. (Yarnall and Gerdts 1986, no. 73300).

101

Winter Scene, the Barn Yard, Cattle, and Figures

c. 1854

Oil on canvas

Location unknown

Grubar no. 78, as
Winter Scene

PROVENANCE: Henry H. Leeds and Company, New York, *Catalogue of Great Annual Sale of Valuable Oil Paintings by American and Resident Artists*, October 31–November 1, 1854, lot 43, p. 3, as Winter Scene, the Barn Yard, Cattle and Figures.

REFERENCES: Henry H. Leeds and Company, New York, sale cat., lot 43. *New-York Daily Tribune*, November 1, 1854, p. 7, mentions sold for $60.

The Leeds sale catalogue describes the work as "a very effective Picture." The *New York Daily Tribune* reported that *Winter Scene*, which sold for sixty dollars, was among the few pictures that brought a high price. This may be the same picture as *Barnyard with Cattle—Winter* (see cat. no. 115). LB

102

The Guide *(pendant to* The Pack Mule)

c. 1854

Oil on canvas

Location unknown

REFERENCE: Henry H. Leeds and Company, New York, October 31–November 1, 1854, *Catalogue of Great Annual Sale of Valuable Oil Paintings by American and Resident Artists*, lot 98, p. 6, lists it as The Guide (pendant to The Pack Mule, no. 99).

103

The Pack Mule *(pendant to* The Guide)

c. 1854

Oil on canvas

Location unknown

REFERENCE: Henry H. Leeds and Company, New York, October 31–November 1, 1854, *Catalogue of Great Annual Sale of Valuable Oil Paintings by American and Resident Artists*, lot 99, p. 6, lists it as The Pack Mule (pendant to The Guide, no. 98).

For a similar subject, see see cat. no. 91. LB

104
Boys Crabbing

1855

Oil on canvas

23 1/4 x 36 3/8 inches
(59.1 x 92.4 cm)

Signed and dated, at center, on edge of dock: Wm Ranney 55

White House Historical Association, Washington, D. C. White House Collection 449. Gift of the Charles E. Merrill Trust, 1972.

Grubar no. 102

PROVENANCE: Charles H. Rogers, Ravenswood, New York; his nephew, Henry N. Corwith, Bridgehampton, New York, early 1930's to 1947; his wife, Dorothy Wooster Corwith, Barre, Vermont, by c. 1947–1972 (Hirschl and Adler Galleries, New York, by 1972).

EXHIBITED: Christian A. Johnson Art Center, Middlebury College, Middlebury, Vermont, 1970, *Art Out of the Attic*, no. 11, as Boys Crabbing [lent by Dorothy W. Corwith].

REFERENCES: Margaret Ranney (wife of the artist), copy of questionnaire for *Appletons' Cyclopedia of American Biography*, about 1883, William Tylee Ranney file, Art Division, New York Public Library, lists it. John Wilmerding, "Discovering American Art," in *Art Out of the Attic* (Montpelier, Vermont: Vermont Council on the Arts, 1970), p. 5. Dorothy Wooster Corwith to Betty Ford, March 27, 1976, with attachment from Mrs. Charles M. Voss, March 28, 1976, provides provenance, Office of the Curator, The White House. William Kloss, *Art in the White House: A Nation's Pride* (Washington: White House Historical Association in cooperation with the National Geographic Society, 1992), p. 125, discusses it.

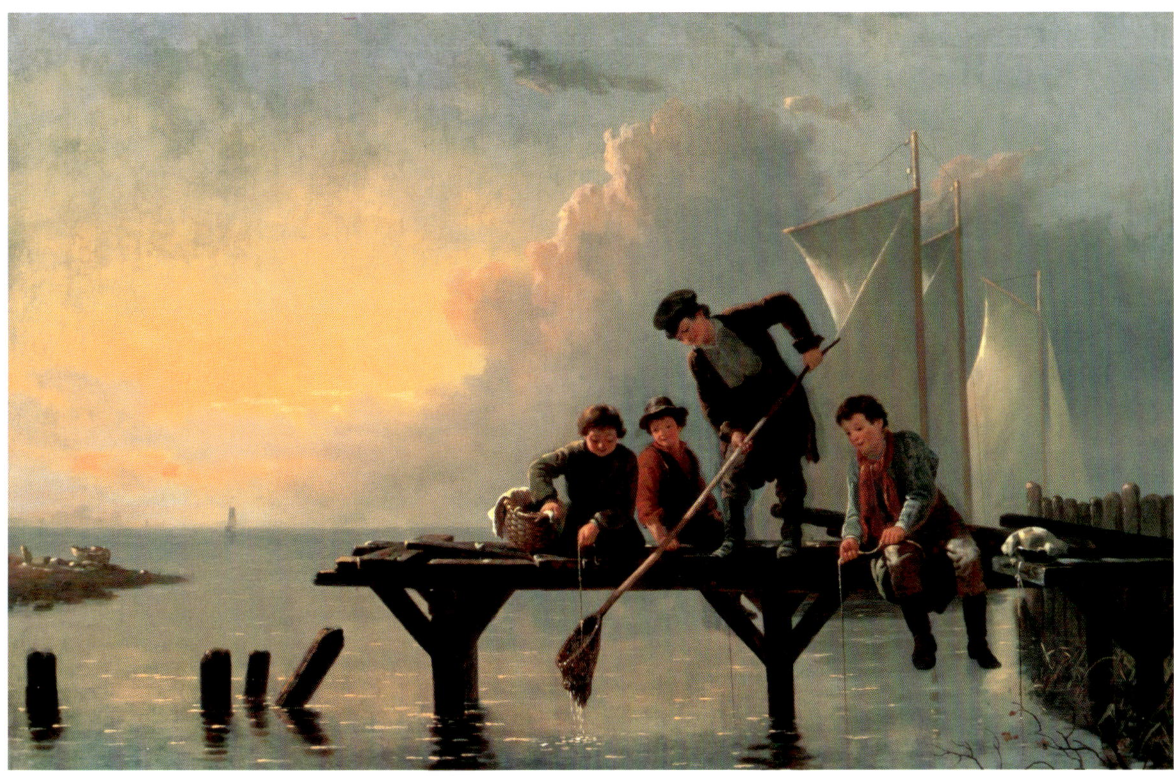

NO. 104

This genre scene, which was recorded by Grubar in 1962 as location unknown, was rediscovered in 1970, when it was exhibited in Middlebury, Vermont. In his introductory essay to that catalogue, art historian John Wilmerding hailed *Boys Crabbing* as "the major discovery of the exhibition." He particularly admired the triangular organization of the figural group which is balanced by a "golden glow of luminous sunlight in the left background."

Rural themes such as this one, which recall bygone days of childhood innocence, enjoyed wide popularity among American painters before the Civil War. Ranney's friend William Sidney Mount, for instance, was one of the leading artists exhibiting these kinds of subjects, which particularly appealed to the nostalgic yearnings of a burgeoning urban populace who had become increasingly weary of the "irksome bondage of a city life" (see Kloss, 1992).

Ranney's genre scene is an affectionate portrayal of four cheerful young boys on a pier where they are involved in a favorite summertime ritual, netting crabs. As his friends look on, one boy raises his dripping net from the water, while another tries to lure the crab onto the string in order to get it into his basket to be cooked later. While there is not enough detail to identify the locale where Ranney might have observed this activity, one assumes it was close to his New Jersey home. In fact, from late July into September, blue crabs, which are superb eating, are found in the Hudson River as far north as Poughkeepsie.

The asymmetry of the composition is accentuated by the series of triangular shapes of the mother-of-pearl colored sails, which dramatically recede into the right background to form a rigorous geometric structure behind the boys. Ranney's delicate palette is comprised of light blues, pinks, and yellows. His skill at mixing and smoothly applying these subtle pastel colors is manifested by the poetic and luminist quality of light and atmosphere that he achieves. LB

105*
Going to Mill

1855

Oil on canvas

19 x 24 inches (48.3 x 61 cm)

Signed and dated, on tree trunk, lower left: W. Ranney/1855

Private collection

Grubar nos. 83, as Going to Mill and 106, as Boy on Horse Fording a Stream

PROVENANCE: Joseph Moreau, by 1856; Mrs. M[ichael] deSherbinin(?); descended through the family to the present owner (sale, Christie's, New York, December 6, 1985, lot 40, as The Young Pioneer) Mr. and Mrs. Edward Nicholson, Hampton Falls, New Hampshire, 1985–1995 (sale, Christie's, New York, January 27 and 28, 1995, lot 836, as Boy on Horse Fording a Stream, illus. and dated 1853).

EXHIBITED: NAD, 1856, cat. no. 22, as Going to Mill and lent by Joseph Moreau.

REFERENCES: New York Tribune, April 12, 1856, p. 4, describes it (quoted in entry). Cowdrey 1943, 2, p. 89.

When this work first came to light in 1985, it had acquired a modern title, The Young Pioneer—probably assigned to it in an effort to place it within the context of Ranney's western pictures. Grubar in 1962 knew of the painting called Going to Mill, exhibited at the National Academy in 1856, and he evidently also knew of, but had not seen, a painting called Boy on Horse Fording a Stream. Since then, two additional pieces of information have emerged to help better identify this picture. One is that a careful examination of this canvas has revealed that the date is actually 1855, not 1853 as previously recorded. The second is that a review describing the painting called Going to Mill when it was exhibited at the National Academy has been discovered. That piece, which appeared in the New York Tribune, described it as "a boy on a horse standing in a pool of water." Based on this new evidence, we feel confident that this canvas is indeed the work that was exhibited at the National Academy in 1856.

In this scene, Ranney portrays an ordinary event in which a young boy crosses a small stream hauling a bag of grain to the mill for processing. While the whole canvas is bathed in an even bright light, the boy and his horse are particularly highlighted in the center of the composition. They are framed by sycamore trees, easily identified by their distinctive mottled bark and early season small leaves. The gently curving branches shelter the boy within a cathedral arch.

This interior-like wooded landscape resembles several compositions by Hudson River school painters, particularly Asher B. Durand's celebrated In the Woods (Metropolitan Museum of Art), which created a sensation when it was exhibited at the National Academy in 1855. One critic called it "a passage of nature uncommonly beautiful," another, "a perfect and sublime wilderness."[1] Indeed, like the leading landscape painters who were inspired by John Ruskin's requirement of observing and meticulously transcribing nature, Ranney faithfully individuates the trees and their forms. But unlike his contemporaries, he does not diminish the figures and other elements in proportion to the landscape; rather he gives equal emphasis to the figure and the setting in his continuing commitment to the narrative genre form.

144

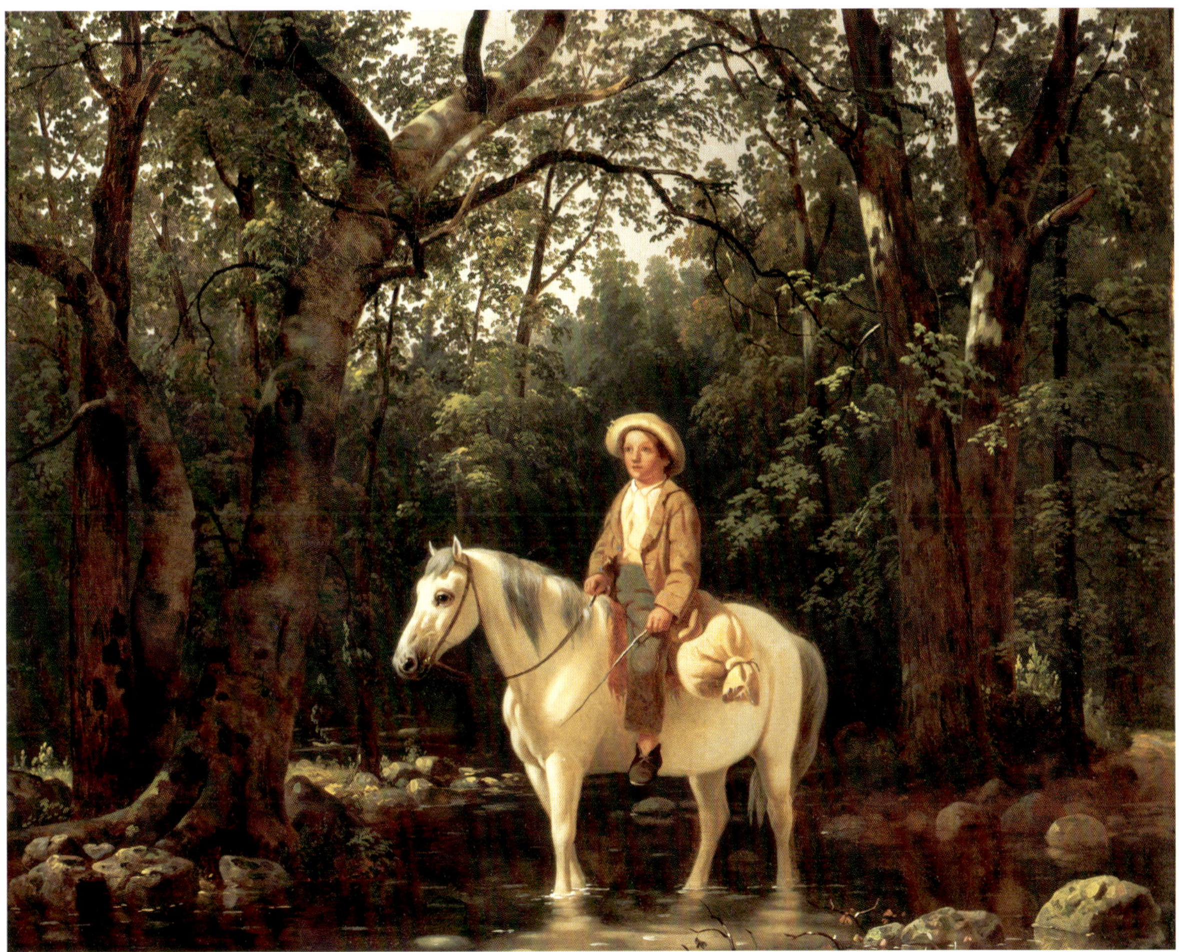

Many of Ranney's patrons may have been drawn to his rural scenes with children (for another example, see cat. no. 104) and nostalgically identified with the boy in this picture. In 1847, one essayist expressed the sentiment of the period as he reminisced about the joys of this seasonal chore: "What proportion of our readers ever bestrode a horse and bag of corn, and trudged off to mill on a bright summer's morning while the birds chanted merrily on bush and tree by the wayside? We have done it so often when a boy, that memory recurs to it as one of our regular morning pastimes to be done before school time."[2]   LB

1. Quoted in John Caldwell and Oswaldo Rodriguez Roque, *American Paintings in the Metropolitan Museum of Art, Volume I: A Catalogue of Works by Artists Born by 1815* (New York: Metropolitan Museum of Art, 1994), p. 424.
2. "The Mill Boy," in *New York Illustrated Magazine of Literature and Art*, vol. 3, no. 6, 1847, p. 95.

106
The Crossing

c. 1855

Oil on canvas

30 x 25 inches (76.2 x 63.5 cm)

Location unknown

PROVENANCE: A. E. Douglass, New York, by 1857.

REFERENCE: A. E. Douglass collection (sale, Henry H. Leeds & Co., New York, March 26, 1857, p. 2, no. 28, as *The Crossing*, provided dimensions, and described as upright oval). *Crayon*, vol. 4 (May 1857), p. 158, indicated in collection of A. E. Douglass and sold for $122.

Grubar (no. 15, p. 27) confused this painting with *Crossing the Ferry* (cat. no. 23), which has different dimensions. LB

107*
Portrait of James Ranney

c. 1855

Oil on canvas

17 1/8 x 13 3/4 inches
(43.5 x 34.9 cm)

Stencil on the back of
the canvas: S. N.
Dodge's/Artist &
Painter's/Supply
Store/189 Chatham
cor/of Oliver
St/[N]York

Private collection

Grubar no. 54

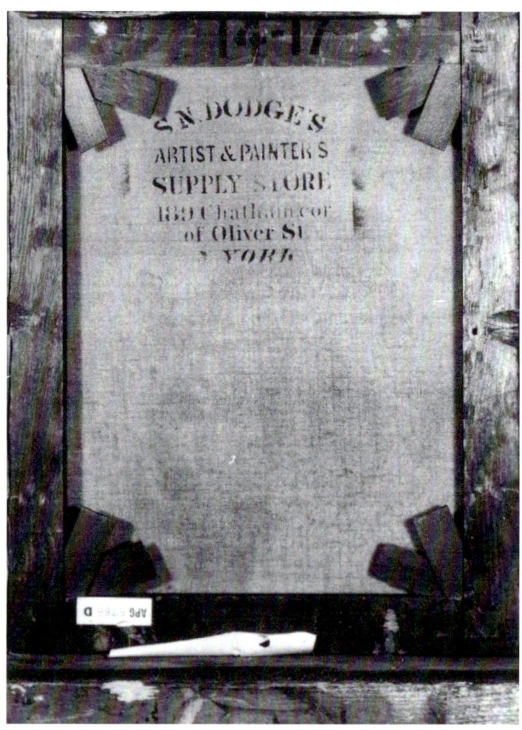
Fig 107.1
Detail of S. N. Dodge canvas stamp.

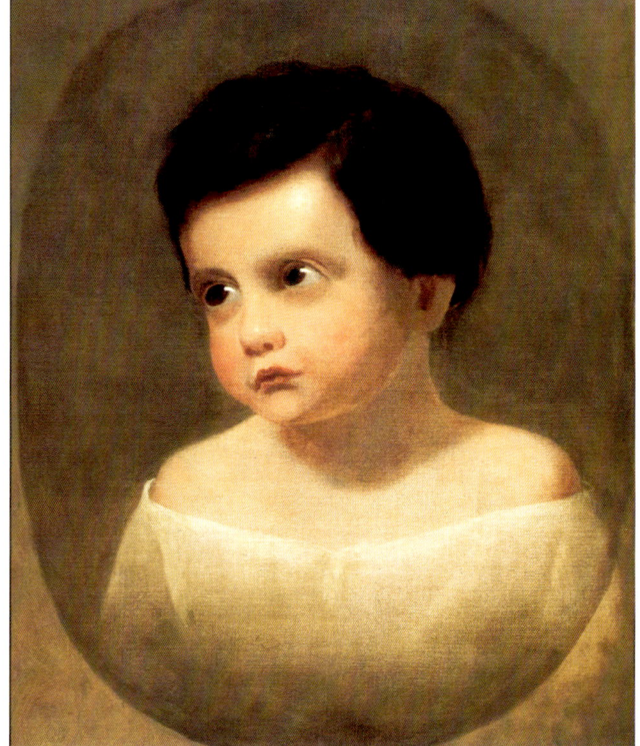
NO. 107

James Joseph Ranney (1853–1928), the youngest of Ranney's two boys, was born in West Hoboken, New Jersey. He and Elizabeth Finer were married in New York on April 24, 1881, and had three children. James worked as an accountant for the Singer Sewing Machine Company until about 1896, when he left to run a summer hotel in Yulan, Sullivan County, New York.[1]

Judging from the apparent age of the child, Ranney probably painted this picture when James was about two or three years old. In this realistic familial portrayal, Ranney, like a proud parent, sentimentally records the likeness of the toddler. In soft, almost pastel colors, he captures the distressed mood of his chubby son whose large doe-like eyes and pouting expression are directed toward a presence outside the picture, as through imploring his mother to release him from the torture of having to sit still while his father records his likeness.

In many of his pictures, Ranney took care to paint a border on the canvas in order to define the general form of its frame. Here, he surrounded the entire image with an oval. This rounded shape seems particularly appropriate to the youth of the sitter and the domestic interior in which the painting is to be displayed. LB

1. Charles Collard Adams, *Middletown Upper Houses,* (1908; repr., Canaan, New Hampshire: Phoenix Publishing, 1983), pp. 401–402.

108
Evening on the Meadows

c. 1855
Oil on Canvas
Location unknown
Grubar no. 82

PROVENANCE: S. N. Dodge, New York, by 1855.

EXHIBITED: NAD, 1855, no. 101, as owned by S. N. Dodge.

REFERENCE: *New York Herald,* March 24, 1855, p. 8, reviews it (quoted in entry).

The following description appeared in the *New York Herald* when the painting was exhibited at the National Academy of Design in 1855: "A good picture, subdued in tone and delicate in finish—the cows are especially well drawn. The only fault we notice is the sky. As [Jacques Louis] David said to the Flemish sign painter, 'there's too much blue.'" There is a small pencil drawing (cat. no. D72) with the inscription "Evening on the Meadows" on the back, which may well be a study for this lost painting.

S. N. Dodge, who lent this painting, as well as *Washington and Gist Crossing the Allegheny River*, to the National Academy's exhibition, is very likely Samuel N. Dodge, who ran an art supply business in New York at the time. Ranney certainly patronized his shop at 189 Chatham Street, because Dodge's stencil mark appears on the back of a number of the artist's canvases (see, for example, fig. 107.1 in cat. no. 107). LB

109*
Self-portrait

c. 1855
Oil on academy board
8 1/2 x 7 1/4 inches
(21.6 x 18.4 cm), cut to
oval shape
Private collection
Grubar no. 87*

NO. 109

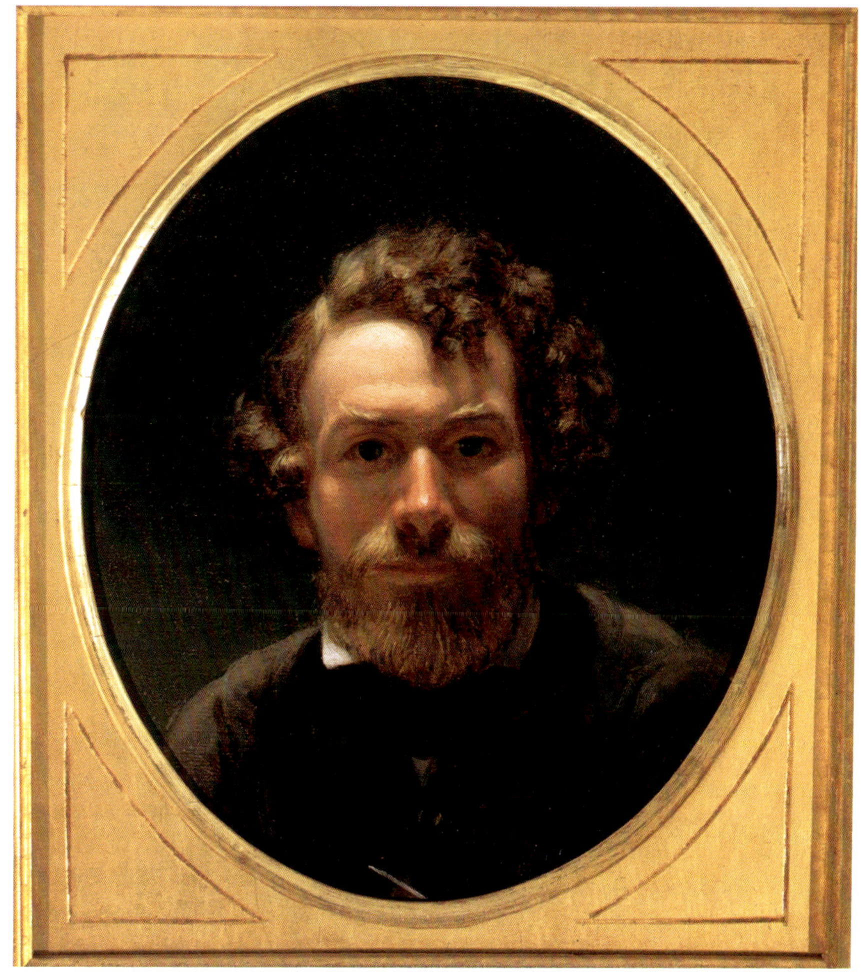

Provenance: Claude J. Ranney, Malvern, Pennsylvania, grandson of the artist (1883-1971).

Exhibited: Chadds Ford 1991, no. 14*

Reference: Thistlethwaite 1991, p. 2, illus., p. 21, discusses.

In his earlier self-portrait, Ranney presents himself as a young man in a somewhat idealized and romanticized pose (see cat. no. 3). Here in this later work, he portrays himself as the mature middle-aged man he had become, with an intensely direct, almost aggressive, gaze. He in fact seems to force himself outside the boundaries of the canvas, toward the viewer.

Within a selective palette of brown tones, Ranney skillfully and dramatically contrasts light and shade so that the almost chiseled facial features result in a captivating three-dimensional presence conveying both a sense of immediacy and a force of personality. Barely visible at the bottom edge of the picture is the wooden end of a paint brush, a traditional attribute emblematic of the artist's profession. While no other portraits by Ranney of this quality and time period have been discovered, the skill of execution and realistic presentation as represented in this example should place him alongside the leading portrait painters of his day. LB

*Gives inaccurate dimensions.

110*
The Pipe of Friendship

c. 1855

Oil on canvas

29 1/2 x 40 1/4 inches
(74.9 x 102.2 cm)

Signed, lower left: Wm
Ranney

Private collection

Grubar no. 61, as The
Scouting Party

Provenance: (Possibly Newhouse Galleries, New York, by 1933); (Kennedy Galleries, New York, by 1939) Claude J. Ranney, Malvern, Pennsyvlania, 1939–1955.

Exhibited: New York, Newhouse Galleries, *The Second Annual Exhibition of American Genre Paintings Depicting the Pioneer Period*, December 22, 1933–January 31, 1934, no. 48, lists it as The Scouting Party. Metropolitan Museum of Art, New York, *Three Hundred Years of Life in America*, April 14–October 29, 1939, pp. 100–101, no. 136, as the Scouting Party lent by Claude J. Ranney. Fort Worth 1987, p. 193, as the Scouting Party.

References: Perry T. Rathbone, *Westward the Way: The Character and Development of the Louisiana Territory as seen by Artists and Writers of the Nineteenth Century* (St. Louis: City Art Museum of St. Louis in collaboration with the Walker Art Center, Minneapolis, 1954), p. 185, illus. as the Scouting Party and p. 268. Grubar, p. 40, inaccurately cites a date of 1851 in signature line and dates it c. 1851. Ayres 1987, p. 98, discusses it.

Mid-nineteenth century writers who accepted the mountain man as a central theme in their works often imbued him as a conflicted personality. On the one hand, the western trappers were portrayed as rough, crude escapees from refined eastern society. Their "manners are blunt and . . . [their] speech is rude," wrote one of their most perceptive observers, Lewis Garrard in 1850. They were "men driven to the western wilds with embittered feeling—with better natures shattered—with hopes blasted—to seek, in the dangers of the warpath, fierce excitement and banishment of care." Yet they showed another side as well. "These aliens from society, these strangers to the refinements of civilized life, who will tear off a bloody scalp with even a grim smile of satisfaction, are fine fellows, full of fun, and often kind and obliging."[1]

Much of the ferocity and swagger of the mountain men were brought to the literature of the day by the men themselves. The Swiss artist Rudolph Friederich Kurz spoke of this when he witnessed their behavior on the Missouri frontier between 1848 and 1851. The "Mountaineers" never tired of distinguishing themselves as extraordinary. They could not "have enough" of attracting attention to themselves "in their highly ornamented buckskin clothes, of performing Indian dances and imitating Indian war cries, in order that they may be regarded as the hardy, fearless, jovial 'Mountaineers,' a name synonymous with famous huntsmen, distinguished warriors, bold and crafty trappers such as are described in books." Despite this, Kurz, like Garrard, viewed them as a "most good-tempered" group of people who, while being boastful and profligate, were essentially generous and humane.[2]

Not surprisingly, Ranney paid tribute to this gentler side of the mountain man's nature in this painting and a smaller version in the Newark Museum (cat. no.141). In these works three trappers form a circle facing one another on their horses. The fellow in a fur cap on the left hands a lighted pipe to the rider closest to the viewer. That rider reaches forward to receive the offering. In the less finished Newark painting, a broad plain reaches out behind the riders. A bank of billowing clouds frames the men with a hint of blue sky to the far left. Here in the larger more finished version the riders are framed instead by the crests of mountains and a pristine alpine lake. In both paintings, a gray mule helps to balance the composition on the left, and in this one a dog sits staring up expectantly at the pipe's recipient. The scene brings to mind a passage in the closing pages of Parkman's *Oregon Trail*. "The horses were saddled in the morning, and the last man had lighted his pipe at the dying ashes of the fire. The beauty of the day enlivened us all."[3]

With this subject Ranney pays tribute to a passing era. By the 1850s the mountain men and fur trappers of the plains and the Rockies were anachronisms. While Kurz had observed that the mountain men were "still the heroes of the day and took great delight in their triumph," their world had altered, for "beaver pelts have fallen in price, the far-famed class of trappers is almost non-existent. Throughout the entire territory of Blackfeet, Crows, Assiniboin, Cree, Chippewa, Herantsa, Arikara, Dakota, the trappers are no longer found at all."[4] When, in 1851, he depicted the western horsemen in one of his deft and spirited academic drawings, *Californians* (fig. 110.1), Kurz's mountaineers had been transformed into gold seekers on their way to the West Coast. Kurz's argonauts, though strikingly similar to Ranney's trappers, represented a new wave of American opportunism. The exchange of a pipe between Ranney's denizens of the wilds represents as much a salute to halcyon days of old as it does a gesture of friendship between comrades.

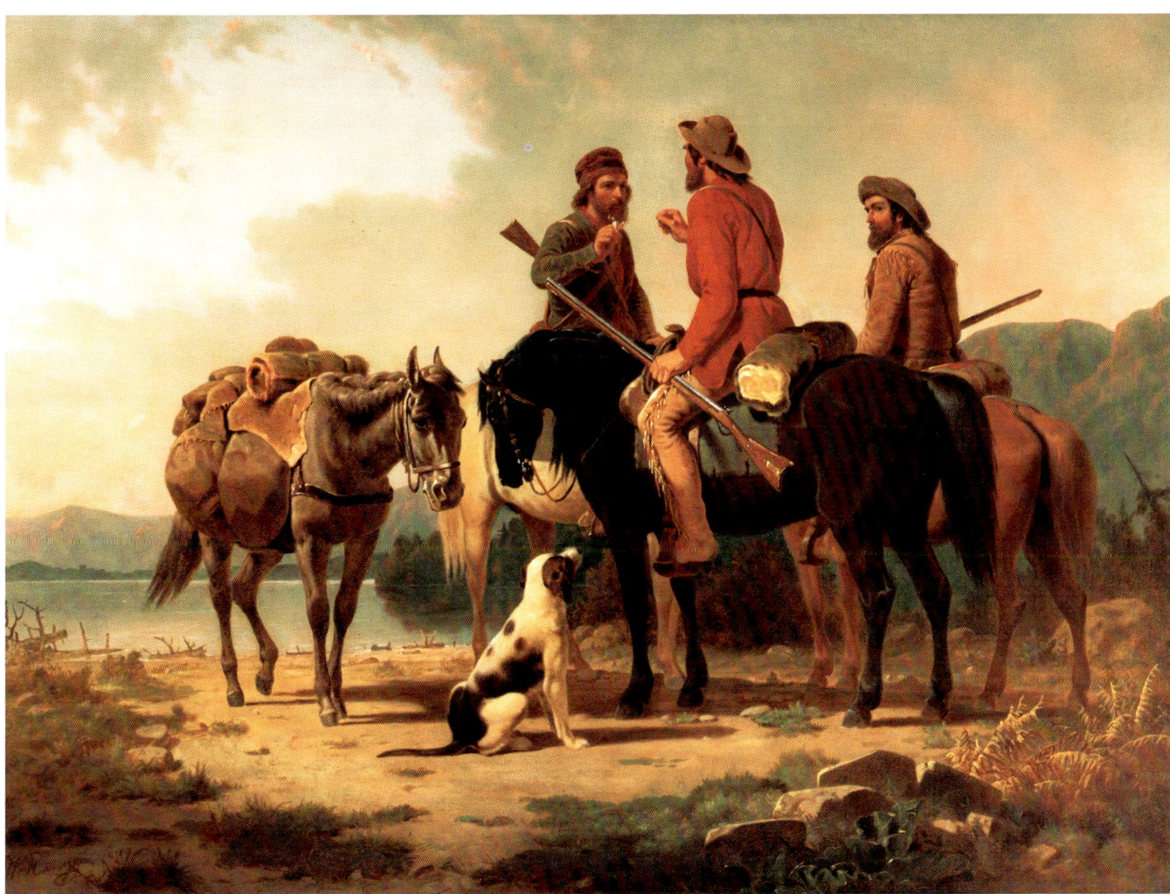

NO. 110

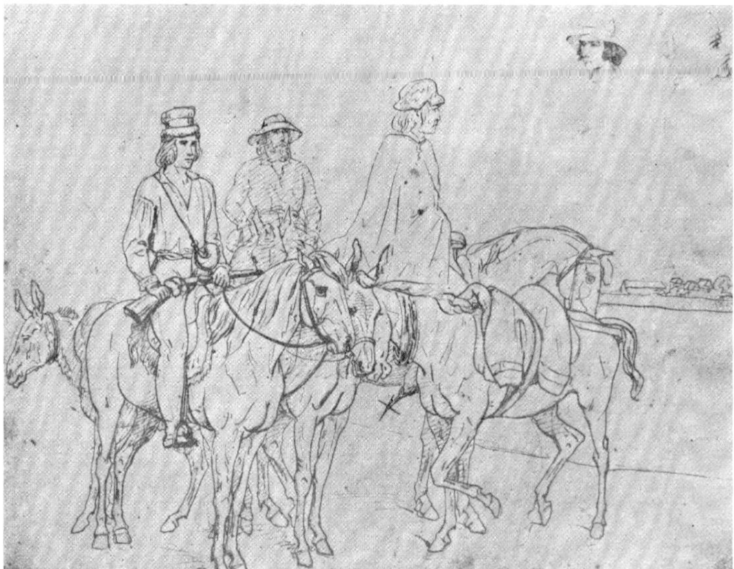

Fig 110.1
Californians . . . From Plate 11 in "Journal of Rudolph Friederich Kurz: An Account of His Experiences among Fur Traders and American Indians on the Mississippi and the Upper Missouri Rivers during the Years 1846 to 1852," *Bureau of American Ethnology Bulletin* 115 (Washington: Government Printing Office, 1937).

Another, somewhat more complex and speculative, reading may be made of these two paintings. Given the contentiousness of the times in which they were produced, these canvases may also speak to the sectional divisions that increasingly manifested themselves in the 1850s and the importance of the West and its resources in determining the future of the Republic. If the painting is read right to left (perhaps indicating east to west), the two figures with their backs to the viewer might represent eastern interests with the most prominent, red-shirted man as the South and the farthest right rider the North. Together they face west, prepared to receive, or at least recognize, its bounty symbolized in the pipe (tobacco being a rare commodity of exchange on the frontier and an emblem of southern economic well-being) and the fully brimming pack mule. The West, revealed in the passive deportment of the third trapper with his rifle hung down, the sunny sky, and the calm waters on the lake, is represented as hospitable, accessible, and richly endowed. The North and South, on the other hand, hold their arms at the ready. The North eyes the South with uncertainty, and the clouds above them augment that tension. It is not known how Ranney personally felt about these issues, whether he supported the antislavery claims that free labor (perhaps symbolized by the trappers) needed to be extended into the West in order to preserve the Union and its principles. But the mood of these two paintings would suggest at least that he held out hope for an amiable resolution to the disputatious issues of his day.

Unlike his contemporary Felix O. C. Darley, Ranney sheltered his themes in promise. Darley, in witness to the literal state of war that existed in the western borderlands during the period of time between the Compromise of 1850 and the Kansas-Nebraska Act in 1854, confronted the conflict pictorially. In his drawings Darley often portrays the frightening realities of life in the West as proslavery Missourians began to invade free territories to press their political agendas and do battle over disputed land claims. His drawings served as illustrations of current events while Ranney's paintings are more of a monument to what once was and might, with a measure of wishful thinking, be again in the future. PHH

1. Lewis H. Garrard, *Wah-to-yah and the Taos Trail* (Cincinnati: H. W. Derby and Co., 1850), p. 66.
2. "Journal of Rudolph Friederich Kurz," trans. Myrtis Jarrell, *Bureau of American Ethnology Bulletin*, no. 115 (Washington, D.C.: Government Printing Office, 1937), pp. 31, 125.
3. Francis Parkman, *The Oregon Trail* (1849; Boston: Ginn and Company, 1910), p. 333.
4. "Journal of Kurz," pp. 31, 125.

111

The Muleteer (also known as the Traveller and the Pioneer)

c. 1855
Oil on canvas
29 1/2 x 24 inches
(74.9 x 61 cm)
Location unknown
Grubar nos. 97, 98, and 99

PROVENANCE: Marshall O. Roberts (1814–1880), New York, by 1864; his widow (sale, Fifth Avenue Art Galleries, New York, Executors' Sale . . . of the Late Marshall O. Roberts, January 19, 20, and 21, 1897, lot 33, p. 16, as the Pioneer and provides dimensions).

EXHIBITED: United States Sanitary Fair, Philadelphia, June, 1864, no. 20, as the Traveller, lent by M. O. Roberts.

REFERENCES: *Catalogue of Paintings, Drawings, Statuary, etc. of the Art Department in the Great Central Fair* (Philadelphia, 1864), no. 90, p. 7, as *The Traveller*. Tuckerman 1867, pp. 431 and 626, as the *Muleteer*. Edward Strahan [Earl Shinn], ed., *Art Treasures in America* (Philadelphia: George Barrie, 1880), vol. 2, p. 16, as the Pioneer. *New York Tribune*, January 20, 1897, p. 6, lists sale price as $55.

112

Hackensack Meadows

c. 1855
Oil on canvas
14 x 20 inches (35.6 x 50.8 cm)
Location unknown
Grubar no. 100

PROVENANCE: Margaret Ranney, granddaughter of the artist, Union City, New Jersey, d. 1965.

REFERENCE: Inventory, Margaret Ranney estate, March 15, 1965, no. 6, listed, and includes undated photograph, copies in Ranney archives.

The appearance of this painting is documented by a photograph probably taken in 1965, the year Margaret Ranney died. LB

113

Cattle Piece

c. 1855
Oil on canvas
Location unknown
Grubar no. 104

PROVENANCE: (sale, Henry H. Leeds and Miner, New York, *Catalogue of a Superb Collection of Fine Modern Pictures*, February 15 and 16, 1866, lot 72, p. 11).

REFERENCE: *New York Tribune*, February 16, 1866, p. 5, notes sold for $65.

114

Pastoral Scene with Cows

c. 1855
Oil on canvas
23 x 26 inches (58.4 x 66 cm)
Signed and dated, lower right: .5 [illegible]/Wm. Ranney
Jane Forbes Clark

PROVENANCE: Descended in the Clark family to the current owner.

Pastoral Scene with Cows is one of several bovine subjects Ranney paint-

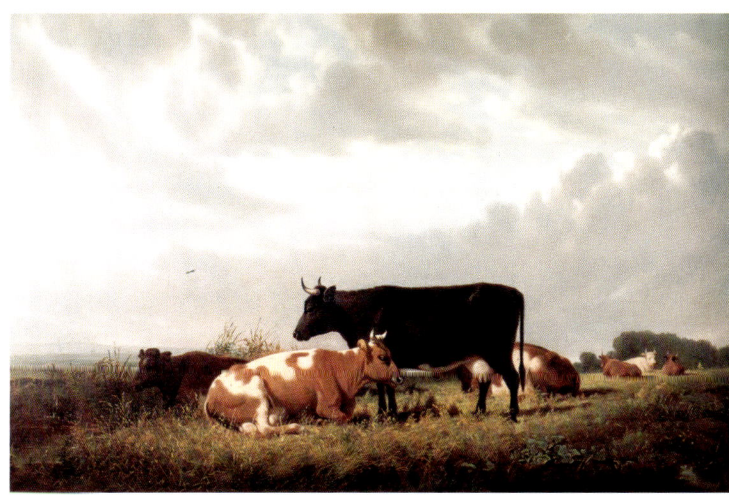

NO. 114

ed during the last years of his life (see, for example, cat. nos. 113, 115, and 117, for instance). This painting may have been commissioned by Edward Clark who raised cattle in the Cooperstown, New York, area. About 1850, he and his wife Caroline had Ranney paint a portrait of their son Ambrose Jordan Clark (see cat. no. 63 for more information on this New York family). LB

115
Barnyard with Cattle—Winter

c. 1855
Oil on canvas
Location unknown
Grubar no. 105

PROVENANCE: (sale, Henry H. Leeds and Miner, New York, *Catalogue of a Superb Collection of Fine Modern Pictures,* February 15 and 16, 1866, lot 57, p. 9).

REFERENCE: *New York Tribune,* February 16, 1866, p. 5, notes sold for $95.

This may be the same picture as *Winter Scene, the Barn Yard, Cattle and Figures* (cat no. 101). LB

116
The Escape

1855–1856
Oil on canvas
Location unknown
Grubar no. 108

PROVENANCE: (sale, Henry H. Leeds and Company, New York, March 24, 1857).

EXHIBITED: Brooklyn Athenaeum, Brooklyn, New York, May, 1856, no. 13, as *The Escape.*

REFERENCES: *Catalogue of the First Annual Exhibition of Pictures at the Brooklyn Athenaeum,* Brooklyn, New York, May, 1856, no. 13, as for sale. *New York Herald,* March 24, 1857, p. 8, documents Leeds sale and calls painting "a superb picture."

117
The Cattle Guard

c. 1855
Oil on canvas
Location unknown
Grubar no. 107

PROVENANCE: Miss Sophia C. V. C. Stevens, Princeton, New Jersey, by c. 1883–1888; W. B. Norman, 1894.

REFERENCES: William Tylee Ranney file, Art and Architecture Division, New York Public Library, copy of Margaret Ranney's questionnaire for Appletons' *Cyclopaedia of American Biography,* c. 1883, lists painting as *Cattle Guard* owned by Sophia C. V. C. Stevens. Grubar, note 184, p. 65, cites will of Sophia C.V. Stevens, Princeton, New Jersey, May 28, 1888, Register no. 5222, Office of Probated Wills, Trenton, New Jersey, which stipulates that Ranney's "cattle scene" should be sold. Claude J. Ranney undated catalogue sheet, Ranney archives, indicates painting was purchased for $25 by W. B. Norman in 1894.

118
Study of a Ledge

c. 1855

Oil on paper mounted
on hardboard

8 3/4 x 11 1/4 inches
(22.2 x 28.6 cm)

Private collection

Grubar no. 110

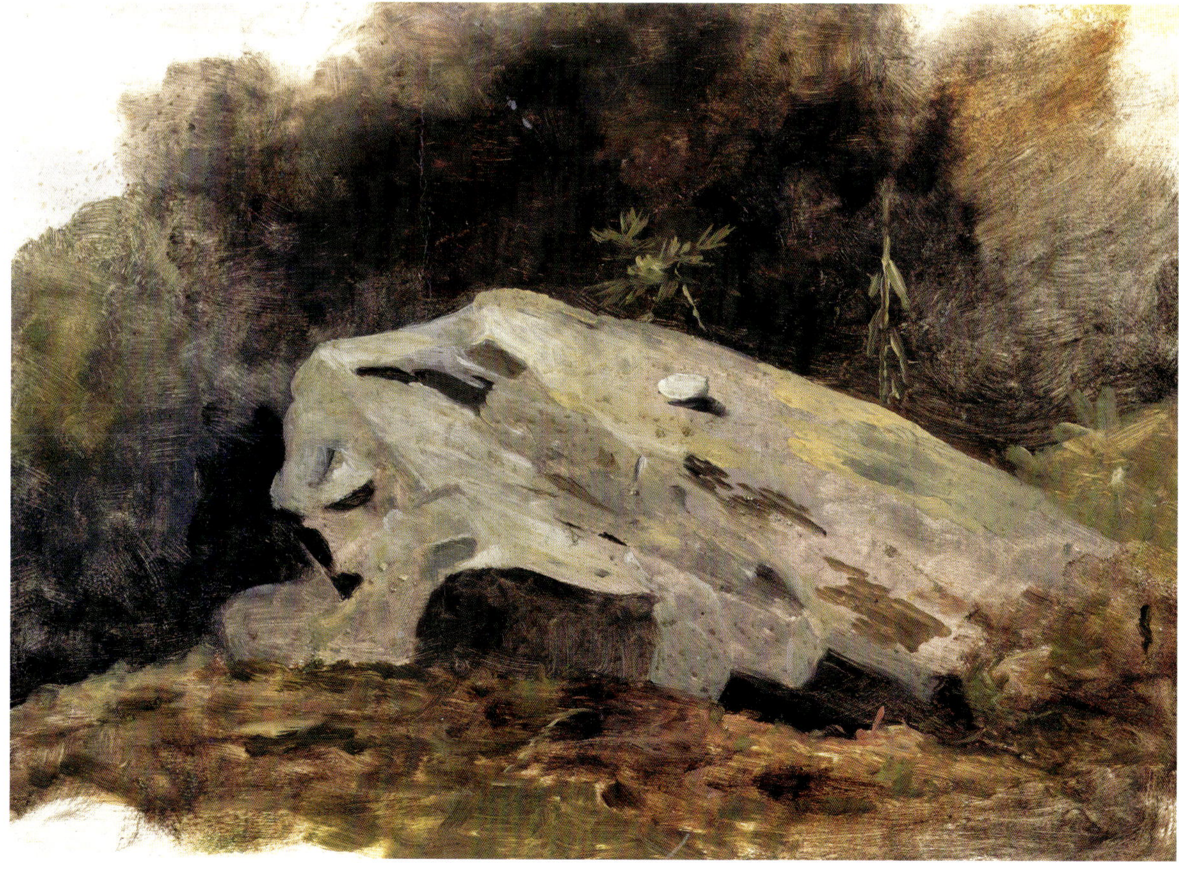

NO. 118

The fortunate survival of this rare, small oil study is evidence that Ranney, like many leading artists by the mid-nineteenth century, followed the practice of painting outdoors directly from nature. These works then became sources for larger compositions completed later in the studio. Boulders such as the one represented here appear as background elements in several of Ranney's paintings (see, for example, cat. nos. 45 and 49). LB

119

Landscape with Pine Tree

c. 1855
Oil on paper
9 x 11 3/8 inches (22.9
x 28.9 cm)
Location unknown
Grubar no. 111

PROVENANCE: Claude J. Ranney, Malvern, Pennsylvania, by 1962.

120

River with Border of Trees

c. 1855
Location unknown
Grubar no. 112

PROVENANCE: Claude J. Ranney, Malvern, Pennsylvania, by 1962.

121

Landscape with Rail Fences

c. 1855
Oil on paper
9 3/8 x 14 1/2 inches
(23.8 x 36.8 cm)
Location unknown
Grubar no. 113

PROVENANCE: Claude J. Ranney, Malvern, Pennsylvania, by 1962.

122

Study of a Horse's Hoof

c. 1855
Oil on paper
9 1/2 x 7 3/8 inches
(24.1 x 18.7 cm)
Location unknown
Grubar no. 114

PROVENANCE: Claude J. Ranney, Malvern, Pennsylvania, by 1962.

123
Dog

c. 1855
Oil on canvas
Location unknown

PROVENANCE: James M. Burt, by 1876.

EXHIBITED: Brooklyn Art Association, New York, *Thirty-first Exhibition*, April 24, 1876–May 6, 1876, no. 197, as possibly by William Ranney owned by James M. Burt.[1]

1. Clark S. Marlor, *A History of the Brooklyn Art Association with an Index of Exhibitions* (New York: James F. Carr, 1970), p. 309.

124
Retriever with Ducks on Rocks Overlooking Water

c. 1855
Oil on panel
5 x 7 1/2 inches (12.7 x 19.1 cm)
Location unknown

PROVENANCE: Margaret Ranney, granddaughter of the artist, Union City, New Jersey, d. 1965.

REFERENCE: Margaret Ranney estate appraisal, March 22, 1965, no. 9, p. 2, listed, and includes undated photograph, copy in Ranney archives.

125
A Bad Egg

c. 1855
Oil on canvas
15 x 17 inches (38.1 x 43.2 cm)
Location unknown

PROVENANCE: John M. Falconer (1820–1903), Brooklyn, New York, c. 1860–1904 (sale, Anderson Auction Company, New York, *Catalogue of the Interesting and Valuable Collection of Oil Paintings, Watercolors and Engravings formed by the Late John M. Falconer* [Brooklyn, New York], April 28 and 29, 1904, no. 613, p. 57, as A Bad Egg, and provides dimensions and medium).

EXHIBITED: Artists' Fund Society of New York, 1860, *First Annual Exhibition*, no. 140, as A Bad Egg, owned by J. M. Falconer.

Born in Edinburgh, Falconer came to the United States in 1848. While he made his living as a hardware merchant, he devoted much of his spare time etching and painting landscapes, genre scenes, and portraits. He also assembled a large collection of works by his fellow artists.[1] In addition to *A Bad Egg*, he collected several drawings by Ranney that are in the M. and M. Karolik Collection at the Museum of Fine Arts in Boston (cat. nos. D3–D7). While no description of this work has yet been discovered, its colorful title suggests that it is probably a genre scene. LB

1. A good abbreviated biography appears in *M. and M. Karolik: Collection of American Water Colors and Drawings, 1800–1875* (Boston: Museum of Fine Arts, 1962), vol. 1, p. 154.

126

Cattle in a Snow Storm

c. 1855

Oil on canvas

Location unknown

PROVENANCE: John Brady, by 1862.

EXHIBITED: Artists' Fund Society of New York, *The Third Annual Exhibition*, 1862, no. 230, as *Cattle in a Snow Storm*, owned by John Brady.

127

The Buttonwood Grove

c. 1855

Oil on canvas

Location unknown

PROVENANCE: Possibly the Ranney Fund sale; William Menzies (sale, *Catalogue of a Collection of Fine Modern Paintings by Celebrated American and Foreign Artists, Belonging to William Menzies, Esq.*, Messrs. Leavitt, Auctioneers, New York, April 18 and 19, 1876, lot 77, as the Buttonwood Grove).

In 1858, William Menzies, a prominent New York book and art collector, bought three works from the Ranney Fund sale: lot 174, *Study of Picture, Virginia Wedding* (cat. no. 97) for thirty dollars; lot 22, *Sketch from Nature* for eight dollars; and lot 44, *Finished Sketch from Nature* for ninety dollars. Only two pictures by Ranney are listed in Menzies's 1876 sale, however—*Virginia Wedding* and this one. It is probable that *The Buttonwood Grove* is one of the nature sketches that Menzies acquired from the Ranney Fund sale. LB

128

Landscape with Cattle

c. 1855

Oil on canvas

Location unknown

PROVENANCE: (sale, Henry H. Leeds and Miner, New York, *Catalogue of a Superb Collection of Fine Modern Pictures . . .* February 15 and 16, 1866, lot 95, p. 15, as Landscape with Cattle).

A picture with this title was sold in 1858 at the Ranney Fund sale (lot 132) to someone named Sullivan for twenty-seven dollars. LB

129*
Spaniel with Woodcock

c. 1855

Oil on canvas

34 x 27 inches (86.4 x 68.6 cm)

Signed, lower left: W. Ranney

Canvas stamp: S. N. [Dodge's]/Art supply [illegible]

The Merestead Painting Collection, Mt. Kisco, New York, Westchester County Department of Parks, Recreation and Conservation.

PROVENANCE: Mrs. George (nee Leah Reese) A. Crocker (1847–1930), New York, her daughter Mrs. William (nee Frances Crocker) Sloane (1877–1962), New York and Mt. Kisco, New York, her daughter Mrs. Robert Lee Patterson, Jr. (nee Margaret Sloane; 1910–2000), New York and Mt. Kisco, New York.

REFERENCE: Gigi Carnes, Curator of Merestead, to Linda Bantel, December 17, 2003, Ranney archives, provides provenance

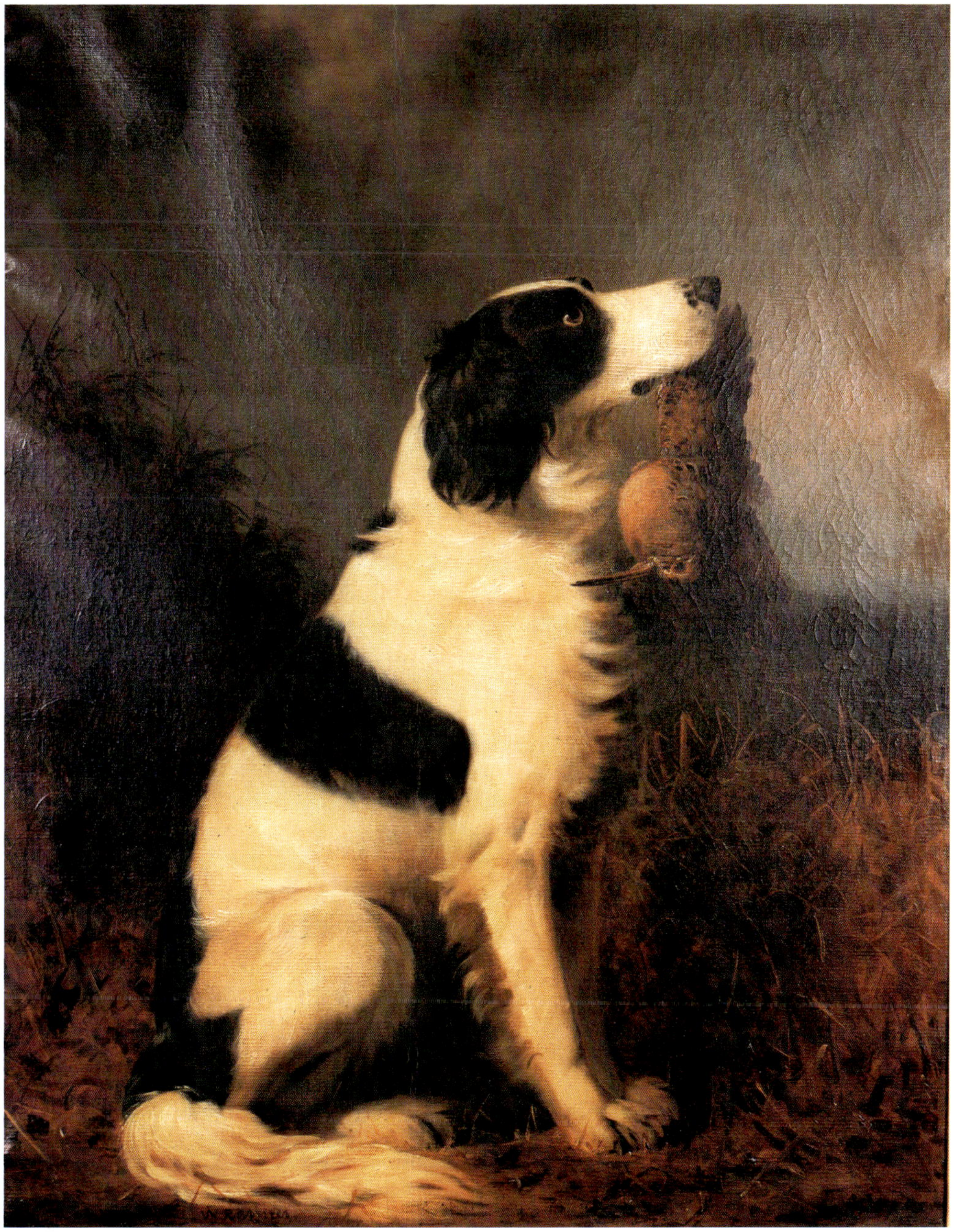

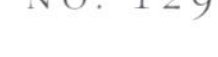

NO. 129

157

Ranney's unique, almost life-sized portrait of this spaniel—a popular game dog of the period—is unquestionably a tribute to a beloved animal. In order to display the breed's distinctive black and white markings and long silky hair, Ranney portrays it in profile, its coloring brilliantly highlighted against the autumnal background. Like his *Fowler's Return* of 1854 (cat. no. 95), Ranney implies the off-canvas presence of the dog's owner. Here, the spaniel, sometimes also called a setter, holds a woodcock in its mouth, as it stares to the right obediently waiting for the hunter to receive it in his hand. According to Frank Forester, the popular sportswriter of the period, a good time to hunt woodcock is in the autumn: "They are still abundant on the proper grounds, particularly among hanging woods of second growth, or chestnut interspersed with evergreens, on the hill-sides, adjacent to water, and in low level maple swamps and alder thickets."[1]

While in his work Ranney often included dogs that played important, but secondary narrative roles, he also portrayed them individually, as in formal portraits, beginning early in his career. In 1846, for instance, he rather shocked the critics when he exhibited *Jack*, a canine portrait, at the National Academy (see cat. no. 24). In the Ranney Fund sale, three images of dogs brought good prices and were probably all oil paintings: *Setter Dog* (lot 36) sold to Walker for thirteen dollars; *Portrait of a Favorite Dog* (lot 60) sold to Jarvis for forty-five dollars; and *Newfoundland Dog* (lot 77), sold to Swan for twenty-one dollars. It certainly seems that *Spaniel with Woodcock* was someone's favorite dog. LB

1. Frank Forester [Henry William Herbert], *Complete Manual for Young Sportsmen* (1856: reprint, [New York]: Westvaco Corporation, 1993), p. 131.

130*
The Trappers

1856

Oil on canvas

23 1/2 x 36 inches
(59.6 x 91.9 cm)

Signed and dated,
lower center: W.
Ranney 1856

Museum of the
American West, Autry
National Center, Los
Angeles

Grubar no. 57

PROVENANCE: (Collins Gallery, New York); (M. Knoedler and Company, New York, by c. 1952–1967) Northern Natural Gas Company, Omaha (later Enron Corporation, Houston), by 1967–1988.

ON LOAN: Joslyn Art Museum, Omaha, 1968–1988.

EXHIBITED: M. Knoedler and Company, New York, *An Exhibition Featuring Paintings from Harold McCracken's Book, Portrait of the Old West*, October 20–November 1, 1952, no. 26. Fort Worth 1987, p. 194, lists collection as Enron Art Foundation/Joslyn Art Museum, Omaha.

REFERENCES: Perry T. Rathbone, ed., *Westward the Way: The Character and Development of the Louisiana Territory as Seen by Artists and Writers of the Nineteenth Century* (Minneapolis: Walker Art Center, 1954), p. 183, illus. and dates it c. 1850, and p. 268, lists it as owned by M. Knoedler and Company, New York; Grubar, p. 39, no. 57, dates it 1851. Ayres 1987, pp. 100–101, no. 64, discusses and identifies trappers as a French Canadian (with fur hat) and an American.

In 1852, that original and impressively loquacious early American romantic novelist James Fenimore Cooper deliberated at some length on the differences between the landscape of Europe and the United States as a subject for art. In an essay for *The Home Book of the Picturesque*, Cooper searched his experience for elements of the national topography that would transcend the familiar Old World artistic fare. He wanted desperately, as an example, to claim the Rocky Mountains as something special. But, having never been there, he demurred. He had heard that they possessed "many noble views," but there were problems that prevented

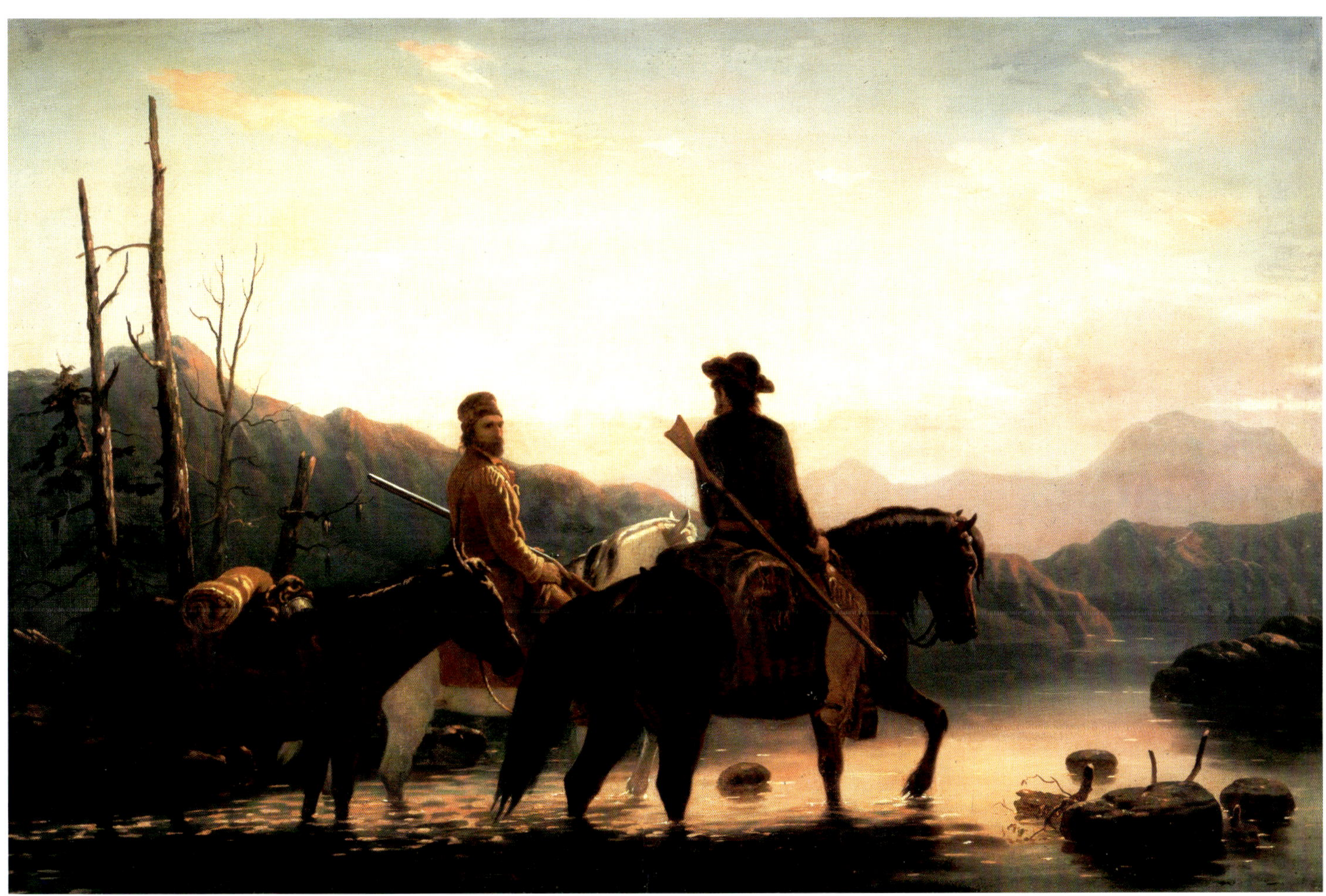

him from including them in his discussion.[1] Ranney saw none of the Rocky Mountain's "noble views" in his lifetime either. The Weehawken bluffs were familiar enough haunts for him and the Hoboken fields as well. By the date of this painting, he had probably visited the Adirondacks, perhaps with his friend Arthur Fitzwilliam Tait, who toured that wilderness area as early as 1851.[2] For Ranney, however, the introduction of the mountain man or trapper into a landscape provided precisely the necessary ingredient to create the idea of life in a distant unknown topography and enchanting wonderland, which was at once patriotic and empyreal.

Henry T. Tuckerman, who visited Ranney's studio in West Hoboken, New Jersey, about this time, commented that the artist "was enamored of the picturesque in scenery and character outside of the range of civilization."[3] In paintings like *The Trappers*, he successfully combined scenery and characters. He could transport New Jersey's meadows to his western dream world. In *The Trappers*, two riders lead their pack mule along the shallow edge of a mountain lake. Surrounded by an ethereal opalescent glow, they glance at one another, perhaps knowing that speech would shatter a holy silence. This was a blessed place, and the trappers, like the heroes of Homer's Elysian fields, were intended to pass through nature's revered sanctuary in exalted fashion. Like Menelaus, these mountain men were to be immortalized. Ranney, who knew full well that the trapper era had slipped into the pages of history, elevated them and their world.

The critics regarded Ranney as "a faithful student of nature," whose "western character and scenery" made for "most interesting pictures."[4] Not all artists who attempted western subjects were so successful at relating the region's picturesque charm. Ranney's fellow artist John F. Kensett ventured west to the Missouri River valley in 1857 and returned with a number of views that were exhibited that fall. The *Crayon* reported on these, claiming in a rather disappointed tone that "the artist brings back several studies of western scenery, which contribute to enlighten the curious about the landscape characteristics of that distant country. According to Mr. Kensett's faithful pencil we should not report very favorable on the picturesqueness of the West in comparison with the East."[5]

It was the symbolic placement of man silhouetted against a luminous cushion of atmospheric grace, enfolding harmoniously with nature that won those accolades for Ranney where Kensett received none. And it was "the temperament of his representations of trappers" as "low keyed but dignified" individuals that brought modern scholars to the conclusion that such paintings as this one were especially "consonant" with the "democratic outlook" of his mid-century American audience's. [6]

Ranney's study (cat. no. 131) for *The Trappers* suggests his initial efforts to connect these men with their exotic milieu. But the study is mostly about the two wilderness hunters and their interaction. It lacks the delicate suffusion of light, the expansive sweep of the mountain backdrop, or the muffled intrusion of mankind found in his more finished works. PHH

1. James Fenimore Cooper, "American European Scenery Company," in Washington Irving, et. al., *The Home Book of the Picturesque, or, American Scenery, Art, and Literature Comprising a Series of Essays* (New York: G. P. Putnam, 1852), p. 56.
2. Warder H. Cadbury, *Arthur Fitzwilliam Tait: Artist of the Adirondacks* (Newark: University of Delaware Press, 1986), p. 28.
3. Tuckerman, p. 432.
4. "Exhibitions," *Crayon*, vol. 5 (December 1858), p. 355.
5. Ibid., 4 (December 1857), p. 377.
6. Glanz 1982, p. 50.

131
The Trappers

c. 1856

Oil on canvas

8 3/4 x 12 inches (22.2 x 30.5 cm)

Warner Collection of Gulf States Paper Corporation, Tuscaloosa, Alabama

PROVENANCE: Possibly the Ranney Fund sale, 1858, lot 97; private collection, New York; (William Stieffel, New York, 1985) (Gerald Peters Gallery, Santa Fe, by 1985–1990).

ON LOAN: Westervelt Warner Museum of American Art, Tuscalosa, Alabama.

EXHIBITED: Gene Autry Western Heritage Museum, Los Angeles, *The West Explored: The Gerald Peters Collection of Western American Art*, 1988–1990, pl. 26.

REFERENCE: Julie Schimmel, *The West Explored: The Gerald Peters Collection of Western American Art* (Santa Fe: Gerald Peters Gallery, 1988), p. 43, discusses, pl. 26.

For a full discussion of this subject, see cat. no. 130. LB

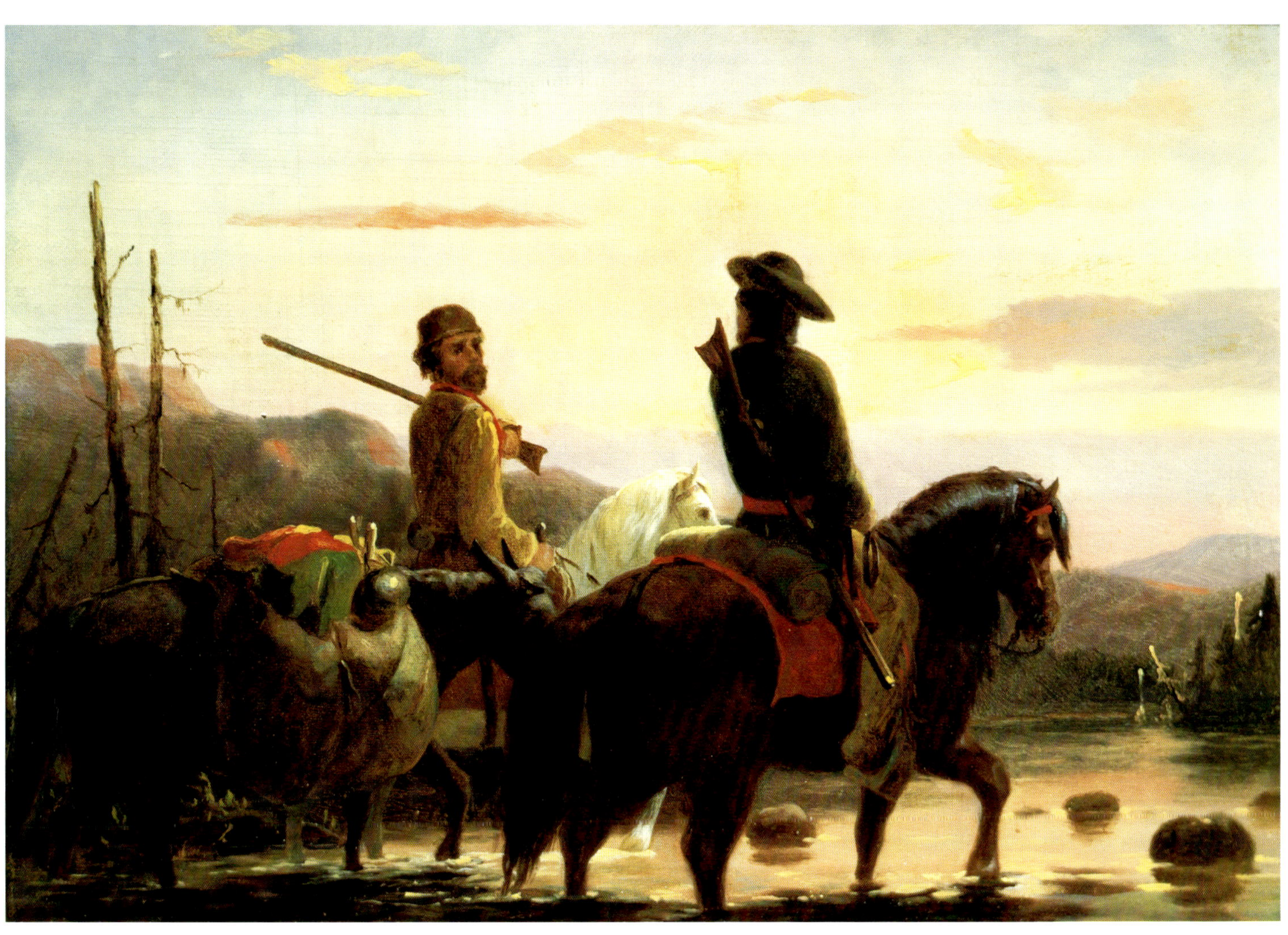

NO. 131

132
A Winter Scene, New Jersey

1856

Oil on canvas

22 x 35 inches (55.9 x 88.9 cm)

Signed and dated, lower right: Wm. Ranney 1856

Anonymous collection

PROVENANCE: Private collection, Hoboken, New Jersey (Richard York Gallery, New York, by 1987) (Alexander Gallery, New York).

REFERENCE: Richard York Gallery, *An American Gallery: Spring 1987* (New York: Richard York Gallery, 1987), no. 4, illus. and provides provenance.

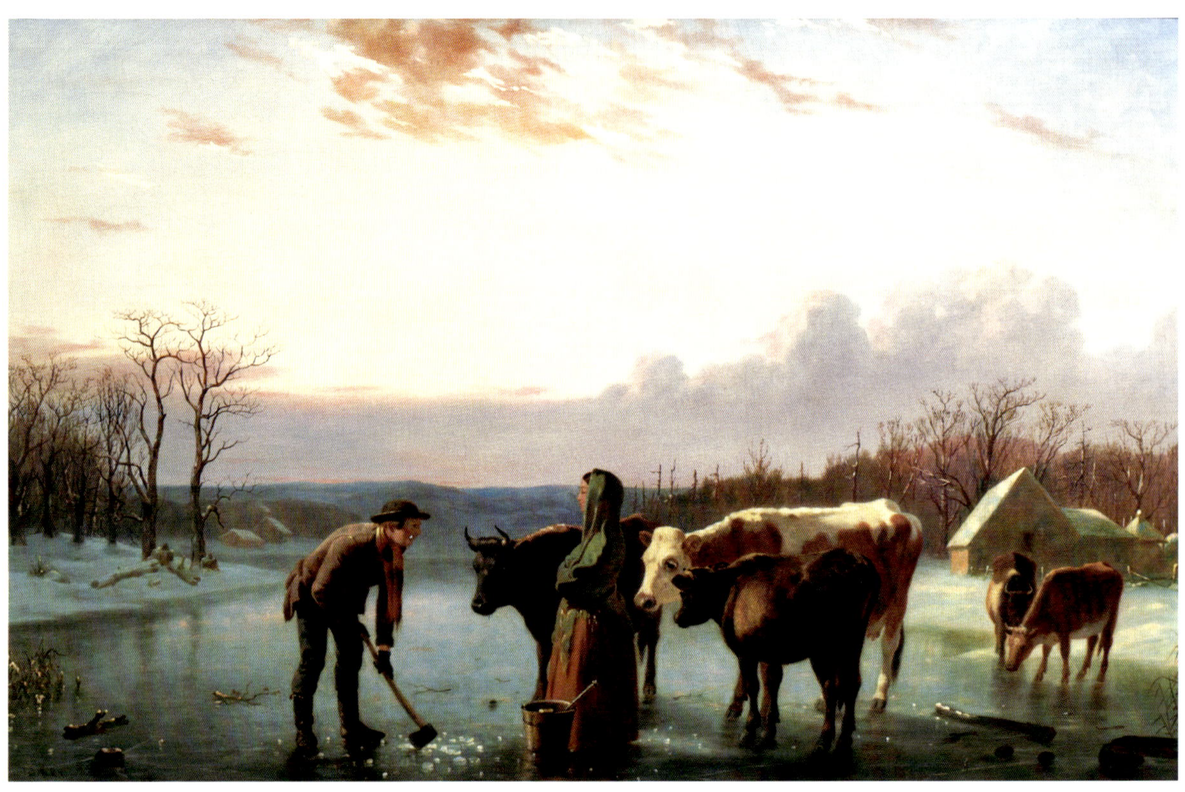

NO. 132

In the mid-1850s, Ranney, who was as skilled at rendering cattle as he was other animals, painted several pictures with titles indicating that cattle were the principal subjects. They were readily available as models at his home in West Hoboken New Jersey, where, according to one contemporary account, Ranney had built a large and commodious studio, "so arranged as to receive animals as the objects of study."[1] This painting, which combines genre and animal painting, may be related to two other works (see cats. no. 101 and 115). LB

1. *Crayon*, vol. 5 (January 1858), p. 26.

133
Haying Time

1856
Oil on canvas
39 1/8 x 55 1/8 inches
(99.4 x 140 cm)
Signed and dated,
lower center: Wm.
Ranney '56
Location unknown

PROVENANCE: (sale, Christie's, New York, December 6, 1985, lot 42, illus.).

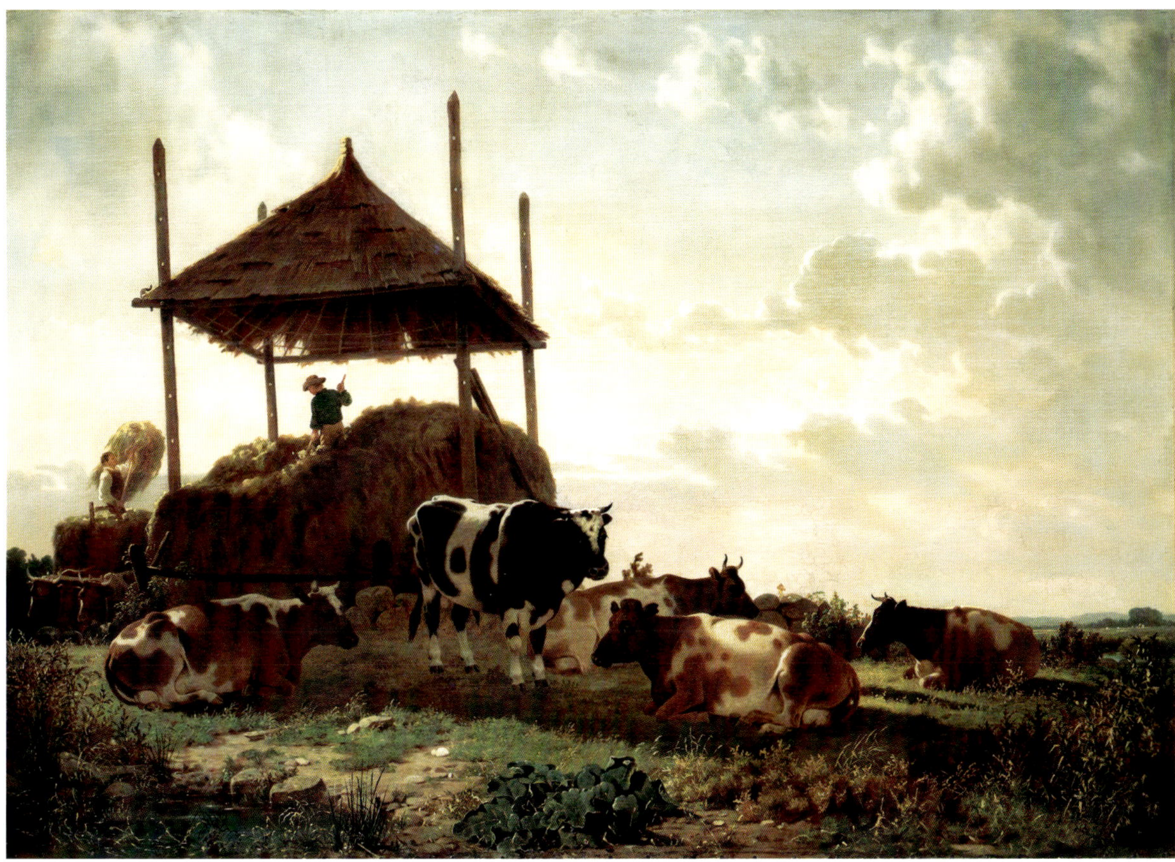

NO. 133

The subject of this painting has a long tradition in Western European art in which the seasons are identified by a particular farm activity. Ranney himself first explored this subject about 1845 (see cat. no. 16). Here in a straightforward manner, Ranney illustrates a rural, autumnal harvest scene. In a characteristically rigorous triangular organization, he depicts the farmhands pitching the hay, the principal fodder for their livestock, which are shown in the foreground. Silhouetted against the dramatic afternoon sunlight is the hayrick crowned by a thatched roof to keep the hay dry. By suffusing the composition with a warm ambient glow, Ranney balanced the forthright anecdotal details with a tranquil mood. His subtle atmospheric effects connects him to the luminist landscape painters of this period.

Nostalgic views of rural life, particularly popular with urban audiences, were frequently exhibited at the National Academy. One writer in the *Knickerbocker*, in reminiscing about his childhood, expressed the sentiments of the era, as he relaxed in Hoboken, New Jersey, gazing "for hours upon the distant city. . . . and think[ing] 'on diverse things foregone,' when we were as yet but a little boy; especially of early days in the country . . . when we used to perch ourselves upon the top of a fresh hay — 'barrack,' (soft and fragrant couch!) and from underneath its straw-thatch roof look out through the gently-falling rain upon the fading yellow woods, the meadows of dim dying green, and russet stubble-fields." After describing several rural scenes, he then pragmatically reminds the reader of the economic interdependence of the city dwellers and their agrarian countrymen: "All these various labors 'In due season' freight the vessels which you see tending to the vast metropolis."[1]

A painting—perhaps related to this picture—entitled *Haystack with Cattle* was sold at the Ranney Fund sale (lot 85) to a man named Howe for fifty-eight dollars. LB

1. *Knickerbocker*, vol. 32 (November 1848), p. 467.

134*
The Victim

1856

Oil on canvas

29 1/4 x 36 1/4 inches (74.3 x 92.1 cm)

Signed and dated, lower center: W Ranney 1856

Inscribed on bottom of stretcher: The "Victim"/W. Ranney

Private collection

Grubar no. 103

PROVENANCE: Possibly Count Pedro Massa (or Pedromassa), Nice, France. George Leca, Island Park, New York, by 1990–c. 1997.

REFERENCES: Margaret Ranney's questionnaire of c. 1883 for *Appletons' Cyclopaedia of American Biography*, William Tylee Ranney file, Art Division, New York Public Library, lists this painting as The Victim and provides provenance. Francis S. Grubar letter to Whom it May Concern, March 10, 1990, Ranney archives, authenticates it.

In this unusual emotional scene, the tranquility suggested by Ranney's typical opalescent sky and grassy landscape is interrupted by the agonizing death struggle unfolding in the foreground where three wolves attack a bull. One of the predators clutches the neck of the prostrate beast, forcing the head to tilt back and the tongue to hang out, as though the animal is gasping for air. To those familiar with Ranney's work, *The Victim* may seem uncharacteristically brutal. A review of the descriptions of at least two unlocated works, however, *The Dead Courser or Charger* (cat. no. 22) and *The Eagle's Nest* (cat no. 32), indicates that, at least from time to time, Ranney did create startlingly violent narratives.

By 1856 when he painted *The Victim*, Ranney had already been suffering—perhaps for as long as two years— from consumption, the nineteenth-century scourge that, with no known cure at the time, killed millions of Americans. Now called tuberculosis, this pulmonary disease attacks the lungs and gradually consumes the entire body. Ranney finally succumbed to the effects of the disease in November of 1857, at the relatively young age of forty-four. Within this biographical context, it is tempting to interpret *The Victim* as a poignant metaphor and visualization of the artist's own futile struggle with a debilitating illness.

Images of animal violence may have been unusual in American art, but by the second quarter of the nineteenth century, they were becoming increasingly popular in Europe. The heightened emotional feelings they engendered particularly appealed to the romantic sensibility characteristisctic of the era. Pictorially, *The Victim* has much in common with works by French sculptor Antoine-Louis Barye (1796–1875), particularly in the bull's pose, which so closely relates to *Bull Attacked by a Bear* of 1839 (Walters Art Museum, Baltimore), commissioned by the duc d'Orleans. While he could not have seen the bronze itself because Walters did not acquire it until 1870, Ranney may have been aware of Barye's work through prints or other publications.

Since *The Victim*, which has only recently been rediscovered, was apparently never publicly exhibited, there is no way of knowing how it would have been received by American audiences. A possible early European owner, who perhaps commissioned the painting, may have appreciated it for the same qualities admired in Barye's work: "a spectacle of the machinations of evil in the world, a spectacle inherently fascinating and moving, yet with an ulimately positive moral lesson."[1]

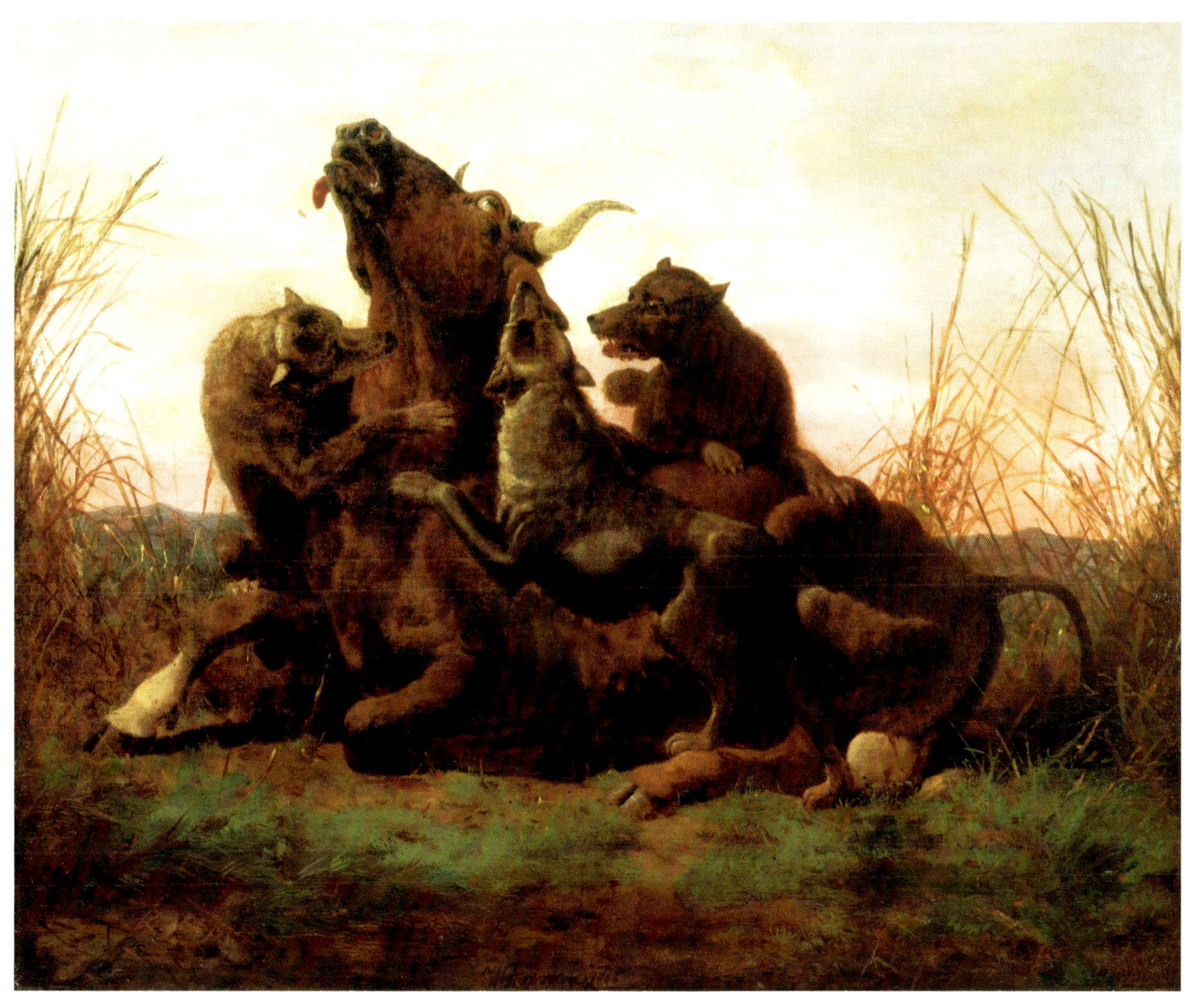

The Dusseldorf Gallery in New York also exhibited some horrific animal paintings, which Ranney could have seen. F. Sigmund Lachenwitz's *A Stag Attacked by Wolves* (location unknown), for instance, was on exhibit there for several years beginning in 1850. It was described in the *Albion* "as a vigorous animal painting, representing a jaded stag run down by wolves."[2] LB

1. Glenn Benge, "Antoine-Louis Barye," in *The Romantics to Rodin: French Nineteenth-Century Sculpture from North American Collections* (Los Angeles: Los Angeles County Museum of Art, 1980), p. 127, provides a succinct intepretation of Barye's animal imagery in terms of French romanticism and aesthetics.
2. Quoted in *Catalogue of a Private Collection of Paintings and Original Artists of the Dusseldorf Academy of Fine Arts* (New York: W. C. Bryant and Company, 1851), no. 111, p. 39.

135*
The Skaters

c. 1856

Oil on canvas, later mounted on hard-board.

23 x 35 1/8 inches
(58.4 x 89.2 cm)

Signed, lower left:
Wm. Ranney

Private collection

Grubar no. 84

PROVENANCE: (Jan Anderson, New York, to 1980) (James Maroney, Inc., New York, 1980).

EXHIBITED: NAD, 1856, no. 104, as *The Skaters*, for sale. Chadds Ford 1991, no. 25.

REFERENCES: *Crayon*, vol. 3 (May 1856), p. 147, calls it *Skater-boys* (quoted in entry). *New York Tribune*, May 3, 1856, p. 9, mentions it. Cowdrey 1943, 2, p. 89. Thistlethwaite 1991, p. 25, illus., p. 26, says Ranney's composition superficially resembles those of George Henry Durrie and Regis Gignoux.

Like *The Sleigh Ride* (cat. no. 75), his celebrated composition of 1852, Ranney focuses the pictorial energy on the triangular grouping of young boys in the foreground, some standing, others seated while they put on their skates. The few adults pictured in the scene are incidental, vaguely defined, and relegated to the background. In keeping with Ranney's interest in narrative content, however, each adult plays an active and distinctive role in creating a realistic ambiance across the canvas—two are skating, one is falling down, and another is tending to his dog. A second group of figures animates the left middle ground. Ranney's liberal use of blues offset by bright reds, whites, and other colors, imparts a carefree charm to the whole scene. A strong light captures the quality of the wintry chill and etches and defines each figure. This crisp atmospheric quality did not, however, impress the *Crayon*'s critic who carped that "Ranney's Skater-boys stiffened under the impossible sunlight."

Rural winter scenes were favorite subjects for many artists of this period. The most prolific and best known for this kind of landscape was the French-born, New York artist Regis-François Gignoux, whose winter scenes, often with ice skaters, were frequently represented in the exhibitions at the American Art-Union from 1842 until its dissolution in 1852, and at the National Academy of Design from 1842 to 1860. While

NO. 135

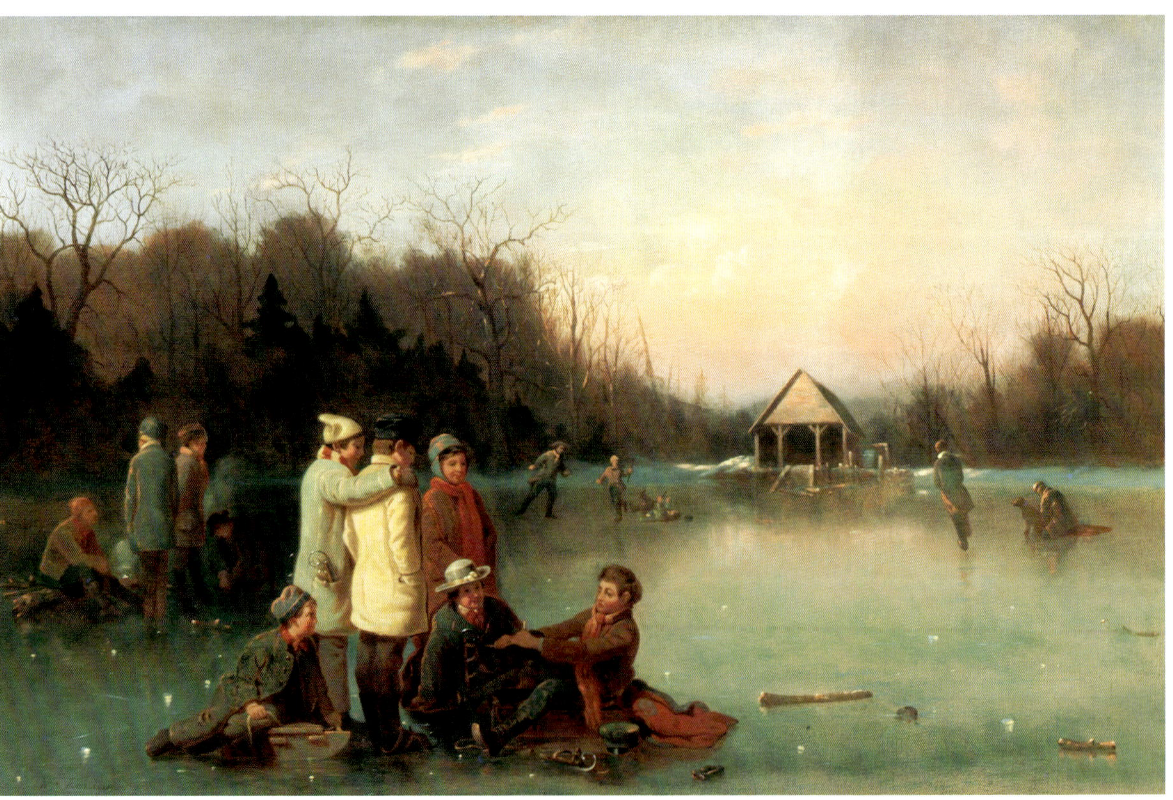

visual elements in Ranney's picture, such as the bare branches of trees silhouetted against the sky and the architectural feature in the background, resemble those in Gignoux's paintings, the large scale of the figures in Ranney's *Skaters* unequivocally places this work in the category of a genre scene rather than a landscape painting.   L B

136
Revolutionary Soldier

c. 1856

Oil on academy board

7 x 5 1/2 inches (14 x 12.7 cm)

Signed

Location unknown

Grubar no. 101

PROVENANCE: British private collector, to 1954 (sale, Parke-Bernet Galleries, New York, March 13, 1954, no. 421).

The Parke-Bernet catalogue described this small work as "a young man, wearing a white shirt and buff breeches, . . . loading his gun, standing on a rocky platform."   L B

137*
Rail Shooting

1856–1859

Oil on canvas

13 3/4 x 19 3/4 inches (34.9 x 50.2 cm)

Signed and dated, on side of boat, lower center: Wm. Ranney 1856 (probably by another hand) & W. S.M. 59. Possible artist's inscription on the back: Rail Shooting

Terra Foundation for American Art, Daniel J. Terra Collection, Chicago, 1992.124

Grubar no. 85

PROVENANCE: J. Ackerman Coles, Newark and Scotch Plains, New Jersey, d. 1925; (Old Print Shop, New York, by 1942); Estate of Carl Badenhausen, Short Hills, New Jersey, to 1982 (sale, Reg[inald] T. Blauvelt, III, Lincoln Galleries, Orange, New Jersey, May 11, 1982) (Berry-Hill Galleries, New York, 1982) Daniel J. Terra Collection, Chicago, 1982–1992.

EXHIBITED: Old Print Shop, New York, April 1942, no. 19. Chadds Ford 1991, no. 24.

REFERENCES: *Art Digest*, vol. 16 (April 15, 1942), p. 18, illus. and notes Old Print Shop exhibit. Thistlethwaite 1991, pp. 34, 35 and 38, illus. and mentions it.

Rail Shooting was presumably one of several works which remained in Ranney's studio after his death on November 18, 1857. While it was not listed in the Ranney Fund sale catalogue of December 1858, it is possible that it was sold in May of that year when Ranney's widow placed all of her husband's art work—"finished pictures, studies for pictures, sketches from Nature, and unfinished works . . . , pen and ink drawings, sketches in pencil, etc."—at S. N. Dodge's New York art supply store in hopes of raising money to help support her young family.[1] Ranney purchased canvas from Dodge, and Dodge himself exhibited two pictures by Ranney at the National Academy in 1855 (see cat. nos. 98 and 108), so he may by that time have been either collecting the works of the artist or acting as his agent.

According to the initialed inscriptions, the painting was finished by William Sidney Mount in 1859, over a year after Ranney's death. While it also bears a Ranney signature and date of 1856, these were probably added by his wife or Mount, for it is unlikely that Ranney would have signed and dated an unfinished work. In any case, this canvas apparently was one of two Mount worked on in 1859 (see cat. no. 141), both of which coincidentally were later owned by J. Ackerman Coles. In his diary entry of February 3, 1859, Mount documents Ranney's painting technique.

> Commenced touching up an unfinished picture by W. Ranney. He appears to make a careful drawing of his design and then glazes over the figure (or whatever he is painting) with red, blue, yellow, brown, green, purple, etc. and then works into the above while wet . . . In some of his skys he changes the tint very often . . . and when the atmosphere is hazzy [*sic*], he also scumbles different tints upon his figures and animals—colors broken—in patches.[2]

Based on Mount's description, one can assume that Ranney sketched in the major compositional elements, including the figures and some of the sky. The delicate handling of the left foreground grasses and the very naturalistic and well-conceived figure of the gray-haired man poling the skiff also seem consistent with Ranney's style. Mount's input, however, may account for the more generalized, almost sketchy, treatment of many of the other details, such as the landscape background, the middle-ground grasses, and in particular the water spaniels, both of which lack the veracity and emotional focus associated with Ranney's dogs. Mount may have also added the boy's blue and orange knit cap with its black and white band, comparable in type to the colorful headgear donned by many of the youths in Mount's own genre scenes, such as, for instance, the yellow hat with a red stripe in *Farmer's Nooning* of 1836 (Long Island Museum of American Art, History and Carriages, Stony Brook, New York).

This is Ranney's only known painting of rail shooting. In the 1850s, these small, short-billed birds, prized by hunters for their sweet taste, were abundant in the fresh and brackish waterways around Ranney's northern New Jersey home, where they fed on aquatic insects and seeds. After wintering in the South, they returned in the spring to the marshy meadows and reed beds to nest and rear their young. Depending on the locale, the hunting season generally began in the early fall, after the young matured. The autumnal scene represented here reflects contemporary hunting practices, such as those codified by Frank Forester, one of the era's leading sporting writers.

> The only method of killing rails, with any success, is from boats, driven over the flats and through the reeds while the tide is rising, as fast as the power and skill of the man who pushes the sportsman with a long punt pole can accomplish. The higher the water, the greater the speed at which the skiff is propelled, the more the sport. The birds will only take wing when the tide is rising, and then only when the boat is forced upon them with such rapidity that they can neither run nor swim away from it. When they have no other choice, they flap up just as the gunwale is run over them, fly awkwardly and lazily away for ten or twenty yards, and then drop again, if not knocked over, which can be done with the merest touch of the shot.[3]

Forester emphasizes the importance of the skill of the man poling, who must not only discover the birds but also mark them when they are shot. All the shooter has to do is "to stand firmly in the boat as it runs over the smooth, moist weeds." He further notes that when the rail rises, the legs hang down.[4] In Ranney's painting, the bird illustrated in the left background plunging headfirst into the marsh is inconsistent with that description. In fact, there is no evidence that Ranney or Mount painted any birds in the sky. According to a conservation report of 1998, that clumsily painted detail was added later, probably by a restorer.[5] It is impossible to know if Ranney's original intent was to include rail either in the sky or arising out of the marshes, or simply to suggest their presence by some clever narrative device alluding to them off canvas, as he did so successfully in *On The Wing* (cat. no. 55). Perhaps because he never completed the picture, *Rail Shooting* lacks the cohesive narrative details so characteristic of the best of his genre work.   L B

1. *Crayon*, vol. 5 (May 1858), p. 148.

2. Quoted in Alfred Frankenstein, *William Sidney Mount* (New York: Harry N. Abrams, 1975), p. 339.

3. Frank Forester [Henry William Herbert], *Complete Manual for Young Sportsmen* (1856; reprint [New York]: Westvaco Corporation, 1993), pp. 128–129.

4. Ibid.

5. Copy of December 8, 1998, memo from paintings conservator to curatorial assistant, Terra Museum of American Art, Ranney archives.

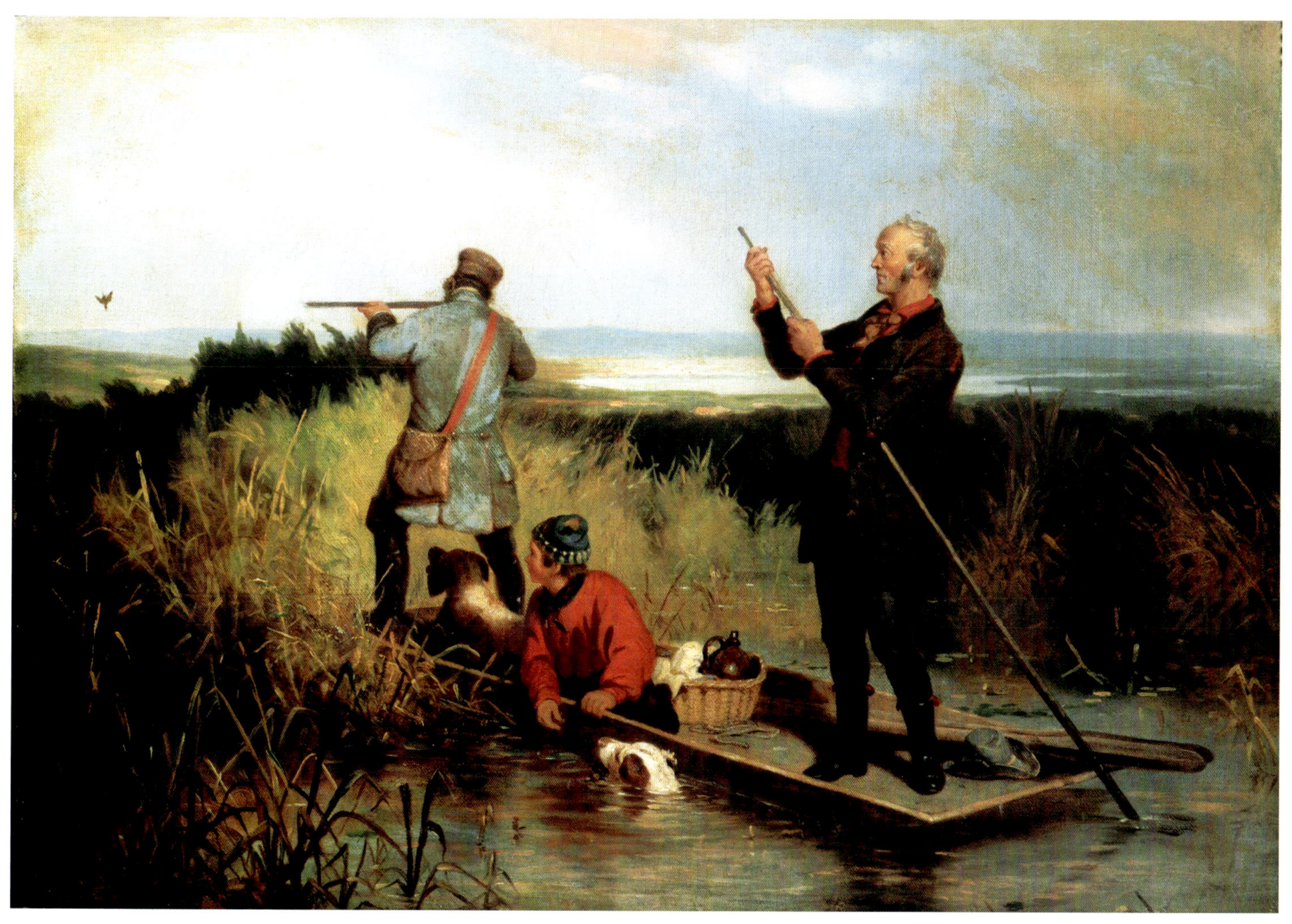

NO. 137

138*
Halt on the Plains

1857

Oil on canvas

46 1/4 x 72 3/4 inches
(117.5 x 184.8 cm)

Signed and dated,
lower left: Wm
Ranney/57

Private collection

Grubar no. 86

PROVENANCE: Everson Museum of Art, Syracuse, New York, to 1948 (Vose Galleries, Boston, 1948) (Gilbert Brouillette, Falmouth, Massachusetts, and New York, 1948); Cornelius Vanderbilt Whitney (1899–1992) New York; his widow, Eleanor (nee Searles, later Mrs. Leonard F. McCollum), Houston, to 1998.

REFERENCES: Vose Galleries to Linda Bantel December 9, 1997, Ranney archives, provides 1948 provenance. Grubar no. 103, p. 47, speculated that this also might be Ranney's last work known as *The Victim*, which has now been located (see cat. no. 134).

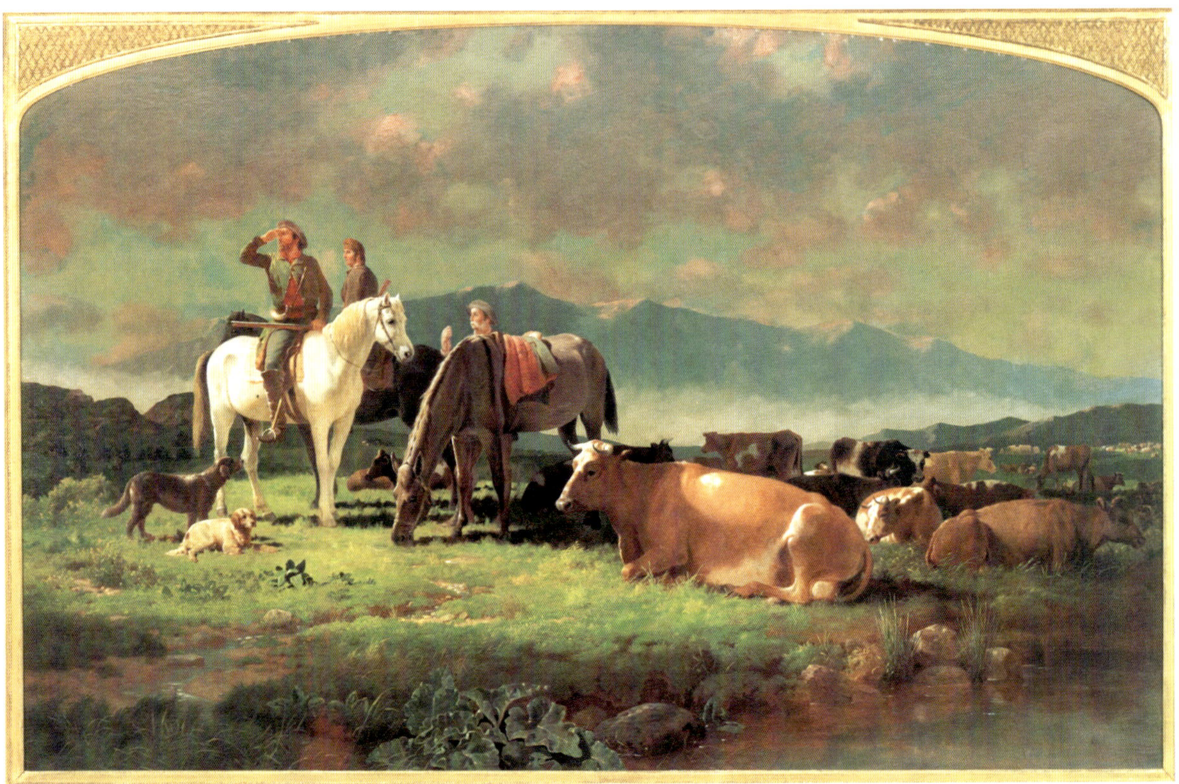

NO. 138

Given the poor state of Ranney's health in 1857, this ambitious canvas presents a remarkably optimistic tableau. In it, high thin clouds float peacefully above a bucolic scene of contentment. The sun breaks through to spotlight what the critic Henry T. Tuckerman had earlier extolled as an essential theme in American art, that "juxtaposition of civilized and savage life."[1] On one side is a gathering of bovine delectation, a group of approximately thirty cows languishing streamside on a warm summer's day. They exude an air of quiescence, sated as they are on the rich verdure provided along the trail. They are well watered, too, though no doubt a bit weary. The path of progress, after all, is not without its fatigues. Yet as portrayed in this work, the trip is replete with rewards and sufficient repasts to continue the march. The quintessence of this halcyon respite, the beefy, reclining repoussoir at the center of the composition, finds its counterpart in the restive gaze of the three men. They are determinedly focused on the distant, unseen horizon, a destination perhaps beyond the reach of their eyes but well within the grasp of their imaginations. In their alert stances, they are ready for the unknown challenges ahead. The wool-lined coat across the saddle, the rifle held ready, and the pair of vigilant hounds attest to the preparedness of these leaders to gather the assets of civilization from the savage domain that lies ahead.

The mahlstick shown in the unusual portrait of Ranney painting this picture (see page XXI) almost perfectly scribes the line separating the two contrasting themes of wilderness and civilization in this tribute to America's pioneers. Ranney produced several smaller studies of westward cavalcades. One drawing, titled *Pioneer Caravan* (cat. no. D13), pictures a host of wagons and animals rounding a large rock outcropping as they head toward a distant mountain ravine. Another, a small oil sketch known as the *Halt on the Prairie* (cat. no. 69), shows a similar troop emerging from a shadowy foreground onto a broad sunny plain with a limitless horizon.

The languorous mood in which Ranney treated this last of his pioneer paintings, *Halt on the Plains*, may find partial explanation in the changing artistic tastes of the day. A call was beginning to be heard for artists to heed the example being set by John Ruskin. Dramatic and theatrical canvases would no longer do, nor would broadly painted landscapes. Artists were beseeched to attend to detail, to the nuances of nature's intricate beauties. A particularly sour review of the National Academy of Design's 1856 exhibition that appeared in the *Crayon* demanded sober attention to earnestness over aspirations of "high Art," and a return to the recognition of the "perfect truth of Nature." The artist who valued the refined study of nature representing a trend referred to by the writer as "pre-Raphaelitism," would know "perfectly the materials of which he builds his art," and thus would be prepared to embark on "the only infallible road to true artistic excellence."[2] Ranney's painting *The Skaters* (cat. no. 135) fell under the critic's censure of almost all of the figure pieces in the 1856 exhibition. It missed the first proclaimed principle of art in that its "only aim is to please the eye, not convey truth."[3] In his painting *Halt on the Plains*, Ranney strove to counter that reproach by demonstrating his regard for an artistic expression in which nature was more closely observed. The particular care in rendering the foreground foliage and rocks and the limpid stream and grassy bed on which the cattle recline is exceptional. So too is the rising mist that speaks of a new day. Clearly those lauded Pre-Raphaelite notions had inculcated the artist, and, despite his failing physical strength, Ranney met the critic's challenge with resolve and masterly adeptness.

On the front page of the March 21, 1857, issue of the new *Harper's Weekly* magazine appeared a story that may also help explain the feeling of stasis within Ranney's *Halt on the Plains*. Titled "Are We as Great a Country as We Think We Are?" the article recounted the findings of Lieutenant G. K. Warren who had recently completed a reconnaissance tour of the northern plains. Warren, a member of the elite Topographical Engineers, had graduated second in his class from West Point and had earned a reputation for the thoroughness of his observations. It was thus rather disconcerting for readers to discover that, according to Warren, the lands west of the 97th meridian were "valueless for agricultural purposes." The conclusion led Harper's editors to wonder what would become of the country's western dream and to pose the question, "How much is left of this treasure once supposed to be inexhaustible?"[4] Ranney's cows stopped in a line, resting perhaps until the veracity of Warren's report can be tested or, more likely, readying themselves for the trip on to Oregon, where the treasure's inexhaustibility was not yet in question. PHH

1. Tuckerman 1847, p. 203.
2. "Exhibition of the National Academy," *Crayon*, 3 (May 1856), p. 145.
3. Ibid., p. 147.
4. "Are We as Great a Country as We Think We Are?" *Harper's Weekly*, 1, no. 12 (March 21, 1857), p. 177.

139*
The Tory Escort

1857

Oil on canvas

36 x 35 inches (91.4 x 88.9 cm)

Signed and dated, lower right: Wm. Ranney/57

Brandywine River Museum, Chadds Ford, Pennsylvania. Gift of Mrs. J. Maxwell Moran, 1997.

Grubar no. 89

PROVENANCE: Margaret Ranney, wife of the artist, (1819–1903); Margaret Ranney, granddaughter of the artist, Union City, New Jersey, d. 1965; Elizabeth R. Moran, great-granddaughter of the artist, Paoli, Pennsylvania, c. 1965–1997.

EXHIBITED: Chadds Ford 1991, cat. no. 26.

REFERENCES: Margaret Ranney, estate appraisal, March 22, 1965, no. 1, lists it, copy in Ranney archives. Claude J. Ranney, undated notes, Ranney archives. Thistlethwaite 1991, pp. 70–71, discusses in terms of elusiveness of subject matter.

In this historical genre scene set within the context of the American Revolution, Ranney depicts a battered patriot in colonial garb, gazing defiantly toward his Tory captor. As though being led to prison, the young man's wrists are bound by a rope attached to the horse's saddle. Visible in the right background is a burning house with smoke rising above it. In addition, there is a creek at the lower left corner. The conflagration is obviously somehow related to the capture of the patriot, but, unlike most of Ranney's genre scenes, the narrative content is vague. Ranney may have been inspired by as an as yet undiscovered account or literary source.

During the war years, Tories, or Loyalists, numbered in the hundreds of thousands, some estimates suggesting as many as one-third of the American populace. Many fought with the British and, to distinguish them from their regulars, were issued green uniforms and cocked hats, just as Ranney shows here.[1] While preferring the stability of English rule to the uncertainty of American independence, the Tories were drawn, like the patriots, from all social classes, the wealthy elite as well as the ranks of men of modest means. Here, in a low-key, nonjudgmental manner, Ranney represents the conflicted political environment in which these ordinary men, who may well have otherwise shared similar backgrounds, now find themselves.

According to Claude J. Ranney's notes, the central figure on the white horse was posed for by Charles Cox, "a descendant of the Cox family who were early settlers of Hudson County, New Jersey." He also identified the figure on the black horse as "Neville." The stallion was said to be owned by the Kerrigan family, neighbors and good friends of the Ranney's in West Hoboken. Grubar notes that according to family tradition, this painting was sold by Ranney's wife after the artist's death to Alfred Corning Clark of New York. Clark, upon learning this was the last painting she owned of her husband's work, apparently insisted upon returning it to her. If that is the case, there seems to be another unlocated version of this subject called *Tories with a Prisoner*, which sold to Pepoon for seventy-five dollars at the Ranney Fund sale (lot 81). There is also a smaller variation of this same theme (see cat. no. 140). LB

1. Ranney could have read a description of the Tory uniform in his copy of Benson J. Lossing, *The Pictorial Field-Book of the Revolution . . .* (New York: Harper and Brothers, 1852), vol. 2, p. 344, n. 1. Ranney's copy is still in the possession of one of his descendants.

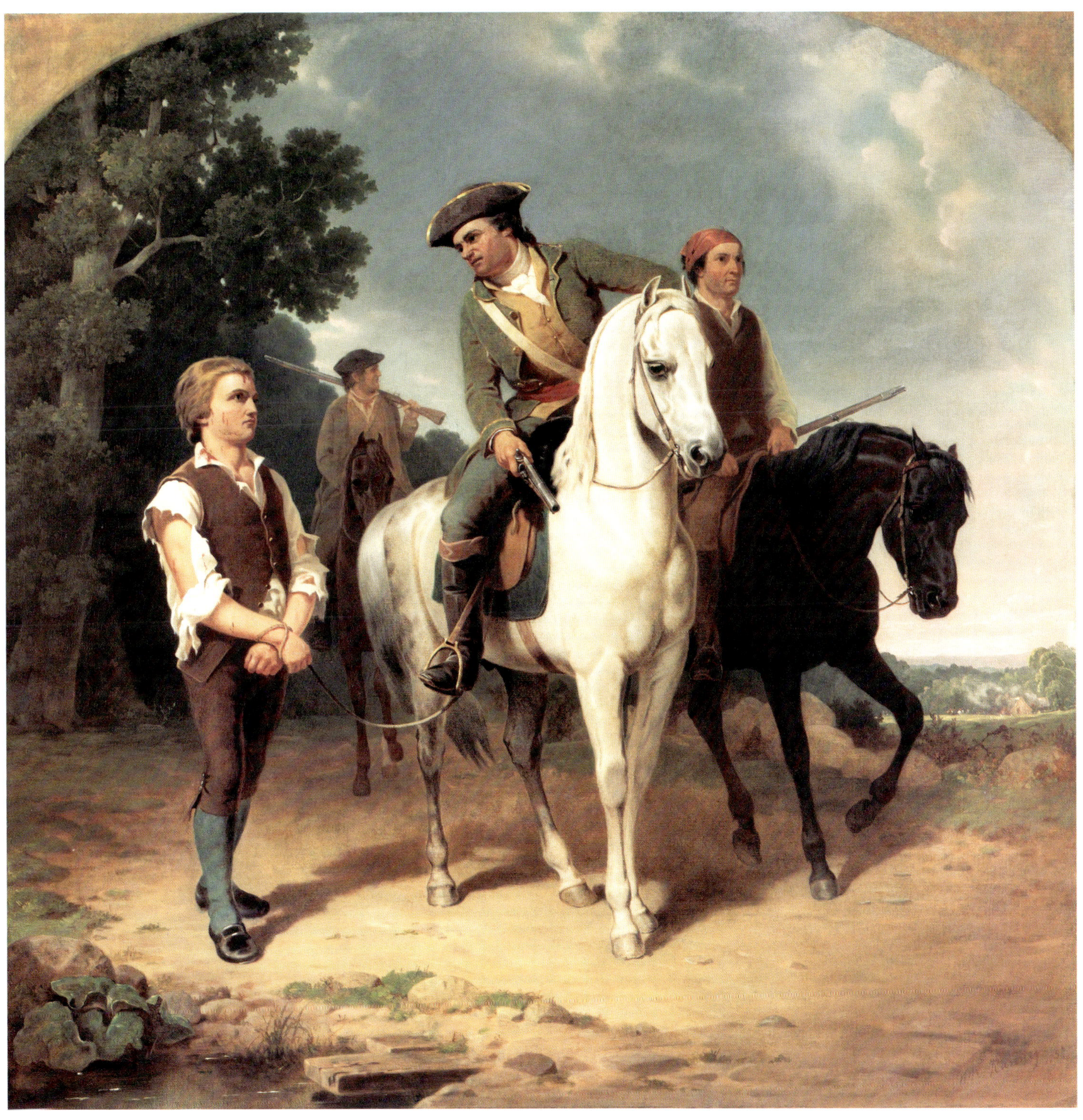

NO. 139

140*
Tories with a Prisoner

c. 1857

Oil on canvas

14 1/4 x 17 1/4 inches (36.2 x 43.8 cm)

Canvas stamp (before relining): S. N. Dodge's/Artists & Painters Supply Store/189 Chatham Cor/of Oliver St., New York

Courtesy of Spanierman Gallery, New York

Grubar no. 90, as *The Tory Escort*

PROVENANCE: Possibly Ranney Fund sale, lot 96, as Tories with a Prisoner, to Wood, for $8.50; Marshall O. Roberts (1814–1880), New York; his widow, to 1897 (sale, Fifth Avenue Art Galleries, New York, *Executors' Sale . . . of the Late Marshall O. Roberts*, January 19, 20, 21, 1897, lot 278, p. 79, as The Tory Escort); Claude J. Ranney, Malvern, Pennsylvania, c. 1950–1971; his daughter, Elizabeth R. Moran, Malvern, Pennsylvania, c. 1971–c. 1991 (sale, Sotheby's, New York, May 15, 1991, lot 37, as The Tory Prisoner.)

Grubar suggested that this painting was a study for *The Tory Escort* (cat. no. 139). Indeed, like many of Ranney's preliminary studies, it is small, unsigned, and undated. It is different enough in composition and other elements, however, that it might equally be considered a variation on the Revolutionary War theme. Compared to the larger signed and dated Brandywine Museum painting on that subject, this work has more details by which Ranney focused the narrative, both emotionally and dramatically. While her home burns in the distant background, a weeping woman clutches her child's hand as she stands helplessly behind her husband, his ripped shirt and bloody brow evidence of a valiant fight. Roped to the white horse, he is being led away by three Tories, forced to leave behind his now homeless family to fend for themselves. Here, Ranney reveals his sympathy for the patriot cause by portraying the Tories, loyal to England, in a far more caricatured and demonized manner than in the larger picture. These men appear to relish their rapacious actions, as they leer down at their captive, seemingly oblivious to the human tragedy they have wrought. In this version of the subject, Ranney sympathetically conveys in pictorial terms the hardships many rural families endured during the war years.

In 1962, Grubar reported that "278" was inscribed twice on the back of the frame and once on a label attached to the back. That number corresponds to the lot number in the Marshall O. Roberts sale. LB

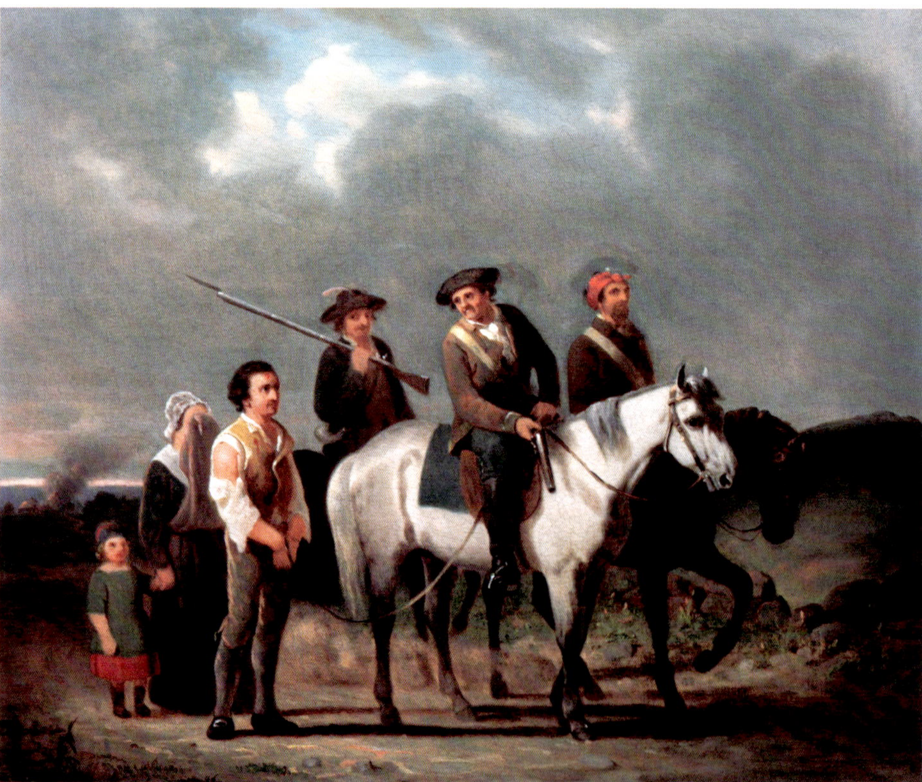

141*
The Pipe of Friendship

1857–1859

Oil on canvas

23 x 36 inches (58.4 x 91.4 cm)

Signed and dated, lower right: W. Ranney 1857. & W.S.M. Feb. 1859. Inscribed on the back of canvas, probably by another hand: The Pipe of Friendship

Newark Museum, New Jersey. Gift of Dr. J. Ackerman Coles, 1920

Grubar no. 92

PROVENANCE: Possibly Ranney Fund sale 1858, no. 159, as Scouts on the Prairie, purchased by Wood for $62.50; Dr. J. Ackerman Coles, Scotch Plains, New Jersey, d. 1915.

EXHIBITED: Newark Museum Association, New Jersey, *The Dr. J. Ackerman Coles Collections: Catalog of a Supplementary Exhibition*, November 1920, no. 41, as The pipe of friendship, Kit Carson and Daniel Boone.

REFERENCES: William Sidney Mount, diary entry, February 3, 1859, in Alfred Frankenstein, *William Sidney Mount* (New York: Henry N. Abrams, 1974), p. 339 (quoted in entry). *American Art in the Newark Museum* (Newark, New Jersey: 1981), p. 366, lists it. Ayers 1987, p. 101, illus. and discusses.

This painting, which is inscribed "Pipe of Friendship" on the back, is a smaller version of a work that had been called *The Scouting Party* and is now also titled the *Pipe of Friendship* (cat no. 110). Evidently, this work was left unfinished at the time of Ranney's death in 1857, and in 1859 was finished by his friend and compatriot William Sidney Mount (1807–1868). Mount completed the work by February 3 of that year, which was very shortly after the Ranney Fund sale. There had been a painting in the sale entitled *Scouts on the Prairie* (lot 159) that sold to someone named Wood for sixty-two dollars and fifty cents (see cat. no. 50 for information on Wood). Another possibility is that that painting was sold earlier by Ranney's widow among a group of "finished pictures, studies for pictures, sketches from Nature, and unfinished works" offered in the shop of Samuel N. Dodge on Chatham Square in New York during the spring of 1858.[1]

In any event, while it is not certain for whom the painting was finished, Mount not only did the work but wrote down his observations of his late friend's technique. In his diary for February 3, 1859, he gives us the following commentary:

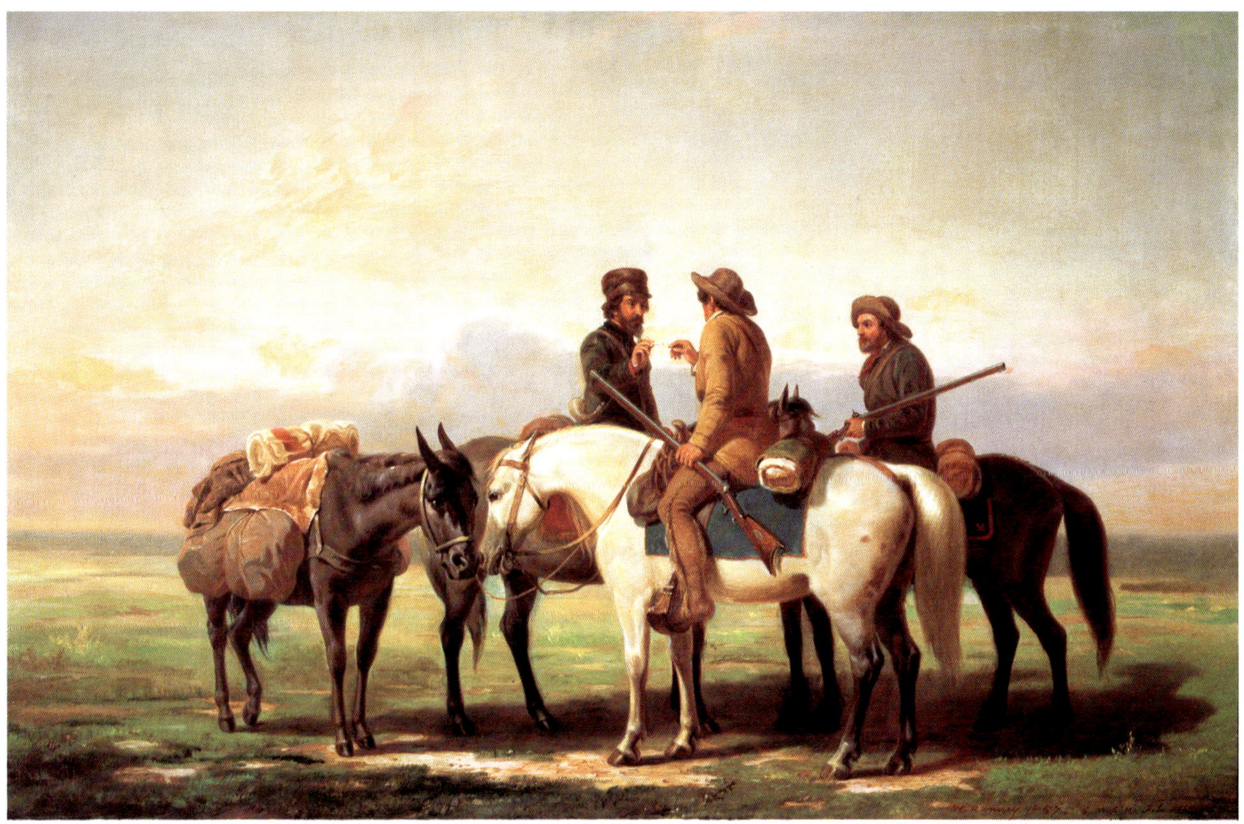

NO. 141

175

Commenced touching up an unfinished picture by W. Ranney. He appears to make a careful drawing of his design and then glazes over the figure (or whatever he is painting) with red, blue, yellow,
brown, Green, purple etc., and then works into the above while wet, or otherwise as the [time] or
case may be.

In some of his skys he changes the tint very often—blue and white, red and white, and yellow and
white—and when the atmosphere is hazzy [*sic*], he also scumbles different tints upon his figures and
animals—colors broken—in patches.

PHH

1. "Domestic Art Gossip," *Crayon*, vol. 5 (May, 1858), p. 148.

142*
Waiting for the Ferry

c. 1857

Oil on canvas

13 1/2 x 18 1/2 inches
(34.3 x 47 cm)

Affixed to the back of
the stretcher is a rem-
nant of an old paper
label with the inscrip-
tion: [Wa]iting for the
Ferry

Private collection

PROVENANCE: Possibly Ranney Fund sale, no. 166, to Riggs for $15; Daniel Riskin, (Gerald Peters Gallery, Santa Fe, by
1990–1995).

REFERENCES: Copy of October 4, 1990, letter from Francis S. Grubar to whom it may concern, authenticates picture, Ranney
archives. *Antiques Magazine*, vol. 139 (March 1991), p. 492, illus. as advertisement in Gerald Peters Gallery, Santa Fe and Dallas.

This recently discovered study is one of at least three recorded examples of Ranney's treating the subject of
water transportation (see cat. nos. 23 and 61). His first such effort, *Crossing the Ferry—Scene on the Pedee* was,
as its title indicates, inspired by views near Fayetteville, North Carolina, Ranney's home during his teen years.
Despite their different dates of execution, both the earlier and later paintings share many details which define
the idyllic eastern landscape—a narrow, curving waterway banked by lush green trees, bluish rolling hills in
the background, and cumulus clouds overhead. Whereas Ranney's earlier scene on the Pee Dee River depicts a
few neighbors apparently making a routine river crossing during the course of their daily lives, *Waiting for the
Ferry* represents an entire family—husband and wife with their children, domestic animals, and a covered
wagon—as though in the throes of moving the household. Seen from behind and conversing with the husband
is a tall frontiersman wearing a fur cap and buckskin leggings, and holding a long-barrel rifle. He seems to be
regaling the husband with stories. Is he a guide or just a fellow traveler? As he talks, the woman, touchingly
surrounded by her children, looks on from the sideline with an intense and anxious expression. Two of the children shown with their backs to the viewer seem transfixed by the scene before them.

This picture can be interpreted within the context of Ranney's several genre scenes documenting episodes of
emigrant families on the overland trail (see, for example, cat. nos. 38, 69, and 138). Statistics show that most
young emigrant families had between three and four children.[1] Women's diaries of the period are often elo-
quent in their descriptions of the uneasiness many experienced at the thought of emigrating west, a decision
often made by husbands which, according to the custom of the times, they felt obligated to honor. One diarist
Mary A. Jones, wrote:

> In the winter of 18 and 46 our neighbor got hold of Fremont's *History of California* and began talk-
> ing of moving to the New Country & brought the book to my husband to read, & he was carried
> away with the idea too. I said *O let us not go.*[2]

Though small and sketchy in execution, this well composed study nevertheless provides a fairly complete and
provocative narrative. In it Ranney expresses the ambivalence and anxiety of easterners as they set out on
the first leg of the arduous journey west, leaving behind the security and familiarity of home to face the
hardships and unpredictability of a new life.

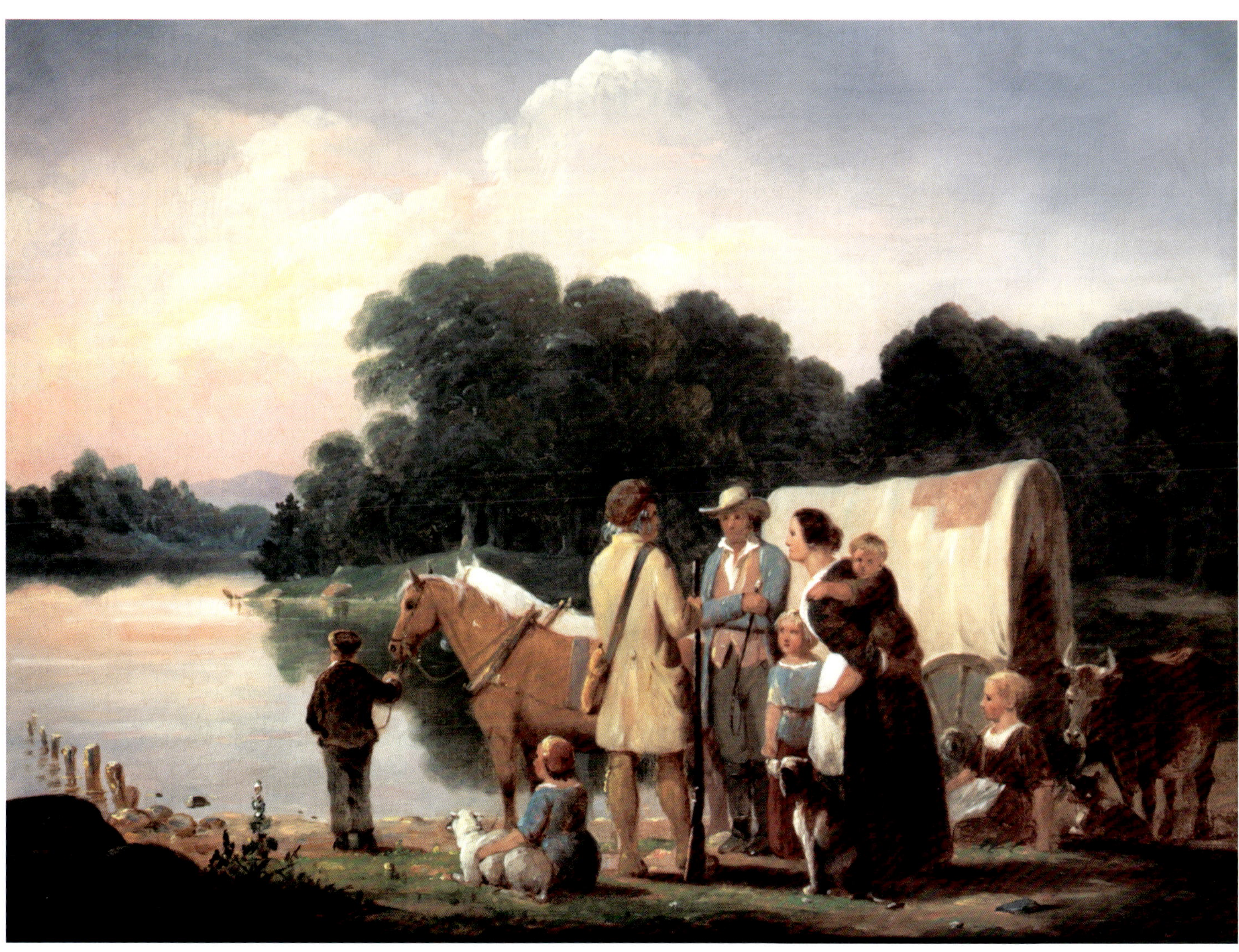

NO. 142

Grubar considered *Waiting for the Ferry* "a final, preparatory oil sketch for a larger painting" on which Ranney was probably working at the time of his death. He further observed that "the treatment of figures, design, color, sense of space and human rapport are all positive Ranney elements." A similarly titled work was sold in the Ranney Fund sale as lot 166 to someone by the name of Riggs for fifteen dollars. Whether this was George Washington Riggs of Washington D.C., as has been suggested, is unknown. A painting simply entitled *The Ferry* was sold (lot 144, p. 8) in a Henry H. Leeds and Company auction in New York sometime in 1860 (precise dates illegible). No dimensions were provided (copy of catalogue in the New York Public Library). LB

1. Lillian Schlissel, *Women's Diaries of the Westward Journey* (New York: Schocken Books, 1982), p. 151.
2. Quoted from Ibid., p. 28.

177

143
The Meadows

c.1857
Oil on canvas
Location unknown
Grubar no. 88

Exhibited: NAD, 1857, no. 494.
Reference: Cowdrey 1943, 2, p. 89.

144
The Spy of War

c. 1857
Oil on canvas
Location unknown
Grubar no. 91

Reference: Jersey City, New Jersey, *Hudson Observer*, October 1927.[1]

Grubar cites the above reference for *The Spy of War* and suggests it may be the same work as *The Tory Escort* (see cat. nos. 139 and 140). LB

1. In a search of this publication for the entire month of October, 1927, no reference to Ranney or this painting was found.

145
The Freshet

1857–1858
Oil on canvas
15 x 24 inches (38.1 x 61 cm)
Signed, lower right: Painted Ranney/Otto Somer
On label affixed to stretcher: The Freshet/Ranney & Sommer
Private collection
Grubar no. 94

Provenance: Possibly the Ranney Fund sale, lot 152; possibly Nason Collins, by 1858; Old Print Shop, New York, to 1957; private collector, 1957–1994 (sale, Sotheby's, New York, December 1, 1994, no. 164).

The Freshet is a small and unusually dark genre painting, its brooding black sky denoting the torrential rains that have swollen the river. Packed at the water's edge at the right side of this ambitious composition are horses and cattle scattered amidst a figurative group whose extensive personal belongings, shown piled on the ground and on the wagon, suggest that they are homesteaders heading west. The picturesque detail of a tray of crystal glasses near the back of the white horse illustrates the kind of household objects some emigrants brought with them. The inclusions of such luxury items here also functions as a poignant reminder of the civilized society they have left behind in the East and are committed to carrying on in the new western settlements. As the travelers bide their time waiting for the river to recede, they watch a man and his two horses swim toward them, while nearby three men occupy themselves giving one of the horses a bath.

The dominant pictorial element, however, is the white horse that faces the water and majestically looms over the scene, imbuing the whole with an evocative sense of fantasy and mystery. While in his early western scenes, Ranney featured a captured white steed which has often been interpreted as a symbol of America's taming the West (see cat. nos. 18 and 19), here the horse appears to bless and oversee the voyage. This image was perhaps inspired by the allegory of the Four Horsemen of the Apocalypse that appears in the New Testament, where the pale horse represents Conquest to some, or to others Christ. Either way, the political and religious overtones parallel American convictions at the time "as expressed in sermons, political speeches, and newspaper editorials that democracy, as planted on the western part of the continent by the United States, was what the world needed, and what God wanted."[1]

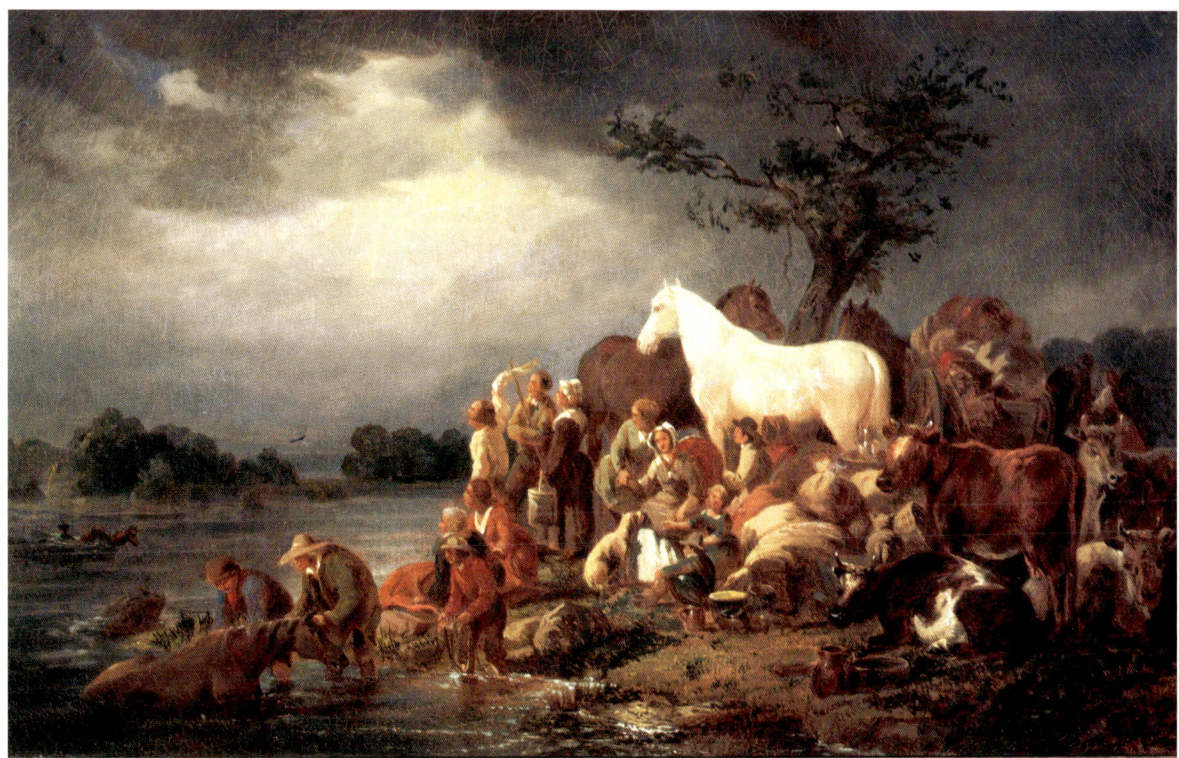

This rather sketchily rendered painting may well have been the one left in Ranney's studio at his death and sold in the Ranney Fund sale to Nason Collins for fourteen dollars (lot 152). According to the signature and the label affixed to the back, it was apparently finished by Otto Sommer, a relatively obscure German artist who worked in Newark and Belleville, New Jersey, in the early 1860s, and later in Chicago. It was reported that by 1871 he had relocated to Munich. In addition to scenes of the West, Sommer painted landscapes, marines, and hunting pictures.[2]

A recently discovered preliminary drawing (see cat. no. D81) relates to this picture. LB

1. See Elizabeth Johns, "Settlement and Development: Claiming the West," in William H. Truettner, ed., *The West as America: Reinterpreting Images of the Frontier, 1820–1920* (Washington: Smithsonian Institution Press, 1991), p. 192.
2. For biographical information, see ibid., p. 367, and William H. Gerdts, *Art Across America: Two Centuries of Regional Painting,1710–1920: The South and the Midwest* (New York: Abbeville Press, 1990), pp. 290 and 292.

146*
Retrieving

c. 1857–1858

Oil on canvas

10 x 13 3/4 inches
(25.4 x 34.9 cm)

Signed with artists'
initials, lower right;
W.R./& A.F.T./&
W.S.M. Inscribed on
the back: Retrieving,
by W. Ranney.
Inscribed on top of
stretcher: Retrieving.

Private collection

PROVENANCE: Possibly Ranney Fund sale, lot 118, as Duck Shooting, to Wood for $27; (Norton Galleries, New York, 1964) Estates of Maude B. Feld and Samuel B. Feld, Esq., 1964–2001 (sale, Sotheby's, New York, November 28, 2001, p. 26, lot 19, illus. and provides provenance).

REFERENCES: Warder H. Cadbury and Henry E. Marsh, *Arthur Fitzwilliam Tait: Artist in the Adirondacks* (Newark: University of Delaware Press, 1986), p. 320, ND. 8, discusses (quoted in entry).

According to Henry E. Marsh's checklist of Arthur Fitzwilliam Tait's works: "This painting was unfinished at the time of William Ranney's death, November 18, 1857. AFT and William Sidney Mount completed the picture so that it could be sold for the benefit of the Ranney estate in December 1858." In addition to that information, a fragment of an original letter, presumably written by Tait, is affixed to the backing and provides the following further information on the history of the painting: "Received from Mr. W[ood?]./for a Painting of Deer . . . /and for finishing a sketch by Ranney— . . . sixty for Deer/and Forty Five for the Sketch/A.F. Tait." If, as Marsh suggests, this painting was indeed sold at the Ranney Fund sale, the only duck shooting picture was lot 118. It was acquired by Wood, who purchased sixteen of Ranney's works from that sale. He may most certainly be the "Mr. W" referred to in Tait's letter.[1] LB

1. Two brothers, Charles B. and David A. Wood, were both New York patrons of William Sidney Mount.

NO. 146

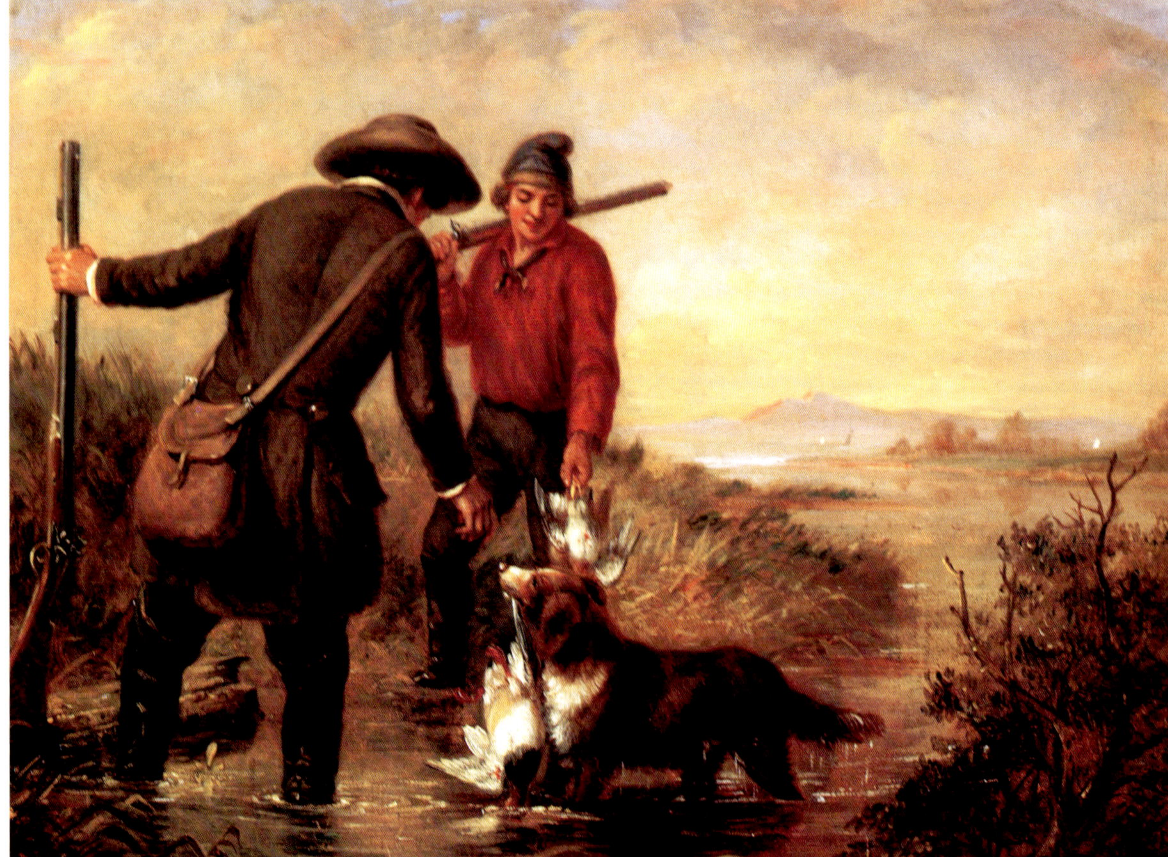

147*
Recruiting for the Continental Army

c. 1857–59

Oil on canvas

53 3/4 x 82 1/4 inches
(136.5 x 208.9 cm)

Inscribed, lower left
(by another hand):
Painted by W. Ranney,
finished by Blauvelt
1859

CANVAS STAMP:
George Rowney & Co
[illegible]./London.

Munson-Williams-
Proctor Arts Institute.
Museum of Art, Utica,
New York. Gift of T.
Proctor Eldred, 58.284

Grubar no. 93, as
Recruiting During the
Revolutionary War

PROVENANCE: Ranney Fund sale, lot 75, as Enlisting During the Revolutionary War; James Topham Brady (1815–1869), New York, 1858; (sale, Anderson Galleries, New York, *Painting by Artists of the 16th to 19th Centuries*, December 9, 10, 11, 1929, lot 78, as Recruiting During the American Revolution, for $150) Moses Tannenbaum (d. c. 1938), by 1929; National Republican Club, New York, by c. 1940 to 1958, as Recruiting for the Continental Army; Thomas Proctor Eldred, Sr., Utica, New York, 1958.

REFERENCES: Intermuseum Laboratory, Oberlin, Ohio, treatment report of May, 1946, (quoted in entry). Letter from Milan R. Hughston, assistant librarian, Amon Carter Museum, to Curator, Munson-Williams-Proctor Institute, December 19, 1980, artist's file, Munson-Williams-Proctor Institute, says annotated copy of Anderson Galleries catalogue in collection of Knoedler Library indicates that painting was sold to Moses Tannenbaum, but was not included in a sale of his collection on January 26, 1938, after his death. Warren H. Metzger, manager, National Republican Club, to T. P. Eldred, November 24, 1958, says he has been a member for 18 years, registrar's files, ibid. *Albany Times-Union*, July 5, 1965, says Thomas Proctor Eldred, Sr., had coveted the painting since he had been visiting the National Republican Club for over twenty-five years, clipping in Ranney archives. Linda Ayres, in Paul E. Schweizer, ed., et al., *Masterworks of American Art from the Munson-Williams-Proctor Institute* (New York: Harry N. Abrams, Inc., 1989), p. 58, illus., p. 59, discusses and draws parallel with short term volunteer enlistments during the war with Mexico in 1846 to 1848.

Recruiting for the Continental Army, also known as *Enlisting or Recruiting During the Revolutionary War*, was left unfinished in Ranney's studio at his death. It was sold in the Ranney Fund sale in December 1858 to family friend and lawyer, James T. Brady. In 1859, it was finished by the portrait and genre painter Charles F. Blauvelt (1824–1900). Born in New York and a pupil of the portrait artist Charles Loring Elliott, Blauvelt, a regular contributor to the exhibitions at the National Academy of Design and the Pennsylvania Academy of the Fine Arts, also specialized in genre themes. His contribution may simply have been adding finishing touches to a virtually complete composition. This opinion is based on evidence reported by a conservator who examined the work in 1946. He observed that the landscape and setting are "strong and unabraded," while "some of the flesh tones and costumes have a thin, rubbed look," an unevenness which is attributable to "the fact that the picture . . . was (rather cautiously) finished by another hand."

This scene, Ranney's last major Revolutionary War subject, is a historical sequel to his *First News of the Battle of Lexington* (see cat. no. 31). Whereas that 1847 work represents a call for volunteers to enlist for a short time in a state militia in response to a specific British threat, *Recruiting for the Continental Army* represents the beginnings of the formation of a large and cohesive national army whose soldiers, in the face of chronic shortages of manpower, were required to make long-term commitments and serve under one commander in chief. During the colonial period, it was the New England region where the major events leading up to the Revolution occurred. Thus it is not surprising that Ranney depicts, atop the wagon at the left, a man holding New England's pine tree flag with its motto, "Appeal to Heaven." Seemingly a visualization of that motto, the nearby recruiter gestures toward the sky as he uplifts his arms.

Art historian Linda Ayres points out that Ranney's picture has much in common with George Caleb Bingham's congested village scenes with their American "types," particularly *County Election* of 1851–1852 (St. Louis Art Museum), which was engraved by John Sartain in 1854. Indeed, a variety of figures and details animate the canvas—men, women, children, dogs, weeping loved ones, soldiers, and enlistees. In the right background, a sign with a crowned head emblematic of British royalty is being pulled down as the innkeeper rushes to save it. With the trio of conspiratorial looking men under the tree at the left[1], Ranney alludes to the complexity of the political situation when, at that time, there was far from ideological consensus among thoughtful Americans about either separating from England or enlisting in the armed forces.

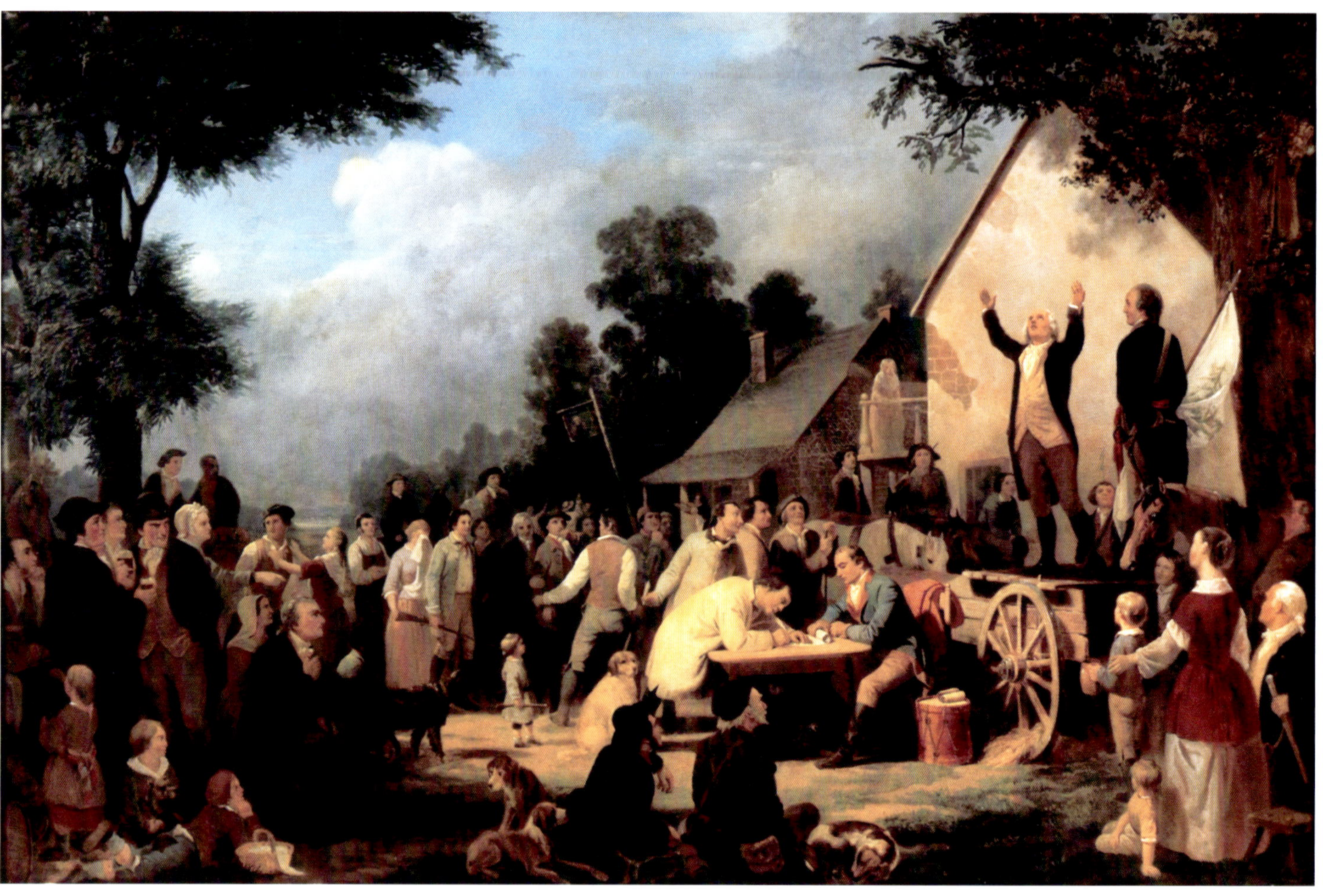

NO. 147

A related work is a *Study for a Large Picture—Revolutionary Enlistment* which was sold to Pepoon for twenty-six dollars at the Ranney Fund sale (lot 63). LB

1. Two of these individuals are also the subjects of a related drawing (see cat. no. D4).

148
Kentucky Scouts

Oil on canvas

14 x 20 inches (35.6 x 50.8 cm)

Location unknown

Grubar no. 95

PROVENANCE: (sale, American Art Association, Anderson Galleries, New York, January 27, 1938, no. 52, p. 36, for $100).

The sale catalogue described *Kentucky Scouts:* "Two hardy frontiersmen in red shirts, buckskin attire and moccasins are holding their guns ready for an encounter as they peer toward the distance from a height where large boulders form quick shelter. Their mounts, chestnut and white respectively, are close to them and seem to share their anxiety. Neutral sky." A postscript to that entry notes that "it has been suggested that the subjects are Daniel Boone and Harrod, after whom Harrodsburg, Ky., is named." LB

149
Cattle

c. 1857

Oil on canvas

Location unknown

PROVENANCE: J. R. Whiting, by 1864.

EXHIBITED: Yonkers Sanitary Fair, Yonkers, New York, *Catalogue of Paintings, on Exhibition in National Guard Armory . . .* February 15, 1864, no. 9, as Cattle owned by J. R. Whiting.

150
Emigrants on the Prairie

c. 1857

Oil on canvas

Location unknown

PROVENANCE: M. Jarvis, by 1862.

EXHIBITED: Artists' Fund Society of New York, New York, *Third Annual Exhibition*, 1862, no. 72, as Emigrants on the Prairie, owned by M. Jarvis.

WORKS ON PAPER CATALOGUE

The works in this section are organized precisely in the order in which Francis S. Grubar listed them in 1962, beginning with items in public collections or documented in the nineteenth century. Because most of the drawings were at that time in the collection of the artist's grandson Claude J. Ranney and because no other provenances are known, it seemed important to retain the sequence in which Grubar first saw them, just in case that order may be useful for future scholars. All newly discovered works have been added at the end. Claude Ranney seems to have been the one who added the initials W. T. R. which appear on most of the drawings in his collection. William Ranney himself never used his middle initial. Many of the drawings that Claude Ranney held at that time have, alas, disappeared since Grubar published his catalogue.

Although many sketches were listed in the Ranney Fund sale (see pp. 207-211), we are certain only in the case of *Study for "Boone's First View of Kentucky, 1769"* (D1)—that it was in fact purchased there. In the nineteenth century, John M. Falconer, artist, hardware merchant, and friend of William Sidney Mount, may have acquired a few drawings directly from Ranney (see D6 and D7).

There are eighty-three works on paper, mostly undated. No chronology for them has been attempted. If a drawing relates to a known painting, it is mentioned in the entry. Some of the works, such as *Study for "The Retreat"* (D35), are remarkably complete; others are mere sketches done in a variety of techniques. Ranney often drew on both sides of the paper, and whenever possible both sides are described and illustrated (since Grubar gave recto and verso separate numbers we have continued his system).

The scope of the subject matter represented in these works on paper is similar to the paintings—genre subjects, landscapes, historical sketches, animals, fanciful scenes, and portraits. Some of the works, such as the sketches for *Gist Rescuing Washington from the Allegheny River* (D21, D65, D80), clearly demonstrate that Ranney was working out his ideas on paper. Most of the landscapes, animal subjects, and portraits confirm his practice of drawing from nature or a live model.

LINDA BANTEL

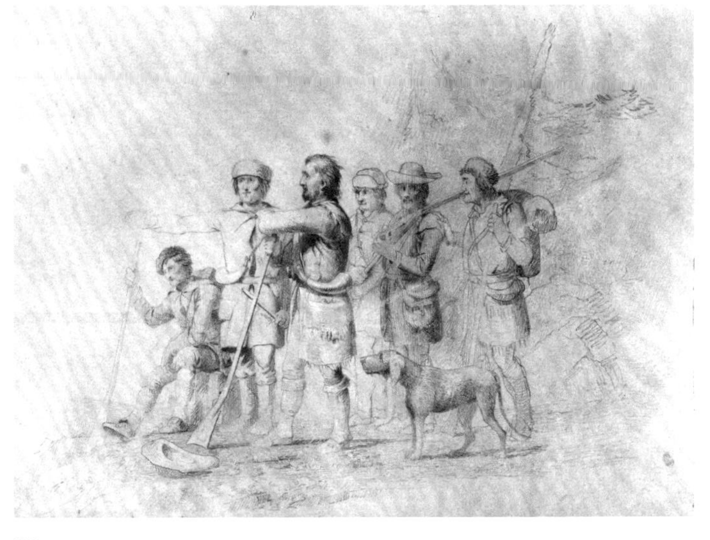

D1

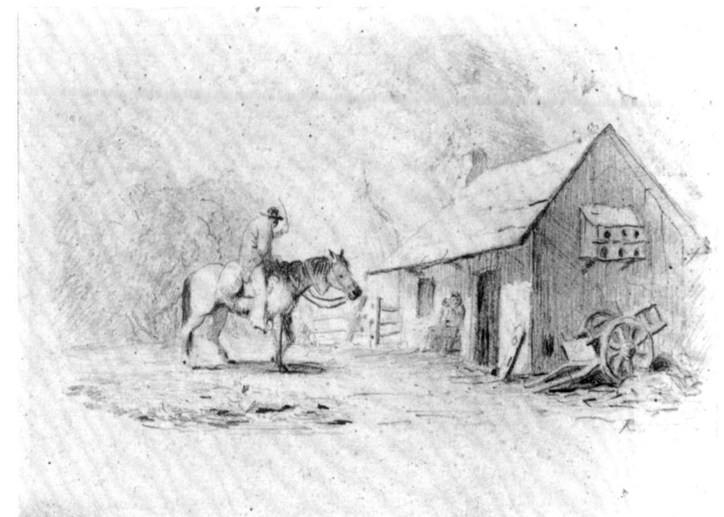

D3

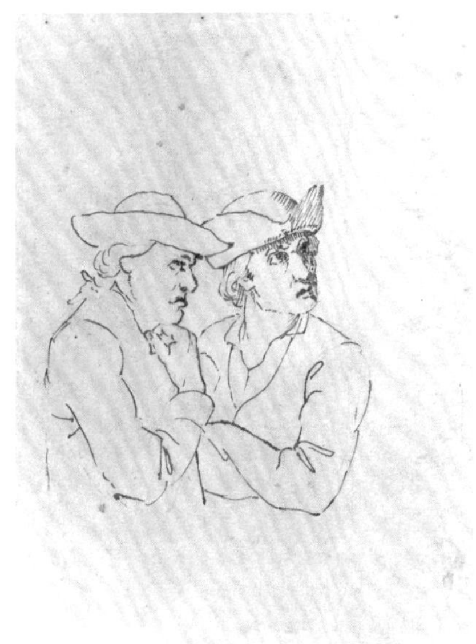

D4

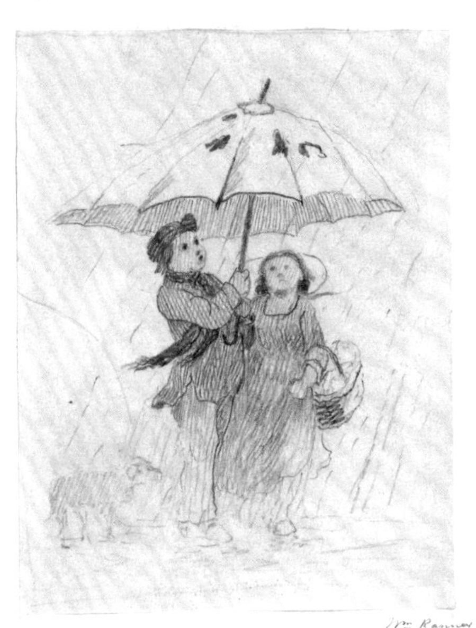

D6

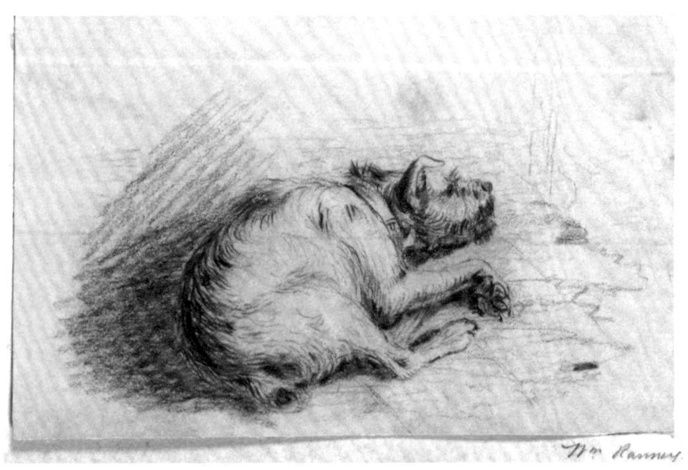

D7

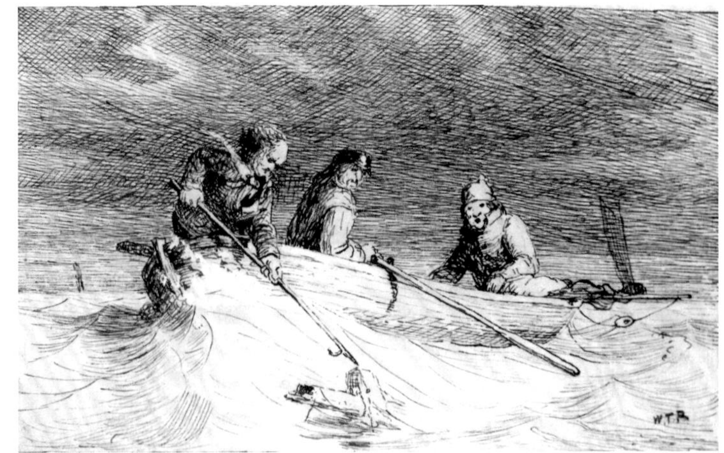

D9

D1*

Study for "Boone's First View of Kentucky [1769]"

c. 1849

Graphite on buff paper, highlighted with chalk

10 x 13 1/2 inches (25.4 x 34.3 cm)

Inscribed on mat, lower right: First thoughts of "Boones view of Kentucky"/ by Ranney; lower left: On the 7th day of June 1769 Daniel Boone, / in company with John Stewart, John Finley [Finlay], / Joseph Holden, James Holden [?], James Mooney [Monay] / and William Cool, found himself on Red / River and from the top of an eminence saw / with pleasure the beautiful level of Kentucky / so wrote John Filson in 1785. / Boone and his companions discovering Kentucky by William T. Ranney A.N.A. 1813–1857.

Speed Art Museum, Louisville, Kentucky. Purchase, Museum Art Fund, 1961.7.

Grubar no. 115

EXHIBITED: Chadds Ford 1991, no. 31.

This may be the drawing called "Study for a Large Picture, Daniel Boon [sic] and Party," which was sold at the Ranney Fund sale (no. 176) to Walker for six dollars. It relates to cat. nos. 45 and 46.

D2

The Sportsman and His Dog

Graphite with washes

About 5 x 6 inches (12.7 x 15.2 cm)

Location unknown

Grubar no. 116

PROVENANCE: John Taylor Johnston, New York (sale, R. Sommerville, New York, *The Collection of Paintings, Drawings, and Statuary, the Property of John Taylor Johnston, Esq.*, December 19, 20 and 22, 1876, lot 316, p. 79.

Reference: *New York Daily Tribune*, December 23, 1876, p. 2, no. 316, lists it and reports sold for $21.

D3

Farmhouse with Dovecote

Graphite on buff paper

3 3/8 x 4 3/4 inches (8.6 x 12.1 cm)

Initialed, lower right: R

Museum of Fine Arts, Boston. Bequest of Maxim Karolik for the M. and M. Karolik Collection of American Watercolors and Drawings, 1800–1875, 1973.381.

Grubar no. 117

D4

Two Disturbed Onlookers

Graphite, pen and ink on paper

7 5/8 x 5 1/2 inches (19.4 x 14 cm)

Museum of Fine Arts, Boston. Bequest of Maxim Karolik for the M. and M. Karolik Collection of American Watercolors and Drawings, 1800–1875, 1973.382

Grubar no. 118.

EXHIBITED: Chadds Ford 1991, no. 42.

D5

Man with Dogs on Leash

Pen and ink on paper

6 1/4 x 7 5/8 inches (15.9 x 19.4 cm)

On the back, in graphite, is a very sketchy image of a dog and a reclining man which may relate to *The Lazy Fisherman* of 1850 (cat. no. 53).

Museum of Fine Arts, Boston. Bequest of Maxim Karolik for the M. and M. Karolik Collection of American Watercolors and Drawings, 1800–1875, 62.221.

Grubar no. 119

EXHIBITED: Chadds Ford 1991, no. 38.

D6

Children Under Umbrella

Graphite on paper

5 x 4 inches (12.7 x 10.2 cm)

Museum of Fine Arts, Boston. Bequest of Maxim Karolik for the M. and M. Karolik Collection of American Watercolors and Drawings, 1800-1875, 60.891.

Bound in a volume of sixty drawings in graphite, pen, wash, watercolor, and gouche by various American artists. compiled by John Makie Falconer (American, born in Scotland, 1820-1903). Falconer Album, no. 54, p. 38.

Grubar no. 120

PROVENANCE: sale, Anderson Auction Company, New York, April 28–29, 1904, *Collection of Paintings, Watercolors, and Engravings, formed by John M. Falconer*, no. 14.

D7

Sleeping Dog

Graphite on paper

3 1/8 x 5 inches (7.9 x 12.7 cm)

Museum of Fine Arts, Boston. Bequest of Maxim Karolik for the M. and M. Karolik Collection of American Watercolors and Drawings, 1800-1875, 60.891.

Bound in a volume of sixty drawings in graphite, pen, wash, watercolor, and gouche by various American artists, compiled by John Makie Falconer (American, born in Scotland, 1820-1903). Falconer Album, no. 55, p. 38.

Grubar no. 121

PROVENANCE: sale, Anderson Auction Company, New York, April 28–29, 1904, *Collection of Paintings, Watercolors, and Engravings, formed by John M. Falconer*, no. 14.

D8
Two Hunters in the West

Pen and ink on paper

10 x 9 inches (25.4 x 22.9 cm)

Location unknown

Grubar no. 122

While Grubar suggested that this drawing belonged to the artist Charles Lanman of Georgetown, D. C., the *Crayon* article he cites (February 28, 1855, vol. 1, p. 137) does not mention a specific work by Ranney. He also speculated that Carl Dentzel of Los Angeles might be the owner. In 1962 when Grubar published his catalogue, Dentzel did own a small work with dimensions (9 x 11 inches) somewhat comparable to this drawing, but it was a painting entitled *Trappers on the Lookout* (cat. no. 48).

D9
Recto: Three Fishermen in a Skiff

Black-brown and red ink heightened with Chinese white on tan paper

4 3/4 x 7 inches (12.1 x 17.8 cm)

Inscribed, lower right: W.T.R.

Grubar no. 123

D10
Verso: Two Men in a Skiff

Corcoran Gallery of Art, Washington, D.C. Gift of Claude J. Ranney, grandson of the artist, 60.49.3.

PROVENANCE: Claude J. Ranney, to 1960.

EXHIBITED: Chadds Ford 1991, no. 41.

REFERENCE: Linda Crocker Simmons et al., *American Drawings, Watercolors, Pastels, and Collages in the Collection of the Corcoran Gallery of Art*, (Washington D.C.: The Gallery, 1983), cat. no. 217, p. 31, suggests it is a study for *Shad Fishing on the Hudson* of 1846 (cat. no. 26).

D11*
Dragoon with His Charger

Graphite and charcoal on cream paper

4 7/8 x 6 1/2 inches (12.4 x 16.5 cm)

Initialed, lower right: R

Corcoran Gallery of Art, Washington, D.C. Gift of Claude J. Ranney, grandson of the artist, 60.49.2

Grubar no. 124

EXHIBITED: Chadds Ford 1991, no. 34.

REFERENCE: Linda Crocker Simmons, et al., *American Drawings, Watercolors, Pastels, and Collages in the Collection of the Corcoran Gallery of Art*, (Washington D.C.: The Gallery, 1983), cat. no. 216, p. 30.

The poses of the horse and its rider relate to those of the *Portrait of Ambrose Clark* of c. 1850 (cat. no. 63). The pose of the horse relates in reverse to the white horse in the foreground of *Marion and His Men* of 1854 (cat. no. 94).

D12
Tooth Extraction

Black wash over graphite on cream paper

8 3/4 x 5 3/8 (22.2 x 13.7 cm)

Inscribed, lower right, in another hand: WTR; and on the back, lower center: Three Boys Wrestling

Corcoran Gallery of Art, Washington D.C. Gift of Claude J. Ranney, grandson of the artist. 60.49.1

Grubar no. 125

PROVENANCE: Claude J. Ranney, Malvern, Pennsylvania, to 1960.

EXHIBITED: Chadds Ford 1991, no. 42.

REFERENCE: Linda Crocker Simmons, et al., *American Drawings, Watercolors, Pastels, and Collages in the Collection of the Corcoran Gallery of Art*, (Washington D.C.: The Gallery, 1983), cat. no. 218, p. 31.

D13
Recto: Pioneer Caravan

Graphite on paper

5 3/8 x 8 3/4 (13.7 x 22.2 cm)

Inscribed, lower right: WTR

Grubar no. 126

D14
Verso: Figure of a Man Sitting (Beggar)

Graphite on paper

Inscribed, lower center: 50 Clinton Place

Private collection

Grubar no. 127

PROVENANCE: Claude J. Ranney, Malvern, Pennsylvania, by 1962.

Presumably, based on the inscription, this drawing was done on the spot at 50 Clinton Place in New York.

D15*
Study for "First News of the Battle of Lexington"

Graphite on paper

7 x 9 inches (17.8 x 22.9 cm)

Inscribed, lower right: WTR

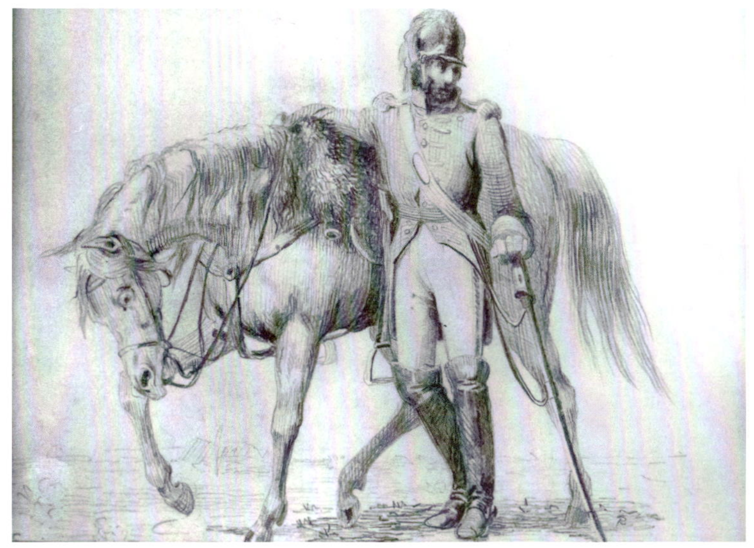

D11

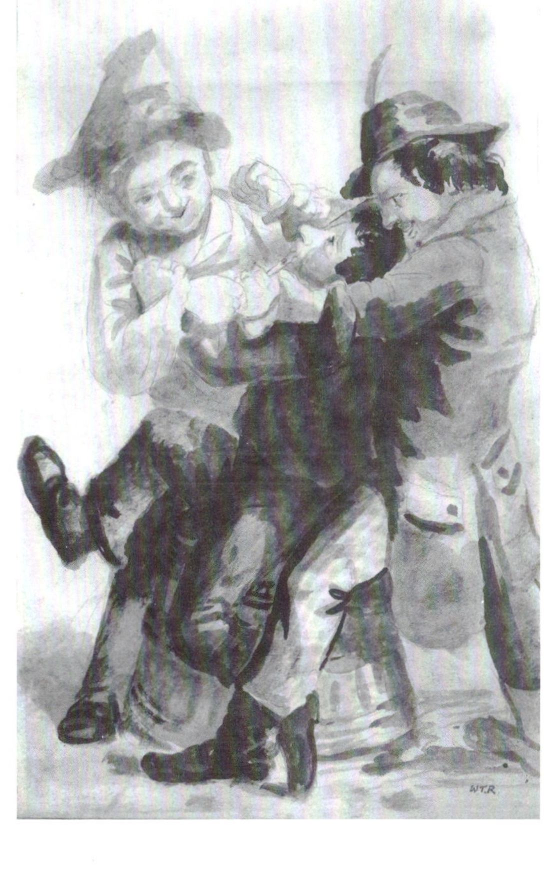

D12

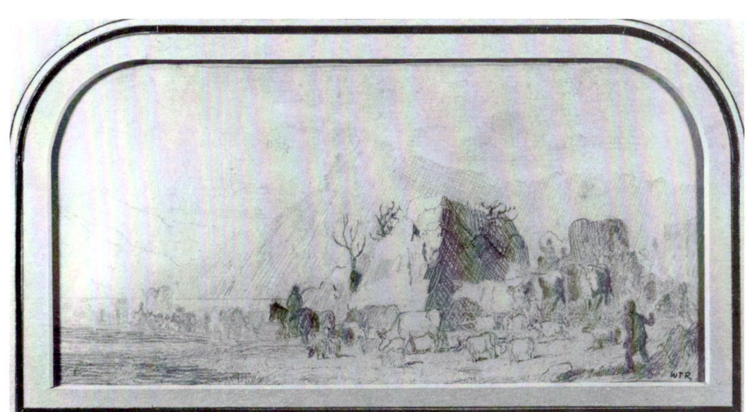

D13

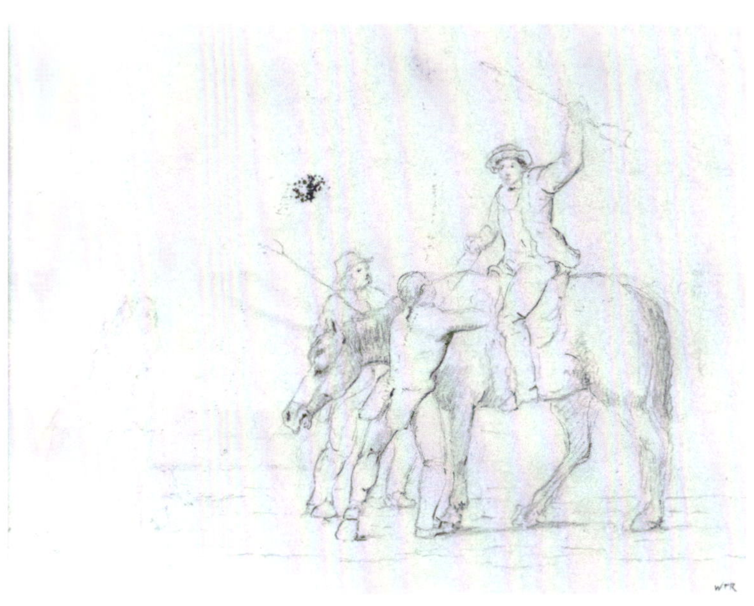

D15

D14

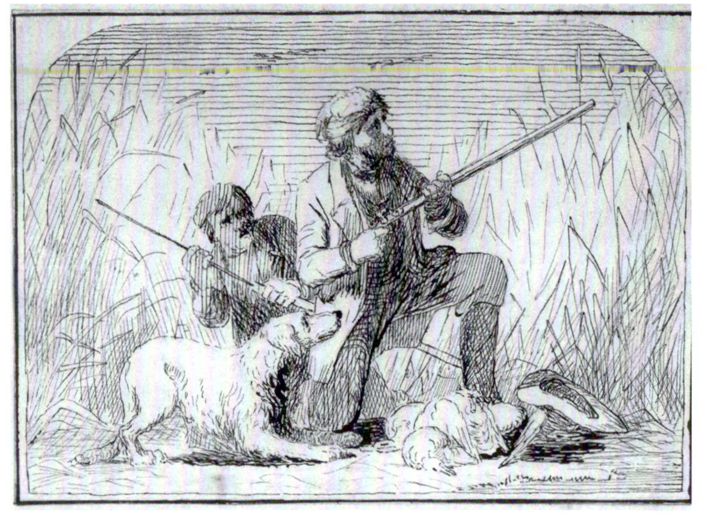

D16

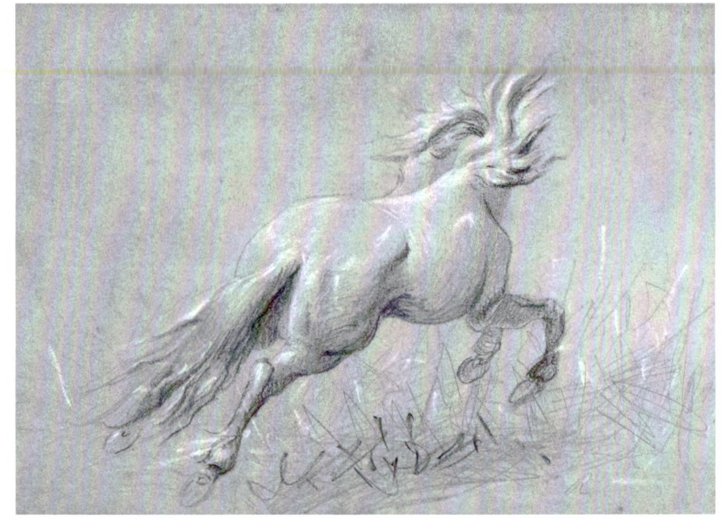

D17

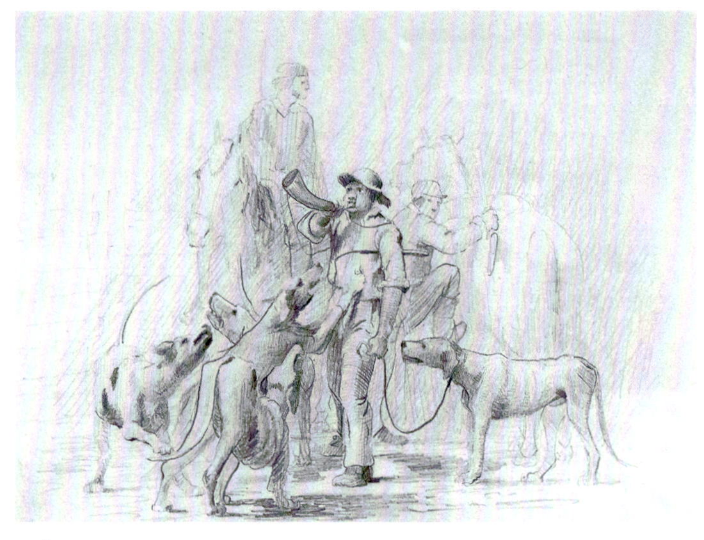

D18

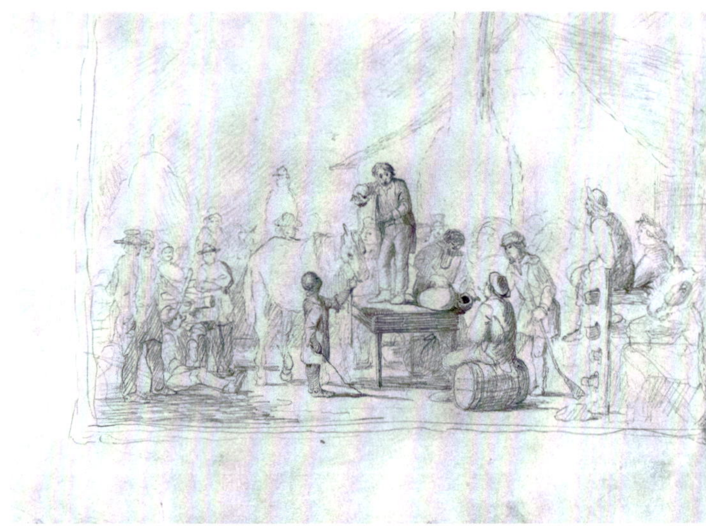

D19

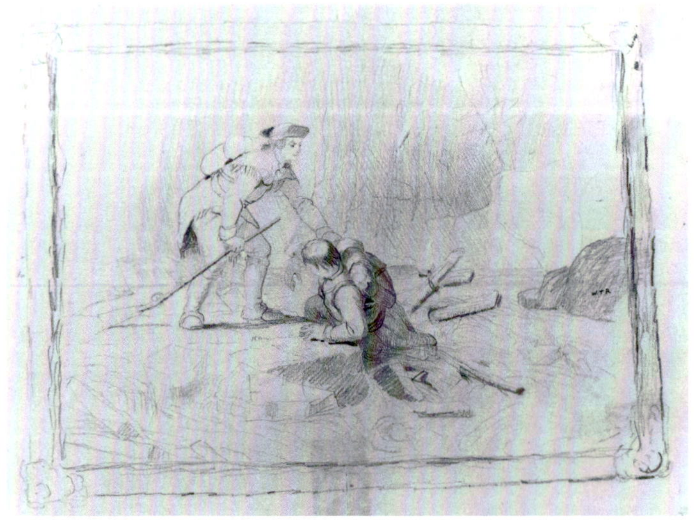

D21

Private collection

Grubar no. 128

PROVENANCE: Claude J. Ranney, Malvern, Pennsylvania, by 1962.

This study relates to *First News of the Battle of Lexington* of 1847 (cat. no. 31).

D16
Study for "On the Wing"

Graphite and ink on paper

4 x 5 7/8 (10.2 x 14.9 cm)

Private collection

Grubar no. 129

PROVENANCE: Claude J. Ranney, Malvern, Pennsylvania, by 1962.

EXHIBITED: Chadds Ford 1991, no. 39.

This study relates to *On the Wing* of 1850 (cat. no. 55).

D17*
Study for "Hunting Wild Horses"

Graphite and black crayon, heightened with white on paper

5 1/4 x 7 3/4 inches (13.3 x 19.7 cm)

Buffalo Bill Historical Center, Cody, Wyoming. Gift of Mrs. J. Maxwell Moran. 22.99.2

Grubar no. 130

PROVENANCE: Claude J. Ranney, Malvern, Pennsylvania, by 1962.

This study relates to *Hunting Wild Horses* of 1846 (cat. no. 19).

D18
Calling the Hounds

Graphite on paper

5 3/4 x 7 3/8 inches (14.6 x 18.7 cm)

Private collection

Grubar no. 131

PROVENANCE: Claude J. Ranney, Malvern, Pennsylvania, by 1962.

EXHIBITED: Chadds Ford 1991, no. 32.

D19
Recto: Frontier Horse Auction

Graphite on paper

8 3/4 x 7 3/8 inches (18.8 x cm 14.6)

Grubar no. 132

D20
Verso: Slight Sketch of "Gist Rescuing Washington from the Allegheny River"

Graphite on paper

This drawing relates to cat. no. 98, Washington and Gist Crossing the Allegheny River of 1854.

Grubar no. 133

Brandywine River Museum, Chadds Ford, Pennsylvania. Museum Volunteers Fund, 1991.

PROVENANCE: Claude J. Ranney, Malvern, Pennsylvania, by 1962; (Hirschl and Adler Galleries, New York, by 1978–1984); E. Mauric Bloch, to 1991 (sale, Christie's, New York, January 9, 1991, lot no. 178).

EXHIBITED: Chadds Ford 1991, no. 35.

D21
Gist Rescuing Washington from the Allegheny River

Graphite on wove paper

8 1/4 x 10 1/4 inches (21 x 26 cm)

Inscribed verso, upper center: Christopher Gist Rescuing Washington from the Allegheny River; lower right: Frontiersman helping another/from the river.

Private collection

Grubar no. 134

PROVENANCE: Claude J. Ranney, by 1962; (Kennedy Galleries, New York, by 1968); (sale, Robert C. Eldred Company, East Dennis, Massachusetts, July 20, 1995, no. 98).

Exhibited: Kennedy Galleries, New York, *American Drawings, Pastel and Watercolors, Part Two: The Nineteenth Century: 1825–1890*, April 16–May 6, 1968.

This drawing relates to *Washington and Gist Crossing the Allegheny River* (see cat. no. 98). Ranney also included in it a sketch for the frame.

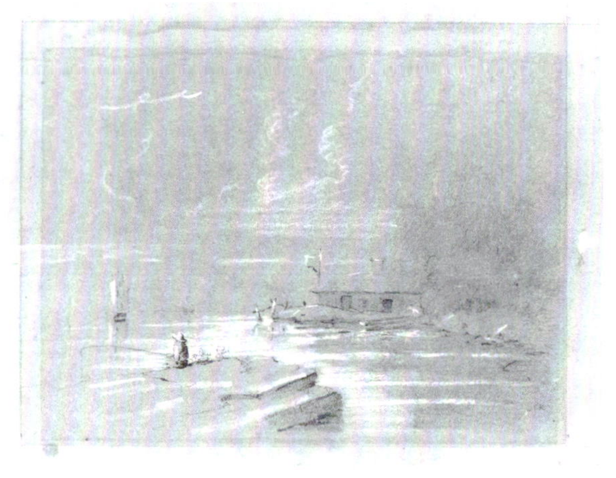

D22

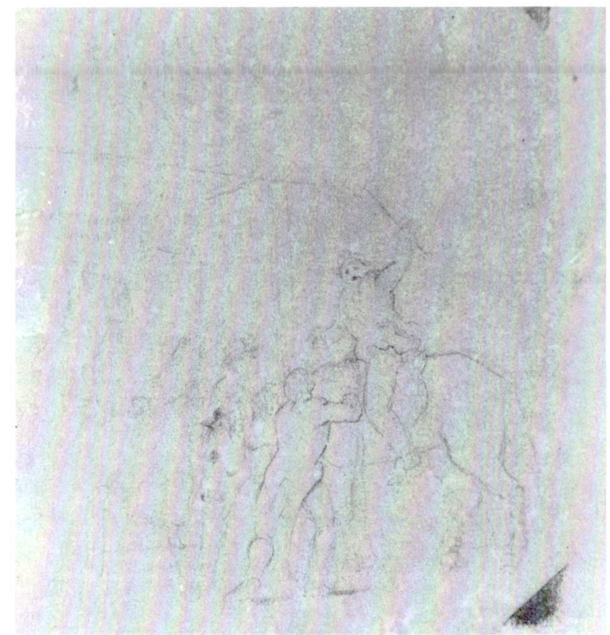

D23

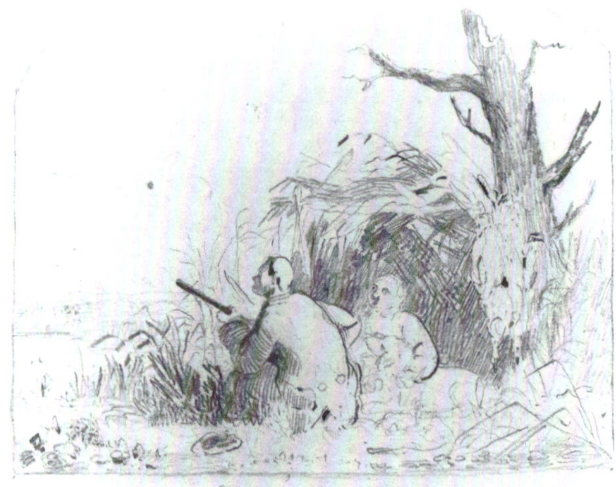

D24

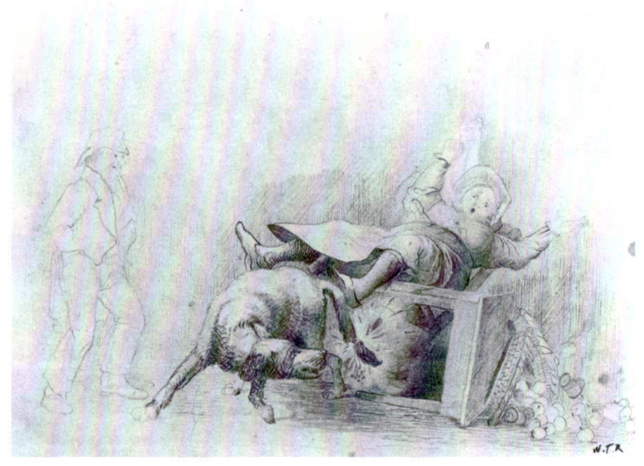

D25

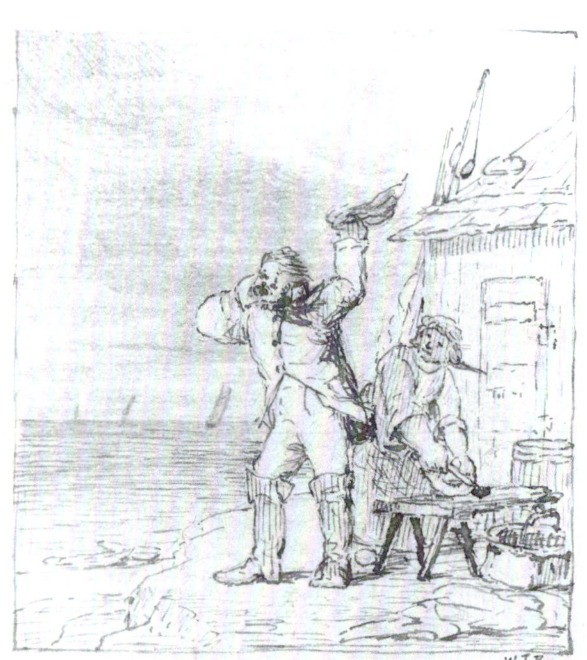

D26

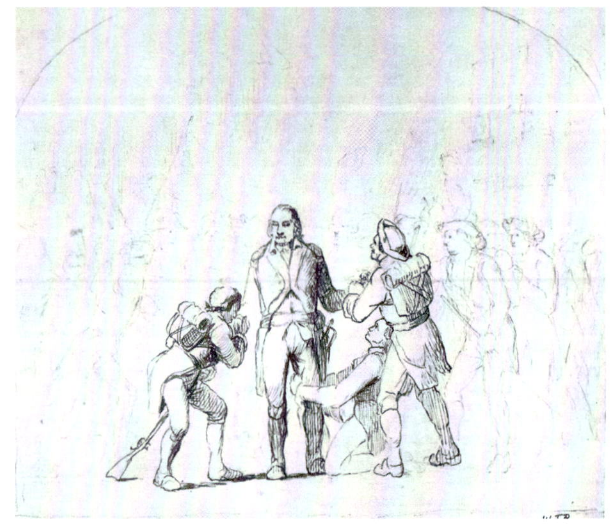

D27

192

D22*

Recto: River Scene with Boy Fishing

Graphite pencil and chalk on brown wove paper

7 x 10 inches (17.8 x 25.4 cm)

Grubar no. 135

D23

Verso: Sketch for "First News of the Battle of Lexington."

Graphite on wove paper

Grubar no. 136

Private collection

PROVENANCE: Claude J. Ranney, Malvern, Pennsylvania, by 1962.

This drawing relates to *The First News of the Battle of Lexington* of 1847 (cat. no. 31).

D24

Duck Shooters

Graphite on paper

7 1/2 x 10 3/4 inches (19.1 x 27.3 cm)

Mr. and Mrs. Francis H. Abbott Jr.

Grubar no. 137

PROVENANCE: Claude J. Ranney, Malvern, Pennsylvania, by 1962.

This drawing relates to the *Duck Shooter's Pony* of 1853 (cat. no. 82).

D25*

The Prankster

Graphite on paper

6 7/8 x 7 3/4 inches (17.5 x 19.7 cm)

Inscribed, lower right (probably by another hand): W. T. R.; inscribed verso: Lady upset by dog

Judith Filenbaum Hernstadt

Grubar no. 138

PROVENANCE: Claude J. Ranney, Malvern, Pennsylvania, by 1962; (Hirschl and Adler Galleries, New York, to 1976).

D26

Coast Scene with Two Figures

Graphite and ink on wove paper

5 3/4 x 5 1/2 inches (12.7 x 14 cm)

Inscribed, lower right (probably by another hand): W. T. R.

Private collection

Grubar no. 139

PROVENANCE: Claude J. Ranney, Malvern,

Pennsylvania, by 1962; (sale, Robert C. Eldred Company, East Dennis, Massachusetts, July 20, 1995, no. 174).

D27

Washington with Soldiers

Pen and ink and graphite on paper

6 1/8 x 7 1/2 inches (15.6 x 19.1 cm)

Inscribed, lower right (probably by another hand): W.T.R.

Location unknown

Grubar no. 140

PROVENANCE: Claude J. Ranney, Malvern, Pennsylvania, by 1962; (Hirschl and Adler Galleries, New York, by 1976).

EXHIBITED: Hirschl and Adler Galleries, New York, 1976, *100 American Drawings and Watercolors*, no. 75; Hirschl and Adler Galleries, New York, 1978, *American Genre Painting in the Victorian Era*, no. 67.

D28*

Three Boats on the Beach

Graphite and chalk on paper

7 x 10 inches (17.8 x 25.4 cm)

Private collection

Grubar no. 141

PROVENANCE: Claude J. Ranney, Malvern, Pennsylvania, by 1962.

EXHIBITED: Chadds Ford 1991, no. 40.

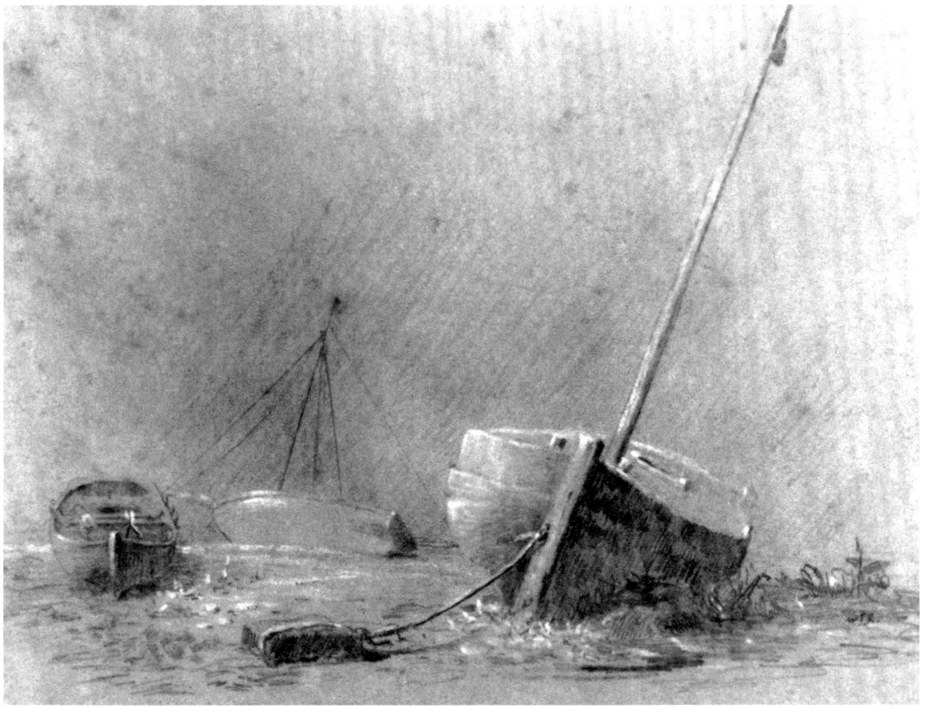

D28

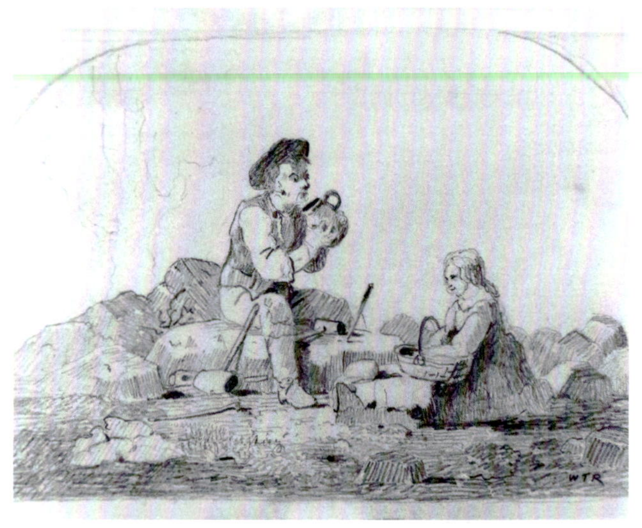

D29

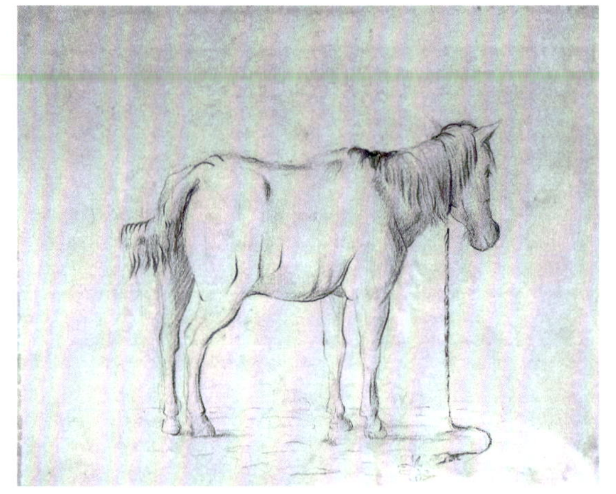

D32

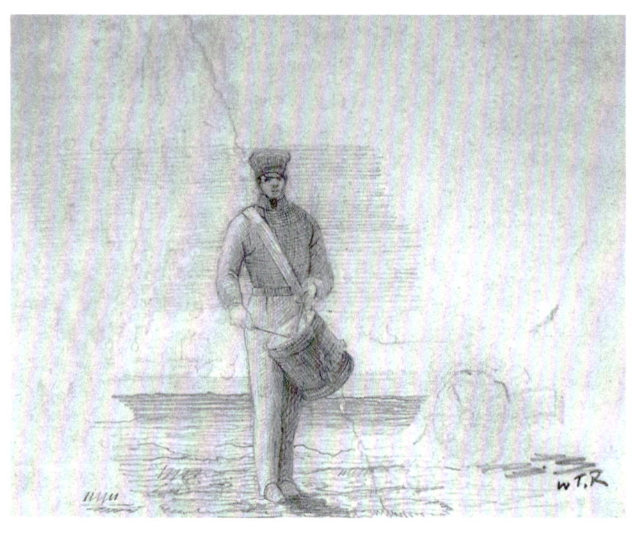

D30

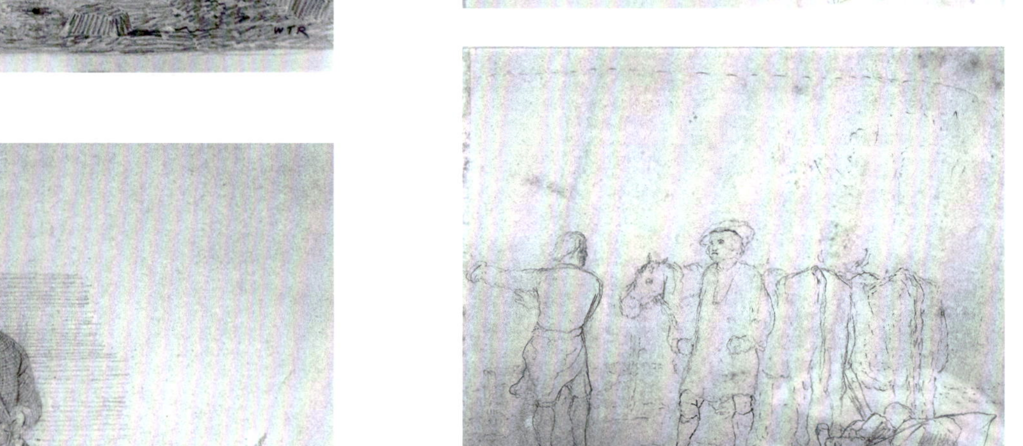

D33

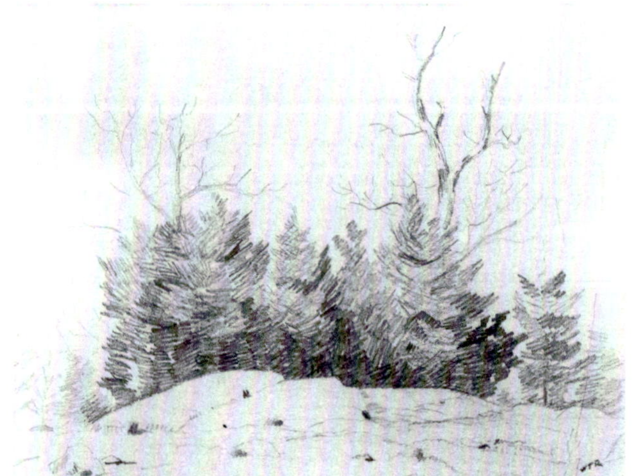

D31

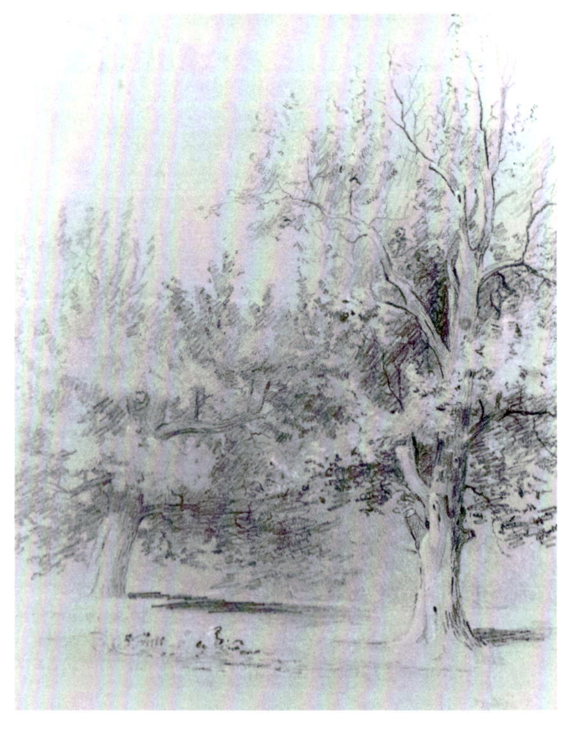

D34

D29

Lunch on the Rocks

Graphite on paper

4 3/4 x 6 3/4 inches (12.1 x 17.1 cm)

Inscribed, lower right (probably by another hand): WTR

Private collection

Grubar no. 142

PROVENANCE: Claude J. Ranney, Malvern, Pennsylvania, by 1962; private collection, New York;

(Hirschl and Adler Galleries, New York, to 1997).

D30

Mexican War Drummer

Graphite on paper

3 x 4 1/2 inches (7.6 x 11.4 cm)

Inscribed, lower right (probably by another hand): W.T.R.

Private collection

Grubar no. 143

PROVENANCE: Claude J. Ranney, Malvern, Pennsylvania, by 1962.

D31

Sketches of Pines

Graphite on paper

5 1/4 x 6 5/8 inches (13.3 x 16.8 cm)

Inscribed, lower right (probably by another hand): W.T.R.

Private collection

Grubar no. 144

PROVENANCE: Claude J. Ranney, Malvern, Pennsylvania, by 1962; private collection, New York, 1976–1997; (Hirschl and Adler Galleries, New York, to 1997).

D32

Recto: Study of a Horse

Brown crayon on paper

8 x 10 inches (20.3 x 25.4 cm)

Grubar no. 145

D33

Verso: Study for a Farmer with Stone Sled and Man Gesturing

Graphite on paper

Private collection

Grubar no. 146

PROVENANCE: Claude J. Ranney, Malvern, Pennsylvania, by 1962.

D34

Study of Two Oak Trees

Graphite, charcoal and chalk on brown wove paper

8 1/4 x 6 3/4 inches (21 x 17.1 cm)

Private collection

Grubar no. 147

PROVENANCE: Claude J. Ranney, Malvern, Pennsylvania, by 1962. (sale, Robert C. Eldred Company, East Dennis, Massachusetts, November 17 and 18, 1995, no. 319).

D35*

Study for "The Retreat"

Graphite and ink on paper

6 1/2 x 9 1/2 inches (16.5 x 24.1 cm)

Private collection

Grubar no. 148

PROVENANCE: Claude J. Ranney, Malvern, Pennsylvania, by 1962.

This drawing relates to *The Retreat* of 1850 (cat no. 60).

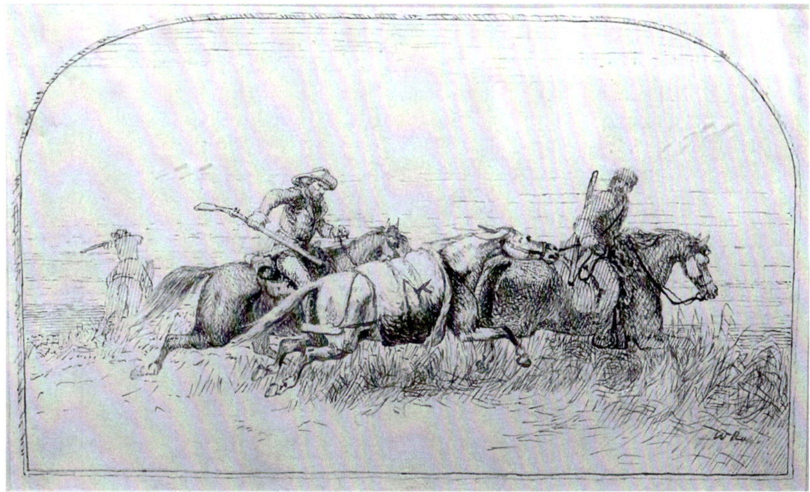

D35

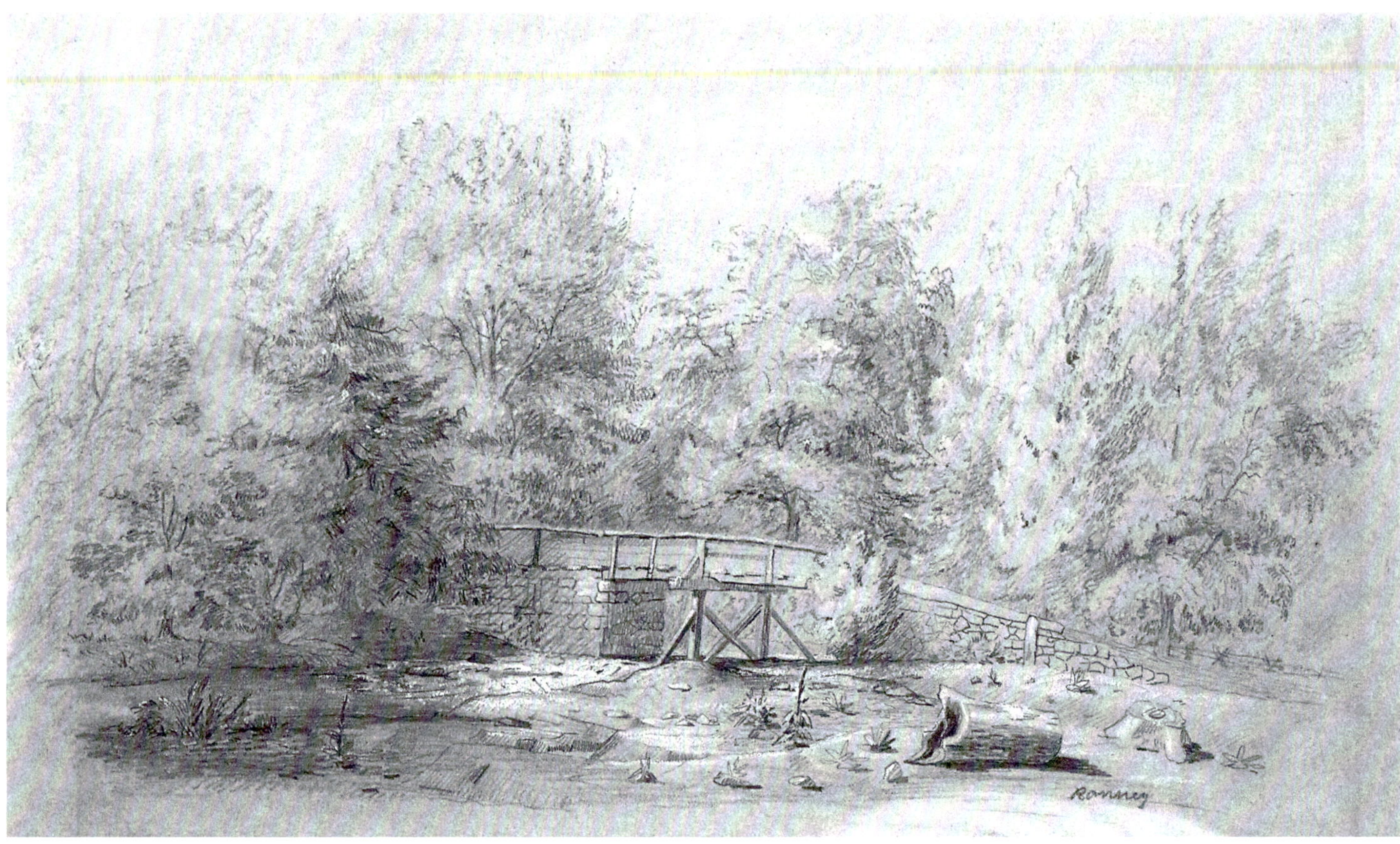

D36

D36
Country Bridge near Middletown, Connecticut

Graphite and chalk on paper

9 1/2 x 14 3/4 inches (24.1 x 37.5 cm)

Signed, lower right: Ranney. Inscribed to the back: [Country Bridge Near Middletown, Conn.]

Private collection

Grubar no. 149

PROVENANCE: Claude J. Ranney, Malvern, Pennsylvania, by 1962.

EXHIBITED: Chadds Ford 1991, no. 33.

This drawing may relate to *Country Bridge near Middletown Connecticut* of 1835–1840 (cat. no. 6).

D37
Recto: Landscape with Trees and Rocks

Graphite on paper

8 3/4 x 12 1/2 inches (22.2 x 31.8 cm)

Grubar no. 150

D38
Verso: Slight Landscape Sketch

Graphite on paper

Grubar no. 151

Location unknown

PROVENANCE: Claude J. Ranney, Malvern, Pennsylvania, by 1962; (Hirschl and Adler Galleries, New York, by 1994); unknown private collection, 1994.

D39
Weeping Willow

Graphite on wove paper

9 x 14 inches (22.9 x 35.6 cm)

Embossed paper maker's mark, lower right: Bristol paper

Private collection

Grubar no. 152

PROVENANCE: Claude J. Ranney, Malvern, Pennsylvania, by 1962; (sale, Robert C. Eldred Company, November 17 and 18, 1995, no. 321)

D40
Recto: A Bone of Contention

Graphite on paper

5 3/8 x 8 3/4 inches (14.3 x 22.2 cm)

Grubar no. 153

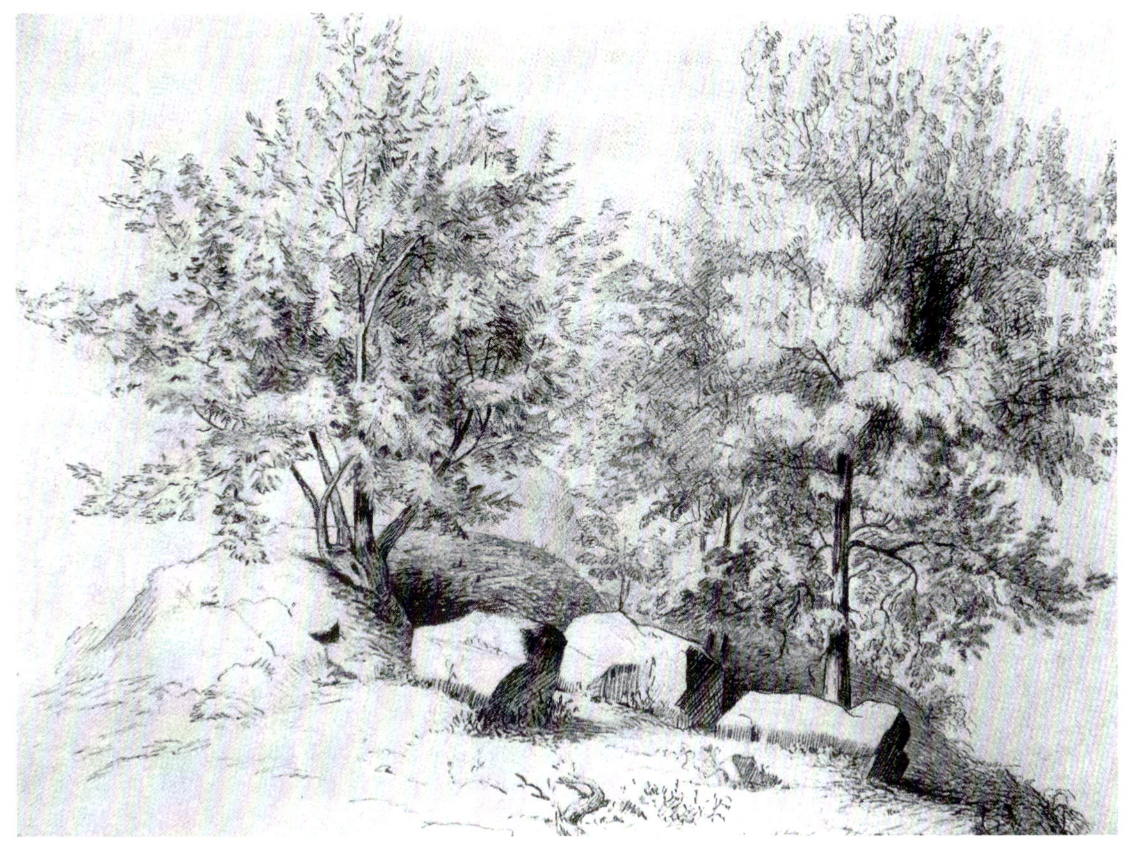

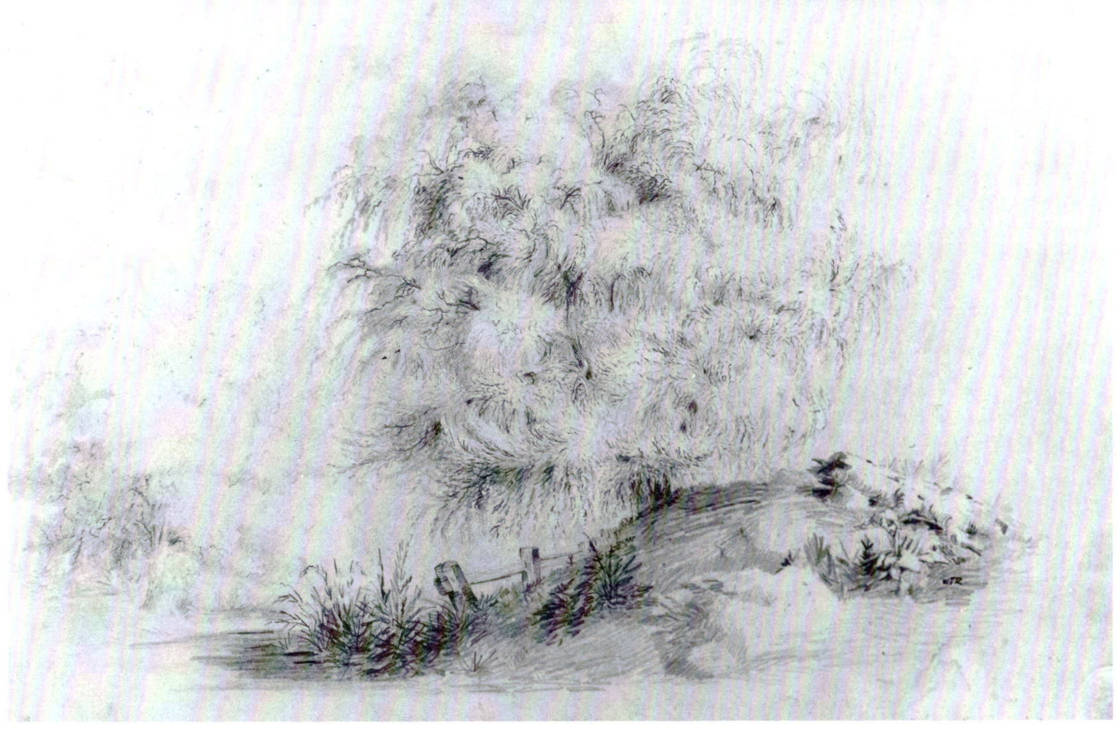

197

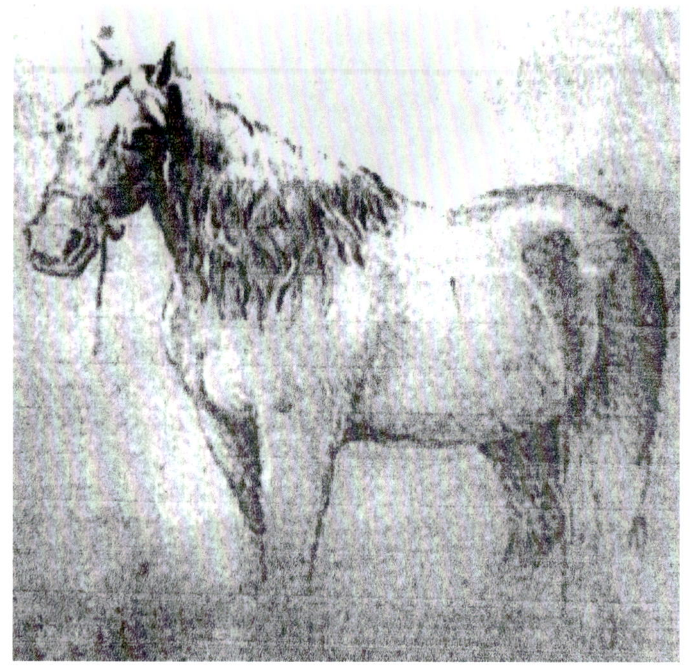

D44

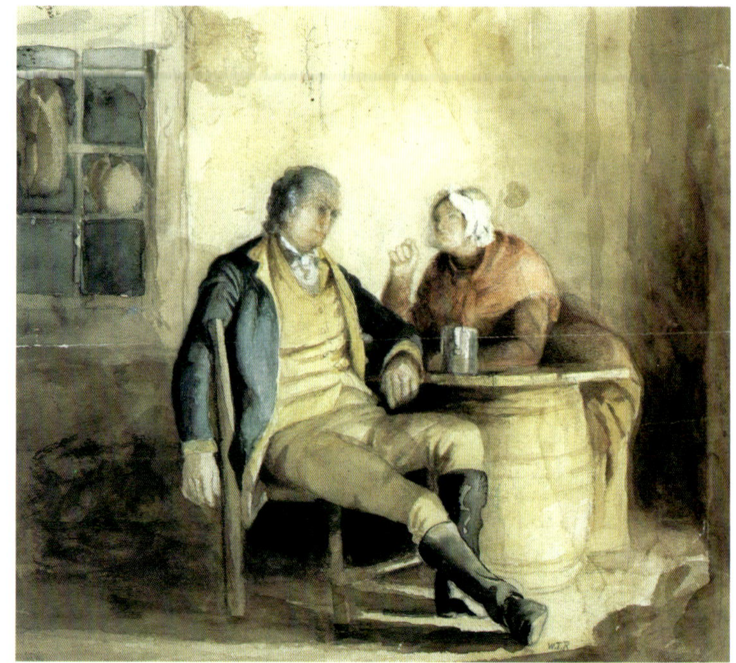

D45

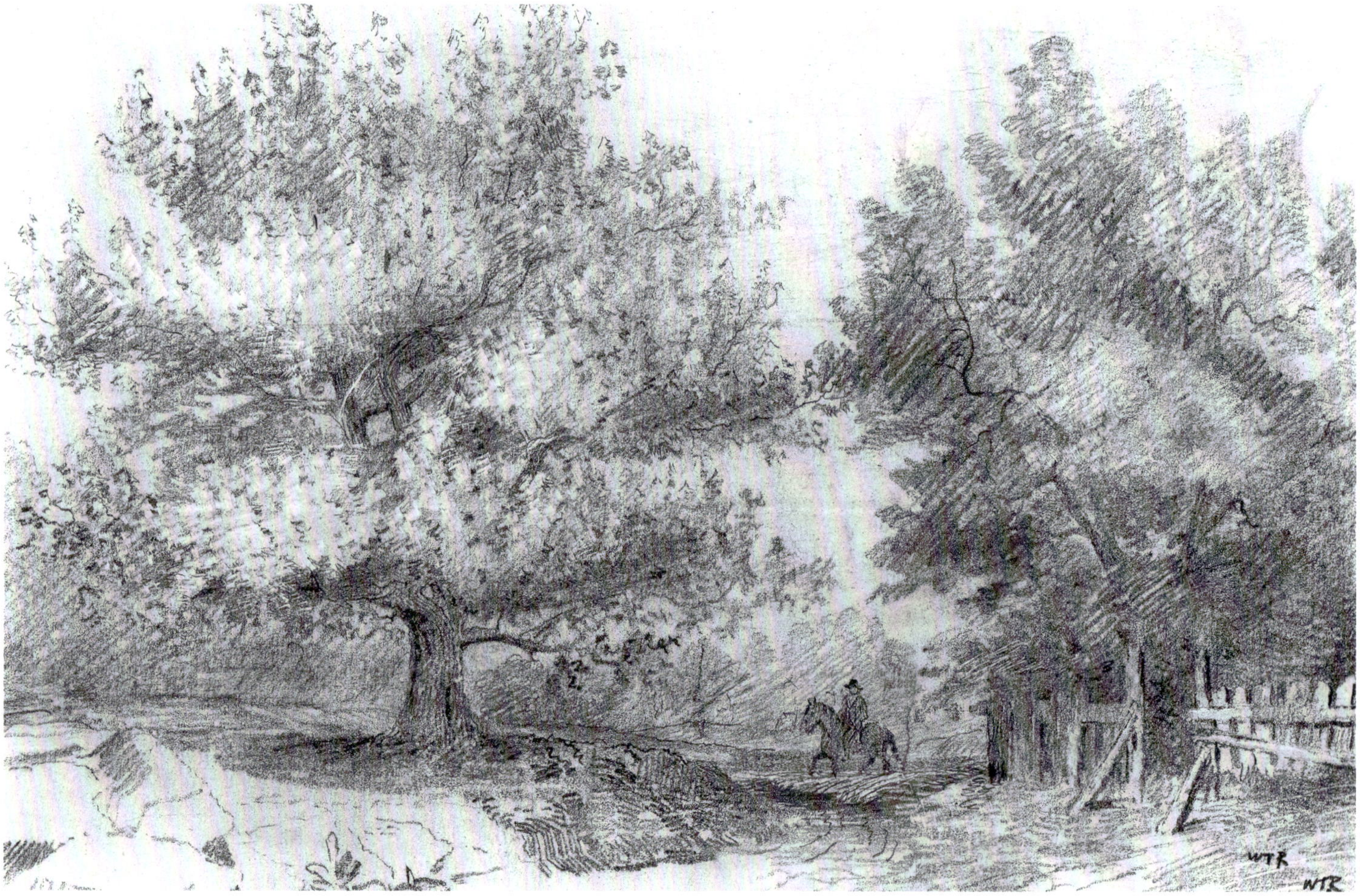

D49

D41
Verso: Sketch of a Young Woman

Graphite pencil on paper

Location unknown

Grubar no. 154

PROVENANCE: Claude J. Ranney, Malvern, Pennsylvania, by 1962.

D42
Recto: Study for "Advice on the Prairie"

Graphite on paper

5 3/8 x 8 3/4 inches (13.7 x 22.2 cm)

Grubar no. 155

This drawing probably relates to *Advice on the Prairie* of c. 1853 (cat. no. 81).

D43
Verso: Hauling the Net

Graphite on paper

Location unknown

Grubar no. 156

PROVENANCE: Claude J. Ranney, Malvern, Pennsylvania, by 1962.

D44
Study of a Horse

Graphite and white chalk

7 x 10 inches (17.8 x 25.4 cm)

Location unknown

Grubar no. 157

PROVENANCE: Claude J. Ranney, Malvern, Pennsylvania, by 1962.

D45
George Washington Conversing with a Woman

Watercolor on paper

9 1/2 x 9 3/4 inches (24.1 x 24.8 cm)

Private collection

Grubar no. 158

PROVENANCE: Claude J. Ranney, Malvern, Pennsylvania, by 1962.

EXHIBITED: Chadds Ford 1991, no. 36

REFERENCE: Thistlethwaite 1991, pp. 59–60, illus. and questions the identity of the subject.

D46
Girl with Bird

Graphite on paper

6 x 5 inches (15.2 x 12.7 cm)

Location unknown

Grubar no. 159

PROVENANCE: Claude J. Ranney, Malvern, Pennsylvania, by 1962.

D47
The Amateurs, and a Taste for Pork

Graphite on paper

8 3/4 x 5 3/8 (22.2 x 13.7 cm)

Location unknown

Grubar no. 160

PROVENANCE: Claude J. Ranney, Malvern, Pennsylvania, by 1962.

D48
Dog Sleeping

Graphite on paper

3 1/2 x 5 1/4 inches (8.9 x 13.3 cm)

Location unknown

Grubar no. 161

PROVENANCE: Claude J. Ranney, Malvern, Pennsylvania, by 1962.

D49
Landscape with Horseman

Graphite on paper

7 1/4 x 10 1/4 inches (18.4 x 26 cm)

Inscribed twice, lower right (probably by another hand): WTR

Location unknown

Grubar no. 162

PROVENANCE: Claude J. Ranney, Malvern, Pennsylvania, by 1962; (Hirschl and Adler Galleries, New York, by 1978); private collection; (Lockwood's Midwestern Galleries, Cincinnati, Ohio, c. 1995).

D50

Head of a Man

Graphite on paper

8 5/8 x 7 inches (21.9 x 17.8 cm)

Location unknown

Grubar no. 163

Provenance: Claude J. Ranney, Malvern, Pennsylvania, by 1962.

D51

Tree

Graphite on paper

7 1/2 x 6 3/4 inches (19.1 x 17.1 cm)

Location unknown

Grubar no. 164

Provenance: Claude J. Ranney, Malvern, Pennsylvania, by 1962.

D52

Weekly Reveille

Graphite on paper

3 x 11 1/8 inches (7.6 x 28.3 cm)

Inscribed, lower right (probably by another hand): WTR

Embossed paper maker's mark, upper right: Bristol paper

Private collection

Grubar no. 165

Provenance: Claude J. Ranney, Malvern, Pennsylvania, by 1962; Olga J. Ledon, Orizba, Mexico; (Hirschl and Adler Galleries, New York, 1975–1977), John Wilmerding, 1978; private collection; (Hirschl and Adler Galleries, by 1997).

Grubar notes that the lettering is probably a design for the masthead of a periodical. There were several newspapers with this title in the nineteenth century.

D53

Franklin in Philadelphia

Graphite on paper

8 3/8 x 6 3/4 inches (21.3 x 17.1 cm)

Private collection

Grubar no. 166

Provenance: Claude J. Ranney, Malvern, Pennsylvania, by 1962.

Apparently based on the popular story of Franklin's arriving in Philadelphia in 1723 with only a Dutch dollar and a copper shilling in his pocket, Ranney represents the young man in colonial dress holding the loaves of bread he was said to have purchased at the time.

D54

Recto: Two Trees

Crayon on machine-made wove paper

10 1/2 x 8 inches (26.7 x 20.3 cm)

Grubar no. 167

D55

Verso: Sketches for Drawing with Stone Sled

Graphite on paper

Grubar no. 168

Private collection

Provenance: Claude J. Ranney, Malvern, Pennsylvania, by 1962; (sale, Robert C. Eldred Company, East Dennis, Massachusetts, November 17 and 18, 1995, no. 318).

The scene in the upper left vignette may relate to *Washington and Gist Crossing the Allegheny River* (cat. no. 98).

D56

Recto: Tree with Rail Fence

Graphite on paper

12 1/4 x 9 1/4 inches (31.1 x 23.5 cm)

Grubar no. 169

D57

Verso: Sketch of Cows Drinking from a Well Sweep

Location unknown

Grubar no. 170

Provenance: Claude J. Ranney, Malvern, Pennsylvania, by 1962.

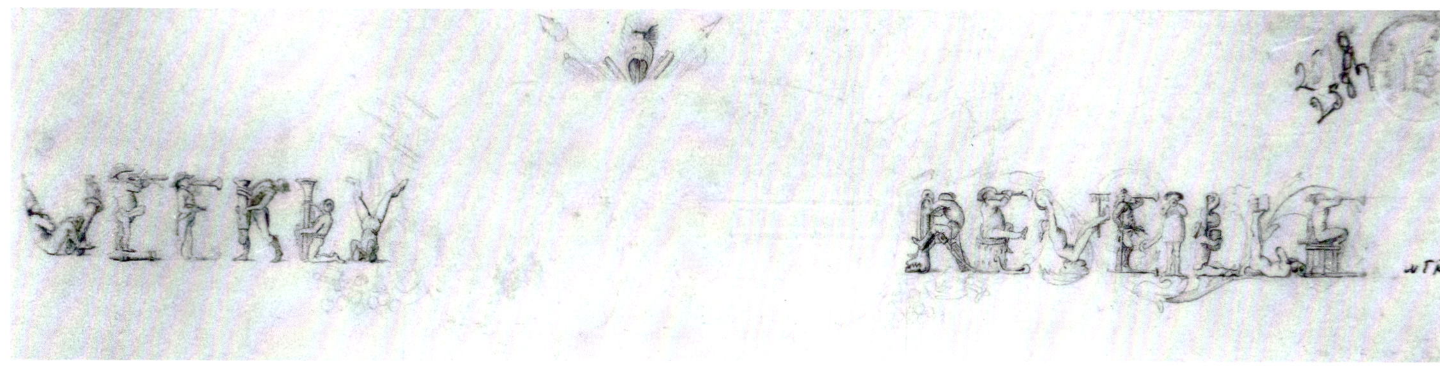

D52

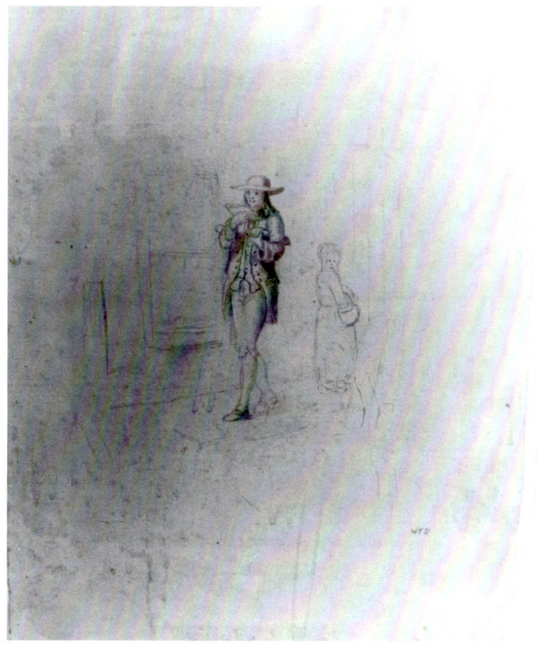

D53

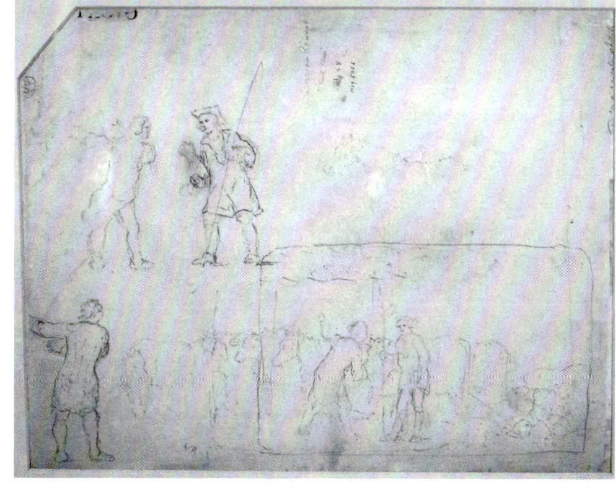

D55

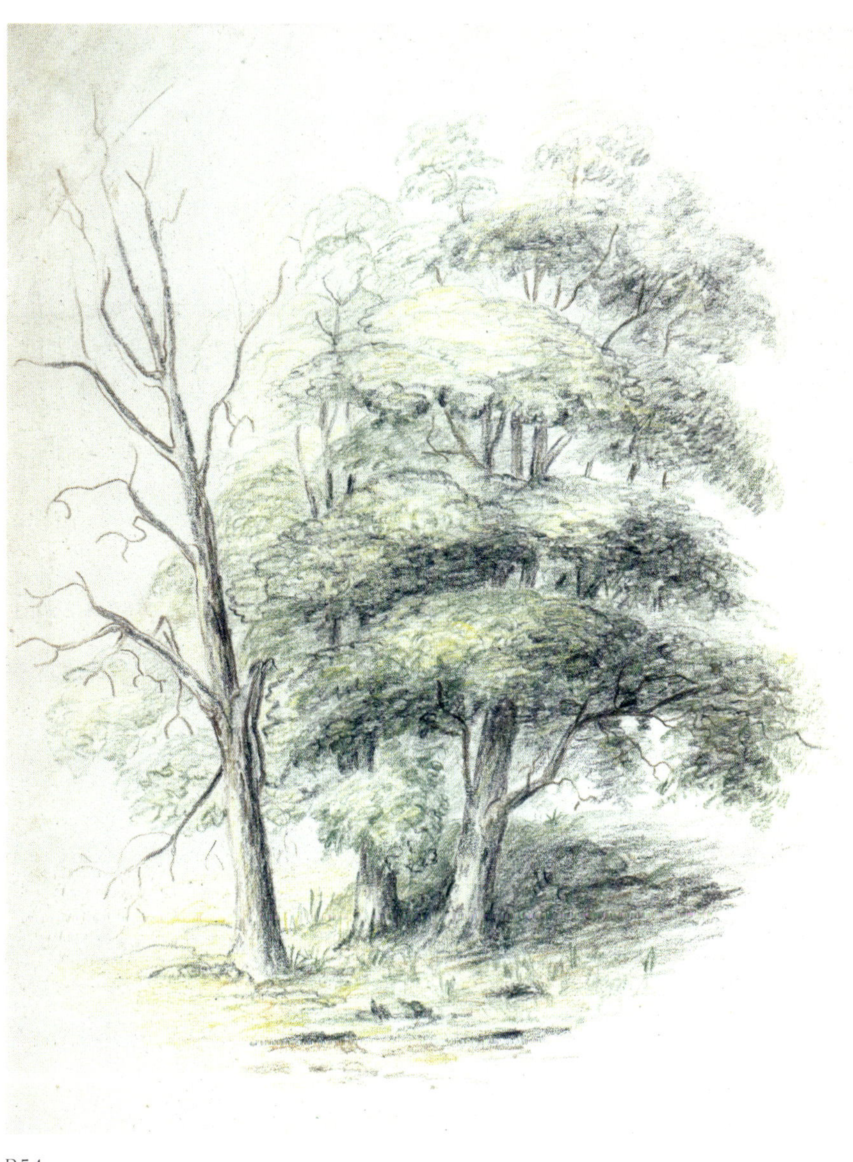

D54

201

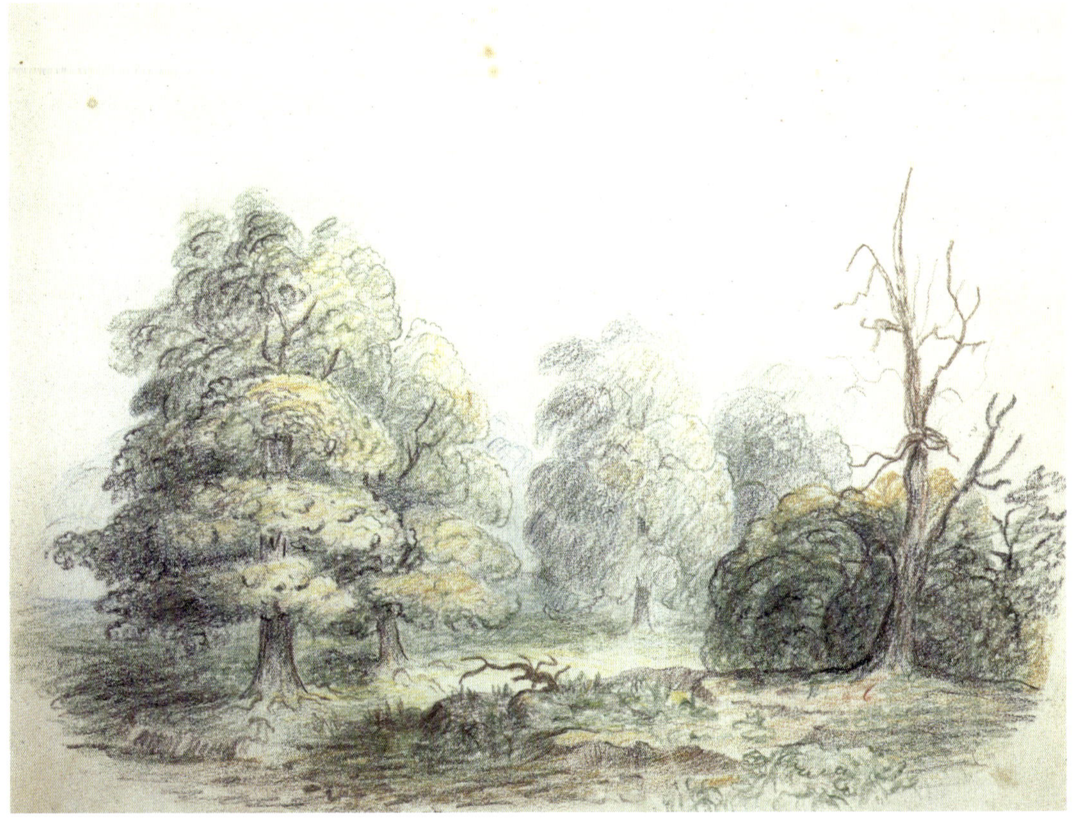

D58

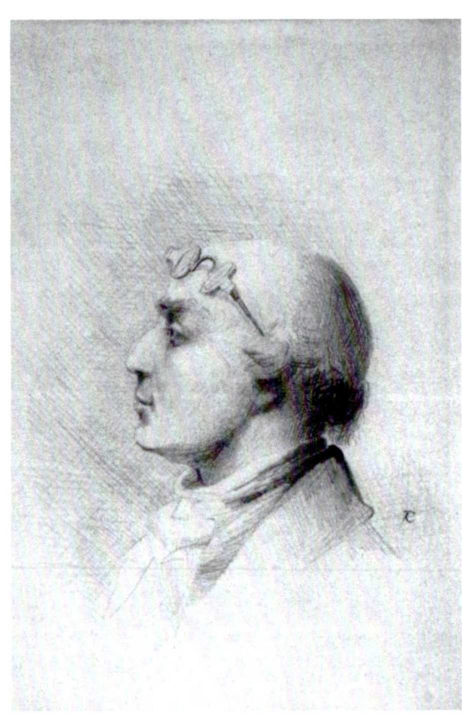

D63

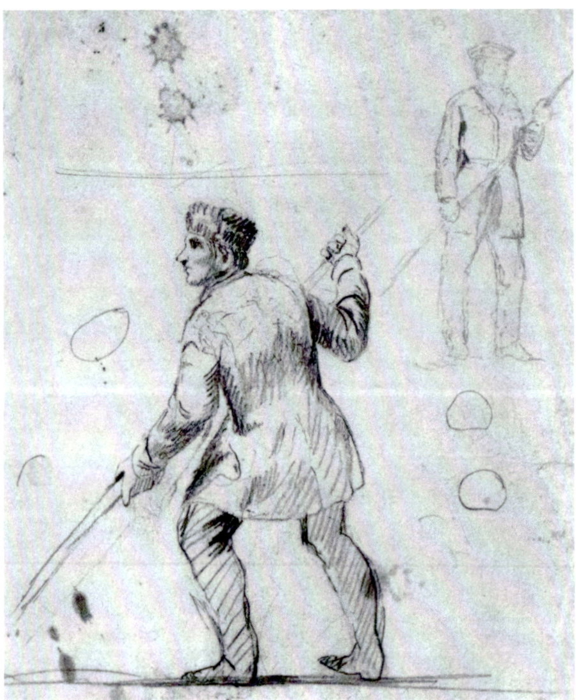

D65   Photograph from Grubar, 1962, no. 178.

202

D58*

Recto: Field with Trees

Crayon on machine-made wove paper

8 x 10 1/2 inches (20.3 x 26.7 cm)

Grubar no. 171

D59

Verso: Study for Farmer with Stone Sled

Graphite on wove paper

Private collection

Grubar no. 172

PROVENANCE: Claude J. Ranney, Malvern, Pennsylvania, by 1962; (Kennedy Galleries, New York, 1968); (sale, Robert C. Eldred Company, East Dennis, Massachusetts, November 17 and 18, 1995, no. 32, as Trees).

EXHIBITED: Kennedy Galleries, New York, *American Drawings, Pastels and Watercolors," Part Two: The Nineteenth Century: 1825–1890*, April 16–May 6, 1968, no. 15, as Study of Trees.

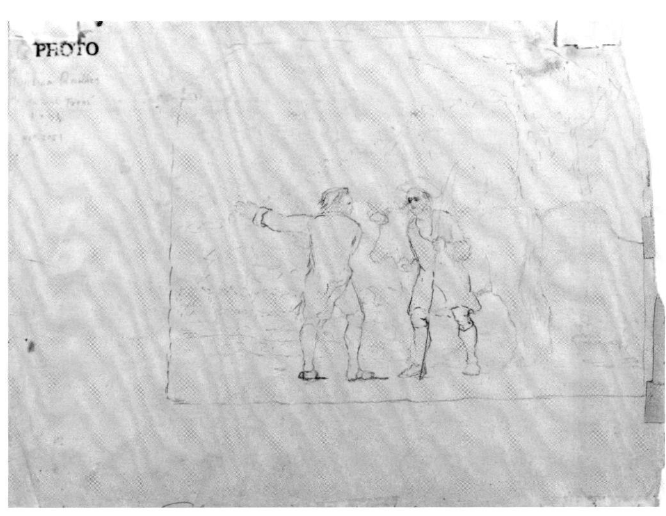

D59

D60

Recto: Study of Rocks

Black crayon heightened with white on paper

7 7/8 x 10 inches (20 x 25.4 cm)

Grubar no. 173

D61

Verso: Composition

Graphite on paper

Location unknown

Grubar no. 174

PROVENANCE: Claude J. Ranney, Malvern, Pennsylvania, by 1962.

D62

Landscape with Stream

Graphite heightened with white on paper

7 x 10 1/8 inches (17.8 x 25.7 cm)

Location unknown

Grubar no. 175

PROVENANCE: Claude J. Ranney, Malvern, Pennsylvania, by 1962.

D63

Head of a Man with Glasses on Forehead

Graphite on paper

6 3/8 x 3 1/4 inches (16.2 x 8.3 cm)

Private collection

Grubar no. 176

PROVENANCE: Claude J. Ranney, Malvern, Pennsylvania, by 1962.

D 64

Study of a Bare Tree

Graphite on paper

13 x 10 3/4 inches (33 x 27.3 cm)

Location unknown

Grubar no. 177

PROVENANCE: Claude J. Ranney, Malvern, Pennsylvania, by 1962.

D65

Two Sketches of a Man Poling

Graphite on paper

10 3/4 x 7 1/2 inches (27.3 x 19.1 cm)

Location unknown

Grubar no. 178

PROVENANCE: Claude J. Ranney, Malvern, Pennsylvania, by 1962; (sale, Christie's East, New York, *American Paintings, Drawings, Watercolors and Scupture*, November 14, 1991, no. 38).

This may be a study for *Washington and Gist Crossing the Allegheny River* of 1854 (cat. no. 98).

D66

Study of an Old Tree

Graphite on paper

7 x 11 inches (17.8 x 27.9 cm)

Location unknown

Grubar no. 179

PROVENANCE: Claude J. Ranney, Malvern, Pennsylvania, by 1962.

D67

Men with Guns

Graphite on paper

Location unknown

Grubar no. 180

PROVENANCE: Claude J. Ranney, Malvern, Pennsylvania, by 1962.

D68

Man with Pitchfork

Graphite on paper

Location unknown

Grubar no. 181

PROVENANCE: Claude J. Ranney, Malvern, Pennsylvania, by 1962.

D69

Sketch of a Woman and Boy

Graphite on paper

Location unknown

Grubar no. 182

PROVENANCE: Claude J. Ranney, Malvern, Pennsylvania, by 1962.

D70

Sketch of a Sluice Gate

Graphite on paper

Location unknown

Grubar no. 183

PROVENANCE: Claude J. Ranney, Malvern, Pennsylvania, by 1962.

D71

The Artist's Wife Reading in Bed

Watercolor with white heightening, graphite underdrawing on wove paper

6 3/4 x 6 inches (17.1 x 15.2 cm)

Private collection

Grubar no. 184

PROVENANCE: Margaret Ranney, Union City, New Jersey, d. 1965; her cousin, Claude J. Ranney, Malvern, Pennsylvania, by 1962.

D72

Recto: Cows in the Hackensack Meadow

Graphite and chalk on wove paper

3 1/2 x 7 1/4 inches (8.9 x 18.4 cm)

This scene relates, in reverse, to *Haying Time* of 1856 (cat. no. 133) and, based on the inscription on the back, possibly also *Evening on the Meadows* exhibited at the National Academy in 1855 (cat. no. 108).

D73

Verso: Sketch for "Duck Shooter's Pony"

Graphite and ink on wove paper

Signed, upper left: William Ranney. Inscribed, upper left: West hoboken, N.J.; lower left: Evening on the Meadows

Private collection

PROVENANCE: Descended in the Ranney family to the present owner.

This drawing relates to *Duck Shooter's Pony* of 1853 (cat. no. 82).

D74

Gathering Chestnuts on the Banks of the Hudson

Graphite on paper

9 x 10 1/4 inches (22.9 x 26 cm)

Inscribed lower left with title and center with date 1840

Private collection

PROVENANCE: Descended in the Ranney family to the present owner.

EXHIBITED: Chadds Ford 1991, no. 28.

D75

Horse's Head

Graphite on paper

8 3/4 x 7 1/4 inches (22.2 x 18.4 cm)

Inscribed, lower right: R

Location unknown

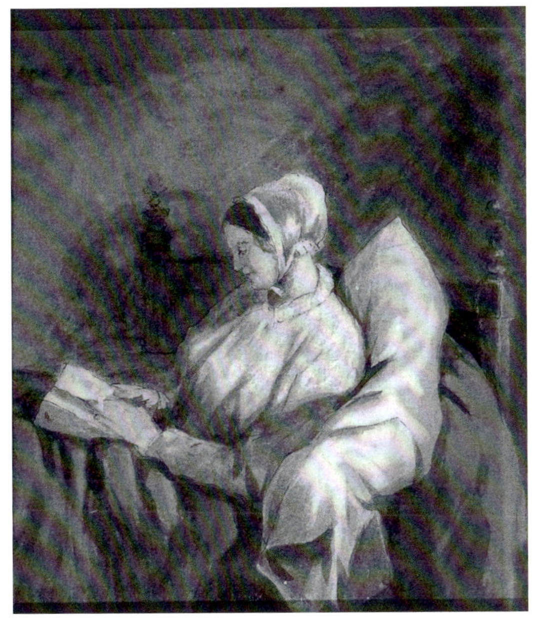

D71

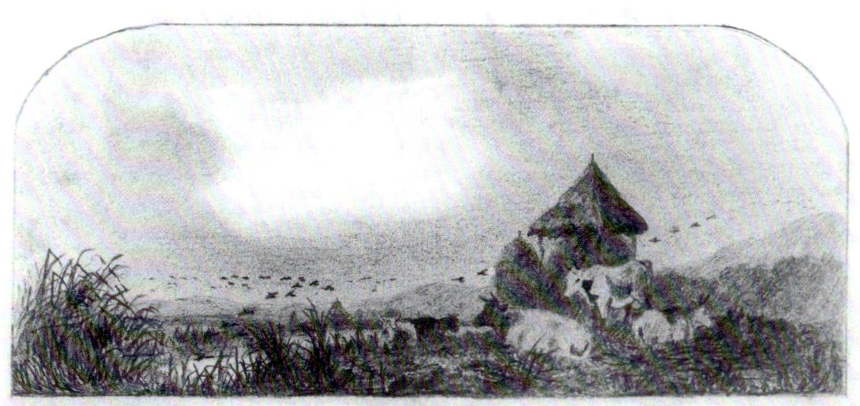

D72

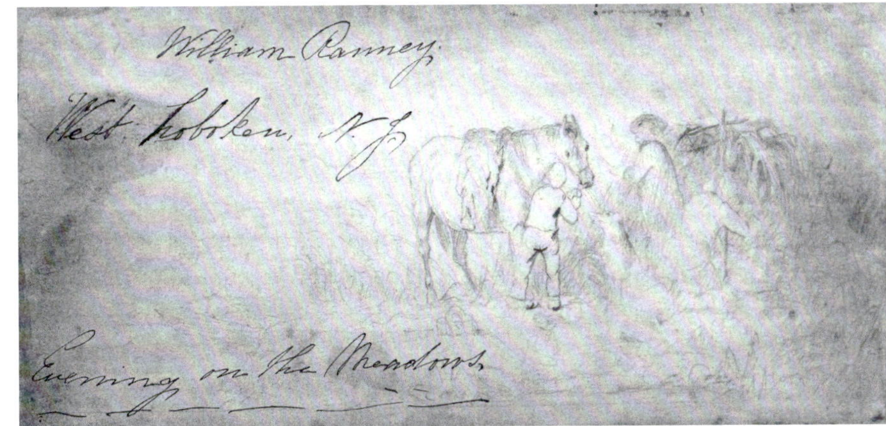

D73

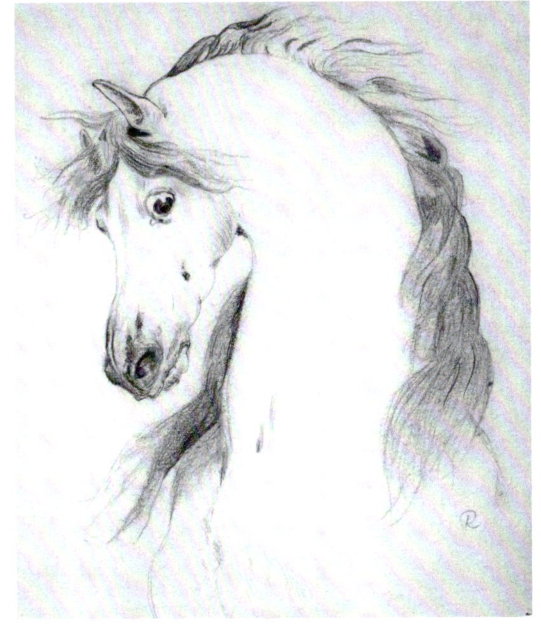

D75

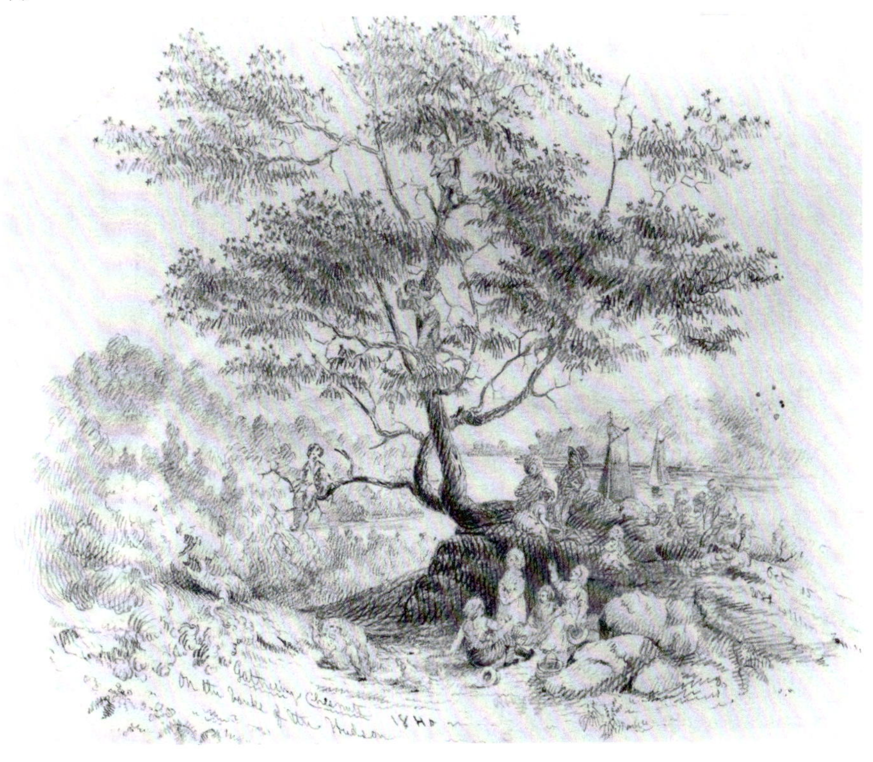

D74

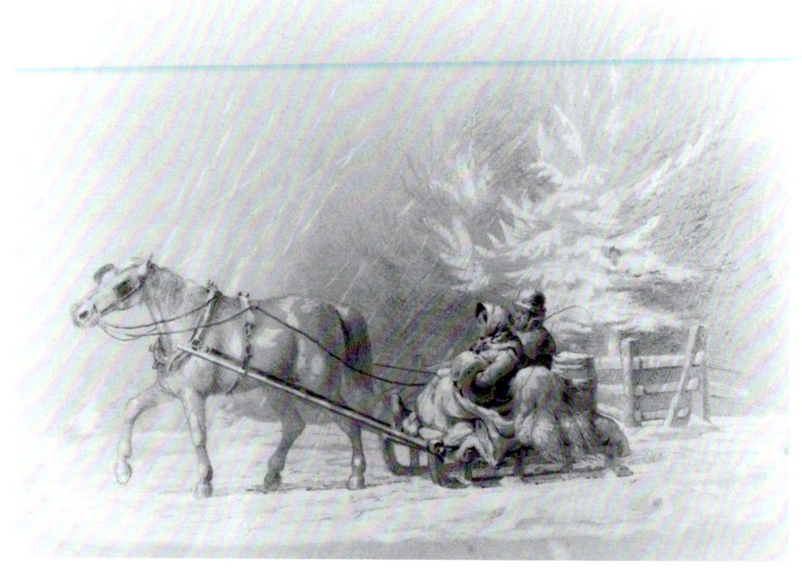

D76

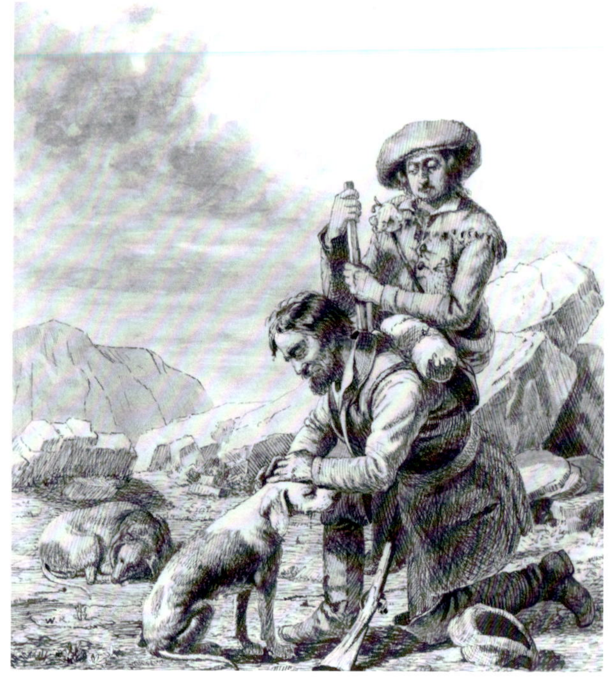

D77

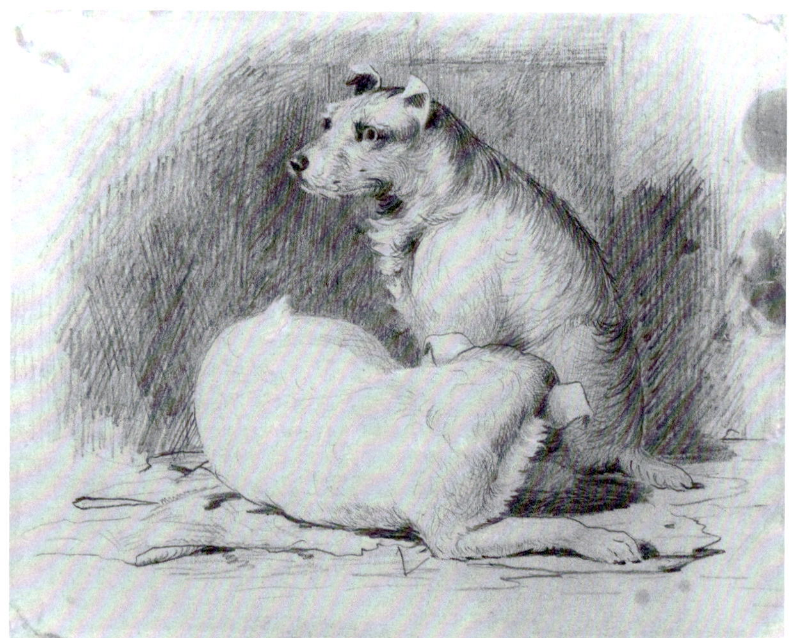

D78

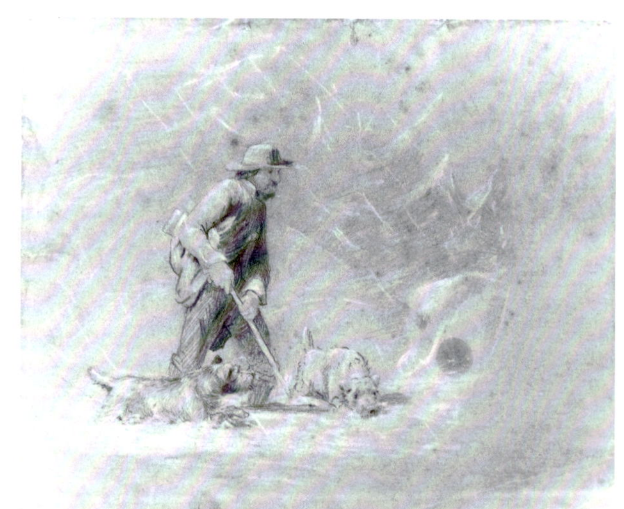

D79

D76
Horse Pulling Sleigh

Graphite heightened with white wash on paper

8 3/4 x 12 1/4 inches (22.2 x 31.1 cm)

Private collection

PROVENANCE: Descended in the Ranney family to the present owner.

Exhibited: Chadds Ford 1991, no. 37.

D77
Mountain Men with Dogs

Ink and ink wash on paper

8 1/2 x 7 3/4 inches (21.6 x 19.7 cm)

Phoenix Art Museum, Gift of the Carl S. Dentzel Family Collection

This drawing relates to the *Wounded Hound* of 1850 (see cat. nos. 49 and 50).

D78*
Two Terriers

Graphite on wove paper

8 x 10 inches (20.3 x 25.4 cm)

Private collection

PROVENANCE: Descended in the Ranney family to the present owner.

D79
Hunter with Two Dogs

Graphite and white chalk on wove paper

8 x 10 inches (20.3 x 25.4 cm)

Private collection

PROVENANCE: Descended in the Ranney family to the present owner.

D80*
Washington and Gist Crossing the Allegheny River

c. 1854

Watercolor, pen and sepia ink on paper

10 3/4 x 14 3/4 inches (27.3 x 37.5 cm)

Brandywine River Museum, Chadds Ford, Pennsylvania. Purchased with funds given anonymously, 1992.

PROVENANCE: Possibly the Ranney Fund sale, no. 89, as Study for Picture, "Washington Crossing the Susquehannah," sold to Wood[1]; private collection, New York State; (sale, Sotheby's, New York, December 1, 1988, no. 4); (Spanierman Gallery, New York, by 1989).

EXHIBITED: Chadds Ford 1991, no. 30, as lent by Spanierman Gallery.

REFERENCE: August 19, 1988, letter to Grubar from Sotheby's says "there is an old strip of paper affixed to the frame on which is printed: 89. Study for Picture, Washington Cross-/ing the Susquehannah, Wm. Ranney," Ranney archives. Francis S. Grubar to Laurene Buckley, Research associate of Spanierman Gallery, August 13, 1989, expresses opinion that this is no. 89 in the Ranney Fund sale, and further notes the "curving spandrels indicated in the upper left and right corners . . . was a favorite device used by Ranney for the frames of his finished paintings and can be found in other sketches as well." Copy in Ranney archives.

This work relates to *Washington and Gist Crossing the Allegheny River* of 1854 (see cat. no. 98).

1. See cat. no. 50 for information on Wood.

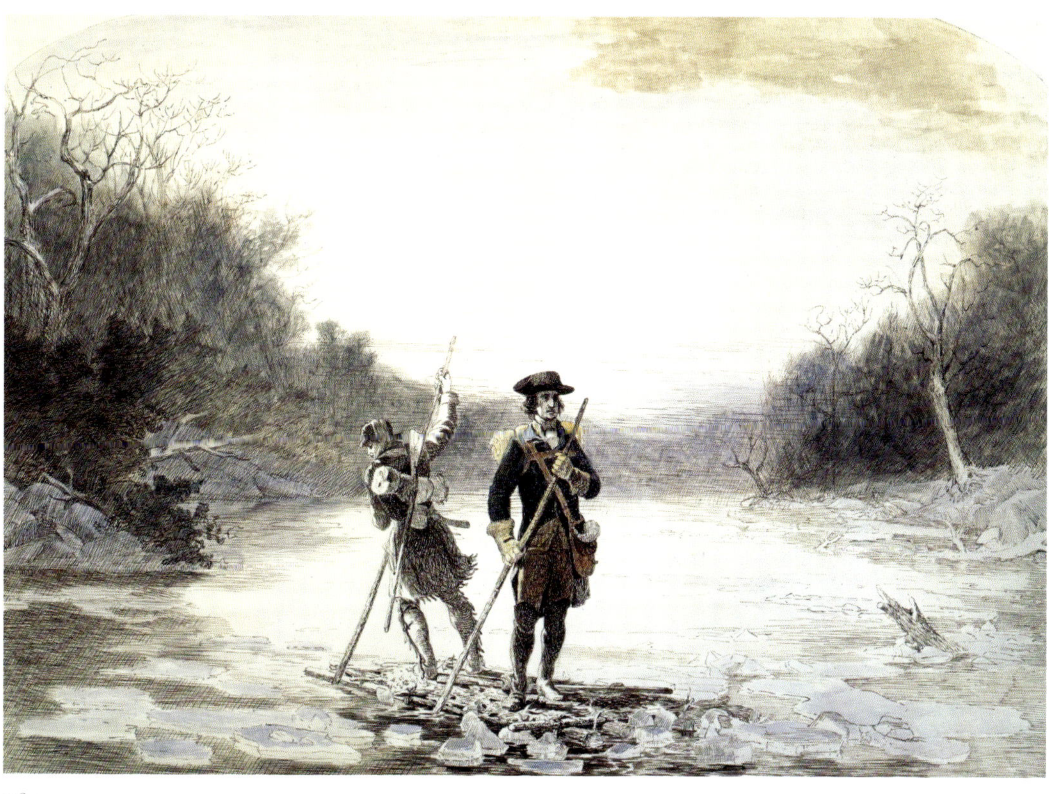

D80

207

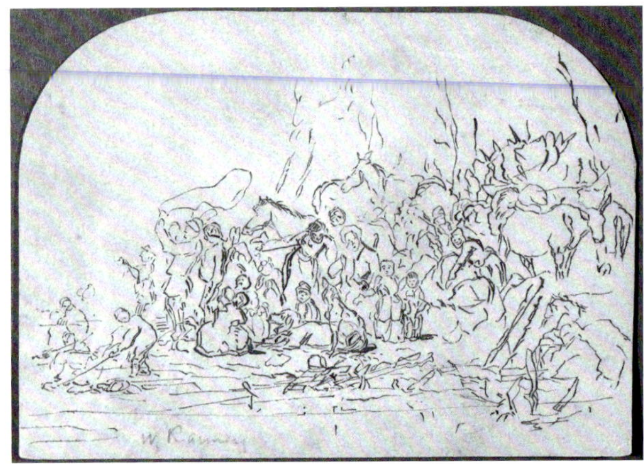

D81

Sketch for "The Freshet"

c. 1856–1857

Graphite on paper

4 3/4 x 6 3/4 inches (12.1 x 17.1 cm)

Inscribed, lower left: W. Ranney

Private collection

This drawing relates to *The Freshet* of c. 1857–1858 (cat. no. 145).

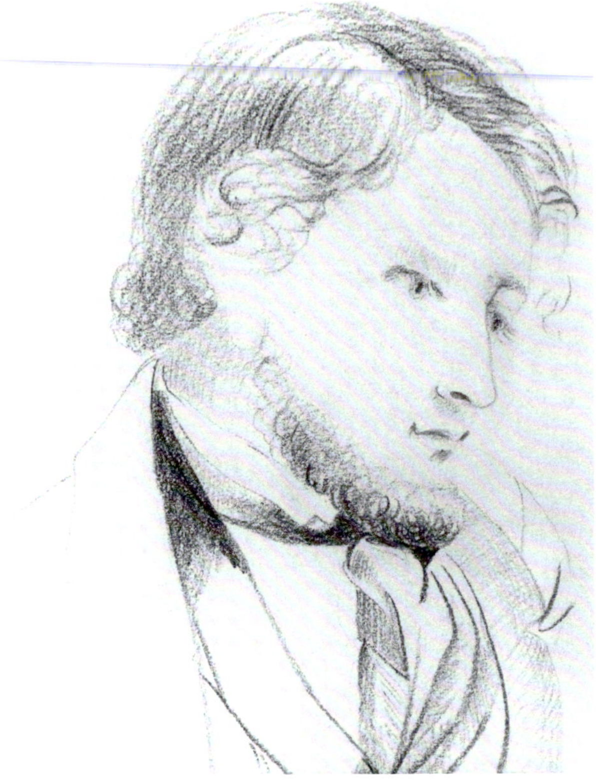

D82

Portrait of a Bearded Young Man

6 1/4 x 5 1/2 inches (15.9 x 14 cm)

Charcoal heightened with red crayon on wove paper

Private collection

PROVENANCE: Descended in the Ranney family to the present owner.

D83

Portrait of a Young Man with Beard

6 3/8 x 5 3/8 inches (16.2 x 13.7 cm)

Graphite on wove paper

Private collection

PROVENANCE: Descended in the Ranney family to the present owner.

D84

At the Well

Drawing

4 x 4 inches (10.2 x 10.2 cm)

Location unknown

PROVENANCE: James M. Burt, Brooklyn, to 1887 (sale, Moore's Auction Galleries, New York, *Catalogue of the Private Collection Belonging to Mr. James M. Burt of Brooklyn*, November 16, 17, and 18, 1887, lot 186).

This drawing may be related to *Hunters at the Well* of 1851 (cat. no. 70).

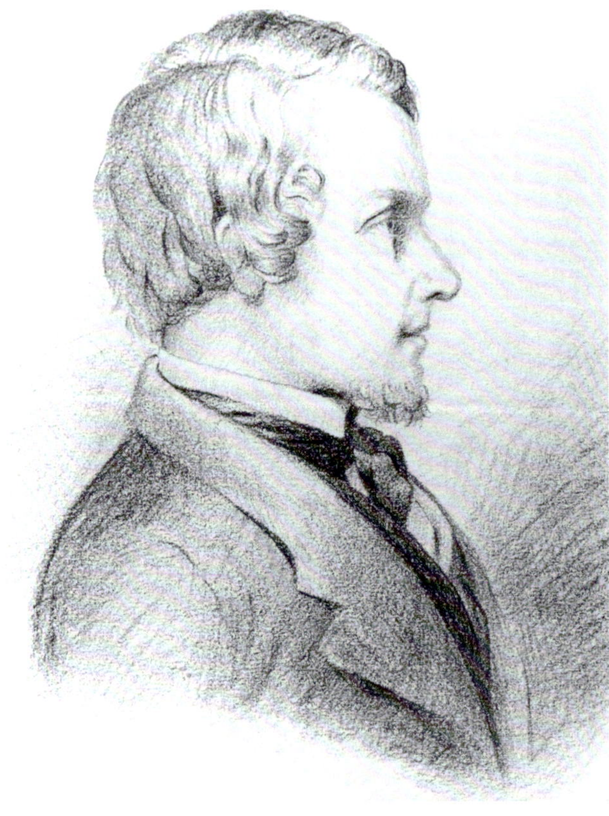

D83

The Ranney Fund exhibition and sale was held at the National Academy of Design, New York, during the month of December, 1858. A valuable source of information regarding this event is in the scrapbook volume entitled "The Ranney Collection," in the New-York Historical Society. All of the material quoted or otherwise referred to in this account is derived from this source, unless otherwise stated. This scrapbook contains a sales catalogue, two printed notices by the fund committee, a ticket to the exhibition (with Nason B. Collins's initials inscribed on it), and various clippings pertaining to the affair or to the artist, mostly from contemporary newspapers.

Prior to the exhibition, a printed form was sent by the committee to various collectors known to have pictures by Ranney, of which the following is an example.

New-York, Nov. 19, 1858.

Jos. Moreau, Esq. [inscribed]
Dear Sir, —

The Artists of New-York will open an Exhibition of Mr. Ranney's Pictures, December 1st, together with pieces painted by themselves, which they have given to be sold for the benefit of Mr. Ranney's widow, at the close of the exhibition.

Hearing that you are the possessor of one of Mr. Ranney's pictures, the Committee take the liberty of requesting you to loan them the said picture to exhibit with the others, they paying all expenses of transportation, & c.

The funds arising from the exhibition will, of course, be appropriated for the benefit of Mrs. Ranney, who, we are sorry to say, is in need of the sympathy and help of all her friends.

If you will send an answer as soon as possible after receipt of this, you will much oblige the Committee.

Direct to
N.B. Collins
23 Wall St. [inscribed]
N. Y.

P. S. — Notice will be given you where to send the pictures, after receipt of your answer.

The exhibition opened on Monday, December 6, 1858, in the rooms of the National Academy of Design on Tenth Street, near Broadway. Admission was twenty-five cents and exhibition hours were from 9:00 A.M. until 10:00 P.M. A statement by the committee regarding the purpose of the event was included with the printed *Catalogue.*

A number of the friends of the late William Ranney, being desirous of expressing in some way their sense of his abilities as an Artist, and his character as a man, decided upon offering a testimonial to his memory, which, at the same time, might be of some permanent value to his bereaved family. The Artists generally, therefore, of the City of New-York, by a mutual understanding, agreed to contribute some works of their own pencils, which being added to the Sketches left by Mr. Ranney, at his decease, might form a collection sufficiently various for an interesting Exhibition, with the ultimate view of selling all these productions at Auction, at the close of the Exhibition. The proceeds to be disposed of as the Artists may direct, for the benefit of the widow and children of the deceased Artist. With this intention the present collection of Pictures has been formed, and it is now respectfully recommended to the attention of the public, not only giving them a chance to procure some works of Mr. Ranney's, which, of course, as every year passes by, becomes more valuable, but also brings before them a collection of our own Artists' Pictures, of real merit, and any buyer can feel, as he looks on the picture after it is purchased, that in becoming a possessor of it, he was helping along a noble act of charity.

The exhibition contained 212 works, of which 108 were by Ranney. The names of many well-known artists of that day, as well as a number of the lesser-known, are found among the remaining 104 items, all of which were contributed. Ranney's work was not listed separately, but interspersed among that of the other artists.

The sale was conducted on the evenings of December 20 and 21, beginning at 7:30 P.M. The following list of works by William Ranney was compiled from the *Catalogue of Paintings to Be Sold for the Benefit of the Ranney Fund.* The original *Catalogue* numbers were utilized, and entries by artists other than Ranney have not been included. In addition, this copy of the *Catalogue* had been carefully ruled in pencil in order that a notation, recorded in ink, could be made before and after each item, pertaining to the price paid and the buyer's last name. In the list which follows, this information will be found in brackets. At the bottom of each page of the *Catalogue* a total was made of the sales and, on the last page, the sum total for the whole auction was computed. In all probability, this was the *Catalogue* used to keep a record during the sale's progress, perhaps by the merchant, Nason B. Collins.

There is little else in the manner of descriptive information for the various works listed and, lacking additional factual data, it would be impossible at this time to make a valid attempt at identifying and classifying most of the items according to their exact place in the artist's *oeuvre*. Many were undoubtedly preparatory sketches and working drawings from his studio. However, judging by the higher prices paid for a few, there must have been some major paintings by Ranney included. Tentative associations, mainly on the basis of title similarities, have been made in Part I [of Grubar's catalogue]. In spite of the present nebulous state of knowledge regarding the Fund sale items, there can be no question but what these works must be considered as a valid and necessary part of his total effort.

[This and the following excerpts from the sale are reprinted from pages 57 to 59 in Grubar 1962.]

1. SKETCH FROM NATURE —
   AMERICAN SCENERY
   [17.50; Russell].

3. COW
   [10; Jarvis].

5. DOCK LEAVES
   [5; Brady].

7. OLD-FASHIONED OVEN
   [10; Jarvis].

9. AUTUMN — A SKETCH
   [10; Wood].

11. THE COW SHED
   [5; Johnson].

13. HORSES
   [27.50; O. Richards].

15. STUDY FROM NATURE
   [5; Barry].

17. HORSE'S HEAD
   [4; Booth].

18. COW'S HEAD
   [16; Putnam].

20. SKETCH FROM NATURE OF GRASS
   [4; Barry].

22. SKETCH FROM NATURE
   [8; Menzies].

24. WOUNDED HOUND
   [21; Wood].

26. LAKE PISACO
   [15; Lord].

28. STUDY FOR LARGE PICTURE OF COW BOYS QUAR-
   RELLING OVER THEIR PLUNDER
   [22; Menzies].

30. STUDY OF A MULE
   [15; Kensett].

32. CATTLE REPOSING
   [17; Jarvis].

34. SKETCH FROM NATURE
   [8; Hoxie].

36. SETTER DOG
   [13; Walker].

38. A TRAPPER CROSSING THE MOUNTAINS
   [17; Walker].

40. ANIMALS
   [10; Bell].

42. ARTIST'S SHANTY, LAKE PISACO
   [6; Worth].

44. FINISHED SKETCH FROM NATURE
   [90; Menzies].

46. SKETCH FROM NATURE
   [40; Russell].

48. RECONNOITERING
   [15; Barry].

50. SALE OF MANHATTAN ISLAND TO THE DUTCH
   [26; Pepoon].

52. SKETCH FROM NATURE
   [9; Barry].

54. PRAIRIE ON FIRE
   [15; Walker].

56. TRAPPERS ON THE LOOKOUT
   [21; Walker].

58. A STUDY — BRADDOCK'S FUNERAL
   [16; Walker].

60. PORTRAIT OF A FAVORITE DOG
   [45; Jarvis].

62. HORSE
   [5; Wood].

134. SKETCH OF TREES
[5; Dodge].

136. THE STANDARD BEARER
[4; Wood].

138. EXPRESS RIDER
[12; N. Collins].

140. DOWNFALL OF MONARCHY
[9; O'Brian].

142. COWS
[5; Havens].

144. THE BARN YARD
[25; Riggs].

146. SKETCH FROM NATURE
[9; Howe].

148. CATTLE
[17; Swan].

150. WATER COLOR DRAWING
[4; Walker].

152. THE FRESHET
[14; N. Collins].

153. RADDISH [sic] GIRL
[11; Hurlburt].

156. HORSE'S HEAD
[10; Hurlburt].

159. SCOUTS ON THE PRAIRIE
[62.50; Wood].

161. THE WOUNDED SCOUT
[25; Walker].

164. MUSK RAT HUNTING
[60; Hurlburt].

166. WAITING FOR THE FERRY
[15; Riggs].

168. SNIPE SHOOTING, (very fine)
[150; Wood].

170. THE TRAPPER'S HALT, (very fine)
[340; Dr. Bissell].

172. BARN YARD
[16; Pepoon].

174. STUDY OF PICTURE, VIRGINIA WEDDING
[30; Menzies].

176. STUDY FOR LARGE PICTURE, DANIEL BOON AND PARTY
[6; Walker].

178. LAST SHOT
[50; Brooking].

180. SOLDIERS IN THE SNOW
[2; Brooking].

182. RABBIT HUNTING
[4; Riggs].

184. DOGS
[8; Eastman].

186. DEAD HORSE
[4; Endicott].

188. SNIPE SHOOTING
[3; Riggs].

190. SKETCH
[2.50; Riggs].

191. SCHOOL BOYS
[6; Eastman].

192. DROVER'S HALT
[5; Waite].

194. RETURN FROM HUNTING
[6; Burt].

196. DEER HUNTING ON THE LAKES
[7; Eastman].

197. PEN AND INK DRAWING
[5; Waite].

198. PEN AND INK DRAWING
[5; Riggs].

199. PEN AND INK DRAWING
[4; Brooking].

200. SKETCH
[7; Waite].

201. SOLDIERS FORDING A RIVER
[2.50; Riggs].

202. WAGON ON THE SNOW
[3; Anderson].

203. FISHERMAN
[6; Riggs].

204. DOG AND DUCK
[2; Ross].

205. DYING HORSE
[2; Anderson].

206. HUNTER WITH GAME
[3; Anderson].

207. CATTLE
[6; Riggs].

OLD (GRUBAR) TITLE	NEW TITLE
Advice on the Prairie	Old Scout's Tale, 85
Battle of Cowpens, The	Battle of Cowpens, 8
Boy on a Horse Fording a Stream	Going to Mill, 105
Cattle Piece	Barnyard with Cattle — Winter, 115
Coast Scene with Figures	Coast Scene, with Figures, 21
Coast Scene, with Fishermen	Coast Scene with Fishermen, 27
Crossing the Ferry — Scene on the Pedee	Crossing the Ferry — Scene on the Pee Dee, 23
Dead Courser, The	The Dead Courser or Charger, 22
Duck Hunters on the Hoboken Marshes	Duck Shooters, 43
Duck Shooting	The Retrieve, 59
Marion Crossing the Pee Dee	Marion Crossing the Pedee, 62
Match Boy, The	Match Boy, 10
Old Oaken Bucket, The	Hunters at the Well, 70
Pennsylvania Teamster, The	Pennsylvania Teamster, 20
Pioneer, The	The Muleteer, 111
Portrait of Clarissa Gaylord Ranney, Mother of the Artist	Portrait of Clarissa Gaylord Ranney, 5
Portrait of James Ranney, Son of the Artist	Portrait of James Ranney, 107
Portrait of Margaret Ranney, Wife of the Artist	Portrait of Margaret Ranney, 66
Portrait of Margaret Ranney, Wife of the Artist	Portrait of Margaret Ranney, 67
Post Rider, The	The Express Rider, 65
Prairie Fire, The	Stampede, 40
Recruiting During the American Revolution	Recruiting for the Continental Army, 147
Sale of Manhattan by The Indians, The	Purchase of Manhattan Island from the Indians by the Dutch in 1626, 87
Scouting Party, The	The Pipe of Friendship, 110
Tory Escort, The	Tories with a Prisoner, 140
Trapper's Last Shot, The	The Last Shot, 52
Traveller, The	The Muleteer, 111
Winter Scene	Winter Scene, the Barn Yard, Cattle, and Figures, 101

ABBREVIATIONS AND SHORT TITLES

Am Art-Union   American Art Union, New York

Am Art-Union *Bulletin*   *Bulletin of the American Art-Union.* New York: Semi-monthly April through December, 1848; monthly April through December, 1849-1851.

Am Art-Union *Transactions*   *Transactions of the American Art-Union* (For a complete listing see Bibilography)

Am Art Union Papers   American Art-Union Papers, Manuscript Collection, New-York Historical Society

Ayres 1987   Ayres, Linda. "William Ranney." In *American Frontier Life: Early Western Painting and Prints.* Fort Worth: Amon Carter Museum; New York: Abbeville Press, 1987.

Chadds Ford 1991   Brandywine River Museum, *William Tylee Ranney, East of the Mississippi.* Chadds Ford, Pennsylvania: Brandywine River Museum, 1991.

Cowdrey 1943, 2   Cowdrey. *National Academy of Design Exhibition Record, 1826-1860.* 2 vols. New York: New-York Historical Society, 1943.

Cowdrey 1953, 2   Cowdrey, Mary Bartlett, ed. *American Academy of Fine Arts and American Art-Union, 1816-1852.* 2 vols. New York: New-York Historical Society, 1953.

FARL   Frick Art Reference Library, New York

Fort Worth 1987   Tyler, Ron, et al. *American Frontier Life: Early Western Painting and Prints.* Introduction by Peter H. Hassrick. Fort Worth: Amon Carter Museum; New York: Abbeville Press, 1987.

Glanz 1982   Glanz, Dawn. *How the West Was Drawn: American Art and the Settling of the Frontier.* Ann Arbor, Michigan: UMI Research Press, 1982.

Grubar   Grubar, Francis S. *William Ranney, Painter of the Early West.* Washington, D. C.: Corcoran Gallery of Art, 1962.

NAD   National Academy of Design, New York

Thistlethwaite 1991   Thistlethwaite, Mark. *William Tylee Ranney, East of the Mississippi.* Chadds Ford, Pennsylvania: Brandywine River Museum, 1991.

Tuckerman 1867   Tuckerman, Henry T. *Book of the Artists: American Artist Life, Comprising Biographical and Critical Sketches of American Artists: Preceded by an Historical Account of the Rise and Progress of Art in America.* New York: G. P. Putnam and Sons, 1867.

Yarnall and Gerdts 1986   Yarnall, James and William H. Gerdts. *The National Museum of American Art's Index to American Art Exhibition Catalogues: From the Beginning through the 1876 Centennial Year.* 6 vols. Boston: G. K. Hall, 1986.

SELECT BIBLIOGRAPHY

AMERICAN ART-UNION PAPERS AND PUBLICATIONS

American Art-Union Papers, New-York Historical Society, New York.

American Art-Union, New York. *Artist's Sale: Catalogue of Very Valuable and Choice Paintings, Recently Selected from the Studios of the Most Distinguished American and Resident Artists*. David Austen, Jr., Auctioneer. December 30, 1852.

American Art-Union. *Catalogue of Pictures and Other Works of Art: The Property of the American Art Union, to Be Sold at Auction by David Austen, Jr. . . . December 15, 16, 17, 1852*.

American Art-Union. *First Annual Sale of Paintings by American and Resident Artists Exclusively: Under the Direction of the American Art-Union*. John H. Austen, Auctioneer. December 15, 1853.

Bulletin of the American Art-Union. New York: Semi-monthly April through December, 1848; monthly April through December, 1849-1851.

Transactions of the Apollo Association for the Promotion of the Fine Arts in the United States, at the First Annual Meeting, December 16th, 1839. New York: Printed for the Association, 1839 [January, 1840].

Transactions of the American Art-Union for the Promotion of the Fine Arts in the United States for the Year 1844. New York: John Douglass, 1845.

Transactions of the American Art-Union, for the Year 1845. New York: Printed at the Office of the Evening Post, 1846.

Transactions of the American Art-Union, for the Year 1846. New York: G. F. Nesbitt, 1847.

Transactions of the American Art-Union, for the Year 1847. New York: G. F. Nesbitt, 1848.

Transactions of the American Art-Union, for the Year 1848. New York: George F. Nesbitt, 1849.

Transactions of the American Art-Union, for the Year 1849. New York: George F. Nesbitt, 1850.

BOOKS, CATALOGUES, PAMPHLETS, AND ARTICLES

Adams, Charles Collard. *Middletown Upper Houses*. 1908. Reprint, Canaan, New Hampshire: Phoenix Publishing, 1983.

Bass, Robert D. *Swamp Fox: The Life and Campaigns of General Francis Marion*. 1959. Reprint, Orangeburg, South Carolina: Sandlapper Publishing Company, 1974.

Blakely, Judith. "The American Art-Union Contribution to American Prints." *Imprint* 1 (October 1976): 6-11.

Blaugrund, Annette. *The Tenth Street Studio Building: Artist Entrepreneurs from the Hudson River School to the American Impressionists*. Southampton, New York: Parrish Art Museum, 1997.

Bloch, E. Maurice. "The American Art-Union's Downfall." *New-York Historical Society Quarterly* 37 (October 1953): 331-359.

Boatner, Mark M. *Encyclopedia of the American Revolution*. Mechanicsburg, Pennsylvania: Stackpole Books

Bode, Carl. *The Anatomy of American Popular Culture, 1840-1861*. Berkeley: University of California Press, 1959.

Boyle, Robert H. *The Hudson River: A Natural and Unnatural History*. New York: W. W. Norton and Company, 1969.

Burnham, Patricia M., and Lucretia Hoover Giese, eds. *Redefining American History Painting*. Cambridge, England: Cambridge University Press, 1995.

Burrows, Edwin G. and Mike Wallace. *Gotham: A History of New York City to 1898*. New York: Oxford University Press, 1999.

Cadbury, Warder H. *Arthur Fitzwilliam Tait: Artist of the Adirondacks*. Newark: University of Delaware Press, 1986.

Caldwell, John, and Oswaldo Rodriguez Roque. *American Paintings in the Metropolitan Museum of Art, Volume I: A Catalogue of Works by Artists Born by 1815*. New York: Metropolitan Museum of Art, 1994.

Callow, James T. *Kindred Spirits: Knickerbocker Writers and American Artists, 1807-1855*. Chapel Hill: University of North Carolina Press, 1967.

Cantor, Jay. "Prints and the American Art-Union." In *Prints in and of the Americas to 1850*. Charlottesville: University of Virginia Press, 1970.

Clark, Carol. "Charles Deas." In *American Frontier Life: Early Western Painting and Prints*. Fort Worth: Amon Carter Museum; New York: Abbeville Press, 1987.

Cooper, James Fenimore. "American European Scenery Company." In Washington Irving et al. *The Home Book of the Picturesque, or, American Scenery, Art, and Literature . . . .* New York: G. P. Putnam, 1852.

Craig, James H. *The Arts and Crafts in North Carolina, 1699-1840*. Winston-Salem, North Carolina: Museum of Early Southern Decorative Arts, Old Salem, 1965.

Crosby, Nathan. *Annual Obituary Notices of Eminent Persons Who Have Died in the United States, for 1857-1858*. Vol. 1. Boston: J. P. Jewett and Company, 1858-1859.

Cummings, Thomas Seir. *Historic Annals of the National Academy of Design, New-York Drawing Association, etc. with Occasional Dottings by the Way-Side, from 1825 to the Present Time*. Philadelphia: George W. Childs, Publisher, 1865.

Currier and Ives: A Catalogue Raisonné. Compiled by Gale Research Company; with an introduction by Bernard F. Reilly, Jr. Detroit: Gale Research Company, 1984.

Dearinger, David, ed. *Rave Reviews; American Art and Its Critics, 1826-1925*. New York: National Academy of Design, 2000.

DeKay, James E. *Zoology of New York or the New-York Fauna: Part IV. Fishes*. Albany: W. and A. White and J. Visscher, 1842.

Dictionary of American Biography. 11 vols. New York: C. Scribner's Sons, 1964.

Durand, John. *The Life and Times of A. B. Durand*. New York. Charles Scribner's Sons, 1894. Reprint, New York. Da Capo Press, 1970.

Encyclopaedia of Contemporary Biography of New York. Vol. 2. New York: Atlantic Publishing and Engraving Company, 1882.

Farnham, Thomas J. *Travels in the Great Western Prairies, the Anahuac and Rocky Mountains, and in the Oregon Territory*. New York: Greeley and McElrath, 1843.

Fifth Avenue Galleries, New York. *By Order of . . . Executors of the Late Marshall O. Roberts; Modern Paintings . . . to Be Sold . . . .* January 19, 20, and 21, 1897.

Flexner, James Thomas. *George Washington: The Forge of Experience (1732-1775)*. Boston: Little, Brown, and Company, 1965.

Forester, Frank [Henry William Herbert]. *Complete Manual for Young Sportsmen . . . .* 1856. Reprint, New York: Westvaco Corporation, 1993.

Francis, John Wakefield. *Old New York: Reminiscences of the Past Sixty Years . . . With a Memoir of the Author by Henry T. Tuckerman*. New York: W. J. Widdleton, 1866.

Frankenstein, Alfred. *William Sidney Mount*. New York: Harry N. Abrams, 1975.

Garraty, John A. *The American Nation: A History of the United States*. New York: Harper and Row, 1966.

Gerdts, William H. *Art Across America: Two Centuries of Regional Painting, 1710-1920*. 3 vols. New York: Abbeville Press, 1990.

Gerdts, and Carrie Rebora. *The Art of Henry Inman*. Washington, D. C.: National Portrait Gallery, Smithsonian Institution, 1987.

Gerdts and Mark Thistlethwaite. *Grand Illusions: History Painting in America*. Fort Worth: Amon Carter Museum, 1988.

Getlein, Frank. *The Lure of the Great West: Painters from Catlin to Russell*. Waukesha, Wisconsin: Country Beautiful, 1973.

Great Central Fair for the U. S. Sanitary Commission. *Catalogue of Paintings, Drawings, Statuary, etc. of the Art Department in the Great Central Fair Held in Logan Square, June 1864, for the Benefit of the U. S. Sanitary Commission*. Philadelphia, 1864.

Groce, George C. and David H. Wallace. *The New-York Historical Society's Dictionary of Artists in America, 1564-1860*. New Haven: Yale University Press, 1957.

Hafen, LeRoy R., ed. *Mountain Men and the Fur Trade of the Far West*. Lincoln: University of Nebraska, 1982.

Harris, Neil. *The Artist in American Society: The Formative Years, 1790-1860*. New York: G. Braziller, 1966.

Headley, J. T. *Washington and His Generals*. Vol. 1. New York: Charles Scribner, 1847.

Herman, Daniel Justin. *Hunting and the American Imagination*. Washington, D. C.: Smithsonian Institution Press, 2001.

Hills, Patricia. "The American Art-Union as Patron for Expansionist Ideology in the 1840s." In *Art in Bourgeois Society, 1790-1850*. Edited by Andrew Hemingway and William Vaughan. New York: Cambridge University Press, 1998.

Hills. "Picturing Progress in the Era of Western Expansion." In *The West as America: Reinterpreting Images of the Frontier, 1820-1920*. Edited by William Truettner. Published for the National Museum of American Art, Washington, D. C.: Smithsonian Institution Press, 1991.

Hills. *The Painters' America: Rural and Urban Life, 1810-1910*. New York: Praeger Publishers, 1974.

Hone, Philip. *The Diary of Philip Hone*. 2 vols. Edited by Allan Nevins. New York: Dodd, Mead, and Company, 1927.

Horry, Peter and Parson M. L. Weems. *The Life of General Francis Marion . . . .* 1854. Reprint, Winston-Salem, North Carolina: John F. Blair Publisher, 2000.

Hubert, Philip G., Jr. *The Merchants' National Bank of the City of New York: A History of Its First Century . . . .* New York: Merchant's National Bank, 1903.

John, Richard R. *Spreading the News: The American Postal System from Franklin to Morse*. Cambridge: Harvard University Press, 1995.

Johns, Elizabeth. *American Genre Painting: The Politics of Everyday Life*. New Haven: Yale University Press, 1995.

Johnson, Deborah. *William Sidney Mount: Painter of American Life*. New York: The American Federation of Arts, 1998.

Nichols, Arlene Katz. "Merchants and Artists: The Apollo Association and the American Art-Union." Ph.D. diss., City University of New York, 2003; Ann Arbor, Michigan: UMI Research Press, 2003.

Kelly, Franklin. *Frederic Edwin Church*. Washington, D. C.: National Gallery of Art, 1989.

Kirsch, George B. *The Creation of American Team Sports: Baseball and Cricket, 1838-72*. Urbana: University of Illinois Press, 1989.

Leavitt, Messrs, New York. *Catalogue of a Collection of Fine Modern Paintings by Celebrated American and Foreign Artists, Belonging to William Menzies, Esq. . . . .* April 18 and 19, 1876.

Lee, W. Storrs. *The Yankees of Connecticut*. New York: Holt, 1957.

Leeds, Henry H., New York. *Catalogue: Great Annual Sale of Valuable Oil Paintings by American and Resident Artists*. October 31 and November 1, 1854.

Leeds, Henry H., New York. *Williams, Stevens and Williams Great Annual Sale . . . .* October 27, 28, and 29, 1852.

Leeds, Henry H., New York. *Williams, Stevens and Williams Second Great Sale of 500 of the Most Valuable Oil Paintings in this Country . . . and about 100 Paintings of the Düsseldorf School . . .* November 10 and 11, 1853.

Lossing, Benson J. *The Pictorial Field Book of the Revolution*. Vol. 2 New York: Harper and Brothers, 1851-1852.

Mann, Maybelle. *The American Art-Union*. Otisville, New York: ALM Associates, 1977.

Marlor, Clark S. *A History of the Brooklyn Art Association with an Index of Exhibitions*. New York: J. F. Carr, 1970.

Marshall, John. *The Life of Washington . . . .* Vol. 4. Philadelphia: C. P. Wayne, 1805.

Matthiessen, F. O. *American Renaissance: Art and Expression in the Age of Emerson and Whitman*. New York: Oxford University Press, 1941.

McClellan, Elisabeth. *Historic Dress in America, 1800-1870*. Philadelphia: George W. Jacobs and Company, 1910.

McPhee, John. *The Founding Fish*. New York: Farrar, Straus and Giroux, 2002.

Miller, Lillian B. *Patrons and Patriotism: The Encouragement of the Fine Arts in the United States, 1790-1860*. Chicago: University of Chicago Press, 1966.

Milner, Clyde A., Carol A. O'Connor, and Martha A. Sandweiss. *The Oxford History of the American West*. New York: Oxford University Press, 1994.

Miner's Art Galleries, New York. *William H. Webb's Collection of Works of Art*. March 29 and 30, 1876.

Mott, Frank Luther. *A History of American Magazines*. 5 vols. Cambridge, Massachusetts: Harvard University Press, 1938-1968.

Novak, Barbara. *American Painting of the Nineteenth Century: Realism, Idealism, and the American Experience*. New York: Praeger Publishers, 1969.

Oates, John A. *The Story of Fayetteville and the Upper Cape Fear.* 1950. Reprint, Raleigh, North Carolina: Fayetteville Woman's Club, 1981

O'Connor, Stephen. *Orphan Trains: The Story of Charles Loring Brace and the Children He Saved and Failed.* Boston: Houghton Mifflin, 2001.

Ornaments of Memory . . . . New York: D. Appleton and Company, 1855.

Parker, Roy, Jr. *Cumberland County: A Brief History.* Raleigh: Division of Archives and History, North Carolina Department of Cultural Resources, 1990.

Parkman, Francis. The Oregon Trail. 1849. Boston: Ginn and Company, 1910.

Pennington, Estill Curtis. *Passage and Progress in the Works of William Tylee Ranney.* Augusta, Georgia: Morris Museum of Art, 1993.

Peverelly, Charles A. *The Book of American Pastimes Containing a History of the Prinicpal Base Ball, Cricket, Rowing, and Yachting Clubs of the United States.* New York: The author, 1866.

Peters, Harry T. *Currier and Ives: Printmakers to the American People.* New York: Doubleday, Doran, and Company, 1942.

"The Pioneers." *Knickerbocker* 43 (November 1841): 390.

Quigley, David. "Southern Slavery in a Free City: Economy, Politics, and Culture." In *Slavery in New York.* Edited by Ira Berlin and Leslie M. Harris. New York: New Press, 2005.

Rathbone, Perry T. *Westward the Way: The Character and Development of the Louisiana Territory as Seen by Artists and Writers of the Nineteenth Century.* St. Louis: City Art Museum.

Reiger, John F. *American Sportsmen and the Origins of Conservation.* 3d ed. Corvallis: Oregon State University, 2000.

Rice, Kathleen. "Representational Images: William Ranney's *Halt on the Prairie.*" Unpublished essay, University of Texas, Austin, 1999.

Robey, Ethan. "The Utility of Art: Mechanics' Institute Fairs in New York City, 1826-1926." Ph.D. diss., Columbia University, 2000.

Saunders, Richard H., ed. *Collecting the West: The C. R. Smith Collection of Western American Art.* Austin: University of Austin Press for the Archer M. Huntington Art Gallery, 1988.

Schimmel, Julie. *The West Explored: The Gerald Peters Collection of Western American Art.* Santa Fe: Gerald Peters Gallery, 1988.

Schissel, Lillian. *Women's Diaries of the Westward Journey.* New York: Schocken Books, 1982.

Sears, Robert. *Pictorial History of the American Revolution with a Sketch of the Early History of the Country . . . .* 1848. Reprint, Whitefish, Montana: Kessinger Publishers, 2004.

Simms, W. Gilmore. *The Life of Francis Marion.* New York: Henry G. Langley and Astor House, 1844.

Spassky, Natalie. *American Paintings in the Metropolitan Museum of Art, Volume II: A Catalogue of Works by Artists Born between 1816 and 1845.* New York: Metropolitan Museum of Art, 1985.

Stewart, Rick with Don Hedgpeth. *The American West: Legendary Artists of the Frontier.* Dallas: Hawthorne Publishing Company, 1986.

Stokes, I. N. Phelps. *The Iconography of Manhattan Island, 1498-1909.* 6 vols. New York: R. H. Dodd, 1915-28. Reprint, New York: Da Capo Press, 1967.

Strahan, Edward [Earl Shinn], ed. *The Art Treasures of America.* Vols. 2 and 3. Philadelphia: G. Barrie, 1879.

Sweeney, J. Gray. *The Columbus of the Woods: Daniel Boone and the Typology of Manifest Destiny.* St. Louis: Washington University Gallery of Art, 1992.

Thistlethwaite, Mark. "The Past into Present: William Ranney's *First News of the Battle of Lexington.*" North Carolina Museum of Art *Bulletin* 16 (1993): 1-12.

Tindall, George Brown. *America: A Narrative History.* Vol. 1. New York: W. W. Norton, 1988.

Truettner, William H. and Alan Wallach, *Thomas Cole: Landscape into History.* New Haven: Yale University Press, 1994.

Truettner, ed. *The West As America: Reinterpreting Images of the Frontier, 1820-1920.* Washington, D. C.: Published for the National Museum of American Art by the Smithsonian Institution Press, 1991.

Tuckerman. "Over the Mountains or the Western Pioneer." In *The Home Book of the Picturesque; or American Scenery, Art, and Literature.* New York: Putnam, 1852.

Voorsanger, Catharine Hoover, and John K. Howat, eds. *Art and the Empire City: New York, 1825-1861.* New Haven: Yale University Press, 2000.

Ward, Harry M. *Between the Lines: Banditti of the American Revolution.* Westport, Connecticut: Praeger, 2002.

Weems, Mason L. *The Life of Washington.* 1809. Reprint, edited by Marcus Cunliffe, Cambridge, Massachusetts: Belknap Press of Harvard University Press, 1997.

Weld, H. Hastings. *Pictorial Life of George Washington: Embracing Anecdotes Illustrative of His Character . . . .* Philadelphia: Lindsay and Blakiston, 1845.

Williams, Hermann Warner. *Mirror to the American Past: A Survey of American Genre Painting, 1750-1900.* Greenwich, Connecticut: New York Graphic Society, 1973.

Wilmerding, John, et al. *American Light: The Luminist Movement, 1850-1875.* Washington, D. C.: National Gallery of Art, 1980.

Young, William. *Lights and Shadows of New York Picture Galleries: Forty Photographs by A. A. Turner . . . .* New York: D. Appleton and Company, 1864.

ARCHIVAL RESOURCES

Frick Art Reference Library. William Tylee Ranney: Artist File: Study photographs and reproductions of works of art with accompanying documentation (two folders).

Gerdts American Art Research Library, New York.

New-York Historical Society.

New York Public Library, Art and Architecture Collection, Artist files.

Ranney Archives, private collection.

PHOTOGRAPHY CREDITS

The majority of the photographs have been provided by the owners or custodians of the works reproduced. The following list applies to those photographs for which a separate credit is due.

Michael Agee, 26

Ali Elai of Camerarts, Inc. New York, D81

Jackie Burns, 53

Campli Photography, D13, D14, D15, D16, D18, D21, D22, D23, D28, D29, D30, D31, D32, D33, D34, D35, D36, D37, D39, D45, D52, D53, D54, D55, D58, D59, D63, D71, D72, D73, D76, D78, D79, D82, D83

Christie's Images Ltd., 133

Rick Echelmeyer, 3, 5, 6, 10, 34, 40, 44, 50, 52, 55, 60, 67, 74, 82, 94, 95, 99, 105, 107, 109, 118, 134, 135, 138, 146

Charley Freiberg, 9

Gerald Peters Gallery, 142

Global Arts, LLC, 66

Rick Hall, 54, 56

Tom LaBarbera, Picture This Studios, 129

William J. O'Connor, 39, 46, 84

Richard Stoner, 98

Vose Galleries, Boston, 51

Richard Walker, 63, 114

Bruce M. White, 36

Unknown Photographer, 87, D27, D75

COLOPHON

Set in Aldus and Sistina types, designed by Hermann Zapf / Darmstadt, Germany.

Printed on Warren's paper by Capital Offset / Concord, New Hampshire.

Design and typography by Jerry Kelly / New York, New York.